KURT WEILL: A HANDBOOK

Kurt Weill

A HANDBOOK

DAVID DREW

University of California Press
Berkeley and Los Angeles

First published in 1987 by
University of California Press
Berkeley and Los Angeles

Phototypeset by Wilmaset Birkenhead Wirral
Printed in Great Britain by
Mackays of Chatham Ltd Kent
All rights reserved

Library of Congress Cataloging-in-Publication Data

Drew, David
Kurt Weill: a handbook.

Includes indexes.
1. Weill, Kurt, 1900–1950—Bibliography. I. Title.
ML134.W4D7 1987   016.78281'092'4   86-25030
ISBN 0–520–05839–9 (alk. paper)

Commissioned by the
Academy of Arts, West Berlin

In memory of
GEORGE DAVIS

4 February 1906, Chicago – 25 November 1957, Berlin

Contents

Foreword   1
Introduction: Report to the Academy of Arts, West Berlin   4
Acknowledgements   48

Weill's Life and Times: A Chronology   53

Catalogue of Weill's Works   69
   Purposes and Organization of the Catalogue   71
   Abbreviations and Editorial Principles   75
   A Note on Weill's Composing Methods   82
   The Catalogue
     Chronological List of Works   86
     Classified List of Works   89
     Juvenilia and Early Works   95
     Opus Numbers and After   127
     Miscellaneous Unidentified Sketches   372
     Doubtful and Chimerical Works   374

Projects: An Outline   379
Brook House Library   425
   Holograph and Autograph Works by
     Other Composers   425
   Printed Music   427
   Recordings   432
   Books on Music, Tutors, etc.   433
   General Literature   434
The Lacunae: A Résumé   436
   An exchange of letters in lieu of a conclusion   440

Appendix I   Kurt Weill Foundation for Music   444
Appendix II   Weill–Lenya Research Center   446
Appendix III   Weill/Lenya Archive at Yale University 448

Indexes: Works; Authors; General   449

*Foreword**

Whether we are accustomed to mentioning Weill in the same breath as Hindemith or as Holländer, as Copland or as Cole Porter; whether we see him as an outstanding German composer who somehow lost his voice when he settled in America, or as an outstanding Broadway composer who somehow contrived to write a hit-show called *The Threepenny Opera* during his otherwise obscure and probably misspent Berlin youth; whether we disagree with both these views and either find evidence of a strikingly original mind at all stages in his career (but at some more than others), or dismiss him as nothing but a gifted amanuensis of Bertolt Brecht; whether we think of him as a 'product of his times' who had his one lucky strike with *Die Dreigroschenoper* and apart from that can safely be forgotten, or whether we believe him to be the creator of a substantial and durable body of work spanning twenty (or even thirty) years; whether we consider him incompetent to write anything but theatre music, or whether we number several of his non-theatrical pieces and at least one of his orchestral works among his finest achievements; in short, whether we feel him to be important or negligible, whether we love his music or detest it, admire or despise it – we may rest assured that we are by no means alone, and that we will not need to look far for some eminent authority who shares our views.

Bertolt Brecht, for instance. His only published assessment of Weill appears in the essay 'On the use of music in the Epic Theatre', and indicates that until Brecht put him on the right track Weill had been composing 'relatively complicated music of a mainly psychological sort, but when he agreed to set a series of more or less banal Song texts [i.e. the *Mahagonny-Gesänge*] he was making a courageous break with a prejudice which the solid bulk of serious composers stubbornly held'. Apart from the fact that Weill had started simplifying his music some considerable time before he met Brecht, and that even while he was composing 'relatively complicated music' he had, for his own and other

---

*Written in London in May 1976, first published in Deutsche Grammophon's three-disc album of music by Weill (1976), and revised in 1986 for this book.

1

people's amusement, written some cabaret songs on texts at least 'banal'
as any of Brecht's for *Mahagonny*, nothing is more remarkable in his post-
1920 music than its withdrawal from those areas which might loosely
be described as 'psychological' – a bad word in Brecht's vocabulary, here
presumably denoting a Straussian or even Schoenbergian ethos. In his
theatrical works prior to the collaboration with Brecht, Weill had already
dissociated most of the characters (or 'figures', to use Georg Kaiser's
term) from their individually characteristic emotions, with the one
significant exception of a 'public figure' (the Tsar in *Der Zar lässt sich
photographieren*) who is stripped down to his private, sensual, self; and in
his non-theatrical works, Weill had concentrated on the moral, the
religious, and the socio-political implications of his chosen texts or
pretexts.

The fact that in these pre-Brecht years he concerned himself not only
with the work of Georg Kaiser and Iwan Goll – both of whom Brecht
admired – but also with Rilke, whose work Brecht disliked, and the
Bible, is revealing only with reference to specific texts and to Weill's
family background. A typically Reform-Jewish upbringing had been
associated with parental influences that were in most respects liberal.
Weill's was a literary as well as a musical family – his mother had wide
literary interests, while his father was a Cantor and a composer of
liturgical music – and Rilke figured prominently among the modern
poets in a family library where the works of Goethe and Heine, of Johann
Gottfried Herder and Moses Mendelssohn, had pride of place, and
where, perhaps, one could have found some writings of Eduard
Bernstein and perhaps even a crumpled copy of the Erfurt Programme of
1891.

Unlike Brecht, Weill never needed to repudiate his early background in
order to define his artistic functions and objectives. Although it is true
that he left the Jewish faith at an early stage in his adult life, there seems
to have been no family dissension on that account. Settings of a
penitential psalm and of the fifth chapter of the Lamentations of Jeremiah
are perhaps the finest of his early works, and Rilke provided a
convenient bridge from the Old Testament to the humanism which was
the only faith Weill professed in later years except inadvertently – for
instance in the chromatically twisted fragment of the Dies Irae which
runs through the first movement of the Violin Concerto, in the
instrumental chorale of the *Mahagonny Songspiel* (and the baleful light it
sheds on the apparent blasphemy of 'Gott in Mahagonny'), in the
Bachian imagery of parts of the *Berlin Requiem*, and even in the amazingly
affectionate irony which distinguishes his settings of real or parodied
Salvation Army texts in *Happy End*. But essentially it is in the
etymological rather than the theological sense that Weill remained to the
end of his life a 'religious' artist. The binding obligation of man to his
fellow men and to society as a whole is implied by the title and

inspiration of his most ambitious stage work, the three-act opera *Die Bürgschaft*; and it is the fundamental theme of all his major works and many of his lesser ones. It is even present in works such as *Happy End* or *One Touch of Venus* which purport to be 'mere' entertainments.

Ten years ago I suggested that we should not worry ourselves about a precise evaluation of Weill's importance or lack of it. Too much had already been spoken and written about Weill while so much of the music was still waiting to be heard again. But without idly pleading the excuse that time alone will tell – for time alone does not tell anything other than the appalling lateness of the hour – I also suggested that we should at least remember with respect a human being whose qualities are reflected in his art: a just, loyal, and friendly man, who knew his own worth and yet dissociated himself from the contemporary cult of genius by preserving – as far as his characteristic irony allowed – a deceptively mild and self-effacing exterior in his everyday encounters; a man for whom democracy was a fundamental and humane truth which should inform every level of activity; a man profoundly aware of the tragedies and follies of his time, but one whose laughter could so convulse him – as he tried to mop away the tears – that it became quite noiseless; a man who was much loved.

Introduction:
Report to the Academy of Arts, West Berlin

Alles was ist, ist Beginnen
und verliert sich noch hinter die Zeit –

Georg Kaiser: *Der Silbersee*

The long and sometimes troubled history of the present volume begins, appropriately enough, with an anomaly: the first critical event was not the death of Weill in April 1950 but that of Arnold Schoenberg fifteen months later.

During the summer of 1956 the distinguished composer and teacher Boris Blacher visited the Schoenberg family's home in Los Angeles. On his return to West Berlin he submitted a report to the Academy of Arts, of which he was then Vice-President. His recommendation that the Academy commission a catalogue of the Schoenberg legacy from Josef Rufer – a member of Schoenberg's Masterclass at the Academy in the pre-Hitler years, and now one of West Berlin's leading music critics – was enthusiastically accepted.

Professor Rufer began his work at the Schoenberg house in the late spring of 1957, and soon discovered that Schoenberg had taken such meticulous care of his autographs that a catalogue of the legacy would not fall far short of a complete Schoenberg catalogue. The Academy's commission was accordingly enlarged in order to enable Rufer to include the few works whose autographs were in other collections. His task of 'gathering together' the manuscripts as well as the 'inspection and cataloguing' of them now acquired a significance that was to have manifold implications for my own work.

It so happened that my first visit to Berlin was in the period immediately following Professor Rufer's return from Los Angeles. The circumstances in which I learned of his project were intimately involved with those attending the genesis of the present volume, and cannot be fully explained without some reference to the personal background.

I first encountered Schoenberg's music as a schoolboy in 1948, when I attended a concert performance of *Pierrot lunaire* (directed from the piano by Peter Stadlen), and became the proud owner of copies of the opus 11 piano pieces and a two-piano reduction of the Piano Concerto. That same year I called on Schoenberg's Spanish-born pupil Roberto Gerhard in his Cambridge house. Somewhere at the back of my mind was the hope that I might find a way of studying composition with him privately during the three years I was due to spend at Cambridge University. But instead – and this was a privilege for which gratitude, however great, would on its own be inadequate – I became, step by informal step, a regular if intermittent member of the Gerhard household, for many more years than three.

At the end of my first Cambridge year I attended the 1951 ISCM Festival in Frankfurt, partly out of general interest, but chiefly in order to hear Gerhard's opera *The Duenna* and the world premiere of Schoenberg's *The Dance Around the Golden Calf*. The latter event brought me to Darmstadt, where the fourth in the series of 'Ferienkurse für Neue Musik' (holiday courses in New Music) was concurrently taking place. The experience was overwhelming.

My firm resolve to return to the Darmstadt Summer School was fulfilled for the first time in 1953. In the two years that had elapsed since the premiere of *The Dance Around the Golden Calf* and the death of its composer, much had changed at Darmstadt: a new generation of composers had emerged under the joint leadership of Boulez, Stockhausen, and Nono, and was in effect proceeding from Adorno's conclusions in his *Philosophy of New Music* (1949) – on the one hand the unqualified rejection of Stravinskian and Hindemithian neo-classicism, on the other the identification of Webern as the key figure for the future of serial music, and the consequent relegation of Schoenberg's twelve-note serial work to a shelf some way above that to which the neo-classical Stravinsky had been consigned, yet structurally related to it.

I returned to Darmstadt in 1954, and found it harder than ever to reconcile the school's dogmatic objections to much that Schoenberg and all that Stravinsky had achieved after the early 1920s with what I heard and was moved by in both composers, throughout their work, irrespective of date, style, or method. I was, however, much consoled by the paradoxical phenomenon of Olivier Messiaen, who was highly esteemed in Darmstadt even though his music was as unthinkable from the standpoint of the Second Viennese School – Webern especially – as it was outrageous from that of Stravinsky. Here, it seemed, was the multiple challenge I had been looking for: the very apotheosis of the unacceptable. During the year 1954–5 I steeped myself in Messiaen's music, and published three long articles on it. The last article stopped at the *Livre d'orgue* of 1951; and it was just there that the constructivist furies Messiaen himself had helped unleash in the immediate aftermath of war were now (or so I felt) threatening to turn on his own intuitive sources of invention. But no representative significance that could be attached to

Messiaen's creative predicament – peculiar to him as it was – could account for the sense of unease with which, in 1955, I reached the end of my third spell at Darmstadt. Despite the continuing influence of such proponents of Schoenberg as Rufer, Steuermann, and Kolisch, it was by now clear that with Schoenberg's death a force had gone from composition – if not from the teaching of it – that was unlikely to be replaced.

In 1956 I went to Venice instead of Darmstadt, and during the return journey decided to write a book on the music of Weill, a composer at the furthest conceivable remove from the ethos and preoccupations of Darmstadt (and indeed of Gerhard, though his own heretical position *vis-à-vis* the Second Viennese School ensured some measure of sympathy for other heresies). In so far as I could comprehend my own interest in Weill at that stage, it was strictly musical; I knew next to nothing of the content of his stage works apart from *Die Dreigroschenoper*, and had no ideological predisposition towards it. What drew me to Weill's music at that time (and still does) was the unique nature of its compositional and idiomatic tensions. These, it seemed to me (and again my present view is fundamentally unchanged), had a unique bearing on the modernist movement in music, and were not seriously discussible except in relation to the consequences of Schoenberg on the one hand and Stravinsky on the other. The fact that Weill was manifestly not a 'great' composer in Schoenberg's sense (or, for that matter, in Stravinsky's rather different one) did not persuade me, on the evidence of what I already knew of his music, that he was necessarily of minor or peripheral significance.

From London's lending libraries and from Universal Edition's hire library I collected every available example of Weill's music. After studying it at the piano for several weeks I repaired to the British Museum's music section, where the assistant librarian was O. W. Neighbour, a noted writer on music and a key figure in post-war Schoenberg studies in England. The help and encouragement I received from him at that stage – and have continued to receive until this day – were of inestimable value.

It was in the British Museum that I first read Weill's three-act opera *Die Bürgschaft*. Plainly a work of major importance, yet almost unmentioned in the standard reference books, it confirmed my impression that nothing less than a book would suffice for any critical study of Weill's music, and that if such a book was to remain within manageable proportions, the biographical matter should be kept to a bare minimum, and was in any case likely to be less helpful than a view of the cultural and political background. By the all-too-simple device of multiplying the length of the Messiaen articles and the time spent on them by a factor of four, I estimated that a book of 120,000 words would take me approximately eighteen months.

In the autumn of 1956 I wrote to Lotte Lenya outlining my project and seeking her approval. Her friendly reply was followed by a long and enthusiastic letter from her husband, the American writer and editor

George Davis, offering assistance of a kind I had not dreamed of. For some while, Davis told me, he and Lenya had been collecting material for a biography of Weill. They now felt that the musical and critical questions which interested me were more urgent, and had therefore decided to renounce their project and offer me the material they had already collected, together with free access to the papers and manuscripts in Brook House, the converted farmhouse in Rockland County (NY) which Weill had bought in 1941 and which had been Lenya's home since his death. Warmly inviting me to come to Brook House at the earliest opportunity, George Davis expressed the hope that we would be able to arrange a preliminary meeting during their forthcoming visit to Germany, where Lenya had various important engagements (including supervision of, and participation in, the complete recording of the *Dreigroschenoper* score). Further letters, in the same extraordinarily friendly vein, followed from Hamburg.

On reading a press report to the effect that one of the main events at the Berliner Festwochen in September 1957 would be a production of *Die Bürgschaft* by Carl Ebert – who had directed the original production in 1932 – I decided to attend, and wrote at once to George Davis. To my delight he replied that he and Lenya would be there too.

Within hours of my first meeting with them, we together attended a reception given by the Festwochen and the Academy of Arts, West Berlin, in the foyer of the Städtische Oper. Professor Rufer, who was one of the guests of honour, was officially welcomed back from the USA by Freiherr von Buttlar, the Secretary of the Academy. During the subsequent interchanges I was greeted by Blacher, to whom Lenya and George Davis had previously mentioned my project. Declaring that the project already implied the 'inspection' and 'gathering together' of Weill's manuscripts, Blacher introduced me to von Buttlar, and without further ado proposed that the Academy commission from me a companion volume to Rufer's. After all, he pointed out, Weill had for three years been a member of Busoni's Masterclass at the Academy – the one Schoenberg had taken over after Busoni's death – and that would provide at least a formal reason for the Academy to interest itself in Weill's artistic legacy.

Overwhelmed by the friendliness and alacrity of Blacher's initiative, I did not perhaps fully appreciate at that stage the sheer boldness of it. Whereas Schoenberg was, by general consent, a towering figure in twentieth-century music, Weill was then widely regarded as, at best, a minor figure redeemed from insignificance only through his brief collaboration with Brecht, at worst, a traitor to the traditions and standards for which Schoenberg had so tenaciously fought. But Blacher – like Karl-Amadeus Hartmann and other leading musical representatives of the 'inner emigration' – had from the beginning recognized Weill as a pathfinder. His gratitude for what that path had signified to him and to some of his fellow composers amid the darkness of the Third Reich, and his memory of the subversive liberties and illegal escapes it had made possible, lent to his advocacy of the Weill project an intensity and an urgency that proved as persuasive as he had hoped. In April 1958 the Music Department and the Senate of the Academy of Arts generously agreed to commission from me a 'Weill bibliography', and to subsidize the necessary journey to America.

At this early and apparently propitious stage the double project had already suffered its first reverse. The death of George Davis in November 1957 was an irreparable loss for Lenya, for his friends, and for all who had recognized the quality of his devotion to Weill's cause. In the few brief weeks of our acquaintance I had come to regard him as the surest guarantee of my ability to fulfil the Academy's commission.

George Davis was the strategist of the so-called 'Weill renaissance' of the 1950s. It was he who convinced the ever-sceptical Lenya that her own contribution as singing actress was indispensable; he who coaxed her back to Europe and into recording studios; and he above all who sensed that an international career would enable her to fulfil, in a manner Weill himself had not foreseen and with an efficacy he could hardly have dared hope for, the responsibilities vested in her as sole executrix of the Weill Estate.

The problem, as George Davis recognized, was global. Weill's death at the age of 50 might not have had the same kind of implications as Mahler's or Berg's at a similarly early age, yet there was a more than merely symbolic significance in the fact that it occurred exactly midway in our century, at a time when Weill's reputation was itself divided in two by the Atlantic Ocean and the Second World War. While the America of 1950 saw him only as a successful and influential Broadway composer, Europe remained ignorant of his American achievements and had forgotten most of his European ones apart from the legendary *Threepenny Opera*.

In 1956 Lenya achieved a breakthrough for Weill and for herself with a commercial recording – her first since the war – devoted to Weill's Berlin theatre songs. Its international success paved the way for the series of recordings that followed; and already there was talk of a 'Weill renaissance'.

Meanwhile Lenya and George Davis had been collecting material for their projected Weill biography, and had started to set in order the papers and manuscripts stored at Brook House. In collaboration with the composer–pianist Marga Richter and the recording-executive Edward Cole, Lenya had examined, and begun to list, most of the musical manuscripts in the legacy. Their work proved an invaluable preliminary to my own.

In the early summer of 1958 I arrived at Brook House. One of my fellow guests was Margarethe Kaiser, the widow of the playwright. Her skill in deciphering German script, and her recollections of the decisive years in which Weill and Kaiser had worked together, were to stand me in good stead.

A cursory inspection of the manuscripts was enough to define a fundamental difference between my task and Professor Rufer's. Whereas Schoenberg had, throughout his relatively long life, prepared for posterity and the honour he was sure it would accord him, Weill, in those middle years that turned out to be his last ones, had professed to scorn posterity, and as a young man had already consciously dissociated himself from romantic notions of the composer as hero, priest, or seer. To design his own monuments and pave the way for future processions of researchers and biographers was wholly foreign to his nature, and to everything he stood for as an American popular composer. It was typical that when Lenya, towards the end of his life, presented him with handsomely bound copies of all the scores published by Universal Edition in Vienna – only a few of which he had brought from Europe or bothered to replace in America – he seemed, according to her account, more embarrassed than gratified. Withdrawal not merely from Europe but from his own European past had become one of the essential conditions of his new identity. In that sense as in others he was profoundly different from Schoenberg, and indeed from Brecht – both of whom, in the course of their circuitous emigrations, had clung tenaciously to whatever manuscripts they could save, as if every line bore witness to the integrity of their work.

There was another difference. Whereas all the completed works of Schoenberg's maturity had been published during his lifetime, and had immediately attracted critical and scholarly attention, the greater part of Weill's output – including almost all the full scores – had remained inaccessible to researchers and general public alike. Critical opinion was therefore uninformed by any sense of what the total *oeuvre* amounted to, let alone what the individual works consisted of.

A list of Weill's known compositions, whether extant or not, was therefore my first priority. George Davis and his assistants had already assembled the various incomplete and inaccurate lists published in American, British, and German reference books. To these had been added further lists from ASCAP and GEMA (respectively the American and the German performing-right societies); from Universal Edition in Vienna, with whom Weill had an exclusive agreement during the years 1924–33; from Heugel et Cie in Paris, who were his publishers from 1934 to 1937; and lastly from Chappell, the Anglo-American publisher of musicals and popular songs with whom Weill was associated from 1937 until his death.

By means of a master list assembled from these sources it was possible to estimate the approximate extent of the gaps in the holograph collection at Brook House, except with regard to the pre-1921 works, of which there was not even a fragmentary list. No works from this period were in the legacy itself, but a few early songs had subsequently been given to Lenya by Weill's relatives, and a copy of the Cello Sonata had been lent by his pupil Peter Bing. Of the works assigned to Universal Edition during the period of the General Agreement with Weill there were no final manuscripts in the legacy and only a handful of sketches and drafts. Like most other publishers during the inter-war period – when hand-copying had suddenly become much more costly and cheap methods of reprography had yet to be invented – Universal Edition had acquired the definitive holographs under the terms of each individual assignment. According to Lenya's information, most of these had survived the war and were safely stored in the UE archives (from which more than one was later to emerge as part of the rental material). There was no reason to suppose that any of the missing sketches were also there.

Apart from a handful of songs apparently given to Lenya and George Davis by Weill's relatives, there were no juvenilia. According to Weill's sister Ruth a packing case containing, among other things, some of Weill's early manuscripts had been accidentally dropped overboard when the ship that brought his parents to Palestine in 1935 was being unloaded. A graver loss – assuming it was not part of the same one – became apparent on my first inspection of the legacy: all the unpublished works from the period 1921–33 were missing, apart from *Die sieben Todsünden*, which Weill himself had taken unusual care of, and the First Symphony, which had been discovered after his death in circumstances that seemed to shed some light on the disappearance of the remainder.

The only known authority on the disappearance was the German critic and musicologist Herbert Fleischer, whom I met for the first and only time during my September 1957 visit to Berlin. His name was already familiar to me as the author of a Stravinsky monograph published in 1929. In 1932 he had been commissioned to write a companion volume on Weill. To his great credit – given the assumptions about Weill's early development which were current at that time and are not unheard of even today – he decided to begin his researches by studying all the early unpublished works that Weill considered significant. With whatever qualms – perhaps with none, for he was apt to be careless in such matters – Weill lent Fleischer a considerable quantity of unique manuscripts.

Shortly before the Nazi seizure of power, Fleischer took the manuscripts to Italy, with the intention of continuing his work there. Some progress was made while he was staying at a hospice run by German-speaking nuns; but before long he decided – perhaps because times were unpropitious – that he had no further need of the manuscripts. He therefore parcelled them up and posted them to Berlin – not however to

Weill's home address, but to the German branch of Universal Edition, which at that time was managed by the young Alfred Schlee.

The fate of that parcel and its contents remains a matter for speculation (and is considered in the final section of this volume). But the sequel to Fleischer's account has some bearing on it. While holidaying in Italy in 1954 he revisited his pre-war refuge, and learned that for more than twenty years the nuns had been waiting to return to him a precious manuscript which he had left behind and which – shorn of its incriminating title page and epigraph – they had hidden away during the German occupation. It was the autograph full score of Weill's First Symphony – in Fleischer's view the most interesting of the scores he had taken to Italy. Fleischer brought the score back to Berlin, and on Lenya's next visit had the great satisfaction of handing it to her personally.

Had I been looking for some guarantee of the accuracy of Fleischer's recollections, I would have found it in the epilogue of his account to me: Fleischer recalled that when he met Weill in Rome in December 1933 and told him of the parcel he had sent to him care of Universal Edition's Berlin office, Weill expressed no surprise at its disappearance, and seemed unconcerned about it.

The further my researches took me, the more Weill's reaction struck me as characteristic. For it was at the end of 1933 that events finally forced him to adjust to the idea that a return to Germany – where his parents and closest relatives were still living – might not be feasible in the foreseeable future. Within a year, not only the hope of a return but even the wish for one seem to have vanished. Thus the parcel could well have symbolized a past that he was already beginning to bury. Yet several more years elapsed before Weill finally succeeded in suppressing the last trace of any conscious preoccupation with his old life and work in Germany. To that gradual and painful process the impoverished European section of the legacy bore silent witness.

By the time I left Brook House in the late summer of 1958 I had drafted the American section of the catalogue, and also the sequence of critical chapters that dealt with the Broadway works one by one. Thus the processes of 'inspection and gathering together' had already become inseparably intertwined with those of criticism and background research. With regard to the American period, the correspondence files and press cuttings in Brook House had provided almost everything I needed at this stage, and the rest was gleaned from publishers and libraries in New York and from a brief sortie to the West Coast. With the European period, however, I could make no start until I had been to Universal Edition in Vienna.

My first visit to Vienna was a turning point. By some miracle of ingenuity coupled with good fortune, Universal Edition had rescued from the twin perils of Nazism and war the holograph final scores of all but one of the works Weill assigned to them. My hopes of finding some trace of Fleischer's precious parcel were neither fulfilled nor immediately extinguished, for it was clear that several more years might yet pass before the full extent of what had been stored away during the war became known. During one of the earliest of my innumerable visits to UE's headquarters there was a knock at the door of the room in which I was working and one of my helpers entered in triumph, bearing a vast load: file upon dusty file of correspondence between Weill and Universal Edition from the years 1924–37.

For the catalogue, the discovery had far-reaching implications. Even greater, and more immediate, was its effect on my plans for the biographical sections of the main book. These, indeed, were trans-formed; for I now had the means of interspersing the critical studies of each work or group of works with a narrative drawn from, and quoting extensively from, Weill's articles and correspondence throughout his entire career. The fact that the UE correspondence was exclusively concerned with Weill's professional life and work was, for my purposes, ideal. I had already decided that his personal life was an area properly left to professional biographers, except in so far as it was directly and demonstrably relevant to musico-critical questions. To judge from my first reading of the personal correspondence in Brook House, most of the private matters were indeed relatively trivial, and the remainder unlikely to occupy as much of my attention as the social and political context of Weill's work plainly should.

It was during my second visit to America, in the winter of 1959–60, that the impertinence of viewing the Broadway musicals from a traditional European standpoint began to dawn on me. In bibliography as in criticism, a method appropriate to *Die Bürgschaft*, for instance, could hardly serve the interests of, say, *Street Scene*. The difference of kind had somehow to be objectively recorded – not an easy task, but one that my first draft for the catalogue had shirked altogether. To pretend that the evolution of a Broadway score follows essentially the same self-critical route as that of a work in the 'classical' tradition is to ignore the real objectives of such a score and to misrepresent the grounds on which, at every compositional stage, ideas might be discarded or replaced.

Prepared though he was by his working experience of commercial theatre in Berlin, in Paris and in London, it was on Broadway that Weill finally renounced the vestiges of that magisterial authority which Wagner had boldly snatched from Beethoven and bequeathed to future generations of German stage composers, however ungrateful to him they might otherwise profess to be. Though I was still some way from comprehending those respects in which Weill remained none the less a master, or even acquired new mastery, I recognized that nothing I had written about the Broadway works was usable, and that the catalogue should be either greatly expanded or drastically compressed.

At this point, my work on the catalogue was overtaken by events, with results that had not been foreseen by the Academy's commission, but were not in principle alien to it. In Weill's case – to a far greater extent than in Schoenberg's – the task of 'gathering together' the artistic legacy had practical implications as well as scholarly ones: it anticipated the performance of major works which for one reason or another had previously been unperformable or else had been available only in versions inconsistent with the composer's verifiable intentions. These practical consequences were already implicit in a discussion – the first of many – which I had in 1959 with Harry Buckwitz, the then Generalinten-dant of the Frankfurt theatres and opera house. To Buckwitz's question as to the most suitable companion piece for the post-war stage premiere of *Die sieben Todsünden* I had replied that in theory the ideal choice was the ballet-opera *Royal Palace*, but the full scores and orchestral parts had been lost, and a new orchestration could not be managed in the time available. The best alternative, we agreed, was the Weill–Kaiser double bill – the only stage works from Weill's German period that presented no major editorial problem.

In the summer of 1960 Lenya sang and acted the role of Anna in the Frankfurt production of *Die sieben Todsünden*, an event sufficiently compelling to induce an otherwise reluctant public to sit through the two Kaiser operas and accord them a polite if unenthusiastic welcome.* During the following season I collaborated with the newly founded opera studio in Gelsenkirchen – today famous as the Musiktheater im Revier – on the first production since the 1927 premiere of the original version of the *Mahagonny-Songspiel*. The restoration of this version was a direct result of my work on the Academy's catalogue; and the Gelsenkirchen production of March 1961 was the very first step towards the present-day acceptance of the work as one of the classics of twentieth-century musical theatre. Meanwhile T. W. Adorno's 30-year-old thesis about the 3-act *Mahagonny* opera had at last been allowed to impinge on the consciousness of the Darmstadt Ferienkurse für Neue Musik. In 1957, Harro Dicks and the Landestheater in Darmstadt had followed their earlier revivals of Honegger's *Antigone* and Křenek's *Das Leben des Orestes* with the first stage production of *Aufstieg und Fall der Stadt Mahagonny* in any country since 1931. At the premiere, Lenya and George Davis were introduced to Wolfgang Steinecke, the director of the Ferienkurse (and of its parent body the Kranichsteiner Musikinstitut). The genuineness of Steinecke's concern for the fortunes of Weill's music in Germany was to be demonstrated on various occasions, but never more provocatively than in 1959, when he

---

* *Der Zar lässt sich photographieren* was later to succeed, unequivocally, in Kassel and elsewhere, but *Der Protagonist* remained an unloved partner until John Eaton's impassioned production of the double bill for the Camden Festival in March 1986.

arranged to integrate one of the Landestheater's *Mahagonny* performances with that year's Ferienkurse für Neue Musik.

While the relatively modest Harro Dicks production of 1957 was the direct precursor of the much more elaborate affair staged at the Hamburg Staatsoper in 1961 by Egon Monk, and hence of the entire *Mahagonny* boom in Germany during the 1960s, Carl Ebert's act of faith in *Die Bürgschaft*, which was almost exactly contemporary with the Dicks *Mahagonny*, remained without issue. One of Ebert's concerns had been to make amends for the injustice that had been done to the work within a year of its first and much acclaimed performance (see p. 235). But the political events that had precluded the revival planned for the 1932–3 season had also prevented Weill from carrying out the extensive revision that he and his co-librettist and stage designer Caspar Neher had decided was essential in the interests of greater clarity and cogency. The composition of a crucially important new scene for the second act, and a handful of incidental improvements, were all Weill had time for before the Nazi seizure of power.

For the 1957 production Ebert and his colleagues made a revision of their own, changing or discarding elements in the work that they felt to be out of keeping with the very different circumstances and mood of Adenauer's Germany. Predictably, the confusions that resulted were greater than any in the original work, while the musical losses – including the whole of the new scene – were severe. At a meeting with Neher and Lenya in Zurich some months later, I suggested that *Die Bürgschaft* was in no need of updating, and that if any posthumous revision was feasible, it could only be on the basis of what was implicit in the structure and expressive content of the music; for it was there that Weill, with an almost Handelian instinct for the strengths and weaknesses of the libretto, had left the clues that might lead to a solution of the dramaturgic problems.

Neher readily agreed that the 1957 version was misguided in its attempt to circumvent the formal and philosophical problems by introducing *Singspiel*-like structures that were foreign to the nature of the work. To my astonishment he not only accepted my alternative proposal, but invited me to carry it out, with whatever assistance from him I might need. Without pausing to consider the long-term implications, but stressing the obvious fact that my grasp of German was inadequate to the task of fitting new words to existing music, I joyfully accepted.

Prior commitments to the catalogue and to the critical biography allowed for little progress with the *Bürgschaft* project during the next two years. Before I had reached any conclusion substantial enough to warrant another meeting, Neher fell ill, and was unable to continue our correspondence. In June 1962 he died.

Whether the *Bürgschaft* project could now survive was a question that I fortunately had no time to consider, for it was at this very moment that I became involved in preparations for the first-ever production of the

Mahagonny opera by a non-German company. The young English director Michael Geliot and the designer Ralph Koltai had won Lenya's support for a London production early in 1963, to be conducted by Colin Davis and mounted by the Sadler's Wells Opera (now the English National Opera).

It was a much more provocative undertaking than any of us realized at the time. In the ever-recurring Grand Prix of twentieth-century music, the United Kingdom has shown a remarkable propensity for falling so far behind on the first laps that for a while it can enjoy the illusion of leading its competitors on the second. Nowhere outside Hitler's Germany had Weill been held in such disfavour as in the United Kingdom during the inter-war years; and the after-effects of that were still discernible in the 1950s. Indeed, the Sadler's Wells *Mahagonny* would have been inconceivable but for the cultural changes that began to make themselves felt during the latter half of that decade. As far as musical life was concerned those changes were confirmed by the appointment in 1960 of William Glock as Head of Music at the BBC. Paradoxically, Weill was benefiting from the same momentum that allowed a new generation of British listeners to become acquainted with the music of the Second Viennese School and the Darmstadt school.

The Wells *Mahagonny* was, however, more than a local phenomenon. For the first time for more than thirty years the work was being staged on the understanding that the fate of the production would depend on the strength of its musical convictions, and that there was no hope of doing justice to the libretto on any other basis. Perhaps only in England and only at that particular juncture could a truth so obviously fundamental to the nature of the work and yet so heretical in relation to its composer's current reputation have emerged into the light of day, have survived throughout the rehearsal period, and have finally triumphed. With the press and with the public the production was a major success.

Meanwhile the Hamburg Staatsoper had mounted Germany's first major post-war production of *Mahagonny* on the different if not opposite understanding that the first duty was to Brecht and specifically to the famous Notes on the work that Brecht and Peter Suhrkamp had published some while after the world premiere. It was characteristic of the profound difference between the British approach and the German one that Davis and his associates were from the start keenly interested in the musical and textual revisions undertaken by Weill and Brecht subsequent to the publication of the work in 1930, whereas the Hamburg authorities had politely returned the marked and annotated score I had offered them, and affirmed that the 1930 score, together with Brecht's *Versuche* edition of the text, was their sovereign authority. While working with Michael Geliot on the English singing translation I was able to discuss with him and with Colin Davis each and every revision that I had so far been able to verify in the course of my researches. All were adopted in the Wells production; some in the subsequent production at La Scala.

But for my practical experience with *Mahagonny* I would not perhaps have been tempted back to *Die Bürgschaft*. But the exhortations of Ernst Hartmann – a director of Universal Edition in Vienna, and a devoted admirer of the work – were, in the circumstances, persuasive. I returned to the work towards the end of 1963, examined the score and the chapter I had written about it, and roughed out in English a revision of the libretto that fulfilled, to the best of my ability, the dramaturgic and philosophical aims I had discussed with Neher. I then collaborated with Hugo F. Garten – an eminent Germanist who as a young man had been a member of Georg Kaiser's Berlin circle – on the much more complex task of integrating a German version with the existing score and with one supplementary passage drawn from the pencil draft in the legacy. After some eighteen months of intermittent but intensive work we had completed the task as best we could, but remained unsatisfied. Although the sad demise of Ernst Hartmann in 1965 had removed from the leadership of Universal Edition the chief advocate of our work, it was not responsible for my decision to shelve the project. The considerations that had determined that decision were identical with those that convinced me of a need to rethink almost everything I had written about Weill, and meanwhile redirect my efforts on behalf of his work.

By the mid-1960s European interest in Weill's music was sharply declining. With Lenya now concentrating her attention on the USA – where the post-Presley revolution in popular music was threatening the musical and other assumptions on which Weill and his Broadway contemporaries had proceeded in the USA – the impulse she had lent the Weill 'renaissance' in Europe ten years before was no longer decisive. Throughout the same period Brecht's posthumous reputation (like the literature that supported or fed on it) had grown prodigiously, while that of Kaiser and of Weill's other collaborators remained static or else declined along with his own. After the initial surge of interest in Weill for his own sake (or, quite legitimately, for Lenya's) the tendency to see him as one of Brecht's 'little lieutenants' had become ever more pronounced, and the difficulty of promoting any work that did not involve Brecht had correspondingly increased.

The labour-saving notion that Weill's characteristic works were as few in number as they were restricted in range had first achieved currency during the 1950s, when the marketing of Lenya's recordings was strongly influenced by the manner in which certain views of pre-Hitler Berlin had captured the popular imagination during that increasingly prosperous decade. But during and after the politico-cultural upheavals of the late 1960s a rebellious new generation – nurtured on Marcuse and Adorno, Chomsky and Lévi-Strauss – was disinclined to accept the marketing men's stressedly apolitical appeals to collective nostalgia, and rightly suspicious of all that pertained to the 'legend' of Berlin. Like their forebears in Germany after the Wall Street Crash and in America in the mid-1930s, the New Left joined with the old avant-garde and discovered in the music of Hanns Eisler a significance they missed in Weill.

The exercise of continuing to think about Weill in the context of the great and the lesser turbulences of the late 1960s should have been salutary. But although contemporary Vietnam and Czechoslovakia had thrown into relief certain aspects of, for instance, *Die Bürgschaft* and the Second Symphony that ten years before had seemed of purely historical interest, and although the closing scene of the *Mahagonny* opera was repeatedly being re-enacted on the campuses and streets of the western world, the spirit of the time seemed profoundly inimical to the publication of what I had so far written about Weill, and indeed to the still unattained academic objectives of the catalogue – whose much revised typescript had by now grown to vast proportions.

With Lenya's concurrence I resolved in 1967 to concentrate for a while on helping to enlarge the general view of Weill by promoting performances, recordings, and editions of works that had hitherto been partially or wholly obscured. In the period 1967–71 I prepared for Universal Edition a revised and annotated vocal score of the *Mahagonny* opera and a performing edition of *Das Berliner Requiem*; for Schott–Mainz – where Ken W. Bartlett proved a stalwart friend of Weill's music – I edited the two symphonies and restored the original version of *Die sieben Todsünden*, of which Colin Davis (with Evelyn Lear as soloist) conducted the first post-war performance at a Henry Wood Promenade Concert in 1968.

Thanks to William Glock, the Second Symphony was included in another Henry Wood Concert that same season; and together with the First it had already been recorded by the BBC Symphony Orchestra under Gary Bertini and issued in the Gulbenkian Foundation's *Music Today* series (of which I was then programme director). Tactically the emergence of the symphonies at this stage in Weill's fortunes was crucial, for each work in its different way cracked open the defence systems that had surrounded received opinion about his music – the Second taking by surprise whatever its brave but ill-equipped predecessor had failed to take by storm. Even the progressivist critics who predictably complained that the Weill of the Second Symphony had somehow betrayed the early promise of the First (and indeed was already heading for a 'commercial' future) failed to notice that they had for the first time acknowledged that the pre-Brecht Weill had promised anything at all.

The first-fruits of promoting the 'symphonic' Weill appeared as early as 1970, when the European Broadcasting Union accepted a proposal from Südwestfunk (South-West German Radio, Baden-Baden) for a worldwide relay of a programme of Weill's concert works, conducted by Ernest Bour and built around the Concerto for Violin and Wind Instruments. In response to a request from Hans Keller, who was then Chairman of the EBU's music section, I suggested a three-part programme in which the Concerto would be followed by the Second Symphony and preceded by the Divertimento, op. 5, or rather – since the holograph orchestral score of the Divertimento had been in the ill-fated Fleischer parcel – by my proposed reconstruction of that work based on the substantial fragments in the Weill legacy. (A similar reconstruction of the *Sinfonia Sacra* was already being undertaken by John Ogdon, but not yet in an orchestral form.)

The EBU accepted both proposals and commissioned from me a new score of the Divertimento – a task on which I collaborated with the British composer Christopher Shaw. For the first time, the Academy's concept of 'gathering together' had acquired a strictly practical and creative function. In its progress from the theocentric world of the Divertimento through the quasi-agnostic abstractions of the Concerto to the demonstrably human-istic concerns of the Second Symphony, the EBU programme – first broadcast in January 1972 – conveyed a fundamental yet unfamiliar truth about Weill's development, and did so in the directest possible way. If there were listeners who heard in the Divertimento a symphonic and polyphonic prefiguration of the theatrical and homophonic *Mahagonny-Songspiel*, theirs was an experience that had a profound bearing on the course Weill took in Europe from 1921 onwards.

It was a course whose decisiveness is not readily apparent at short range. Weill's changes of tack from work to work are an exact projection of those within the works, and show consummate skill and daring in the art of sailing against the wind – technically, aesthetically, and culturally. With Weill, the roles of memory and foresight and the use of accumulated experience in response to new information are always intensely idiosyn-cratic. (The holographs considered in the present volume contain some vital clues.) While there are few kinds of musical folly that have not been falsely attributed to Weill by the foolish, his intelligence is of such a rare order that it is generally underestimated by intelligent musicians of other sorts, and even, in its American manifestations, overlooked altogether.

The symphony that in effect closed Weill's career as a self-aware German composer was precisely complementary to the one that stood at its threshold. Invisible though that symmetry was to Weill's contempor-aries, it derives its sense from impulses and tensions that were implicit in his early stage works and became manifest as soon as he evolved his own kind of tonality and associated it with closed forms. From the *Mahagonny-Songspiel* to *Die sieben Todsünden*, every dramatic score strives to reconcile the demands of the theatre with a calculated and in some cases ostentatious tendency towards the conditions of the concert hall. Music stripped of decor but boasting its own incomparably suggestive lighting schemes, it takes issue with all its texts and dramatic pretexts, and asks for little more than a bare stage, sympathetic performances, and an attentive public; and yet it is the music of a composer more intimately, multi-fariously, and significantly involved with the theatre than any other of his generation.

With the unfinished and, for the time being, unfinishable *Bürgschaft* project still looming in the background, I was conscious of a simpler obligation towards *Royal Palace*, the earliest casualty among Weill's stage works and the only one that was structurally intact yet, for practical purposes, unperformable. After a vain attempt to interest a celebrated team of duo pianists in arranging a suite from the dance episodes, I suggested to Gunther Schuller that he consider an orchestral suite, perhaps with optional chorus. He, however, was so impressed by the vocal score that he proposed arranging all but the purely operatic sections as a choral and orchestral dance suite, and including it in a programme he was to conduct for the San Francisco Opera in 1967. It was a happy idea: his orchestration was brilliant and the so-called 'dance fantasy' was well received.

Three years were to pass before I found a further opening for *Royal Palace*. Meanwhile I had become involved, willy-nilly, in a much more complex theatre venture initiated by Josef Heinzelmann, a freelance *régisseur*, writer, and broadcaster, with a special interest in Offenbach and Weill. Among his current responsibilities was the German promotion of Heugel's stage catalogue, in which *Der Kuhhandel*, an operetta by Weill with original German libretto by Robert Vambery, had been slumbering since the disastrous premiere in 1935 of an English adaptation entitled *A Kingdom for a Cow*. Heinzelmann now informed me that the city theatre in Dortmund was planning to present the German premiere, and had invited him to direct it.

It was not, at that particular juncture, the most welcome of news: *Der Kuhhandel* was musically unfinished, and *A Kingdom for a Cow* a makeshift that had very properly been shelved. On hearing of the Dortmund plan, Lenya asked me to prepare a performing version of the *Kuhhandel* score, and to collaborate with Heinzelmann, Vambery and Dortmund on the consequent – or associated – textual revisions. Vambery, whose home was in California, was not able to join our preliminary discussions, but seemed content to await developments. Work on the musical structure and then on the text occupied us for many months. Finally we were joined by Christopher Shaw, who volunteered to orchestrate those passages that Weill had left in voice and piano score.

With the completion of Shaw's masterly orchestration in March 1970 the performing version of *Der Kuhhandel* was ready for production – or rather, it would have been if Vambery had not rejected it out of hand, and substituted a version of his own that cleverly ignored all the musical problems, shifted the tendency of the satire in the opposite direction, removed from its American location the nefarious armaments firm that precipitates the entire action, and introduced to the grand finale some pronouncements that any present-day White House spokesman with a bent for satire would be proud to lend his name to. Stoutly maintaining that his version corresponded precisely to Weill's mature intentions,

Vambery refused to contemplate any alternative. On every ground – musical and dramatic, ethical and ideological – the disagreement was complete. Reluctantly, Dortmund cancelled its production.

Given the insecure status of Weill's music in Germany in those years, the cancellation was preferable to an ill-starred production. Nevertheless, I had lost several months that could have been spent on stage works of more central and urgent importance – for instance *Der Silbersee*, an indispensable link between the '*Stücke mit Musik*' and the operas. It had not been performed in its original orchestration since 1933.

As soon as the dust from *Der Kuhhandel* had begun to settle I conferred with Jo Elsendoorn, who had succeeded Peter Diamand as Director of the Holland Festival. He was much attracted by the idea of a concert performance of the *Silbersee* music at the 1971 Festival, and recommended it to the Residentie orchestra in The Hague.

The Hague orchestra rightly prided itself on its success in finding a new public for its adventurous and attractive programmes. In responding to the socio-political changes of the late 1960s, it had profited greatly from its association with Bruno Maderna. Since the time of our first encounter in Darmstadt, Maderna had emerged as one of Weill's few champions among the post-war avant-garde; and from a recent conversation I knew him to be keenly interested in *Der Silbersee*. But since the Holland Festival dates available to the Residentie orchestra were not convenient for him, he could only lend his moral support to the enterprise.

Not that the orchestra's management needed convincing. Such was their enthusiasm that my relatively modest plan for a concert performance of the *Silbersee* music was transformed into an ambitious, not to say over-ambitious, double bill involving theatrical elements and television: *Royal Palace*, reorchestrated in its entirety, was to be the curtain-raiser for a semi-staged version of *Der Silbersee* in which the musical numbers would be framed by the original dialogue and linked by specially written narrations. Lenya agreed to combine the role of narrator with that of one of the leading figures in the play, and Heinzelmann was commissioned to prepare the text and direct the production.

Plans for the Festival were already far advanced when I learned from O. W. Neighbour of an extraordinary discovery he had made while browsing through a box of unidentified miscellanea in a Parisian music store: a perfect copy of the long-lost *Recordare*. On account of its biblical text and musical associations I had always assumed it to be one of the most important works in the missing Fleischer package. Neighbour alone was aware of that assumption, for he alone had read my draft of the critical biography. One could well ask whether there was another musician in Europe who would at that time have recognized the priceless value of that insignificant-looking copyist's manuscript.

Overjoyed by the discovery – the first major one since I had started work nearly fifteen years before, and, as I now hoped, a portent of others – I immediately despatched a copy of *Recordare* to Jo Elsendoorn. By some miracle of organization which only he could have accomplished at such short notice, the world premiere was scheduled for the same 1971 Festival.

Despite the presence of Lenya and ample coverage in the Festival literature, the double bill was sparsely attended, and neither it nor the premiere of the *Recordare* aroused much public interest. With the notable exception of Hans Heg – a champion of New Music, but by no means an orthodox one – the Dutch critics missed the point of Elsendoorn's bold initiative, and quite failed to grasp that it was ahead of its day.

In Berlin at that time the director of the Festwochen was Nicolas Nabokov, who had been a friend of Weill's in the Weimar years and, as a naturalized American, was very much at home with that section of the Manhattan intelligentsia that had added its own lustre to Lenya's New York success with *The Seven Deadly Sins* in 1959. Rightly chary of imposing Weill's music on the Festwochen during a period when the tides in Germany were manifestly against it, he was none the less convinced that its time would come. After his retirement from the Festwochen directorship in 1972 he retained an advisory function that was no mere formality and was certainly valued by his successor, Dr Ulrich Eckhardt. Eckhardt's flair as a festival planner had first attracted attention in the Rhineland, where his collaborations with Mauricio Kagel, among others, had been widely praised. Although Nabokov had already laid the basis for a major Festwochen retrospective to mark the Schoenberg centenary in 1974, Eckhardt was to bring his own distinctive style to it.

Just as the death of Weill had been followed a year later by that of Schoenberg, so, conversely, was the centenary of Schoenberg's birth to be followed a year later by the 25th anniversary of Weill's death. Early in 1973 Dr Eckhardt invited me to Berlin for discussions about a Weill retrospective which he had in mind for the 1975 Festival. The guest of honour would be Lenya; and the programme was to cover the entire range of Weill's work, with stage productions of European and American works at the centre, and around them, concert and radio performances, open-air music, a cabaret, a musicological conference, an exhibition, and to open it all, a popular Weill revue for stage and TV.

That was the original framework of our discussions (in which we were joined by Helmut Kotschenreuther, a Berlin music critic, and the author of a Weill monograph published in 1960). But Berlin's annual festival, like other such festivals including Holland's, had only limited resources for initiating its own musical productions, and was thus to a large extent dependent on the co-operation of local institutions, and on the funds available for engaging artists, ensembles and orchestras from elsewhere.

Much work had still to be done on the preparations for the Schoenberg retrospective. But it was clear that an immediate start would have to be made on the Weill project.

The practical implications were daunting. Apart from her personal advisers in legal and financial matters Lenya had no formal base from which to administer and promote her copyrights, and was accustomed to rely on such trusted friends as Lys Symonette and Anna Krebs for those musical, archival, and secretarial services that from time to time were found to be necessary. On the advice of the distinguished theatre lawyer John F. Wharton – who had become a close friend of Weill's while acting as attorney to the Playwrights' Company – she had, however, established in 1962 the Kurt Weill Foundation for Music.

Created primarily for tax reasons, the Foundation had no staff or premises, and no extensive programme. During the early 1960s the legally mandated AGM was held at the offices of Wharton's firm and was the occasion for justifying the Foundation's charitable status by voting grants to suitable causes – among them, William Bolcom and Bruce Mather, two young composers who had been recommended to Lenya by Darius Milhaud. There were also grants to Lys Symonette for editorial work, and to myself for certain promotional services (though not, at my request, for any form of writing).

For various reasons that need not concern us here, the Foundation had come to a standstill by the end of the 1960s, and by 1973 was in no condition to respond to the Berlin initiative. In view of these and other problems in Europe, Lenya, after due consultations with her advisers, decided that the Weill Estate should have a European representative and that I should fulfil that function from an office in my London home.

An agreement to that effect was signed during my visit to New York in June 1973. Since its provisions were not intended to relate to circumstances and needs in America, the future of the Foundation was one of the main topics I raised with Lenya and her associates during that visit. Lenya was in no doubt about the need for an altogether more active organization, one that would concern itself not only with promoting knowledge and under-standing of Weill, but also with such vital questions as establishing a proper home for the archives (which for many years had been stored in a warehouse in Manhattan). I therefore promised to outline my proposals for an entirely new constitution, and for an appropriate Board of Trustees.

On my return to London I prepared a paper whose contents were closely modelled on those of the published documents relating to the Paul Hindemith Foundation in Blonay. The paper was duly forwarded, but to the best of my knowledge neither it nor my subsequent suggestions regarding the composition of a new Board were ever formally discussed. Although I had been a member of the Board ever since Lenya became its first President, I had not been receiving minutes for some while past (and none have since been traced).

My contract as the Estate's European Representative was annually renewable, and was integrated with the two-year consultancy agreement I had previously concluded with the Berlin Festival. In November 1973 both Lenya and I were guests of the Academy of Arts at the symposium *Theater im Exil* organized by Dr Walter Huder, the Academy's Archivist and (in his original role as organizer of the Academy's Georg Kaiser Archive) one of the earliest and most helpful supporters of the present volume. Our visit provided a welcome opportunity for discussing with Dr Eckhardt the overall plan for the Weill Portrait, with particular reference to the placing and the content of a *chanson*-evening which Lenya was to give at the Academy of Arts. At a subsequent meeting with Blacher, I expressed the hope that he might find some way of making his own purely musical contribution to the 1975 Weill programme. He nodded his assent; and then, with the gentlest of reproachful smiles, remarked that after waiting patiently some thirteen years, the Academy of Arts might welcome a contribution from myself, in the shape of a Weill catalogue. Sympathetic though he was to my account of the palimpsest-like draft, and to the reasons (which I had discussed with him previously) for my having interrupted work on it, he urged me to reduce the scope and size of the catalogue drastically, and finally to renounce the by now forlorn hope of being able to include most or all the 'lost' works.

Fortified by this sensible advice, I returned to London and began the catalogue afresh. With help from my friend and colleague Malcolm MacDonald, a new and much simplified version was completed during the course of 1974. But having eagerly offered it to the prospective publishers of the critical biography (Little, Brown and Co. of Boston) I felt a sense of guilty relief when they replied that they would prefer to begin with the first volume of the critical biography, which I hoped to finish the following year. Seeing the catalogue through the press would have added another factor to an already overcrowded timetable. Urgently required work on *Die Bürgschaft* – in which Dr Drese, the Zurich Intendant, was interested – was already having to be deferred because of a serious problem that had emerged in Berlin: one by one, the major institutions were regretfully informing the Festwochen that they were unable to contribute to the Weill retrospective. This meant, in effect, that their concert halls, stages, and television studios would not be available to us. Undaunted, Eckhardt and his team, together with their allies at the Academy of Arts, abandoned the idea of a full-scale retrospective and decided to concentrate on a simpler 'Portrait'. Since there was no practical possibility of producing even one of the twenty-seven extant stage works, every programme would have to be hand-made, and related to the 'Portrait' as a whole.

The chilly effect of the first negative replies from the Berlin institutions led me in April 1974 to approach Siegfried Unseld, the head of Suhrkamp Verlag in Frankfurt, and offer to edit an anthology of important writings

on Weill, to be published in time for the 1975 'Portrait'. Dr Unseld's
reply was affirmative and challenging: there should be two anthologies
not one, and the companion volume should be a collection of Weill's
own writings.

During the autumn and early winter of 1974–5 I compiled and
annotated both collections. For the first of them, *Über Kurt Weill*, I wrote
an extensive introduction, 'Weill and his Critics' (also published separately in the *Times Literary Supplement*, 1975, nos. 2838/9). Its final
section, concerning the antithetical and occluded relationship between
Schoenberg and Weill, was completed in one of the studios at the
Academy of Arts in the early morning of 30 January 1975. Outside my
window, the Tiergarten was shrouded in mist. I recalled with pleasure
the previous evening in Blacher's home, when his young son Kolya had
played, marvellously, his solo violin sonata, and his wife Gerty had
reported encouraging news from the hospital. But as I descended the
Academy stairs on the way to the breakfast room there was a sound
from below of hushed yet agitated voices. During the night, Blacher had
died.

The Academy had by then emerged as the Festwochen's principal ally
in the fight to rescue the Weill project from official lethargy. The only
other institutional collaborator was Sender Freies Berlin, which, thanks
to the enthusiasm of its music director Walter Hart, had undertaken to
mount a major choral and orchestral concert. The plan for a conference
of critics and musicologists had already been abandoned, and the
hoped-for exhibition was about to suffer the same fate. Lack of television support for Dr Eckhardt's idea of a full-scale Weill revue modelled
on the highly successful New York production *From Berlin to Broadway*
(1972) had threatened to deprive the whole venture of a suitably eye-
catching start; but Eckhardt had fortunately been able to engage the
Italian *diseuse* Milva for an opening celebrity concert at the Academy of
Arts. Since Milva was a renowned Brecht singer and needed no guidance as to choice of programme, I was free to concentrate on the four
main sections of what was now advertised as a 'Kurt Weill Portrait'.

Three of the sections were reserved for the Academy's main auditorium. The first, which was due to follow the Milva evening, was
designed in two self-contained parts: a short and ostensibly 'academic'
concert of early chamber works and songs, followed by a 40-minute
programme for Lenya, accompanied by Aribert Reimann and devoted
largely to 'The Unknown Kurt Weill' (to borrow a title later adopted by
Lenya's protégée Teresa Stratas). The extreme contrasts of style and
tendency between the two halves of this programme were then to be
projected on to the larger canvas of the two succeeding programmes,
which had the superscriptions 'In Times of War' and 'In Times of
Peace'. Borrowing an idea of Harrison Birtwistle's, I designed these as
musically continuous structures in which the interplay of large and

small ensembles was part of the dramaturgy, and there were no pauses for exits, entrances, or applause.

These two programmes called for a virtuoso mixed ensemble of a sort that in those days and those conditions could be provided only by the London Sinfonietta. On practical grounds – which happened to suit the requirements of a 'Songspiel' drawn from the *Johnny Johnson* music – we therefore decided on a cast of London-based singers, and dismissed from our minds the unworthy thought that inviting a group of classically trained British musicians to perform Weill in Berlin might be analogous to inviting a team from the Berliner Ensemble to perform a Britten opera in Aldeburgh. There were, however, two special factors: the first was Lenya's eager acceptance of the proposal that she come to London to coach the singers, and the second was the spirit and the versatility of the London Sinfonietta under its conductor David Atherton.

A visit to New York in the spring of 1975 enabled me to give Lenya a full progress report, and to discuss with her the final shape of her own contribution to the 'Portrait'. I was also able to present her with an advance copy of *Über Kurt Weill*, whose Introduction I had dedicated to her. Some days later I learned that the book, and especially the Introduction, had aroused some controversy among Lenya's friends and colleagues. Lenya herself admitted to me that parts of it had distressed her; but when she quoted, as a prime example, my observations about the musical *Lady in the Dark* I was able to convince her – or so she assured me – that there had been a far-reaching misunderstanding of my intentions. In the eighteen years we had worked together it was the first moment of discord. I left for Europe in the belief that it had been happily resolved.

There was still much to be done – not least for the Sender Freies Berlin programme, which was to end with a new concert version of the *Silbersee* score, almost complete, but this time without dialogue or narrations.* Altogether there would be seven world premieres of substantial works or arrangements of works – not to mention sundry songs and choruses – and for each of these the responsibility of producing the performance material was directly or indirectly mine. Meanwhile Hans Werner Henze, who had admired Weill's music since his first discovery of *Die Dreigroschenoper* soon after the war's end, had become so incensed by the apparent indifference of most of the West Berlin institutions that he had marshalled the young composers associated with the militant *Hinz und Kunz* collective, and encouraged them to compose 'homages to Weill' for inclusion in the London Sinfonietta programmes. Independently, the British composer Robin Holloway was writing his own homage, in the form of a Concertino – his third – for chamber ensemble.

---

* The other works in the programme were *Der neue Orpheus* – receiving its first German performance for nearly fifty years, with Anja Silja as soprano soloist – and the Berlin premiere of the Second Symphony.

The first of the homages were arriving from various corners of Europe during the summer weeks, at about the time when word was received that Lenya had withdrawn from the Academy concert for reasons of health, and would not even be able to attend the Festwochen. Barry McDaniel and Aribert Reimann courageously undertook to complement the group of *Lieder* they were preparing for the first half of the Academy concert with another group selected from the American songs Lenya had intended to include in the second half. With equal fortitude the British singers accepted that they would have to appear before a Berlin audience without the inestimable benefits of Lenya's coaching. There was a still greater challenge implicit in the welcome news that almost immediately after the Festival they and the Sinfonietta would record the main works from their Berlin programme for Deutsche Grammophon – from whose vast catalogue of 'serious music' Weill had hitherto been notably missing.

Apart from the painful absence of Lenya, the omens for Berlin were good: *Über Kurt Weill* and *Ausgewählte Schriften* had received wide and favourable coverage in the German press; Dr Eckhardt and his colleagues had ensured that the 'Weill Portrait' was publicized with maximum effectiveness; and the Academy of Arts had assembled a fine team of collaborators and technicians under the leadership of Nele Hertling, the Academy's Music Director (and today its Secretary).

Final rehearsals in London prevented me from attending the Milva evening, but its success was a foregone conclusion. Less predictable was the programme itself, for it had been billed merely as a selection of Weill's songs, and was so described – with no specified titles – in the notes provided for the audience. Without notice or announcement, Milva had however interpolated in the Academy programme several Brecht settings by Hanns Eisler. The surprise this occasioned among those who recognized the authorship of the songs was perhaps misplaced. International recording stars tend to be a law unto themselves. Moreover, the ideological climate of the 1970s favoured those elements of Brechtian orthodoxy from which the naïve might infer that it was immaterial which 'composer' was nominally involved, since the songs were to all intents and purposes Brecht's . But according to the less naïve and more prevalent view, Eisler in any event merited pride of place. This was manifest in the work of the *Hinz und Kunz* collection: while none of the younger composers had shown any discernible interest in the official object of their homages, several had submitted Eisler imitations so starry-eyed as to constitute a subform of the newly fashionable New Romanticism.

As the audience arrived for the first of the Sinfonietta's concerts – the one entitled 'In Times of War' – supporters of a radical socialist 'Union of Creative Artists' stood in the forecourt of the Academy of Arts distributing broadsheets that bore the headline 'Kurt Weill, or the Marketing of the Misunderstood'. Prompted by an article in the

Festwochen brochure that made light of the complex question of the Weill–Eisler–Brecht relationship, the broadsheet sought to protect both composers from the embraces of 'official' culture. Although the authors were careful to distinguish between the Marxist Eisler and the 'democratic humanist Weill' they ended with a summons, in the name of *both* composers, to an anti-war demonstration the following Sunday. Since no one had thought to distribute the broadsheet outside the artists' entrance, the British singers and players knew nothing of all this, and were greatly puzzled by some sporadic demonstrations during the first half of their concert.

Two years later in that same auditorium the Hanns Eisler Choir and Ensemble of West Berlin gave a programme of political music as part of the 1977 Festwochen's comprehensive survey of the 1920s. There were several works by Weill, including *Das Berliner Requiem*, which had been arranged for mixed chorus because the sopranos and altos were so enamoured of the piece that they insisted on being allowed to take part. After the concert, which was as enthusiastically and respectfully applauded as any Fischer-Dieskau recital, the performers repaired to a *Kneipe* in Moabit and talked, until the small hours, of every imaginable topic, but also, more than once, of their gratitude to the London Sinfonietta for the programmes of 1975 and the recordings made a fortnight later.

Such a rapprochement would have been unthinkable at any time before the 1975 Festwochen. For Weill in Europe, 1975 marked a watershed from which positive consequences are still flowing, ten years later. For my own work, however, it was the end of an era.

I returned to London from Germany in time for the Sinfonietta's recording sessions in September 1975, and found waiting for me a registered letter from Alfred Rice, a New York attorney, who informed me that he was now representing Lenya's interests. The letter instructed me to return, forthwith, all the materials and documents I had been lent for my work on the critical biography, the catalogue, and the performing editions.

The timing was not ideal. After consultation with Lenya in the spring of that year, I had agreed to join the music-publishing firm of Boosey & Hawkes in October, on the express understanding that I could continue to fulfil existing commitments to the Weill interests, and in the belief that by then the first volume of the critical biography would be ready for print. I had not anticipated that preparations for the Festwochen events, together with performances and recordings that followed from them, would consume every available moment from then until October, and that renewed pleas from Universal Edition for *Die Bürgschaft* would have to be dealt with during any time that remained at my disposal before the year's end.

Early in 1976 I visited New York on personal business, and prolonged my stay in order to discuss Weill matters with Lenya and with her new associates Alfred Rice and Margo Harris. To Lenya, with whom my meetings were as amicable as ever, I gave a copy of my finally completed

Bürgschaft revision, and promised that I would not return without the completed typescript of Volume I of the critical biography.

With that indeed completed, I returned to New York in November 1976, hoping to present Lenya with the first copy of the typescript. Unfortunately, events conspired against our meeting, and attempts to re-establish contact during the remainder of my brief stay were of no avail. The subsequent silence spoke for itself, and it was clear that my official duties for the Weill Estate should forthwith cease. In my letter of resignation I expressed the hope that Lenya would not hesitate to turn to me if circumstances were to change and my help was again required. A few weeks later I received word that the Board of the Kurt Weill Foundation for Music was to be reduced in size, and that the place I had nominally occupied on it since the beginning was now superfluous. I was not, however, informed of the appointment to the Board of Margo Harris and several others, nor of the engagement of Alfred Rice as the Foundation's counsel. Soon afterwards I learned from Heugel that the strenuous objections to Vambery's new version of *Der Kuhhandel* which I had made in 1970 on grounds of principle had now, all of a sudden, been discounted, and that a publication agreement had been concluded which even ignored Shaw's exemplary orchestrations. Equally representative of the time was a letter in which my American publishers, with whom I had been on the best of terms, renounced their claim on the critical biography – the first volume of which was to have been forwarded to them as soon as Lenya had read and approved it.

It was during this very period – March 1977 – that the London Sinfonietta presented at the Queen Elizabeth Hall a quartet of concerts containing most of the pieces from their Weill repertory, in combination with new works commissioned from British composers. Peter Maxwell Davies's *A Mirror of Whitening Light*, Harrison Birtwistle's *Silbury Air*, and Robin Holloway's Concertino No. 3, 'Homage to Weill' (which had proved too demanding to be adequately rehearsed in time for Berlin), were among the works receiving their first performance in this untoward context. The risks were considerable: not only was the Sinfonietta experimenting with an entirely new programme structure, but it was doing so in the dark. No one had any means of telling whether there was a public for Weill among London's concert-goers, or whether the known public for new works would accept Weill's very different hypotheses.

The experiment attracted large audiences and was so well received that it established a pattern for the Sinfonietta's concert promotions that has been followed and extended ever since. In the history of the European reception of Weill's music since 1950 the series merits a place of its own, for it showed how barriers of prejudice that had existed for half a century could be demolished at a stroke: directly confronted by various forms of non-tonal music, Weill's forms and illusions of tonality emerged neither as an implied critique of modernism nor as a casualty of it, but as saboteurs and bridge-builders from an earlier stage of the same fight.

The only major score that was played in Berlin but omitted from the London series (and also from the Deutsche Grammophon recording) was *War Game*, a 'Songspiel' based on the *Johnny Johnson* war music. Since the case for omitting it was unanswerable on practical grounds there was nothing to be gained from discussing it on other ones, though these were in fact fundamental: only in *Johnny Johnson* had the Sinfonietta musicians sensed something alien to their training, their traditions, and their instincts. For all its manifest Europeanisms, the score necessarily and knowingly includes something of Broadway. Had we thought of adding to the Berlin programmes a framework of selections from, say, *Anything Goes* or *Girl Crazy*, we might all have recognized that what offended the musicians in *Johnny Johnson* was not the Broadway style as such; it was Weill's decision to make use of it.

That was the one old barrier the Sinfonietta series had left untouched. The risk of unwittingly strengthening it had already become apparent to me while editing the two Suhrkamp volumes, for in both of them the European contributions had inevitably outnumbered and outweighed the American ones – an imbalance I had tried to correct in the Introduction to *Über Kurt Weill*.

A much graver risk, as I now realized, was inherent in my plan to publish a first instalment of the critical biography that ended with Weill's flight from Germany. Whether it ran to a single very large volume or two more manageable ones, the structure and scale were such that there was no possibility of including even the early American years.

After the withdrawal of my American publishers I had the immense benefit of the advice and support of their prospective British partners, Faber and Faber. Since the early 1960s the music and music books divisions of Faber had been under the wing of the author and scholar Donald Mitchell. In his Notting Hill Gate home in 1956 I had written my first letter to Lenya, together with a specimen chapter that owed much to his and Hans Keller's writings on Mahler and Britten, and to their joint admiration for Weill.

With Dr Mitchell's agreement I decided in the spring of 1977 to separate the biographical from the critical chapters, and to publish the former first, with the catalogue as an extensive appendix. The necessary adaptations and revisions occupied most of my spare time from then until the late autumn. Meanwhile Dr Mitchell had informed Lenya of the new plan, and had arranged with her to deliver the typescript of the biography and the catalogue in person during his forthcoming visit to New York. On his arrival at the end of November 1977 he learned that Lenya had suddenly been taken to hospital, and that there would be no chance of seeing her. He left the completed typescript with Margo Harris.

A New Year cable from Lenya expressing her delight at what she had by then read of the biography prompted Dr Mitchell to write to her requesting formal confirmation of her agreement to my copious quotations from Weill's letters and articles. In a reply that was notably cooler in tone than her cable, Lenya explained that while she had found nothing to take exception to in the first part of the biography, she would have some points to raise about the second (American) part, but meanwhile had had to interrupt her reading in order to examine a book on Weill which, she said, was due to go to press.

Two months later Dr Mitchell received a formal letter signed by Lenya and dated 14 March 1978. On the grounds that some manuscript corrections to my typescript were illegible, that no bibliography had been included, and that a few pages seemed to be missing from the catalogue, permission to quote copyright material was withheld for the time being – a tolerable delay (it was suggested) in view of the number of years Lenya had patiently waited for the book's completion. The copy of my typescript was retained, and a fortnight later – on 27 March 1978 – the *New York Times* carried a feature article by Donal Henahan under the banner headline 'Gottfried Wagner Doing Life of Weill'. Mr Henahan explained that the subject of his article was 'not just any 30-year-old named Wagner, but a great-grandson of the composer of *The Ring*', and that his acquaintance with Lenya had arisen from his dissertation on Weill and Brecht (with which he had obtained his doctorate from the University of Vienna in February 1977). Work on the biography was to start immediately. 'It is all very pleasant,' Wagner was quoted as saying: 'Lenya has promised me her exclusive assistance until 1981. There is no authoritative life of Weill now.' Wagner was duly furnished with a grant from the Foundation, whose Board of Trustees he now joined.

Wagner and his dissertation were by no means unfamiliar to me. I had first heard from him in October 1973, when he wrote to say that he was starting work on a 'dissertation about the stage plays of Brecht and Weill', and had been inspired to undertake this task by the philosopher Ernst Bloch, who was a close friend of his father Wolfgang and his uncle Wieland.* His first need was for 'important literature' on Weill, and at the suggestion of the Academy of Arts, he was now asking me to recommend some.

Our correspondence continued amicably for several months. I informed Lenya of it at once, and before long suggested to her that Wagner might eventually prove a suitable addition to the Foundation's Board of Trustees. I had been hoping to arrange an early meeting with him in Vienna, but circumstances prevented this. Fortunately a television

---

*See the present author's introduction to Ernst Bloch, *Essays on the Philosophy of Music*, trans. Peter Palmer (Cambridge University Press, Cambridge, 1985).

assignment brought him to London in the first week of June 1974, and allowed him sufficient time to join me at home for lunch and an afternoon's discussion. Although it was soon clear that for him the music of Weill – though not the Broadway music, about which he was wholly dismissive – held some special significance that was not to be found in Eisler or other composers in Brecht's circle, almost everything he said that afternoon confirmed my growing impression that his fundamental concerns had more to do with the theatre than with music, with Brecht than with Weill. When I visited Lenya in the USA shortly after my meeting with Wagner I felt obliged to sound a note of caution about my previous recommendation, at least as far as the Foundation was concerned.

'It was very important for me having met you', wrote Wagner on 15 July, 'and I do thank you very much for your help and good will.' The remainder of his letter and the whole of its successor gave some grounds for disquiet, but he accepted my expression of it with good grace. Finally, on 22 April 1975, he briefly acknowledged receipt of the copy of *Über Kurt Weill* which I had sent him on publication, and offered to write an article for the programme book of the Berliner Festwochen. As his proposed topic was unsuitable, I offered him an alternative platform. I did not hear from him again.

In November 1977 – four months before the *New York Times* announcement of his biography – a slightly revised version of his dissertation was published by Kindler (Munich) as *Weill und Brecht. Das musikalische Zeittheater*, with a foreword signed by Lenya and dated March 1977. Wagner's own preface began with the following statement (my translation, incorporating in italics what is a footnote in the original):

> Source research was gravely impeded, and often made impossible, through the destruction of important autobiographical documents as a result of the National Socialist dictatorship, and through the lack of constructive collaboration with the Weill Archive on the part of the executor [*sic*] David Drew, *despite two years of intensive and fruitless endeavour and a research visit to the executor in London.*

If there is any substance in the reference to Nazi depredations it is so exaggerated as to serve no useful function other than helping to mask the intimate relationship between the second clause, the footnote, and the chain of events which began with my abortive visit of November 1976 and culminated in the *New York Times*'s announcement of March 1978. Paradoxically the authority lent to Wagner's allegation by Lenya's apparent endorsement of it in her Preface derived not from her artistic eminence but from the fact that she was the sole executor of Weill's will; and as such she had very properly exercised her exclusive right to decide – at least until September 1975 – who should or should not have access to the research material that belonged to her. As my correspondence with

Wagner amply demonstrates* there had never been any obstacles to his progress other than intellectual and temperamental ones of his own making. It would nevertheless be rash to suppose that the words with which he began his foreword to *Weill und Brecht* were simply a product of local exigencies. Students of Weill affairs in the latter half of the 1970s would be well advised to refer to an almost exactly contemporary article by the West Berlin critic and composer Jürgen Engelhardt: 'Fragwürdiges in der Kurt-Weill-Rezeption', in Dietrich Stern (ed.), *Angewandte Musik der 20er Jahre* (*Das Argument*, AS 24, W. Berlin, August 1977, pp. 118–37). Like most of the contributors to this volume and to its predecessor (*Hanns Eisler*, AS 5) Engelhardt was an associate of the West Berlin Hanns Eisler Choir. But since in his opinion everything that was most 'questionable' in the 'Weill reception' – notably the nature and 'marketing' of the two Suhrkamp anthologies, the 1975 Festwochen Portrait, and the London Sinfonietta album – stemmed from the 'English administrator of the Kurt Weill legacy', and had culminated, after eighteen years of malfeasance, in the denial of research facilities to such scholars as Gottfried Wagner, the intended critique seemed to lack its proper measure of dialectical objectivity, and did not, I gathered, represent the collective view of the Eisler Choir. So numerous were Engelhardt's errors of fact and interpretation and so transparent his intentions that I declined the editor's offer of space to reply – noting that some attempt at least to check the facts beforehand would have been helpful – and contented myself with the often convenient thought that time is truth's best ally and foolish polemics are best forgotten.

My complacency in that respect long outlived my memories of Engelhardt's article. Indeed it survived until as late as February 1986, when his central allegation about the blocking of access to primary sources was unwittingly quoted to me by a German friend who knew nothing of the background but described it as 'common knowledge' in certain Berlin circles, and cited the case – hitherto unknown to me – of a musicologist who had finally been forced to abandon a major research project on émigré German composers after despairing of any adequate response to requests for assistance with access to Weill's papers. The irony that this unhappy episode seemed to have occurred during a period when I myself had no access to the Weill archives only emphasized the extent of the confusion and of Wagner's responsibility for it.

The announcement of Wagner's biography project in March 1978 coincided with a period when my music-publishing commitments

---

* In April 1986 I gave to the Weill–Lenya Research Center copies of nine letters from Gottfried Wagner to myself (9 October 1973 – 11 October 1974) and eleven in reply (5 December 1973 – 16 May 1975).

fortunately left me with little time for work on Weill or even for further thought about it. The one link that held fast during the next eighteen months was the German translation of the Catalogue, which the Academy had commissioned from Ken W. Bartlett in 1976. From time to time Bartlett would ply me with questions that had arisen during the course of his work. His meticulousness was matched by a tact and good humour that I had every reason to cherish during that dark time. Without perhaps realizing it, he had become the nightwatchman of my entire work.

Appropriately enough it was *Mahagonny* that eventually drew me back into the penumbra of Weill affairs in New York. In the spring of 1979 I received an urgent message from the Metropolitan Opera regarding their forthcoming production and its hitherto unforeseen dependence on the English version Geliot and I had prepared for Sadler's Wells eighteen years before. A few days' work in London with the Met's emissary initiated a notably happy collaboration which was resumed during the first rehearsal period at the Met that autumn. As always, *Mahagonny* disturbed and challenged everyone concerned with the production, and provoked its own special kinds of inquiry and self-examination. The fierce curiosity with which Teresa Stratas approached the role of Jenny and questioned every action, word, and nuance was an example to us all.

Prior to my arrival at the Met, Lenya had been a frequent visitor and much appreciated counsellor. Her absence during the days I was working there was therefore keenly felt; and to my great regret there was no opportunity of meeting her when I returned for the gala premiere that November.

In the early spring of 1980 the national Music Critics Association sponsored in New York a two-day colloquium about Weill and *Der Silbersee* in conjunction with the City Opera's production of *Silverlake*, a free adaptation of Kaiser's play by Hugh Wheeler. The colloquium was jointly chaired by myself and Professor Kim Kowalke, whose reputation as a leading Weill scholar had been established by the recent publication of his *Kurt Weill in Europe* (UMI Research Press, Ann Arbor, 1979) – the book version of the invaluable dissertation he began shortly after our first meeting in Lenya's New York apartment in 1973. To remark that there was no one with whom I would more gladly have shared that platform is to pay tribute to his personal and scholarly integrity, and also – considering how unsteady the platform was – to his sang-froid; for the Wheeler version of *Der Silbersee* was, in my view, wellnigh indefensible.

Thanks to the imperturbably genial Kowalke, the first day of the colloquium – which concerned Weill in general – passed without major disturbances (though not without impalpable dissonances from the row where Lenya and her associates had prominently seated themselves). The opening session on the next day was devoted to the original *Silbersee*, without direct reference to *Silverlake* but with all possible relevance to it.

Whatever the value of our prepared papers, it was far surpassed by the impromptu address delivered towards the end of the morning by the eminent conductor Maurice Abravanel, who had been a lifelong friend of Weill's and, alone in the profession, had championed his music from the early years through to Broadway. Of the man and his music Abravanel spoke with such fire, such dignity, trust, and intelligent good humour, that it seemed as if he were standing before the judgment seat from which both Hans Sachs and Jack O'Brien* were about to deliver their verdicts on *die ewige Kunst*. It was salutary to be reminded that in him, as in Lenya, 'knowledge' of Weill belonged to realms of experience that could, on such an occasion, be revealed to the rest of us, but would never be conquered by the forces of research and criticism. As Kowalke remarked when our applause had at last died down, further academic formalities were now superfluous. The afternoon was accordingly declared an open forum.

During the adjournment I was working alone in a secluded corner when Lenya appeared. It was our first meeting for almost exactly four years, but a witness would hardly have guessed that as many hours had passed. Yet Lenya's first words recalling my remarks that morning about *Der Silbersee* and its connection with Schiller's *Die Räuber* were by no means as casual as they sounded. Inviting me to spend a day at Brook House when the colloquium was over only to learn that I was due to return to Europe immediately, she urged me to contact her during my planned visit to Tanglewood that summer. In the same spirit I invited her, and she agreed, to join us on the platform for the final session of the colloquium.

Lenya's public demonstration of a new accord, like her private reservations about the adaptation of *Der Silbersee*, sprang from the same reawakened perceptions that now led her to invite Kim Kowalke to join the Foundation's Board of Trustees (from which Margo Harris had resigned). It was only at this stage that the Board, while still confined to a purely advisory role, began to involve itself in questions of principle and policy.

During the summer of 1980 I took a day's leave from Tanglewood and drove to Brook House in the company of the Austrian composer Heinz Karl Gruber, whose orchestral *chanson*-cycle *Frankenstein*!! had already been widely acclaimed, and less widely attacked, in terms of its supposed relationship to Weill and Eisler. Our conversation with Lenya on the veranda at Brook House was so light-hearted and *gemütlich* that her friendly inquiries about progress on 'the book' could only be answered in the same tone. Of the four lost years there was no mention; nor could there be any reference to the new and quite extraneous complications

---

* *Aufstieg und Fall der Stadt Mahagonny*, Act I scene vi.

that had hindered – and would continue to hinder – my response to the fresh encouragement provided by our meeting at the New York colloquium. From January 1980 until far into 1981 circumstances in the music-publishing world – at least in my corner of it – were scarcely favourable to spare-time activities.

After our visit of August 1980 there was no further news from Lenya herself. But reports of her condition during the winter of 1980–1 were disquieting. It was not until my return visit to Tanglewood in the summer of 1981 that I reached her by phone. Though much weakened from the effects of major surgery, she urged me to visit her, and when she received me next day, it was without a sign that she knew it might be for the last time. Indeed she spoke mainly of her firm resolve to recover her strength as soon as possible, with a view to setting her affairs in order – first by obtaining new legal counsel and then by once again reorganizing the Foundation, which she hoped to be discussing with me soon.

On a more personal note, but still in relation to a clearly envisaged future, Lenya reaffirmed her intense admiration for the work of Teresa Stratas. As a parting gift she presented me with Stratas's new recording, *The Unknown Kurt Weill*, and laughingly advised me against letting anyone see it as I left the house.

During the last months of her life Lenya was devotedly cared for by Margo Harris, first in Brook House and then in Miss Harris's own Manhattan apartment. It was there that I visited Lenya a fortnight before her death. She was too exhausted to speak or to do more than very slowly raise her hand in greeting.

From the *Nebelszene** of Lenya's last days there emerged a controversial new will which had grave implications with regard to archival materials and to the administration of copyrights; Alfred Rice remained a co-executor, while the attorney of Brecht's son Stefan was named in the document as successor executor and trustee. At a special meeting, the Foundation engaged new counsel to replace Alfred Rice, and at the Annual General Meeting following Lenya's death the Board of Trustees recognized as imperative the need to secure its own survival in such a way as to protect Weill's and Lenya's artistic legacy. In accordance with Lenya's wishes Kim Kowalke was elected President. Gottfried Wagner was not re-elected as a Trustee.

Lenya's confidence in Kowalke was amply justified. With an acumen and sensitivity worthy of George Davis, and qualities of leadership equal to the demands of a situation immeasurably more complex and hazardous than any foreseeable in the happy days of the 1950s, Kowalke,

---

* *Die Bürgschaft*, Act I scene ix.

with the aid of a united Board of Trustees, had achieved by November 1983 most of the aims I had outlined for the Foundation ten years before, and much else besides. The first issue of the *Kurt Weill Newsletter* appeared in November 1983. Kowalke's introduction to it began as follows:

> It's hard for me to believe that Lenya has been gone nearly two years. When she asked me [in 1981] to succeed her as President of the Foundation, I had no inkling that these two years would be the most hectic, frustrating, rewarding and exhilarating of my life . . .
>
> The first year was consumed by legal battles. Although Lenya had specifically bequeathed to the Foundation all royalties and had named it the beneficiary of a remainder trust, her will made no mention of copyright ownership or disposition of archival materials that weren't already on loan at Yale. Finally in August 1982, the New York Surrogate's Court decreed the Foundation heir to all copyrights that Lenya had owned and awarded it the remaining archival materials.
>
> This enabled us to work out a comprehensive archival agreement with Yale, whereby it would house, catalogue, and service a Weill/Lenya Archive containing nearly all of the original documents, with the exception of visual and audio-video materials. The Foundation established a Research Center and Business Office in New York City that will house photocopies of materials at Yale and other collections, an audio-video and oral history archive, and satellite references for Weill–Lenya research. We were fortunate that David Farneth agreed to join us as Archivist in April 1983.

The Foundation's Research Center was officially opened on 1 November 1983. Next day, the first-ever Kurt Weill Conference was to open at Yale under the joint sponsorship of the Foundation and the Yale University Music Library. Professor Kowalke had told me of his plans for the conference many months before and had most graciously invited me to deliver the keynote address. Reminded of Blacher's advice to me ten years before, I had suggested to Professor Kowalke – and he had agreed – that the conference might be an appropriate occasion for publishing the original English version of the catalogue. By now my impressions of the catalogue were dominated by Ken Bartlett's German version (which was finished apart from some questions I had not yet been able to answer and some gaps I had yet to fill).

When I began to reread the original, I saw at once that the opening entries would have to be rewritten and strengthened, if only to counteract the false impression of Weill's beginnings that might arise as a result of the lamentably fragmentary state of our knowledge – a state almost unchanged since 1958. With that alone in mind I began to rewrite these entries, and warned Ken Bartlett that a few new pages would be forwarded to him shortly. But the further I proceeded the clearer it became that a catalogue designed with a view to Berlin's 1975 'Weill Portrait' was, by definition, ill suited to the very different circumstances of 1983 – quite apart from the specific needs of the Yale Conference. Knowledge of Weill in the English-speaking world had been greatly increased in 1979 by the publication of Kim Kowalke's analytical and documentary volume *Kurt Weill in Europe*; that same year had seen the publication of a full-length popular biography by Ronald Sanders, *The Days Grow Short*; and from somewhere in the background, the proliferating sky-scrapers of Brecht criticism were throwing multiple shadows across the entire field of Weill studies. None of this was reflected in the 1975 version of the catalogue.

During the spring and summer of 1983 I expanded and largely rewrote every entry – the last of them only a few days before the Yale Conference. The implications for Ken Bartlett were so grave that I would have lacked the will to continue had it not been for the boundless forbearance and generosity of his response to the sheaves of fresh pages I was sending him.

On the eve of the opening of the Weill–Lenya Research Center in New York, Professor Kowalke confided in me that he had prepared a paper for the conference whose intentionally cryptic title – 'Lost and Found' – related to a topic so fraught with legal problems that he had not until now been free to divulge it. A substantial holograph collection of early works by Weill – most of them quite unknown – had been in the possession of Rita Weill (the composer's sister-in-law), together with a considerable number of letters and postcards. Professor Kowalke had himself been allowed briefly to inspect the entire collection; and thanks to the good will of Hanne Weill-Holesovsky, the Foundation already held photostat copies of some of the holographs.

Despite numerous other commitments, David Farneth and his assistant managed to duplicate those copies for me in time for my return to London. At last I had what I had been seeking since 1959: a selection of early scores that was sufficiently large and coherent to provide – in conjunction with contemporary references to other scores still missing – a basis for critical judgements, and hence a structurally defensible starting point.

Meanwhile, the head of the Music Library at Yale, Harold E. Samuel, had introduced me to the members of his staff and in particular to Adrienne Nesnow, who had been commissioned, with funding from the National Endowment, to catalogue the manuscripts and documents in the Weill/Lenya Archive. The Archive had of course seen many changes in the seven years since I last had access to it. When the Conference was over I was able to verify points that had arisen in the process of rewriting my own catalogue – a copy of which I left with the Library.

The task of writing the entries on the newly discovered works was completed during the early weeks of 1984. Owing to other commitments – notably, expanding and preparing for print the paper I had delivered at the Yale Conference – no further work on the catalogue was possible until the beginning of 1985, when I returned to the Research Center for several days and again visited the Weill/Lenya Archive in Yale. By the early summer I had added the Chronology and Projects sections to the main body of the present volume.

At this point Professor Kowalke arrived in London, bearing some fascinating news. In New York there was renewed hope that the Foundation would acquire photostat copies of the remaining uncatalogued holographs from the Rita Weill Collection; and in Berlin Professor Kowalke had discussed with Ulrich Eckhardt a second and enlarged 'Weill Portrait' to be mounted during the 1987 celebrations in honour of Berlin's 750th anniversary. The sense of cyclic renewal was heightened by Dr Eckhardt's subsequent letter to me on this same subject. The concept of a large-scale Weill revue which Eckhardt had first formulated in 1973, and which had been successfully realized on a smaller scale at the Schiller Theater seven years later, had at last been fulfilled by the new team at the Theater des Westens. (It was in the foyer of that same theatre, in its earlier guise as the Städtische Oper, that Blacher had mooted the idea of the present catalogue, at the time of Ebert's new production of *Die Bürgschaft*.) Produced by Helmut Baumann and choreographed by Jürg Burth, *Von Bilbao, Youkali und Alabama* was a major popular success, first in Berlin and later in Hamburg.

Kowalke left London in the summer of 1985 expecting that the Foundation would soon receive copies of the uncatalogued autographs. Predictably, perhaps, new complications arose almost at once, and there was still no sign of the vital photostats by the end of August, when the typescript of the present book's Catalogue section was delivered to the publishers. There had however been one consolation: in June a hitherto unknown holograph of a version of *Ofrah's Lieder* significantly different from the one in the Rita Weill Collection was auctioned at Sotheby's and acquired by the Library of Congress in Washington. From the Library's Music Division I received by special courier a photostat copy. Without it, the present Catalogue would have lacked an essential source of enlightenment.

In December 1985 I left for New York on an assignment for the Foundation. By then I had reconciled myself to the seemingly unavoidable fact that some of the early pages of the Catalogue consisted of the merest speculations about the character and significance of the items so tantalizingly glimpsed by Kim Kowalke in 1983. But at the Weill–Lenya Research Center that first evening Kowalke and Farneth greeted me with the astounding news that next morning the representatives of Rita Weill's Estate would hand over to the Foundation photostats of all the remaining musical items from the Collection.

Although the originals were still not available even for inspection, and although negotiations for numerous uncopied letters from Weill had yet to be concluded I was able, for the second time in twelve months, to take back to London a large package containing material of vital importance to the Catalogue. The outstanding items from a bibliographical point of view were the two songs that Elisabeth Feuge and the composer had performed at their *Lieder* recital in June 1920 – 'Abendlied' and 'Die stille Stadt'. The bare facts that were already known to us had given no hint that a boundary line missing from the jigsaw map of Weill's pre-1921 compositions is located precisely in the area between the two songs. Whereas 'Abendlied' still belongs to the conventional world of *Ofrah's Lieder*, 'Die stille Stadt' is the earliest-known song in which Weill projects his own individual vision in a form powerful enough to overcome structural inconsistencies. So strikingly characteristic are the tone and gait of the song that the pairing with 'Abendlied' in Weill's *Lieder* programme seems to confirm the growing evidence that his early vocal output – unlike Berg's before him or Britten's after – was neither voluminous nor prodigious, and that whatever early manuscripts may have been among the family belongings that apparently sank to the bottom of Tel Aviv harbour in 1935, few are likely to have been of real musical value.

The light shed by 'Abendlied' and 'Die stille Stadt' seemed finally to banish the *ignis fatuus* of a 'definitive' catalogue. Other discoveries will certainly follow in the coming years. Each will alter the proportions between knowledge and speculation. But none, I believe, could provide a better substitute for completion than these two discoveries, or more fitting symbols of Weill's artistic legacy than the timeless ostinato and unresolved dissonances that close his setting of Stefan George's 'Die stille Stadt'.

Michael Gilbert's recent dissertation *Bertolt Brecht and Music* contains a useful reminder of how easily the value of such discoveries, and the purpose of analysing them, can still be misunderstood by those whose only natural approach to Weill is by way of a partisan reading of Brecht.* According to Gilbert,

> the 'Kurt Weill establishment' has sought in recent years to de-emphasize the ultimate significance of Weill's association with Brecht by focusing primarily on 'the unknown Weill' (particularly his symphonic and chamber music, as well as his early operatic works), and by taking a more narrowly musicological (that is, formalistic and analytical) view of all of Weill's output.

Instead of asking himself how these activities could conceivably be thought to 'de-emphasize the ultimate significance' of anything whatsoever, Gilbert throws scholarly caution to the winds:

> In a sense, Drew and his followers have attempted to create an image or understanding of 'Weill without Brecht', which in many respects is as unconvincing and problematic as a recent attempt by a Chicago theater company to stage Brecht without Weill in a fashionably punkish, new-wave rock musical production of *Mahagonny*.

---

*Michael John Tyler Gilbert, *Bertolt Brecht and Music: A Comprehensive Study* (A thesis submitted in partial fulfilment of the requirements for the degree of Doctor of Philosophy (German) at the University of Wisconsin-Madison, 1985) pp. 95ff.

Logic is not the only absentee from these remarks. Gilbert fails to recognize that Weill had to make do 'without Brecht' for nine-tenths of his adult life. Whatever one may think of the results, an 'image or understanding' of them is surely a legitimate aim for those who care at all for his work, and a 'fashionable punkish' staging of *Mahagonny* without Weill is irrelevant.

Like some of his predecessors in 'Brecht–Weill' studies, Gilbert is immediately suspicious of the motives of any critic whose interest in Weill differs from his own. Question-begging assumptions, ironic asides, and selective quotation serve their customary purpose. When, for example, the present author is credited with attempting 'to shelter Kurt Weill from Brecht's "harmful" influence' the word 'harmful' mischievously conceals its authorship behind prophylactic quotation marks. The resulting travesty is then illustrated by what Gilbert describes as a 'particularly blatant example'. This turns out to be the partial quotation of a single sentence that has been wrenched from its musical context in order that a reference to the ideologically light-weight *Happy End* score can be misconstrued in terms of Gilbert's fantasies about the 'attempt' to portray 'Weill without Brecht'. 'At the root of this effort', Gilbert confidently maintains, 'is an ideological bias which is not hard to detect.' Not content with one 'particularly blatant example' he snatches at a 'similar' one and promptly impales himself on his own ideological railings:

> In a rather undisguised indictment of Brecht's move towards Marxism and the Communist Party in the late twenties, Kim Kowalke has written that 'Weill never shared this shift from a moral system of humane, non-political socialism to an overt political identification'.

Naturally the 'harmful' influence of Brecht to which Gilbert ironically alludes is (in part) seen to be a Marxist one. It is not hard to 'detect' – as Gilbert himself seems to sense – that Weill remained open to Marxist influences from 1919 until towards the end of the 1930s. But the notion that such influences made him any kind of political thinker is absurd. What Kowalke writes is the simple truth, and Brecht was never in any doubt about it.

A catalogue of Weill's work – or for that matter a Weill Archive or Foundation – is by definition dedicated to 'the whole Weill' and cannot therefore be unresponsive to the ideological implications that have been thrust upon an intrinsically neutral and indeed commonplace concept. Whenever one of the domestic radiators of Brecht scholarship threatens to overheat at the very mention of Weill's independence from Brecht it is perhaps prudent to glance at the central furnaces and reactors, and ask why the comparable concept of Eisler's and Dessau's independence has been circulating for years with manifest encouragement and benefit on both sides of the East–West border. It is not enough to remark that between Brecht and the two gifted composers who can justly be called his 'collaborators' there was an indissoluble treaty and no cause for serious disagreement. The fact remains that of all the creative artists who were close to Brecht for any length of time, only Weill won for himself the kind of reputation and success that could, in the narrow view, be thought to constitute the slightest threat to Brecht; and that is another simple truth that Brecht was clearly aware of.

For lack of corroborative evidence we may, if we choose, disbelieve Lenya's often repeated stories of how Brecht, in 1927, objected to the prominence given to the composer's name in a billing for the *Mahagonny-Songspiel* and declared that Weill had to 'learn' that this would not be 'acceptable' in the future; or how, during the preparations for the Berlin premiere of the *Mahagonny* opera, he attacked a press photographer who was attempting to photograph him and Weill together. We can even argue that in 'bourgeois' society authors had for too long been seen as the butlers and valets of composers; and that it is only an accident of history that there are so few photographs of Weill and Brecht in conversation, and that even these are relatively recent discoveries. The fact remains that after more than two generations of worldwide research into every aspect of Brecht's life, there has yet to be discovered a single instance of his having spoken or written kindly of Weill, or having acted generously towards him whether as colleague or ex-colleague. 'I . . . recall things Brecht would say about Weill,' writes Eric Bentley in *The Brecht Memoir* (New York, 1985, p. 83); 'He was catty on that subject, not only hinting that he himself composed the best tunes . . . but indicating that Weill had gone wrong where BB had gone right in the handling of American exile.' Bentley's tone is better attuned to the pettiness of Brecht's behaviour than to the seriousness of the artistic issues. To feel wounded on Weill's behalf, or even on music's, is already to risk attributing to Brecht's creative achievement defects of character which are properly those of the author. Bentley himself, in an essay of 1961 appropriately entitled 'Homage to BB', fell into the opposite side of the trap and allowed himself to perpetrate one of the earliest examples of a folly that has today become gospel in orthodox Brechtian circles:

> Brecht had no talent at all for collaboration if the word carries any connotation of equality, of give and take. [. . .] [His] collaborators were always people who wanted and needed to be dominated and exploited. That this should be true of friends and mistresses who never wrote anything notable of their own goes without saying. It is also true of the Big Names, including the biggest name of all – that of Kurt Weill. Weill has no more enthusiastic and enthralled listener than myself: the success of his music for *Mahagonny* and the other Brecht works is not in question. But how was that success achieved? Brecht sometimes intimated that he himself contributed some or all of the tunes of *The Threepenny Opera*. For years I considered this a boast. Later I came to believe it . . . Weill took on the artistic personality of any writer he happened to work with. He had no (artistic) personality of his own.*

---

* Eric Bentley, 'Homage to BB', Introduction to *Seven Plays by Bertolt Brecht*, edited by Eric Bentley (New York, 1961), p. xxxiv.

As we pass the thirtieth anniversary of Brecht's death, his reputation stands higher than ever. No poet or playwright of our century has established so strong a hold on the minds and imaginations of readers and theatregoers throughout the world; none has commanded such fanatical loyalty from scholars, critics, and journalists; and none has been better placed to reap the benefits of shrewd and intensive marketing conducted by a formidable network of publishers and official organizations, and astutely guided by ever-watchful heirs and their legal representatives. Despite its immensity and apparent diversity, the entire structure is essentially monolithic. No exit or entrance is left unguarded. Within the perimeter, questions and criticism are warmly welcomed, arguments encouraged, theory and practice endlessly gone over. But woe betide the backsliders, the doubters and the unbelievers beyond the walls. Among the earliest of them was Weill.

At the point where Brecht ceased to be a self-determined cause and became a legend he acquired a strange likeness to the greatest of all his natural enemies, Richard Wagner. On the lower levels of their exceptional genius both men were masters of the entrepreneurial and manipulative skills; and both had established before their death everything that was needed for the continuity and security of their work, including the conditions conducive to a posthumous and worldwide cult. It is not from Brecht's 'influence', and still less from his genius, that Weill needs 'shelter', but from the cult's effect on critical standards, and from the sheer obfuscation that occurs as soon as the jealousies and petty rivalries of long ago are handed down to later generations and solemnly re-enacted in forms that purport to be ideological but plainly are not.

The natural link between marketing strategies and critical attitudes is illustrated on the one hand by such titles as *Brechts 'Die Dreigroschenoper'* and *Brechts 'Aufstieg und Fall der Stadt Mahagonny'* – chosen by Suhrkamp for recent (1985) and forthcoming (1986–7) volumes in their series of Brecht *Materialien* – and on the other by Albrecht Dümling's 700-page study of *Brecht und die Musik* published in 1985 by Kindler Verlag of Munich. A pupil of Carl Dahlhaus and a creative associate of West Berlin's Hanns Eisler Choir, Dümling has accomplished a considerable feat: his book is superbly researched, attractively written, and at heart genuinely musical. For Weill, both as man and as musician, he shows more initial respect and affection than is customary among the younger West German critics. But as soon as Brecht makes his entry, Dümling's 'image and understanding' of Weill begins to blur, and emotion takes over from common sense (see p. 202 below). Despite some incidental insights that are unprecedented in Brecht literature, Dümling ends by endorsing the traditional view of Weill as essentially a creation of Brecht and one who inadvertently or by design betrayed the intentions of his Maker.

If there is a lesson to be learned from the vagaries of Vulgar Brechtism it is one that Brecht's own work points to: the clandestine relationship between hero-worshippers and iconoclasts is always consummated under cover of darkness, and often goes unrecognized even by those who are caught up in it. Were Weill to be rescued from his detractors only to become an object of adulation, the rescue itself would be illusory and the damage greater than any that could deliberately be inflicted on him. So few criteria are applicable to his European and his American work in equal measure that a failure to discriminate between different kinds as well as different orders of quality attacks the very basis of any defensible evaluation of 'the whole Weill'. To deny, out of misplaced loyalty, the very existence of the rift that divides his work in two is not only to flout all musical sense; it is culpably to conceal that rift's first cause.

The image or understanding that still needs to be brought into sharper focus is that of Weill *without Germany*. Behind it looms an incommensurable tragedy for Western man, and no serious discussion of Weill is conceivable without reference to its significance for him as a German composer of Jewish descent. Had he been a consciously Jewish composer who happened to be born in Germany the nature and realities of his exile would have been very different. It was the fundamentally German nature of his creative and intellectual loyalties, and the consequent attenuation of his Jewish links, that gave the specifically anti-semitic indictments of him as one of the 'representatives of Jewish-Marxist culture' a power to wound, and wound deeply, which they never attained with non-Jewish intellectuals like Brecht – for whom, indeed, such indictments were legitimately a source of pride.

The circumstances and considerations that led Weill in 1934–5 to identify himself with the Judeo-messianic content of *Der Weg der Verheissung* were those that led Schoenberg formally to renew his religious obligations after his expulsion from the Prussian Academy of Arts and his flight to Paris in the early summer of 1933. The parallel was a function of movement, of flight in both senses of the word: long before the Nazi seizure of power the two composers had been proceeding on widely separate paths, at different altitudes, and in opposite aesthetic directions; and yet the forces that drove them to Paris had not in any respect differentiated between the Austrian master and the first German composer to disavow – in principle and by precept – the accolade 'verehrter Meister', which had already and deservedly been bestowed on Hindemith.

The discovery that '*tout Paris*' was lionizing the composer of *Die sieben Todsünden* (first performed in Paris in June 1933) while ignoring the plight of less fashionable refugees must therefore have been almost intolerable to the 59-year-old Schoenberg and his loyal adherents (Eisler among them). But before the year was out, Weill too was suffering the pangs of rejection and had retreated from metropolitan Paris to his hideout in Louveciennes.

He was now at the threshold of the third and most difficult of the seven-year periods that subsume his creative development after 1919. The second period had likewise, but in a different sense, begun with a rejection, indeed, with two related ones: in 1927 Schoenberg had unsuccessfully recommended Weill for membership of the Prussian Academy of Arts* at the very point when Weill was finally renouncing Pierrot's moon in favour of Alabama's, and thereby seeming to dissociate himself from much that he had held dear since 1919. Considerably greater, however, were the implications of his efforts in 1934 to uproot himself from Germany and its now abhorrent 'culture' – beginning with the explicitly anti-Fascist *Der Kuhhandel*,† and continuing with *Der Weg der Verheissung*. A revulsion that on the emotional level was simple and wholly understandable became on the creative and intellectual levels increasingly complex, until in the end it affected the entire linguistic and intellectual structure of Weill's creativity.

Precisely what was at stake can be heard in the Second Symphony and *Die sieben Todsünden*, the last two works that presuppose the German audience Weill had made his own since 1927. As two forms of unconscious leave-taking they are consummate.

Something of the inner life of these works may be gleaned from the profoundly searching portrait photograph of Weill taken by Hoyningen-Huene in Paris during the preparations for *Die sieben Todsünden*.‡ Among the numerous portraits of Weill in his thirties the Hoyningen-Huene is unique. It alone has the kind of historical and psychological authenticity that allows it to stand beside the Man Ray and the Florence Homolka portraits of Schoenberg. In that respect its complete and cruel antithesis is the portrait photograph of Weill taken by the fashionable Canadian photographer Yousuf Karsh at the time of *Street Scene*. By far the most widely reproduced of all Weill photographs,‡ it shows him seated at his Brook House desk, immaculately dressed and freshly coiffured, with chin thrust forward as in no other photograph, and pen poised over a page that could almost be a balance-sheet but reveals itself, in the better reproductions, as a page from the rehearsal score of *Street Scene*. There is no remotely comparable picture, and yet it is impossible to imagine one better suited to the purposes of documenting the 'image and understanding' of 'Weill in America' that has been so vigorously promoted by Brecht scholars in recent years – the image, that is, of one who was at home on Broadway but would have been equally so in the boardrooms of Wall Street or Madison Avenue.

In the transparent mendacity of the Karsh portrait lies its only truth.

---

* See H. H. Stuckenschmidt, *Arnold Schoenberg* (London, John Calder, 1977) p. 325.
† See Drew, 'Reflections on the Last Years: *Der Kuhhandel* as a Key Work', in Kowalke (ed.), *A New Orpheus: Essays on Kurt Weill* (New Haven, Yale University Press, 1986).
‡ See plate section.

The figure at the desk is no mere *Doppelgänger*, but an impostor who can at once be unmasked by reference to a random sample from several hundred photographs of Weill taken during the 1940s. The imposture becomes 'genuine' through Weill's endorsement of its impersonal conformity in preference to the introspective and enigmatic figure portrayed not only by Hoyningen-Huene but also, with uncharacteristic insight, by Karsh himself in a second, and quite unknown, portrait taken at the same session in Brook House. It shows Weill in profile, standing by the stone staircase and reading a book whose author – or so the tone of the picture declares – is more likely to be Heine than O. Henry.*

The incongruity between the 'official' portrait and the European works with which it has so often been associated in concert programmes and record albums is manifest. To all outward appearances the Weill portrayed by Karsh has been as successful in disposing of his German past as the Weill who composed *Down in the Valley* and 'Wouldn't you like to be on Broadway?'. The fact that Schoenberg – no less than Thomas Mann or Brecht – was inseparable from his native culture and fiercely affirmed it in America is enough to explain why there was no possibility of Weill – with or without the intermediacy of Gershwin – renewing in Hollywood the acquaintance with Schoenberg he had briefly enjoyed in Berlin. With Stravinsky, whom he had also known in Berlin, there was no such problem. Stravinsky's backstage congratulations to Weill on the opening night of *Lady in the Dark* were not out of character; Schoenberg's would have been unthinkable.

It was Stravinsky – with an eye on Schoenberg, whom he was never to meet in Hollywood though they lived within easy reach of each other – who first declared his indifference to posterity; but it was Weill who was notoriously identified with the same sentiment. The date of Weill's pronouncement on that subject was 3 February 1940; the place, an interview with William G. King in the *New York Sun*; and the context, the end of the 'phoney war' in Europe and the start of Weill's collaboration with Moss Hart on *Lady in the Dark*. 'I'm convinced', he declared,

> that many modern composers have a feeling of superiority towards their audiences. Schoenberg, for example, has said he is writing for a time fifty years after his death [. . .] As for myself, I write for today. I don't give a damn about writing for posterity.

The apparent antagonism derives its strength from the suppressed remnants of an admiration that twenty years earlier had been boundless. Reformulated for Adorno's benefit in the early 1940s† it became a polarity

---

* Although there are purely technical reasons why the staircase portrait may have been unacceptable, the imagery and tone are so at odds with the 'official' portrait – as I hope to show in a future publication – that better results would surely have made no difference.
† The topic of Weill and Schoenberg was raised by the present author in conversation with Adorno in 1962, and elicited this recollection of Weill's remark.

indicative of two mutually exclusive routes for music – the only two that Weill was still prepared to defend. His rationalization had at least the merit of simplicity, and it was only towards the end of his life that the threats to it in his own field of music-theatre began to emerge on almost every side – Britten and Orff, Bernstein and Menotti, to name but four of the most widely publicized.

The full extent of what his own route in the 1940s excluded is most apparent from the vantage point of the two Ben Hecht pageants, *We Will Never Die* and *A Flag is Born*. Exactly opposite them on the Schoenberg side stand *A Survivor from Warsaw* and the unfinished modern Psalm, *Israel Exists Again*. While Schoenberg's versions of the Holocaust and its aftermath are propaganda only to the extent that his essentially artistic aims permit, Weill's and Hecht's never pretended to be anything other than propaganda, and since all propaganda is by its very nature self-eliminating it seems grimly appropriate that most of the music for them is lost.

The Weill–Hecht pageants exemplify in an extreme form the fundamental condition of Weill's Broadway work, which is that it rejects – as no work by a Schoenberg pupil, including Eisler, ever could – the concept and aura of 'das Kunstwerk'. But the kind of atrocities described in *We Will Never Die* have certainly played their part in the waning of European man's confidence in the entire tradition of 'high' art; and the extent to which Weill's Broadway work is a conscious reaction to a universal tragedy should not be underestimated – least of all in his last completed work, *Lost in the Stars*.

The conditioned reflexes of intellectualist opposition to Broadway that Schoenberg overcame in the case of Gershwin but few critics have managed to cope with in the comparable but different case of Bernstein have always been, and continue to be, the principal obstacle to a fair assessment of Weill's American achievement. To remark, as Europeans in particular are prone to do, that his American achievement is inferior to the European is to condone the kind of hierarchical comparisons by which Gershwin's music would be judged 'inferior' to Schoenberg's rather than as generically different.

The chances of Weill's American achievement being fairly assessed in Europe were never great and until quite recently have been diminishing. Today, as the Broadway musical prices itself out of its natural habitat and is deflected from its more serious (post-Weillian!) aims by a combination of economic, political, and social factors, it looks to Europe and especially to London for a temporary refuge. In these precarious circumstances it is just possible that some of the shows Weill wrote with little or no thought of tomorrow may find new audiences.

The American Weill's celebrated scorn for posterity was surely one of the factors that caused Lenya to hesitate for so long over the nature and timing of any formal provisions for the future of his work (and indeed of her own). Yet the words Maxwell Anderson had spoken at Weill's graveside are legible in so many of her actions during the ensuing thirty years that they can never have been far from her mind:

> I could wish that the times in which he lived had been less troubled. But these things were as they were – and Kurt managed to make thousands of beautiful things during the short and troubled time he had. [. . .] He left a great legacy in his music and in our memory of him. [. . .] But what he left must be saved, and we who are still here must save it for him.

Thanks above all to Lenya and to George Davis, much has indeed been saved, and all of it bears witness to that which has yet to be saved, not only from Weill's own work but also from the still scattered and damaged legacies of many other creative artists less fortunate than he.

D.D.

Berlin, August 1981
London/New York, August–December 1985
Moscow/London, 6 April–15 July 1986

Acknowledgements

The preceding Report describes the circumstances in which the West Berlin Academy of Arts commissioned this book; but the gratitude it expresses both to that institution and to its individual representatives requires ampler definition here. In again recalling Boris Blacher's decisive role with regard to the commission I must also pay tribute to the manner in which, after his death, his widow Gerty Herzog-Blacher and his friend and pupil Gottfried von Einem continued to involve themselves in the book's fortunes.

My first researches in Germany would have been very much slower and more difficult without the help of Dr Walter Huder, today the head of the Academy's archives. Frau Nele Hertling, in her present capacity as Secretary of the Academy, and previously as head of its music division, has been in charge of arrangements for the book and its German translation during the past two decades, and has been most generous with her time, her wise counsel, and her sympathetic support.

As the Report explains, my links with the Academy cover a period of thirty years and came about in the first place through Lotte Lenya and her husband George Davis. To do justice to the extent and character of Lenya's personal commitment to the objectives of this book and its companion volumes is a task that would merit a book to itself. From her lively understanding of the priorities discerned by George Davis as from her natural warmth and generosity of spirit there sprang so much encouragement and practical assistance that everything I wrote was in some sense informed by it.

As Lenya's successors since 1982 in administering Weill's artistic legacy, the Kurt Weill Foundation for Music has unequivocally re-affirmed the spirit of collaboration that had facilitated my work throughout the 1960s and the first half of the 1970s. Its President, Dr Kim Kowalke, has on countless occasions afforded me the immense benefits of his guidance, his scholarship, and, not least, his humour. Weill and Lenya would both have rejoiced to know that under his leadership the Foundation's Research Center in New York is an eminently serious but not a solemn place, and that among the sounds that have reverberated

48

from its high ceilings during the past three years, that of helpless laughter has been by no means infrequent. The Foundation's Archivist, David Farneth, has responded with impeccable efficiency and seemingly imperturbable geniality to the innumerable demands I have made upon his time and patience, and in this he has been ably assisted by his staff. Together with Dr Kowalke, he has supplied me with important material and information I could not otherwise have known of or had carelessly overlooked. He has also accompanied me on research forays, and has fulfilled, often with breathtaking swiftness, my manifold requests from the opposite side of the Atlantic.

The Foundation's Musical Executive and Vice-President of the Board of Trustees, Lys Symonette, has played a valued role in many of our round-table discussions at the Research Center, and has been especially helpful over points of transcription and translation. Like Mrs Symonette, Professor Guy Stern was closely associated with Lenya and George Davis from the early days, and is today a member of the Foundation's Board of Trustees; my thanks are due to him for many courtesies and for the opportunity of availing myself of his great knowledge of German literature. To Milton Coleman, one of Lenya's most trusted advisers and today the Foundation's Treasurer, I owe a special debt of gratitude for expressions of friendship and support during the past fifteen years. Another loyal friend of Lenya's, Milton Caniff, was like myself a member of the Foundation's board until 1976; to him and to his wife I am most grateful for help and hospitality during my early visits to South Mountain Road. The late John F. Wharton, who helped bring the Foundation into being in 1962, was a friendly supporter of my work from the start.

Quotations from all letters and articles by Weill and by Lenya are © copyright by the Foundation, and appear in the following pages by kind permission of the Foundation. Translations from the German are by the present author except where otherwise noted.

To my valiant publishers, Faber and Faber, to my old and my new friends in that firm, and above all to Dr Donald Mitchell, Chairman of Faber Music, and his wife Kathleen, I owe an immeasurable debt. Peter du Sautoy, the predecessor of Matthew Evans as Managing Director of Faber and Faber, was an early supporter of my entire Weill project; and from the vantage point of his well-earned retirement has continued to take a kindly interest in it. The powerful encouragement and gentle persuasiveness, the critical insight and, not least, the magnanimous forbearance of my editor, Patrick Carnegy, have been an inestimable asset: in the fields of copy-editing, proofing and design, Jill Burrows, Jane Robertson and Louise Millar have been his tireless partners.

Drafted and written in an age before the very concept of a word-processor was known to the author and twice re-written in a later age when hopes of domesticating that animal had seemed merely fanciful, the present book owes an untold amount to the selfless labours of Pauline Gardiner, whose fair-copying of my own hand-corrected typescript, and whose readiness to cope with emergencies at all hours of the day and any day of the week were truly heroic. In that she followed a tradition already established by Jill Kirkpatrick and Malcolm MacDonald during the production of the final copy of the 1974 version.

When books of this kind are written by those of us who follow careers outside the academic field they tend, alarmingly, to draw benevolent colleagues into their vortex no less surely than hapless members of the author's family. Just as the early phases of my Weill work were indebted to the understanding of my editors at the *New Statesman*, John Freeman and Karl Miller, so were the final ones indebted to that of Tony Fell, Managing Director of Boosey & Hawkes Music Publishers. Two Boosey & Hawkes colleagues, Jane Burwell and Paul Meecham, have sacrificed innumerable evening and weekend hours to the cause of completing this book. Almost every page carries for me reminders of their work, and also that of Ken Bartlett – my translator and unofficial guardian–editor in Germany. Another part of the same constellation of collaborators is formed by my wife Judith, my daughters Lucy and Flora, my son Thomas, my mother, my stepfather the late Charles Mactaggart, and my grandmother, the late Grace Violet Hicklin, whose generosity enabled me to meet some of the costs of research and travel that would otherwise have been beyond my means.

The structural links between the present volume and the biographical and critical works associated with it are so numerous and so close that in most cases it is impossible to apportion between the projects those contributions of active or moral support for which my thanks are due. The appended list of my debts to institutions and individuals does not discriminate in this respect or with regard to relative scale: irrespective of size, each contribution has been invaluable and the cumulative effect vast. Later volumes will provide opportunities for more detailed definition and for mentioning these few individuals whose contributions did not or could not overlap with my work on the present volume.

Meanwhile, the opacity of a mere register of names can perhaps best be alleviated by selecting some representative figures from typical categories. Walter Kaempfer was a fellow-student with Weill at the Berlin Hochschule für Musik in 1919–20, and the only musical friend from that period to remain close to him throughout the German years and resume contacts with Lenya in the 1950s; Maurice Abravanel was one of Weill's composition-pupils in the mid-1920s, and became a lifelong friend and advocate of his work. I owe much to him and to Professor Kaempfer. Among Weill's relatives and personal friends, his brother Hanns, who died in 1946, played a role matched only by that of his sister Ruth. She and her husband Leo Sohn were exceptionally helpful to me. The doyen of Weill's publishers is Hans W. Heinsheimer. He joined Universal

Edition in Vienna shortly after Weill signed his first contract with that firm, was soon appointed head of its opera department, and remained in that post until 1938. After a decade in New York with Boosey & Hawkes – where Weill had hopes of placing *Street Scene* – he was appointed Director of Publications of G. Schirmer Inc., and in that capacity published one of Weill's most successful stage works, *Down in the Valley*. Although the number of times I have coupled Dr Heinsheimer's name with Weill's over the past twenty-five years must vastly exceed the number of times I have had the pleasure of meeting him, memory somehow allows those two orders of encounter to become indistinguishable.

My early and urgent need for contacts with Weill's publishers was paralleled by a comparable need to explore the worlds of his European collaborators; here, Martin Esslin and John Willett – the pioneers of Brecht studies in England – were unfailingly helpful. During the same period Margaret Rostock, librarian of the German Institute (as it then was) in London went to endless trouble on my behalf, as did Margaret Haferd of the United States Information Service.

Weill's professional associates and colleagues

Maurice Abravanel, Charles Alan, T. W. Adorno, George Antheil, Claudio Arrau, Ernst and Margot Aufricht, Peter Bing, Marc Blitzstein, Frank Cahill, Edward Clark, Cheryl Crawford, Carl Ebert, Hanns Eisler, Herbert Fleischer, Yvonne de la Casa Fuerte, Max Gobermann, Walter Goehr, Berthold Goldschmidt, Claire Goll, Walter Geiser, Ira and Lee Gershwin, Paul Hindemith, Felix Jackson (Joachimson), Edward James, Philipp Jarnach, Walter Kaempfer, Arthur Kistenmacher, Karl Koch, Maurice Levine, Muir Mathieson, Burgess Meredith, Darius and Madeleine Milhaud, Hans Nathan, Caspar Neher, Erwin Piscator, Lotte Reiniger, Feri Roth, Hermann Scherchen, William Steinberg, Henry Schnitzler, Fritz Stiedry, H. H. Stuckenschmidt, Anthony Tudor, Heinz Unger, Robert Vambery, Günther Weisenborn, Louise Zemlinsky.

Relatives and friends of Weill and of Lenya

Edward Cole, Mary Daniels, Martus Granirer, Anna Krebs, Marie Laure de Noailles, Henri Monnet, Paul Moor, William and Julie Sloan, Jo Révy.

Friends, colleagues, and associates of the author

Francis Burt, Regina Busch, Martin Esslin, Sidney Fixman, Peter and Suzanne Florence, Alexander Goehr, Paul Hamburger, Peter Heyworth, Josef Heinzelmann, Stephen Hinton, Sylvia Hirst, Bruce Hunter, Ian Kemp, Miles Krueger, R. O. Lehmann, William Mann, Jacques-Louis Monod, O. W. Neighbour, Andrew Porter, Hans F. Redlich, Willi Reich, Harold Rosenthal, Albi Rosenthal, Michael Rubinstein, Matyas Seiber, Christopher Shaw, Ronald K. Shull, Nicholas Slonimsky, John Warrack, J. Randall Williams, Eric Walter White, Harriett Watts, John Willett.

Weill's publishers

Universal Edition, Vienna: Karl Heinz Füssl, Ernst Hartmann, Stefan Harpner, Elena Hift, Elisabeth Molner, Alfred Schlee, Helmut Wagner. Universal Edition, London: Mia Herrmann, Alfred Kalmus, Tony Wright. Schott-Söhne, Mainz: Ken W. Bartlett. Heugel et Cie, Paris: François and Philippe Heugel, Manfred Kelkel. Chappell Inc., New York: Max Dreyfus, Lou Brunelli. G. Schirmer, New York: Hans W. Heinsheimer.

Institutions and Archives

Bertolt Brecht Archive, East Berlin: Helene Weigel-Brecht, Hertha Ramthun, Günter Glaeser. Bibliothèque Nationale, Paris. British Library. Deutsche Staatsbibliothek, East Berlin. German Institute, London (later Goethe Institute): Margaret Rostock. Institut für Theaterwissenschaft der Universität Köln: Helmut Grosse. Library of the Performing Arts, Lincoln Center, New York. Library of Congress, Washington. Österreichische Nationalbibliothek. United States Information Service (London): Margaret Haferd. Yale University Music Library: Victor Cardell, Adrienne Nesnow, Dr. Harold E. Samuel, Helen Bartlett.

D.D.
19 January 1987

Weill's Life and Times:
A Chronology

1900

2 March Born in the North German town of Dessau (Leipzigerstrasse 59), the third son of Albert Weill (1867–1955) Cantor of the Dessau synagogue, and Emma Weill née Ackermann (1872–1957); his brothers Nathan and Hanns are respectively two years and one year older. The Weill family has its roots in South Germany (Baden), and traces its origins back to the thirteenth century.

1901

6 October Birth of Weill's sister Ruth.

1907

18 February Dedication of the new Dessau synagogue in the Steinstrasse; Albert Weill and his family move to the Cantor's ground-floor apartment adjoining the synagogue.

c. **1909**

After three years at the elementary school (Vorschule) Weill now moves to the secondary school (Oberrealschule) where he is to remain until he is eighteen.

1913

1 October The 28-year-old conductor Albert Bing (who had studied conducting with Arthur Nikisch and composition with Pfitzner) takes up his appointment in Dessau as first Kapellmeister, under Franz Mikorey, at the Court Opera of the Duchy of Anhalt. He and his wife Edith – sister of the Expressionist playwright Carl Sternheim – are later to become close friends of the Weill family and 'second parents' to Kurt, who will be his private pupil during the years 1915–17.

1914

28 June　The assassination in Sarajevo of the heir to the Austrian throne precipitates the outbreak of the First World War.

1915

Having completed two or three years of elementary piano studies (first with the synagogue organist, Albert Brückner, and latterly with a French-born pianist, Margaret Schapiro), Weill now starts studying piano, theory, and composition privately with Albert Bing.

18 December　At a benefit concert sponsored by the Dessau Youth Section of the 'Verein für das Deutschtum im Ausland' (Society for Germans Abroad) and given in the palace of Duke Friedrich of Anhalt, Weill performs a Chopin nocturne and Liszt's *Liebestraum* No. 3.

1916–17

First serious attempts at composition (*Ofrah's Lieder*, September 1916); gives piano lessons to Duke Friedrich's nephews, Joachim and Eugen, and to his niece, Marie-Auguste; his studies with Bing now include conducting; Bing arranges for him to work part-time, on a voluntary basis, as coach at the (by now understaffed) Court Theatre.

Winter 1917–18　Intensive studies with Bing – instrumentation and orchestration, score-reading, piano.

1918

6 February　Weill is the piano accompanist in a *Lieder* and aria recital given in Dessau by pupils of the court opera singer Emilie Feuge; the second part of this programme opens with his own 'Abendlied' and 'Maikaterlied'.

March　Obtains his matriculation.

April　Leaves Dessau for Berlin and three months of study divided, experimentally, between philosophy at the University (under Max Dessoir and Ernst Cassirer) and music (piano, organ and theory) at the Hochschule für Musik. Under the terms of a pact devised by Albert Bing and agreed with his parents, he decides at the end of the three months to concentrate on his musical studies.

September　Enrols full-time at the Hochschule für Musik, studying conducting under Krasselt, counterpoint under F. E. Koch, and composition under Humperdinck.

November　Abdication of the Kaiser; armistice signed.

December　Spends Christmas vacation with his family in Dessau.

1919

January–July   Continues studies at the Hochschule für Musik.

July   Despite the award of a Felix Mendelssohn-Bartholdy award for composition, Weill agrees with his parents that he should leave the Hochschule at the end of the present semester on 26 July and gain more practical experience as a vocal coach and conductor, while continuing composition lessons (with Hermann Wetzler in Cologne or even, as Bing suggests, with Pfitzner in Munich). Two factors seem to have contributed to this decision: on the one hand growing dissatisfaction with the intensely conservative outlook of the present staff at the Hochschule (including Humperdinck), and, on the other, changes in family circumstances. Albert Weill is nearing the end of his tenure as Cantor in Dessau and in the autumn will move to a new home in Leipzig.

August   Having failed as yet to find a suitable post elsewhere, Weill (with private misgivings) enrols once again as a volunteer coach at the Dessau Opera, but now on a full-time basis. Albert Bing's new Chief Conductor is Hans Knappertsbusch.

4 September   In the concert hall of the Friedrichs-Theater, Dessau, Weill accompanies Elisabeth Feuge in a recital of arias (Meyerbeer, Rossini, Thomas) and *Lieder* (Pfitzner, Liszt, Wolf, Reger, Weill, etc.). According to a press report the house was full and the evening a great success.

December   As a result of a recommendation from Humperdinck, Weill is engaged as assistant conductor at the newly formed Municipal Theatre in the Westphalian town of Lüdenscheid.

1920

January   Following the resignation of the chief conductor, Weill takes over the responsibility for a mixed repertoire of operettas and popular opera.

May   At the end of the Lüdenscheid season Weill goes to Leipzig where his father has just been appointed director of the B'nai B'rith Children's Home. He stays with his parents for several weeks at their new home in the Leipzig suburb of Klein Steinberg.

22 June   Introduces and plays the piano in a programme of twentieth-century songs and piano music (Reger, Trunk, Schreker, Pfitzner, Marx, Schoenberg) sponsored by the Jewish cultural society in Halberstadt, whose musical activities are partly or wholly the responsibility of his brother Hanns. The singer is Elisabeth Feuge.

September   Returns to Berlin; his first lodgings are in Zehlendorf (Beerenstrasse 48); later he moves to Lichterfelde (11 Flensburgerstrasse).

December   Busoni interviews Weill, examines a portfolio of his compositions, and admits him as the sixth and last member of his (newly
reconstituted) Masterclass in Composition at the Prussian Academy of
Arts in Berlin.

1921

Supplementary studies with Philipp Jarnach; seeks part-time employ-
ment as synagogue organist; plays piano in a *Bierkeller* cabaret.

1922

18 November   *Zaubernacht*, a dance pantomime for children, to a scenario
by Wladimir Boritsch, has its successful premiere at the Theater am
Kurfürstendamm, Berlin.

1923

Four first performances in one year: Divertimento and *Sinfonia Sacra*
(Berlin Philharmonic), String Quartet, Op. 8 (Berlin and Frankfurt), and
the Suite from *Zaubernacht* (Dessau).

December   Weill completes his third and last year in the Masterclass;
Busoni writes to Universal Edition (Vienna), commending Weill to their
attention with particular reference to his opus 8 String Quartet.

1924

January   Premiere of *Frauentanz* at a Berlin ISCM concert conducted by
Fritz Stiedry; first meetings with the Expressionist playwright Georg
Kaiser (1878–1945).

February–March   Holiday in Switzerland and Italy followed by a visit to
Universal Edition in Vienna, where he accepts the offer of an exclusive
publishing contract.

May   Moves to new lodgings on the Winterfeldplatz; composition pupils
include Claudio Arrau, Maurice (de) Abravanel, and, rather later, Nikos
Skalkottas.

27 July   Death of Busoni.

Autumn   Through Kaiser, meets the actress Lotte Lenja (Lenya)
(1898–1981).
November   Starts regular work as chief music correspondent of *Der
deutsche Rundfunk*, the principal radio journal in Berlin.

1925

May   Moves to the Pension Hassforth, Luisenplatz 3, where Kaiser has a *pied-à-terre* and the poet–playwright Rudolph Leonhardt lives permanently. This is to be Weill's and Lenya's home for the next four years.

11 June World premiere of the Concerto for Violin and Wind Orchestra in Paris.

27 December American premiere of *Zaubernacht* (*Magic Night*), presented by Wladimir Boritsch in a special series of five Christmas matinées at the Garrick Theater, New York, with a company of children including Felicia Sorel (later to make her name on Broadway).

1926

28 January Marries Lenya.

27 March At the Dresden Opera, Fritz Busch conducts the first performance of Weill's and Kaiser's one-act opera *Der Protagonist*; its success, both with the press and with the public, establishes Weill's reputation as one of the outstanding composers of his generation in Germany.

1927

February–March First discussions with Brecht regarding a future collaboration take place under the shadow of the unsuccessful premiere at the Staatsoper unter den Linden (conductor, Erich Kleiber) of *Der neue Orpheus* and *Royal Palace*, both to texts by the surrealist poet–playwright Iwan Goll (1891–1950), a friend of Kaiser's and admired by Brecht for his Jarry-esque farces. Brecht begins work with Weill on the opera that is to become *Aufstieg und Fall der Stadt Mahagonny*.

18 July *Mahagonny*, a *Songspiel* to pre-existing texts by Brecht, is sung and acted by Lenya and a quintet of opera singers, and played by an ensemble from the Baden-Baden orchestra, as part of an opera programme commissioned and presented by the festival of 'Deutsche Kammermusik 1927' organized by Hindemith, Hans Flesch, and Heinrich Burkhard.

1928

18 February *Der Zar lässt sich photographieren*, Weill's and Kaiser's second one-act opera, is successfully launched at the Leipzig Opera and is taken up by numerous other companies in German-speaking territories.

3 August Premiere at the Theater am Schiffbauerdamm, Berlin, of *Die Dreigroschenoper* (*The Threepenny Opera*), a 'play with music' based on Elisabeth Hauptmann's translation of John Gay's *The Beggar's Opera*; text and lyrics by Brecht.

1929

Early in the New Year, Weill and Lenya move to an apartment at Bayern-Allee 14.

2 September Happy End, a 'play with music' by Brecht and Elisabeth Hauptmann, opens at the Theater am Schiffbauerdamm. It completely fails to match the success of *Die Dreigroschenoper*, and is withdrawn, never to be seen again in the lifetimes of either Weill or Brecht.

October The Wall Street Crash rocks the economies of the Western World, and heralds the Depression – whose effects are particularly severe in Germany.

1930

9 March After various ugly interruptions, the Leipzig premiere of the opera *Aufstieg und Fall der Stadt Mahagonny* ends in tumult; though not overtly political, the hostile demonstrations are representative of the forces which, before the year is over, will have ensured – whether by violence or by intrigue – that the favourable effects of the productions in Leipzig and elsewhere are nullified.

23 June Triumphantly successful premiere of Weill's and Brecht's 'school opera' *Der Jasager* – which was to have taken place as part of Hindemith's 'Deutsche Kammermusik 1930' festival in Berlin but was withdrawn in protest against the Festival's rejection of Brecht's and Eisler's *Die Massnahme*, and presented under the auspices of the Prussian Academy of Church and School Music.

1931

21 December The *Mahagonny* opera has its Berlin premiere at the Theater am Kurfürstendamm, in a commercially backed production by Ernst Josef Aufricht, directed by Caspar Neher and conducted by Alexander von Zemlinsky.

1932

10 March Amid the uproar of the presidential elections, in which Hitler is a candidate, and under direct political attack from the Nationalist and Nazi press, the Städtische Oper, Berlin, presents the world premiere of *Die Bürgschaft*, an opera in three acts with libretto by Caspar Neher and the composer. Weill's most ambitious work to date, it becomes a rallying point for the remaining defenders of the Republic's artistic policies.

March Weill moves from the Bayern-Allee to the modern house he has purchased in the suburb of Klein-Machnow (Wissmannstrasse 7). He and Lenya have now broken up, but are not yet formally separated. (Lenya is in Russia, where she has a role in Piscator's film of Anna Seghers's novel *The Revolt of the Fishermen of St Barbara*.)

Midsummer   Approximately 5½ million unemployed in Germany.

11 December   A semi-staged performance of the *Mahagonny-Songspiel* and *Der Jasager*, sponsored by the Vicomte and Vicomtesse de Noailles and given at the Salle Gaveau in Paris, takes the fashionable audience by storm, and is an immense personal success for Weill; Second Symphony commissioned by Princesse de Polignac.

1933

30 January   Hitler becomes Chancellor.

18 February   Triple premiere (Leipzig, Magdeburg, Erfurt) of the 'Wintermärchen' *Der Silbersee*, text and lyrics by Georg Kaiser; enthusiastic reception by general public and most of the press, including the Hugenberg chain; the Communist press is lukewarm, the Nazi press alone is hostile.

22 February   In Nazi demonstrations at the second *Silbersee* performance in Magdeburg, Weill is the subject of anti-Semitic abuse.

27 February   Reichstag fire.

28 February   Emergency decrees herald Nazi seizure of power.

21 March   Caspar and Erika Neher take Weill across the German border in their car, and head for Paris.

23 March–c. 10 July   Weill remains in Paris (first at the Hôtel Splendide, then at the Noailles residence), supported by continuing but reduced advances from his publishers and by a commission fee from Edward James for *Die sieben Todsünden*, a spectacle (or choral ballet) with text by Brecht. During the spring Lenya is in Berlin. Her correspondence with Weill is wholly amicable.

7 July   The premiere of *Die sieben Todsünden* at the Théâtre des Champs-Elysées is coolly received.

July–August   Italy, Switzerland; poor health.

September   Weill's and Lenya's divorce is formally completed.

3 October   Weill's contract with Universal Edition is suspended.

31 October   New publishing contract with Heugel (Paris).

November   Weill acquires a three-year lease of the first-floor apartment in a simple house in Louveciennes, near Paris. His house in Berlin is to be sold, but the formalities will not be concluded for some while.

26 November   Pro-Hitler and anti-Semitic demonstration, led by the composer Florent Schmitt, at concert performance in Paris of three songs from *Der Silbersee*, sung by Madeleine Grey and conducted by Maurice Abravanel. Weill is deeply shocked.

29 December   Attends the first performance in Italy of *Der Jasager* and the *Mahagonny-Songspiel* at the Accademia di Santa Cecilia in Rome. He returns to France by way of Vienna and Carlstadt (where he is briefly reunited with his parents).

1934

January–June   In Louveciennes; completes Second Symphony; begins the operetta *Der Kuhhandel*, and is encouraged by Heugel's popular-music department to enter the *chanson* market.

18 June   In Venice for a meeting with Max Reinhardt, Meyer Weisgal, and Lord Melchett regarding Weisgal's project for a large-scale musico-dramatic work by Franz Werfel and (it is hoped) Weill. Entitled *Der Weg der Verheissung* (*The Road of Promise*) it will set its account of the Jewish people (from the time of Moses' birth to that of the destruction of the Second Temple) in the context of racial persecution in modern times. The likely venue for the first performance is the Royal Albert Hall, London.

August   On returning to Louveciennes from his summer holiday in Italy Weill finds that he is obliged to write at very short notice the songs and incidental music for *Marie Galante*, a stage adaptation by Jacques Deval of his best-selling novel.

22 December   The Paris premiere of *Marie Galante* is a failure. Weill has already drafted nearly two hours' music for *Der Weg der Verheissung*, and is eager to return to *Der Kuhhandel*.

1935

January–June   In London – with expeditions to Alexander Korda's film studios in search of film work. Weill's first objective in London is to arrange for a production of *Der Kuhhandel*, in an English adaptation, which will be entitled *A Kingdom for a Cow*. When this is achieved he leaves his West End hotel and rents a small flat at Bramham Gardens, Earls Court, where he later finds a room for Lenya.

28 June   Premiere of *A Kingdom for a Cow*. The high expectations aroused by the previous day's trouble-free dress rehearsal are not fulfilled, and the critics, though favourably impressed by the play, the music, and the serious intentions of the authors, are doubtful whether the production will appeal to the London public, and certain that it cannot compete with recent imports from Broadway. The box-office response is indeed disastrous, and *A Kingdom for a Cow* suffers the same swift fate as *Happy End* and *Marie Galante*.

August Final discussions in Salzburg with Reinhardt, Werfel, and Weisgal regarding the premiere of *Der Weg der Verheissung*, which is now due to take place in New York in January 1936. Weill is to be a member of the production team, and will be required to write some new and more 'popular' numbers for the American adaptation, which is now entitled *The Eternal Road*. Lenya has been offered a part, and will join Weill and Weisgal on the voyage.

September Weill arrives in New York with Lenya and is immediately embroiled in the production difficulties of *The Eternal Road*. The St Moritz Hotel on Central Park is to be his home for the next three months.

10 October Meets George and Ira Gershwin after the premiere of *Porgy and Bess*.

November Meetings with Brecht, who is in New York (with Eisler) for the Theatre Union production of *The Mother* (*Die Mutter*); and with Marc Blitzstein, whom Weill had first met earlier in the year in Paris.

December An all-Weill concert of operatic and theatre music is mounted in New York by the League of Composers, and meets with a frosty reception. Some frankly popular numbers from *A Kingdom for a Cow* and *Marie Galante* give particular offence to more than one faction.

1936

January A fortnight before the planned opening of *The Eternal Road*, the production company is declared insolvent; Werfel returns to Europe immediately, but Weill decides that it would be wiser to remain in America until the premiere, unless a hoped-for commission from Les Ballets de Monte Carlo materializes (which it does not).

February Obtains a new passport from the German Consulate, establishes a new base at the Hotel Park Crescent, and explores various openings – notably the offer of a commission from American Ballet.

26 March Heugel gives notice that their 'financially disastrous' contract with Weill will be terminated on 31 December; meanwhile Meyer Weisgal is planning a September opening for *The Eternal Road*, and Weill is developing his contacts with the Group Theatre and with Jed Harris.

May Cheryl Crawford, who is a director of the Group Theatre (together with Lee Strasberg and Harold Clurman), arranges for Weill to visit the playwright Paul Green in Chapel Hill, North Carolina, in order to plan with him a musical play for production during the following season.

Late June–August Weill is at the Group Theatre summer camp in Nichols, Connecticut, lecturing, and sketching music for the Paul Green play, *Johnny Johnson*.

July   Start of the Spanish Civil War.

September   Weill returns to New York, where his and Lenya's home for the next twelve months is to be Cheryl Crawford's apartment at 455 East 51st Street.

19 November   The premiere of *Johnny Johnson* is moderately successful in general, and highly so as far as Weill is concerned; among the 'backers' of the production are the film producer Lewis Milestone and the playwright Clifford Odets, whose wife Luise Rainer had in 1933 been studying the role of Fennimore for the projected production of *Der Silbersee* at the Deutsches Theater, Berlin.

1937

7 January   *The Eternal Road* opens at the Manhattan Opera House and is generally acclaimed by press and public; although in the coming weeks it attracts large audiences, the overheads are vastly in excess of the box-office receipts, and stringent economies prove insufficient.

19 January   Weill and Lenya remarry.

May   After 153 performances, *The Eternal Road* is forced to close, leaving a trail of unrecoverable debts, and a reputation of having been one of the costliest failures in the history of show business; Weill's reputation is relatively unscathed, since the extent of his musical contribution had from the start been deliberately minimized – to his extreme annoyance.

Late January–July   Film work in Hollywood; Weill stays first at 6630 Whitley Terrace, and later moves to 686 San Lorenzo Drive, Santa Monica; further contacts with the Gershwins, renewed friendship with the composer George Antheil (whom Weill had first met and befriended in Berlin in 1929); work with Sam and Bella Spewack and E. Y. Harburg on a musical play about refugees from a German theatre, for which a Broadway production by Max Gordon seems imminent (but does not materialize).

August   Discussion in North Carolina with Paul Green regarding *The Common Glory*, a musical pageant about the origins of American democracy, designed for the Federal Theatre.

26/27 August   Having originally entered the USA on a temporary visa, which has since been extended, Weill takes the first step towards American citizenship, and re-enters from Canada in order to establish immigrant status. His lease on the apartment in Louveciennes has lapsed; Madeleine Milhaud arranges for the transportation of his belongings to New York.

September   Thanks to his Hollywood work, Weill is now able to exchange his rooms in Cheryl Crawford's Manhattan apartment for a duplex apartment at 231 East 62nd Street.

September–December Work on *The Common Glory* gradually slows down; the actor Burgess Meredith interests Weill in a Davy Crockett play by Hofmann (H. R.) Hays, who two years before had collaborated with Hanns Eisler on the political show, *A Song about America*; the Federal Theatre is attracted by the idea of a musical version of the play, with Meredith playing the role of Crockett. Weill and Hays start work.

1938

January–April After weeks of work on the text and the music, the Davy Crockett project peters out for want of a backer. But meanwhile Burgess Meredith's friend and neighbour Maxwell Anderson has enthusiastically responded to the idea of collaborating with Weill on a historical play based on Washington Irving's satirical history of New York; and the organizers of the 1939 New York World's Fair have commissioned Weill to compose an elaborate score for the pageant *Railroads on Parade*. Weill and Lenya rent a small country retreat at the end of a wooded lane leading off the Haverstraw Road, Suffern – some 35 miles from central Manhattan and within easy reach of Maxwell Anderson's and Burgess Meredith's homes in South Mountain Road, New City.

10 April Hitler's annexation of Austria; before long, Weill's erstwhile publishers, Universal Edition, are taken over by Nazi interests; only Alfred Schlee remains to guard the remnants of the Hertzka tradition.

April–May Weill is in Hollywood for the final editing and dubbing of his score for Fritz Lang's film *You and Me*; on his return to New York he is confronted with Maxwell Anderson's completed book and lyrics for *Knickerbocker Holiday* together with plans for a production in September or October. The entire score has to be written and orchestrated in a few weeks.

19 October *Knickerbocker Holiday* opens on Broadway and is a success.

1939

30 April *Railroads on Parade* opens at the World Fair, and is judged one of the Fair's outstanding successes.

June–July Weill in Malibu, working with Anderson on *Ulysses Africanus*, a drama of the American South, originally planned for Paul Robeson.

3 September Two days after the German invasion of Poland, Britain and France declare war on Germany.

1940

3 February In an important interview published in the *New York Times*, Weill unreservedly commits himself to Broadway and to the development of its musical sector.

March Starts work with Moss Hart on *Lady in the Dark*.

1941

23 January *Lady in the Dark* premiere in New York; it is an unqualified success.

February Paramount buys the film rights for *Lady in the Dark*.

5 April Weill buys Brook House, a converted farmhouse on South Mountain Road, close to the homes of Maxwell Anderson and Burgess Meredith. The first home of his own since he left Germany, it is a source of much happiness to him for the remainder of his life, and an immediate consolation for the difficulties he now experiences in finding a basis for a new Broadway collaboration. (Two years are to pass before any further collaboration takes wing.)

7 December Pearl Harbor is attacked by the Japanese; America declares war on the Axis powers.

1942

In the face of continual frustrations with his Broadway projects, Weill devotes much of his time to work connected with the war effort.

April Begins working for 'Lunch Hour Follies' (an organization modelled on such British ventures as 'Workers' Playtime') with the aim of entertaining munitions workers during their midday break.

June Cheryl Crawford, now an independent producer, agrees to back Weill's proposed collaboration with Sam and Bella Spewack on a musical adaptation of F. Anstey's Victorian novella *The Tinted Venus*, for which Ogden Nash will write the lyrics. Weill offers title role to Marlene Dietrich.

September (first three weeks) Drafts some songs for *The Tinted Venus*.

Late September – early October In Hollywood for talks with Dietrich; visits Brecht in Santa Monica.

November Resumes work for 'Lunch Hour Follies'; *Tinted Venus* collaboration is not going smoothly, but Tilly Losch is now being considered for the title role.

1943

January–March Owing to the difficulties of commuting to New York in wintry wartime conditions, Weill stays at the Hotel Ambassador, New York, latterly working with Ben Hecht on the Jewish memorial pageant, *We Will Never Die*.

April Finally despairing of the Spewack *Venus* script, Cheryl Crawford engages the celebrated humorist S. J. Perelman to write an entirely new 'book'; at last there is real and encouraging progress. The *Venus* show is now to be called *One Touch of Venus*.

Late April or early May Brecht and Ruth Berlau stay at Brook House for several days, principally in order to work with Weill (see *Projects*).

June Weill returns to Hollywood and visits Brecht again.

27 August Takes the oath as an American citizen.

7 October *One Touch of Venus* opens on Broadway, and is an instant 'hit'.

1 November Having accepted a film offer on condition that he works with Ira Gershwin, moves to 881 Moraga Drive, Hollywood; apart from brief visits to New York, he is to remain there for the next six months.

1944

January–March Further negotiations with Brecht (see *Projects*) regarding *Der gute Mensch von Sezuan*.

April Begins collaboration in Hollywood with Edwin Justus Mayer and Ira Gershwin on an operetta based on Mayer's Benvenuto Cellini play, *The Firebrand*.

August Rents house at 10640 Taranto Way, Bel Air, Los Angeles, for eight weeks; attends recording sessions for his musical film with Ira Gershwin, *Where Do We Go From Here?*

October Completes rehearsal score of *The Firebrand* and reluctantly renounces the Brecht project, having failed to find a Broadway producer for it.

1945

22 March *The Firebrand of Florence*, with Lenya in the leading role of the Duchess, opens on Broadway, and is poorly received; the production closes at the end of April – Weill's first and only Broadway failure.

April–June Hollywood again, this time for work on the long-delayed film of *One Touch of Venus*; on 18 April meets Brecht; corresponds with Paul Robeson concerning a 'black Oedipus' opera; meetings with Jean Renoir and René Clair.

7 May   End of war in Europe.

6 August   Atomic bomb on Hiroshima; surrender of Japan a week later.

1946

A year in Manhattan and South Mountain Road, largely occupied with *Street Scene*, a 'Broadway opera' based on Elmer Rice's play of the same name.

1 August   Elected a member of the Playwrights' Company – the first new member since the Company's foundation in 1938.

16 December   Pre-Broadway opening in Philadelphia of *Street Scene*, which plays to almost empty houses for three disastrous weeks; Weill devotes all his energies to saving the production for Broadway.

1947

9 January   *Street Scene* opens on Broadway, and is acclaimed by audience and press alike; but the running costs are dangerously high.

March   First discussions with Alan Jay Lerner.

6 May   Sails for England on the liner *Mauretania*; after an evening in Liverpool – where his first experience of a music-hall delights him greatly – he spends a week in London renewing old acquaintances and developing his links with the film industry (Alexander Korda, Muir Mathieson, Hubert Clifford) and with the BBC (in the person of Herbert Murrill, an eminent but not prolific composer once associated with Rupert Doone's Group Theatre and now in charge of the BBC's music department). He then proceeds to Paris – where he spends a shorter and less happy time – and from there, via Switzerland, to his principal destination, Palestine. There he visits his parents and relatives in Naharia, is introduced to Chaim Weizmann and shown round his Institute, and is formally introduced to the Palestine Symphony Orchestra.

12 June   Returns to New York, and holds an angry *post mortem* on the closure of *Street Scene* (on 17 May), which in his view was unwarranted.

June–July   First discussions with Herman Wouk regarding a future adaptation of his best-selling novel *Aurora Dawn*; start of collaboration with Alan Jay Lerner on a new Cheryl Crawford show for September.

Late August   Brecht writes from Hollywood inviting Weill to write the music for the first production of *Schweik im 2. Weltkrieg*, which Wolfgang Langhoff is planning to produce at the Deutsches Theater in the Russian sector of Berlin; Brecht also reports on the recent Losey–Laughton production of his *Galileo*, and mentions a Swedish film project for *Die*

Dreigroschenoper, which, he hopes, will pay for his forthcoming trip to Zurich.

September Postponement to spring 1948 of the Weill–Lerner show (provisionally entitled *A Dish for the Gods*); Weill tells Brecht that because of his present commitments he could not undertake the *Schweik* score before next summer, and offers to help raise funds for his trip to Zurich.

24–26 September In Washington Hanns Eisler appears before the House Committee on Un-American Activities (HUAC), which is investigating Communist infiltration in Hollywood; his case is referred to the Justice Department.

12 October Caspar Neher writes to Weill from Zurich (where he is awaiting the arrival of Brecht, though he does not mention this) regarding *Die Bürgschaft*.

27 October Weill and Maxwell Anderson are among the sixty-six signatories of a solidly Democrat protest against the current HUAC hearings.

30 October Brecht appears before the Washington HUAC Committee, is commended for his good behaviour, and leaves for Switzerland the next day.

1948

Early spring Hans Heinsheimer, who was head of Universal Edition's opera department from 1926 until the Anschluss in 1938, and then moved to New York as the assistant to Ralph Hawkes in the new Boosey & Hawkes American office, approaches Weill in his new capacity as Director of Publications at Schirmer with a request for an opera in the tradition of *Der Jasager*, for production by the opera department of the University of Indiana in Bloomington, whose director is Hans Busch, the son of Fritz Busch; Weill offers to adapt the unpublished ballad opera *Down in the Valley* which he had composed in 1945 for an abortive radio series.

15 July Together with Alan Jay Lerner, Weill attends the highly successful Bloomington premiere of *Down in the Valley*.

7 October *Love Life* opens on Broadway; moderate success.

1949

January–February Correspondence with Brecht regarding proposed updating of the text of *Die Dreigroschenoper* for German productions and with others regarding proposed updating of the music. To both proposals Weill is adamantly opposed. Begins work with Maxwell Anderson on *Lost in the Stars*, an adaptation of Alan Paton's *Cry the Beloved Country*.

July Collapses while playing tennis with Alan Lerner, but soon recovers and dismisses the incident as unimportant.

31 October *Lost in the Stars* opens on Broadway; success.

1950

January Weill begins work with Anderson on a musical adaptation of *Huckleberry Finn*; writes to Brecht of his plans to visit Europe with Lenya in the spring.

3 March Celebrates fiftieth birthday quietly at home.

15 March Coronary.

3 April Dies in Flower Hospital, New York.

5 April Buried, without religious rites, in the cemetery at Haverstraw overlooking the Hudson River.

Catalogue of Weill's Works

Purposes and Organization
of the Catalogue

Purposes

The immediate purposes are twofold: first, to list Weill's known works and their constituent elements; second, to locate, list, and describe the extant holographs. On the assumption that specialized catalogues will eventually be forthcoming and that in the meantime there is a need for a compendium to which the interested general reader as well as the specialist can turn, the present catalogue's bibliographic functions have been somewhat curtailed in order to leave room for more broadly informative ones. Value judgements are in principle excluded, but exceptions are made where a practical problem demands. Since the space and treatment allotted to each composition are determined solely by the nature of the material, a forgotten by-work may figure more prominently than some major composition. Such imbalances have no critical significance, except in so far as they demonstrate a certain objectivity implicit in the whole undertaking. For the ultimate purpose of the catalogue is to present a view of Weill's *work* – in the sense of handicraft, labour, and industry – which concentrates on essential data and is relatively undisturbed by the aesthetic categories his achievement so often calls in question. Although conceived as being strictly complementary to the 'critical biography' with which it has from the start been associated, the catalogue shares with that work a fundamental preoccupation with chronology, as a function of creative evolution. Not only the sequence of entries, but also the subheadings, from 'inception' to 'first performance' and beyond, are chronologically ordered.

Order of Entries

Entries are arranged chronologically according to the starting date of each composition. Major revisions, adaptations, or rearrangements (e.g. suites) are treated separately if in the interim any new work has been started. Discontinued projects on which Weill is known to have made a musical start are included in the main body of the catalogue at the appropriate points; those that had no direct musical consequences are considered in the *Projects* section.

Structure of Entries

TITLES

The main titles of unpublished works correspond to those given on the autograph title-page or first-page heading unless otherwise noted. In the case of published works the printed title page has priority, but discrepancies between that and the autograph are identified in the *Notes*. Translations given in round brackets are in general use; those in square brackets are the author's.

SUBTITLES AND DESCRIPTIONS

Subtitles or generic descriptions provided by the composer appear in quotation marks beneath the main title, translated if necessary.

TEXT AUTHOR

Whenever appropriate, the name of the author is incorporated in the subtitle or generic description. Pre-existing texts are (unless self-evident) denoted by the preposition 'on' or 'after' – the latter in cases where Weill is (apparently) responsible for some elements of adaptation.

DURATION

All durations are approximate.

DRAMATIC ROLES AND VOCAL SPECIFICATIONS

Roles are listed in approximate order of prominence. Vocal specifications correspond with the lists in published scores of works written for more-or-less traditional operatic or concert organizations. Of Weill's other work for the musical stage, only the 'winter's tale', *Der Silbersee*, the operetta *Der Kuhhandel*, and the 'Broadway opera' *Street Scene* allow for a comparably specific listing. To outward appearances at least, Weill accepted the principle that vocal music written for actors or other non-professional singers is freely transposable according to the exigencies of casting. Although in practice his orchestration and (during the European period) his sense of key characteristics suggest that the freedom has limits, the fact remains that, in casting works of this kind, the tension between purely musical and purely theatrical considerations is acute, and will be resolved according to the personalities involved and the resources available, rather than to any prescriptions. The present catalogue therefore follows the composer's example, and remains non-committal.

INSTRUMENTATION

Details of instrumentation are given at this juncture except where they are few enough to be included in the descriptive subtitle. The means of signifying instrumentation are described below, under *Abbreviations*.

SYNOPSIS

The subject matter and action are outlined.

MUSICAL NUMBERS, ROLE DISTRIBUTION, AND SCENE CHANGES

Apart from the three stage works on texts by Kaiser and Goll, every score for the stage and the cinema is summarized in terms of 'numbers'. Although such summaries fail to distinguish between closed forms and open or overlapping ones, and although they necessarily ignore the existence of various types of recitative (which have a significant role in Weill's European music), they do help indicate the approximate extent of the score, while providing a means not only of indexing the entire output of arias, duets, choruses, songs, and song-type ensembles, but also of cataloguing Weill's numerous self-borrowings. Identifying and placing those numbers omitted from stage works prior to completion, first performance, or publication, or added thereafter, proved to be one of the most challenging tasks implicit in the responsibility of 'gathering together' Weill's artistic legacy. 'Cut' numbers whose exact placing cannot be deduced from internal or other evidence are listed as appendices to their parent work; the final status of all cut numbers (e.g. vocal score or orchestrated) is codified.

MANUSCRIPTS

These are described under four headings corresponding to the main evolutionary stages discussed below (*Weill's Methods of Composition*):

Sketches
Ranging from thematic memos through substantial fragments to complete paragraphs or stanzas. Pencil only.

Draft
Complete continuity draft or particell. Pencil only.

Rehearsal Score
Fair copy of draft made only when a vocal score is urgently required for rehearsal purposes. Usually ink.

Orchestral Score
Always ink, except for late additions to Broadway scores.

The *quantity* of material in each of these categories is indicated either by the author's calculation of the number of holograph pages (irrespective of completeness) or, in the case of orchestral scores and some rehearsal scores, by reference to the composer's own pagination.

Instead of the folio measurements customarily given in manuscript catalogues under each entry, the present catalogue uses a code system referring to the brand-names of every manuscript paper Weill is known to have used. The codes and papers are listed, together with measurements and approximate dates of use, under *Abbreviations*.

All inks are black unless a colour is mentioned.

FIRST PERFORMANCE

Dates are derived from (or have been checked against) contemporary newspaper and periodical sources, from which come the partial cast lists where complete ones have not been traced. In the case of Broadway musicals, 'out of town' openings are no less significant than the actual premiere. Both are noted.

PUBLICATIONS

The only posthumous publications noted under this section are first publications or significant new editions. No attempt has been made to list the considerable quantity of popular arrangements and reprints published in Weill's lifetime.

PERFORMING VERSIONS

Under this heading are noted the existence and (where appropriate) the first performance and publication of posthumous editions prepared from remnants of works that would otherwise be unperformable, or from complete works whose performance has been hindered by inherent practical problems.

NOTES

Commentaries and marginalia are reserved for the end of the entry except where they have a direct bearing on an earlier section.

Abbreviations and Editorial Principles

Location of primary sources

AdK   Akademie der Künste, West Berlin

BBA   Bertolt Brecht Archive, East Berlin

DSBA   Deutsche Staatsbibliothek (East Berlin) Ferruccio Busoni Archive

EHA   Engelbert Humperdinck Archive, University of Frankfurt

KWF   Kurt Weill Foundation for Music

LOC   Library of Congress, Washington DC

LPA   Library of the Performing Arts, Lincoln Center, New York

ONC   O. W. Neighbour Collection

PHI   Paul Hindemith Institute, Frankfurt-am-Main

RWC   Rita Weill Collection

UEA   Universal Edition Archive; the extant holograph full scores etc. of works assigned to UE are deposited in the music collection of the Austrian National Library in Vienna; with effect from February 1986 Weill's correspondence with Universal Edition is available for research purposes – together with the correspondence of other leading composers in the UE catalogue – through the Stadt- und Landesbibliothek in Vienna. A project for the computerization of all references is due to be completed in January 1988.

WLA   Weill/Lenya Archive – The Papers of Kurt Weill and Lotte Lenya; Yale University Music Library Archival Collection, MSS 30. This collection – the catalogue of which is noted below, under AN.WL – includes most of the items originally in the Weill legacy. Inquiries should be addressed to the Yale University Music Library, P.O. Box 2104A, Yale Station, New Haven, CT 06520-7440.

WLRC   Weill–Lenya Research Center, 7 East 20th Street, New York, NY 10003; see p. 446 below.

Unless otherwise mentioned, all musical manuscripts described in the catalogue section of the present volume are in WLA, all correspondence with Universal Edition is in UEA, and all correspondence between Weill and Lenya is in WLRC.

Secondary sources

AD.BM   Albrecht Dümling. *Lasst euch nicht verführen. Brecht und die Musik*. Munich: Kindler. 1985

AN.WL   Adrienne Nesnow. *Kurt Weill and Lotte Lenya papers*. New Haven: Yale University Library. 1984

BB.AJ   Bertolt Brecht. *Arbeitsjournal*. Frankfurt-am-Main: Suhrkamp. 1974

BB.GBL   Bertolt Brecht (ed. Fritz Hennenberg). *Das grosse Brecht-Liederbuch*. Frankfurt-am-Main: Suhrkamp. 1984

BB.GW   Bertolt Brecht. *Gesammelte Werke*. Frankfurt-am-Main: Suhrkamp (Werkausgabe). 1967

DD.UKW   David Drew (ed.). *Über Kurt Weill*. Frankfurt-am-Main: Suhrkamp. 1975

HM.WL   Henry Marx (ed.). *Weill–Lenya*. New York: Goethe House. 1976

JS.KW   Jürgen Schebera. *Kurt Weill*. Leipzig: VEB Deutscher Verlag für Musik. 1983

KK.ANO   Kim H. Kowalke (ed.). *A New Orpheus: Essays on Kurt Weill*. New Haven: Yale University Press. 1986

KK.LF   Kim H. Kowalke. 'Lost and Found'. A paper on Weill's redis-covered manuscripts, delivered at the Kurt Weill Conference, Yale University, 5 November 1983. Text in WLRC.

KK.WE   Kim H. Kowalke. *Kurt Weill in Europe*. Ann Arbor: UMI Research Press. 1979

KW.AS   Kurt Weill (ed. David Drew). *Ausgewählte Schriften*. Frankfurt-am-Main: Suhrkamp. 1975

KWN   *Kurt Weill Newsletter*. Published twice a year by the Kurt Weill Foundation for Music. Inc., 142 West End Avenue, Suite 1-R, New York, NY 10023

PH.OK   Peter Heyworth. *Otto Klemperer. His life and times*. vol. 1. London, New York: Cambridge University Press. 1983

RS.DGS   Ronald Sanders. *The Days Grow Short. The Life and Music of Kurt Weill*. New York: Holt, Rinehart and Winston. 1980

RS.MWB   Ronald K. Shull. *Music and the Works of Bertolt Brecht: A Documentation*. Ph.D. dissertation, University of Kansas, 1985

Publishers

EAM   European American Music Inc.

UE   Universal Edition, Vienna

Instrumentation

In the case of works for small ensembles, the instrumentation is given in full. In the case of works written in Europe and involving standard orchestras it is indicated by figures according to the customary layout, with doublings in parentheses. Thus '1.1.1(bcl)1, 1.1.0.0.' means one flute, one oboe, one clarinet doubling bass clarinet, one horn, one trumpet, and no trombones or tubas. Where string dispositions are given, the figure indicates players, not desks; four figures instead of the usual five indicates that the violins are not divided. In the case of scores written for Broadway, the self-explanatory reed-book system indicates the wind-instrument doublings.

acdn.	=	accordion	ob.	=	oboe
band.	=	bandoneon	org.	=	organ
BD	=	bass drum	perc.	=	percussion
bcl.	=	bass clarinet	picc.	=	piccolo
bjo.	=	banjo	pno.	=	piano
bsn.	=	bassoon	qt.	=	quartet
ca.	=	cor anglais	sax.	=	saxophone
cbsn.	=	contrabassoon	SD	=	side drum
cel.	=	celesta	str.	=	strings
cl.	=	clarinet	tamb.	=	tambourine
cnt.	=	cornet	tba.	=	tuba
cym.	=	cymbal	tbn.	=	trombone
db.	=	double-bass	TD	=	tenor drum
dr.	=	drum	timp.	=	timpani
fl.	=	flute	tpt.	=	trumpet
flhn.	=	flugelhorn	trgl.	=	triangle
glock.	=	glockenspiel	vib.	=	vibraphone
gtr.	=	guitar	vla.	=	viola
harm.	=	harmonium	vlc.	=	cello
hn.	=	horn	vln.	=	violin
mdln.	=	mandolin	wbl.	=	woodblocks

Orthography

Certain American forms that are variable even in matters of official nomenclature – for instance Theater versus Theatre – have been standardized according to British usage. The sometimes quaint orthography of song titles in the published vocal scores of Weill's Broadway musicals of the 1940s has only been followed in the cataloguing of each work. The name 'Lenya' is used throughout in that American form, except for the dedication of *Der Protagonist*, which preserves the original German spelling, 'Lenja'. 'Švejk is the name of Hašek's hero; 'Schweyk' is Brecht's version of it.

Numeration

In the main text of the catalogue numerals below 100 are spelt out, except for bar numberings and page references. The lists of musical numbers are based as far as possible on any numbering adopted or approved by Weill himself, but inconsistencies in the numbering and lettering of principal and subsidiary (e.g. incidental or reprised) numbers have been corrected wherever the interests of easy cross reference allow. Musical numbers omitted from the final or published score are listed in their original location, where this is known, and numbered accordingly. The letters x, y, or z are suffixed to the numbering of each omitted item: x denotes that the number was orchestrated by Weill; y, that there is only a voice and piano score; z, that there is only a rough draft or serviceable sketch.

Collation

Where there is no pagination by the composer or his assistants the author's calculations do not include blank pages or those on which non-autograph workings are musically insignificant. Manuscripts are described as 'bound' where stitching and/or glueing is relatively secure, and 'disbound' where the binding has broken loose or is seriously damaged. Covers may be paper, thick paper, card, thick card, or board. For the manuscript papers, the following terms are used:

side: a page not paginated by the composer or his assistants
page: a paginated side
sheet: a standard four-sided sheet or bifolium, sides *a* (recto), *b* (verso), *c*,
    and *d*
leaf: half a sheet, torn off
single sheet: printed as such, and generally single-sided
title sheet: a bifolium with titling on side *a*, used instead of a binding for
    the manuscript pages enclosed in it
folding: a folding of sheets, one inside the other, sometimes with
    interspersed leaves
gathering: a folding stitched or gummed at the fold

Manuscript papers

Papers bearing a maker's name, brand-mark, or colophon are identified throughout the catalogue by means of a simple code indicating commercial origin together with the number of 'lines' (staves or staffs) per page. Thus A^{20} signifies a 20-line paper with the brand-name Ashelm, Am^{12} a 12-line paper with the name American Brand. Unless otherwise noted the format is upright; whether it is that or landscape (oblong), the measurements for uncoded papers mentioned in the main text give the height first.

The following table of codifications proceeds from the papers purchased in Germany (1913–33), to those from England (1933–5), and finally to the American papers (1936–50). Since the 'gathering together' of scattered untitled manuscripts has been greatly aided by analysis of paper types, the first and last years in which paper was used are given in the fourth column of the table, except in those cases where the paper is not known to have been used for more than one or two works (which are then specified). Column two gives a short form of the maker's name or brand-mark, column three the dimensions in centimetres, height before width.

GERMANY

A^{18}	Ashelm 263	34 × 27	*Die Bürgschaft* 1930
A^{20}	Ashelm 262	34 × 27	1929
$B^{6 \times 2}$	Beethoven 2 [six systems]	33.6 × 27	1921
B^{10}	Beethoven 54	20 × 17	1921
B^{12}	Beethoven 31	33.7 × 27.5	1920–8
B^{14}	Beethoven 32	33.8 × 27.7	1921–30
B^{16}	Beethoven 33	34 × 27	*Divertimento* 1921
B^{18}	Beethoven 34	34 × 26.5	1923–32
B^{20}	Beethoven 35	34 × 27	1921–30
B^{22}	Beethoven 36	34.4 × 27	1922–30
B^{24}	Beethoven 37	33.7 × 26.7	1924–9
B^{26}	Beethoven 38	33.7 × 26.7	1924–32
B^{28}	Beethoven 38a	34.9 × 26.2	1923–31
B^{30}	Beethoven 39	33.7 × 26.7	1927–30
BH^{24}	B&H Nr.14.A (+colophon)	(reproduction)	*Andante* (Weber) 1918
BC^{24}	B.C. No.8.1.	34.3 × 27	*Dreigroschenoper* 1928
F^{12}	Festa 680	34 × 27	*Die Weber* 1920
Fa^{12}	Fabrikmarke No. 28^B	18 × 15	*String Quartet* 1918
Fe^{12}	Festa 680	34 × 27	*Vom Tod im Wald* 1927
N^{14}	Nr. 15	35 × 30.2	1922–3
N^{16}	Nr. 16	35 × 30.2	*String Quartet Op. 8* 1923
P^{14}	'pawnshop' colophon	33.8 × 29.2	1929–30
P^{16}	P.K.S 8133	35 × 27.3	*Petroleuminseln* 1928
R^{20}	Edition Ruth	38.8 × 27.3	*Frauentanz* 1923
R^{24}	Edition Ruth	34.1 × 27.2	*Pantomime* 1924
R^{28}	Edition Ruth	34 × 27	1926–7
S^{18}	Sunova no 19	34 × 27	*Mahagonny* 1927
S^{20}	Sunova nr. 8	33.5 × 26.7	*Lindberghflug* 1929
S^{26}	Sunova nr. 11	33.8 × 29.2	1928–32
S^{30}	Sunova nr. 14	42 × 32	1929–30
S^{32}	Sunova nr. 15	41.9 × 31.8	*Happy End* 1929
T^{14}	triangular colophon + 265	33 × 26.2	*Zaubernacht* 1922
Won^{12}	W.O.N.i.H. No 402a L.C.G. (with rearing horse colophon)	(photocopy, reduced size)	1916–19
Wo^{12}	W.O.N.i.H. Nr 402b M.12 (with colophon as above)	(photocopy, reduced size)	Cello Sonata

FRANCE

D^{16}	Durand	35.4 × 27	1933–4
D^{24}	Durand	35.3 × 26.6	1933–4

D^{28}	Durand	34.6 × 27.2	1933–4
Ku^{12}	no maker's name	31 × 24	*Der Kuhhandel* 1934
Ku^{16}	no maker's name	35 × 27	*Der Kuhhandel* 1934
Ku^{28}	no maker's name	34.6 × 27.2	1934–5

ENGLAND

Co^{10}	no maker's name	30.5 × 24.5	*Kingdom for a Cow* 1935
Co^{12}	no maker's name	38 × 24.8	*Kingdom for a Cow* 1935
Co^{20}	no maker's name	37 × 27	*Kingdom for a Cow* 1935
Ch^{16}	J & W Chester no. 16	36.5 × 27	*Der Weg der Verheissung* 1935–6
Ch^{24}	J & W Chester no. 24	36.5 × 27	1935–7

USA

AB^{12}	American Brand	32 × 24	1937–8 (Paramount film studios)
C^{12}	Chappell 2	33.5 × 26.2	1941–7
C^{22}	Chappell 5 (scoring paper)	37 × 26/5	1944–8
Cb^{12}	Circle Blueprint	34.3 × 28	*Love Life* 1947–8
CMC^{25}	Chappell Musical Comedy	39.5 × 26.8	*We Will Never Die* 1943
Cp^{12}	Chappell Professional	31.8 × 23.8	1937–46
F^{12}	Carl Fischer 4	31.5 × 24	1938–49
F^{14}	Carl Fischer 6	32 × 23.2	1939–40
F^{21}	Carl Fischer 21 (scoring paper)	34.3 × 27.4	*We Will Never Die* 1943
F^{24}	Carl Fischer 22	34.5 × 27.5	*Der Weg der Verheissung* 1935–6
Fsp^{12}	Carl Fischer 104 (spiral bound)	32 × 24	1938–40
K^{10}	King 2	31.8 × 23.5	*Propaganda Songs* 1942
K^{12}	King 1	31.8 × 24	1937–48
K^{20}	King 4 (scoring paper)	35.8 × 25.7	*Lost in the Stars* 1949
Km^{10}	King M.2	31.7 × 24.3	*Lost in the Stars* 1949
M^{12}	Maestro 115	32.5 × 24	1938–49
M^{20}	Maestro 106	38 × 27.6	*Love Life* 1947–8
MM^{14}	MM5	31.5 × 24	1938–49
MM^{24}	MM10	34.2 × 27.2	1938–9
NBC^{12}	NBC Chicago no. 1	31 × 24	1942–4
Ns^{22}	NBC–5 (scoring paper)	34.2 × 27.4	*3 Walt Whitman Songs* 1942
O^{12}	O. Saporta	31.7 × 24.3	1939–49
P^{12}	Paramount Pictures Inc. 86–X–54	34 × 27.2	1937–9
Psp^{22}	Paramount (scoring paper) 35–X–15	35.5 × 27.3	1938–40
Pa^{14}	Parchment 16	31.8 × 24.2	1937–8
Pa^{16}	Parchment 14	34.3 × 27.3	*Knickerbocker Holiday* 1938
Po^{12}	Passantino 1	31.8 × 24.5	*Lost in the Stars* 1949
Pre^{12}	Premier 102–12	31 × 24	*One Touch of Venus* 1943
Pr^{12}	Premier 101–12	31.8 × 24.2	1940–8

Psk[12]	Presser 912 sketch book	31.4 × 23.7	*Lady in the Dark* 1940
RM[12]	Robbins Music Corp. 2–12	27.4 × 17.2	1939
Sc[12]	Schirmer Imperial 10	31.5 × 24	*Where Do We Go From Here* 1943
Sc[14]	Schirmer 23	31.8 × 24	1937–49
Sch[20]	Schirmer Imperial 19	34.3 × 27.4	1937–44
Sc[24]	Schirmer 61	33.7 × 27.3	*Lost in the Stars* 1949
Sch[12]	Schirmer Royal 54	31.8 × 24	1937–49
Sch[14]	Schirmer 59	32 × 24.2	1936–40
Sch[16]	Schirmer 4	33.2 × 26.5	*Der Weg der Verheissung* 1935–6
Sch[24]	Schirmer 6	35.2 × 26.6	1935–50
Scs[24]	Schirmer 13 (scoring paper)	34.4 × 27.2	*Lost in the Stars* 1949
S[20]	Schirmer Style 19	34.25 × 27	*Knickerbocker Holiday* 1938
Wh[12]	no maker's name (single sided)	30 × 27	*Where Do We Go From Here* 1943–4

A Note on Weill's
Composing Methods

Weill was not accustomed to compose at the piano and tended to be critical of those who were. According to Lenya he used the piano only for checking completed sections or numbers. The expanded-tonal and non-tonal music of the periods between 1918 and 1927 may have required him to make more frequent and localized checks; but signs of keyboard influence are rare, and less prevalent than in comparable music by most of Weill's contemporaries outside the Schoenberg circle. The graphic evidence provided by the manuscripts of these early works seems conclusive: however dense the texture or chromatic the writing, the sketches appear fluent and confident.

The visual aspect of the later manuscripts reflects the precision of musical thought and the efficiency of the technique. Only during the period 1937–9, when Weill was learning a new language, did the sketches and even the drafts become definably tentative, not only in appearance, but also in substance, style, or tone. In all other periods Weill seems to have preferred to solve problems before rather than after embarking on each stage of composition. These stages remained distinct in function throughout his career, and merit separate consideration.

Sketches

PRE-COMPOSITIONAL MEMORANDA

Examples surviving from the German period are few, but sufficient to confirm what could be deduced from the completed works: it was in this pre-compositional stage that Weill's methods were to change most radically. During his time with Busoni at the Berlin Academy of Arts (and probably also in earlier years) he confined most of his preliminary work to sketchbooks, which were large enough to record the evolution of several substantial pieces. With each work his first step was to assemble a collection of melodic, harmonic, and rhythmic motifs interspersed with verbal memos and a few contrapuntal workings. Although the latest surviving examples date from 1928, Weill would surely have continued the practice in a modified, and doubtless simplified, form until the time of the Second Symphony. After 1934, motivic memoranda of any kind became irrelevant except in response to the special requirements of radio or film music. With that exception, the first step became the one that had previously been a (sometimes dispensable) link between memos and drafts.

FRAGMENTARY SKETCHES

In the case of works for the theatre, these are primarily a means of establishing a fund of ideas as swiftly as possible, often in shorthand. The sketches break off either when the continuation is self-evident or when there is a compositional obstacle. The order of sketching tends at the start to be determined by a sense of what will be decisive with regard to style or character; thereafter it becomes more or less arbitrary. While the visual impression of a rapid flow of ideas is the rule in most periods, an exception must be made for sketches dating from 1937–9, when Weill was learning the language of Broadway and Hollywood. It is significant that during this period he reverted to the use of sketchbooks, and set himself occasional exercises – whether in the identification and handling of conventional pop-song tags (harmonic and rhythmic) or in the setting of a given song-text in a variety of conventional ways. Not until 1940 and *Lady in the Dark* are the new materials sketched with something akin to the old mastery and verve. The sketchbook used for that first Broadway triumph seems to have been the last he ever used.

Drafts

PRELIMINARY DRAFTS

These are relatively rare, and relate only to individual numbers. They are distinguished from their successors by some degree of sketchiness or structural incompleteness.

FINAL DRAFTS

These give the substance and the continuity of each individual number. The total continuity of any number-form work is not necessarily assured at final-draft stage. While the three surviving drafts of European number-form works proceed from start to finish – as of course do drafts of through-composed works – the Broadway musicals, apart from *Lady in the Dark*, were drafted piecemeal, in whatever order convenience or whim dictated. (*Street Scene*, though ostensibly through-composed, is no exception.) *Happy End* would certainly have been drafted in the same casual way, and parts of *Die Dreigroschenoper* likewise; but perhaps not *Der Silbersee*, and certainly not *Die sieben Todsünden*.

As a rule, two staves suffice for the accompaniment in drafts of vocal or dramatic works of any period after 1927. Purely instrumental or orchestral drafts may extend to three or four staves. In pre-1927 drafts, Weill tended to include many incidental details of orchestration and even of playing mode (*sul pont.*, *con sord.* etc.). Post-1927 drafts are less informative in all respects, except where a specific harmonic or contrapuntal process calls for more precise detail. In drafts of any vocal music for the popular stage, Weill allows for the necessity of a subsequent rehearsal score; accompaniments are therefore less fully characterized than in drafts for works requiring no such score.

Rehearsal Scores (voice and piano)

Properly speaking, voice and piano scores of this kind do not belong in the sequence of compositional stages, since Weill undertook them only when the practical exigencies of a performance-deadline left him with no alternative. In the commercially funded theatre of Berlin or Paris, London or New York, that was the inevitable rule, since any work or show conceived for the commercial theatre is identified with a specific production and its timetable, almost from the moment of conception. Suitable material for auditions, learning, and rehearsal is therefore a much higher priority than the orchestral score. That the state theatre system of Germany allowed Weill to follow his natural bent and proceed directly from draft to orchestral score is well illustrated by the example of *Der Silbersee*. Even though the work was written for singing actors, Weill was able to proceed as if he were writing an opera, and leave to a specialist the task of making a piano reduction from his orchestral score.

Full Scores (orchestral, etc.)

Until 1933 the orchestration stage of any work generally overlapped with the planning and first sketching of the next work. Thereafter, the demands of the commercial theatre imposed their own rhythm and tempo, and precluded any overlapping. On Broadway, it was not only the production system but also the practical and showman-like functions Weill chose to fulfil within it that lengthened the gaps between the completion of one of his musicals and the inception of the next. These gaps were never less than six months and sometimes very much longer. This change in the 'natural' flow of Weill's creativity was associated with a change in his attitude to orchestration. The task of orchestration was one that all his Broadway contemporaries, and every predecessor since Victor Herbert, delegated to professional arrangers – generally because they themselves were not competent to undertake it. Those few who did possess the necessary expertise – such as Vernon Duke, or Gershwin in his later years – were, with good reason, daunted by the pace of Broadway production and the risks of orchestrating anything before the casting was complete and the show ready for rehearsal. Weill's own desire to supervise and participate in rehearsals was at least as strong as theirs from the very start, and it grew with the years. But stronger still was his professional pride and his instinctive awareness that only through the orchestral score could he fully articulate the individuality and the expressive nuances latent in the bare outlines of his voice-and-piano drafts. The barer those outlines were, the more sure he was that he alone knew their secret. Thus the task of making an orchestral score acquired for him an altogether new significance. Whereas in his German years it had simply been a matter of realizing on paper what was already clear in his mind, now it became a creative opportunity in its own right – an opportunity for invention, fantasy, and therefore self-expression. No wonder he clung to it so fiercely and was prepared to share it only in last-minute emergencies or on the very rare occasions when he felt that a typical Broadway effect, rather than a typically personal sound, was called for.

The Catalogue

CHRONOLOGICAL LIST OF WORKS

[1913]	Mi addir
[1913]	Es blühen zwei flammende Rosen
[1914]	Ich weiss wofür
[1914]	Reiterlied
[1915]	Gebet
1916	Sehnsucht
1916	Ofrah's Lieder
[1916]	Zriny
[1916]	Im Volkston
[1917]	Volkslied
[1917]	Das schöne Kind
1917–18	[Two Duets on poems by Otto Julius Bierbaum]
1917	Intermezzo [in B flat]
1918	Andante aus der A-Dur-Sonate von C. M. v. Weber [orchestral arrangement]
1918	String Quartet in B minor
[1918–19]	Suite in E for Orchestra
1918–19	[Orchestral Work]
1919	[Die Weise von Liebe und Tod]
[1919]	Schilflieder
1919–20	Sonata for Cello and Piano
1919	Die stille Stadt
1919–20	Ninon von Lenclos
[1920]	Sulamith
[1920]	Die Weber
1921	Symphony [No. 1, in one movement]
[1921]	[Cabaret Number]
[1921]	[Polka]
1921	Die Bekehrte
1921	[Rilkelieder]
1921–2	Divertimento, op. 5

[1922]	Psalm VIII
[1922]	Divertimento für Flöte und Orchester, op. 52, von Ferruccio Busoni [arrangement for flute and piano]
1922	[Sinfonia Sacra]/Fantasia, Passacaglia und Hymnus, op. 6
1922	Zaubernacht [op. 7]
[1922–3]	String Quartet [first version of String Quartet, op. 8]
1923	String Quartet, op. 8
1923	Quodlibet, op. 9 (Suite from *Zaubernacht*)
1923	Frauentanz, op. 10
1923	Recordare, op. 11
[1923–4]	Stundenbuch [op. 13]
1924	[Pantomime, op. 14]
1924	Concerto for Violin and Wind Orchestra, op. 12
[1924]	[Foxtrot and Ragtime]
1924–5	Der Protagonist, op. 15
1925	Der neue Orpheus, op. 16
1925	Ich sitze da un' esse Klops
1925–6	Royal Palace, op. 17
1926–7	Na und ?
1926	Herzog Theodor von Gothland
1927	Der Zar lässt sich photographieren, op. 21
1927	Mahagonny-Songspiel
1927–9	Aufstieg und Fall der Stadt Mahagonny
1927	Vom Tod im Wald, op. 23
1927	Gustav III
1928	Leben Eduards des Zweiten von England
1928	Konjunktur
1928	Katalaunische Schlacht
1928	Die Dreigroschenoper
1928	Berlin im Licht
1928	Petroleuminseln
1928	Das Berliner Requiem
[1928–9]	Kleine Dreigroschenmusik
1929	Der Lindberghflug [original version, with Paul Hindemith]
1929	Happy End
1929	Zu Potsdam unter den Eichen; Die Legende vom toten Soldaten
1929	Der Lindberghflug
1930	Der Jasager
1930–2	Die Bürgschaft
1931	Mann ist Mann
1932–3	Der Silbersee
1933–4	Symphony [No. 2]
1933	Die sieben Todsünden

1933	Der Abschiedsbrief
1933	Es regnet
1933	La grande complainte de Fantômas
1934	Der Kuhhandel
1934	Complainte de la Seine
1934	Je ne t'aime pas
1934–5	Der Weg der Verheissung
1934	Marie Galante
1935	A Kingdom for a Cow
1936	High Wind in Jamaica
1936	The Fräulein and the Little Son of the Rich
1936	Johnny Johnson
1936	The Eternal Road [interpolations]
1937	The River is Blue (Castles in Spain)
1937	[Musical play: Mannheim Opera]
1937/8	You and Me
1937	[Two Chansons for Yvette Guilbert]
1937	The Common Glory
1937	Albumblatt für Erika
1938	Two Folksongs of the New Palestine
1938	Davy Crockett
1938–9	Railroads on Parade
1938	Knickerbocker Holiday
1939	[Songs of Discovery]
1939/45	Ulysses Africanus
1939	Madam, will you walk?
1939	Two on an Island
1939	Nannas Lied
1939	Stopping by Woods on a Snowy Evening
1940	The Ballad of Magna Carta
1940	Lady in the Dark
1941	Fun to be Free
1942	Three Walt Whitman Songs
1942	Your Navy
1942	[Propaganda Songs]
1942	Und was bekam des Soldaten Weib?
1942	Mine Eyes Have Seen The Glory
1942	The Pirate
1942[–3]	Six Songs
1942–3	One Man's Venus
1942	Russian War Relief
1943	We Will Never Die
1943	One Touch of Venus
1943–4	Where Do We Go From Here?
1944	Wie lange noch?

1944	Salute to France
1944	The Firebrand of Florence
1945[–8]	One Touch of Venus [film version]
1945	Down in the Valley
1946	Street Scene
1946	Kiddush
1946	A Flag is Born
1947	Come up from the Fields, Father
1947–8	Love Life
1947	Hatikvah
1948	Down in the Valley
1949	Lost in the Stars
1950	Huckleberry Finn

CLASSIFIED LIST OF WORKS

It is characteristic of Weill's works in general that they resist classification, and of his stage works in particular that some of them defy it altogether. For instance, *Der Weg der Verheissung* is at once opera, oratorio, and play-with-music, *Royal Palace* is opera and ballet in almost equal measure, the *Mahagonny-Songspiel* and *Die sieben Todsünden* are stage works that are nearly concert pieces (of an unusual sort!), and among the 'Broadway Musicals' only *One Touch of Venus* approximates to the conventional understanding of that term. The following classifications should therefore be studied with more caution than the handful of cross-references might suggest. With regard to performance requirements, the categories 'Plays with Music', 'Operetta' and 'Broadway Musicals' need some definition. The first derives from *Die Dreigroschenoper* and its Viennese ancestors (Raimund, Nestroy) and calls for a fully-fledged theatre company with singing actors, a musical director of more than average competence, and instrumental resources ranging from *ad hoc* ensembles of upwards of a dozen players to the full orchestras required by *Der Silbersee* and *Der Weg der Verheissung* – both of which also require trained singers and a chorus (a double chorus in the latter case). 'Operetta' signifies the Offenbach–Johann Strauss tradition and commensurate forces; 'Broadway Musicals' presupposes the intensively rehearsed casts, and more or less luxurious conditions, of the 1940s 'star system' for which each work in its different way was tailor-made.

Operas

Ninon von Lenclos (1 act, Ernst Hardt) 1919–20, lost
Der Protagonist (1 act, Georg Kaiser) 1924–5
Royal Palace (1 act opera–ballet, Iwan Goll) 1925–6
Na und ? (2 acts, Felix Joachimson) 1926–7, lost

Der Zar lässt sich photographieren (1 act, Georg Kaiser) 1927
Aufstieg und Fall der Stadt Mahagonny (3 acts, Bertolt Brecht) 1927–9
Der Jasager (2 acts, Bertolt Brecht) 1930
Die Bürgschaft (3 acts, Caspar Neher) 1930–1
Der Weg der Verheissung (4 acts, see *Plays with Music*) 1934–5
Down in the Valley (radio/college opera, Arnold Sundgaard) 1945/48
Street Scene (2 acts, see *Broadway Musicals*) 1946

Songspiel

Mahagonny (Bertolt Brecht) 1927
(see also under *Arrangements of Works by Weill*)

Plays with Music

Die Dreigroschenoper (John Gay, E. Hauptmann, Bertolt Brecht) 1928
Happy End (E. Hauptmann, Bertolt Brecht), 1929
Der Silbersee (A Winter's Tale, 3 acts, Georg Kaiser) 1932
Der Weg der Verheissung (Biblical Drama, 4 acts, Franz Werfel) 1934–5
   American version in 3 acts by Ludwig Lewinsohn: The Eternal Road
Marie Galante (Jacques Deval) 1934
Johnny Johnson (Paul Green) 1936
Davy Crockett (H. R. Hays) 1938, incomplete

Operettas

Der Kuhhandel (Robert Vambery) 1934–5, incomplete
   English version: A Kingdom for a Cow' (Reginald Arkell, Desmond
   Carter) 1935
Knickerbocker Holiday (see *Broadway Musicals*) 1938
The Firebrand of Florence (see *Broadway Musicals*) 1944

Broadway Musicals

Knickerbocker Holiday (quasi-operetta, Maxwell Anderson) 1938
Ulysses Africanus (musical, Maxwell Anderson) 1939–45, incomplete
Lady in the Dark (musical play, Moss Hart, Ira Gershwin) 1940
One Touch of Venus (musical comedy, S. J. Perelman, Ogden Nash) 1943
The Firebrand of Florence (operetta, E. J. Mayer, Ira Gershwin) 1944
Street Scene (Broadway opera, Elmer Rice, Langston Hughes) 1946
Love Life (Vaudeville, Alan Jay Lerner) 1947–8
Lost in the Stars (musical tragedy, Maxwell Anderson after Alan
   Paton) 1949
Huckleberry Finn (Maxwell Anderson) 1950, incomplete

Pageants

Railroads on Parade (Edward Hungerford) 1938–9
Fun to be Free (Ben Hecht) 1941, lost

We Will Never Die (Ben Hecht) 1943, lost
A Flag is Born (Ben Hecht) 1946, lost

Incidental Music

THEATRE

Die Weber (Gerhart Hauptmann) *c.* 1920, part lost
Gustav III (Strindberg) 1927
Leben Eduards des Zweiten von England (Brecht) 1927
Konjunktur (Leo Lania, Felix Gasbarra, Erwin Piscator) 1928, part lost
Katalaunische Schlacht (Arnolt Bronnen) 1928, lost
Petroleuminseln (Lion Feuchtwanger) 1928, part lost
Mann ist Mann (Bertolt Brecht) 1931, lost
Two on an Island (Elmer Rice) 1939, lost
Madam, will you walk? (Sidney Howard) 1939

RADIO

Herzog Theodor von Gothland (Grabbe) 1926, lost
Your Navy (Maxwell Anderson) 1942, lost

FILM

The River is Blue (Lewis Milestone) 1937
You and Me (Fritz Lang; lyrics by Sam Coslow) 1937–8
Where Do We Go From Here? (William Perlberg; lyrics by
   Ira Gershwin) 1943
Salute to France (Jean Renoir) 1944

Radio Works

Das Berliner Requiem (cantata for 2 male voices, male chorus, and wind
   orchestra, on poems by Bertolt Brecht) 1928
Der Lindberghflug (cantata for soloists, chorus and orchestra, jointly
   composed with Paul Hindemith, text by Bertolt Brecht) 1929;
   withdrawn; see *Vocal and Choral with Orchestra*
La grande complainte de Fantômas (Robert Desnos) 1933
The Ballad of Magna Carta (Maxwell Anderson) 1940

Dance Works

Zaubernacht (children's pantomime, scenario by Wladimir Boritsch)
   1922, part lost
Untitled work (pantomime in 3 acts for large orchestra, scenario by
   Georg Kaiser) 1924; incomplete, part lost
Die sieben Todsünden (soprano voice, male quartet, orchestra, text by
   Bertolt Brecht) 1933

Choral Music a cappella

Ich weiss wofür (Guido von Güllhausen) 1914
Gebet (Emanuel Geibel) 1915
Psalm VIII (Latin Vulgate) 1921
Recordare (Lamentations V) SATB chorus, 3-part children's chorus, 1923
Zu Potsdam unter den Eichen (Bertolt Brecht) male voice choir, 1929
Die Legende vom toten Soldaten (Bertolt Brecht), SATB, 1929
Kiddush, tenor solo, SATB, organ, 1946

Vocal and Choral with Orchestra

Sulamith (cantata for soprano solo, female chorus, orchestra),
    text unknown, 1920, lost
Das Stundenbuch (Rainer Maria Rilke), 6 songs for baritone or (mezzo-)
    soprano and orchestra, 1923–4, part lost
Der neue Orpheus (Iwan Goll), soprano solo, violin, orchestra, 1925
Vom Tod im Wald (Bertolt Brecht), ballad for bass solo, ten
    wind instruments, 1927
Das Berliner Requiem (Bertolt Brecht), cantata for tenor and baritone
    soloists, male chorus, and wind orchestra, 1928
Der Lindberghflug (Bertolt Brecht), cantata for three soloists, chorus,
    and large orchestra, 1929

Orchestral

Suite in E for Orchestra, 1918–9
[Die Weise von Liebe und Tod] (symphonic poem after Rilke's 'Cornet')
    1919–20, lost
Symphony no. 1, 1921
Divertimento, for string orchestra with wind instruments and male
    chorus, 1921–2, partly lost
Sinfonia Sacra (Fantasia, Passacaglia, Hymnus), 1922; orchestral score lost
Quodlibet (Suite from 'Zaubernacht'), 1923
Concerto for violin and wind instruments, 1924
Berlin im Licht, for military band, 1928
Kleine Dreigroschenmusik, 1928–9
Symphony no. 2, 1933–4

Chamber

String Quartet in B minor, 1918
Sonata for Cello and Piano, 1919–20
String Quartet, op. 8, 1923

Piano

Intermezzo, 1917
Albumblatt für Erika, 1937

Lieder

CYCLES WITH PIANO OR INSTRUMENTAL ENSEMBLE

Ofrah's Lieder (Jehuda Halevi), for voice and piano, 1916
Schilflieder (Nikolaus Lenau) *c.* 1919, lost
Rilkelieder, 1921, part lost
Frauentanz (medieval texts), for soprano and five instruments, 1923

CYCLES WITH ORCHESTRA

Stundenbuch, for baritone or (mezzo-)soprano and orchestra,
    1923–4, part lost

INDIVIDUAL, WITH PIANO

Reiterlied (Hermann Löns), *c.* 1914
Sehnsucht (Joseph Freiherr von Eichendorff), 1916
Im Volkston (Arno Holz), 1916
Volkslied (Anna Ritter), 1917
Das schöne Kind, 1917
Maikaterlied (Otto Julius Bierbaum), canon for two sopranos, 1917
Abendlied (Otto Julius Bierbaum), duet for two sopranos, 1917
Die stille Stadt (Richard Dehmel), 1919
Die Bekehrte (Johann Wolfgang von Goethe), 1921

Berlin Songs, and Chansons

Ich sitze da un' esse Klops (trad.) for voice, 2 piccolos, bassoon, 1925
Die Muschel von Margate (Felix Gasbarra), 1928
Berlin im Licht (Kurt Weill), 1928
Petroleum-Song (Lion Feuchtwanger), 1928
Der Abschiedsbrief (Erich Kästner), 1933
Es regnet (Jean Cocteau), 1933
Fantômas (Robert Desnos), 1933
Complainte de la Seine (Maurice Magre), 1934
Je ne t'aime pas (Maurice Magre), 1934
Two Chansons for *L'opéra de quat' sous* (Yvette Guilbert), 1937
Nannas Lied (Bertolt Brecht), 1939
Und was bekam des Soldaten Weib? (Bertolt Brecht), 1942
Wie lange noch? (Walter Mehring), 1943

American Songs

Stopping by Woods on a Snowy Evening (Robert Frost), 1939
Song of the Free (Archibald MacLeish), 1942
Four Songs of Walt Whitman, 1942/7 (also with orchestra)
Propaganda songs for war workers, 1942–4

Arrangements

Carl Maria von Weber, Andante aus der A-dur Sonate
  von C. M. v. Weber, for orchestra, 1918
Ferruccio Busoni, Divertimento for flute and orchestra,
  piano reduction, 1922
Two Folksongs of the New Palestine, for voice and piano, 1938
Mine Eyes Have Seen The Glory (including 'Battle Hymn of the
  Republic', 'The Star-Spangled Banner', and 'America'), for reciter
  and orchestra, 1942
Hatikvah, for orchestra, 1947

Arrangements of Weill

ORCHESTRA

Divertimento, op. 5 (Drew/Shaw)
Suite from *Aufstieg und Fall der Stadt Mahagonny* (Brückner–Rüggeberg)
Suite from *Die Bürgschaft* (Brückner–Rüggeberg)
Suite from *Der Silbersee* (Karel Solomon)
Bastille Music (suite from *Gustav III*; arr. Drew)

SINGERS AND ENSEMBLE (*Songspiele*)

Happy End (Drew)
War Game (from *Johnny Johnson*) (Drew)
Öl-Musik (from *Konjunktur*) (Drew)

SOLOISTS, CHORUS, ORCHESTRA

Der Silbersee (Drew)
Der Weg der Verheissung (in preparation)
Railroads on Parade (in preparation)
Four American Songs (from *Railroads on Parade*) (in preparation)
Lost in the Stars (in preparation)

SEMI-STAGED SHORTENED VERSIONS

Royal Palace (Gunther Schuller)
Der Silbersee (Heinzelmann/Drew)

Juvenilia and
Early Works

On 5 November 1983, during the last day of the Kurt Weill Conference at Yale University, Professor Kim Kowalke, the President of the Kurt Weill Foundation, announced the discovery of fourteen early manuscripts, eleven of them relating to compositions unknown to have existed or presumed lost. Two years earlier Dr Hanne Weill-Holesovsky, daughter of Weill's brother Hanns, had informed the Vice-President of the Foundation, Lys Symonette, that her mother Rita Weill might possess various letters and manuscripts relating to Weill. Following the death of Rita Weill in 1983 the Foundation was able to obtain photocopies of [some of] the manuscripts. These are now available for study at the Weill–Lenya Research Center in New York. The original manuscripts are sealed in a bank vault awaiting a probate settlement, after which the Foundation will begin negotiations for their purchase.

Kurt Weill Newsletter, vol. 2, no. 1 (spring 1984); quoted by permission of the
Kurt Weill Foundation

The problems and limitations inherent in the study of manuscripts from photocopies rather than from the originals are obvious; my descriptions of the Autographs in the Rita Weill Collection, and the comments on handwriting ventured in the subsequent *Notes*, are therefore to be treated as provisional until the originals are available for examination. In that respect the first section of the Catalogue is already distinct from the rest. But it is also distinct in a fundamental sense that affects the procedures, the character, and the tendency of the entire section. Since most of the manuscripts are undated and few are mentioned in the known contemporary sources, the cataloguing process cannot ignore any factors relevant to chronology. Those that loom largest in the products of childhood and adolescence are handwriting and notation. Both are reflections of intellectual development and technical training, and therefore neither is a discrete category: they direct attention towards the fields of musical description and critical evaluation that have expressly been excluded from the remainder of the Catalogue. The value judgements implicit in the very concept of 'juvenilia and early works' cannot be shirked – least of all at the frontier where they threaten to invade the areas beyond; and where, perhaps, they begin, surreptitiously, to do so.

[1913], Dessau

Mi addir

'Mi addir al hakol' – medieval Ashkenazic wedding psalm
For high voice[s] and piano [or organ?]

Autograph (RWC)

A leaf of 12-line paper (33.5 × 27), torn from a ring binder, carries on one side a pencil draft, presumably holograph, of a 28-bar setting of 'Mi addir al hakol' ('He who is mighty/Blessed and great above all beings/May He bless the bridegroom and the bride'). Bars 18–21 have no accompaniment.

While the musical hand is too immature to be attributable with any certainty to Weill, the signature 'Kurt Weill Dessau' is unquestionably Weill's, and by no means childish. The title and the German script subtitle 'Jüdischer Trauungsgesang' (Jewish wedding song) are less clearly identifiable, and the text underlay is still rougher. At the start of the third system is a gratuitous signature 'Weill', which must be non-autograph.

Notes

Unless the autograph signature was added later – which seems unlikely, and cannot be judged without access to the original – it tends to preclude any dating much earlier than 1913. That being so, *Mi addir* serves the one useful purpose of demolishing any sentimental notions about Weill's beginnings: so far from being remarkable – let alone prodigious – the composition is in every respect juvenile; only the barest rudiments of harmony, form, and notation have been mastered, and nothing resembling a genuine musical idea is yet discernible.

[1913], Dessau

Es blühen zwei flammende Rosen

Fragment of an untitled *Lied* for voice and piano

Autograph (RWC)

On the reverse side of the leaf carrying *Mi addir* is the unsigned pencil draft of the first ten bars of a B flat minor *Lied* in 12/8 time. The nuances, and the German script of the underlay, are strikingly mature, and must be autograph. The musical script remains juvenile, but is better formed than that of *Mi addir*, and has the same backward slope that is characteristic of the holographs of 1915–17.

Notes

In eight out of the ten bars of tonic–dominant harmony the same chromatic scale rises, *con fuoco*, to the same grief-laden 6–5 appoggiatura. Too naïve to qualify as a musical setting of the words, it serves well enough as a graphic depiction of them:

> *Es blühen zwei flammende Rosen*
> *auf einer Doppelgruft*
> *im lauen Windeskosen*
> *umschlungen sich die Rosen*
> *und küssen sich über der Gruft.*

[August 1914, at the earliest], Dessau

Ich weiss wofür

For 4-part male chorus *a cappella*
Text: Guido von Güllhausen

Autographs (RWC/WLRC)

The earlier of the two extant versions (RWC) is on one side of a leaf of 12-line paper (34.5 × 26.5 cms). The autograph heading reads: 'Ich weiss wofür für Männerchor von Kurt Weill/Guido Von [*sic!*] Güllhausen'; the text underlay is also autograph, but in German script. The musical hand is surely Weill's, and very much better formed than that of *Mi addir*. The copy of the second version (WLRC) is written on a leaf of the same 12-line paper and is non-autograph throughout.

Notes

In its high-flown patriotism and shamelessly militaristic sentiments the poem was as well suited to the mood in which Germany entered the First World War (on 28 July 1914) as Weill's 32-bar setting was suited to the kind of Gesangsverein for which it was doubtless written. (A document in RWC, noted by Kowalke (KK.LF) but yet to be released, indicates that as late as 18 December 1915 Weill was associated with the 'Verein für das Deutschtum im Ausland. Jugendgruppe Dessau'.) The autograph version in B flat major clearly precedes the non-autograph version in A flat. Both structurally and in its part-writing the latter has been corrected – perhaps by Weill's father – in such a way as to affirm the composition's all-embracing indebtedness to the hymn-book conventions of the day. The fair copy gives the archaic spelling 'weisz'.

First Modern Performance

13 September 1975, Akademie der Künste, West Berlin; RIAS Kammerchor conducted by Uwe Gronostay.

[1914], Dessau

Reiterlied

For voice and piano
Text: Hermann Löns

Autograph

Non-autograph copy on four sides of a sheet of 12-line paper measuring 34.5 × 26.5 cms. The signature 'Kurt J. Weill' is autograph, as is the partly illegible opus number 'Werk 2 [Nummer] 1'. Some nuances added to this piano part on sides *a* and *b* may be autograph. The manuscript is one of a set of four acquired from Weill's family in the mid-1950s – the others being the holograph of 'Volkslied' and the non-autograph copies of *Ich weiss wofür* and 'Im Volkston'. All four were once preserved in a ring binder, and accordingly have punch-holes in the margins (cf. *Mi addir*).

Notes

The novelist and poet Hermann Löns (1866–1914) was a leading advocate of so-called 'Heimatkunst' – a form of regionalist nationalism, which, in Löns, is centred mainly on the life and legends of the Lüneburg Heath. Like many of his poems, his 'Horseman's Song' is in the manner of a folk song. Weill's setting is aptly marked 'einfach, volkstümlich' ('simple, in the folk style'), and within its very modest limits it is effective and charming. However much help Weill received while writing it, he has advanced some way since *Mi addir*. The naïve pretensions of an opus numbering argue for an early date – there is no other example among the juvenilia – and the substitution of the Germanic 'Werk' for 'opus' could be taken for a childish prank were it not in tune with the philosophy of Löns. Between that homage to *Deutschtum* and the patriotic fervour of *Ich weiss wofür* there can be no large gap of time or experience.

First Modern Performance

9 September 1975, Akademie der Künste, West Berlin; Barry McDaniel (baritone), Aribert Reimann (piano).

[Jewish Pentecost, 1915], Dessau

Gebet

'Herr, den ich tief im Herzen trage'
For SATB chorus, *a cappella*
Probably written for the Confirmation of Ruth Weill
Text: Emanuel Geibel

Autographs (RWC)

A non-autograph ink copy – possibly in the same hand as the second version of *Ich weiss wofür* – is on two sides of a leaf of 14-line paper (33.5 × 27 cms). The text underlay is autograph, but the title and signature are in the copyist's hand; another hand has noted, roughly, the occasion for which the piece was composed. The complete title reads, 'Gebet. von Em. Geibel. Zu Ruths Confirmation. Kurt Julian Weill'. An incomplete set of chorus parts in various hands contains several autograph tempo and expression marks. The tenor part has the non-autograph signature 'K. J. Weill'.

Notes

Had Weill himself written the heading 'Zu Ruths Confirmation' it could have referred only to his sister; since he did not, the remote possibility of a coincidence casts a shadow of doubt on what is otherwise a useful if problematic clue to the dating of the composition.

Ruth Weill was born on 6 October 1901. According to Orthodox Jewish Law, girls attain their religious majority at the age of twelve years and one day – automatically, and without public rites. But the Reform movement, which originated in North Germany in the second decade of the nineteenth century, established a ceremony of Confirmation for girls, generally on the second day of their fourteenth year or at the subsequent Pentecost; sometimes, however, one or even two years later than either of those dates. The use of the word 'Confirmation' rather than the Neo-Orthodox *bar mitzvah* in the heading of *Gebet* is consonant with Weill's choice of a North German Christian poet – one who had enjoyed the patronage of the Prussian and Bavarian courts, and the widespread popularity that went with it. (At the 1984 centenary of his death, Geibel was remembered chiefly through Hugo Wolf's *Spanisches Liederbuch*.) The choice of terminology and poet are both representative of the Reform tendency, which in Dessau, the birthplace of its spiritual father Moses Mendelssohn, was inseparable from the life and worship of the Jewish community. The mixed chorus is also a typical manifestation of Reform (though Weill's father, the Cantor, had been an advocate of male choirs on practical rather than Orthodox grounds). Musically *Gebet* reveals no Judaic traits; its style is indistinguishable from that of the standard church anthem in Germany and most other parts of northern Europe from about 1880 until well into the twentieth century. Technically as well as stylistically *Gebet* bears comparison with some of the liturgical pieces by Weill's father that found a publisher.

Whether Weill's youthful *Gebet* had undergone revision at the hands of Albert Weill or his organist is a question essential to any accurate dating, and at present there is no means of answering it. If, however, it is reasonable to argue from the compositional mishaps in the holograph version of *Ich weiss wofür* that some more experienced hand must have been at least partly responsible for the improved non-autograph version, then the improvement must be the axis of any comparison between its predecessor and the almost painfully correct *Gebet*. Assuming, for the sake of argument, that *Gebet* has likewise benefited from professional attentions, a direct comparison between the two versions of *Ich weiss wofür* serves as a means of hypothesizing an original, uncorrected, version of *Gebet*. But with all due allowance for the primitive sentiments of Güllhausen and the lofty ones of Geibel, the very conception of *Gebet* testifies to a later stage of development. Even if we discount such refinements as the two snatches of imitative counterpoint – typical as these are of the Cantor's own compositional endeavours – the motivic and phraseological structure, and their broader tonal implications, override the effects of any hypothetical revisions.

Pending the discovery of the date of Ruth Weill's Confirmation, together with incontrovertible evidence of its connection with the composition of *Gebet*, several widely divergent datings are equally tenable. If the extant version of *Gebet* is an adult's revision of some lost original, a period of between six months and a year after the composition of *Ich weiss wofür* would account for the hypothetical advance; and that, assuming a late 1914 dating for *Ich weiss wofür*, would allow *Gebet* to have been written either before the Jewish Pentecost of 1915 (19 May) or else before Ruth Weill's fourteenth birthday in October of that year. If, on the other hand, the non-autograph manuscript of *Gebet* is merely a copy of Weill's unaided work, any dating before Pentecost 1916 (7 June) would be hard to support in the face of technical evidence provided by 'Sehnsucht' and *Ofrah's Lieder* (see below).

1916, Dessau

Sehnsucht

'Es schienen so golden die Sterne'
Lied for voice and piano [unfinished?]
Text: Joseph Freiherr von Eichendorff

Autograph (RWC)

An incomplete ink holograph draft, without text underlay, tempo markings or nuances, is on two sides of Won[12]. At the head of side *a* are title, poet's name, and the signature 'Kurt Julian Weill 1916'.

Notes

The inexact dating is open to several interpretations: if retrospective, it would tend to suggest either that Weill had lost the final version of the draft or, more probably, that he never made one; if contemporary with the composition but prior to the September 1916 dating of *Ofrah's Lieder*, it is the earliest autograph dating we know of. In any case the ambitions and the influences (in this case Loewe and Mendelssohn) are akin to those of the song-cycle, and quite distinct from those of the simpler and obviously earlier undated compositions. In the answer to the opening D major phrase, and more extensively in the second verse's turn to the relative minor, some roots of the post-1933 European Weill can just be discerned.

[Spring 1916] – September 1916, Dessau

Ofrah's Lieder

Cycle for voice and piano on modern German translations of Hebrew poems by Jehuda Halevi (*c.* 1080 – *c.* 1145).

Note 1

A physician by training, Judah ben Samuel ha-Levi was the foremost Hebrew poet of medieval times, and also an important neo-platonic Arabic philosopher. He spent his early years in his native Spain, and then emigrated to Palestine, where he died. The poems chosen by Weill are moralities and fables drawing for their imagery on nature and the animal kingdom. 'How astonishing forsooth, and wonderful,' begins 'Wie staunenswert', 'the gentle dove catches the eagle'.

Drafts A *and* B

(Partly missing?)

A		B	
1	'In meinem Garten steh'n zwei Rosen'	1	ditto
2	'Ich bin dir mehr als Sonnenglanz'	2	'Nur dir, fürwahr'
3	'Nur dir, fürwahr, mein stolzer Aar'	3	'Wie staunenswert'

Autographs (RWC)

Draft A is on seven sides of a 12-line paper (oblong format without maker's name). Each song begins on a new page and has a heading in the same style: *Ofrah's Lieder 1*, etc. If the eighth side of the original manuscript, rather than the first, is the one that is blank, this would confirm the impression left by the character of 3 and its tonal relationship to the preceding songs – namely that Weill was originally planning a three-part cycle. In version B 'Nur dir, fürwahr' is shifted to second place, with the result that its E flat major tonality is made to sound as if it were a subdominant consequence of the first song's B flat major. In this context the C major of 'Wie staunenswert' could not have been intended as conclusive; nor indeed could its vapid Wagnerisms. If Weill was now planning a set of five, the fourth song could have been 'Ich bin dir mehr als Sonnenglanz', from draft A. Not only would the Schubertian F minor of its opening have made an effective contrast, but the tentative cadence in A flat major, beneath which Weill has written 'oder auch gleich nach Es' (or alternatively straight to E flat), would have allowed for several different tonal conclusions to the cycle. The first page of a slightly revised version of the E flat major 'Nur dir, fürwahr' is headed by the Roman numeral V, and might seem to indicate a further stage in the evolution of draft B towards the definitive version of the cycle; but since it is identical with the final version of that song, it is more likely to be a second copy for singer or accompanist.

Definitive Version

1. 'In meinem Garten steh'n zwei Rosen'
2. 'Nichts ist die Welt mir'
3. 'Er sah mir liebend in die Augen'
4. 'Denkst du des kühnen Flugs der Nacht'
5. 'Nur dir, fürwahr, mein stolzer Aar'

Autograph (LOC)

Written in blue ink on twelve sides (non-autograph pagination) of Won[12], the manuscript was in the possession of the soprano Elisabeth Feuge and her heirs until its purchase in 1985 by the Music Division of the Library of Congress in Washington. Except in 2, the underlaid texts are in modern arabic script. On the title page is an oblong octagonal label, with the autograph date 'September 1916' (in the left-hand corner) and autograph titling as follows: 'Ofrah's Lieder/Ein Liederzyklus nach Gedichten von/Jehuda Halevi/von/Kurt Julian Weill'.

Note 2

'Nichts ist die Welt mir' is so much more accomplished than any of the four songs in the two preceding drafts that it suggests a lapse of weeks or even months before Weill put the cycle into its final form; yet there has been no technically significant revision of the two songs Weill has preserved. The weakest of the new songs is 'Er sah mir liebend in die Augen'. Clearly intended to replace 'Wie staunenswert', it likewise attempts to establish a quasi-operatic contrast to the cycle's predominantly lyrical manner. But although it is compositionally more sharply focused than 'Wie staunenswert' it is quite as naïve in its histrionic attitudes, and sounds all the more so after the relatively sophisticated 'Nichts ist die Welt mir'. If, at a second look, one is disconcertingly reminded of the attitudes Weill was to poke fun at fourteen years later, in Lucy's 'Eifersuchtsarie' – the only *Dreigroschenoper* number that lives up to that work's reputation as a parody – that is a tribute to the revelation afforded by the next song in the cycle. In the ambivalence of the very first harmony, as in the semitonal processes by which it is dissolved prior to the exorbitant F sharp major resolution, one hears the *ferner Klang* of the Weill to come; and then, as if to prove that this uncanny prefiguration is real rather than fanciful, the piano, in bar 6, suddenly glimpses Seeräuberjenny's eight-sailed ship as it emerges from the chromatic mists with Wagner's Flying Dutchman still aboard.* The telescopic effect is so pronounced that one has to remind oneself that the musical substance is hardly such as to overwhelm listeners unfamiliar with what lay ahead. Only a teacher as sympathetic and discerning as Albert Bing might have recognized the promise latent in that first page of 4, and forgiven the romantic effusions that follow.

Between the first two versions of *Ofrah's Lieder* and the definitive one runs the line that divides adolescent works that were of interest chiefly within the family circle from those that began to reach out for a wider audience. Judged on its own intrinsic merits, without the distortions of sentiment or hindsight, the definitive version is simply a step in the right direction: at the age of 16½ Weill still had much to learn about harmony and composition, but was learning fast. The fact that he was prepared to offer *Ofrah's Lieder* for public performance a whole year later† may raise

---

* What an astonishing vindication of Ernst Bloch's insight – see his famous essay 'Lied der Seeräuberjenny in *Die Dreigroschenoper*' (reprinted in *Bertolt Brecht's Dreigroschenbuch*: Frankfurt, 1960).
† See Weill's letter of 15 November 1917 to his brother Hanns (copy in WLRC).

questions about his powers of self-criticism; yet he had good reason to regard *Ofrah's Lieder* as his true starting point. Small wonder that he unconsciously returned to its polyglot Jewish–Romantic modes in *Der Weg der Verheissung* and *The Eternal Road*. For all their gleanings from Schubert and Schumann, from Loewe and Mendelssohn and Wagner, *Ofrah's Lieder* contain the first glimpses of the mature Weill, and the only ones before he had discovered Mahler and modern music.

[1916], Dessau

Zriny

'Opera' after the tragedy by Theodor Körner (1791–1813)
(Missing)

Notes

In the interview with Louis B. Simon published in the *New York Times* on 13 April 1941 under the title 'Up the Rungs from Opera', Weill is reported as saying that his first attempt at opera was based on Körner's *Zriny* (1812). No further details are given; nor are there any references elsewhere to the work. As *Zriny* was standard reading in German schools on account of its patriotic and militarist virtues, it would certainly have recommended itself to the composer of *Ich weiss wofür*, not least because the repertory of bellicose 4-part male choruses included Weber's Körner settings, *Leyer und Schwert*, op. 42. According to Weill's sister Ruth (in conversation with the present author), a domestic production of *Der Freischütz* was one of several that Weill put together during the war years for the entertainment of family and friends. *Zriny* might well have been designed for such an evening; but not after Albert Bing had encouraged Weill to question the legitimacy of Prussian ideals. In that sense, 1916 is the latest possible date; an earlier one seems unlikely on technical grounds. The would-be operatic gestures in *Ofrah's Lieder* give some indication of what *Zriny* might have amounted to.

[late 1916], Dessau

Im Volkston

'Das Scheiden, ach das Scheiden'
Song for voice and piano
Text: Arno Holz (1863–1929)

Autograph

A non-autograph fair copy is on four sides of a sheet of 12-line paper measuring 34.5 × 26.5 cms. The signature 'Kurt J. Weill' and the first tempo indication are autograph.

Notes

At least in its copied version the song has a formal cogency and a consistency of style and tone absent from *Ofrah's Lieder* and 'Sehnsucht'. Some sturdy contrary motion and purposeful root progressions seem to herald a more enlightened view of harmonic functions and their relevance to poetic expression. Once again, guesswork has to provide the dating for which there is so urgent a critical and biographical need; and once again the process is imperilled by the lack of holograph sources. At first glance there seems to be no obvious reason why, with a little expert assistance, the song in its present form could not have been written before *Ofrah's Lieder*. The narrow frame of harmonic reference (modelled on the simpler Schubert) excludes the kind of technical and stylistic mishaps that arise from the greater ambitions of *Ofrah's Lieder*. Moreover, the intensity that singles the song out from the other juvenilia might well be cited as evidence of something discovered in Holz's poem that was conducive to a premature eloquence. Although Holz was a poet of the same generation and North German origin as Hermann Löns, 'Im Volkston' has no connection with the bucolic simplicities of 'Reiterlied'. It speaks, with appropriate simplicity and candour, of the anguish of separation from a loved one. The graveside grief of 'Es blühen zwei flammende Rosen' is the only precedent in the poems Weill had chosen previously.

In that relationship lies a clue to the dating of 'Im Volkston'. It is not only Weill's mature music that repays analysis in terms of the hermeneutics of his tonal, motivic, and intervallic preferences: the tonal and motivic link between 'Es blühen zwei flammende Rosen' and 'Im Volkston' shows that the underlying compositional instincts were already active at a prenatal stage. The conventional 6–5 melodic motif in the minor mode, which in 'Es blühen zwei flammende Rosen' achieves only a childish repetitiveness, reappears as the characteristic and genuinely musical *Affekt* in 'Im Volkston'; and it does so in the same key of B flat minor. That evidence of consanguinity is also, however, the evidence of the growth that has occurred, and the time that has elapsed, between the puerile composition and the youthful one. Whereas the fragment of 'Es blühen zwei flammende Rosen' generates no formal energy from its mechanical alternations of tonic and dominant, 'Im Volkston' is mobile enough to make the narrowness of its tonal ambit expressive of the poet's climactic cry, 'Ach Gott, wie lang wird's dauern/ bis wir uns wiedersehn!' Modest though it is, this is not an achievement that could be attributed solely to technical improvements made by another hand. Moreover, no adult musician capable of making such improvements would have left untouched some of the more precarious harmonic and structural developments in the song; nor is it likely that Weill, having witnessed in his fifteenth or sixteenth year the beneficial effects of someone else's revisions, would have been content with the weaker songs in *Ofrah's Lieder*.

Perhaps the most important clue to the dating of 'Im Volkston' lies in a musical influence that would surely have made itself felt in *Ofrah's Lieder* if Weill had yet been open to it: that of Gustav Mahler. It is by no means a pervasive influence. But without it, such details as the piano's imitations of flute and piccolo in the last verse are barely thinkable.

As the first sign of Weill's discovery of Mahler's 'Wunderhorn' world, 'Im Volkston' testifies to a growing maturity and must, I believe, be regarded as the unaided work of its composer. The period after the completion of the definitive version of *Ofrah's Lieder* seems the most likely one for such a song.

[early 1917], Dessau

Volkslied

For voice and piano
Text: Anna Ritter (1865–1921)
(Partly missing)

Anna Ritter was a follower of Arno Holz in the German Naturalism movement.

Autograph

Ink sketch, on one side of a 24-line paper (34 × 24.5 cms), with title, poet's name, and signature ('Kurt Weill'). The vocal line is incomplete, the German-script text underlay tentative. Comparisons with the much neater fair copy of 'Das schöne Kind' are unhelpful, except in so far as both songs are signed in the same way – that is, without the intermediary 'Julian' or 'J.' characteristic of every previous autograph apart from that of *Mi addir*. Neither the middle name nor the initial appears in any known signature of later date.

Notes

Like the 'flute and piccolo' embellishments in 'Im Volkston', the rotating thirds of 'Volkslied' are an echo from Mahler. The sketch is not sufficiently formed to provide a basis for judgements about the song's precise chronological relationship to 'Im Volkston', but there can be little doubt that it belongs to the same two- or three-month period.

[1917, first half], Dessau

Das schöne Kind

'Wie war ich doch so wonnereich'
Song for voice and piano (author unknown)

Autograph

An ink holograph fair copy on four sides of Won[12], titled 'Das schöne Kind' and signed 'Kurt Weill', is in the possession of an anonymous collector who bought it from a London music dealer in the early 1960s. A photostat is in WLA.

Notes

The fact that Weill is using, for the last known time, the same manuscript paper that carries the holographs of *Ofrah's Lieder* and 'Sehnsucht' may well be significant, since wartime conditions deteriorated sharply during the winter of 1916–17 and affected supplies of all inessentials. However, the musical evidence is incompatible with a lapse of much less than half a year between the definitive *Ofrah's Lieder* and 'Das schöne Kind'.

Redolent as it is of the drawing-room repertoire of the 1900s, the song is so unabashedly sentimental that even the Straussian implications of its semitonal side-slips can be absolved from the charge of precocious knowingness, and accepted as innocent accessories to Mendelssohnian and Tchaikovskian cliché. Isolated or no, the song is, in its modest way, a landmark: though not in any respect original, it is the earliest known piece in which can be discerned the hand of one who has the makings of a professional composer. We may legitimately prefer the adolescent heartbreak of 'Im Volkston', on the grounds that it is keenly felt and perhaps more 'genuine'; but there is no denying which is the more shapely, varied, and proficient piece. A few inept passages reminiscent of those in 'Im Volkston' tend to confirm that the Holz setting was not many months earlier and that it was indeed Weill's unaided work. But the predominant impression left by 'Das schöne Kind' is of strikingly increased technical command. Many a worse song found its way into print in the golden era of the recital ballad.

before November 1917/before February 1918, Dessau

[Two Duets on Poems by Otto Julius Bierbaum]

for two sopranos and piano

   1   Maikaterlied (Tomcat Song)
   2   Abendlied (Evening Song)

Note 1

Weill subsequently arranged the 'Abendlied' for solo soprano (see *First Performances*).

The poet, editor, and journalist O. J. Bierbaum (1865–1910) figured prominently in the German *Jugendstil* movement, and decisively in the development of literary cabaret (*Überbrettl*) in Berlin during the early 1900s.

Autographs (RWC)

The photostats in WLRC show two markedly different manuscripts on the same unnamed 12-line paper (nine sides and five sides respectively). *1* is headed 'Maikaterlied (Bierbaum)/Kanon für 2 Sop. Stimmen/von Kurt Weill', followed by the expression mark 'Lustig u. neckisch' (merry and roguish). The underlaid text is in German script, and the musical manuscript is an excellent fair copy suitable for any of the three performers. That it was not the original copy seems likely in view of the purely mechanical copying error that forced Weill to strike out one complete system before he began the next. To judge from the photostat, the 'Abendlied' holograph is much less meticulous, and suggests at first glance an earlier date – partly because of the crowded piano part, and partly because of the roughness of the German script underlay. If this was the copy Weill himself played from, these defects would be of no account. The first sign, and the only non-musical one, that the holograph is of later date than that of 'Maikaterlied' is in the signature, and specifically in the letter 'K': it is the first example known to us of a form that Weill retained, with minor modifications, until he left Germany.

First Performances

The first known public performance of the duets was given in Dessau on 6 February 1918 by Clara Ohent and Gertrud Prinzler, accompanied by the composer, at a recital mounted in the Protestant Community Hall by pupils of Emilie Feuge, a leading figure at the Court Opera in Dessau, and a holder of the title 'Herzogliche Kammersängerin'. It was Frau Feuge's daughter Elisabeth – herself destined for a notable career – who gave the first verifiable public performance of the solo version of 'Abendlied' (the programme for her recital, with Weill, at the Casino Hall in Halberstadt on 22 June 1920 is reproduced in JS.KW, p. 23). On this occasion the song was paired with Weill's Dehmel setting, 'Die stille Stadt'. Since 'two Lieder' by Weill are mentioned in a press notice (copy in WLA) of Frau Feuge's and Weill's previous concert in Dessau on 4 September 1919 it seems reasonable to suppose that the solo version of 'Abendlied' was performed on that earlier occasion (and 'Die stille Stadt' also, if it had been composed by then).

Note 2

In a letter to his brother Hanns dated 15 November 1917 (copy in WLRC) Weill replies to a request for some of his music, and specifically, it seems, for 'Maikaterlied' and *Ofrah's Lieder*. Remarking that he has no duplicates of any of his works and that he is reluctant to part with unique manuscripts, he goes on to say that he must copy out 'Maikaterlied', and concludes: 'With the "Ofrah" songs it is not so serious; but I myself am too fond of the canon [to part with it], and moreover it will also be having its premiere at the farewell concert of [for?] Frau Feuge.' His affection for 'the canon' is understandable, as is the implied sense that he has left *Ofrah's Lieder* behind him. Stylistically the companion piece is 'Das schöne Kind'; but the canonic disciplines help exclude the cloying harmony of that song, just as the 'merry and roguish tone' guards against sentimental indulgence. Albert Bing and his wife have evidently introduced Weill to the *Berliner Luft* and enabled him to respond with a light touch to the erotic comedy of Bierbaum's Tomcat. This is the side of Bierbaum that Schoenberg had encountered in 1901 when he set 'Gigerlette' for Wolzogen's 'Bunte Bühne' in Berlin, and there is nothing in Weill's setting, either technically or stylistically, that would have disqualified it for performance in that same theatre during that same period. If sheer poise and professionalism were the only criteria, 'Maikaterlied' could stand as Weill's first wholly successful composition (and the last for some while). What it lacks are those moments of prophetic intensity which fleetingly illuminate *Ofrah's Lieder*. As in 'Das schöne Kind', increased expertise is achieved at the cost – indeed, the necessary cost, at this stage – of suppressing an instinctive, untutored, originality. If 'Maikaterlied' is prophetic, it is only in a very general sense: just as 'Das schöne Kind' had looked forward to Weill's earliest attempts at popular love songs for the American stage – for instance in *Johnny Johnson* (1936) and, more especially, in *The Ballad of Davy Crockett* (1937) – so does 'Maikaterlied' anticipate the lighter side of *Der Kuhhandel* (1934) and related passages in *Knickerbocker Holiday* (1938).

Weill's letter to his brother Hanns of 15 November 1917 clearly implies that the 'Maikaterlied' was still without a companion piece. The *Jugendstil* lyricism of 'Abendlied' has nothing in common with the slightly risqué humour of the 'Maikaterlied', and the only link between the two poems is in their nocturnal background. Weill's setting of 'Abendlied' seems at the start to acknowledge the previous existence of the 'Maikaterlied', in so far as the voices begin in close imitation. Meanwhile the D flat major tonality has instantly and effectively banished the light-heartedness of the canon's F major, and introduced a Straussian colouring that calls to mind (only in that tonal sense) Strauss's early Bierbaum settings. A misleading impression of the song is given by the layout of the manuscript and by the extraordinarily clumsy and unimaginative keyboard writing – extraordinary, that is, in a young pianist–composer who certainly knew the relevant literature. One would prefer to think it was a hasty draft made with a view to subsequent elaboration or even orchestration. But in fact the arrangement for solo voice provided the only occasion for improvements: the incorporation of the second voice part would have forced Weill to remove some of the cluttered accompaniment. (A solo voice arrangement of the canonic 'Maikaterlied' would not have been feasible without calling for an obbligato instrument.) In all other respects 'Abendlied' is much more proficient than the Eichendorff and Halevi settings. Harmonically it lacks the security of 'Maikaterlied', but chiefly because it ventures further: for the first time, as far as we know, parallel fifths are used extensively, and the structural possibilities of enharmony are tentatively explored. As in all the music of 1915–16 – but not in 'Maikaterlied' – the main problems stem from the handling of the bass. But even here the advance since the time of *Ofrah's Lieder* has been considerable; and it is thanks to structural pressure from the bass that 'Abendlied' achieves at several points an eloquence to which 'Maikaterlied' never aspired.

Given the musical relationship between the 'Abendlied' and the B flat *Intermezzo* of December 1917, the date of the 'Abendlied' is probably November–December of that year.

December 1917, Dessau

Intermezzo [in B flat]

[for piano]
Duration: 4 minutes

Autographs (RWC)

Ink score on four sides of a 14-line paper measuring 33.5 × 27.5 cms. The manuscript is dated beneath the signature. There are no tempo indications, nuances, or phrasings, nor is there any specification of instrument.

Notes

Although two passages are not strictly playable by only one pair of hands at a keyboard, and although other passages read like the short score of an orchestral or string-orchestral piece – even of a quartet movement, which would tie up with a reference (see p. 114) in an undated letter of this time to his brother Hanns – there can be little doubt that Weill had the piano in mind, probably with himself as performer. We know from another undated letter to his brother that he had been studying at least one of the Brahms Intermezzos during the summer of 1917, and was considering adding op. 119 no. 2 to his repertoire. For recital purposes in Dessau during the following season an Intermezzo of his own might well have been useful. Since the composition is finished in every detail apart from those the composer–pianist could have left to the spur of the moment, the RWC copy may have been the last.

As the earliest instrumental composition to have survived and the only known piano piece (apart from transcriptions) in Weill's entire output, the *Intermezzo* may attract attention for the wrong reasons; for it is no mere curiosity. To judge from the harmonic language and also from some of the keyboard writing its immediate forebear is the 'Abendlied'. But it is highly significant for the future that Weill's musical invention is stimulated rather than hindered by the absence of a text. Though not an unqualified success, the *Intermezzo* is much more freely inventive than 'Abendlied', and also more consistent, more expressive, and above all more original. With unexpected suddenness and completeness, though not, as we have seen, without previous warning, Weill has found a voice of his own, and sustained it from start to finish. The quintessence is in the first eight bars of the second idea – where Peachum's errant daughter Polly can already be heard, calling for Macheath. But from the opening chord of the piece to the final cadence there is nothing that does not relate to some aspect of the later Weill, either technically or expressively. The richness of the harmony arises, paradoxically, from a process of simplification as radical as that which helped ensure the success of 'Maikaterlied', yet quite different in its functions. While the A sections of the ternary form consist of explorations and elaborations of a 'tonic' pedal whose implications are ambiguous from the start and remain so throughout, the B section roves far and wide on the simplest of scalar planks – a bass line rising chromatically through the octave, then slipping sideways and rising again; and so on. Without reference to Schoenberg's revolution and probably without knowledge of anything of his apart from some early songs and *Verklärte Nacht*, Weill has discovered, in microcosm, a world of possible and desirable freedoms. Had he written nothing else during the winter of 1917–18, the *Intermezzo* would be enough to explain why Albert Bing was emboldened to plead his cause in the family circle, and persuade his parents to let him continue his musical studies in Berlin.

March 1918, Dessau

Andante aus der A-Dur-Sonate von C. M. v. Weber

Arrangement for orchestra
Instrumentation   2.1.2.1.   2.2.2.0.   timp. str.

Autograph (RWC)

Ink holograph on nineteen sides of BH[24], dated by the composer beneath his first-page signature.

Notes

The *Andante* of Weber's second Piano Sonata (1816) is not as obvious a candidate for orchestration as many of that composer's lesser piano solos and duets. Weill's version is doggedly faithful to the keyboard textures, and seems to have profited little from the example of Weber's own orchestral style. In view of the date, it seems likely that the orchestration was a holiday task set by Albert Bing, and that Weill's special affection for Weber's music was merely an added inducement. On 2 March 1918 Weill celebrated his eighteenth birthday, and that same month he completed his studies at the Dessau Oberrealschule. In April he was due to begin a trial term in Berlin, divided equally between the Hochschule für Musik and the University. Since Albert Bing had been largely responsible for persuading Weill's parents that their son should be given the chance of testing his aptitude for a musical career, he would have had every interest in ensuring that Weill put his brief vacation to good use.

1918, Berlin/Leipzig

String Quartet in B minor

  1 *Mässig*
  2 *Allegro ma non troppo (in heimlich erzählendem Ton)*
  3 *Langsam und innig*
  4 *Durchaus lustig und wild, aber nicht zu schnell*
Duration: c. 20 minutes

Autographs

SKETCHES AND DRAFTS

Missing.

SCORE A (RWC)

Ink manuscript on fifty-four sides of unnamed 10-line paper, oblong format. The photostat copy (WLRC) shows that the score is unbound but in good condition. The first page is headed 'Streichquartett in H-moll. Kurt Weill 1918'. There are also autograph violin parts in RWC, but these correspond to the copy of score B which has been in the possession of Frau E. Happe and her heirs since 1920. Annotations in the RWC score (e.g. in the final cadence of the first movement) confirm that the Happe score is the later one.

SCORE B Heirs of E. Happe, Lüdenscheid

The score was inspected by the present author in 1961. It is neatly bound, with autograph titling on the front-cover label and again on the first page. There is no date. Weill uses a miniature-format 12-line paper (18.5 × 15.2 cms) of which there are no other examples among his known manuscripts; beside the colophon is the serial number 28B. The manuscript runs to fifty-seven numbered pages. Apart from some wise modification of the tempo markings (2 was originally *Allegro*, and 4, *Vivace*), the only major revision is in 3, where the florid second violin part has been much simplified in the interests of clarifying the texture.

First Performance

Hidden among the few musical manuscripts in the legacy that survived from the later Berlin years was an insignificant-looking sheet of poor-quality paper on which was a (German script) letter to Weill (WLRC) written from the Westphalian city of Hagen on 2 July 1920 – when Weill would either have been conducting in Norderney or else staying with his parents in Leipzig. It happens to be the only pre-1933 letter to Weill that survives in the legacy, and it has an important bearing both on the first performance of B minor Quartet, and on the dating of the subsequent Cello Sonata. Its author, Martin Missner, was the cellist in a quartet based in Hagen and presumably drawn from the municipal orchestra. Hagen is only a short train ride from Lüdenscheid, and its musical and other resources would have been useful to Weill during the 1919–20 season when he was conducting opera and operetta at the Lüdenscheid Stadttheater. Missner reports that he and his colleagues are looking forward to resuming their study of the quartet after the summer vacation, and clearly implies that a performance is in view. Whether it was to be a public one, and whether in fact anything further happened, has yet to be discovered. It is worth recalling, however, that conditions in Germany after the onset of inflation became increasingly chaotic; and it may also be relevant that there is evidence in the RWC violin parts that the work has been read through at least once, but no evidence that it has been intensively studied.

First Modern Performance

9 September 1975, Akademie der Künste, West Berlin; Melos-Quartett of Stuttgart.

Notes

In a letter to his brother Hanns written towards the end of 1917, Weill speaks of a string quartet on which he is now engaged, and comments on the viola part ('die Schwierigkeiten mit der Bratsche sind nicht allzu gross') in a way that seems to presuppose a question about the possibility of performing the work, perhaps in Halberstadt at one of his brother's concert programmes for the Behrend-Lehmann-Verein. If the quartet as it now stands was conceived and begun during the winter that saw the composition of the B flat *Intermezzo*, the remarkable breakthrough already announced by the piano piece becomes almost incredible, given that little more than a year had passed since the definitive version of *Ofrah's Lieder* (a work Weill suggests to his brother for the next Halberstadt concert). Not only is the command of form and style far greater than in the known works up to and including the *Intermezzo*, but the very idiom is unprecedented. Taking as his first model the Reger of the Mozart Variations and the lighter chamber music, and incorporating elements from Mendelssohn and even Mahler, Weill arrives at a structurally simplified form of North German neo-classicism, which he somehow succeeds in making his own. Precarious though the structure is at certain points, there are enough formal inspirations to hold it together, and enough melodic-harmonic ones to help redeem even the garrulousness of the fugal finale – where Weill's obvious inexperience with the quartet medium allows him finally to abandon all caution (in the key of B major!).

From a strictly contrapuntal point of view the fugal pretensions are pure theatre. As such the finale is enjoyable until the fugue returns after an (inspired) interruption and overstays its welcome. Whatever else it may be, the finale is not academic, and in that respect it is typical of the work as a whole. Therein lies another reason why the dating is so problematic. The style and outlines of the quartet are broadly consistent with what might have been expected from Weill after his first (part-time) term at the Berlin Hochschule für Musik – that is, some six months after the B flat *Intermezzo*. Yet the sheer power to communicate which it retains to this day – much more convincingly than its successor of 1924 – is not a product of teaching, but is innate, and therefore hard to pinpoint in time. Should a precise date for the quartet ever be established, it will not alter the fact that it is the earliest large-scale work of Weill's that merits performance in standard-repertoire concerts.

Borrowings

Ideas and even whole sections from the quartet reappear in *Zaubernacht* (1922) and in the *Quodlibet* (1924).

Publication

EAM: score and parts on hire.

[1918–19]
orchestration nearly complete 27 March 1919, Berlin/[?Dessau]

Suite in E for Orchestra

(Orchestersuite E-Dur)

1 *Andante con moto – Allegro vivace* (4/4)
2 *Adagio* (3/4)
3 *Scherzo. Sehr schnell* (3/4)
4 *Intermezzo* (5/8) *Ziemlich langsam* (5/8)
5 *Menuetto* (3/4)
6 *Finale* (2/4) [no tempo marking]
Dedication: 'To my father, in grateful devotion'
Duration: 22 minutes
Orchestra: 2.1.2.1. 2.2.2.0. timp. str.

Autograph (RWC)

Ink holograph on sixty-one numbered pages (two systems a page) of a 24-line paper (33 × 26 cms); the fifth movement has no title or tempo indication at the start, but its 'trio' ends with the words 'Da Capo il Menuetto al Fine'. Dedication, title, and signature are given only once on the oblong octagonal label (8.5 × 12.2 cms) affixed to the front cover of the score, and read as follows: 'Meinem Vater in dankbarer Verehrung./ Orchestersuite E dur/von Kurt Weill'. Formally speaking, the composition is complete; practically, it is not. Except for the first movement and the opening of the (very sketchy) second, there are no dynamic or expression marks. (Orchestral parts could have been extracted only from the first movement.) Autograph corrections and emendations are few; non-autograph ones – all of them minor and most of them confined to the *finale* – are more numerous but too desultory to suggest that the score was examined closely by a teacher or a conductor.

Notes

At the time of writing, the holograph in RWC and a letter of 27 March 1919 (RWC, copy in WLRC) are the only known sources of information about a work whose very existence was unsuspected until 1983. It is clear from the manuscript that Weill abandoned the Suite unheard, and did not plan a revision. The dedication to his father clearly signifies something. But what? The salient impression is that the score was designed to add substance and bulk to an academic portfolio whose contents, until then, were somewhat slender.

In matters of technique Weill had been a slow starter, and it was not until his eighteenth year that he began to tackle the fundamental problems. The breakthrough achieved in 'Maikaterlied' and the B flat *Intermezzo* must therefore have been associated with an acute sense of time lost – a sense reinforced by the challenging prospect of academic life in Berlin. One can imagine with what eagerness Weill might now have begun to steep himself in the history and practice of thorough-bass, and devour the contents of Ludwig Thuille's *Harmonielehre* (which, only fifteen months later, he was to commend with such enthusiasm to Peter Bing, his first pupil). Since everything was propitious for a technical and creative advance as rapid as the early development had been slow there is no reason why a start should not have been made on the Suite at the end of his first term at the Hochschule für Musik (where the formidable F. E. Koch was in charge of the counterpoint course). Perhaps it was a holiday task set by Humperdinck or even by Kretzschmar, the Hochschule's ultra-conservative Principal; perhaps it was a submission for the Mendelssohn Prize. In any event, Weill was clearly at pains to display evidence of skills attained and objectives defined, together with those qualities of diligence, seriousness, and good behaviour which the guardians of conservatories and the dispensers of prizes and bursaries are accustomed to look for.

Harmonically he avoids the liberties of the *Intermezzo*, and risks nothing that might offend disciples of Pfitzner or the recently deceased Max Reger. Pfitzner and the *Tristan* harmony are already present in the slow introduction to the first movement, and there are echoes of him elsewhere. But it is the romantic playfulness and the classicizing romanticism of Reger's two late-period orchestral suites, opus 125 and (more particularly) the six-movement opus 130, that seem to be at the forefront of Weill's mind.

Something, though not quite everything, of Weill's own emerging personality has been lost to view as he pursues his academic objectives. Recognizing an urgent need to tackle his problems at source he becomes almost obsessive in his concern for establishing and developing bass-oriented textures. This is the only feature of the work itself that seems consistent with the (inconclusive) extra-musical evidence that the composition of this Suite followed rather than preceded that of the much more personal and successful B minor String Quartet.

Comparison of the two works is complicated both by the possibility that the Suite was subject to academic pressures, and by the fact that Weill's inexperience with the orchestra had effects that are disproportionate to those stemming from his inexperience with the quartet medium. It is nevertheless hard to imagine the composer of the third movement of the quartet proceeding to write anything quite so shapeless and colourless as the second movement of the Suite; nor would one expect the youthful contrapuntist who boldly makes his bow in the finale of the quartet to have lost his nerve at the very next turning and foregone the opportunities for polyphonic display that are implicit in the Reger-like aspirations of the Suite. Given that Reger has also left his mark on the quartet, the absence of even a token fugato in the Suite can only be attributed to orchestral worries, if indeed the Quartet came first. Conversely, the meeting Weill arranges in the Quartet between Reger on the one hand, and Mendelssohn and Mahler on the other, is one from which a later work should have benefited. But there are no traces of it in the Suite.

Weill's letter to his brother Hanns of 27 March 1919 refers to the fact that the orchestration of the Suite is still not finished, and does so with some annoyance as he is impatient to start his next orchestral work. In conjunction with Weill's own dating of the String Quartet, this is incontrovertible evidence that the Quartet was finished first; but not that it was started first. Final judgement about the chronology of the two works must await conclusive evidence. Meanwhile, we have all the purely musical evidence needed for a judgement about their relative status. While the orchestral work is demonstrably a student piece, the Quartet, as the composer of *Zaubernacht* well knew, was much more than that.

1918–19, Berlin (Hochschule für Musik)

[Orchestral Work]

(Missing)

In a letter of February 1919 written to his parents from the Hochschule für Musik, Weill mentions a recent performance of 'an orchestral work' of his, by the Hochschule orchestra. He reports that the performance was attended by teachers and students, but says nothing about the work or their reactions. For reasons noted above (Suite in E for Orchestra, *Autograph*) allowance must be made for the possibility that the 'work' in question was the first movement of the Suite.

[March–September] 1919, Berlin/Dessau

[Die Weise von Liebe und Tod]

'Symphonic Poem' after Rainer Maria Rilke's *Die Weise von Liebe und Tod des Cornets Christoph Rilke*

Rilke's narrative prose-poem was written in 1899 and first published in 1903. It tells of the 18-year-old Christoph von Rilke of Langenau, his arduous ride to join an Austrian regiment during the Turkish war of 1663, his arrival and appointment as standard-bearer, the dancing in a great castle on the eve of battle, his night in the arms of a nameless countess, the lovers' awakening as the castle is set on fire, and finally the half-clothed Cornet's desperate ride to the battlefield, where he bears the standard into the very heart of the enemy's ranks, and is slain.

Notes

The first precisely datable reference to *Die Weise* is in a letter of 17 March 1919 from Weill (in Berlin) to his brother Hanns (in Halberstadt). Ten days later he writes of the work as if it had only now begun to take shape in his mind (original in RWC; photostat copies in AdK and WLA):

> I want to divide the whole piece into three sections, that is to say, in a single movement, of course. The first part depicts the dark mood of the knights, which will be interrupted only now and then by a shaft of light – the boy's courageous thirst for action; the second part will be lyrical and will depict the night of love, giving way to the sudden bursting into flames of the castle, the terror, and in the third part, battle and death. Naturally I will not proceed in a purely programmatic way. My music will certainly be stimulated by the various moods of the poem but it will also be comprehensible without any programme.

In a letter to Hanns of 3 July Weill reports that the draft of *Die Weise* (as he calls it) is finished ('Die Weise ist bis auf den letzten Schlussakkord in der Skizze fertig') and that he will now turn to the orchestration. There is another reference to *Die Weise* in a letter from which at least the first page is missing. Lys Symonette's translation of this important fragment was first published in KWN 3.1, spring 1985, where it is conjecturally dated spring 1919. If that dating is correct, Weill's reference to his orchestrating one of his works without supervision must refer to the Suite in E, not *Die Weise*.

The only contemporary reference to *Die Weise* is in Strobel's article on Weill, which *Melos* published in October 1927 (DD.UKW, pp. 28–35). Strobel's claim that the work was influenced by Schoenberg's symphonic poem *Pelleas und Melisande* was probably suggested by Weill himself. In any case it is the earliest work Strobel mentions, and presumably the earliest that Weill thought worth mentioning.

In a conversation with the present writer in Berlin in the early 1960s,

Arthur Kistenmacher recalled that during the season of 1919–20 (when he was directing the Stadttheater in Lüdenscheid) Weill told him, in great excitement, that a conductor in Dresden (whose name Kistenmacher could no longer recall) had just accepted one of his orchestral works for performance the following season. *Die Weise* was surely the work in question; no doubt the economic chaos of the following year put paid to the performance. As for the conductor, the most likely name is that of Fritz Reiner, to whom Weill refers in a letter written soon after his arrival in the USA as being someone he had known since the very start of his career.

An important footnote to Kistenmacher's recollection is provided by a recently discovered letter (EHA) which Weill wrote to Humperdinck from Lüdenscheid on 16 March 1920. In the final paragraph he tells his former teacher that he has sent the score of *Die Weise* to Arthur Nikisch, and is awaiting his reactions. Since the 65-year-old Nikisch was as unlikely to have accepted a work by an untried 20-year-old as Kistenmacher was to have forgotten his world-famous name and confused Berlin (or Leipzig, where Nikisch conducted the Gewandhaus orchestra) with Dresden, the most probable course of events – given that Weill would certainly not have made a second copy of so large a work, and assuming that *Die Weise* was the work in question – is that Nikisch promptly returned the score and Weill immediately sent it on to Dresden.

[July 1919, Dessau]

Schilflieder

Song-cycle
Text: [Nikolaus Lenau]
  [1   Drüben geht Sonne
  2   Trübe wird's, die Wolken jagen
  3   Auf geheimem Waldespfade
  4   Sonnenuntergang
  5   Auf dem Teich, dem regungslosen]

Notes

Rudolf Kastner's 1925 article on Weill (first published in *Musikblätter des Anbruch*, 7, and reprinted in DD.UKW, pp. 10–13), refers to 'ein Zyklus *Schilflieder*, Klavierstückchen usw.' ('a cycle of *Reed Songs*, little piano pieces, etc.') as being the culmination of a period, beginning soon after Weill's 'tenth birthday' (*sic!*), when he was struggling, quite untaught, to put down on paper the music that came into his head. Since the cycle and the 'little piano pieces' are the only compositions prior to *Zaubernacht* (1922) that Kastner mentions, it is clear either that he had not troubled to question Weill (with whom he was well acquainted) or – perhaps more likely – that Weill had fobbed him off with some suitably dismissive remarks and a token mention of one specific work. Although his information about Weill's pre-Busoni years can have come only from Weill, Kastner does not attempt even approximate datings, and is mistaken about the order of events. But his reference to *Schilflieder* is surely reliable, for it is not a title about which a German musician would easily be confused. Presumably the poet's name goes unmentioned because Kastner took it for granted that his readers would not need to be told it.

The five 'Schilflieder' of Nikolaus Lenau (1802–1850) are justly celebrated, for they epitomize in a mere two pages the lyric melancholy of that unhappy poet. Though their diction and imagery are quite simple, the content is much too highly charged for the juvenile composer described by Kastner and represented by such things as *Mi addir* and 'Reiterlied'.

Writing to his brother Hanns from Berlin on 3 July 1919, Weill reports that he is about to start the orchestration of *Die Weise*, and will not embark on a new large-scale work until that task is done. Instead he will just write 'a few songs' ('ein paar Lieder'). The idea of composing a cycle of *Schilflieder* while orchestrating a tone poem based on Rilke's *Cornet* is not so extravagant that we can afford to dismiss it – least of all when there is no indication of any other date or opportunity.

Late Summer 1919/Summer 1920, Dessau

Sonata for Cello and Piano

    1   *Allegro ma non troppo*
    2   *Andante espressivo*
    3   *Allegro assai*
Dedication: 'For Fritz Rupprecht and Albert Bing'
Duration: 23 minutes

Autographs (RWC/WLA)

A complete and fluent draft of the first movement is in RWC. Headed 'Cellosonate' but unsigned, it is written on twenty sides of Won[12] and is followed by a 12-bar sketch (for an interpolation), which ends on the first system of a new side. There are no workings on the remainder of that side, or on the next. Evidence that Weill broke off at this point and did not resume work for some months is considered below. There is no sign of that break in the copyist's score of the complete work which was in the possession of Albert Bing's son Peter at the time of Weill's death, and is now in WLA. To the title 'Sonate für Violoncello und Klavier' Weill has added his signature and the dedication 'für Fritz Rupprecht u. Albert Bing'. He has also made a few minor corrections and annotations in the score itself (which is written on forty-one pages of an 18-line paper, Klemm No. 5).

Notes

In a letter of spring 1919 (WLRC, photostat of an undated fragment) Weill writes to his brother Hanns from Berlin about his creative ideals and difficulties. At the start of the WLRC fragment – probably following an account of the pressures and frustrations of his academic work – he writes: 'Not even so much as a little song is taking shape; today I had a very beautiful idea for the beginning of a cello sonata, and immediately noted it down; now, once again, I'd already like to destroy it.' If this was indeed the beginning of the present Sonata, there was added reason for Weill to lose interest in his Suite for Orchestra: harmonic possibilities latent in 'Abendlied' and manifest in the *Intermezzo* had scarcely been touched upon in the Suite, but are fundamental to the first movement of the Sonata, which dismisses at one stroke the academic neo-classicism of the Suite and carries on with those late-Romantic elements in the B minor Quartet which are amenable to early modernist and impressionist treatment. Certainly there are missing links between the Quartet and the Sonata; and some may have been destroyed by Weill himself, as his letter to Hanns Weill suggests. But much the largest must have been the missing tone poem *Die Weise von Liebe und Tod*. In that same letter to his brother, Weill declares that for his own generation, the Mahler–Schoenberg line is decisive, and that for him personally, Schoenberg has become the lodestar. In the very next sentence he speaks of *Die Weise* and how 'this music' is what he is now living for and living through. It therefore seems unlikely that he returned to his 'beautiful idea' for a cello sonata – or found another one – until after he had finished at least the composition and perhaps also the scoring of *Die Weise*, which would have been during the summer of 1919. Since Weill was about to start working under Albert Bing at the Dessau opera, and since Bing and Rupprecht (who was cellist in the Dessau orchestra) were already established as a recital team, the incentive and the opportunity were at hand.

So why did Weill break off after the first movement of the Sonata, and begin work on an opera? There is a ready-made answer in his letter to Hanns Weill of spring 1919, where he describes his inhibitions about writing 'absolute music'; but it is clear from the thoroughly uninhibited Sonata that the description was exaggerated, and that the real answer is not psychological but purely musical. The clue to it is in the setting of Richard Dehmel's poem 'Die stille Stadt', which Weill must have written soon after the first movement of the Sonata. Here, the tonal functions which had been the *raison d'être*, the subject matter, and the intolerable burden of the Suite in E are becoming so attenuated as even to call in question the much looser principles on which the sonata movement was based. It is not hard to imagine how the discovery that he had unwittingly invalidated his own premisses brought home to Weill that there was a linguistic and dialectical problem that had to be tackled before he could consider continuing the sonata. In such a situation, older and wiser composers had gratefully turned to the lyric stage. Having followed their example – how far, we do not know, for the opera has vanished without trace – he did indeed return to the sonata and complete it according to new tonal premisses that were broad enough to take some account of the old. The ecstatic transfigurations of the coda finally discover the tonality which is at the furthest possible remove from that in or around which the Sonata began.

In his letter to Weill of 2 July 1920 (see p. 113) Martin Missner expresses keen interest in the Cello Sonata which Weill is 'currently' writing ('die in Arbeit befindliche Cellosonate') and begs him to send it to him as soon as it is ready, as he would have many opportunities to play it during the coming winter, and would like to begin studying it in mid-September, before the start of the (opera) season. Unless Weill had neglected to mention a prior obligation to Bing and Rupprecht, we may assume that there was no such obligation at this stage, and that the dedication which Weill added to the copyist's score is evidence that nothing came of Missner's plans. Economic conditions in Germany during the winter of 1920–1 were hardly favourable to performances of modern chamber music.

First Performance Plans

According to a letter from Weill to his brother Hanns (17 October 1920) Bing hoped to give the premiere in Hanover in February 1921. There was then to have been a performance in Berlin. No evidence that either of these performances materialized has yet been traced; but the absence of any reference to the Sonata in the first biographical notes on Weill to appear in concert programmes tends to suggest that the work remained unperformed.

First Modern Performance

9 September 1975, Akademie der Künste, West Berlin; Siegfried Palm (cello), Aloys Kontarsky (piano).

Publication

EAM, 1984: score and cello part (on sale).

[August] 1919

Die stille Stadt

Song for voice and piano
Text: Richard Dehmel

Note 1

Despite his North German connections with Arno Holz, Dehmel (1863–1920) is in a very different category from the contemporary poets whose work Weill is known to have set during his adolescence. Dehmel's best work has outlived its time, as has that of his younger and more celebrated contemporary, Rilke.

As one of the leading contributors to the Berlin periodical *Pan* (founded in 1894 by Otto Julius Bierbaum), Dehmel had played an important role in the literature of *Jugendstil*; and it is the musical consequences of that movement that are so strongly reflected in the Halberstadt recital given by Weill and Elisabeth Feuge on 22 June 1920. A Dehmel setting – even more than the Bierbaum one (p. 109) with which Weill had paired it – was in principle well suited to a programme featuring *Lieder* by Reger and Pfitzner, and ending with the 'Song of the Wood Dove' from Schoenberg's *Gurrelieder*. Dehmel settings figure in the *Lieder* of all three masters, but it was Schoenberg for whom Dehmel had acquired a pivotal significance – first at the start of his public career, and then again in the 'revolutionary' years before the First World War. (For Dehmel's part in the Symphony for soloists, chorus and orchestra with which Schoenberg was occupied between 1912 and 1914, see Josef Rufer, *The Works of Arnold Schoenberg* (London: Faber, 1962), pp. 115–18.) Through Feuge and Bing, Weill may well have known the Dehmel settings in Schoenberg's opus 2 and opus 3; and he would certainly have been aware that *Verklärte Nacht*, op. 4, is based on a poem by Dehmel.

Whereas Schoenberg's place in the Halberstadt programme reinforces the contemporary significance of Weill's Dehmel setting, Pfitzner's is a reminder that Albert Bing was his pupil and that several works of his – including the music-drama *Der arme Heinrich* – had been performed in Dessau during the war years. Since Pfitzner would almost certainly have met and worked with Elisabeth Feuge after she won fame at the Bavarian State Opera – if not already at the Dessau Court Theatre – it is of more than coincidental interest that he made his own setting of 'Die stille Stadt' in 1922.

Autograph (RWC)

An unsigned draft, musically complete and headed by the title of the poem and the surname of the author, covers four sides of Won[12] and the first system of the fifth side. The paper is the same as that which Weill had used for the first movement of the Cello Sonata, and the musical manuscript is so similar as to rule out any significant lapse of time between the two compositions.

First Performance

Assuming that the first movement of the Cello Sonata was finished by the beginning of August 1919, Weill would have had enough time to make the solo arrangement of 'Abendlied' and compose 'Die stille Stadt' while he and Elisabeth Feuge were working on the *Lieder* programme which they gave at the Dessau Opera on 4 September 1919. If the two songs mentioned in the press review of that concert (WLRC) were in fact 'Die stille Stadt' and 'Abendlied' the arrangement of a duet song already heard, and presumably enjoyed, in Dessau would not only have been a time-saver – perhaps after he and Feuge had decided against a selection from *Ofrah's Lieder* – but would have cushioned the effect of a song considerably more 'advanced' in its harmony than anything the Dessau audience was accustomed to. (In a letter to Hanns Weill of 5 September Weill speaks of the audience's incomprehension of the 'strenge Modernität' of his two songs, a remark that rules out *Ofrah's Lieder* and needs to be taken with a pinch of salt as far as 'Abendlied' is concerned.)

Note 2

'Die stille Stadt' extends the harmonic fields of the sonata movement still further beyond the boundaries of traditional tonality, incorporating strangely personal and quite un-Schoenbergian fourth-chord progressions which are to become one of the hallmarks of his style in the early 1920s – with implications for the future that reach as far as *Die Bürgschaft*, the Second Symphony, and even *Der Weg der Verheissung*. While the key signature and the initial root-position triad proclaim that tonality is not yet in abeyance, everything that follows suggests that for Weill its days are numbered; and sure enough, key signatures are abandoned in the second and third movements of the Cello Sonata and not restored until *Die Dreigroschenoper*.

1919–20, Dessau/Lüdenscheid

Ninon von Lenclos

One-act opera after the play (1905) by Ernst Hardt (1876–1947) (Missing)

The only known reference is in a letter from Weill to his sister, written from Lüdenscheid on 28 January 1928. He does not mention the name of the opera, but simply expresses a fervent desire to finish his 'setting' (Vertonung) of 'the Ernst Hardt one-acter'. The only one-act play by Hardt – who in 1919 was appointed director of the German National Theatre in Weimar, and in 1928 was to direct the first performance of *Der Lindberghflug* – is *Ninon von Lenclos*. The play is a neo-Romantic gloss on the historical figure of Ninon (or Anne) de Lenclos (1620–1705), celebrated in her time for her literary *salon*, her wit and intelligence, and her numerous *liaisons*. The play is not, however, concerned with the literary and historical background, but only with the tragedy of a great love which the heroine discovers to be incestuous. Weill's decision to 'set' the play was surely influenced by his current interest in the operas of Schreker – to which that same letter to his sister bears witness.

[August–September 1920], [Leipzig/Berlin]

Sulamith
(*The Sulamite*)

'Chorfantasie' for soprano, female chorus, and orchestra

Autographs (WLRC)

Three fragments of a short-score draft, written in mauve pencil. A sheet of 12-line paper measuring 18.5 × 15 cms carries the first fragment on sides *a* and *b*, and the second on the remaining two sides. The discontinuity of *b* and *c* indicates that this section of the draft must have been continued on one or more sheets enclosed in the extant one. The third fragment is musically closely related to the second, but is not a direct continuation and is written on a different-sized sheet (B¹²). Covering the first three sides and ending at the top of the fourth, it consists of the final sixty-one bars of the work.

Notes

The title and subtitle of the work are given by Strobel in his 1927 article (DD.UKW, p. 29). A misleading clue to the authorship of the text is hidden in Louis M. Simon's interview with Weill published three months after the premiere of *Lady in the Dark* (*New York Times*, 13 April 1941, 'Up the Rungs from Opera'). Here Weill is reported as stating that one of his apprentice works was an opera based on Hermann Sudermann's novel *Das hohe Lied* (The Song of Songs). Among the principal figures in the novel is the composer of an unfinished setting of the Old Testament Song of Songs. Since Weill does not mention the Hardt opera or *Sulamith* in the Simon interview, and since an adaptation of Sudermann's novel (published in 1908) would have been so complex an undertaking that some trace of it would surely have survived if Weill had made any headway with it, it seems likely that an early memory of operatic ambitions inspired by the novel had become confused with a later one of the cantata – whose text is not from the Old Testament, but could well be the work of some young contemporary of Weill's, under the influence of Franz Werfel.

Strobel describes *Sulamith* as 'impressionistic', but this is not borne out by the surviving fragments. Harmonically they are in the direct line of succession from the second and third movements of the Cello Sonata. This alone would be enough to suggest a dating in the second half of 1920. But a more precise hypothesis becomes possible in the light of Weill's excited reaction to the announcement, that summer, of the appointment of Franz Schreker as director of the Hochschule für Musik in Berlin. The idea of studying with Schreker had been on Weill's mind since January or earlier, but he had regarded it as impracticable so long as Schreker remained in Vienna. Now that he was coming to Berlin, everything changed – including, perhaps, his own creative decisions. Given the likely direction of *Ninon von Lenclos*, *Sulamith* was a logical and self-justifying development; but it also remained an expedient one so long as there was no desirable alternative to the prospect of returning to the Hochschule für Musik simply in order to study with Schreker. If the Cello Sonata was finished in July, Weill would have had the whole of August and the beginning of September for *Sulamith*. But once Busoni had entered Weill's life, such a work would have been almost inconceivable. Aesthetically it marks the end of the era that had its tentative beginnings in *Ofrah's Lieder*.

[Autumn 1920], [Berlin]

Die Weber
(*The Weavers*)

Music for the play (1892) by Gerhart Hauptmann (1862–1946)
(Partly missing)
1   Weberlied I
2   Weberlied II

Hauptmann based the play on his father's accounts of the Silesian weavers' riots of 1844, and used the historical background to mirror the social and political tensions of his own day. In the aftermath of the failed German revolution of 1918 *Die Weber* acquired new significance, and was recognized as one of the models for the radical-activist theatre developed by Ernst Toller and Friedrich Wolf, among others. The play's protagonist is collective – the weavers themselves, reduced to abject poverty and

near-starvation by the businessman Dreissiger. Under the leadership of
the ex-soldier Moritz Jäger they storm and loot Dreissiger's house, and
beat off the military detachment sent to quell them.

Autographs

The two settings of the Weavers' Song from Act II are suitable only for
stage use; each is in black ink on a leaf of F^{12}, is headed 'Kurt Weill:
Weberlied', and has a simple accompaniment on one system only
(instrumentation unspecified).

Note 2

Weberlied I is in the style of a chorale, and follows Hauptmann's own
suggestion in using the melody generally associated with the folk song
'Es liegt ein Schloss in Oesterreich'. The second appears to be an original
melody, but is strikingly suggestive of the songs of revolutionary Russia,
and hence of the *Kampflieder* that were influenced by them. Hermann
Scherchen, who had been a prisoner of war in Russia at the time of the
revolution, made choral arrangements of several Soviet songs, and
introduced them to Germany soon after his return. A letter from Weill to
his brother Hanns of 3 July 1919 shows that he was already in touch with
Scherchen at that time. Research into the performance history of *Die
Weber* after 1918 may yet uncover information relevant to the precise
dating of Weill's two settings. Meanwhile the hypothetical dating given
above seems consistent with the graphic and musical evidence, and with
what we know of Weill's life and interests in 1920.

OPUS NUMBERS AND AFTER

In German-speaking countries the generation of composers born during
the 1900s was the last to maintain the practice of opus numbering which
had begun to evolve in the early eighteenth century and became
universal in Beethoven's time. For nearly a century it was taken for
granted that numbering starts with the first published work, and follows
the order of publication, not of composition. So long as the business of
publishing and the art of composition were developing on parallel lines
to their mutual profit, 'opus 1' was at once a commercial label and a
certificate of artistic achievement. But as soon as composers began to
attack the roots of a generally accepted musical language, the tradition
that publishers determine what should qualify as a composer's 'opus 1'
began to disintegrate.

Like Hindemith before him, Weill claimed the freedom to decide for himself where his *oeuvre* began; but, unlike Hindemith, he failed to advertise the fact in any list or reference book (or at least, in any that has yet come to light). Opus 8 was his first published work, while his opus 5 of 1922 is the earliest to which a definitive number can be given. Since the two substantial works surviving from 1919–20 do not have numbers, it seems likely that Weill began the series in September 1920, at the start of his three years as a member of Busoni's Masterclass in Composition.

In the formal sense, the series ends seven years later, soon after Weill began his collaboration with Brecht (though the precise point at which it stops is just as unclear as the precise point at which it starts). In spirit, however, the series continues for another seven years – that is, until the completion of the Second Symphony in January 1934. The subsequent attenuation, and the final dissolution, of his links with the European concepts of 'opus' and '*oeuvre*' are surely the salient events in his later development.

April–June 1921, Berlin

Symphony [No. 1, in one movement]

Grave – Allegro vivace – Andante religioso – Larghetto
Duration: 24 minutes
Orchestra: 2(picc.).1.2.2.   2.2.2.0,   timp. perc. str.

Autographs

FULL SCORE

The score (on B²⁴) has been neatly bound in a blue cartridge paper and paginated 1–64 by the composer. There is no title or signature on page 1, presumably because both were on the separate title page, which was removed during the Second World War. (See p. 11.) The autograph is dated at the end.

ARRANGEMENT FOR PIANO (four hands)

Twenty unbound pages of B⁶ˣ², without title page or signature. The *primo* and *secondo* parts are separated, on facing pages. The score is incomplete: the *primo* part ends at bar 217, the *secondo* at bar 239.

Notes

According to Strobel (DD.UKW, p. 29), the 'socialist–pacifist' motto of the work (presumably written on the title page) was taken from Johannes R. Becher's *Arbeiter, Bauern, Soldaten*. The original version of this *Festspiel* (published in Leipzig in 1921) was subtitled 'Der Aufbruch eines Volkes zu Gott' ('A People's Awakening to God'). In a letter to his brother of 7 November 1920 Weill reports that he has been commissioned to write a score for the play. The project – musically a demanding one – is not mentioned again, and presumably did not materialize.

First Performance

1956: studio recording by North-West German Radio, Hamburg, with the NWDR Symphony Orchestra conducted by Wilhelm Schüchter. The recording was relayed on 20 February 1957, and subsequently listed by ASCAP under the title *Berliner Symphonie*.

Publication

Schott, 1968: full score and study score edited, with an introduction, by David Drew. The editor advises increasing the number of horns to four.

[1921]

[Cabaret Number]

Slow foxtrot for piano with vocal refrain (anonymous satirical text)
Duration: 3 minutes

Autographs

The draft – which is incomplete – is written on both sides of a leaf of 18-line paper measuring 34 × 27 cms; it is without title or signature, but has the tempo indication 'Langsamer Fox'. There are two scribal clues to the dating of the composition: first, the preponderance of German script, which does not appear in any of Weill's manuscripts after 1922; second, the fact that prior to Weill's use of this sheet for his pencil draft, another hand had inscribed time signatures that correspond to those required for the Cello Sonata at the end of its first movement and the start of its second. (Bing and Rupprecht would have required playing copies of the Sonata during the season 1920–1.) Names listed (upside-down) at the top of the first side are those of friends from Weill's early 'Busoni' years – Gratenau, Lasoli, Manzi, as well as Jarnach and Kaempfer.

Notes

The first two sections are for piano alone: 18 bars in D major, and 32 in B flat. The third section is a 16-bar vocal refrain in D major, ending with a first-time bar. At that point the manuscript breaks off; but the proportions and musical character suggest that a quick-tempo variation of the refrain will follow, and there is certainly no reason to suppose that the piece was left unfinished. It is remarkably assured, considering its early date. Weill seems aware of Parisian as well as Viennese and cabaret idioms. Compared to the text, which harmlessly parodies an advertisement for soap powder, the music seems almost too sophisticated. But it is hard to judge without the context. If, as is probable, the number was written for one of the programmes given in the *Bierkeller* cabaret where Weill played the piano, it may well be the only survivor from a considerable quantity of such *rudes saloperies* (as Satie would have called them). In any case it is an indispensable document, for it shows not only that Weill made popular idioms his own very early in his career, but also that the mastery of such idioms was within his reach only because for him musical substance transcended any idiomatic considerations. Thus, a variant of the cabaret number's neo-Schubertian foxtrot tune in B flat is used to very different effect in *Zaubernacht* and *Quodlibet*; and its D major refrain is later to be transformed into one of the elements of the *Zaubernacht* waltz (34). (The relationship between text and music in the cabaret number is too close for there to be any possibility that *Zaubernacht* was written first.)

[1921], Berlin

[Polka]

(Unfinished)
For piano

Autograph

Forty-two bars, indelible pencil, rough draft only, incomplete on a single sheet of 14-line paper, 34 × 27 cms. At the head of the second side Weill has sketched a three-note figure, with the legend 'Andante ⁶/₄/[illegible] in der Fantasia [illegible] (Stretta)'. Appended to the same page and written in ordinary lead pencil (possibly at a later date) is a memorandum of a one-bar figure. It recurs as an ostinato in the unfinished intermezzo for *Frauentanz* (see p. 149) whose theme is in fact derived from the Polka.

[October] 1921, Berlin

Die Bekehrte
['The Convert']

Song for voice and piano
Text: Johann Wolfgang von Goethe
(Partly missing)

Autographs

SKETCHES

On sides *a* and *c* of a sheet of B^{10} are the beginnings of two settings unrelated to the later and near-complete draft; on *b* are the first two bars of the drafted setting.

DRAFT

Sides *c* and *d* of a sheet of B^{20} carry a setting that is complete except for dynamic nuances and an uncopied repeat. Autograph paginations 5–6 and 15–16 are inverted on this sheet, which seems to have been part of a volume of early compositions: the page numbered 5 carries a fragment of full score for the First Symphony (bars 22–23), together with three sketches for the Divertimento and a harmonic progression related to one of the abortive settings of 'Die Bekehrte'. The page numbered 6 carries three sketches for the finale of the Divertimento.

FINAL COPY

Missing.

Notes

In the autumn of 1921 Busoni gave Goethe's poem to the members of his Masterclass as a composition task (without telling them that he had set himself the same task). After he had seen the results, he chose Vladimir Vogel's setting as the most representative of what he called 'the new road' in music, and published (in *Faust*, No. 2) a short note about it entitled 'Der Kampf um den neuen Stil'. Though implying that Vogel's setting, for all its qualities, is not the most 'masterly' of those submitted to him, Busoni mentions no others. Weill, who must have known Wolf's setting of the same poem, clearly found the task difficult. The extant draft is adequate, and not without personal touches. But was it final?

[November] 1921, Berlin

[Rilkelieder]

For voice and piano
Poems by Rainer Maria Rilke (*Das Stundenbuch*, 3)
(Partly missing)

1 Vielleicht, dass ich durch schwere Berge gehe
2 Mach mich zum Wächter deiner Weiten

Autographs

A complete pencil draft of *1*, and an incomplete draft of the beginning of *2* (headed '*II*' and reaching the poem's twelfth line by the end of the page) are on a leaf of B²⁰. The pages are numbered 17–20, which may indicate that Weill began the *Rilkelieder* immediately after 'Die Bekehrte' – the draft of which, we have seen, is written inverse on pages of the same paper, numbered respectively 16 and 15.

Notes

Related settings of the same poems open *Stundenbuch*, a cycle of six Rilke settings for voice and orchestra that Weill wrote in 1923–4.

[November] 1921–2, Berlin

Divertimento op. 5

For small orchestra with male chorus
(Partly missing)

  1   Fantasia
  2   [Ostinato]
  3   Aria
  4   [Waltz]
  5   Scherzo
  6   Chorale-Fantasy
Duration: *c.* 25 minutes
Orchestra: 1.0.1.1.   1.0.2.0.   [?solo str. qt.], str.

Autographs

SKETCHES

On side *b* of the sheet of B²⁰, which carries the draft of 'Die Bekehrte' and a full-score false start of a page of the First Symphony, there are several sketches for the sixth movement of the Divertimento. On *a* there are precise notations of three ideas – one that appears in the fifth movement of the Divertimento, and two others plainly intended for the same work: a *grazioso* waltz tune in E flat, and a short motif in 2/4 time labelled 'als basso ostinato': these may be the only extant sources for the second and fourth movements.

FINAL DRAFT

A complete draft of the fifth movement in short score is on eight sides of B²⁰, paginated 7–14. At the top of the last page of the folding – from which the lower half has been removed – is a full-score draft in another hand (probably Jarnach's) of the last four bars of a rapid movement in 2/4 time. Since the instrumentation (clarinet, horn, bassoon, string quartet) is the same as in the *Scherzo*, this is doubtless a suggested scoring for the conclusion of the 2/4 'ostinato' movement. Beneath are two sketches, by Weill himself, for the *Sinfonia Sacra*.

FULL SCORE

Missing.

PARTS

The original orchestral parts of the last movement are headed 'Schluβatz aus dem Divertimento op. 5 v. Kurt Weill'. The brass parts are in Weill's hand in purple ink, while the remainder have been extracted by a professional copyist. They are in black ink, but have purple ink corrections by Weill.

ARRANGEMENT FOR TWO PIANOS

Missing, except for one piano part for the fifth movement (headed 'V. Satz'), ink autograph on six sides of a two-sheet folding of B^{16}.

Notes

Strobel (DD.UKW) writes of two 'fantasia-type' movements for the full orchestra enclosing a group of short dance movements for chamber ensemble. Press notices mention '*Aria*' and '*Scherzo*'; one critic writes that there are five movements. The text of the *Chorale-Fantasy* is an old Danish psalm, thought to have originated in Germany. It is quoted at the end of Jens Peter Jacobsen's novel *Frau Marie Grubbe*, which explains why the text is erroneously attributed to Jacobsen himself in the programme leaflet (WLA) provided at the first performance of the *Chorale-Fantasy*.

First Performances

Chorale-Fantasy only: 7 December 1922, Singakademie, Berlin; choir of the Kaiser-Wilhelm-Gedächtniskirche and the Berlin Philharmonic Orchestra conducted by Heinz Unger. The premiere of the complete work was given by the same orchestra and conductor in the Berlin Philharmonic Hall on 10 April 1923.

Performing Version

By David Drew and Christopher Shaw, 1971; commissioned by the European Broadcasting Union, and first performed on 10 January 1972 by the orchestra of Südwestfunk, Baden-Baden, under Ernest Bour. The first two movements of this four-movement version are adapted from the unpublished movements of opus 8.

[?1922], Berlin

Psalm VIII

For 6-part (SSATTB) chorus, *a cappella*
Text: Latin Vulgate
(Unfinished or partly missing)

Autographs

Discontinued pencil draft on one side of an 8-line paper, oblong format
6.5 × 16.5 cms.

Notes

The two principal ideas recur in the *Allegro deciso* of the String Quartet,
op. 8 (first version).

First Performance

January 1972, BBC Chorus conducted by Peter Gellhorn; BBC studio
recording.

[1922], Berlin

Divertimento für Flöte und Orchester, op. 52, von Ferruccio Busoni

Arrangement for flute and piano

Autograph

The original was presumably lodged in the archives of Busoni's
publishers, Breitkopf & Härtel (Leipzig) after publication. Neither this,
nor any copy, has yet come to light.

Publication

Breitkopf & Härtel, 1923: flute and piano score, with flute part.

Notes

The performances and the subsequent recording by the distinguished
Italian flautist Severino Gazzelloni in the 1960s were largely responsible
for establishing Weill's arrangement as a concert work in its own right.
Whether Busoni himself saw the arrangement as anything other than an

adjunct to study and rehearsal may seem questionable, given his own supreme qualifications as a keyboard transcriber. We should not, however, forget how poor his health was during the last years, and how great the pressure to complete his opera *Doktor Faust*.

February–May 1922, Berlin

[Sinfonia Sacra] op. 6

Fantasia, Passacaglia, und Hymnus
For orchestra
(Full score missing; draft incomplete)
Dedication: Philipp Jarnach
Duration: 18 minutes

Note 1

The dedication does not appear in the surviving material but was recalled by Philipp Jarnach himself, in conversation with Lenya and George Davis in Hamburg in 1955. (At Busoni's suggestion Weill had been studying counterpoint with Jarnach during the previous year.) The advantages of a title less ponderous than the original – with its echoes of Reger and the deterrent tripartite title for Schumann's opus 52 – were suggested to Lenya by the present writer, and a new main title agreed to in the light of the three quotations from settings of Rilke which appear in the outer movements. The central Passacaglia was evidently written first; for on 13 February 1922 Weill wrote to Busoni (original in DSBA): 'With great joy and much urgency I am working on a Passacaglia for orchestra, which I hope will be ready before your return.'

Autographs

SKETCHES

Two brief memoranda appear at the end of the short-score draft of the Divertimento's scherzo (see p. 133). The first is a version of the Passacaglia theme which has the same ground bass as in the final draft but a different harmonization; the second, below it, is headed interrogatively 'Fugato Thema?' and bears only a general character relationship to the fugal material in the final draft. The other item in WLA is more significant, for it shows that the entire material for the opening stages of the Hymnus is derived from an uncompleted setting for high voice and (apparently) piano of the poem 'Ich will ihn preisen' from Rilke's *Das Stundenbuch*. The draft, which is on a leaf of B^{24}, breaks off after thirty-six bars – at the end of the poem's fifth line. The fact that there are no signs of Weill having encountered compositional difficulties, and the further fact that the draft is immediately followed by memos and sketches for later stages of the Hymnus (including a stretto for the fugal development) already tend to suggest that he was not planning to write another Rilke song as such, but was simply using the poem as a means of defining the expressive content of the Hymnus and helping himself formulate some of the basic musical ideas. The final draft lends support to that theory. As noted below, there is a direct link from the 1921 *Rilkelieder* (see p. 131) to the Hymnus. But it does not seem likely that 'Ich will ihn preisen' belonged to the set: not only is there a difference of style and language, but the leaf of B^{24} carrying the draft bears the pagination 92–3, whereas the drafts of the 1921 songs are on similar pages of B^{20} numbered (in similar style) 17–20.

SHORT-SCORE DRAFT

The draft is written in pencil, with occasional notes of instrumentation in ink. It is badly damaged and lacks four of the original sixteen sides. The Fantasia is the only complete movement: it covers the first four sides, which are two leaves of B^{24} (not a matching pair). At the foot of the first two sides, inverted and therefore reversed, are the paginations 94 and 93. This suggests that the draft of the Fantasia was begun immediately after the few sketches of the Hymnus described above. Like the first four sides, the last two (which carry the conclusion of the Hymnus) are written on a leaf of B^{24}. The remaining sides are gathered in a single folding of intact B^{24} sheets. The lacunae, which occur near the start of the Passacaglia and towards the middle of the fugal section of the Hymnus, must be due to the loss of the outermost sheet of this folding (that is, the original pages 5–6 and 13–14). The entire draft is in a title sheet of B^{24} signed and headed: 'Kurt Weill: Fantasia, Passacaglia u. Hymnus f. Orchester'.

FULL SCORE AND PERFORMANCE MATERIAL

Missing.

ARRANGEMENT FOR TWO PIANOS

A single sheet of B^{14} carries the first thirty bars of one of the piano parts, written neatly in ink.

First Performance

12 March 1923, Philharmonie, Berlin, Berlin Philharmonic Orchestra, conducted by Alexander Selo.

Performing Version

John Ogdon has composed replacements for the passages missing from the Passacaglia and the Hymnus, and is planning to arrange the whole work for two pianos.

Note 2

The work is a direct successor to the 1921 Symphony and at the same time an implicit criticism of its late-Romantic and early-Expressionist rhetoric. Weill seems to have found in Rilke a means of retracing the spiritual pilgrimage of the First Symphony without repeating its characteristic attitudes or gestures. The Fantasia defines his objectives by extensive motivic reference to the two *Rilkelieder* of 1921: 'Vielleicht, dass ich durch schwere Berge gehe' ('Maybe, through heavy mountains I am wending') and 'Mach mich zum Wächter deiner Weiten' ('Make me a watchman of your spaces'). The Hymnus struggles for, and finally achieves, the jubilation which in Rilke's 'Ich will ihn preisen' sounds 'like the trumpets going before an army' but which in the corresponding section of the 1921 Symphony is only a brief and swiftly suppressed summons.

Summer 1922, Berlin

Zaubernacht [op. 7]
(*Magic Night*)

'Children's Pantomime' (*Kinderpantomime*) in one act
Scenario, with song text, by Wladimir Boritsch [Boritch]
Duration: 50 minutes
Orchestra: fl. bsn. harp. pno. perc. str. qt. solo soprano
(Unpublished; orchestral score and material missing)

The scenario is lost. The following outline is culled from press reports and from notes in the piano score.

As 'the Girl' and 'the Boy' fall asleep, the Fairy enters and sings her magic spell. One by one the children's toys, and the characters from their story books, are brought to life. Presently, the children themselves become involved in a phantasmagoria where, for instance, Andersen's Tin Soldier helps rescue Hansel and Gretel. At the end, the Witch is hunted by the assembled company, and at last disposed of. The Fairy then vanishes, the children sink back into a dreamless sleep, and their mother tiptoes into the room to close the curtains.

Note 1

The musical form of *Zaubernacht* is continuous, and even such set pieces as the two Marches, the Waltz, and the Gavotte are open-ended. In the following schematic outline, the main and subsidiary units are numbered and identified (by tempo and metre) in such a way as to facilitate cross reference with the orchestral suite *Quodlibet* which Weill composed some months later. The musical content of the score is not, however, implicit in the outline, since few of the units have material that is all their own. There are two dozen recurrent themes and motifs, only a few of which function as traditional *Leitmotive*. How far their appearances, in various guises, were intended to have a precise dramatic function cannot be accurately gauged from the piano score. Numerous non-autograph stage directions have been roughly and sometimes illegibly entered in blue and in red crayon, but they are quite unsystematic with regard to exits and entrances, and leave many extensive or musically decisive passages unaccounted for. (A few neater directions are in Weill's hand, but have no special significance.) All decipherable stage directions that help fill out the scenario are included in the right-hand column of the following outline, and are preceded by the corresponding (non-autograph) cue numbers – an incomplete series, generally coinciding with a formal division in the music and perhaps relating to lighting cues. Passages recurring in *Quodlibet* – see p. 147 – are denoted by the symbol [Q].

1	*Sostenuto* (2/4) [Q]		
2	Lied der Fee (*Etwas bewegt*) 9/8 'Mein Spielzeugvolk muss sein am Tage starr und stumm!'		
2a	coda 3/4 [Q]		
3	*Allegro molto* 2/2 [Q]		Verwandlung
4	*Langsamer Walzer* 3/4	1	Ball heraus gerollt
4a	*Langsamer Walzer* 3/4 [Q]	2	Hampelmann
5	*Breit u. gewichtig* 3/4 [Q]	3	Kochhand – Hampelmann
6	*Ziemlich rasch* 6/8	4	Pferdchen
7	*Etwas zögernd* 2/4 [Q]	5	Der Junge erwacht – Pferd stampft
		6	Mädchen erwacht . . . läuft (zum) Pferd
8	*Molto allegro* 6/8 [Q]	8	Pferd stampft. Knabe läuft weg. Pferd ab.
9	*Sehr zögernd* 2/4 *poco a poco string.*	10	Knabe springt auf, läuft hinaus. Er fällt auf die Betten zurück.
9a	*Poco sost.* 3/4		Knabe hinkt. Mädchen tröstet ihn. M. spricht v. der Puppe Vorhang hoch.
10	*Allegro non troppo* 2/4	11	Mädchen merkt die Gegenstände im Puppenzimmer
10a	*Etwas schleppend* 3/4		
11	[*allegro*] 3/8	13, 14, 15	
12	*Molto allegro* 4/4 [Q]	16	Mädchen versucht auf [?] . . . holt Peitsche. Puppe fällt
		17	Mädchen läuft Mädchen weint
13	*Moderato* (Die kranke Puppe) 3/4		
14	*Andante* 3/4	18, 19	Hampelmann
15	[*Breit und gewichtig*] 3/4	20	—
16	*L'istesso tempo* – *Misterioso* 3/4 [Q]	21	Der Bär

17	Andantino 3/4	22	—
18	Ben sostenuto e marcato 3/2 + 4/4	23	—
19	Allegro 3/4		
20	Vivace 3/2 + 4/4		
21	Furioso 3/2		
22	Tranquillo 2/4		
23	Doppio movimento 2/2		Bär Verbeugung
24	[foxtrot]		
25	Allegro 4/4		
26	Etwas ruhiger [coda] 4/4	25	Mädchen läuft zum Bären, Ball kommt zum Mädchen. Sie gehen zum Vorhang. Mädchen klopft.
26b	[molto agitato] [Q]		
27	Quasi Recitativo [Q]		
28	Tranquillo 3/4 [Q]		Vorhang auseinander. Verbeugung
			Chines.[ischer] Arzt richtet sich auf. C. [A.] nimmt Hörrohr. Mädchen klagt ihm. Zeigt Puppe mit Bär. Arzt denkt nach . . .
28a	[andantino] 3/4 + 2/4 [Q]		
29	più tranquillo 3/4 [Q]		
30	Langsamer Marsch 4/4 [Q]	28	Prozession
			Die Puppe erwacht. Arzt gibt Medizin
30a	Più allegro 2/4 [Q]		Bär wird stutzig
31	Quasi doppio movimento (Cancan) [Q] 2/4		Die Bärenjagd
			Bär läuft ins [Schilderhäuschen]
32	Im strengen Marschtempo 4/4 [Q]	30	Das Bein. Alles ist gespannt. Soldat erscheint.
32a	Trio [Q]	31	Exerzieren. Soldat zeigt Gewehr. Puppe läuft weg. Knabe versucht das Gewehr.
32b	[Marsch] [Q]		Allgemeiner Marsch.
33	Allegro molto 2/4		Das Stehaufmännchen [. . .] fordert den Soldat heraus. Soldat stürzt sich auf ihn. Mädchen zum Bär. Bär stürzt auf ihm. Stehaufmännchen freut sich. Knabe und Hampelmann stürzen auf ihn.
33a	Dolente 2/4 [Q]	33	Knabe zieht Stiefel aus. Bär zieht 2. Stiefel. Es gelingt.
33b	Moderato 2/4 [Q]		Stehaufmännchen versucht aufzustehen . . . Kochhand führt ihn ab.
34	Vivace – Tempo di Valse 3/4	34	Knabe nimmt Harmonika
35	Andantino. Etwas schwermütig 6/8	35	H[ansel] und Gr[etel] treten heraus. Sie begrüssen den K. [Knabe?]

36	*Gavotte* 4/4	36	Hexe. Grosse Verwirrung. Tanz der Hexe. Sie zieht H. und Gr. hinaus.
37	*Molto furioso* 4/4 [Q]		Allgemeine Verfolgung
38	*Presto* 2/2		
39	*Ruhig, schwebend* 2/4 [Q]		Glocke–6 Schläge Kinderfrau . . . öffnet Fenster. Kinder schnuggeln sich einander. Vorhang sehr langsam.

Autographs

SKETCHES AND DRAFT

Missing.

REHEARSAL SCORE (Piano)

An unbound and untitled folding of sixty-eight numbered pages of T^{14} and B^{12} carries the whole score, written in blue ink. Pages 65–6 have been removed, and a musical link from page 64 inserted at the top of page 67. Indications of instrumentation have been added by the composer at various points and in such a way as to confirm that the piano score is merely a fair copy of the draft, not a reduction of the orchestral score. References to the stage action are largely non-autograph; numerous non-autograph indications of cuts and changes have been made in pencil and in red and blue crayon.

FULL SCORE AND MATERIAL

Missing. According to Weill's letter to Universal Edition of 3 June 1924 the orchestral material but *not* the full score was by then in New York, where the pantomime was due to be staged (see p. 57). The work may have been conducted from the piano score.

Other Sources

A non-autograph copy of the rehearsal score was in the possession of the widow of Wladimir Boritsch in New York in 1960, when the present author inspected it. Some seven years later Mrs Boritsch declared that she had given it to an American library; attempts to trace it have been of no avail. The score omits the 'Lied der Fee', but contains the music missing from pages 65–6 of the holograph score. This score is also the only known source for the instrumentation details given above.

First Performance

18 November 1922, Berlin, Theater am Kurfürstendamm; conductor George Weller, stage director Franz-Ludwig Hörth, choreographer Mary Zimmermann, designer Rafael Lasto; with Frau Marker-Wagner

(soprano) and dancers from the Zimmermann school including Erika Klein (the Doll) and Elsa Gramholtz (Gretel).

Note 2

The score contains several self-borrowings. From the second movement of the B minor Quartet come the motifs of the Boy, the Girl, and the Bear, and much of the music of sections *7*, *9*, *10* and *12*. The same work's idealized waltz theme appears speeded up in *11*. The Cabaret Number (see p. 129) provides material for *24*, *32a* and *34* (second section) – almost note-for-note in the first two instances, freely in the last. There is also one anticipation: *32* reappears as the *Alla marcia* of the opus 8 Quartet.

First American Performance

27 December 1925, Garrick Theatre, New York. Choreographer: Micho Ito.

Note 3

In April 1923 Weill composed an orchestral work in four movements based on music from *Zaubernacht* (see *Quodlibet*, p. 147). Exactly a year later (22 April 1924) he informed Universal Edition that he would arrange the entire *Zaubernacht* for full orchestra if Boritsch succeeded with his plans for a New York production. On 3 June he wrote again to UE, saying that the orchestral parts were now in New York but that he had retained the score, and had decided upon a 'Mozart orchestra'. This sounds like a word of advice from Busoni. No stranger to New York and its public, Busoni had armed the emigrant Boritsch with a letter of recommendation that praised his production of *Zaubernacht* and the music Weill had written for it; and he would surely have warned them both that a nine-piece chamber ensemble was not what New Yorkers and their children would expect to hear at Christmas time. The letter, which was still in the possession of Wladimir Boritsch's widow in 1954, is dated February 1924 and signed Dr Ferruccio Busoni, Senator and Professor at the State Academy of Arts in Berlin:

> In *Magic Night* Dr Boritsch has composed a pleasing and effective production, particularly suited for children's and Christmas plays. In addition Mr Kurt Weill has written an orchestral accompaniment which I consider admirably successful, melodious, and in character. The production is earnestly recommended to all stages wishing to offer their public a light yet artistic piece.

Whatever the orchestral forces, Boritsch apparently failed to raise the financial backing for a 1924 production. During the early months of 1924 Weill worked on a second pantomime (see p. 154), and although the size of the orchestra, and the sometimes aggressively dissonant language of the music, rule out the possibility that it was designed for Boritsch's purposes in New York, some potential link between it and *Zaubernacht* was probably in view. Weill did not inform Universal Edition of the second pantomime – at least in writing – but he would hardly have revealed and underlined his intentions about the first one unless he had decided that the ensemble version was provisional. Sure enough, UE never asked to see it.

There is no firm evidence that the New York performances of *Zaubernacht* were conducted from the full score, rather than from the piano score that remained in the possession of the Boritsch family. Since score and parts would normally have remained together they were probably lost together.

[Winter 1922–3], Berlin

String Quartet

First (unpublished) version of the opus 8 Quartet

1   *Allegro deciso*
2   *Andantino*
3   *Presto*
4   *Andante non troppo*
Duration: *c.* 20 minutes

Autographs

SKETCHES

Missing.

DRAFT

As drafted, the Quartet begins with the *Andantino* (here marked *Allegretto quasi Andante*) and continues with the *Allegro deciso*. Immediately after the draft of the *Andantino* come two fragmentary drafts: an abortive *Alla marcia*, and an *Allegro maestoso*, which produces the basic ideas for the ensuing *Allegro deciso*.

A title sheet of B^{22} encloses the entire draft. Side *a* bears the inscription 'Kurt Weill/Fantasia, Passacaglia u. Hymnus [cancelled]/Streichquartett op. 8'. Sides *b* and *c* are blank. Side *d* carries, inverse, a sketch for part of the fugal section missing from the draft of the Hymnus – a 10-bar episode with the fugal subject inverted; beneath are ink sketches for the *Allegro deciso* of the Quartet (second-group material), together with two unidentified pencil sketches.

SCORE

The first two movements (in the order given above) are written on thirty numbered pages of N^{14} mostly in blue-black ink; pages 1–6 and 22–30 are written in purple ink. Each of the first six pages is cancelled in blue crayon. (The manuscripts of the third and fourth movements are described under String Quartet, op. 8, p. 144.)

Note 1

In a letter to Busoni dated 'Leipzig, 31 March 1923' (original in DSBA) Weill alludes to his current preoccupation with the 'revision' (die Änderung) of the String Quartet, and does so in a way that presupposes Busoni's knowledge of his intentions in that respect. Indeed his only reason for mentioning it seems to be that he has heard from 'Donaueschingen' that 'the programme' is nearly complete, and that in view of the pressure of time he is proposing to send the first version of the Quartet 'provisionally' (vorläufig). It is clear from his tone that the idea of including a Weill quartet in the Donaueschingen 'Neue Musik' festival had already been accepted in principle, presumably on the strength of a recommendation from Busoni and on the understanding that important revisions were in progress. Weill would not have wished Busoni to hear from one of his ambassadors at the Donaueschingen court – either Jarnach or Erdmann – that an unapproved version of the Quartet had been submitted. The version played by the Amar Quartet on 24 June – not in Donaueschingen but in Frankfurt – was certainly the later one. For Weill's comments on that event, and for notes on movements 3 and 4, see pp. 145–6.

The first movement of the present version incorporates material from *Psalm VIII* (see p. 134). The recurrence of a substantial section of the movement in a fragment of the orchestral score of the untitled and unfinished pantomime of 1924 (see p. 154) suggests that, whatever reservations Busoni may have had about the movement, Weill was prepared to defend it in another context. The second movement may also have been destined for the pantomime. But although it is musically well matched to its predecessor, it does not in the same way call out for orchestral treatment. Together, the two movements are so much stronger and more personal than the single one that replaced them in opus 8 that Busoni's commendation of the later version (see p. 147) is almost incomprehensible.

FIRST MODERN PEFORMANCES

See *Divertimento* (p. 133) for orchestral versions of 1 and 2. The original versions of these movements were first performed on 7 March 1977 by the Curtis Chamber Ensemble at a concert given at the Lincoln Center, New York, in conjunction with the Weill–Lenya Exhibition sponsored by the Goethe House.

March–April 1923, Leipzig

String Quartet op. 8

1 Introduktion (*Sostenuto, con molto espressione*)
2 Scherzo (*Vivace*)
3 Choralphantasie (*Andante non troppo*)

Dedication: Albert Weill
Duration: 17 minutes

Autographs

SKETCHES

Missing.

DRAFTS

1 is missing. Since the music of *2* and *3* is identical with that of *3* and *4* of the unpublished version there was no need for further drafts.

SCORE

Seventy-one numbered pages of N^{16}, N^{14} and B^{14}. These are contained in a cover sheet of B^{26}; the inscription reads 'Meinem Vater gewidmet'. The manuscripts of *2* and *3* have been transferred from the score of the unpublished version.

First Performance

24 June 1923, Frankfurter Kammermusikwoche 'Neue Musik' (Frankfurt-am-Main), Amar Quartet.

Publications

UE, 1924: pocket score; parts.

Notes

The week of modern chamber music in Frankfurt was organized by Hermann Scherchen. Weill's quartet opened a morning concert that continued with Schoenberg's *Das Buch der hängenden Gärten*, and ended with Rudi Stefan's *Musik für Saiteninstrumente*. (Schoenberg, whose *Friede auf Erden* ended the evening concert on the same day, was unable to attend – see his letter to Scherchen of 23 June 1923, in Arnold Schoenberg, *Letters*, ed. Erwin Stein, London, 1964.) Described by Karl Holl in *Die Musik* (XV, August 1923, p. 813) as a 'not very interesting attempt at a string quartet', Weill's opus 8 was overshadowed by the works of such established masters as Schoenberg, Stravinsky and Bartók, and by those of younger composers, notably Hindemith (his song-cycle *Das Marienleben*).

During 1923 the Amar Quartet (Licco Amar, Walter Caspar, Paul Hindemith, and Maurits Frank) consolidated their links with Busoni and his circle. One of their major successes was with the Quartet by Philipp Jarnach, which they performed in the Donaueschingen programme of 19 July (together with quartet pieces by Weill's friend Max Butting) – probably the programme Weill had had in mind when he wrote to Busoni about submitting the unrevised version of his quartet provisionally (see p. 143). Whether the Frankfurt performance of his opus 8 was a substitute for the Donaueschingen one or a 'try-out' necessitated by the late arrival of the revised score and some prior obligation to Busoni and to Jarnach (who had been Weill's teacher in 1921–2) it is clear that Hindemith and his colleagues were disappointed with the work. On 21 June 1923 – three days before the first performance – Weill wrote to Busoni about his musical experiences in Frankfurt so far: the performances of Busoni's *Fantasia Contrappuntistica* and (for the first time in Germany) of Stravinsky's *L'histoire du soldat* (which Busoni himself was to hear in Weimar two months later).* He then turned to the rehearsal which he had just attended:

> Today I heard my quartet for the first time, because the Hindemith people are very overworked. Strangely enough the last movement – for me as well as for you the most mature – seems to have been the least well received by the four gentlemen. I'm afraid that Hindemith has already danced his way too far into the land of the foxtrot.

The 'Hindemith people' did not play the Quartet again. Its second and faithful advocates were the Roth Quartet, who took the work into their repertoire after giving a private performance in Busoni's house in November 1923.

In the late 1950s the exact circumstances of the Frankfurt premiere had yet to be ascertained, and there was some doubt as to whether the performers on that occasion were the Amars or the Roths. During the present author's conversation with Hindemith in Berlin *c.* 1960, Hindemith denied that the Amar Quartet had ever played a quartet by Weill, paid a fulsome tribute to the composer of *Die Dreigroschenoper*, and added, with a smile, 'but he couldn't write quartets'.

Had Hindemith known the B minor Quartet of 1918 or the two movements rejected from its successor (p. 143) he might not have been quite so dismissive. But as far as Weill's opus 8 is concerned his remark seems less unjust than Weill's about 'the land of the foxtrot'. Hindemith's brief sorties into that territory in *Tuttifäntchen* and opus 24 no. 1 cannot

---

*Weill described *L'histoire* as a 'Volksstück' somewhere between 'pantomime, melodrama and farce'. The score, he wrote, was 'masterly'. With the required genuflexion towards Busoni and his aristocratic tastes, he then confessed that even 'the sidelong glance at the aesthetic of the street-corner' had seemed 'tolerable'. (Letter in DSBA.)

have had any bearing on his view of the *Choralphantasie*, a movement that is as confused in its formal and stylistic aspects as it is misjudged in the textural ones. Admittedly it contains the happiest passage in the entire work (rehearsal figures 52+1 to 59); but the lessons from France which Weill has taken to heart at that point and nowhere else should have dissuaded him from basing the rest of the movement on the chorale fantasy of the First Symphony – which is much the weakest section of that work but nevertheless has some fine moments that are manifestly conceived for orchestra and unsuitable to the quartet medium. One can understand why Busoni would have preferred the formalities of the Symphony's chorale fantasy to the Expressionist abandon of the earlier sections. But how can he and Weill have supposed that the opus 8 version of it was the most 'mature' movement in a work from which the two best (and most mature) movements had been removed? The so-called *Introduktion* that replaces them is so desultory in its effect that the ensuing Scherzo is left without any formal justification (whereas in the first version of the Quartet it was, among other things, a foil to the two serious and intense movements that preceded it). The main scherzo material, though not strikingly original, is better judged in terms of the quartet medium than most of opus 8, but the *alla marcia* trio is a borrowing from *Zaubernacht* (32) which has no logical connection with the scherzo and no reason to lead back to it (hence the inept *poco tranquillo* codetta).

In any chronological survey of Weill's European work, and especially in a catalogue such as this, the opus 8 Quartet should be treated as an exception and an anomaly, for it is the only work of Weill's European years that belies its chronological placing, locally and in the longer term. As a 'revision' of the original version it was already topsy-turvy: if the *first* pair of movements from the original version had been retained, instead of the second pair, and a new finale of comparable strength and originality had been added, the revision would have been a notable improvement. But it would still not have brought the work anywhere near the level of the 'Passacaglia' in the *Sinfonia Sacra*, the finale of the Divertimento, or – above all – the *Recordare*. These movements, and the *Recordare* as a whole, reflect the five years of experience and study that had elapsed since the composition of the B minor Quartet. Apart from a few short-lived flights of harmonic inspiration – about which T. W. Adorno delivered a characteristically brilliant aperçu when he mentioned the work in the course of a 1923 review (*Zeitschrift für Musik* Berlin, Jg. 90, Nr. 15/16, p. 316) – the opus 8 Quartet reveals no significant advance in the technical field, and seems to have lost the spontaneity as well as the quirky bravado of its predecessor.

Nevertheless it was the first work of Weill's to which Busoni gave his official imprimatur. In a letter written towards the end of Weill's three years in the Masterclass, Busoni warmly commended his young charge to

Emil Hertzka (Director of Universal Edition) and spoke of the opus 8 Quartet as 'a work of splendid qualities, in skill as in invention'.* Why Busoni should have denied that accolade to the far more deserving *Recordare* is a less puzzling question than how so fine a musician can have accepted, let alone encouraged, the evisceration of the first version of the String Quartet, and then recommended Weill to the world's foremost publisher of New Music on the strength of the flimsiest score he had written since the Suite in E for orchestra.

The opus 8 Quartet was duly accepted for publication, together with *Frauentanz* and *Quodlibet*. All the other works that preceded the signing of a general agreement between Weill and Universal Edition remained in manuscript and very soon disappeared from view.

April 1923, Berlin

Quodlibet op. 9

Suite for orchestra from the children's pantomime *Zaubernacht*

1 *Andante non troppo – Allegro molto*
2 *Molto vivace – Allegretto scherzando – Allegro non troppo*
3 *Un poco sostenuto, misterioso – Recitative – Andantino – Più mosso – Più tranquillo – Alla marcia funebre*
4 *Molto allegro – Tempo di marcia – Molto vivo – Furioso – Tempo di marcia – molto vivo*

Orchestra: 2.2.2.2. 2.2.2.0. timp. perc. str.
Dedication: Albert Bing
Duration: 20 minutes

Autographs

FULL SCORE (UEA)

158 numbered pages of B^{18}, bound in grey board cover, stitching loose. The original dedication 'Albert Bing und der Kapelle des Friedrichs-Theaters in Dessau gewidmet' has been cancelled and the words 'An Albert Bing' substituted. Beneath is the title 'Quodlibet/Vier Orchester-stücke aus einer Kinderpantomime/op. 9'.

ADDITIONAL MATERIAL (UE)

Copyist's full score used for first performance and giving original title 'Orchestersuite aus der Kinderpantomime Zaubernacht'.

---

*The part of this letter concerning Weill and his Quartet was reproduced in the catalogue of Hans Schneider, the German music dealer who sold the original letter to a private collector in 1970. The exact date and the complete text of the letter have yet to be divulged.

Publication

UE, 1926: full score; title page 'An Albert Bing/QUODLIBET/(Eine Unterhaltungsmusik)/von/KURT WEILL/Op. 9/PARTITUR'.

First Performance

15 June 1923, Dessau, Friedrichs-Theater, municipal orchestra conducted by Albert Bing.

Notes

Quodlibet is not a conventional suite. In its free relationship to the original score, and in its complete independence from scenario, situation, or dramatis personae (except at the start and again at the end), it is somewhat akin to the Divertimento from Stravinsky's *The Fairy's Kiss*. Each of the four movements juxtaposes widely disparate elements from *Zaubernacht*, according to considerations that are purely musical. The following schematic outline uses the numberings adopted from the *Zaubernacht* score in the present catalogue:

> 1st movement: 1–2a–3–39
> 2nd movement: 8–7–8–33a,b
> 3rd movement: 16–27–28–28a–30a–5–4a–5–29–30
> 4th movement: 26b–12–37–32a,b–38–31

June–July 1923, Heide, N. Germany/Berlin

Frauentanz op. 10

Seven Medieval Poems
For soprano, flute, viola, clarinet, horn and bassoon
1 Wir haben die winterlange Nacht (Dietmar von Aiste)
2 Wo zwei Herzenliebe an einem Tanze gan (Anon)
3 Ach wär' mein Lieb ein Brünnlein kalt (Anon)
4 Dieser Stern im Dunkeln (Der von Kürenberg)
5 Eines Maienmorgens schon (Herzog Johann von Brabant)
6 Ich will trauern lassen stehn (Anon)
7 Ich schlaf, ich wach (Anon)

Dedication: Nelly Frank
Duration: 13 minutes

Autographs

SKETCHES

Missing.

SHORT SCORE

Four sides of B¹² carry 3 and 6 and part of 1. The fourth side also has the first eighteen bars of an instrumental intermezzo for flute, clarinet, horn and bassoon – presumably one of the four discarded intermezzos mentioned by Weill in an undated letter to Busoni (DSBA). Weill there writes of '7 Lieder mit Bläserbegleitung' (seven songs with wind accompaniment); the scoring of the surviving intermezzo confirms that at this stage there was no viola (which raises questions about 5, since that song is accompanied by viola alone). The theme of the surviving intermezzo is borrowed from the *Polka* (p. 130); a variant of the entire fragment is the basis of the 'Zodiac Dance' in *Royal Palace* (p. 162).

FULL SCORE

Two copies (both in UEA). The first is on sixty-seven sides of B²⁸, and has 4, 5, 6 in another order. The first five songs are dated, and 1 has the place name 'Heide'. (There are two towns of that name in Germany.) The order and dates are: 1, Heide, 29 Juni 1923; 2, 2 Juli 1923; 3, 3 Juli 1923; 6, 5 Juli 1923; 4, 8 Juli 1923; 5; 7. The second copy, on twenty-nine pages of R²⁰, establishes the published order but is otherwise identical with the first copy; the title page (B²⁸) carries the dedication 'Nelly Frank gewidmet' (substituted for the cancelled 'Der Barbara zu eigen').

PIANO REDUCTION

The composer's reductions of 1, 2, 4–7 are missing; the holograph of Busoni's reduction of 3 – a sheet of R²⁰ titled *'Kurt Weill/Frauentanz III/Op. 10/Klavier Auszug/von/Ferruccio Busoni'*, signed and dated *'Ferruccio Busoni/nach Weill/13 februar 1924'* – is in WLA.

Publication

UE, 1924: score.
UE, 1925: piano reduction: No. 3 bears the legend 'Die Klavierbearbeitung dieser Nummer ist die letzte Arbeit von Ferruccio Busoni'. ('The piano arrangement of this number is Ferruccio Busoni's last work.')

First Performance

January 1924, Berlin, concert of ISCM, German section; Nora Pisling-Boas, with ensemble conducted by Fritz Stiedry.

Note

Weill's undated letter to Busoni (see *Short Score*) refers to his search for a suitable singer, and contains a crucial observation (italicized here) which could equally well have been made by the future composer of *Der Silbersee* (Fennimore's role) and *Die sieben Todsünden*: 'If I bear in mind that the *Lieder* must be sung *without any sentimentality, with a slender, light, and yet expressive voice*, then there is hardly anyone suitable in Berlin apart from Artôt de Padilla.' The Franco-Spanish soprano Lola Artôt de Padilla (1876–1933) was one of the leading opera singers in Berlin – where she was engaged from 1909 until her retirement in 1927.

September 1923, Berlin

Recordare op. 11

For 4-part chorus and children's chorus, *a cappella*
Text: Lamentations V (Latin Vulgate)
Dedication: Hanns Weill
Duration: 17 minutes

Autographs

All holograph material is missing. A professional copy of the complete score, initialled and dated by Weill at the end, is written on thirty-four pages of a 16-line paper, stitched and bound in a plain blue cover without titles. In the copyist's hand, at the head of the first manuscript page, is written the following: 'Meinem Bruder Hanns Weill/Recordare/(Der Klagelieder Jeremiae V. Kapitel)/Vierstimmig mit Kinderchor/von/Kurt Weill/Op. 11'.

First Performance

2 July 1971, Pieterskerk, Utrecht, NCRV Vocal Ensemble, children's choir 'Cantasona', Boxtel, conducted by Marinus Voorberg.

Publication

EAM, 1983: score (with piano reduction for rehearsal purposes).

Notes

The copyist's score was discovered in 1970 among the unmarked miscellany of a Parisian music dealer. The finder, O. W. Neighbour, gave it to the present author. On 16 February 1924 Weill told his publishers that he had heard that the *Recordare* would be performed at the next Tonkünstlerfest in Kassel. Copies of the score must by then have been in circulation. The performance did not materialize.

[October 1923]/[August] September 1924, Berlin

Stundenbuch op. 13
[*Book of Hours*]

Song-cycle for baritone and orchestra
Texts: Rainer Maria Rilke
(Partly missing)

1 Vielleicht, dass ich durch schwere Berge gehe
2 Mach mich zum Wächter deiner Weiten
3 Manchmal steht einer auf beim Abendrot
4 Bei Tag bist du das Hörensagen
5 Lösch mir die Augen aus
6 In diesem Dorfe steht das letzte Haus

Note 1

The first two poems are from book 3 of Rilke's *Das Stundenbuch*, 'The Book of Poverty and Death', the remainder from book 2, 'The Book of Pilgrimage'. The dating of the cycle, the opus number and the number of songs are all in doubt. The work is first mentioned in a letter from Weill to UE of 10 September 1924. There he calls it 'Stundenbuch – sechs Dichtungen für Bariton und Orchester' and reports that he is just finishing it. The programme book for the concert in which *Stundenbuch* was first performed begins by announcing 'Stundenbuch/Dichtungen Rilkes für Bariton und Orchester/op. 13', and continues with the texts of the four 'Book of Pilgrimage' poems only, beneath the same title and subtitle but now with the opus number 14. Finally the programme note by Hugo Leichtentritt is headed 'Sechs Gesänge für Bariton und Orchester op. 13'. But in an article on Weill published in a Dessau newspaper on or about 24 October 1924 his ex-pupil Peter Bing writes of 'four orchestral songs op. 12'. Weill himself uses the same number in a brief list of works which he sent to Bing in 1925. In that same list the Violin Concerto, which was published in 1925 as opus 12, is opus 13. Weill's confusion must have arisen because of a lapse of time between the composition of *Stundenbuch* and the scoring. Strobel (in DD.UKW) pushes *Stundenbuch* back to opus 11; but that, as we have seen, belongs to *Recordare* (which Strobel does not mention).

Autographs

No holographs or copies of *3, 4* and *5* have survived. For sketches of earlier versions of *1* and *2*, see *Rilkelieder* (p. 131).

Non-Autograph Copies

Scores, parts and vocal scores of *1* and *6* are in the Talbot Library, Westminster Choir College, Princeton, NJ. The full scores are littered with copying errors; the vocal scores are not reductions but uncorrected copies of drafts – *1* is gravely defective.

First Performance

22 January 1925, Berlin, Philharmonic Hall; Manfred Lewandowsky, Berlin Philharmonic Orchestra, conducted by Heinz Unger.

Later Performances

16 and 18 December 1926, The Hague and Utrecht; Myra Mortimer, soprano, and the Residentie orchestra under Piet van Anrooy. Cancelled owing to Miss Mortimer's illness.

Note 2

The non-autograph material of *1* and *6* in the Talbot Library was previously in the possession of the late Myra Mortimer, an American-born singer who spent her last years in Spokane, Washington. The parts do not appear to have been used in performance, and the scores are unmarked. If these were the songs omitted from the Berlin premiere, Miss Mortimer may also have decided to omit them in Holland. But since neither song is suitable for a soprano, and since *2* already existed in an earlier version for high voice (see p. 131) it is also possible that transposed and re-orchestrated versions of both songs were included in the material forwarded to the Residentie orchestra (whose archives were destroyed during the Second World War).

The least likely explanation for the survival of these songs is that both were rejected on grounds of quality. Had *7* survived on its own, there would have been grounds for such a conclusion. Effective and even powerful though it is in general outline and in certain specific gestures, it is technically insecure in its relationship to the 1921 setting of the same text: too often the speculative conclusions that Weill now tries to draw from the relatively traditional harmonic formulations of the original lack any clear structural function, and seem merely wilful. *6* is in another class. The best composed and the most imaginative of Weill's post-1920 *Lieder*, and a direct counterpart to 'Die stille Stadt' (p. 123), it is not an achievement that would have been possible without the experience and the technical disciplines of the *Recordare*.

A conjectural dating of *Stundenbuch* based on only two of the six songs has to take into account the opus numbering, the schedule of Weill's creative activities, and not least the incentives for composing a new Rilke cycle or continuing the one begun in 1921. Busoni had dedicated his revolutionary *Entwurf einer neuen Ästhetik der Tonkunst* of 1907 to 'Rilke, the musician in words', and Weill had based his first major orchestral work on Rilke (see p. 118). But wherever musicians of Busoni's generation and of Weill's were gathered together, a common bond was likely to be found in Rilke, who was by far the most widely admired German poet in the era before Brecht.

The relationship between the *Stundenbuch* version of 'Vielleicht, dass ich durch schwere Berge gehe' and the original 1921 setting suggests that a cycle that may have begun as a Masterclass project – like the setting of Goethe's 'Die Bekehrte' – later acquired a life of its own, perhaps through the mediation of the *Sinfonia Sacra* (see p. 135). If Weill regarded the 1921 project as potentially important but failed to complete it, there would have been an incentive for taking it up again before his spell in the Masterclass ended. But the decisive element, perhaps, was the premiere in Donaueschingen on 17 June 1923 of Hindemith's large-scale Rilke cycle *Das Marienleben*. Four days later Hindemith and his three Amar Quartet colleagues were to give the first rehearsal of Weill's opus 8 Quartet in the composer's presence (see p. 143). Until then the only signs of potential rivalry had been the accidental correspondence between *Zaubernacht* and Hindemith's 'Christmas Tale' *Tuttifäntchen*; but henceforth it was to be a palpable influence on the work of both composers until the time of *Die Bürgschaft* and *Mathis der Maler*. Both as an answer to *Das Marienleben* and as the consolidation of a cycle begun at least a year before Hindemith's, *Stundenbuch* would have been a timely project during the final stages of Weill's period with Busoni. Since *Recordare* was written in September 1923 and bore the opus number 11, the opus 12 numbering given to *Stundenbuch* by Weill in his list for Peter Bing may indeed have been the one with which the cycle began. Although little is known about Weill's life during the last three months of 1923, the series of major premieres that had dominated the previous nine had come to an end, and there should have been ample time to complete in short score the six *Stundenbuch* songs we know of, or else to attempt a voice and piano cycle on the scale of *Das Marienleben*. Whichever was the case, all the evidence suggests that the composition of *Stundenbuch* was finished by the end of 1923, and that Weill's reference to his completing the work, in his letter to Universal Edition of 10 September 1924, can only have related to the full score. In 1924 his life and his music took a new turn. The meeting with Georg Kaiser – which came about through Fritz Stiedry, the conductor of the January premiere of *Frauentanz* (see p. 149) – had immediate creative consequences, and these in turn were associated with Weill's partly conscious effort to ratify his independence from the dying Busoni. The radical changes of harmonic and melodic language that occurred in the compositions of 1924 already rule out the possibility that the *Stundenbuch* setting of 'In diesem Dorfe steht das letzte Haus' belongs to that year. Examination of the timetable of Weill's collaboration with Kaiser – including the composition of the Concerto for Violin and Wind Orchestra (p. 156) which interrupted it – confirms on the practical side what the aesthetic of the Rilke cycle suggests on the creative side: there was no 'room' for the *composition* of such a cycle in 1924. On the other hand there was one compelling reason for returning to the cycle and completing the orchestral score: the death of Busoni on 27 July 1924. Weill's deeply troubled anticipation of this event is manifest in both the tone and the content of an undated postcard to his family (WLRC). A sense of personal bereavement such as he had not previously experienced in his adult life and was not to know again until the death of his brother Hanns many years later must surely have found some kind of musical expression; and yet there is no published work dedicated to Busoni's memory. If the work in question was *Stundenbuch* the completion in September 1924 of a work that compositionally and aesthetically belongs to the previous year would be explained, as indeed would the confusion over opus numbers (with the Concerto usurping the original opus 12) and the speed with which Heinz Unger – as a close associate of Busoni – mounted the first performance. Among the audience at that performance was Lotte Lenya, whom Weill had met through Kaiser. After attending a performance of the First Symphony fifty years later, she remarked to the present author that the 'sound' of it reminded her of *Stundenbuch*.

Voice and Piano Arrangement

In 1975 Malcolm MacDonald – in consultation with Christopher Shaw and the present author – made an arrangement of 1 which took full account of the orchestral texture, and tackled the problems inherent in the widely differing and obviously inaccurate sources. Barry McDaniel (baritone) with Aribert Reimann (piano) gave the first performance at the Akademie der Künste, West Berlin on 9 September 1975.

February–July 1924, Berlin

[Pantomime op. 14]

Unfinished work for dance theatre, in three acts
Scenario: Georg Kaiser
Orchestra: 3(3 picc.)2.3.bcl.3   3.3.3.0.   timp. perc. harp str.
Partly missing

Note 1

In his first letter to Universal Edition – 16 February 1924 – Weill reports that he is planning 'a new (comic) opera' with Georg Kaiser. There is no further reference to the opera project in any later correspondence or documents. The pantomime is not mentioned in any of the UE correspondence. In an undated postcard to his sister and her husband (WLRC) written in the early summer of 1924 Weill expresses pleasure at being 'at last' able to resume work on the pantomime, now that he has finished the Concerto for Violin and Wind Orchestra. Since he had started the Concerto when Kaiser's temporary absence from Berlin forced him to interrupt work on the pantomime, it follows that Kaiser's availability had little or nothing to do with the change from opera to pantomime. But why was the pantomime abandoned after it had advanced as far as it did? In his programme note for the Dresden premiere of *Der Protagonist* Weill states that *two whole acts* of the pantomime were already complete in full score when he and Kaiser suddenly became frustrated by the voicelessness of their characters, and turned to opera – in fact to *Der Protagonist* (which contains two pantomime scenes, though not without voices). In itself this is a remarkably unconvincing explanation, and a quite unnecessary one since there was no need to mention the pantomime in the first place. The 'comic' opera, which he does not mention, would have been more relevant; but that would have required yet another explanation. Pending further discoveries (especially with regard to Kaiser's activities and associations in 1924) we can only surmise that an opportunity and possibly a commission for writing a large-scale dance piece arose in February or March, but suddenly evaporated five or six months later – by which time Weill and Kaiser may indeed have begun to find the medium frustrating.

Autographs

SKETCHES (WLA)

An untitled leaf of B^{22} carries (*recto* and *verso*) memos of no fewer than twenty-three motifs. Some of these recur in the fragment of the full score of the pantomime. The heading 'Oper' appears above the third and seventh motifs on *a* and the first on *b*; the last motif on *a* is headed 'Schluss 1.Akt'. A chorus is indicated for the eighth motif on *b*; and the tenth motif has a vocal treatment of the syllable 'ha'. At the foot of *b* is the heading 'Konzert' (concerto) and beneath it an 8-bar sketch for violin and orchestra surely intended for (though it was not actually used in) the Concerto which was written during a lull in the composition of the pantomime.

FULL SCORE (WLA)

The surviving fragment is on a 40-page folding of R^{24}. The manuscript breaks off mid-way on the thirty-eighth side. If Weill's statement that he *completed* two acts in full score is taken literally, he had also composed a large part of the third act. However, the last nine bars of the existing full score are musically identical with bars 126–35 of the *Allegro deciso* movement in the unpublished version of the opus 8 String Quartet (see p. 142). Since an earlier episode in the fragment is based on the first twenty-three bars of that same movement, a conjectural ending for the fragment can be supplied without great difficulty. If the fragment comes from the end of the second act rather than the beginning of the third, the actual end was already there in principle, and Weill was not greatly exaggerating.

Note 2

The appearance of the word 'Oper' in the sketches suggests the possibility that the pantomime had an operatic centre rather as *Der Protagonist* has a pantomimic one. In that case Weill may have been deliberately underplaying the experimental nature of the form when he told UE he was working with Kaiser on a comic opera. The general character of the pantomime cannot safely be judged from the surviving fragment, except in so far as the high norm of dissonance precludes the possibility that the pantomime was designed for the same audience as *Zaubernacht*. Grotesque and phantasmagoric rather than merely 'comic', the music owes something to Busoni's imaginative world and orchestral technique, but almost nothing to his methods of composition. What is more surprising is that it has very little bearing on *Der Protagonist*. The fact that only one of the twenty-three motifs on the sketch-sheet has any counterpart in the opera is of more than merely statistical interest. Except for a few isolated passages in *Royal Palace*, the pantomime fragment has no close parallel in Weill's early music. If it evokes any scenario that Kaiser was likely to write at that stage, it would be one that relates in general character to *Die Kaiserin von Neufundland*, the Wedekind pantomime Weill was eager to write in 1936 (see p. 397).

April–May 1924, Berlin

Concerto for Violin and Wind Orchestra op. 12

1   *Andante con moto*
2   *Notturno – Cadenza – Serenata*
3   *Allegro molto un poco agitato*
Duration: 32 minutes
Orchestra: 2.1.2.2.   2.1.0.0.   timp. perc. db.

Autographs

SKETCHES

Missing (but see *Notes* on *Foxtrot and Ragtime*, p. 157).

FULL SCORE (UE)

Ninety-six pages of B¹⁴, with title page in composer's hand, 'Konzert für Violine u. Blasorchester/(Concerto pour violon et orchestre d'instruments à vent)/Op. 12/(Partitur)'. Dated at the end, 'April–May 1924', and bound (post-1950) in the publisher's standard grey cover for use as hire material.

PIANO REDUCTION (UE)

Fifty-seven pages of B^{14}, with title and dedication to Josef Szigeti in another hand.

Publication

UE, 1925: violin and piano score (reduction, by the composer, unattributed).

UE, 1965: study score (without editorial commentary; there are discrepancies with violin and piano score).

First Performance

11 June 1925, Paris, Théâtre de l'exposition des arts décoratifs; Marcel Darrieux (violin), Orchestre des Concerts Straram conducted by Walther Straram.

[?Spring 1924], [?Berlin]

[Foxtrot and Ragtime]

Light music, probably not by Weill; incomplete
Orchestra: 1.1.1.1.   0.1.1.1.   pno. harm. timp. perc. 2 vlns.

Autograph

FULL-SCORE DRAFT

Nothing else survives. There is no other example among Weill's manuscripts of a full score in draft form. Rapidly written in pencil, it covers thirteen sides of B^{26}, two systems a side. The G major Foxtrot has no introduction, but otherwise is complete on the first seven sides of a folding whose eighth and last side carries the start of the B flat major Ragtime. The continuation of the Ragtime is on sides *b–d* of a separate sheet of B^{28} (side *a*, described below, is not connected with this work); the conclusion is on sides *a–c* of another such sheet. The final cadence of the Ragtime prepares for a third piece; but a change of key signature to three flats is all that follows.

Notes

If Weill was the composer as well as the orchestrator of these pieces they are a unique example in his entire output of conventional light music without trace of a personal fingerprint. Given that he never made drafts of his own full scores, and that the instrumentation has obviously been determined by some extraneous factor – for it is neither as conventional as the music nor as personal as Weill would surely have made it – it seems probable that these are arrangements for theatre or cinema orchestra of popular material that had been supplied to him for that purpose. Although there is no record of Weill undertaking commercial work of this kind, his piano reduction of Busoni's Divertimento for Flute and Orchestra had been his first published work, and may well have led to copying jobs, which in turn might have led to undertakings such as this.

The dating 'spring 1924' is inferred from side *a* of the first separate sheet, which carries a coherent sketch of the first thirty-five bars of a non-tonal *Allegro non troppo* for unidentified solo instrument (clearly a violin), with accompaniment of wind instruments and double-basses. Although none of the music found its way into the opus 12 Concerto for Violin and Wind Orchestra, it must have been an early sketch for that work, since the second concerto, which Weill promised to write for Stefan Frenkel and began to sketch in 1925 (see *Der neue Orpheus*, draft score, p. 160), would hardly have been in the same style as the first, or for the same ensemble. There can be no doubt that the sketch predates the full-score draft of the Ragtime, for the manuscript of the latter gives no evidence of an interruption.

September 1924 – March 1925, Berlin

Der Protagonist, op. 14

Opera in one act
Libretto: Georg Kaiser
Dedication: Lotte Lenja
Duration: 75 minutes
Cast: The Protagonist (tenor), Sister (soprano), the Young Lord (baritone), Major-domo (tenor), Innkeeper (bass), 3 actors (alto, baritone, bass).
Orchestra: 0.2.0.bcl.2. 3.0.3.0. perc. timp. str.; stage orchestra: 2.0.2.2. 0.2.0.0., starting and finishing in the orchestra pit.

Shakespearian England. A troupe of strolling players rehearse a bawdy comedy – a wordless pantomime in the style of Boccaccio – which they are planning to present that evening for the entertainment of the Duke and his court. The Protagonist, still transported by his role, amazes his apprehensive sister by receiving the news of her long-concealed love affair light-heartedly yet incredulously. She leaves, assuring him that she will prove the truth of her story by returning with her lover. The Major-domo now brings word that a Bishop has unexpectedly joined the Duke's party, and that the comedy must therefore be replaced by a serious play. The Protagonist promptly orders his reluctant players to re-rehearse the same scenario, transposing comedy to tragedy. This time the Protagonist is so carried away by his role as a deceived husband that the other players, and the stage musicians, break off in embarrassment. His sister reappears, knowing nothing of the transformation, but eager to introduce her lover, the Young Lord. The Protagonist, still confusing illusion with reality, stabs her. As she lies dead at his feet he asks to be spared arrest till after the evening's performance; for this is his 'best part'.

Autographs

SKETCHES

Missing.

FINAL DRAFT (WLRC)

Fifty-two sides of B^{28}, in three foldings, are contained in a title sheet that reads: 'Diese vollständigen Skizzen zum/"Protagonist"/gehören/Peter Bing/Weihnacht 1925./ Kurt Weill.' The draft is indeed complete. There are very few corrections, and only a handful of incidental sketches (mostly at the foot of the page).

FULL SCORE

307 pages of B^{26}, bound in hardboard cover, with some autograph corrections, and cancellation by another hand of certain instrumental doublings. Title page: 'Der Protagonist/Ein-Akt-Oper von/Georg Kaiser/Musik/von/Kurt Weill/Partitur'.

Publication

UE, 1925: vocal score (reproduction of anonymous arranger's manuscript, corrections in another hand; dedication 'für Lotte Lenja' corrects erroneous dedication to Lotte Leonard).
UE, 1926: vocal score (engraved).
UE, 1926: full score (manuscript copies, hire only).

First Performance

27 March 1926, Dresden State Opera; conductor Fritz Busch, director Josef Gielen, designer Adolf Mahnkes; with Kurt Taucher (Protagonist), Elisa Stünzner (Sister); Paul Schöffler (Young Lord), Adolf Schöpflin (Innkeeper).

July–September 1925, Berlin

Der neue Orpheus op. 15

Cantata for soprano, solo violin and orchestra
Text: Iwan Goll
Dedication: Lotte Leonard
Duration: 16 minutes
Orchestra: 2.2.2.2.   0.2.2.0.   harp perc. str. without vlns.

Autographs

SKETCHES

Missing.

DRAFT SCORE

The complete draft is on eleven sides of a 6-sheet folding of B^{28}, dated at the end '18 August 1925'. The twelfth and last side of the folding carries a 12-bar sketch for solo instrument and orchestra. Unrelated to *Der neue Orpheus*, it is probably an initial idea for a second violin concerto, which Weill was planning to write for Stefan Frenkel. Other sketches for this are in the *Na und?* material.

FULL SCORE (UEA)

Forty-seven numbered pages of B^{28}, with title page stamped 'Leih-material/Universal Edition'; disbound and in poor condition.

Publication

UE, 1925: full score (hire only).
UE, 1926: vocal score (piano reduction by Arthur Willner).

First Performance

2 March 1927, Berlin, Staatsoper, unter den Linden, Delia Reinhardt (soprano), Rudolf Deman (violin), conducted by Erich Kleiber. (Concert performance in lieu of projected staging.)

Notes

In a letter to Universal Edition dated 17 July 1925, Weill refers to the work as a 'Concertino'. The vocal score gives the same opus number as the previously published *Der Protagonist* – an error corrected to opus 16 in two advertisements published in 1926–7 in UE's house magazine, *Anbruch* (see KK.WE, p. 393).

[?September] 1925, Berlin

Ich sitze da un' esse Klops
(Traditional Berlin text)

For high voice, two piccolos, and bassoon
Duration: 45 seconds

Autographs

Sketches and drafts, if any, are missing. The score is in the possession of
R. O. Lehmann, and belongs to a collection of his manuscripts on loan to
the Pierpont Morgan Library, New York. It was originally part of an
album of manuscripts by Universal Edition composers, which was
presented to Emil Hertzka on the occasion of the firm's 25th anniversary
in 1926; but like Schoenberg's canon 'Tapfer sind solche, die Taten
vollbringen', which is also in the collection, it has been torn out. (Not all
the presentation copies were in the album itself – the other item at the
Pierpont Library, Bartók's *Tót nepdál*, dated '1925', is on a different-sized
paper.) The 'Klops' song is written in black ink on two sides of an oblong
sheet (25 × 38 cms) of 14-stave paper. The paper is handmade, of high
quality, with watermark.

A holograph copy of the score, inscribed 'für Thea und H. H.
Stuckenschmidt zur Hochzeit', was in Professor Stuckenschmidt's library
in Prague at the outbreak of the Second World War, but has not been
seen by its owner since then.

First Performance(?)

14 December 1927, Berlin, at the Stuckenschmidts' wedding reception at
Viktoria Luiseplatz 4. The first modern performance, and probably the
first public one, was at the Akademie der Künste, West Berlin, on 12
September 1975; the soloist was Philip Langridge, with members of the
London Sinfonietta.

Posthumous Publication

EAM, 1982: in *The Unknown Kurt Weill: A Collection of 14 Songs*
(anonymous voice-and-piano arrangement).

Notes

Any date between 1924 and the end of 1927 would be defensible on
purely musical grounds, but the September 1925 date of Schoenberg's
canon is probably the most reliable evidence. In September 1925 Weill
had just finished *Der neue Orpheus* – in which, it so happens, he alluded
to another popular song of 'old Berlin'. But his delightfully tipsy setting

of the 'Klops' song is more in the style of parts of the first pantomime in *The Protagonist*. At the end of it, Weill has written, 'Dies wünscht Ihnen, verehrter Herr Direktor Hertzka/Ihr ergebener Kurt Weill'.

October 1925 – January 1926, Berlin

Royal Palace op. 17

Opera[-ballet] in one act
Text: Iwan Goll
Dedication: Georg Kaiser
Duration: 50 minutes
Cast: Dejanira (soprano), the Husband (bass), Yesterday's Lover (baritone), Tomorrow's Enamoured One (tenor), the Young Fisherman (tenor), the Old Fisherman (bass), head waiter, boy; soprano solo and female chorus (behind the stage). Part of the action shown on film.
Orchestra: (details from piano reduction – all orchestral material lost) 2.2.2.alto sax.3. 4.2.2.1. timp. perc. str.; stage orchestra: glock. 5 bells. cel. pno. harp perc.

A luxurious hotel on the edge of an Italian lake. The world-weariness and dissipation of the guests contrast with the idyllic landscape and the 'far-off sound' of church bells mingling with the runic songs of fisherfolk. Three men are vying for Dejanira's love; each makes his pleas in an extended 'vision' – the first, cinematically, the other two choreographically. The Husband can only think of offering Dejanira still more of the very things she has tired of – money, travel, possessions. Her past lover counters with nocturnal and erotic memories – a ballet of the stars and the signs of the zodiac, combined with the ecstatic song of a distant couple. Finally, the prospective lover apostrophizes the natural world and Orpheus appears, attended by a retinue of forest creatures. As the last vision fades Dejanira denounces her three suitors. Dismissing their promises and their fine words – behind which she sees nothing but naked egotism – she renounces the world and plunges into the dark waters of the lake. To the strains of a surreal tango, she is transformed into a mermaid-like shape. Her uncomprehending husband stands on the shore, shouting for help.

Autographs

No musical holographs have survived. A 9-page carbon-copy typescript of the libretto (UEA) contains corrections in Weill's hand, as does the piano reduction (also in UEA) by Arthur Willner. In Willner's manuscript no action is indicated for the third of the dance scenes, which is simply entitled 'Tiersymphonie' (Animal Symphony); the Orphic element added by Weill (and included in the typescript libretto) may therefore have been an afterthought, determined by the decision of the Staatsoper to produce *Der neue Orpheus* as a curtain-raiser to *Royal Palace*.

Publication

UE, 1926: libretto.
UE, 1926: vocal score (piano reduction by Arthur Willner).

First Performance

2 March 1927, Berlin, Staatsoper unter den Linden: conductor Erich Kleiber, designer Franco Aravantinos, choreographer Max Terpis; with Delia Reinhardt (Dejanira), Leo Schützendorf (Husband), Leonhard Kern (Yesterday's Lover), Karl Joken (Tomorrow's Enamoured One), Marcel Noë (Young Fisherman), Rudolf Watzke (Old Fisherman), Gitta Alpar (soprano), Rudolf Kölling (head waiter), Harald Kreutzberg (boy). Film directed by F. L. Hörth, produced by Phoebus-Film AG. *Royal Palace* was the central piece in a triple bill that opened with a concert performance of *Der neue Orpheus* and closed with Falla's *Master Peter's Puppet Show*.

Performing Versions

1966–7: Dance version (omitting most of the operatic scenes and slightly reordering the others) devised and orchestrated by Gunther Schuller, who conducted the first performance at the San Francisco Opera in 1967.
1971: orchestration of the entire work in its original form, by Gunther Schuller and Noam Sheriff; two concert performances at the 1971 Holland Festival, conducted by Gary Bertini.

Notes

The original performance material was last used in a production at the Essen Opera in 1929, conducted by Rudolph Schultz-Dornburg. The publishers' records show neither that it was returned nor that it was lost. The Essen records were destroyed in the Second World War.

March 1926 – March 1927, Berlin/Alassio/Berlin

Na und ?

Number opera in 2 acts and 17 numbers
Libretto: Felix Joachimson (Felix Jackson)
(Mostly lost)
Duration: full evening
Orchestra: full, including saxophones, flexatone, two mandolins, and piano solo.

No libretto or scenario has survived. In a discussion with the present author in 1960, the librettist declared that he had only the haziest recollection of the plot. It concerned, he said, an Italian of humble birth who makes his fortune in America and then returns to his native village to find that his erstwhile fiancée is about to marry another. He abducts her to his mountain retreat, which is then besieged by the outraged villagers.

Jackson was unable to recall the denouement or indeed any other details, except that he had based the libretto on a newspaper story. While that may seem to confirm the impression that *Na und ?* was some sort of latterday *verismo* opera – a slice of Menotti before its time – surviving sections of the voice-and-piano draft (with barely legible text) give a very different impression. So too does the brief description provided by Weill himself, in a letter to his publishers (4 April 1927) enclosing a copy of the libretto:

> It is the first operatic attempt to throw light on the essence of our time from within, rather than by recourse to the obvious externals. The theme is the actions and reactions of contemporary man. [. . .] It is a type of light-hearted opera that has not been developed since *Der Rosenkavalier*. [. . .] not grotesque or parodistic but cheerful and *musikantisch*. The form is: seventeen closed numbers, linked by recitatives or melodramas accompanied by piano or chamber ensembles.

Technically and stylistically, the extant music is a direct development from *Royal Palace*, and has no leanings towards neo-*verismo* (or indeed towards *Der Rosenkavalier*). The Italianate aspects are similar to those in *Royal Palace* and are consistent with what Busoni had regarded as desirable in modern opera. Although the jazz elements relate to the hero's American experience they avoid the more obvious Americanisms of *Royal Palace*, while retaining a broadly Expressionist character (notably in the 'Shimmy-song'). Much of the music is still highly dissonant, but the links with traditional tonality have been strengthened, and not only in relation to the frankly popular idioms associated with the milieu. Ideas that Weill was later to use, note for note, in *Aufstieg und Fall der Stadt Mahagonny* are representative of a general tendency that would surely be confirmed by the complete score. *Na und ?* (rather than the Kaiser operas, and more clearly than *Royal Palace*) was both the precursor and the prerequisite of the *Mahagonny* opera.

Autographs

SKETCHES

Missing.

DRAFTS

Approximately a third of the entire draft survives in three separate foldings of 28-line paper. There is also a separate sheet of similar paper which merits prior consideration. It appears to have been the outer sheet of a lost folding that carried the greater part of the draft of Act I. The evidence of that lies in the heading 'Ouverture' on side *a*, and in the musical character of the *allegro molto* that ensues on sides *a* and *b*. The overture was presumably completed on the next sheet of the folding. It is not a final draft, but a continuity sketch, giving the bare outlines of the polyphonic opening section. The contrasting section begins, in a more homophonic style, with a *molto rubato appassionato* theme (later to be used in *Der Zar lässt sich photographieren*) which is still in full spate at the end of what was probably the last available system (the remaining two staves being taken up by a 13-bar sketch of a tarantella idea that recurs in *Gustav III*). The workings on *c* and *d* have no connection with the previous material or with any of the other *Na und ?* drafts; they appear to be memos and sketches for *Herzog Theodor von Gothland*.

The earliest of the three extant foldings carries most of the Act I finale on eight sides of R^{28}. The start of the finale is missing and was presumably written on the previous folding; otherwise this finale is intact; and it concludes with the words 'Ende I. Akt'.

The legend 'II. Akt' heads the twenty pages (numbered 1–20) of manuscript in a second folding of R^{28}. Unlike the draft of the Act I finale, this substantial fragment gives a clear picture of the kind of formal processes Weill alluded to in his letter to Universal Edition. Although the so-called 'closed forms' are identifiable, it is misleading to suggest that they are merely 'linked', for in fact the musico-dramatic development is continuous, and through-composed in a sense that owes nothing to neo-classical symmetries (and almost nothing to traditional tonality). In the following numbering, the 'intermezzi' are denoted by dashes and the word 'Interlude' is reserved for purely orchestral sections. The first two numberings are Weill's:

I   Aria
II   Duet
     –Interlude–
[3] Duet scene and recitative
     –Melodrama and Interlude–
[4] 'Shimmy' (trio)
     –Chorus–
[5] Duet (*alla turca*)
     –Interlude–

The 'Shimmy' – a trio sung by the hero, Alexander, the Bridegroom, and someone identified simply as 'Amerikaner' – has a doggerel refrain beginning with the words 'Lady Lili You'. The final interlude is a 5/8 time presto for solo piano which is still in progress at the end of the twentieth and last page of manuscript.

The fragment contains several ideas later used in the *Mahagonny* opera. After a hint at one of the characteristic *Mahagonny* ostinatos in the first interlude, the Duet scene has a note-for-note anticipation of the *dolce espressivo* counter-melody at rehearsal figure 127 in Jim Mahoney's *Mahagonny* aria 'Wenn der Himmel hell wird'. The second interlude introduces separately two motifs which in the *Mahagonny* boxing scene (and perhaps elsewhere in *Na und ?*) are combined: the quasi-glissando horn motif, and the syncopated answer to it. These too are at the same pitch level as in *Mahagonny*, but the first is in triple rather than common time. Finally the *alla turca* duet adumbrates the driving ostinato rhythm of the final section of the Act I finale of *Mahagonny*.

The third folding of R^{28} includes a leaf of B^{28} and carries six sides of discontinuous drafts. The first three of these are headed respectively 'Nach I' ('after I'), 'Nach II', and 'Nach V'. The final item has been partitioned from the others by a horizontal line, and is marked 'Schluss 1. Akt' ('end of the first act'). The fact that this is musically identical with the ending (a humming chorus – *cf. Mahagonny!*) given in the draft of the complete finale indicates that the interpolations were made before the completion of the draft of Act I. It follows that the idea of linking the seventeen 'closed forms' with recitatives and melodramas, and also with choruses (as 'Nach II' suggests and the item before the *alla turca* duet confirms) arose during the course of composition.

In a recently discovered letter of 15 June 1927 – to which there is further reference in *Note 1* – Weill mentions three of the seventeen numbers as follows, and describes them as suitable for non-theatrical use:

> das Banjo-Duett Nr. 5
> das Couplet Nr. 7
> der Nigger-Song Nr. 12

Since the 'Nigger-Song' is presumably the 'Lady Lili You' refrain from the 'Shimmy' it is possible to deduce the proportions between the two acts. As already noted, the 'Shimmy' is the fourth of the five numbers in WLA's Act II fragment. There are therefore seven numbers missing prior to the Act I finale, and another four, including of course a second finale, after the second act's *alla turca* duet.

Notes

Felix Joachimson was born in Berlin in 1903 and studied composition with Weill in 1925–6. After some early experience as a freelance music critic and writer he was appointed Chefdramaturg at the Viktor Barnowsky theatre in Berlin, where he was responsible for the engagement of Weill as composer for the innovatory production of Strindberg's *Gustav III* (see p. 187). Joachimson had his first major success in September 1927 with *Fünf von der Jazzband*, a comedy directed by Brecht's lifelong collaborator Erich Engel, designed by his and Weill's friend Caspar Neher, and enthusiastically reviewed by Brecht's apostle Herbert Ihering (*Berliner Börsen-Courier*, 23 September 1927, reprinted in Ihering, *Von Reinhardt bis Brecht*, Bd. II, Berlin, 1959, pp. 28off.). Joachimson continued his career in the German theatre until the advent of Hitler, and then, under the name Felix Jackson, began a second and even more successful career in Hollywood as producer, screenwriter, and novelist.

Universal Edition, in the person of its director Emil Hertzka, expressed some disquiet about the libretto of *Na und ?* which Weill had posted from Berlin on 4 April 1927, and asked Weill to come at once to Vienna and play the whole score through. The poor reception of *Royal Palace* in March of that year had undoubtedly put Hertzka and his assistant Hans Heinsheimer on their guard, and the play-through – no easy task for Weill – did not persuade them to accept the work for immediate publication. A letter confirming that Weill was free to negotiate with other publishers followed almost immediately, and on 15 June 1927 – just a month before the Baden-Baden premiere of the *Mahagonny-Songspiel* – Weill submitted libretto and score to Schott's in Mainz, with a covering letter in which he described *Na und ?* as 'ein Werk leichteren Genres' and cannily selected the three numbers that he thought could be promoted separately. It is important to recall that the rebuff from UE and the approach to Schott took place in the immediate aftermath of the immensely successful world premiere of Krenek's opera *Jonny spielt auf*, which contained several numbers that very soon became popular 'hits'. Schott's publishing policy was centred on the work of Hindemith, and a stray opera from the UE stable would not have been an attractive proposition. Hindemith had already written *Hin und Zurück* with the Berlin revue writer Marcellus Schiffer, and before long was to embark on *Neues vom Tage*, also with Schiffer, and also, in its way, 'ein Werk leichteren Genres'. On 9 July 1927 Schott wrote to Weill politely rejecting *Na und ?*, and returning the manuscript.

The premiere of the *Mahagonny-Songspiel* at Baden-Baden later that month was attended by Otto Klemperer and Hans Curjel, Klemperer's Chefdramaturg at the newly formed Oper am Platz der Republik, or Kroll-Oper as it was popularly known. Since Universal Edition had intimated that they would reconsider *Na und ?* if Weill succeeded in gaining the interest of a major opera house, we may assume that once Schott had turned down his offer, Weill took the earliest opportunity of approaching the Kroll administration – certainly at Baden-Baden, if not before.

According to Curjel – in a verbal account to the present author – the score and libretto of *Na und ?* were delivered to his office at the Kroll and remained there for some months. But meanwhile Curjel had become one of the leading advocates of *Aufstieg und Fall der Stadt Mahagonny*, over which Klemperer was later to hesitate so painfully (see PH.OK, *passim*). According to Curjel, Weill continued to press the case for *Na und ?* until he, Curjel, produced the score from a cupboard in his office, and persuaded Weill to re-read it there and then. At the end of the reading, or so the story goes, Weill quietly closed the score, and with a shrug of his shoulders and a sheepish grin, tucked it under his arm, and left.

The story has at least a ring of truth, which is more than can be said of the popular legend that Weill had already dropped the score from his train window into the Danube after Universal Edition had rejected it. (In fact Weill was not in the habit of destroying his scores – losing them or giving them away suited his temperament better.) Herbert Fleischer (see p. 10) was sure that *Na und ?* was not among the early unpublished scores he took to Italy in 1933; and Lenya was equally certain that after the Nazi seizure of power she entrusted it once again to Curjel. But Curjel's own recollections of the score did not extend into the 1930s. *Na und ?* is not only the largest of Weill's lost works. In terms of his creative evolution – as the fragments of the draft demonstrate – it is by far the most important.

So long as there remains any hope for its discovery, there can be no last word on the subject. It therefore seems more appropriate to end these notes with the two words with which Weill and Joachimson began. In his letter to Schott, Weill declared that 'the title is not yet final' ('Der Titel ist noch nicht endgültig'). '*Na und ?*' is generally translated as the German equivalent of 'So what?'. But the Americanism misses its various resonances. Among them is 'What next?'. In that sense it was not an altogether inappropriate title for the predecessor of *Der Zar lässt sich photographieren* and *Aufstieg und Fall der Stadt Mahagonny*.

Summer 1926, Berlin

Herzog Theodor von Gothland

Music for a radio production of the 5-act tragedy by Christian Dietrich Grabbe, adapted by Klabund and Alfred Braun; for soloists, chorus and orchestra.

Autographs

All material is missing, with the possible exception of the untitled sketches on the second half of the B[28] sheet that carries the incomplete drafts of the *Na und ?* overture. These appear to relate to the 'Battle Song' and 'Turkish March' mentioned by Weill, and to involve the wordless chorus mentioned by Camilla Stiemer (see *Notes* below for both references).

First Performance

1 September 1926, chorus and orchestra of Radio Berlin, conducted by Bruno Seidler-Winkler, with Theodor Loos (Olaf), Werner Krauss (Theodor), Lothar Müthel (Friedrich), Johanna Hofer (Cäcilia).

Notes

In a letter to Peter Bing of 3 September 1926 Weill says he is particularly pleased with a 'little Turkish March', a 'Song with obbligato harp and saxophone', a 'Battle Song', 'War Music' and 'a large-scale Funeral March'. The only other reference to the score is an enthusiastic review by Camilla Stiemer in *Der deutsche Rundfunk* (12 September 1926). She mentions a wordless chorus, which apparently was used as a ritornello device ('in the manner of Greek drama') and also 'a beautiful *Lied* whose words are spoken by the rejected wife while the saxophone carries the melody'. She describes the score as 'highly impressive in its own right'. It is probably the earliest example of a radio score commissioned from a notable modern composer.

March–August 1927, Berlin

Der Zar lässt sich photographieren op. 21
(*The Tsar has his photograph taken*)

Opera buffa in one act
Text: Georg Kaiser
Duration: 60 minutes
Cast: the Tsar (baritone), Angèle (soprano), the Assistant (tenor), the Boy (alto), the False Angèle (soprano), the False Assistant (tenor), the False Boy (alto), the Leader (tenor), the Tsar's Aide (bass), two detectives, conspirators, officers, policemen. Male chorus in pit.
Orchestra: 2.2.2.2. 3.2.2.0. timp. perc. pno. str.; gramophone for the prerecorded *Tango Angèle*.

Paris, 1914; the fashionable photographer Angèle has no sooner been informed that the Tsar is already on his way to her studio than a gang of revolutionaries breaks in. While she and her two assistants are being trussed up and dragged away, three members of the gang disguise themselves as their doubles. In due course the False Angèle ceremoniously receives the Tsar, and ushers him into the studio. The camera's black cloth now conceals a lethal weapon; but the Tsar – a peace-loving democrat with an eye for the ladies and a hearty dislike of his imperial role – is more interested in the False Angèle than in posing. He gives orders that they be left alone. Unable to restrain him for long enough to aim the camera-gun at him, and not, perhaps, altogether resistant to his unexpected charm, the False Angèle is finally frustrated in her murderous endeavours by a warning that the plot has been discovered by the police. With the aid of a gramophone recording of the seductive *Tango Angèle* she extricates herself from the Tsar's clutches and, in the nick of time, escapes with her fellow conspirators. Order is restored and the Tsar, with heavy heart, consents to have his photograph taken by the 'real' Angèle (who lacks, alas, the attractions of the impostor).

Autographs

SKETCHES

Missing.

FIRST DRAFT

Sixteen pages of B^{30} in a single folding carry the greater part of the draft; the remainder – from the third bar on page 59 of the published vocal score to the end – is missing.

FULL SCORE (UEA)

230 numbered pages of a 26-line paper, bound in a black cover. A non-autograph footnote to the first page indicates that the orchestral piano part can, in places, be omitted at the conductor's discretion, and that lightness and clarity in the orchestral sound should be the rule throughout. This note does not appear in the published full score. Both in the autograph full score and in the published score the *Tango Angèle* appears only in a piano version: the dance-band accompaniment for the duet of the Tsar and the False Angèle was recorded by the Dobbri Saxophone Orchestra at a session in Berlin on 11 January 1928 in the composer's presence and perhaps under his direction (and was later released on the Beka label, B.6313.11). On 11 December 1928 Weill informed UE that the orchestral material was available from the record company (Carl Lindström AG). The material is lost, but the original recording is still available as part of the Universal Edition hire material. Its sound quality could be improved by modern technology, but on no account should its period character be lost.

Publication

UE, 1927: vocal score (piano reduction by Erwin Stein), full score, libretto, and gramophone record.

First Performance

18 February 1928, Leipzig Opera at the Neues Theater, Leipzig, with the Gewandhaus orchestra conducted by Gustav Brecher. Director Walter Brügmann; with Theodor Horand (Tsar), Ilse Kogel (Angèle), and Maria Janowska (False Angèle).

Notes

Although *Der Zar lässt sich photographieren* was expressly written as a new companion piece for *Der Protagonist* – *Royal Palace* having been judged a failure – it was paired on this occasion with one of the early *verismo* operas, Nicola Spinelli's *A basso porto*, whose world premiere had been given in Hamburg in 1894. *Der Zar* was combined with *Der Protagonist* for the first time at the Reussisches Theater, Gera, on 22 April 1928; the conductor was Maurice Abravanel.

May 1927, Berlin

Mahagonny

Songspiel after texts by Bertolt Brecht
Commissioned by Deutsche Kammermusik Baden-Baden 1927
Duration: 25 minutes
Cast: Charlie (tenor), Billy (tenor), Bobby (bass), Jimmy (bass), Jessie
   (soprano), Bessie (soprano).
Orchestra: 2 vln. 2 cl. (bcl.). 2 tpt. alto sax. tbn. pno. timp. TD. SD. BD. jazz
   dr. woodblock. cym. bells

There is no individual characterization, and no dialogue or action apart
from what is present or implied in the poems: the fleshpots of Mahagonny
attract many visitors, but prove disappointing and expensive; God orders
the inhabitants to Hell, but they revolt, claiming they are there already.

   1   'Auf nach Mahagonny'
   2   Kleiner Marsch (orchestra)
   3   'Alabama Song'
   4   Vivace (orchestra)
   5   'Wer in Mahagonny blieb'
   6   Vivace assai (orchestra)
   7   'Benares Song'
   8   Choral (orchestra)
   9   'Gott in Mahagonny'
   10 Finale: 'Dieses ganze Mahagonny'

Note 1

The placing of the present entry on the *Mahagonny-Songspiel* is an
exception to the chronological rule observed elsewhere in this catalogue.
Strictly speaking *Aufstieg und Fall der Stadt Mahagonny* should precede it,
for the opera was the first to be conceived and also the first to be started
(see p. 181). But the sense in which the *Songspiel* was a by-product of the
opera has to be weighed against the broader and deeper sense that it could
not have been composed *after* the opera, and cannot be understood in the
light of it.

Autographs

SKETCHES

Advanced sketches of 5 and 7 are on two leaves of B^{26} and B^{28} respectively.
The last seventeen bars of *10* are among the sketches for *Gustav III*.

DRAFT

Missing.

Seventy-eight numbered pages of B²⁸, disbound, without title page, but with the end date 'Berlin-Charlottenburg May 1927'. The binding has been damaged by the insertion, in 1932, of several numbers from the printed full score of *Aufstieg und Fall der Stadt Mahagonny* together with the holograph full score of the so-called 'Havana-Lied' from the 1931 version of that opera. These insertions (removed in 1960) were made, with Weill's consent, for the specific needs of the semi-staged concert performance of the *Songspiel* at the Salle Gaveau in Paris in December 1932. Associated pencil and crayon markings are in the hand of the conductor of that performance, Maurice Abravanel, who was responsible for some necessary adjustments to the numbers from the opera, and of Hans Curjel, who was responsible for the staging. Significant musical additions to the 'Alabama Song' and to the closing bars of the whole work have been made in pencil at an earlier date and in another hand – probably that of Ernst Mehlich, the conductor of the first performance. The autograph originals of these insertions are in one of the non-autograph vocal scores (see below).

A non-autograph vocal score by an unnamed arranger is written on sixty-seven pages of S¹⁸. It bears the stamp 'Universal Edition Archiv' and the title 'Mahagonny/Ein Songspiel/Text von Bert Brecht/Musik von/Kurt Weill/Klavierauszug'. Numerous stage directions in pencil are in the hand of Hans Curjel and not, as the present writer assumed in 1960, that of the original director, Walter Brügmann. The preliminary note about the staging (title page, *verso*) is not consistent with the first production at Baden-Baden, where Brügmann was himself 'directed' by Brecht; but in so far as it envisages a stylized production with identical costumes for all six singers, it accords with the holograph full score of the 'Alabama Song', in which (as in this vocal score) the song text, as originally underlaid, is identical with Brecht's 'Hauspostille' text and thus ignores the fact that it is to be sung by two women.

A vocal part for the role of Bessie was extracted from this vocal score by a professional copyist, and was for many years in the possession of the late Irene Eden, the original Bessie. In 1970 or thereabouts it was offered for sale by a German music dealer and inspected by the present writer before its acquisition by Universal Edition, in whose Archive it now is. The importance of this copy derives solely from two autograph insertions in pencil: the first, presumably suggested by Irene Eden herself, is a coloratura embellishment to the second refrain of the 'Alabama Song'; the second is an extended instrumental line – almost certainly intended for solo violin – which seems to have been written during rehearsal in order to resolve a practical problem that jeopardizes the effectiveness of the work's closing bars. While the embellishment for the 'Alabama Song' was eventually confirmed in the operatic version, the second insertion has no corroboration other than the equally hasty and imprecise notation in another hand in the holograph full score (see above).

Publication

LIBRETTO

UE, 1927: the title page reads: 'Kurt Weill/Mahagonny/(Textbuch)/ Gesangstexte entnommen aus Brecht's "Hauspostille"'. There are no texts other than these song texts, and no stage directions or preliminary notes. The vocal numbers are in the order given above, but are titled, numbered and paired as follows:

1 Mahagonny Song/Alabama Song
2 Mahagonny Song/Benares Song
3 Mahagonny Song/Finale

VOCAL SCORE

UE, 1927: 'Alabama Song' only (beginning with cadential bars of 2).

UE, 1963: edition attributed to David Drew and based on the 1927 vocal score; with symbolic references to production notes which the author had never intended for publication and which, by a happy mischance, were accidentally omitted by the publishers. The notes were based on annotations in the non-autograph vocal score, mistakenly attributed to the original director (see *Other Sources*, above).

UE, 1967: second edition, again attributed to David Drew, but again published without his prior knowledge. Innocent of any corrections, it contained the production notes that had mercifully been omitted from the 1963 edition. After this second mishap, the text for a corrected edition was prepared immediately, on the understanding that the 1967 publication would be replaced as soon as a reprint was due. Nineteen years later the 1967 score is still in print.

FULL SCORE

UE, 1963: hire material only.

First Performance

18 July 1927, Kurhaus, Baden-Baden; directed by Walter Brügmann, in unofficial collaboration with Brecht; projections and costumes by Caspar Neher; the City Orchestra was conducted by Ernst Mehlich; with Lotte Lenya (Jessie), Irene Eden (Bessie), Erik Wirl (tenor), Georg Ripperger (Billy), Karl Giebel (Bobby), and Gerhard Pechner (Jimmy).

Note 2

Although the premiere was highly successful, the *Songspiel* was not published or promoted after its solitary performance – presumably because of the decision to incorporate all the vocal numbers in the large-scale opera that Weill and Brecht had been discussing since March 1927. There is no evidence that Weill gave any further thought to the *Songspiel* until 1932, when representatives of La Sérénade, the Parisian modern music organization, questioned him about a suitable programme for the Salle Gaveau in December. Prompted by his friends Maurice Abravanel and Hans Curjel, he suggested combining *Der Jasager* with an expanded version of the *Songspiel*, which would serve the double purpose of providing Lotte Lenya and the principal tenor, Otto von Pasetti, with more vocal opportunities than did the original, and of filling out a programme that would otherwise have been too short. Abravanel and Curjel incorporated four numbers from the opera *Aufstieg und Fall der Stadt Mahagonny*, and substituted the opera's version of the 'Alabama Song' for the original and more dissonant one. The resulting 'Paris version' (as it is sometimes called) was repeated in London and in Rome during 1933 under Abravanel's direction, and revived, against the composer's wishes, by Curjel in 1949, at the Venice Biennale.

After the first performance and publication of the opera *Aufstieg und Fall der Stadt Mahagonny*, the *Songspiel* tended to be referred to as 'Das kleine Mahagonny'.

For the 1960–1 season of the Städtische Bühnen, Gelsenkirchen, the present author prepared an edition of the 1927 *Songspiel*, shorn of its later accretions, but furnished with production notes. This putative 'Originalfassung' was performed for the first time at Gelsenkirchen on 2 March 1961. As far as text and music were concerned, it did in fact correspond almost exactly with what had been performed in Baden-Baden in 1927. However, on 10 February 1963 the Berliner Ensemble presented a so-called 'theatre version' (Bühnenfassung) by Manfred Wekwerth, Manfred Karge, and Matthias Langhoff, which purported to be authentic, and bore the title 'Das kleine Mahagonny'. Acclaimed by critics and hugely enjoyed by theatre audiences, first in East Berlin and then in many Western cities during the Ensemble's tours, this version is also available on gramophone records and has become a rich source of confusion. Whatever its interest as an example of Brechtian theatre, it bears no relation to the *Songspiel* or indeed to the art of musical composition as Weill understood it. It is, in fact, a 60-minute play with incidental music; the play burlesques the libretto of *Aufstieg und Fall der Stadt Mahagonny*, and is faithful enough to the spirit of Brecht's famous 'Anmerkungen' on that work; the music is a primitive and deservedly anonymous arrangement of snippets from the opera and the *Songspiel*. Bereft of structure and musical sense, it sounds as if it were conceived at one committee meeting, and ripped, untimely, from its author's pen at the next. As conductor of the performance and the recording, and as Music Director of the Berliner Ensemble, the composer and conductor Hans-Dieter Hosalla had much to answer for.

The Berliner Ensemble's 'Das kleine Mahagonny' was probably the first and is certainly the most celebrated of those bastardizations of Weill that owe their existence, and their spurious legitimacy, to the claim that Brecht himself fathered the music in those works where he collaborated with Weill (as distinct from Eisler and Dessau, who have mercifully been spared paternity-suits of this kind, and the indignities that follow). Especially in literary and dramatic circles the *Mahagonny-Songspiel* was for many years seen as the classic instance of cohabitation, since the 'music' for the five 'Mahagonny-*Lieder*' had been printed in the appendix to the 1927 edition of Brecht's *Hauspostille*. The fact that three of the five *Lieder* had no bearing at all on Weill's settings, and that the other two merely provided a pre-compositional framework, seems to have been overlooked even in Weill's day: with a firmness that would otherwise have been unnecessary, the composer himself put the matter in its proper perspective during the course of his 1929 essay 'Über den gestischen Charakter der Musik' (KW.AS. pp. 40ff).

April 1927 – April 1929/various revisions 1929–31

Aufstieg und Fall der Stadt Mahagonny
[*Rise and Fall of Mahagonny City*]

Opera in three acts
Text: Bertolt Brecht (with Weill)
Cast: Leokadja Begbick (alto or mezzo-soprano), Fatty (tenor), Trinity Moses (baritone), Jenny Hill (soprano), Jim Mahoney (tenor), Jack O'Brien (tenor), Pennybank Bill (baritone), Alaska Wolf Joe (bass), Tobby Higgins (tenor), men and girls of Mahagonny.
Orchestra: 2 fl. ob. cl. alto sax. ten sax. 2 bsn (cbsn). 2 hn. 3 tpt. 2 tbn. tba. pno. timp. harm. (*ad lib*). banjo. bass guitar. bandoneon. cym. BD. SD. TD. gong. tom-toms. str.; stage orchestra: (2 picc. 2 cl. 3 sax. 2 bsn. 2 hn. 2 tpt. 2 tbn. tba. perc. zither *or* xyl. banjo. bandoneon).

Note 1

In the holograph full score (see below) Weill specifies a string strength of six violins, three violas, two cellos, and two basses. This is confirmed by the score that his publishers prepared and printed well before the rehearsals for the first productions, and so far as we know it was never officially contradicted. The problems created by following Weill's recommendation are altogether disproportionate to the occasional advantages. While the scoring of certain passages is indeed consistent with a 6.3.2.2 string section, that of many others requires a minimum of two or three times as many players, whatever the acoustic conditions. In view of the general character of the scoring, Weill's reasons for defining a string strength so precisely are obscure (but might be less so if we possessed the full score of *Na und ?*, with its chamber-orchestral subdivisions). Given the character of the tuttis, which is by no means chamber orchestral, Weill would have been wiser to set certain limits and leave the final decision to the conductor. Since the variables in a work of this scale are so numerous, the probable explanation of his manifest under-estimation is that on the one hand it was a way of announcing to the larger opera houses that the string forces required for *Elektra* (and probably for *Royal Palace* too) were inappropriate, and on the other of assuring the smaller ones that *Mahagonny* was not beyond their reach. Some allowance should perhaps be made for a bad conscience over his own miscalculations of voice-and-orchestra balance in the two Georg Kaiser operas – both of which he heard during the period when he was scoring *Mahagonny*. But a composer as experienced as he in the field of opera could never have supposed that there is a direct correlation between the number of string players and the audibility of singers and their words – unless, that is, he were dealing with some factor of which he had no experience. One must therefore ask whether there is any substance in the popular belief that *Mahagonny* was not primarily intended for opera singers – as its earliest opponents insisted – but rather for the kind of cast so cleverly assembled by Ernst Josef Aufricht for his privately funded Berlin production in December 1932. The answer to that question can be read in the score itself, and also, at greater length, in Weill's correspondence with his publishers before and after the series of productions in German opera houses in 1930. In no sense – except perhaps a polemical one – was the work conceived for institutions that took their lead from the Charlottenburg house in Berlin or the Bayerische Staatsoper in Munich. But from start to finish it was written for the numerous houses which until 1930 were firmly committed to a 'progressive' policy. In these, the initiatives of Max Reinhardt and the younger directors had ensured that the concept of the singer–actor was developing swiftly and on the highest musical level. There is no reason of any kind to suppose that Weill determined the string strength for *Mahagonny* out of deference to the voices of more or less untrained singers. Equally without foundation, and wholly unmusical, is the notion that an undernourished string section will ward off the perils and seductions of 'romanticism'. Faulty balance remains a fault until it is corrected by the appropriate technical means, and cannot be justified in other terms. How little the string writing in *Mahagonny* has to do with Romantic conceptions, and how supremely irrelevant to those conceptions (see Richard Strauss!) is the actual number of strings employed, is clear from related passages in *Der Lindberghflug* and *Der Jasager*, where Weill specifies string sections that are, respectively, 'large' and 'as large as possible'.

Aside from all extra-musical arguments and ideological glosses, the orchestral requirements for *Mahagonny* undoubtedly constitute an obstacle to many organizations that would like to perform the work but lack the necessary resources. To remark that the same is true of every relatively large-scale opera that has achieved popularity under the protection of modern copyright laws is strictly relevant, but insufficient. The chief difference is that Weill himself became aware of the problem as soon as Germany's opera houses began to give way to the forces of political reaction, and even contemplated rescoring *Mahagonny* for a 15-piece chamber orchestra (see letter to UE of 14 March 1930). Whether he would have had the heart to persevere had the opportunity arisen seems questionable, not so much because of the time and effort involved as because the task itself would have entailed demolishing an irreplaceable element in the musico-dramatic structure – the stratified orchestration. There are no conceivable substitutes for whatever Weill himself might have supplied by way of compensation for that.

The desert city of Mahagonny is the creation of three fugitives from justice – Begbick and her accomplices Fatty and Moses. Advertised as a paradise for pleasure-seekers, it soon attracts the discontented from every continent. Some are disappointed with what they find and make their getaway. Among those who remain, only the lumberjack Jim Mahoney dimly senses that something is amiss. Yet it is he who eventually expounds Begbick's underlying tenets in radical form. Inspired by an approaching hurricane, he advocates an end to all legal or moral constraints. When the hurricane miraculously bypasses Mahagonny, the inhabitants celebrate, in the spirit of Jim's proposal. Jim is eventually ensnared by Begbick, brought to trial for failing to pay his debts, and executed. Alarmed and confused by a fate that portends their own, the inhabitants set fire to Mahagonny and march forth in futile protest, each against his neighbour, all against all.

Note 2

Like *Na und ?* – to judge from the surviving drafts – *Mahagonny* is a number opera in which the inner momentum owes much more to the experience of through-composed forms than the mere outlines suggest. So far from being the naïve 'juxtaposition' of song-type numbers that some early critics took it for and every badly paced and unmusical production makes it out to be, the total form is a remarkably flexible and versatile combination of diverse elements. The following summary of the numbers and their constituent elements is as unresponsive to the formal strengths of the score as to its weaknesses. The numbering is the one adopted in the 1969 edition of the score; the alphabetical subdivisions indicate critical stages in the musico-dramatic development, but also include, for purposes of cross-reference, certain crucial refrains.

ACT I

Scene i: A Desolate Region
 1 a   orchestral prelude
   b   melodrama (Fatty, Moses, Begbick)
   c   'Darum lasst uns hier eine Stadt gründen' (Begbick)
   d   'Sie soll sein wie ein Netz' (Begbick)
   e   'Aber dieses ganze Mahagonny' (Begbick, Fatty, Moses)

Inter-scene in Front of the Half-curtain
 2   Alabama Song: 'Oh show us the way to the next whiskey bar'
         (Jenny, girls)
         refrain: 'Oh Moon of Alabama'

Scene ii: A Metropolis
 3 a   'Wir wohnen in den Städten' (chorus)
   b   'Fern vom Getriebe der Welt' (Fatty, Moses)

Inter-scene
 4   'Auf nach Mahagonny' (Jim, Jack, Bill, Joe)

Scene iii: Pier
 5 a   'Wenn man an einen fremden Strand kommt' (Jim, Jack, Bill, Joe)
   b   'Ach, meine Herren, willkommen zu Hause' (Begbick)
   c   'Heraus, ihr Schönen von Mahagonny' (Jim, etc.; Jenny, etc.)
   d   'Ach bedenken Sie, Herr Jack O'Brien' (Jenny)
   d¹ Havanna-Lied: 'Ach bedenken Sie, Herr Jakob Schmidt' (Jenny)
   e   'Ich kenn' die Jimmys aus Alaska schon' (Jenny, Jim and ensemble)

Inter-scene
 6 a   'Ich habe gelernt' (Jenny–Jim)
   b   'Bitte, Jimmy' (Jenny–Jim)

Scene iv: Hotel 'Zum reichen Mann'
 7 a   'Ach dieses ganze Mahagonny' (Begbick, Fatty, Moses)
   b   'Auch ich bin einmal an einer Mauer gestanden' (Begbick)

Scene v: Pier
 8 a   melodrama (Jim, Jack, Bill, Joe)
   b   'Wunderbar ist das Heraufkommen des Abends' (Jack, Bill, Joe)
   c   'Ich glaube, ich will meinen Hut aufess'n' (Jim)
         refrain: 'Ihr habt gelernt das Cocktail – Abc.'

Scene vi: Hotel 'Zum reichen Mann'
 9 a   The Maiden's Prayer (Gebet einer Jungfrau) – piano solo
   b   'Tief in Alaskas schneeweissen Wäldern' (Jim)
   c   'Sieben Jahre' (Jim/full ensemble)

10 a   fugato – orchestra
   b   'Oh furchtbares Ereignis' (ensemble, chorus)
   c   'Ach mit eurem ganzen Mahagonny' (Jim)

Scene vii: A wall
11   Finale
   a   'Haltet euch aufrecht' (male chorus)
   b   'Oh Moon of Alabama' (Jenny, girls)/'Es nutzt nichts' (Jack)
   c   'Siehst du, so ist die Welt' (Jim)
         refrain: 'Wir brauchen keinen Hurrikan'
   d   'Wenn es etwas gibt, das du haben kannst für Geld' (Jim)
   e   'Zerstört ist Pensacola' (Fatty, Begbick, Jim, ensemble)
   f   'Denn wie man sich bettet, so liegt man' (Jim, full ensemble)

ACT II

Scene i: Country road outside Mahagonny
12   a   orchestral prelude
     b   'Oh wunderbare Lösung' (chorus)

Inter-scene
13   a   'Erstens, vergesst nicht, kommt das Fressen' (male chorus)

Scene ii: A table
     b   'Jetzt hab' ich gegessen zwei Kälber' (Jack, men)
     c   'Sehet, Jack ist gestorben' (male chorus)

14   a   'Zweitens kommt der Liebesakt' (male chorus)

Scene iii: In Front of the Mandelay Brothel
     b   'Spucke den Kaugummi aus' (Begbick)
              refrain: 'Rasch, Jungens, he' (men)
     c   'Ich bitte, die Herren, sich in Geduld zu fassen' (Moses)
     d   'Sieh jene Kraniche' (Jenny, Jim)

Inter-scene
     e   'Drittens, das Boxen nicht vergessen . . .' (male chorus)

Scene iv: A Boxing Ring
15   a   Quick March (Flotter Marsch) (wind band on stage)
     b   'Wer jemals den Kopf über Fäuste gestellt' (Joe)
     c   'Joe, du stehst mir menschlich nah' (Bill)
              refrain: 'Die sieben Winter' (Bill, Joe)
     d   'Moses, mach Hackfleisch' (male chorus)

Inter-scene
     e   '. . . viertens, Saufen laut Kontrakt . . .' (male chorus)

Scene v: A Bar
16   a   'Freunde, kommt, ich lade euch ein' (Jim)
     b   'Wer in Mahagonny blieb' (male chorus)
     c   'Jenny, komm' her!' (Jim)
     d   'Der Schnapps in die Toiletten geflossen' (Jim, male chorus)
     e   'Stürmisch die Nacht' (Jenny, ensemble)
     f   'Meine Herren, meine Mutter prägte' (Jenny)
              refrain: 'Denn wie man sich bettet, so liegt man'
     g   'Wer in seinem Kober bleibt' (male chorus)
     h   'Lasst euch nicht verführen' (full chorus)

ACT III

Scene i: A Street
17   'Wenn der Himmel hell wird' (Jim)
              refrain: 'Nur die Nacht darf nicht aufhör'n'

Scene ii: A Courtroom
18   a   'Haben alle Zuschauer Billette?' (Moses, Fatty, Begbick,
              Tobby Higgins, male chorus)
     b   'Jim, du stehst mir menschlich nah' (Bill)
              refrain: 'Die sieben Winter' (Bill, Jim)
     c   'Er hat kein Geld' (chorus)
     d   Benares Song: 'There is no money in this land' (Jenny, Begbick,
              Fatty, Bill, Moses)
              refrain: 'Let's go to Benares'

Scene iii: A Primitive Gallows
19 a 'Liebe Jenny . . . Lieber Jimmy' (Jim–Jenny)
    b melodrama with reprise of *6b* (Jim, Jenny) (alternative to reprise: *14d*)
    c 'Und jetzt empfehle ich dich meinem letzten Freunde Billy' (Jim)
    d 'Erstens, vergesst nicht, kommt das Fressen' (male chorus)
    e 'Lasst euch nicht verführen' (Jim, Jenny, chorus)

Inter-scene: 'God in Mahagonny'
    f 'An einem grauen Vormittag' (Fatty, Tobby, Bill)
    g 'Sauft ihr wie die Schwämme' (Moses)
    h 'Ansahen sich die Männer von Mahagonny' (Jenny)

Finale: Mahagonny in Flames
    i 'Aber dieses ganze Mahagonny' (full ensemble) [=*1e*]
    j 'Wir brauchen keinen Hurrikan' (full ensemble) [=*11c*]
    k 'Denn wie man sich bettet, so liegt man' (full ensemble) [=*11f*]
    l 'Oh Moon of Alabama' (full ensemble) [=*2*]
    m 'Können ihm Essig holen' (full ensemble)
        refrain: 'Können einem toten Mann nicht helfen'

Note 3

Derivations from the *Mahagonny-Songspiel* are as follows: *1e* (and its reprises *10c* and *19i*) = *Songspiel 10*; *2* = *Songspiel 3*; *4* = *Songspiel 1*; *8a* = *Songspiel 6*; *16b* = *Songspiel 5*; *18d* = *Songspiel 7*; *19c* = *Songspiel 8*; *19f–h* = *Songspiel 9*.

Autographs

SKETCHES

A few isolated items have by chance survived, thanks to their being scattered among Weill's unpublished manuscripts. The first twenty-nine bars of *1d* and fourteen bars of *9b* are on a quartered sheet of B^{30}; a fragment of *13a* is on one side of a 26-line paper; and a 30-bar setting for 4-part chorus *a cappella* of the first three stanzas of 'Lasst euch nicht verführen' (see *19e*) is on one side of B^{28} – it is unrelated to the version in the 1930 score, and is certainly of earlier date. Another setting of the first stanza of the same text, for two unidentified voices, is sketched on one side of a half of B^{28} and dates from the last weeks of 1931, as does the other item on this sheet – a complete sketch of $5d^1$, the 'Havanna-Lied': both were written towards the end of 1931 for the Berlin production of *Mahagonny* at the Theater am Kurfürstendamm.

FINAL DRAFT

Missing.

FULL SCORE

Each of the three acts is written on leaves of B^{30} enclosed in a title sheet of the same paper. On the first title page the non-autograph heading 'Herrn

Dr Roth von Greissle' records the transmission of the score from Felix Greissle's office in Universal Edition to Dr Ernst Roth's. The second and third autograph titles are precisely modelled on the layout and orthography of the first, which reads as follows: 'Aufstieg u. Fall der Stadt/Mahagonny/Oper in 3 Akten/von/Kurt Weill/Text/von/Bert Brecht/1. Akt/Partitur'. The autograph pagination is continuous: Act I, pages 1– 206; Act II, pages 207–331; Act III, pages 332–449. At the foot of the last page is the note: 'Ende der Oper/April 1927 – April 1929'.

The first discussions about the opera took place in March 1927, and Brecht's first story outline (BB.AJ 329/60) dates from that same month. Weill, according to his own testimony, began making sketches for the opera almost immediately. See AD.BM pp. 136ff. for a detailed account of the origins of the work, with particular reference to Weill's little-known rebuff to a playwright named Gilbricht who was wrongly claiming that Brecht had plagiarized the Mahagonny idea ('Kurt Weill zum Fall Brecht–Gilbricht', in *Der Montag-Morgen*, Berlin, 10 June, 1930). For further comments on the starting point of the opera, see p. 188 of the present catalogue. Weill's end date of April 1929 is not, of course, the final one. It was only at this stage that he sent the libretto to his publisher. The director of Universal Edition, Emil Hertzka, immediately expressed doubts about the propriety of various passages, notably of the Brothel Scene (Act II scene iii). At his insistence Weill and Brecht undertook various revisions during the summer of 1929. These proved insufficient at a time of general alarm about censorship and the growing threat to artistic freedom. In September 1929, Weill composed 14d, the duet 'Sieh jene Kraniche' – sometimes known as the 'Kraniche-Duett' or 'Cranes' Duet' – and offered it as a temporary alternative for 14a–c, in order to fulfil a specific condition of the Leipzig contract. Reluctant to remove 14a–c altogether, he then recomposed the ending of the original scene to allow a transition to the 'higher' plane of the 'Kraniche-Duett' (the orchestral score of which dates from the last week of October 1929). All these revisions are incorporated in the full score, most of them by means of pasted-in insertions. Fortunately these have not obliterated the original manuscript beneath; but a few of the original vocal lines have been erased by Weill himself.

There is no evidence, and no reason to suppose, that Weill returned to the holograph full score after October 1929. Together with the typescript libretto described below, it provided Universal Edition with the master copies for performance material and for the publications that were issued in time for the March 1930 premiere.

LIBRETTO

(1)   Typescript on forty-one numbered pages (20.8 × 20.1 cms) with a few autograph additions and corrections in pencil, but no other markings. The title-page legend exactly corresponds to the one on the

holograph full score. The whole typescript appears to have been typed by Weill himself on his own machine. It certainly predates the completion of the full score and may well have been based on the final draft score: the 'Benares Song' (18d) is not yet included, and the Act III finale follows the example of the *Songspiel* and consists only of the single stanza of 'Aber dieses ganze Mahagonny' (19i). The text of the Brothel Scene is identical with the unexpurgated version originally underlaid in the holograph full score, apart from a provocatively sexual reference excised by Weill himself:

STIMME DER BEGBICK: Introducto pene frontem in fronte ponens requiescat.
MÄNNER (*in hochster Ungeduld*): Ewig nicht stehet der Mond über dir,
Mandelay.

Two appendices to the libretto, each typed on the same paper and each with an autograph note to the printers requesting that the text be followed exactly, give subsequent versions of the Brothel Scene, dating from September and October 1929 respectively. The first, on a single page, establishes the 'Kraniche-Duett' as the sole item in that scene; the second, on two pages, is the version that went into print.

(2)   Act III only, carbon copy on flimsy paper, paginated 1–11. There are many autograph corrections in pencil. There is also a solitary correction in Brecht's hand, revising the text for one of the placards in the Act III finale, which appears here in its complete form, as published in 1930. But the 'Benares Song' is still missing from this version of the libretto; the text appears in a typewritten appendix (top copy) with Weill's autograph annotations. A fair-copy carbon of the whole of T2 is also in UEA, and was probably made by the publishers. There are no annotations.

PRODUCTION NOTES (UEA)

Typescript, paginated 1–22, with the following title page: 'Caspar Neher und Kurt Weill./Vorschläge zur szenischen/Ausführung der Oper/ Aufstieg und Fall der Stadt Mahagonny'. Undated, but written in November 1929. The first page has a manuscript superscription in Weill's hand, referring to the article 'Vorwort zum Regiebuch der Oper Aufstieg und Fall der Stadt Mahagonny' published in *Anbruch* 12 (January 1930), pp. 5–7. There are no other manuscript annotations. Pasted to page 1 is a typewritten addition to the opening remarks, which reads 'Wichtig für Bühnenbild und Kostüme: Jede Annäherung an Wildwest-und Cowboy-Romantik und jede Betonung eines typisch amerikanischen Milieus ist *zu vermeiden*.' ('Important for scenery and costumes: any suggestion of Wildwest or Cowboy romanticism and any emphasis on a typically American milieu is to be avoided.') This note, together with attendant suggestions for changes of nomenclature, was written too late to be incorporated in the published vocal score, but appears in the full score. The notes themselves remained unpublished (apart from the

Anbruch foreword) and would in fact have required radical revision in the light of the first stage productions and Weill's reactions to them.

Publication 1

PRIOR TO THE FIRST STAGE PRODUCTION

UE, 1929: vocal score, reduction by Norbert Gingold; full score, containing preliminary notes postdating the vocal score.

UE, 1930: libretto, textually identical with full score; vocal album, with cover design by Caspar Neher, and the numbers in an arbitrary order: 4, 2, 19a–b, 15, 17, 19m.

First Performance

9 March 1930, Leipzig, Neues Theater: conductor Gustav Brecher, director Walter Brügmann, designer Caspar Neher; with Paul Beinert (Jim), Marga Dannenberg (Begbick), Mali Trummer (Jenny), Hans Fleischer (Bill), Walter Zimmer (Moses), Hanns Hauschild (Jack), Theodor Horand (Bill), Ernst Osterkamp (Joe), Alfred Hollander (Tobby).

Revisions 1930–1

Minor musical and textual changes were made during rehearsals for the premiere, and some were incorporated in the production in Kassel which followed a few days later. Weill and Brecht made further changes immediately after the premiere, in the interests of clarifying Act III. Thus far the revisions were confined to cuts, transpositions and text changes, and apparently did not involve any significant recomposition. The first major musical revision – or, at least, the first we know of – is referred to in a letter from Weill to Universal Edition dated 6 October 1930: for the production then in rehearsal at the Frankfurt opera he had made a new orchestration of the chorale 'Lasst euch nicht verführen', and sent it direct to the conductor, Wilhelm (William) Steinberg. Presumably this revision was made because the original had been composed for its Act III location (*19e*) and was not altogether suitable for its new, post-Frankfurt, function as the conclusion of Act II (*16h*). Whatever the case, no material relating to it has survived.

The Frankfurt production, which had the first of its twelve performances on 16 October 1930, was the last in a German opera house during Weill's lifetime, but not the last in Germany. Ernst Aufricht's privately financed production opened at the Theater am Kurfürstendamm on 21 December 1931. It was directed and designed by Caspar Neher and conducted, at Weill's suggestion, by Alexander von Zemlinsky. The significance of the latter choice lay in the musical authority it lent to a production that could not afford to cater for a primarily musical or opera-going audience, but needed, for reasons Weill well understood, to attract the kind of public that had flocked to *Die Dreigroschenoper* at

Aufricht's Theater am Schiffbauerdamm. With Harald Paulsen as Jim, Lenya as Jenny, and Trude Hesterberg as Begbick, Aufricht had shrewdly tipped the balance away from the opera house; with Zemlinsky as conductor, Weill had no less shrewdly tipped it halfway back again. Even without the presence of Brecht, who quarrelled with Weill during rehearsals and distanced himself from the whole project, a conflict of interest would have been inevitable. To judge from Weill's contemporary correspondence, that conflict was reflected in the revisions made specifically for this production. Some, he felt, should be incorporated in a definitive edition; others pleased him less. But which? And why? No performance material used in that production, or in its four predecessors, survived the Second World War. The holograph full score of the 'Havanna-Lied' ($5d^1$), which was written expressly for Lenya, survived only because it had been incorporated in the material for the 'Paris version' of the *Mahagonny-Songspiel* (see p. 174); an entirely new setting of 'Lasst euch nicht verführen' survives only in a pencil draft; and there is no trace whatsoever of the 'extraordinary orchestral interlude' ('ausser-ordentliches Orchesterzwischenspiel') which, according to T. W. Adorno's review in *Anbruch*, 14 (February–March 1932, p. 53), replaced one of the cut passages and functioned as a kind of survey and summation of the whole '*Mahagonny*-style'.

The last production of *Mahagonny* in Weill's lifetime was mounted at the Raimund Theater, Vienna, on 26 April 1932 – directed by Hans Heinsheimer, conducted by Gottfried Kassowitz, and witnessed (at a rehearsal) by Alban Berg. With Lotte Lenya as Jenny and Otto von Pasetti as Jim, it was strongly influenced by the Berlin production, but involved even more drastic cuts. Weill's only contribution was to warn Heins-heimer against reducing the work to a succession of songs or song-type numbers. That, however, was exactly how it turned out; and it lasted just over an hour.

Publication 2

POST-1950

UE, 1969: vocal score, edited, with an introduction and notes, by David Drew. This edition is a revision of the 1930 vocal score incorporating every verifiable revision undertaken by Weill himself, with or without Brecht's collaboration. The principal sources were: *A*: holograph full score; *B*: T1, T2; *C*: published score with autograph corrections (WLA); *D*: the same, with notes by Alexander von Zemlinsky (author); *E*: the same, with notes by Caspar Neher (Neher Estate); *F*: composer's correspondence with his publishers (UEA); *G*: production notes (UEA); *H*: Brecht, 'Aufstieg und Fall der Stadt Mahagonny' in *Versuche* 1–12, vol. 2 (1930, reprinted 1959). The only purely editorial contribution is the exact location of the 'Kraniche-Duett' – this is discussed below in Notes 8–9.

Notes 4–10

(4) Returning to the *Mahagonny* problem in 1983 for the first time for several years I was reminded yet again of its fascination, and its intractability. What fascinates is the collision of two congenial yet incompatible minds; what is hard to deal with are the unwelded fragments they left behind.

(5) There is no 'ideal' production of *Mahagonny*, just as there is no 'definitive' edition. Because the work is not only unfinished but unfinishable, Weill continued it in *Die Bürgschaft*, which is equally unfinished and unfinishable, and which therefore is continued in *Der Silbersee* and yet again in the *Der Weg der Verheissung*; which is the apotheosis of the unfinished.

(6) Those who choose to stage *Mahagonny* in the spirit of Brecht's 'Anmerkungen' of 1930 are unlikely to observe or care that Weill had no hand in them, and that he demonstrably had very different ideas about opera in general and *Mahagonny* in particular. Such directors may safely be left to their Brechtian devices, which will either punish them with a disaster or reward them with a theatrical success. The work itself is beyond their reach.

(7) Even if Weill had not played an active and in some respects decisive role in the forming and writing of the libretto, its structural and other weaknesses are primarily his responsibility, not Brecht's. Improvements are always possible, but seldom transferable from one production to the next.

(8) The 'Kraniche-Duett' lies at the heart of a problem that becomes manifest in the collapsing episodic structure of Act III: musically and aesthetically it aspires to the very heights from which Act III has to fall but on which Act II has no reason to dwell.

(9) The truthfulness of *Mahagonny* may well be greatest when the 'Kraniche-Duett' is omitted. It was omitted in the Berlin 1930 production. But not for that reason. The conventional, and therefore theoretically unacceptable, context for the valedictory sentiments of the 'Kraniche-Duett' is in Act III scene iii. That interpolation can best be justified if it is supported by another which is equally conventional: Jim's aria 'Wenn der Himmel hell wird' (17), which Weill moved from the end of Act II to the start of Act III, must be moved a step further, to the dangerous position occupied by the 'Benares Song'. The 'Benares Song' must then replace 'Wenn der Himmel hell wird' as 17, or else be quietly dropped and allowed once again to fulfil its unique and indisputable role in the *Songspiel*, from which it belatedly came.

(10) The very nature of the work compels us to continue searching for ideal solutions long after we have recognized that there are none to be found.

[?September] 1927, Berlin

Vom Tod im Wald op. 23

(Bertolt Brecht)
Ballad for bass solo and ten wind instruments
Duration: 10 minutes
Instrumentation: 2 cl. 2 bsn. 2 hn. 2 tpt. 1 tbn. 1 bass tbn.

Autographs

SKETCHES

Missing.

DRAFT

Complete on four sides of B²⁶, titled in ink, *c.* 1955, by Lenya. At the foot of the fourth side is a memo of the 2-bar motif that opens *Der Lindberghflug*.

VOCAL SCORE

Eight pages of Fe¹², headed 'Vom Tod im Wald/Bert Brecht/Ballade von Kurt Weill op 23 für eine Bass-Stimme u. 10 Bläser/Klavierauszug'; the score is stamped 'Universal Edition Archiv'.

FULL SCORE

Missing; non-autograph copy in UEA.

First Performance

23 November 1927, Berlin, Philharmonic Hall; Heinrich Hermanns (bass) with members of the Berlin Philharmonic Orchestra conducted by Eugen Lang.

Publication

UE: score and parts for hire.

Notes

Vom Tod im Wald is the last work to which Weill gave an opus number. Unless he misnumbered it, there is a 'missing' Opus 22, which at that stage he may well have associated with *Mahagonny*, whether *Songspiel* or opera. By 1928 the idea of giving an opus number to a work written in collaboration with Brecht would have seemed unduly provocative. Thus the series was allowed to lapse, several years before Weill himself parted company with the concept of 'Opus-Kunst'.

Vom Tod im Wald is also the last work in which Weill used a predominantly non-tonal language. Both for that reason and because it is a singularly uncompanionable piece, it proved quite unsuited to the role he sought for it a year later, when he made it the starting point for his neo-tonal radio cantata *Das Berliner Requiem* (p. 207).

The version of Brecht's poem is from the *Hauspostille* (1927).

October 1927, Berlin

Gustav III

Music for the play by Strindberg
Orchestra: 2.picc.0.2.2. 2.2.1.0. BD. TD. 2SD. cym. tam-tam. trgl. tamb. wbl. rifles glock. vln. harm. pno. unison chorus.

1   Introduction and Fanfare
2   Interlude (Acts I and II) *Allegro non troppo*
3   Interlude (Acts III and IV) *Alla marcia*
4   *Tempo di minuetto*
5   *Allegro – Allegretto – Allegro*
6   *Allegro giusto*
7   *Allegro non troppo*
8   *Allegro molto*
9   *Vivace* (with chorus, 'Carmagnole')

Autographs

SKETCHES AND DRAFTS (ONC)

Four sheets of R^{28} carry a few memos and a nearly continuous rough draft (with marginal memos) of most of the score; all the material was used apart from a march song accompanied by two piccolos. (The composer's name appears in blue crayon near the foot of one of the leaves as if it were a signature, though in fact it is in the hand of Walter Goehr, the conductor of the first performance.) A leaf of the same paper carries further sketches for *8* and *9*, including the quasi-glissando brass motif later used in the Boxing Scene of the *Mahagonny* opera, Act II. On the last two staves of the same leaf – after nine blank staves and, presumably, some lapse of time – Weill has written a memo of the main theme of another of the Act II *Mahagonny* tableaux – the Brothel Scene. A more tenuous connection between *Gustav* and *Mahagonny* is established by a fully worked sheet of B^{28} that dates from April or May 1927: motifs from *Der Zar lässt sich photographieren* are at the head of *b* and halfway down *c*; at the foot of *c* is a fragment of the introduction to the 'Alabama Song' and on *d* is a complete sketch of the last bars of the *Mahagonny-Songspiel*. The second item on *c*, however, is the source of *3* in *Gustav*, while the first on *c* gives the 12-note build-up used at the start of the *Gustav* finale. The most likely inference, given the known dates of the *Songspiel* sketches, is that both of these were rejected ideas for *Der Zar*.

FULL SCORE

Thirty-nine numbered pages of B^{22}, disbound and without title page. There are several contradictory non-autograph paginations in pencil, in red, and in blue crayon. End date '16–19 Oktober/1927'. Affixed to the last page, on the back of a postcard, is a caricature in black ink of a conductor (not Walter Goehr), signed: 'A. 1927'.

Publication

None.

First Performance

29 October 1927, Berlin, Theater in der Königgrätzerstrasse; director Victor Barnowsky, designer Traugott Müller, conductor Walter Goehr; with Rudolf Forster (Gustav III), Karl-Ludwig Achaz (Anckarström), Hans Leibelt (Armfelt), Ernst Stahl-Nachbaur (Schröderheim), Annamarie Steinsieck (Queen Sofia), Maria Fein (Lady Schröderheim).

Notes

The sketches and drafts in the O. W. Neighbour Collection were originally in the music library of Walter Goehr, to whom Weill had given them at the time of the Berlin production. The timing of that gift has a bearing on the composition of the *Mahagonny* opera which is certainly interesting and perhaps of considerable importance. Whereas the sketch for the ending of the *Mahagonny-Songspiel*, like the sketches for *Der Zar*, must date from April or May 1927 and therefore predates the Strindberg sketches on the same R^{28} sheet by five or six months, there can be no doubt that the thematic memo relating to the Brothel Scene in the *Mahagonny* opera is contemporary with the Strindberg drafts on the B^{28} sheets (at this time Goehr was studying with Schoenberg and was close to Eisler; his path was not to cross with Weill's again). To argue that the *Mahagonny* motif was sketched for the Strindberg play and subsequently incorporated in the second act of the opera would be to ignore both the visual evidence and the musical context. The memo has the appearance of a footnote, and in close proximity to it is the trumpet motif used in item 7 of the *Gustav III* music but destined for the orchestral ritornello in the second act of *Mahagonny*. Before we draw any conclusions, one caveat must be entered: the presence in the *Gustav III* music of several ideas from *Na und ?* – including one that later reappeared in the *Mahagonny* opera – does suggest the possibility that the trumpet motif likewise derives from the Joachimson opera. Stylistically there is nothing to preclude such an origin, given the jazz influences at work in *Na und ?* (see p. 164). But the Brothel Scene motif has no obvious precedents in the surviving sections of the Joachimson opera, and is therefore in that sense more questionable. On grounds of probability therefore – and pending the unearthing of the complete *Na und ?* – we must conclude that Weill was already giving serious thought to the second act of the *Mahagonny* opera in October 1927. This tends to confirm that the April 1927 starting date that Weill gives for the *Mahagonny* opera is independent of the *Songspiel*, and that Hans Curjel's memory must have been at fault when he claimed, in discussions with the present writer and with Klemperer's biographer Peter Heyworth, that the idea of the opera arose only from the experience, and the success, of the *Songspiel* at Baden-Baden in July 1927. (See PH.OK, p. 246.)

Posthumous Arrangements

A suite devised by David Drew was first performed on 17 May 1970, at the University of Aberdeen, by an ensemble under the direction of Ian Kemp. The definitive version of this Suite, entitled *Bastille Music*, had its first performance at a Berlin Festival concert at the Akademie der Künste on 13 September 1975. The London Sinfonietta was conducted by David Atherton.

[February] 1928, [Leipzig]

Leben Eduards des Zweiten von England

Music for the play by Bertolt Brecht and Lion Feuchtwanger
(after Marlowe)
(Largely missing)

Brecht follows the broad outlines of Marlowe's plot, but makes considerable changes in the motivation, alters and simplifies the detail, and adopts a rougher tone. The play is summarized at the start, in the manner of travelling theatre:

Here will be publicly presented the History of the troubled reign of Edward the Second, King of England, and his wretched death/As well as the Good Fortune and End of his favourite Gaveston/Further, the unruly Destiny of Queen Anna/ Likewise the Rise and Fall of the great Earl Roger Mortimer/All of which came to pass in England, chiefly in London, six hundred years ago.

Note 1

It is unlikely that Weill's score was extensive. There is no reference to it in his extant correspondence, and no trace of it in WLA.

Autograph

The only known holograph is in BBA (930/22) and was discovered by the archivist Herta Ramthun in a copy of Weill's *Song-Album* (UE, 1929) which belonged to Helene Weigel (see RS.MWB). A leaf of 16-stave music paper (without maker's name) measuring 16.4 × 12.6 cms carries a pencil manuscript of a 16-bar melody, with underlaid text, for the song of the ballad-seller (Balladenverkäufer) in Act I scene ii: 'Edis Kebsweib hat einen Bart auf der Brust' (Eddy's strumpet has hair on his chest).

Note 2

Weill's tune for 'Edis Kebsweib' is oddly suggestive of *Der Kuhhandel* and *Knickerbocker Holiday*. It has no connection with other and earlier melodies for the same ballad, which are in BBA and are tentatively ascribed to Brecht. The first production of the play (Munich 1924) was directed by Brecht himself, and designed by Caspar Neher. There were at least two further productions before the one for which Weill provided music. This was directed by Alwin Kronacher and presented for the first time on 10 March 1928 at the Altes Theater, Leipzig. Less than a month earlier – on 18 February – the Leipzig opera had given in the Neues Theater the world premiere of Weill's *Der Zar lässt sich photographieren* (p. 169).

March 1928, Berlin

Konjunktur

Music for the play by Leo Lania
Song texts by Felix Gasbarra
(Partly missing)
Orchestra: 2 fl., cl., sax., 2 tpts., tbne., pno., timp., perc., vln.

'The hero of this play', wrote Lania in his note for the 1928 Piscator production, 'is petroleum'; and the purpose, he continued, is to portray 'the political and economic forces' governing its development and distribution. The action begins in a backward Balkan-style country. Three local hoodlums strike oil. International speculators move in, and finally the bosses of Royal Dutch Shell, Standard Oil and the Pan-Russian Naptha Syndicate. Thus the stage is set for what Morus, in *Die Weltbühne* (Berlin, 1928, 24/16), described as 'the struggles of the strong and the exploitation of the weak, manslaughter and murder, grandiose fraud and primitive trickery – all for oil's sake'.

The full extent of the musical score is unknown. The sources in KWA and UEA are obviously incomplete. Individual items, though titled, are unnumbered, and the following order is to some extent arbitrary.

    1 Anfang   [Opening]
    2 Landungsbrücke [Jetty]

3 Kleiner Marsch [Little March]
4 Oelblase (Film) [Oil Bubble]
5 Petroleum-Musik [Petroleum-music]
6 Arbeitsrhythmus [Work-rhythm]
7 Arbeiterlied (I. Fassung) [Workers' song, first version]
8 Arbeiterlied (II. Fassung) [Workers' song, second version]
9 Nachtszene [Night-Scene]
10 Muschelsong – Die Muschel von Margate [Mussel-Song. 'The Mussel of Margate']. 'In Margate bei der Promenade'

Autographs

SKETCHES

A single badly damaged leaf on B^{28} carries sketches for 5, 9, and 10. On two of the three available staves at the foot of the first side, directly beneath the opening of 10 (continued on the next side), is an unaccompanied 8-bar melody. In form, in key, and in almost every rhythmic and intervallic detail it is identical with the tenor saxophone's neo-Bachian obbligato in the arrangement of the 'Anstatt-dass Song' (*Die Dreigroschenoper*) which Weill wrote nine months later for the *Kleine Dreigroschenmusik*. The melody does not appear in *Die Dreigroschenoper* itself. The version in the *Konjunktur* sketches is without heading or annotation.

Note 1

The simplest explanation of the apparent intrusion of the *Dreigroschenmusik* obbligato in the *Konjunktur* sketches would be that it post-dated the sketches by eight or nine months. But apart from the graphic evidence – which lends no support to the notion of a later date – such an explanation would require us to accept that at a time when Weill was writing the *Dreigroschenmusik* the only blank staves he could find for a melody that came to him uninvited were at the foot of some old sketches. (The back of an envelope would have served him almost as well, and a vocal score of *Die Dreigroschenoper* very much better.) Assuming, therefore, that the melody belongs to the *Konjunktur* complex, we are left with the much more interesting possibility that in one way or another the 'Anstatt-dass Song' originated in *Konjunktur*. Compositionally the most likely route is the one that would have led Weill to sketch a 12-bar entity corresponding to the 4-bar introduction to the 'Anstatt-dass Song' and its 8-bar accompanimental continuation, and then to conceive the 'unaccompanied' melody as a descant for the continuation. As the *Kleine Dreigroschenmusik* version demonstrates, the resulting counterpoint does not require, or indeed presuppose, the vocal part. It is only in the (homophonic) refrain that the voice parts become formally significant. And yet – as so often in Weill – it is not the melodic developments that ultimately determine the strength and unity of the song, but the harmonic and tonal ones. For that reason, no one familiar with the musical structure of the song – and hence conditioned by the effect of its central masterstroke – will find it easy to dissociate the introduction from the refrain, and imagine the former as twelve bars of open-ended incidental music. It is almost equally hard to imagine it as the introduction to something else, unless the harmonic structure of whatever followed was more or less the same as in the 'Das ist der Mond über Soho' refrain. Since the expressive implications of that structure would have been wholly compatible with a companion piece for the 'Muschelsong', or another militant 'Arbeiterlied', it is certainly possible that *Konjunktur* contained a formal prototype of the 'Anstatt-dass Song', and that the addition of a vocal part to the hitherto instrumental introduction necessitated the omission of the descant melody – which was held in reserve for the Suite. Although the awkward rhythmicization of the 'Anstatt-dass' refrain has an effect that is at once comical and menacing in the context, it could well be the calculated result of imposing a new text whose versification was more free than that of the original work-song (or whatever). Since Brecht was one of Gasbarra's colleagues in the 'collective' that worked on *Konjunktur* (see *Note* 2) we may be sure that he knew all or most of the music Weill wrote for it; and the plan for a 'Beggar's Opera' followed soon afterwards.

VOCAL SCORE (UEA)

10 only, on two sides of B²⁴. Only the first of the four stanzas is in Weill's hand.

FULL SCORE

Fourteen sides of B²⁴, without binding or numbering, carry all the items listed above apart from *3, 5,* and *9. 1* and *2* are on four sides of what looks as if it was originally a gathering of six sides, but the third leaf has been torn off. *10* covers six-and-a-half sides of a damaged folding.

Publication

UE, 1929: *10* only, in *Song-Album*.

First Performance

8 April 1928, Berlin, Piscator-Bühne at the Lessing Theatre; director Erwin Piscator, designer Traugott Müller, conductor Edmund Meisel; with Roma Bahn, Renée Stobrawa, Leonhard Steckel, Curt Bois (Dictator and Monk), Ewald Balser, and Tilla Durieux.

Posthumous Arrangement

Öl-Musik, a suite devised by David Drew and comprising *9, 6, 7, 8* and *10* (in that order) was first performed at the Akademie der Künste, West

Berlin, on 13 September 1975, by the London Sinfonietta under David Atherton, with Meriel Dickinson (mezzo-soprano) and Benjamin Luxon (baritone).

Note 2

Lania's play is sometimes listed under the title *Öl-Konjunktur*. The political background to the premiere – notably the intervention of Soviet emissaries – is described by Piscator in his classic work *Das politische Theater* (Adalbert Schulz, Berlin, 1929).

Brecht had been associated with the Piscator-Bühne since the previous autumn, and had already worked with Lania, Gasbarra, and Piscator on the Hašek adaptation *Die Abenteuer des braven Soldaten Schweyk* – staged in January 1928, and so successful that a second theatre had to be found for *Konjunktur*.

The documentary elements in Lania's play included film; some of Weill's score related to this, and is cued accordingly – e.g. the *ad lib* ostinatos of 6. The extended 'Nachtszene', which survives only in sketch form, was used twenty years later as the introduction to the second act of *Street Scene*.

[March] 1928, Berlin

Katalaunische Schlacht
[*Defeat of the Huns*]

Music for the play by Arnolt Bronnen
(Missing)
  Act I: The German Lines on the Western Front
  Act II: A Paris Cinema
  Act III: An Ocean Liner

First Performance

25 April 1928, Berlin, Staatstheater; producer Heinz Hilpert; designer Traugott Müller; with Maria Bard (Hiddie), Lothar Müthel (Kennedy), Walter Frank (Karl).

Notes

The score was described as 'masterly' by Herbert Ihering in the *Berliner Börsen-Courier* (H. Ihering, *Von Reinhardt bis Brecht*, vol. I: Berlin, 1959, pp. 331–4). The play is typical of Bronnen's post-Expressionist style. Its motivation is implicit in the superscription to Act II: 'The war is finished, but not the people who made it.'

May–August 1928, Berlin/St-Cyr-sur-Mer/Berlin

Die Dreigroschenoper
(*The Threepenny Opera*)

Play with music; text by Bertolt Brecht, after John Gay's *The Beggar's Opera* in the German translation by Elisabeth Hauptmann.
Duration: full evening; 55 minutes music
Cast: singing roles: Macheath, J. J. Peachum, Mrs Peachum, Polly Peachum, Brown, Lucy Brown, Jenny Smith, Street Singer, chorus; other roles: Filch, the Revd Kimball, the gang, beggars, whores, constables.
Orchestra: alto sax. (fl. cl. baritone sax.). tenor sax. (soprano sax. bcl. bsn.) 2 tpt. tbn. (double-bass), bjo. (vlc. gtr. Hawaiian gtr. band. mdln.), timp. perc. harm. (cel.). pno-conductor.

The action closely follows Gay. The gangster Macheath 'marries' Polly Peachum, whose father is boss of London's beggars; flees Peachum's wrath; is betrayed by the whore Jenny, captured, and imprisoned; escapes; is recaptured, taken to the gallows, and miraculously reprieved.

Note 1

The order of numbers given below corresponds to that of the holograph scores except that Weill begins his numbering not with the Ouvertüre but with the Moritat. The 'Eifersucht' aria of Lucy (22y) was omitted from both the holograph scores. It was intended for Act II scene ii, and was presumably written with a trained singer in mind.

    1 Ouvertüre

Prologue: The Annual Fair in Soho
    2 Moritat vom Mackie Messer (Street Singer): 'Und der Haifisch, der hat Zähne'

ACT I

Scene i: Jonathan Jeremiah Peachum's Wardrobe-room
    3 Morgenchoral des Peachum (Peachum): 'Wach auf, du verrotteter Christ!'
    4 Anstatt-dass-Song (Mr and Mrs Peachum): 'Anstatt dass sie zu Hause bleiben'
       refrain: 'Das ist der Mond über Soho'

Scene ii: An Empty Stable
    5 Hochzeitslied (chorus): 'Bill Lawgen und Mary Syer'
    6 Seeräuberjenny (Polly): 'Meine Herrn, heut sehn Sie mich Gläser aufwaschen'
       refrain: 'Und ein Schiff mit acht Segeln'
    7 Kanonen Song (Macheath, Brown): 'John war darunter und Jim war dabei'
       refrain: 'Soldaten wohnen auf den Kanonen'

8 Liebeslied (Polly, Macheath): 'Siehst du den Mond über Soho?'
    refrain: 'Und gibt es kein Schriftstück vom Standesamt?'

Scene iii: Peachum's Wardrobe-room
9 Barbara Song (Polly): 'Einst glaubte ich, als ich noch unschuldig war'
    refrain: 'Ja da kann man sich doch nicht nur hinlegen'
10 I. Dreigroschenfinale (Polly, Peachum, Mrs Peachum): 'Was ich möchte,
    ist es viel?'

ACT II

Scene i: The Stable
11 Melodrama (Macheath): 'Die Liebe dauert oder dauert nicht'
11a Polly's Lied (Polly): 'Hübsch als es währte'

Interlude
12 Ballade von der sexuellen Hörigkeit (Mrs Peachum): 'Da ist man einer
    schon der Satan selber'

Scene ii: A Brothel in Wapping
13 Zuhälterballade (Macheath, Jenny): 'In einer Zeit, die jetzt
    vergangen ist'

Scene iii: The Old Bailey – a Cage
14 Ballade vom angenehmen Leben (Macheath): 'Da preist man uns das
    Leben grosser Geister'
    refrain: 'Das simple Leben lebe, wer da mag!'
15 Eifersuchtsduett (Lucy, Polly): 'Komm heraus, du Schönheit von Soho'
    refrain: 'Mackie und ich, wir lebten wie die Tauben'
16 II. Dreigroschenfinale (Macheath, Mrs Peachum and chorus): 'Ihr Herrn,
    die ihr uns lehrt, wie man brav leben'
    refrain: 'Denn wovon lebt der Mensch?'

ACT III

Scene i: Peachum's Wardrobe-room
17 Lied von der Unzulänglichkeit menschlichen Strebens: 'Der Mensch lebt
    durch den Kopf'

Interlude
18 Salomon Song (Jenny): 'Ihr saht den weisen Salomon'

Scene ii: A Room in the Old Bailey

Scene iii: The death cell
19 Ruf aus der Gruft (Macheath): 'Nun hört die Stimme, die um
    Mitleid ruft'
20 Grabschrift (Macheath): 'Ihr Menschenbrüder, die ihr nach uns lebt'
20a Gang zum Galgen (orchestra)
21 III. Dreigroschenfinale (Chorus, Brown, Macheath, Polly, Mrs Peachum,
    Peachum): 'Horch! wer kommt?'
    chorale: 'Verfolgt das Unrecht nicht zu sehr'

Cut number
22y Arie der Lucy (Lucy): 'Eifersucht! Wut, Liebe und Furcht zugleich'

Autographs

SKETCHES

Missing.

DRAFT

Missing.

REHEARSAL SCORE AND PRODUCTION MASTER (UEA)

The unpaginated manuscript has been assembled piecemeal, one number to a sheet or folding, except for *8* and *12*, which are paired. It covers some forty-six sides of various papers – B^{12}, B^{14}, and B^{24} – and has no title page, binding or cover wrap. Not all the manuscript is Weill's: the holograph was subsequently worked over by Norbert Gingold, and became the production master for the published vocal score (in which the piano reduction is ascribed to Gingold, although by far the greater contribution is Weill's, and is not in fact a 'reduction' at all). Gingold has signed the first page of each number in red crayon at the top, noting that it has been 'eingerichtet' (put in order). The 'putting in order' is partly editorial; largely, however, it is a matter of amending and elaborating Weill's manuscript in the light of the subsequent full score. Where the full score alters or amplifies characteristic figurations in any fundamental sense, Gingold adapts the holograph accordingly. *17* is the only number for which he supplies a complete reduction of his own to replace Weill's rehearsal score. Other reductions are called for only when Weill has restricted his rehearsal score to a single stanza (or verse and refrain), and reserved the variants for the full score. *2, 7, 10* and *14* have Gingold's reductions of later stanzas. Two items are missing altogether: the 'Barbara Song', and the very brief 'Gang zum Galgen'.

At the close of the third finale Weill has written the words 'Ende der "Beggars Opera"'. It is a reminder that the final title of the play was a late addition. Among the provisional titles noted by Brecht were *Gesindel* ('Rabble') and *Die Ludenoper* ('The Rascals' Opera' or 'Lewd-fellows' opera'). For more details see Werner Hecht (ed.), *Brecht's 'Dreigroschenoper'*, Frankfurt, 1985, pp. 17ff.

Evidence that the music was composed while the play was still incomplete may be found in the numbering of the rehearsal score. But in this respect as in others, caution is advisable. It is certainly significant that Weill stops his numbering at *14* and leaves blank spaces for the subsequent numbering (which has been filled in by Gingold in red crayon). This, however, may merely have been in anticipation of the belated interpolation of the 'Salomon Song'. Yet the earlier numbering – including the misnumbering of *5* and *6* – is not necessarily contemporary with the musical manuscript. In one case it almost certainly is not: in the folding that tellingly pairs the 'Ballade von der sexuellen Hörigkeit' (*12*) with the Polly–Macheath 'Liebeslied' (8), the later number precedes the earlier one.

Holograph rehearsal scores of 9, in an earlier version, and of 11a in its original form as 'Marie, Fürsprecherin der Frauen' (after Rudyard Kipling) are in the legacy of Kate Kühl (AdK, 72.70), the creator of the role of Lucy. Both manuscripts are described and critically assessed by Fritz Hennenberg in his essay 'Weill, Brecht und Die Dreigroschenoper' in the Oesterreichische Musik-Zeitschrift (Vienna), Jg. 40/6, June 1985, 281ff.

FULL SCORE (UEA)

Fifty pages of B^{22}, B^{14}, B^{30}, S^{26} and BC^{24}; the original binding has been destroyed and the score is now stored in a folder. It is dated at the end '23 August 1928 Charlottenburg', and is without a title page.

LIBRETTOS (UEA)

Typescript

Fifty-four numbered pages (the first two acts are top copies, the third carbons), plus four unnumbered preliminary pages including title page: 'Die Dreigroschenoper/(nach 'The Beggars Opera' von John Gay)/von / Brecht/Musik von Kurt Weill'. There are numerous manuscript corrections and additions, mostly in the hand of Brecht; Weill has inserted the music cues in red crayon.

Galley Proofs

These have been set from the typescript copy described above; there are numerous manuscript corrections by Weill and (?)Elisabeth Hauptmann. Weill again inserts the music cues in red crayon. There is evidence of second thoughts about the precise cue for 11; the typescript has it at Macheath's words 'Und jetzt adieu mein Herz', but Weill's manuscript shifts it to 'bin ich schon hinter dem Moor von Highgate'. An entirely new cue, inserted by Weill in pencil rather than crayon, suggests playing the Moritat very quietly in 3/4 time at the entry of Brown shortly before the second finale (16).

First Performance

31 August 1928, Berlin, Theater am Schiffbauerdamm; director Erich Engel, designer Caspar Neher, conductor Theo Mackeben; with Harald Paulsen (Macheath), Roma Bahn (Polly), Kate Kühl (Lucy), Lotte Lenya (Jenny), Erich Ponto (Peachum), Kurt Gerron (Brown), Ernst Busch (Smith, and Street Singer).

Publications

UE, 1928: vocal score, omitting 12, reduction by Norbert Gingold; piano-conductor score – anonymous arranger, copious errors; single numbers – 2, 6, 7, 8, 9, 13; libretto.

Ullstein, 1929: condensed piano score, with vocal lines incorporated on the two systems, and parallel texts; subpublished by Ullstein, Berlin, in the *Musik für Alle* series, with article by Paul Wiegler, illustrations from the stage production, and a reproduction of part of a draft of *14*, differing from the rehearsal score in UEA.

UE, 1930: vocal score of *12*, in *Song-Album*.

Die Musik, 1932: vocal score of *22y*, published as a supplement to the November 1932 issue of *Die Musik* (Berlin, vol. 25 no. 2) together with a brief 'Anmerkung zu der unterdrückten Arie der Lucy' (Note on the suppressed Lucy-aria).

SUITES AND (AUTHORIZED) ARRANGEMENTS; ADDENDA

1928: jazz arrangements of *2* by Isko Thaler and *7* and *13* by Jerzy Fitelberg.

1929: *Kleine Dreigroschenmusik für Blasorchester* (see p. 211), Weill's arrangement for wind orchestra of Ouverture, *17/1, 4, 14, 11a, 13, 7, 19, 20, 21* in that order.

1929: *Sieben Stücke aus der Dreigroschenoper* – Stefan Frenkel's virtuoso arrangement for violin and piano of *2, 19, 14, 11a, 13, 6* and *7* in that order. Though opposed in principle to arrangements of his music by other hands, Weill rightly regarded Frenkel's Suite as exceptional and commended it to UE.

1937: two songs specially composed for Ernst Aufricht's production of *L'Opéra de quat' sous* at the Théâtre des Etoiles, Paris. The songs were written for the Mrs Peachum (Yvette Guilbert), and the texts were by Guilbert herself. Although Weill assured Aufricht that they were 'zwei sehr gute Dreigroschenoper-Chansons', the one that has survived (see p. 293) is so far removed from his 1928 style that he cannot have considered it appropriate to anything other than the requirements of the Paris production.

1938: *The Judgement of Paris*, ballet by Antony Tudor, first performed by the Ballet Club at the Mercury Theatre, London, July 1938; first American production by Ballet Theatre, New York, 23 January 1940; often revived since 1945, notably by Ballet Rambert. The score for *The Judgement of Paris* was compiled by Tudor himself and arranged for two pianos by his musical assistant John Cooke. Although the circumstances of 1938 seem to have precluded consultations with Weill or with Universal Edition, Weill was invited in 1940 to prepare an orchestral version of the score for the Ballet Theatre production. Not surprisingly he declined. The anonymous orchestration used by Ballet Theatre is probably the work of Harold Byrns, the German-born conductor who was at that time the company's musical director. The score was registered for copyright purposes at the Library of Congress.

1942: 'Kanonen Song' and 'Barbara Song', arranged by the composer for Lenya's recording of *Six Songs* (p. 327).

Note 2

CONTEMPORARY PERFORMANCE PRACTICE AND CURRENT RESEARCH

Dr Fritz Hennenberg, the Leipzig musicologist and author of the standard work on Paul Dessau, has since the early 1980s been at the forefront of European research into the work of composers associated with Brecht. As editor and compiler of *Das grosse Brecht-Liederbuch* (Berlin/Frankfurt, 1984) and as contributor to *Brecht's 'Dreigroschenoper'* (Frankfurt, 1985; ed. Werner Hecht) he has significantly enlarged the area of knowledge about Brecht in general and *Die Dreigroschenoper* in particular. With regard to Weill his most important publication to date has been the essay 'Weill, Brecht und die "Dreigroschenoper"' (*Oesterreichische Musik-Zeitschrift*, Jg. 40/6, Vienna, June 1985). As well as providing useful examples of the numerous discrepancies between holograph, typescript, and printed sources, Hennenberg touches on the complex topic of performance practice. Until recently the principal sources for research in this field have been the commercial recordings of 1929–30, and especially those conducted by Theo Mackeben. In 1984 these were supplemented by the discovery of a set of orchestral parts used and marked by Mackeben himself – not an official UE set, but a manuscript set diverging from Weill's full score in numerous details. (The originals are in the possession of Mackeben's heirs in Berlin; photostat copies are in WLRC.) A detailed study of the Mackeben material is now (1986) being prepared by the British conductor and musicologist Geoffrey Abbott; his report on it will be included in the 'Cambridge Opera Handbook' on *Die Dreigroschenoper* which Dr Stephen Hinton is editing for Cambridge University Press.

An examination of Mackeben's role before and after the premiere of *Die Dreigroschenoper* has long been overdue. Mackeben's own musical ambitions and his eventual success as a composer of operetta, revue and film music in Germany after 1933 need to be taken into account, for whatever the nature and extent of his influence on Weill during the composition of *Die Dreigroschenoper*, his natural tendency would have been to adapt the score to the exigencies of the moment once the production had become a box-office success. Dr Hennenberg has noted the gradual accretion of 'incidental music' in *Die Dreigroschenoper*, but has failed to remark that waltz-time and *alla funebre* versions of the Moritat, for example, are as foreign to the original form and spirit of the score as they are appropriate to the atmosphere of a box-office hit and the distribution of an internationally financed film version. It was in defence of that form and spirit that Weill brought his case against the producers of Pabst's *Dreigroschenoper* film (whose musical director was Mackeben); and it was in the same cause that ten years later he rejected T. W. Adorno's arguments in favour of a free jazz improvisation.* At the very

---

*See KK.ANO, pp. 248–9, for the present author's account of Weill's dispute with Adorno.

end of his life Weill was refusing to countenance changes to the *Dreigroschenoper* score proposed by the Munich Kammerspiele and apparently backed by such authorities as Carl Orff and Karl-Amadeus Hartmann. When the Kammerspiele nevertheless went ahead with the changes, ostensibly in the interests of 'updating' the score, Weill took legal action.* He was equally adamant in his opposition to Brecht's 'updatings' of the song texts. There too he found himself defending the universality of the original against the claims of actuality.

Weill's instinct was right. If the *Dreigroschenoper* score and text had needed modernizing in 1949, they would have needed it again four or five years later and at similar intervals ever since. While Brecht's case for topicalizing the text had at least the merit of clarity, recurrent pleas for permission to modernize the score are often blurred by an underlying and unacknowledged financial or commercial interest. In the theatre – whether public or private – such interests deserve acknowledgement. The problem is clear: in 1928 the twenty-three instruments of Weill's orchestra (counting percussion as one) were allotted to a mere eight players; in today's professional conditions about twice that number might be called for if the letter of Weill's score is to be observed. As the cost of fidelity to his declared intentions increases, so does the need to understand the musical sense of it. As that understanding increases in its turn, so does the possibility of making allowances for changed conditions.

Note 3

Marc Blitzstein's 'English adaptation' – begun shortly after Weill's death and first heard on 14 June 1952 at Brandeis University in a concert performance conducted by Leonard Bernstein – played an indispensable role in the Weill revival of the 1950s. Its success made possible the off-Broadway production of *The Threepenny Opera* which opened at the Theater de Lys on 10 March 1954, with Lotte Lenya as Jenny (a renascence already witnessed at Brandeis). The Theater de Lys production, by Carmen Capalbo, became one of the longest-running musical shows in the history of the American theatre. It was the springboard for Lotte Lenya's international career, and – with powerful help from Louis Armstrong's recording – the source of one of the major 'hits' of the century, 'Mack the Knife'. Blitzstein's contribution to that 'hit' is characteristic of his version as a whole. Vulnerable though the version is from several points of view, and superseded as it has been by more faithful and academically respectable renderings, it remains unmatched

---

*See Weill to Brecht, 14 February 1949; Karlheinz Gutheim to Weill, 18 February 1949; and Weill to Brecht, and also to his German agent, in May 1949. (Copies of all letters and cables are in WLA.)

in its musicality – its instinctive response to the gist, the gait, and the timbre of Weill's music. It is not a response likely to pacify scholars who find more Blitzstein than Brecht in the adaptation; but it is certainly one of the reasons why Blitzstein's version captured the popular imagination at that decisive moment – a moment that would never return – and why, in consequence, it has become part of the 'legend' of *The Threepenny Opera*. Whatever the superior merits of its successors in whatever language, its historic role is unchallengeable.

Blitzstein's titles and first lines are given below according to the numbering system adopted for the German original:

1   Overture
2   The Ballad of 'Mack the Knife': 'Oh the shark has pretty teeth, dear'
3   Morning Anthem: 'Wake up all you godless, wake up'
4   Instead-of Song: 'Instead of staying home at night behaving'
5   Wedding Song: 'Bill Lawgun and Mary Sawyer'
6   Pirate Jenny: 'You gentlemen can watch while I'm scrubbing the floors'
7   Army Song: 'Johnny joined up and Jimmy was there'
8   Love Song: 'You see the moon over Dock Street'
9   Barbara Song: 'I used to believe, in the days I was pure'
10 First Threepenny Finale – The World is Mean: 'All I'm asking, isn't much'
11 Melodrama
11a Polly's Song: 'Sweet while it lasted, and now it is over'
12 The Ballad of Dependency: 'Now there's a man, a living tool of Satan'
13 Tango-Ballade: 'There was a time, and now it's all gone by'
14 Ballad of the Easy Life: 'They tell you that the best in life is mental'
15 Jealousy Duet: 'Come on out, you gutter-lily you'
16 Second Threepenny Finale – How to Survive: 'Now those among you full of pious teaching'
17 Useless Song: 'If first you don't succeed, then try and try again'
18 Solomon Song: 'Remember wise old Solomon'
19 Call from the Grave: 'Oh hear me calling to you, come and save'
20 Walk to the Gallows (orchestra)
21 Third Threepenny Finale: 'Hark! Hark! Hark! Victorious messenger riding comes'

Addendum

The 'Bilbao Song' from *Happy End* was translated by Blitzstein and incorporated in the 1956 London production of his version, under the title 'Bide-a-wee in Soho'.

Note 4

HOW WAS WEILL'S SUCCESS ACHIEVED?

The success of [Weill's] music for *Mahagonny* and the other Brecht works is not in question. But how was that success achieved? Brecht sometimes intimated that he himself contributed some or all of the tunes of *The Threepenny Opera*. For years I considered this a boast. Later I came to believe it.

Eric Bentley, 'Introduction: Homage to B.B.' (*Seven Plays by Bertolt Brecht*, edited by Eric Bentley, Grove Press, New York, 1961, xxxiv)

Eric Bentley was by no means the first to whom Brecht had imparted some such view of Weill's success. As far as *Mahagonny* was concerned (see p. 175) a comparable view had been circulating since the late 1920s. But *Die Dreigroschenoper* was at that time much bigger game; and the fact that Brecht's claim to co-authorship of the music is not known to have been aired in public during Weill's lifetime may simply indicate our need for further research. The speed with which the claim was beginning to circulate at the time of Brecht's death in 1956 – the very time when Blitzstein's *Threepenny Opera* adaptation and Louis Armstrong's 'Mack the Knife' recording were bringing Weill his first posthumous success – already suggested what the letter and the spirit of Bentley's 1961 'Homage' confirmed: the theory that Brecht himself 'contributed some or all of the tunes' had been part of the Brechtian folklore 'for years', if not for decades, and had now been assimilated by the posthumous cult. In 1961 Bentley already seemed to accept it as an article of faith rather than as something requiring verification, and until the 1980s that faith remained the only basis for acceptance, apart from the doubtful testimony of those who were claiming to have witnessed the collaboration at first hand.

Musicologically and in other respects the picture was transformed in the 1980s by the discovery of some early Brecht settings by Franz Servatius Bruinier, a cabaret musician who was born in the Rhineland in 1905 and worked closely with Brecht between 1925 and 1927. Among these settings are versions of two songs later used in *Die Dreigroschenoper*: 'Seeräuberjenny' (6) and the 'Barbara Song' (9). The latter need not detain us here, as its bearing on Weill's setting is insignificant. 'Seeräuberjenny' is very much more interesting. The material in the Brecht Archive (BBA 249/53–9) consists of a vocal part and an incomplete set of band parts – trumpet, alto saxophone, banjo, and percussion. The voice part is titled 'Seeräuber-Jenny/Text u. Musik von B. Brecht/Arrangement von F. S. Bruinier', and dated 8 March 1927 – the very month when Weill began working with Brecht on the *Mahagonny* opera.

The basic character-contrast between verse and refrain in the Brecht–Bruinier version has been adopted by Weill and immeasurably enhanced by his recomposition of the verse and his transformation of the refrain in terms of what has preceded it and what is yet to come. The fact that he follows the 11-bar outline of Brecht's refrain almost exactly in his own 5-bar version of it was, for many Brecht scholars, a revelation of the truth they and their forebears had taken more or less on trust for so many years. Fritz Hennenberg's pioneering researches into the Bruinier–Brecht collaboration (BB.GBL vol. 1) have been continued by Albrecht Dümling, who proves less circumspect than his predecessor when he writes (AD.BM. p. 133),

> The astonishing refrain, which is one of the most celebrated melodic ideas that occurred to Brecht, was in 1928 transferred by Weill to *Die Dreigroschen-*

oper almost unchanged. It is not out of the question that other melodies in *Die Dreigroschenoper* also derive from Brecht.

Certainly it is not out of the question. But until we have further evidence, Dümling's conjecture belongs to the same department of quasi-mystical faith as Bentley's 1961 'Homage'. In his excitement at the discovery of Brecht–Bruinier, Dümling seems to have lost his grip on musical and other facts. For what is both 'astonishing' and 'celebrated' is not Brecht's serviceable but in itself unremarkable idea; it is Weill's composition of it. Bruinier may have been the first musician to board Brecht's 'Schiff mit acht Segeln' but it was Weill who took it to sea and steered it to its destination with all its cannon blazing.

Ultimately the discovery of the Brecht–Bruinier song can do nothing but good. The stir it created in 1984 is already shown to be as naïve as the consternation Diaghilev allegedly expressed on being shown that the well-loved tunes in Stravinsky's *Firebird* were exactly what any 14-year-old might have guessed they were: Russian folk tunes. On a humbler level the same is true of 'Seeräuberjenny': whether the pirate ship is sailing under Brecht's flag or Weill's, the contour, ictus, and intervallic structure of the refrain proclaim a Slavonic origin (and it is one that Weill in no way disguises). Innumerable parallels could doubtless be found in Russian folk song up to and including the time of the October Revolution. One example that was in its day considerably more 'celebrated' than Brecht's melody is the tune used by the Soviet composer Lev Knipper for his 'Cavalry of the Steppes'. Its contour relationship with the 'Seeräuber' refrain would hardly have escaped Weill's amused attention when he made his orchestral arrangement of Knipper's tune in 1943 (see p. 331).

Since most of the melodically distinctive passages in Brecht's tunes are borrowed from popular sources, it is by no means 'out of the question' that the 'Seeräuber' refrain is another borrowing, and will sooner or later be identified as such. In that event a song already rich in associations will have acquired a further layer of them, and the credit due to Brecht for the inspiration of combining these particular words with this particular melodic line will be increased accordingly.

Whatever has yet to be revealed, the decisive inspiration in the song is Weill's and Weill's alone. The very fact that at a structurally crucial point the melodic line is a borrowing confirms the evidence of our ears: as so often in Weill, the structural priorities are harmonic and tonal, not linear. The refrain, as Dümling remarks, is 'astonishing'; but only because of the tonal events that have preceded it and the harmonic ones that then explode its own cadential structure.

Nevertheless Brecht–Bruinier compels one to ask what mysterious force drew Weill to the refrain and prompted so powerful a reaction to its East European melos. For a while it seemed as if another cryptic clause had been added to the song's anarchic–revolutionary programme –

without loss to its messianic associations, but also without enriching them. But quite soon after the discovery of the Brecht–Bruinier song a complementary discovery on the Weill side solved the riddle – at no expense to the song's fascination – by adding to the broadly Russian resonances of the refrain a specifically Jewish one. In 1985 the definitive version of Weill's *Ofrah's Lieder* of 1916 was acquired by the Library of Congress (see p. 102). Among the songs that were not in the draft versions previously available in the Weill–Lenya Research Center was a setting of Jehuda Halevi's 'Denkst du des kühnen Flugs der Nacht', a passionate nocturnal invocation to the beloved. At the very start a precipitously chromatic progression from somewhere in the region of G minor affords a longer glimpse of the mature Weill than any other passage in this adolescent cycle. With the arrival at F sharp major, the Late Romantic vistas in which the heavenly bridegroom and the earthly became indistinguishable seem once more to be opening out. At this point, and at the words 'Sie schmückten nur mein Angesicht' (starting on an unaccompanied F sharp upbeat), the piano inserts a B minor root-position triad, and voice and piano together outline a 7-note motif identical with the head-motif of the 'Seeräuberjenny' refrain; not however in Brecht–Bruinier's version and key, but in Weill's slightly altered version and in the same key.

At the unconscious level where his mature imagination is always most deeply stirred, Weill has returned to his origins, his home, and his earliest creative experience. This is the world of which Ernst Bloch had so profound an intuition when he wrote his classic essay on 'Seeräuber-jenny' (1929) and dedicated it to Weill and Lenya. It was not a world that Weill needed or would have wished to share with Brecht, but the values that were part of it were also a part of everything he contributed to *Die Dreigroschenoper*.

The marriage Weill has arranged between Halevi's ecstatic bride and Brecht's apocalyptic pirate leaves the artlessness of Brecht–Bruinier and the artiness of *Ofrah's Lieder* far behind. But since the motif that united them is still the merest cliché, the validity of the contract might well be in question had the banns been announced only once. How, then, does Weill treat the 'Barbara Song', and the rather less permanent domestic arrangements it records? About them, Brecht and Bruinier have nothing of any musical account to say. Weill on the other hand discovers a refrain no less 'celebrated' than that of 'Seeräuberjenny'. Melodically its head-motif is also a cliché; and it too has very strong East European associations. Its first appearance in Weill – or at least the first we know of – is in his setting of Eichendorff's 'Sehnsucht' (p. 101), which dates from 1916. The motif reappears that same year at the very start of the second of *Ofrah's Lieder* – 'Nichts ist die Welt bei mir'.

'The world is nothing to me.' The means whereby Weill repeatedly expresses that sentiment in his *Dreigroschenoper* music, but only and always in order to refute it, are characteristic of his own peculiar dialectic. In them will be found the true secrets of his success.

October 1928

Berlin im Licht

(a) Song for voice and piano (text by Weill)
(b) March for military band
   Commissioned by the sponsors of the 'Berlin im Licht' Exhibition, 13–16 October 1928
Duration: 3 minutes
Orchestra: 1.1.Eb cl.3.1.   2flhn. 2 tenor hn. 2 baritone hn. 2.2.1.   perc.

Autographs

No holographs of the song have yet been traced. The full score of the military-band version is in UEA. The first three sides of a folding of B³⁰ carry the introductory section. Swiftly written in another hand, it resembles an assistant's realization of a short-score draft rather than an orchestrator's version of a voice-and-piano version. The refrain, or trio, is scored by Weill himself and covers the fifth and sixth sides of the folding. As the refrain is simpler to arrange as well as shorter, pressure of time is the likeliest explanation for the division of labour. The non-autograph script somewhat resembles that of Jerzy Fitelberg.

Publication

UE, 1928: the song was published in a popular voice-and-piano edition; the military-band version was available on hire.

First Performances

13 October 1928, Berlin, Wittenberg Platz: open-air concert given by a military band conducted by Hermann Scherchen; 16 October 1928, song version performed by Paul Graetz at a late-night revue at the Kroll Opera.

Arrangement

1928: by Otto Lindemann, for jazz band and singer.

Notes

Weill signed his publishing agreement with Universal Edition for *Berlin im Licht* on 17 October 1928. Added to the typescript agreement are the (non-autograph) words 'Text von Weill selbst'. Since the agreement itself is based on the express understanding that no other copyright is involved, the addition seems superfluous. On the other hand, there is no doubt that Brecht helped with the text: BBA (452/63) holds Brecht's fair-copy typescript of three stanzas.

November 1928

Petroleuminseln
(*The Oil Islands*)

Music for the play by Lion Feuchtwanger
(Partly missing)

Deborah Gray is President of the Island Oil Company and owner of most of the Brown Islands. She describes herself as 'hideous to look at, living entirely on oil, creating wealth out of society's blunders, quite unmoved by the thrills of the class war, and uninterested in God'. Her share of the international oil markets is already great, and she intends to increase it. To that end she starts an intrigue with H. B. Ingram, an international oil agent in the pay of Moscow. Her rival is Charmian Peruchacha, a dazzling beauty whom the islanders regard as their 'good angel'. Miss Gray swindles Ingram, has Charmian disposed of, and emerges from the struggle more powerful then ever.

Note 1

The play contains three songs:
1   Das Lied von den Braunen Inseln – 'Petroleum Song'
2   Lelio Holyday's Song (Act II scene i)
3   The Producer's Song (Act II scene ix)

'Das Lied von den Braunen Inseln' is first heard as a gramophone record played by passengers on a ship bound for the Brown Islands. It is subsequently used by other characters, and by the islanders in chorus, as a means both of mocking Miss Gray and of deploring the spoliation of the once beautiful islands.

Autographs

SKETCHES

Recto of a leaf of P[16] carries a rough sketch of the refrain of *1* in an arrangement for 3-part *a cappella* chorus, together with a 16-bar melody entitled 'Heilsarmee'. (As there is no evident occasion for Salvation Army music in the play, the latter may have been destined for another purpose.) Random accidentals have been playfully added by another hand to the 3-part setting; there are also some non-autograph notes of dramatic cues. On the reverse side there is a non-autograph notation of 'Yankee-Doodle'.

REHEARSAL SCORE

1, on a single side of B²⁶, is in UEA. *2* and *3* are missing.

FULL SCORE

Missing (*1* only? – *2* was to be accompanied by guitar, *3* has no specification).

Publication

UE, 1929: *1*, in *Song-Album*.

First Performance with Weill's Music

28 November 1928, Berlin, Staatstheater; producer Jürgen Fehling, designer Caspar Neher; with Maria Koppenhöfer (Deborah), Lotte Lenya (Charmian), Eugen Klöpfer (Ingram), Lothar Müthel (Holyday)

Note 2

According to the Staatstheater programme, Weill wrote only the songs; the incidental music was improvised by a jazz band, Sidney Kay's Fellows. The gramophone recording of *1* was made by the Lewis Ruth Band, and released commercially (Paloma 3502). A setting of *2* under the title 'Ballade des Herrn B. W. Smith' was the third number in Walter Goehr's radio cantata *Pep* (Baden-Baden, 1929).

November–December 1928, Berlin

Das Berliner Requiem

'Little Cantata after poems by Brecht'
For tenor, baritone, male chorus (or tenor, baritone and bass soloists
   only) and wind orchestra
Commissioned by the Reichs-Rundfunkgesellschaft
Dedication: Frankfurt Radio
Duration: (performing edition) 18½ minutes
Orchestra: 0.0.2.2 sax.2.   2.2.2.1.   timp. gtr. perc. org. or harm.

Note 1

Although the commission was fulfilled and the Cantata performed, subsequent borrowings and insertions left the work in some disarray; and the loss of both the holograph full score and the original performance material has meant that the precise nature of the minor revisions Weill made during rehearsals (such as the introduction of a male chorus where previously there had been three male soloists) can only be surmised. A more radical revision was planned but never carried out. The first five items in the following list represent the vestiges of the Cantata in a performable order approximating as closely as possible to Weill's intentions, but requiring a conclusion – for which a repeat of the opening chorale is an adequate substitute, and one that corresponds to Weill's thoughts about that number.

1   Grosser Dankchoral (Great Chorale of Thanksgiving) for chorus:
     'Lobet die Nacht!'
2   Ballade vom ertrunkenen Mädchen (Ballad of the drowned girl) for trio
     or chorus: 'Als sie ertrunken war und hinunterschwamm'
3   Marterl (Memorial Tablet) for tenor and chorus: 'Hier ruht die Jungfrau
     Johanna Beck'
3a   [alternative to 3] Grabschrift 1919 (Gravestone 1919) for tenor and
     chorus: 'Die rote Rosa schon lang verschwand'
4   Erster Bericht über den unbekannten Soldaten (First Report on the
     Unknown Soldier) for tenor and chorus: 'Wir kamen von den Gebirgen'
5   Zweiter Bericht über den unbekannten Soldaten (Second Report)
     for baritone and chorus: 'Alles, was ich euch sagte'
6y   'Zu Potsdam unter den Eichen' (To Potsdam under the Oak Trees)
     for trio
7x   'Können einem toten Mann nicht helfen' (Can't help a dead man)
     for trio

Note 2

The poems are from various stages in Brecht's development. Since most of them were unpublished or inaccessible, Brecht must have 'collaborated' at least to the extent of making them available. Whether his contribution went further than that is doubtful. Like the title, the selection of poems lacks the kind of precision that was characteristic of Brecht, and the original idea of opening the Cantata with Weill's 1927 setting of *Vom Tod im Wald* (p. 186) is one that cannot conceivably have been suggested by Brecht: striking as it is, the Expressionist manner of the setting emphasizes how remote the poem is from Brecht's preoccupations of 1928. Even from Weill's point of view, it was an eccentric idea: *Vom Tod im Wald* is so fiercely self-contained that it defies incorporation in another work, and seems even to resist inclusion in a concert programme. Weill's failure to foresee the risks was a miscalculation from which the Cantata never recovered. His first plan was for *Vom Tod im Wald* to be followed by 'Können einem toten Mann nicht helfen' and then the sequence 2–5 with a concluding 'Grosser Dankchoral'. Shortly before the premiere he realized that *Vom Tod im Wald* was incompatible, and decided to substitute 'Zu Potsdam unter den Eichen' (see p. 222). This, apparently, was the version of the Cantata broadcast from Frankfurt. It was not performed again. Weill's subsequent decision to remove 'Können einem toten Mann nicht helfen' and convert it into the closing statement in the *Mahagonny* opera meant that another substitute would have to be found, and also that the vocal score of the Cantata announced for publication in 1929 could not appear. Early in 1930 Weill proposed introducing the *a cappella* chorus *Die Legende vom toten Soldaten* (see p. 222), regardless of the fact that it called for a mixed chorus. Again the order of numbers was to be changed, and now there was also talk of a new and more convenient orchestration. But Weill was busy with other projects; and he was still busy a year later, when he next thought of the work. As far as we know he had no opportunity to work on the Cantata before he fled from Germany in March 1933; thereafter, he had no incentive. The Cantata was not heard again until the mid-1960s, when the present writer prepared a performing edition, first published in 1967 (with introductory notes more detailed than these).

Autographs

SKETCHES AND DRAFTS

Missing except for pencil draft of 3 ('Marterl') on the first side of a single sheet of 22-line paper (35.2 × 27.2 cms) with non-autograph pagination 39–40. The draft was in UEA, probably because of an oversight on Weill's part as there is no apparent reason for him to have sent it to his publishers. It is numbered '4' and carries some notes of instrumentation.

FULL SCORE

Missing, except for 1, on four sides of B^{26}. The separation of this number from the rest of the holograph may well have come about if – as is conceivable – Weill rescored the chorale following his decision to use a full male chorus.

Non-Autograph Material (UEA)

FULL SCORE

A contemporary fair-copy full score, including *Vom Tod im Wald* and *7x*, but not the full score of *6y*, which is lost. The title page reads: 'Dem Frankfurter Sender gewidmet/Das Berliner Requiem/Kleine Kantate/ für/3 Männerstimmen u.Blasorchester/nach Texten von Bert Brecht'.

VOCAL SCORE

1929, by Norbert Gingold.

Publication 1

UE, 1929: 3 only, in *Song-Album*.

First Performance

22 May 1929, Radio Frankfurt; Hans Grahl (tenor), Johannes Willy (baritone), Jean Stern (bass); with Reinhold Merten (organ) and the Frankfurt Radio Orchestra, conducted by Ludwig Rottenberg.

Posthumous Arrangements

In 1960 Walter Goehr made two versions of 'Zu Potsdam unter den Eichen', as replacements for the lost full score: the first was for the same forces as indicated in Norbert Gingold's vocal score; the second was transposed and arranged for Lotte Lenya alone; Lenya sang it for the first time in 1961 at a Musica Viva concert in Munich conducted by Miltiades Caridis.

Publication 2

UE, 1967: vocal score of a performing edition edited, with an introduction, by David Drew; reduction by Karl Heinz Füssl.
UE, 1977: study score of the 1967 edition.

Note 3

The holograph draft might be thought to prove that 'Marterl' was the original composition and 'Grabschrift 1919' an afterthought. Yet the internal evidence – musical and literary – suggests an alternative possibility. Only in the 'Grabschrift 1919' version does 3 define and fulfil its structural function as the axis between the 'Ballade vom ertrunkenen Mädchen' and the two 'Reports on the Unknown Soldier'. If, for the purposes of *Das Berliner Requiem*, the 'drowned girl' of the Ballad is identified with 'Die rote Rosa', the fact that in 1919 Rosa Luxemburg's body was found in the Landwehr canal some time after her murder by right-wing paramilitary fanatics has a crucial bearing on the pacifism of the two Reports on the Unknown Soldier. Whereas the tone of Weill's setting is perfectly judged in relation to the overt and the concealed content of 'Grabschrift 1919', its profoundly quietist irony loses both its depth and its edge when associated with the apolitical 'Marterl' – which has no bearing on the ensuing Report. 'Grabschrift 1919' has all the marks of being the 'lost' poem that Brecht is known to have written after hearing the news of Rosa Luxemburg's death but before her body was discovered. If not the actual poem, it could be an accurate recollection of it, but surely not a new poem written for the tenth anniversary of Luxemburg's death, let alone something written to 'fit' already existing music and bolster the Requiem's Armistice Day reflections. Until further evidence comes to light there can be no final verdict. But it is worth bearing in mind the possibility that 'Grabschrift 1919' was the first idea for 3; that the number was *sketched* in that form; and that 'Marterl' was substituted at draft stage after Weill or Brecht had been given some indication that the radio authorities would be unlikely to countenance so provocatively political a text. In those circumstances a tactical compromise would naturally have implied the aim of reinstating 'Grabschrift 1919' as soon as the conditions of the radio commission had been fulfilled. In the non-autograph copy of the full score the text had been underlaid in a different hand. When 3 was chosen for Universal Edition's 1929 *Song-Album* (see below) Weill insisted on the inclusion of 'Die rote Rosa' (letter to UE of 6 January 1930).

[December 1928 – January 1929]

Kleine Dreigroschenmusik
(*Little Threepenny Music*)

Suite from *Die Dreigroschenoper* for wind ensemble
Duration: 22 minutes
Orchestra: 2fl. 2cl. alto sax. tenor sax. 2tpt. tbn. tba. timp. perc. bjo. gtr. (or harp). band. pno.

1 Ouverture (*Maestoso*)
2 Die Moritat von Mackie Messer (*Moderato assai*)
3 Anstatt-dass-Song (*Moderato*)
4 Die Ballade vom angenehmen Leben (Foxtrot: *Molto leggiero*)
5 Pollys Lied (*Andante con moto*)
6 Tango-Ballade (minim = 58)
7 Kanonen-Song (Charleston-Tempo, minim = 92)
8 Dreigroschen-Finale (dotted minim = 60)

Note 1

Two of Weill's movement titles are not self-explanatory: the second number combines 'Die Moritat von Mackie Messer' with the 'Lied von der Unzulänglichkeit menschlichen Strebens' in a simple A–B–A–B form; the eighth (Finale) comprises 'Ruf aus der Gruft', 'Grabschrift', and 'Chorale'.

Autographs

SKETCHES AND DRAFTS

Apart from the sketch for the saxophone counter-melody in 3, which inexplicably appears among the sketches for *Konjunktur* (see p. 191), nothing has survived. Two or three such sketches were probably all Weill needed before starting the full score.

FULL SCORE (UEA)

Forty-two manuscript pages, on B^{28}, are bound in a brown-paper cover (stitching broken) with title page: 'Kurt Weill/Kleine Dreigroschen-Musik/für Blasorchester'.

First Performance

7 February 1929, Berlin, Staatsoper am Platz der Republik; Preussisches Staatskapelle, conducted by Otto Klemperer.

Note 2

The present writer is to blame for the legend that the first performance of the *Kleine Dreigroschenmusik* was given (by the same forces as above) at the Berlin Opera Ball in January 1929. This was certainly the first plan – Weill refers to it, in a letter to his publishers, as if it were definitive – and it would therefore have been the occasion for which Weill was induced by Klemperer to write the Suite. However, Klemperer's biographer Peter Heyworth has established beyond reasonable doubt that there was no performance of the *Kleine Dreigroschenmusik* at the Opera Ball. The concert on 7 February included the Sixth Brandenburg Concerto, Hindemith's *Kammermusik*, op. 6 no. 2, for cello and chamber orchestra, and Stravinsky's *Pulcinella* Suite. *Kleine Dreigroschenmusik* was billed as a premiere.

====

April–May 1929, Berlin

Der Lindberghflug
(*The Lindbergh Flight*)

(Original version, with Paul Hindemith)
Radio cantata, for alto, tenor, baritone, and bass soloists, chorus and
    orchestra
Text: Bertolt Brecht
Commissioned by Deutsche Kammermusik Baden-Baden 1929
(Unpublished: withdrawn and replaced by Weill's complete setting)
Duration: 30 minutes
Orchestra: 1.0.2.alto sax.1.   0.2.1.1   bjo. pno. timp. perc. (reduced) str.
Each of the sixteen numbers has a narrative superscription, which may
be spoken:

1	Aufforderung an die amerikanischen Flieger, den Ozean zu überfliegen (chorus)	[Weill]
	(Invitation to the American aviators to fly across the ocean)	
2	Vorstellung des Fliegers Charles Lindbergh (tenor solo)	[Weill]
	(Introduction of the aviator, Charles Lindbergh)	
3	Aufbruch des Fliegers Charles Lindbergh in New York zu seinem Fluge nach Europa (tenor)	[Weill]
	(Charles Lindbergh's departure from New York on his flight to Europe)	
4	Die Stadt New York befragt die Schiffe (baritone, chorus)	[Weill]
	(The city of New York questioned the ships)	
5	Fast während seines ganzen Fluges hatte der Flieger mit Nebel zu kämpfen (melodrama)	[Hindemith]
	(Throughout almost the entire flight the aviator had to contend with fog)	
6a	In der Nacht kam ein Schneesturm (bass)	[Hindemith]
	(In the night came a snowstorm)	
6b	'Es geht nicht mehr' (tenor)	[Weill]
7	Das Wasserrauschen kommt näher	[—]
	(The roar of the waves gets nearer)	

8 Schlaf (alto and tenor) [Hindemith]
(Sleep)
9 Während des ganzen Fluges sprachen alle amerikanischen Zeitungen
unaufhörlich von Lindberghs Glück (baritone, chorus) [Weill]
(Throughout the entire flight the American papers spoke
unceasingly about Lindbergh's luck)
10 Die Gedanken des Glücklichen (recitation) [—]
(The thoughts of the lucky one)
11 Schrieben die französischen Zeitungen: 'So fliegt er, über sich
die Stürme, um sich das Meer, unter sich den Schatten
Nungessers' (chorus) [Hindemith]
('So he flies', write the French newspapers, 'with the storms above him,
the sea around him and beneath him the shadow of Nungesser')
12 Lindbergh's Gespräch mit seinem Motor (tenor) [Weill]
(Lindbergh's conversation with his aero-engine)
13 Endlich, unweit Schottlands, sichtet Lindbergh Fischer (baritone, bass)
[Weill]
(Finally, not far from Scotland, Lindbergh sights fishermen)
14 Auf dem Flugplatz Le Bourget bei Paris erwartet in der Nacht des
21. Mai 1927, abends 10 Uhr, eine Riesenmenge den amerikanischen
Flieger (chorus) [Hindemith]
(At 10 p.m. on the night of 21 May 1927, a vast crowd is waiting at Le
Bourget airfield near Paris for the arrival of the American aviator)
15 Ankunft des Fliegers Charles Lindbergh auf dem Flugplatz Le Bourget
bei Paris [—]
(Arrival of the aviator Charles Lindbergh at Le Bourget airfield
near Paris)
16 Bericht über das Unerreichbare (soloists and chorus) [Hindemith]
(Report on the Unattainable)

Note 1

The numbering and German titling given above follows the programme
booklet for 'Deutsche Kammermusik Baden-Baden 1929', where the
entire text is printed and footnoted thus: 'Die Nummern 1, 2, 3, 4, 6b, 12,
und 13 sind von Weill.' The implication that the remaining numbers were
by Hindemith is misleading. *7, 10,* and *15* were spoken numbers,
probably with sound effects. The background and holograph sources are
comprehensively examined by Rudolf Stephan in his edition of the
Hindemith–Weill score: Paul Hindemith, *Sämtliche Werke, Band 1, 6,
Szenische Versuche* (Schott–Mainz, 1982). Ronald K. Shull is a more recent
and equally important authority (RS.MWBB, 128.00). Remarkably little
attention, however, has been paid to the nature and motivation of the
so-called collaboration between Weill and Hindemith. The essential clue
is the title under which Brecht's text was first published in April 1929
(*Uhu*, Berlin, year 5, vol. 7, pp. 10ff.): 'Lindbergh, ein Radio-Hörspiel für
die Festwochen in Baden-Baden. Mit einer Musik von Kurt Weill'
(Lindbergh, a radio play for the Baden-Baden Festival, with a score by
Kurt Weill). Stephan notes that a proof copy of this is dated 8 February
1929. If there was still no thought of Hindemith's participation by the

time *Uhu* went to press, it is clear that what was later advertised as an 'experiment' was, to some extent at least, a rescue operation. Weill was so meticulous with regard to deadlines, and so accurate in his prognostications, that the cause of the emergency must have been unforeseen. We know that he finished the full score of the *Mahagonny* opera in March 1929, and can assume that he would have done so two or three weeks earlier but for the last-moment decision to extend the Act III Finale. Although he could not have given *Der Lindberghflug* his undivided attention until April, he may well have begun sketching it in March while attending not only to the full score of the opera but also to those non-musical matters that any new opera entails when it is nearing completion. In that case he should have had no difficulty in drafting the twelve numbers of the *Uhu* version before the end of April, and producing the rehearsal scores for soloists and chorus by the middle of May. That would have left two months for orchestration, and for the extraction of parts in time for the first orchestral rehearsals. It was a tight schedule, because of the delay with the full score of the *Mahagonny* opera; but not in itself an impossible one.

To judge from the musical and manuscript evidence, Weill composed the first four numbers in the *Uhu* text as a single unit, and then turned to the first of the numbers with which Brecht was now supplementing the *Uhu* text (9 as it eventually became). These he then scored and numbered 1–5.

The arrival of Brecht's additional texts at a time when Weill was also having second thoughts about *Das Berliner Requiem* may already have constituted an emergency; but the decisive factor was surely Ernst Josef Aufricht's desire to celebrate the first anniversary of *Die Dreigroschenoper* with a new musical play written by Brecht and Weill for his ensemble at the Theater am Schiffbauerdamm. In his memoirs (*Erzähle, damit du dein Recht erweist*, Frankfurt, 1966) Aufricht implies that the project had first been mooted during the heady days following the triumph of *Die Dreigroschenoper*. If so, the atmosphere and the circumstances would have ensured that it remained nebulous at that stage. Weill's programme for the next six months was already alarmingly full and Brecht's cannot have been much different. Vague promises would soon have been forgotten; but if Aufricht returned in, say, the early spring of 1929, to propose and plan for an August opening, he would have created precisely the kind of emergency that might have persuaded even Weill to accept the idea of sending an SOS to Hindemith – the one German composer whose gifts and fame represented a fundamental threat to him. The idea surely came from Brecht. Not only was it characteristic of him; it was also, from his point of view, thoroughly expedient. The culminating event in the Baden-Baden Festival was to be the premiere of his *Lehrstück* (later known as the *Badener Lehrstück vom Einverständnis*), a 50-minute music-theatre work with a major score by Hindemith. The text of *Lehrstück* was certainly not complete by the spring of 1929 (when Brecht was, among other things, co-directing the production at the Theater am Schiffbauerdamm of a new play by Marieluise Fleisser). For him at that moment there was every advantage in inviting Hindemith to join *Der Lindberghflug*; Hindemith for his part had at least two manifest incentives in addition to the perhaps unconscious one of stealing a march on the composer of *Die Dreigroschenoper*: first, he could demonstrate his renowned professionalism in a context that combined the medieval ideals of the craft association – the 'mutual aid' of the *Musikantengilde* – with the newly fashionable if dimly comprehended concept of the collective; and, secondly, he could treat *Der Lindberghflug* either as an exercise for the battle course of *Lehrstück*, or as an adjunct to it. On that basis, it is not hard to imagine Hindemith and Weill agreeing to a dual-control system that divided the fifteen musical numbers (out of the total of sixteen) equally between them. From piecing together the known dates and the likely practical requirements, it becomes clear that Weill must have completed his seven-and-a-half numbers in rehearsal score, and probably also in full score, by the time he left Berlin in the third week of May 1929. Hindemith may by then have begun his contributions; but the fact that he wrote no more than five-and-a-half numbers, coupled with the perhaps deliberate vagueness of the note in the Baden-Baden programme, suggests that he undertook to write only as much as he had time for, and that at least some of his *Lindberghflug* music postdated the completion of his much more important score for the *Lehrstück*. As far as Weill was concerned, the cut-off point was surely the middle of May. While it would be interesting to know exactly when it was that he and Brecht agreed to leave Berlin for a working holiday in the South of France, there can be no doubt that the decision presupposed Hindemith's understanding and co-operation. The project to be broached in the South of France had nothing to do with Baden-Baden: it was *Happy End*, the new musical play for performance at the Theater am Schiffbauerdamm in August.

Autographs

SKETCHES

Side *a* of a sheet of B^{30} carries the complete vocal line of *1*, without the two supporting harmonies. Near the foot of the page, and written at right-angles to it, is a book list: 'Döblin: *Wang-lun* [Alfred Döblin's novel *Die drei Sprünge des Wang-lun*, 1915], Voltaire, *Sämtliche Werke* /Commenius /Nestroy (*30 Jahre aus dem Leben eines Lumpen*)/Mehring *Gedichte*/Lao-Tse'. Lower down, and written across the page, are Döblin's and Leo Lania's addresses. The remaining sides are blank, apart from the title 'Mahagonny' placed centrally at the head of side *d*.

REHEARSAL SCORE (UEA)

This is incorporated in the vocal score of the definitive version of *Der Lindberghflug* (see p. 223).

FULL SCORE (UEA)

The holograph of *13* is in WLA, headed 'Nr. 13 Lindbergh sichtet Fischer/ Weill: Lindberghflug (Brecht)': it is written on the first three sides of a sheet of S²⁰. The remaining seven numbers are in the Paul Hindemith Institut (PHI). They are written on thirty-two sides of S³⁰, paginated in another hand. There is no cover or title page, and although the foldings have been sewn together, most of the pages are now loose. The autograph heading to *1*, 'Kurt Weill: Lindbergh-Flug (Brecht)', is consistent with the evidence of the *Uhu* publication of the text (see *Note 1*); the heading to *12*, 'Aus "Lindberghflug" von Kurt Weill', could indicate that some form of facsimile reproduction was envisaged – perhaps for a magazine (or even for a newspaper, as the number is very short).

The numbering of *1–4* is autograph, as is that of *9*, which, however, bears the number '5'. *6b* has the non-autograph number 'VII', and *12* is unnumbered, but has the non-autograph note appended to it, 'folgt: Fischerduett' ('the Fishermen's duet follows' i.e., *13*).

First Performance

27 July 1929, Kurhaus, Baden-Baden: Frankfurt Radio Orchestra conducted by Hermann Scherchen; with Betty Mergler, alto (Sleep), Josef Witt, tenor (Lindbergh), Johannes Willy, baritone (Fog, and the City of New York), Oskar Kalman, bass (Snowstorm), and the choir of the Hugo Holles Madrigal Society; production for radio by Ernst Hardt, for concert audience by Brecht.

Publication

B. Schott Söhne, Mainz, 1982: in Paul Hindemith, *Sämtliche Werke, Band 1, 6, Szenische Versuche*. Edited with an introduction and notes by Rudolf Stephan.

Note 2

At the time of writing (June 1986) the contractual basis of the 1982 publication awaits clarification. In a letter to Hans Curjel HCA of 2 August 1929 (Curjel archive) Weill gave an extremely negative view of Hindemith's contribution, and left no doubt that he intended to complete the work himself. On 20 September 1929 he reacted unfavourably to an inquiry from Universal Edition regarding the joint version. As soon as he had finished his own version (see p. 223) the joint version was contrary to his interests, though not of course to Hindemith's or to Brecht's. In 1930 Hermann Scherchen conducted a shortened version (*1–3, 5, 6a, 8, 12–14*) of the joint version for a recording produced by Berliner Funkstunde and subsequently relayed by Radio Paris and by the BBC in London, with French and English narrations respectively. The copy of this recording, which Professor Scherchen kindly made available to the present author, is now in WLRC, and is a unique document with regard to Weill's vocal requirements for the tenor part – superbly sung by Erik Wirl, whom Weill regarded as the ideal Jim Mahoney in *Aufstieg und Fall der Stadt Mahagonny*.

[June]–August 1929, Le Lavandou/Unterschondorf/Berlin

Happy End

Comedy with music, in three acts
Book by 'Dorothy Lane' (Elisabeth Hauptmann)
Lyrics by Brecht
Duration: full evening – 40 minutes music
Cast: singing roles: Bill Cracker, Sam Worlitzer, Hannibal Jackson, Lilian Holiday, Lady in Grey, Jane; SATB chorus; other roles: Dr Nakamura, Jimmy Dexter, Bob Berker, Johnny Flint, Salvation Army Captain, Mary.
Orchestra: Alto and tenor saxophones, two trumpets, trombone, banjo (= Hawaiian guitar, bandoneon, bass guitar), percussion, piano, harmonium.

Bill Cracker's dance hall in Chicago serves as the headquarters of the gang led by the mysterious Lady in Grey. The first attempts of the local Salvation Army to reform the gangsters are notably unsuccessful, until Lilian Holiday, influenced by the charms and the whisky of Bill Cracker, sings the 'Matrosen-Tango'. For this indiscretion she is temporarily disgraced. But since none of her colleagues can offer comparable box-office attractions she is soon reinstated. On Christmas Eve the gang carry out a spectacularly successful burglary, and then discover an unexpected bond with the Salvationists. Joining forces with them, they open a splendid new headquarters in the city's wealthiest district; for it is there, they reckon, that souls to be saved are most numerous.

ACT I

Scene i: Bill's Dance Hall
1   Bilbao Song (Bill): 'Bills Ballhaus in Bilbao'
2   Der kleine Leutnant des lieben Gottes (Lilian): 'Obacht, gebt Obacht!'
3   Heilsarmeelied I (Lilian, Salvationists): 'Geht hinein in die Schlacht'
4   Matrosen-Tango (Lilian): 'Ja, das Meer ist blau, so blau'

ACT II

Scene i: The Salvation Army Hall
 5   Heilsarmeelied II: 'Bruder, gib dir einen Stoss'
 6   Heilsarmeelied III: 'Fürchte dich nicht'
 7   Heilsarmeelied IV: 'In der Jugend gold'nem Schimmer'
 8   Das Lied vom Branntweinhändler (Vorbildliche Bekehrung
       eines Branntweinhändlers) (Hannibal Jackson): 'Hinter Gläsern, an
       dem Schanktisch'

ACT III

Scene i: Bill's Dance Hall
 9   Mandelay Song (Sam Worlitzer): 'Mutter Goddams Puff in Mandelay'
10   Surabaya-Johnny (Lilian): 'Ich war jung, Gott, erst sechzehn Jahre'
11   Das Lied von der harten Nuss (Bill): 'Wer will einen grossen
       Mann hab'n'
12   Die Ballade von der Höllen-Lili (Lady in Grey): 'Wenn ich in der
       Hölle brenne'

Scene ii: The new Salvation Army Hall
13   Hosianna Rockefeller (full cast): 'Reiche den Reichtum den Reichen'

Note 1

No overture or prologue has been traced and none is mentioned in the
list of musical numbers Weill sent to Universal Edition on 3 June 1932.
Apart from one counting error (three *Heilsarmeelieder* instead of four),
Weill's list is accurate, though not methodically ordered.

Autographs

SKETCHES AND DRAFTS

Missing, except for a pencil draft of *11* on four sides of B²⁴, paginated 7–9
in another hand.

REHEARSAL SCORES

9,13 (two sides each), and *5–7* on a single sheet of B²⁴. UEA holds a vocal
score of 'Surabaya-Johnny' which is filed among the manuscripts used as
masters for the 1929 *Song-Album*. An autograph note to the effect that it
must be transposed from E major to E flat – the key of the orchestration –
suggests that it may have been the original rehearsal score. The rehearsal
score of *4* was in the Legacy in the early 1970s, but is not in WLA and is
presumed lost.

FULL SCORES

4, 9, 11 are missing (scores have been reconstructed from a contemporary
set of parts). On 7 June 1932 Universal Edition told Weill that its set of
autograph full scores (of which, clearly, no copies had yet been made)
was incomplete: *2, 8, 12, 13* and the four *Heilsarmeelieder* were all they

possessed. In his reply of 11 June Weill expressed astonishment at this news and suggested that UE may have sent *1, 4, 9* and *11* to Electrola (which had recorded them with the Lewis Ruth Band in 1929) and never recovered them. He had evidently forgotten that Lenya had recorded *1* and *10* with an orchestra conducted by Theo Mackeben in 1930. The autographs of these did not come to light until the 1950s, when Lenya purchased them from the conductor Bruno Seidler-Winkler during one of her first post-war visits to Berlin. In his letter of 11 June 1932 Weill wrote that as far as he knew the orchestral parts for *1, 4, 9* and *11* were still with the conductor of the Lewis Ruth Band, Ludwig Rüth. He suggested that Rüth might know of the whereabouts of the scores, and that if he did not, scores should be made from the parts. It therefore seems likely that the parts of all four numbers were recovered from Rüth, but that the scores of *4, 9* and *11* have been missing since the 1929 recording.

The ten holographs now in WLA are written on various papers, mostly in separate foldings: *1* (nine sides S^{30}), *2* (fourteen sides B^{24}), *Heilsarmeelieder* I–IV (continuous on three sides B^{24}), *8* (seven sides S^{32}), *10* (eight sides S^{30}), *12* (ten sides A^{20}) and *13* (seven sides S^{32}).

Publications

UE, 1929: voice and piano arrangements of *1, 4, 10,* issued separately.
Felix Bloch-Erben, 1929: theatre text (duplicated).

First Performance

2 September 1929, Berlin, Theater am Schiffbauerdamm. Director Erich Engel, designer Caspar Neher, conductor (of the Lewis Ruth Band) Theo Mackeben; with Carola Neher (Lilian), Oskar Homolka (Bill), Kurt Gerron (Sam), Helene Weigel (Lady in Grey), Peter Lorre (Dr Nakamura), Albert Hoerrmann, Theo Lingen, Erich Harden.

Note 2

The play is primarily the work of Brecht's assistant, Elisabeth Hauptmann. Its first act was well received at the premiere but the evening as a whole was a fiasco. Apparently thrown together at the last moment, the third act ended in uproar. The press was unanimously scornful, and the production closed after a few days. Since the score had been almost as poorly received as the play, Weill's publishers had no great incentive to concern themselves with it. But Weill himself was never in any doubt about the importance of the musical numbers in relation to the post-*Dreigroschenoper* development of his song style. In his view – first expressed in a letter to UE of 14 October 1929 – the fault lay with the play and its primitive musico-dramatic structure.

Apart from a vain attempt to popularize four of the numbers with the aid of commercial recordings, nothing further happened until June 1932.

On the 3rd of that month Weill gave UE the 'very interesting' news that Brecht and Hauptmann had produced a 'definitive, depoliticized, version of *Happy End*'. He had yet to see it, but the stage publishers Felix Bloch-Erben had already informed him of their wish to include the songs with the inspection material, and inquired whether the manuscripts were in his possession – which they were not. Assuming that they had been returned to Vienna, he now asked UE to send them to him, and added that he had broached with Bloch-Erben his idea of making a condensed version of the play, in which 'the scaffolding of the whole thing' ('das Gerüst des Ganzen') would be the musical numbers. This he would like to offer to 'Wiener Opernproduktion', the company Hans Heinsheimer and Max Brand had formed and inaugurated with their production of a condensed version of the *Mahagonny* opera. It would, he felt, be an ideal vehicle for Lenya. On 15 June he wrote to report that he had now read the new version of *Happy End* and was astounded to discover that 'Brecht and Frau Hauptmann have left the play *completely untouched*'. He now intended to inform Bloch-Erben that unless Brecht undertook a fundamental revision that reduced *Happy End* to a total running time of about two hours, so that the play was simply 'the scaffolding' ('das Gerüst') for the music, he would dissociate himself from it. How Weill can have supposed that Brecht would do any such thing is hard to imagine: only two months before, on 11 April, Berlin Radio had broadcast, as a first performance, Brecht's *Die heilige Johanna der Schlachthöfe* (*St Joan of the Stockyards*), a play written in collaboration with Hans Hermann Borchardt (see p. 406), Emil Burri, and Elisabeth Hauptmann, and described in its first edition (*Versuche 5*, Berlin, 1932) as having been 'derived from the play *Happy End* by Elisabeth Hauptmann' (an official statement that attracted so little attention that the 'Dorothy Lane' pseudonym retained its mystery for half a century). Is it conceivable that Weill was by this time so far removed from Brecht and his activities that he had confused the reports of *Die heilige Johanna der Schlachthöfe* – certainly a 'fundamental' revision, but also a deeply politicized one – with the expected laundering of *Happy End*? One would hardly credit it, but for the naïvety of the expectation itself.

Predictably, nothing came of Weill's hopes for *Happy End*. Yet he still cherished them, and on 26 December 1932 he wrote to UE about his 'old plan' for arranging the *Happy End* songs as a 'a kind of *Songspiel* with short spoken scenes' and establishing it as a companion piece to the *Mahagonny-Songspiel*. This, he thought, he could easily work out with Neher: 'but that would cause endless troubles with Brecht' ('aber das würde ja endlose Scherereien mit Brecht geben'). *Happy End* was neither seen nor heard again in his lifetime or Brecht's. But on 19 December 1956 – just three months after Brecht's death – Elisabeth Hauptmann wrote to Lenya from Berlin, enclosing a copy (WLRC) of the *Happy End* text in the version currently promoted by Bloch-Erben. 'It strikes me as somewhat garbled' ('Es kommt mir etwas verstümmelt vor'), she remarked, promising to look among Brecht's papers in case there was anything else there. In this version the play is arranged in two acts, and is shorn of the agitprop insertions that offended the critics in 1929 (and especially the Marxists). The 'Hosianna Rockefeller' finale is dropped altogether – a sacrifice Weill had already contemplated in 1932, when conditions were even less favourable for it than they were in the Bundesrepublik in 1956.

Posthumous Publication

1958: piano–conductor score. The anonymous editor gives no account of his activities. Sources are not identified; no reference is made to the fact that the piano–conductor scores of 4, 9 and 11 had had to be assembled from the band parts, in the absence of holograph or copied full scores; an 8-bar instrumental episode has been removed from 2 without explanation; and a reprise of 2 serves to conceal the omission of the finale to *Happy End*, 'Hosianna Rockefeller' (13).

1980: study score, with American versions of the lyrics by Michael Feingold, and music 'edited and corrected in accordance with the composer's manuscripts by Alan Boustead'. 1–12 are reproduced from Boustead's own excellent manuscript; mysteriously 13 is appended to the score in a reproduction of the holograph score, so reduced as to be almost illegible (which perhaps was the intention). Instead of the necessary editorial notes there is a brief, unsigned, introduction in German and in English, giving the theatrical background and attempting a brief characterization of the music. While Boustead's participation in this edition is an assurance of high musical standards, the publication itself does not bear comparison with the study score of *Die Dreigroschenoper*. With support from the Kurt Weill Foundation, a new critical edition of score and parts has been prepared by Gary Fagin and will be available from EAM in 1987.

Posthumous Arrangement

'SONGSPIEL' VERSION

Since the songs and choruses are interpolations that owe nothing to their dramatic context in conception and derive little benefit from it in practice, a version of the score that can stand on its own and represent the 'argument' of the play (such as it is) without reference to its action or characters is feasible (as Weill himself seems to have recognized – see *Note 2*). In 1975 the present writer prepared just such an abstract; it was first performed by Mary Thomas (soprano), Meriel Dickinson (mezzo-soprano), Philip Langridge and Ian Partridge (tenors), and Benjamin Luxon (baritone), with the London Sinfonietta under David Atherton at the Akademie der Künste, West Berlin, on 13 September 1975. Subsequently it was recorded, and also used as the basis for a television film.

The score is divided into a Prologue (Bilbao Song) and three sections: I 'Songs of Hellfire and Repentance' (*6, 12, 8, 4, 5*); II 'Songs of Innocence and Experience' (*9, 7, 10*); III 'Songs of the Rival Armies' (*2* (first half), *3, 11, 13, 2* (second half)).

Note 3

Bettina Jonic, who was a memorable Lilian Holiday in the 1965 production of *Happy End* for the Traverse Theatre in Edinburgh and the Royal Court Theatre in London (director: Michael Geliot), is the author of *The Ladies*, a play about Lotte Lenya and Helene Weigel, with music by John Rushby-Smith, staged for the first time at the French Institute's Théâtre Artaud in London, in May–June 1986. The advance publicity for this production included the following statement:

> On the opening night of Brecht's *Happy End* Helene Weigel pulled a political manifesto from her pocket and began to shout Marxist slogans at the audience. Lotte Lenya, her co-star, never spoke to her again. It had ruined her career in Berlin.

On the opening night of *Happy End* Lotte Lenya was playing the role of Lucille in Karlheinz Martin's historic production for the Berliner Volksbühne of Büchner's *Dantons Tod* (see p. 375).

[?September] 1929

[Workers' Choruses]

    1   Zu Potsdam unter den Eichen (TTBB *a cappella*)
    2   Die Legende vom toten Soldaten (SATB *a cappella*)

Texts: Bertolt Brecht
Duration: 7 minutes

Autographs

SKETCHES AND DRAFTS

Missing.

SCORES

1 is missing; *2* (in UEA) is on eight sides of A²⁰, headed 'Die Legende vom toten Soldaten/(Brecht)/für gemischten Chor von Kurt Weill'.

Publication

UE, 1930: published separately, but in the same choral series. *1* is titled: 'Zu Potsdam unter den Eichen aus "Berliner Requiem"/Text von Bert Brecht'.

First Performance

November 1929, Berlin, Schubertchor, conducted by Karl Rankl; performance sponsored by 'Interessengemeinschaft für Arbeiterkultur'.

Notes

The arrangement of 'Zu Potsdam unter den Eichen' (whose original version was written in 1928 for *Das Berliner Requiem*) and the composition of 'Die Legende vom toten Soldaten' were undertaken in response to a request from Erwin Stein of Universal Edition for material suitable for the red-cover choral series promoted by UE under the title 'Die rote Reihe'.

The series was designed for the amateur choral movements in Germany and Austria, and was, on the Marxist wing, associated with the pioneering work of Hanns Eisler, whose compositions dominated the programme in which Weill's two choruses were first performed. 'Die Legende vom toten Soldaten' is the only known example of a Brecht setting by Weill in which the principal melodic idea is taken, note for note, from a melody used, if not composed, by Brecht. The Ballad was written in 1918 and was a favourite of Brecht's in his early ballad-singing days. He included it in his play *Trommeln in der Nacht*, and published it together with its tune in the *Hauspostille* (1927). The ballad became notorious in right-wing and pro-censorship circles, because of its allegedly blasphemous and unpatriotic content.

September–November 1929, Berlin

Der Lindberghflug
(*The Lindbergh Flight*)

Cantata for tenor, baritone and bass soloists, SATB chorus (with children's choir *ad lib.*) and orchestra
Text: Bertolt Brecht
Duration: 35 minutes
Orchestra: 2.0.2.2.   0.2.2.0.   timp. pno. perc. str.

The text, including the narrative captions, is identical with that of the original Baden-Baden version, apart from the omission of the seventh number. The numbers are here identified by their first lines; Baden-Baden numberings are given in square brackets.

1	[1]	'Hier ist der Apparat' (chorus)
2	[2]	'Mein Name ist Charles Lindbergh' (tenor)
3	[3]	'Ich habe bei mir' (tenor)
4	[4]	'Hier spricht die Stadt New York' (baritone, chorus)
5	[5]	'Ich bin der Nebel' (chorus); 'Das tue ich nicht' (tenor)

6	[6a, 6b]	'Seit einer Stunde' (chorus); 'Es geht nicht mehr' (tenor)
7	[8]	'Schlaf, Charlie' (bass)
8	[9]	'Ganz Amerika glaubt' (baritone); 'Wenn der Glückliche' (chorus)
9	[10]	'Zwei Kontinente warten auf mich' (tenor: spoken)
10	[11]	'Auf unsern Kontinent zu' (chorus)
11	[12]	'Jetzt ist es nicht mehr weit' (tenor)
12	[13]	'Da ruft etwas, horch!' (baritone, bass)
13	[14]	'Jetzt kommt er' (tenor, chorus)
14	[15]	Ankunft des Fliegers (orchestra)
15	[16]	'Zu der Zeit, wo die Menschheit' (soloists, chorus)

Note 1

The numbers that Weill had already composed for the Baden-Baden version – that is 1–4, 6 (second part), 8, 11 and 12 – do not undergo any substantial alterations in the definitive version. Only the scoring is changed. A large string section is specified; at the first performance the chorus-strength was 100 (Weill to UE, 26 October 1929).

Autographs

SKETCHES AND DRAFTS

Missing.

According to a letter to his publishers, dated 8 October 1929, Weill planned to complete the draft during the second week of October.

REHEARSAL SCORE (UEA)

Omitting only 9 and 14 (which have no singing parts) Weill sent the complete vocal score to Universal Edition on 23 October 1929, less than a fortnight after he had finished the draft. Seven of the numbers, however, had only to be slightly adapted from the rehearsal score he had already written out for Baden-Baden. The score now in UEA is unbound and without title page. Its 56 pages of P[14] include 9 and 14. 2 ('Vorstellung des Fliegers') has been removed, presumably at the time when it was needed as a production master for the 1931 *Song-Album*; it is now stored with the other UEA manuscripts relating to that album. One of the two latecomers, 9, is non-autograph, as are 1, 4, and the choral section of 8 imported from the Baden-Baden score, together with a fragment of Hindemith's choral setting of 10, which had been numbered '11' in the Baden-Baden version.

FULL SCORE

Because of changes of instrumentation, the full score does not incorporate any pages from the Baden-Baden version. It was completed on 10 November 1929 – a remarkable feat unless at least some of it was written concurrently with the rehearsal score. It runs to 119 numbered pages of A[20], and is bound in a blue cardboard cover. The title page reads: 'Kurt

Weill/Der Lindberghflug/Text von Bert Brecht/Partitur'. The score was
used by Otto Klemperer for the first performance, and contains a few of
his markings. Two passages have been struck out from 5: a 4-bar solo
after the present rehearsal figure 25, and a 20-bar development of this
prior to the present figure 29 and Lindbergh's 'Ich fürchte dich nicht'. So
slender is the significance of the text for these cut passages – in which Fog
mockingly challenges Lindbergh to venture further out from the
American coast – that one can only assume that the lines were added to
the Baden-Baden version simply in order to provide Weill with a musical
opportunity that Hindemith had not required. The results, however, did
not justify the effort. The passages do not appear in the published scores.

First Performance

5 December 1929, Berlin, concert at the Staatsoper am Platz der Republik
(Kroll-Oper) conducted by Otto Klemperer; with Erik Wirl (tenor), Fritz
Krenn (baritone), Martin Abendroth (bass) and the chorus and orchestra
of the Kroll-Oper.

Publication

UE, 1930: vocal score, with piano reduction attributed to Norbert
 Gingold; full score, with an English translation by George Antheil; title
 page: 'Der Lindberghflug /Lindberghflight/Worte von Brecht/English
 translation by George Antheil/Musik von Music by Kurt Weill/Partitur
 Score'; vocal score, second edition, with Antheil translation.

Note 2

Towards the end of 1930 Brecht published the first of his collections of
'Versuche' (*Versuche* 1–3, Berlin, 1930, Gustav Kiepenheuer Verlag). The
first of these 'Versuche' ('Attempts') is entitled *Der Flug der Lindberghs*
(*The Flight of the Lindberghs*), and subtitled 'Ein Radiolehrstück für Knaben
und Mädchen'. It contains three new texts (one of which, 'Ideologie', is
crucial) and various revisions, notably the substitution of a collective
(choral) Lindbergh for the individual (solo). These additions and changes
are independent of any musical considerations. Their tendency is
confirmed in the 'Erläuterungen' appended to the text and signed by
Brecht and (Peter) Suhrkamp.
    In January 1950, Brecht revised the text once again, eliminating all
mention of Lindbergh – for reasons cogently expressed in a new Prologue
– and retitling the work *Der Ozeanflug*. There is no evidence that Weill
knew anything of this revision prior to his death a few weeks later.
    On 26 May 1967 Südwestfunk, Baden-Baden, broadcast *Der Ozeanflug*
in a 'production' directed by Peter Schulze-Rohr. The score was
attributed to Weill but had in fact been very freely arranged by Friedrich
Scholz after the manner of Hosalla's version of the *Mahagonny-Songspiel*

(see p. 174). Since the stylistic obstacles were greater than in the *Songspiel*, this process entailed rendering the original score almost as unrecognizable as Lindbergh himself. Authorization for further performances was withheld by Lotte Lenya.

January, March–May 1930; revised version: Autumn, 1930, Berlin

Der Jasager
[*The Yes-Sayer*]

School opera (Schuloper) in two acts
Text: Bertolt Brecht after the Japanese play *Taniko* (English by Arthur Waley, German by Elisabeth Hauptmann)
Written at the invitation of Neue Musik Berlin 1930
Dedication: Gustav Brecher
Duration: 35 minutes
Cast: The Boy, the Mother, the Teacher, Three Students, SATB chorus
Orchestra: fl. cl. alto sax.; 2 pno. harm. perc *ad lib*; plucked instruments *ad lib*; vlns. vlcs. dbs. (all strings maximum strength).

The Teacher is about to take a group of students on a dangerous journey across the mountains to visit a famous scholar. Against his better judgement he allows the Boy to go with them to fetch medicine for his sick Mother. After the long and arduous climb, the Boy too becomes sick. The Three Students remind the Teacher of the 'ancient custom'. The Teacher asks the Boy whether they should on his account turn back; but in deference to the ancient custom, the Boy consents to be hurled into the valley.

ACT I

The House of the Mother
  1 Chorus: 'Wichtig zu lernen vor allem ist Einverständnis'
  2 Teacher ('Ich bin der Lehrer') – Boy
  3 Teacher ('Ich bin länger nicht hier gewesen') – Mother
  4 Boy ('Ich muss etwas sagen') – Teacher
  5 Teacher ('Ich bin noch einmal zurückgekommen') – Mother ('Seit dem Tag, an dem uns dein Vater verliess') – Boy (Trio: 'Ich werde die gefährliche Wanderung machen')
  6 Chorus ('Sie sahen, dass keine Vorstellungen ihn rühren konnten') – Mother, Teacher

ACT II

In the Mountains
  7 Chorus ('Die Leute haben die Reise in die Berge angetreten')
  8 Teacher ('Wir sind schnell hinangestiegen') – Students – Boy
  9 Students ('Wir wollen es dem Lehrer sagen!') – Teacher – Chorus
  10 Teacher ('Höre gut zu') – Boy – Students ('Er hat ja gesagt') – Chorus
  11 Chorus – reprise of 1

Autographs

SKETCHES

Missing.

DRAFT

Twenty pages of B³⁰, in a title sheet of B²⁸ inscribed 'Diese erste Nieder-schrift des "Jasagers"/gehört der Vicomtesse und Vicomte de Noailles/In dankbarer Erinnerung an den/10. Dezember 1932/Kurt Weill'. The draft is in the possession of the heirs of the Vicomtesse de Noailles; the date is that of the Paris premiere of *Der Jasager*, which was financed by the Noailles.

REHEARSAL SCORE (UEA)

Fifty pages of mixed B¹⁴ and P¹⁴, in a damaged title sheet of P¹⁴. The autograph title 'Text nach dem Japanischen/von Brecht' has been changed by another hand to 'Text aus dem Japanischen/bearbeitet von Brecht'. The dedication 'Gustav Brecher gewidmet' is also in another hand.

FULL SCORE

Eighty-four pages of B²² (forty pages of Act I, forty-four of Act II, in separate gatherings, bound with white tape). A title sheet of the same paper reads 'Kurt Weill/Der Jasager/Schuloper in 2 Akten/Text nach dem Japanischen/von/Brecht/Partitur'.

Note 1

The first musical sketches were made in January 1930. Progress was then interrupted for several weeks by preparations for, and the immediate consequences of, the world premiere of the *Mahagonny* opera on 9 March. The rehearsal score must have been written concurrently with the draft – which was finished early in April – since it was needed even more urgently than the full score (completed 16 May).

Publication

UE, 1930: vocal score (inexpensive production, at the composer's request); full score.

Note 2

Doubtless with Brecht's encouragement, Weill withdrew *Der Jasager* from Neue Musik Berlin 1930 after the Festival organizers had decided against performing Brecht's and Eisler's *Die Massnahme* (a decision taken on the basis of the text only). Through Leo Kestenberg, arrangements were made with the State Academy for Church and School Music for a premiere immediately after the close of the Festival.

First Performance

23 June 1930, Radio Berlin, live broadcast; 24 June, stage premiere at the Zentralinstitut für Erziehung und Unterricht, Berlin; the conductor, Kurt Drabek, the singers, including Otto Hopf as the Teacher, and the orchestral players, were students from the Staats-Akademie für Kirchen-und Schulmusik, and from other Berlin schools.

Note 3

REVISED VERSION, AUTUMN 1930

The first production to benefit from Brecht's presence and advice at rehearsal stage was the one prepared by students at the Karl-Marx School in Berlin-Neukölln during the autumn term of 1930. In the light of reactions to the June performance, and probably with a view to the production at the Karl-Marx School (a stronghold of progressive education, established by the Social Democrats after the First World War), Brecht and Weill made two interpolations. The first is in 2, and follows the words 'Reise in Berge' (rehearsal figure 9): 'Es ist nämlich eine Seuche bei uns ausgebrochen, und in der Stadt jenseits der Berge wohnen einige grosse Ärzte' ('An epidemic has broken out here, and in the city beyond the mountains there are some great doctors'). The second and much longer interpolation is in 10, the finale. The text for it (BB.GW 2, p. 621) extends from the Three Students' words 'Er hat ja gesagt' (rehearsal figure 69) to the Teacher's question 'Seid ihr bereit, ihn ins Tal hinabzuwerfen?' Minor textual changes prior to this passage are not incorporated in any of the extant musical holographs, but may well have been in the printed scores used by the first performers of this 'neue Fassung', as Weill termed it.

Autographs of Revised Version

SKETCHES

The sketches for both passages are interspersed with the earliest surviving sketches for the opera *Die Bürgschaft*, which Weill began during the late summer of 1930.

REHEARSAL SCORE

Missing.

FULL SCORE (UEA)

The two interpolations are on nine sides of a folding of B^{20}, signed and headed 'Kurt Weill: Jasager (neue Fassung)'.

Note 4

BRECHT'S REVISIONS

True to the educational principles of the Karl-Marx School, *Der Jasager* was presented as material for discussion, criticism, and classroom projects rather than as a 'school opera' in the didactic sense. In response to criticisms voiced by the students, Brecht made further revisions, and when these did not suffice, he prepared the complementary play *Der Neinsager (The No-Sayer)*. Up to the point where the fateful question is put to the Boy, the text of *Der Neinsager* is identical with that of the June 1930 *Jasager*. But this time the Boy refuses to submit to the 'old custom' and proposes a new and better one – that of thinking afresh in each new situation. His comrades concur and resolve to carry him home. In his prefatory note to the editions of *Der Jasager* and *Der Neinsager*, which he published towards the end of 1930, Brecht recommends that the two 'little plays' are, wherever possible, presented side-by-side: 'Die zwei kleinen Stücke sollten womöglich nicht eins ohne das andere aufgeführt werden.' This, however, is practicable only if they are indeed presented as 'little plays', for Weill was not involved in the later revisions, and provided no music for *Der Neinsager*. Given that he would have had to recompose the nine-tenths of the text he had already set in *Der Jasager* if *Der Neinsager* was to make any musico-dramatic sense, he could well have been excused on the grounds of his involvement with *Die Bürgschaft*. But the perfunctory nature of the two interpolations he had composed in the autumn helps suggest a much more powerful reason for his failure to respond either to *Der Neinsager* or to Brecht's later revisions of *Der Jasager*: at some level he must have recognized that if *Der Jasager* is studied and performed with true understanding, the original text requires no 'corrections' beyond those which the music itself so eloquently supplies.

August 1930 – October 1931; new scene: February 1932, Berlin

Die Bürgschaft
[*The Pledge* or *The Surety*]

Opera in three acts
Text by Caspar Neher and the composer, after Herder's *Der afrikanische Rechtsspruch (The African Judgement)*
Dedication: Walter Steinthal
Duration: 3½ hours
Cast: Johann Mattes (high baritone), his wife Anna Mattes (mezzo), his daughter Luise (soprano), David Orth (high bass), his son Jakob Orth (tenor), Three Creditors (tenor, baritone, bass) and their subsequent

transformations as Highwaymen, Blackmailers, Bailiffs and Agents, Judge (tenor), Scribe (tenor), Commissar (tenor), Adjutant (tenor); Herald (tenor); commenting chorus (semi-chorus) on raised platform with important alto solo; large chorus on stage.

Orchestra: 2.(2picc.).2.2.2(cbsn.). 0.3(2cnt.).2.1. timp. perc. 2 pnos. full str.

The mythical land of Urb, in pre-colonial times (Prologue and Act I), and after its invasion by the Great Power (Acts II and III).

PROLOGUE

The cattle dealer Johann Mattes returns in despair from the gambling dens of the capital city, and confesses to his wife that all is lost and that the Creditors are after him. She advises him to seek help from the corn dealer David Orth, who lives on the other side of the great river. Mattes leaves. By the time he returns with Orth, the Creditors are already removing the furniture from his house. Orth declares that since he regards Mattes as his 'best customer', he will, for a given period, stand surety for him. The Creditors agree, and before long Mattes discharges his debts.

ACT I

Mattes buys from Orth two sacks of grain, in which he later finds a hidden hoard of money. Assuming, from misconstrued evidence, that the money was not Orth's and has not been missed, he decides to keep it and tell nobody. Three Blackmailers uncover his secret and start to threaten him, whereupon he hastens back to Orth. But Orth questions his own right to the money, and persuades the astonished Mattes to let the case be decided by the Judge, whose wisdom is renowned throughout Urb.

ACT II

In Solomonic fashion, the Judge decrees that the money shall be divided between Jakob Orth and Luise Mattes when they are older.

The Great Power, whose actions, according to the Judge, are determined solely by the laws of money (*Geld*) and of power (*Macht*), now invades the land of Urb. While the Commissar announces the 'new order', and defines its political and economic objectives, the Judge is heard advocating passive resistance. To discredit him and at the same time to demonstrate his own absolute power, the Commissar re-examines the case of Orth and Mattes, declares both men to be criminals, and releases them on condition that they serve the new regime – a task in which they will be assisted by the Three Blackmailers, whom he had already recruited as his Agents when they stopped him at the City Gates.

ACT III

Six years have passed. Urb is now industrialized. But the Great Power has fulfilled no promises other than those implicit in the twin laws of Money and Power. The rich – Mattes and Orth – have grown richer, the poor, poorer. In a succession of four apocalyptic visions, Urb is visited by War, Inflation, Famine and Disease. When at last the people seek to overthrow the system and destroy their oppressors, Orth saves his own life by offering Mattes as a sacrifice to the mob – who lynch him. As the curtain falls, Orth proclaims the triumph of Money and Power.

Note 1

The number form of *Die Bürgschaft* is more complex and close-knit than
that of the *Mahagonny* opera, and is correspondingly less susceptible to
schematic representation. The following outline is intended chiefly as a
means of identifying the main dramatic (and thematic) events, and
approximately indicating the vocal texture of each number. First lines are
cited as indications of crucial or static moments, but are not given in the
case of ensembles or fast-moving dialogue scenes. Subsections are not
musically self-contained (as several are in the *Mahagonny* opera).

PROLOGUE

Mattes's House
  1 Johann and Anna: 'Weh uns! Wir sind verloren'
  2 Anna: 'So war er immer'; semi-chorus: 'Es ändert sich nicht der Mensch'
  3 Anna, Three Creditors, semi-chorus, David Orth

ACT I

  4   (i) Semi-chorus: 'Seit diesen Ereignissen sind sechs Jahre vergangen'

Orth's House
         (ii) Orth ('Wir wohnen im Lande Urb') Mattes, small chorus, Jakob

A Narrow Defile
  5 Three Highwaymen: 'Auch im Lande Urb'; Mattes

Orth's House
  6   (i) Semi-chorus: 'Seht dort die Lastschiffe auf dem Fluss'
         (ii) Orth: 'Sicher spät in der Nacht war's'; Jakob

Mattes's House
  7 Anna, Luise: 'Er spricht mit mir kein Wort'
  8 Mattes: 'Sie soll nichts wissen' (recitative and aria)

On the River
  9   (i) Semi-chorus, alto solo: 'Jetzt ist es Abend'
         (ii) Semi-chorus, Orth, Mattes

Close by Mattes's House
 10 First Finale:
         (i) Three Blackmailers: 'Die Verhältnisse von Mein und Dein'
         (ii) Mattes, semi-chorus, Orth
         (iii) Semi-chorus, Mattes, Orth, Jakob Orth: 'Gehet zum Richter'

ACT II

 11 *Allegro giusto* (orchestra)

The Judge's Room
 12   (i) Judge, Mattes, Orth, townspeople
         (ii) Herald: 'An die Bevölkerung der Stadt!'
 13   (i) orchestral interlude: Kleiner Marsch

A Street, Outside the City
         (ii) Anna and Johann Mattes, David and Jakob Orth
         (iii) Three Blackmailers: 'Das ist ein Zustand, wie wir ihn brauchen'

14   (i)   Blackmailers: 'Oh lassen Sie uns leben'
       (ii)   Judge, chorus (offstage): 'Seid klug und wehret euch nicht'
       (iii) Commissar: 'Ich will nicht ruhen'

The Judge's Room
       (iv)   Judge: 'Seht, wie das Ende ausgereifter Dinge'
       (v)   Chorus: 'Länger als eine Stunde'

In Front of Mattes's House
15   (i)   Anna: 'Oh meine Tochter, warum kommst du nicht zurück?'
       (ii)   Three Agents (dialogue)

The Market Square in the City
16   (i)   Commissar: 'Das Wohlbefinden des Landes'
       (ii)   Agents; Mattes, Orth, chorus: 'Wir sind verhaftet'
       (iii) Anna: 'Wo ist meine Tochter?'
       (iv)   Commissar, Adjutant, Mattes, Orth, Three Agents, Judge

ACT III

17   (i)   alto solo: 'Und wieder sind sechs Jahre vergangen'
       (ii)   Semi-chorus: 'Es ändert sich nicht der Mensch'
       (iii) alto solo, semi-chorus: 'So schieden sich die Armen von
                 den Reichen'
       (iv)   alto solo, semi-chorus: 'So kamen sie zu den vier Toren'

I: War
18   Orchestra (Barbarischer Marsch); chorus ('Tag und Nacht
                 marschiert die Armee')
18a   Semi-chorus: 'Johann Mattes aber und David Orth wurden reich'

Mattes's House
19   (i)   Anna and Johann: 'Die Jahre sind vergangen'
       (ii)   Chorus: 'Tag und Nacht marschiert die Armee'
19a   Chorus: 'Der Krieg ist aus'

II: Inflation
20   Chorus: 'Wo ist unser Geld?'

Orth's Granary
21   (i)   Chorus (women): 'Gib uns Mehl'
       (ii)   Jakob, David

III: Hunger
22   (i)   Semi-chorus: 'Da kam der Hunger'
       (ii)   Chorus, Mattes, Agents
22a   Semi-chorus: 'Und viele blieben am Wege zum vierten Tor'

IV: Disease

Double scene: A Beer-Garden in the City, with Dance Floor; a Hospital Ward
23   Luise Mattes, a man, Jakob, dancers (beer-garden scene)
                 Anna, chorus (hospital scene): 'Sie stirbt!'
23a   Semi-chorus: 'Sie begannen zu zweifeln an allem'

24   Second Finale

       (i)   Ritornello for orchestra

A City Street
  - (ii)   Chorus (the people of Urb): 'Halt! Sind das denn nicht die Männer?'
  - (iii) Agents: 'Nein, wir sind es nicht'
  - (iv)   Chorus: 'Schafft Mattes her!'

In Front of Mattes's House
  - (v)   Mattes: 'Sie sind schon hinter mir her'
  - (vi)   Agents: 'Wir waren beim Kommissar'

Orth's Granary
  - (vii) Mattes: 'Hilf mir, Orth'
  - (viii) Mattes, Orth: 'Hilf mir, Orth . . . Wie soll ich dir helfen?'
  - (ix)   Semi-chorus: 'Jetzt kämpfen beide'
  - (x)   Mattes, Orth: 'Bringst du mich fort? . . . Ja, ich bringe dich fort'
  - (xi)   Chorus, 'Schlagt Mattes tot!'
  - (xii) Orth: 'Wem du auch begegnest'

Note 2

14 (*i*)–(*iii*) is the new scene written in January 1932, shortly before the premiere and after the vocal score had gone to print. Although it replaced the closing part of 13 and the beginning of the original 14 (which are therefore excluded from the outline above) it was not given a numbering of its own. The dramatic function of the Judge throughout this scene is such that Weill had also to expand the final ensemble in Act II (16), in order to allow the Judge to make a final and, in principle, decisive appearance.

Autographs

SKETCHES

Miscellaneous preliminary sketches are on a leaf of A^{18} and another leaf of a 14-line paper without maker's name. A full sheet of B^{30} carries on *a* and *b* the sketch of an opening aria for Johann Mattes which did not reach draft stage, but is the source of the musical material for Orth's final pronouncement, 'Wem du auch begegnest' (24 (*xii*)). *c* carries sketches for the 'neue Fassung' of *Der Jasager* (see p. 228); *d* has further sketches for *Die Bürgschaft*, and a note of instrumentation which – unless it related to a later work, e.g. *Der Silbersee* – differs significantly from the orchestra in *Die Bürgschaft*: 2.1.2.1.   0.3.3.0.   pno. perc. str. 4.3.2.1 (no second violins). A sketch for the choric final section of 17, 'So kamen sie zu den vier Toren', is on the first side of a sheet of B^{26} whose three other sides carry sketches for *Der Silbersee*. The remaining *Bürgschaft* sketches in WLA are afterthoughts. All of them postdate the final draft. Apart from those written on the back page of the draft, they are on an assortment of B^{28} and B^{30} papers. Among them are, for example, contrapuntal elaborations of material that is homophonically presented in the draft.

FINAL DRAFT

126 sides of B^{30}; the foldings are contained in a cover sheet of the same paper bearing the non-autograph title 'Die Bürgschaft'. The draft breaks

off at bar 1320 – 215 bars before the end. Weill and Neher struggled for some weeks with the ending of the opera; no sketches or drafts for it have survived. Despite the lacunae this is by far the most substantial draft of a European work to have been preserved in the legacy.

FULL SCORE (UEA)

518 pages of B²⁸, in unbound foldings without title page or signature. Act I is paginated 1–224 and dated at the end '6 Aug 1931'; the second act is paginated 225–367 and dated '2 Sept 1931'; the third 1–151, and dated '19 Oct 1931'. The two passages added in January 1932 – *14 (i)–(iii)*, and the interpolation in *16* – are missing; but there is no sign, nor any reason to suppose, that they were ever incorporated. In view of the late date of composition and the lack of any covering documents in the Universal Edition files, the originals were probably inserted in the printed full score used by Fritz Stiedry (the conductor of the first performance), after orchestral parts had been extracted locally, and copies forwarded to Wiesbaden and Düsseldorf where the regional premieres were to take place three days later.

VOCAL SCORE

14 (i)–(iii)

Whereas the vocal score of the published version of *Die Bürgschaft* is by Erwin Stein – whose pencil manuscript, on 331 pages, is in UEA – that of the new scene (*14 (i)–(iii)*) was made by Weill himself. The holograph is in the possession of Carl Ebert. It is written on ten pages of B¹⁸ (the paper supplied and stamped by the Berlin publishers Bote und Bock, then at Tauentzienstrasse 6). The holograph is contained in a title sheet bearing the dedication 'Für Carl Ebert/in herzlicher Freundschaft/Kurt Weill/ Louveciennes Oktober 1934'. (The paper, which has the serial number 681 but no maker's name, is clearly of French origin.) In a covering letter to Ebert, Weill affectionately recalled their troubles with 'that damned second act' and expressed his gratitude to Ebert for his part in persuading him and Neher to write the new scene.

Publication

UE, 1932: vocal score, reduction by Erwin Stein; full score, hire only, not including *14 (i)–(iii)* or additions to *16*; libretto, unrevised; processed vocal score of inserts, for second printing of vocal score.

First Performance

10 March 1932, Städtische Oper, Berlin: conductor Fritz Stiedry, director Carl Ebert, designer Caspar Neher; with Hans Reinmar (Mattes), Charlotte Müller (Anna), Irene Eisinger (Luise), Wilhelm Rode (Orth), Paul Feher (Jakob), Bjorn Talén (Judge), Josef Burgwinkel (Commissar),

Ruth Berglund (alto, in choir), and Wilhelm Gombert, Rudolf Gonszar, and Eduard Kandl (Creditors, Blackmailers, etc.).

Note 3

LATER PERFORMANCES AND REVISIONS

Weill took a keen interest in the two provincial productions that opened on 13 March 1932 – the Wiesbaden one under Karl Rankl and the Düsseldorf one under Jascha Horenstein – and attended performances of both. Some of the incidental revisions made during the rehearsal period and perhaps also in the immediate aftermath of the performances are noted by Weill in his own copy of the printed vocal score (WLA) and also in the copy belonging to Fritz Stiedry (whose own markings, of course, preponderate). Thanks to the intercession of David Josef Bach (see p. 385) a production at the Vienna Staatsoper, conducted by Clemens Kraus, became a possibility during the summer of 1932. On 15 June 1932 Weill informed Universal Edition that he and Neher had 'firmly resolved' to write a new Act II for Vienna, should the work be taken up by the Staatsoper. It was not taken up; but with the apparent improvement of the political situation in Germany in the latter half of 1932, Carl Ebert and the Städtische Oper in Berlin became more confident about the prospects of reviving the work in 1933, and contracts were signed for new productions in Hamburg-Altona and Königsberg (Scherchen). The events of February 1933 put an end to all plans for *Die Bürgschaft* in Germany; and once Weill's hopes for France (Paris Opéra) and the USA (Philadelphia, through Stokowski) had been extinguished the incentive for resuming work on *Die Bürgschaft* was certainly not strong enough to overcome the practical difficulties. A public 'pledge' that the Städtische Oper would eventually revive *Die Bürgschaft* had, however, been given in an appropriately gnomic form by Max von Schillings after the Nazi seizure of power.* It was fulfilled twenty-four years later.

Posthumous Revisions

On 6 October 1957 the Städtische Oper, Berlin, presented a so-called 'Neufassung' of *Die Bürgschaft* (conductor Arthur Rother, director Carl Ebert, designer Neher), which had been prepared by Neher, Ebert, and Horst Georges, with the musical assistance of Gottfried von Einem and Francis Burt. Dramatically, the results were not altogether to Neher's liking.

A new and quite different basis for revision was discussed a year later by Neher, Lotte Lenya, and the present writer, and agreed in principle. A draft revision on that basis was completed by the present writer in 1976.

---

* Recounted by Berthold Goldschmidt at the Kurt Weill Conference at Yale, November 1983.

Lacunae

Irrespective of the need for posthumous revisions – which is open to a wide variety of opinions – the importance of the two additions to Act II seems indisputable. However, no orchestral material of any kind, whether scores or parts, has been traced since 1945. It is thought to have been among the performance materials confiscated from Universal Edition after the *Anschluss*.

[January] 1931, Berlin

Mann ist Mann

Comedy (*Lustspiel*) by Bertolt Brecht
Music for the 1931 Berlin production
(Vanished – though not without trace)

The play is set in a rough-and-ready imitation of British India, supposedly in the year 1925. Galy Gay, an Irish porter incapable of offending anyone except by his sheer inoffensiveness, says farewell to his wife and sets off to buy a fish for their supper. On the way he meets three British soldiers who have lost the fourth member of their party, Jeraiah Jip, while looting a temple, and will need a substitute for him when they return to barracks and their fearsome Sergeant, 'der Blutige Fünfer' (Bloody Five). Galy seems a perfect choice. Ever gullible, he accepts their offer of a drink in the army canteen run by Widow Begbick. Once inside the barracks, there is no escape for him. Step by step he is forced to adopt the identity of the missing soldier. At last he is transformed into Jeraiah Jip, 'the human fighting-machine'.

First Performance

6 February 1931, Berlin Staatstheater; with Peter Lorre (Galy Gay), Helene Weigel (Begbick), and Theo Lingen, Alexander Granach and Wolfgang Heinz as the three soldiers.

Notes

The Staatstheater programme does not name any musicians or musical director, and refers only to three incidental items by Weill – 'Nachtmusik', 'Schlachtmusik', and 'Marschmusik'. There is no mention, in the programme or in the Berlin press notices, of the 'Begbick Song', also known as 'Das Lied vom Fluss der Dinge' ('The Song about the Flux of Things'), which Brecht added to the text in 1931. Given the celebrity and notoriety of the 'Brecht–Weill' combination, the extent to which Weill's music escaped attention on this occasion would seem to argue either that his contribution was very slight, or that it was pushed so far into the background that it seemed so. There is, however, incontrovertible evidence that he wrote at least one song for the production; and it is evidence of a kind that provides a clue as to the nature of the rest of the score.

Autograph

After Helene Weigel's death in 1971 her script for the 1931 Berlin production of *Mann ist Mann* was acquired by the BBA. In it, the archivist Hertha Ramthun discovered a notation in pencil of an 8-bar melody for the refrain of 'Das Lied vom Fluss der Dinge', beginning with the words 'Beharre nicht auf der Welle' ('Cling not to the wave'). It is written on an inserted leaf of 6-line paper, landscape format, measuring 9.7 × 17.7 cms. At that stage the manuscript was tentatively attributed to Weill. The present writer inspected a copy in 1983, confirmed the attribution and identified the melody as that of Anna's song, 'Oh meine Tochter, warum kommst du nicht zurück?' in the second act of *Die Bürgschaft* (15 (i)).

Those eight bars of unharmonized melody suggested an explanation not only for the mysterious 'disappearance' of Weill's *Mann ist Mann* score, but also for the equally mysterious fact that he troubled to undertake it at a time when he and Brecht had drifted apart, and when in any case he was completely immersed in *Die Bürgschaft*.

By the beginning of 1931 Weill must have been well into the draft of the second act of *Die Bürgschaft*. If he had not yet reached 15 (i), he would surely have reached 13(i), the 'Kleiner Marsch', whose militaristic aspirations are heightened in the draft version by the quotation of the 1912 music-hall song 'Tipperary' which was adopted by the British Expeditionary Forces during the First World War. Significantly, Weill removed the 'Tipperary' quotation from *Die Bürgschaft*, where the Anglo-Indian references are more obvious though less urgent than those to European fascism. With or without the quotation, the 'Kleiner Marsch' would have served admirably for the 'Marschmusik' in *Mann ist Mann*, just as the instrumental introduction to Anna's 'Oh meine Tochter' would have served for the 'Nachtmusik'. As for the 'Schlachtmusik', nothing could have been more pertinent to the world of 'Bloody Five' than the 'Barbarischer Marsch' that dominates the 'War' scenes of *Die Bürgschaft* (Act III, 18 and 19 (ii)).

Trumpet, saxophone, piano duet and percussion would have been quite sufficient for all this, and a full score unnecessary. Armed with a copyist and the sketches and early drafts for *Die Bürgschaft*, Weill would have needed little more than a day or two for cobbling together a *Mann ist Mann* score that nicely matched Neher's scenery and costumes and, like them, would soon be taken to pieces and vanish. That, of course, would explain the absence of any reference to the score in the correspondence between Weill and his publishers. Kept within those limits, the task would not have entailed any significant interruption of work on *Die Bürgschaft*, and would have had the advantage of preserving good relations with Ernst Legal – who had been a proponent of the *Mahagonny* opera at the Kroll.

August 1932 – January 1933, Klein-Machnow

Der Silbersee
Ein Wintermärchen
[*The Silver Lake – A Winter's Tale*]

Musical play in three acts
Text: Georg Kaiser
Duration: 3 hours; 65 minutes music
Cast: singing roles: Severin (tenor), Fennimore (soprano), Olim (bar-
    itone), Frau von Luber (mezzo-soprano), Baron Laur (tenor), Lottery
    Agent (tenor), Two Gravediggers (baritones), Two Shopgirls (sopra-
    nos), Two Young Men (basses), chorus (SATB); speaking roles: a portly
    country policeman, two doctors, a nurse, etc.
Orchestra: 2.1.2.1.   2.2.0.0.   timp. perc. pno. harp str.

A legendary country, resembling Northern Germany, at a time of acute social and
economic distress. The wooded banks of the Silbersee provide shelter for a few of
the many who have despaired of finding work in the nearby metropolis.
Returning from a raid on a suburban grocery store, Severin and his comrades are
fired upon by the country policeman Olim. The others escape, but the wounded
Severin is arrested and taken to the prison hospital. While preparing the official
report, Olim undergoes a crisis of conscience, changes the report so as to secure
Severin's release, and resigns from the force. With the proceeds of a lottery win
he purchases a castle, and there, in the guise of a mysterious benefactor,
dedicates himself to Severin's wellbeing. But Severin is obsessed with thoughts of
revenge.
    Thanks to the innocent and other-worldly Fennimore, whom Olim's châtelaine,
Frau von Luber, has engaged with a view to discovering the secrets that unite and
divide the two men, Severin learns of Olim's real identity. So murderous is his
rage that Olim flees to an attic room. While pretending to offer comfort and
friendly advice Frau von Luber dupes him into assigning to her (and to her friend
the Baron Laur) the castle deeds, and his entire fortune. The *coup de grâce*, she
hopes, will now be administered by Severin. However, her plan is foiled by
Fennimore, who effects a reconciliation between the two men. Furious, von Luber
drives her niece out into the wintry night, and then turns to Olim and Severin,
teasing, goading, and finally humiliating them with the evidence that the tables
have been turned at last. Dispossessed, they too are cast out. Together they set off
towards the Silbersee, intending to drown themselves. But the voices of
Fennimore and the chorus are heard, reminding them of their duties to each other
and to their fellow men. When they reach the Silbersee, winter miraculously turns
to spring; but the lake is still a solid sheet of ice. With new confidence, they start
to walk across.

[1a]   Ouverture (*Allegro assai*)

ACT I

The Wooded Banks of the Silbersee
1   'Gräbst du?' (two young men) [Gravediggers' Duet]
2   *Alla marcia funebre* – 'Wir tragen den Toten zu Grabe' (four young men)

3   'Der Bäkker bäckt ums Morgenrot' (Severin, four men)
             [Hunger Song]

A Grocery Store
4   'Wir sind zwei Mädchen, die an jedermann verkaufen' (two shop-
             girls) [Song der beiden Verkäuferinnen (Song of the Shopgirls)]
4a   Walzer (orchestra)

Police Station
5   [melodramas, choruses]
   (i)   *Sostenuto* (orchestra)
   (ii)   'Olim! Tut es dir nicht leid?' (chorus)
   (iii) 'Jetzt bist du auf dem Wege' (chorus)
   (iv)   'Wenn du nicht schiltst' (chorus)
   (v)   'Immer weiter dringen' (chorus)
   (vi)   'Noch hast du das Geld nicht' (chorus)
6   'Was zahlen Sie für einen Rat?' (Lottery Agent) [Song von der
             Krone des Gewinns]
6a   [development and conclusion of 5]
   (i)   'Olim! was willst du tun?' (chorus)
   (ii)   'Olim! Willst du vergessen?' (chorus)
   (iii) 'Du hast dich zum Aufbruch entschlossen' (chorus)
   (iv)   Nachspiel (orchestra)

Prison Hospital
[7a]   Melodrama (Severin) [Severin's Delirium]
7   'Was soll ich essen in der Morgenfrühe?' (Severin, Olim)

ACT II

[8a]   *Moderato assai* (orchestra)

Olim's Castle
8   'Ich bin eine arme Verwandte' [Fennimore's Song: 'Die arme
             Verwandte' ('The Poor Relation')]
9   'Rom hiess eine Stadt' (Fennimore) [(Ballade von) Cäsars Tod
             (Ballad of Caesar's Death)]
10   *Allegro moderato* (orchestra) [Fennimore's Dance]
11   'Erst trifft dich die Kugel' (Severin) [Rache-Arie (Revenge Aria)]
12   'Auf jener Strasse' (Severin, Fennimore) [Silbersee-Duett]
12a   Reminiszenz (chorus) [shortened reprise of 11]

ACT III

Olim's Castle
13   *Allegro assai* (orchestra) [shortened reprise of 1a]
14   'Wie Odysseus an den Mast des Schiffes' (Severin) [Odysseus-Arie]
15   Totentanz (orchestra) [Fennimore's Dance of Death]
15a   'Es wächst uns in den Mund der Wein' (Frau v. Luber,
             Baron Laur) [Schlaraffenland-Song (Song of Cockaigne)]

The Walk to the Silbersee (Finale)
16   (i)   *Andantino* (orchestra) – melodrama (Severin, Olim)
      (ii)   'Ihr sollt den Weg nicht finden' (chorus)
      (iii) *Allegretto* (orchestra) – melodrama (Severin, Olim)
      (iv)   'Alles, was ist, ist Beginnen' (Fennimore's voice; chorus)

Autographs

SKETCHES

The only surviving sketches are on sides *b–d* of a sheet of B²⁶ whose first side carries a sketch for the alto solo 'So kamen sie zu den vier Toren' in the third act of *Die Bürgschaft* (17 (*iv*)). *b* carries canonic workings for 16 (*i*) and a sketch of 16 (*ii*); *c* carries four items in the following order: a tentative sketch for *15*; coda of *3*; definitive sketch for *15*; waltz refrain of *4*. The fourth side is the most interesting, for it carries orchestral sketches discarded from *Der Silbersee* but resumed in later works. There are two fully formed paragraphs, the first in E major and the second in the relative minor. Both were to recur, almost note for note and obviously from memory, in the sketches for *Marie Galante* (August 1934). Again, both failed to qualify for inclusion. That appears to have been the end of the E major idea; but not of its C sharp minor relative. This idea – whose general character is surprisingly, and no doubt fortuitously, similar to that of Satie's *Gnossiennes* – continued to haunt the composer; it followed him to America and first reappeared in the sketches for *Johnny Johnson* (summer 1936). Yet again it was rejected. But before long, persistence was at last rewarded: in a remote stretch of *The Eternal Road* a passing caravan required a supply of incidental music and was duly provided with a development and orchestration of the C sharp minor idea.

FINAL DRAFT

Missing.

FULL SCORE (UEA)

226 pages of B²⁶ (1–3 only) and S²⁶, unbound, without title page, and paginated act by act (respectively ninety-two, seventy, and fifty-six pages, plus seven pages of S²⁶ for the Overture). The final page of the score is inscribed 'Ende Klein-Machnow 1. Dezember 1932'. The Overture was composed later that same month.

Publications

UE music; Felix Bloch-Erben, text.
1933: (1) *Sechs Stücke aus 'Der Silbersee'*: voice-and-piano album containing numbers *3*, *4*, *6*, *8*, *9*, and *16b*. There is no reference in the album to the existence of any other music for *Der Silbersee*. The cover design is not the one submitted by Caspar Neher, but is the work of the Viennese artist Mopp. (2) Vocal score. The anonymous piano reduction is by Erwin Stein (whose manuscript is in UEA). The six numbers included in the vocal album have been engraved, as has the 'Silbersee-Duett' (*12*), which Universal Edition withdrew from the album at proof stage, when Weill discovered, to his amazement, that 'The Ballad of Caesar's

Death' was not among the selected numbers, and insisted on its inclusion. (3) Manuscript copies of the full score, hire only.

First Performance and Simultaneous Local Premieres

18 February 1933

Leipzig, Altes Theater: conductor Gustav Brecher, director Detlef Sierck (Douglas Sirk), designer Caspar Neher; with Alexander Golling (Severin), Erhard Siedl (Olim), Gretel Berndt (Fennimore), Lina Carstens (Frau von Luber), Ernst Sattler (Baron Laur), Albert Garbe (Lottery Agent), Grete Henschke (soprano solo).

Magdeburg, Stadttheater: conductor Georg Winkler, director Helmut Götze, designer Ernst Rufer; with Ernst Busch (Severin), Eduard Wandrey (Olim), Elisabeth Lennartz (Fennimore), Ruth Baldor (Frau von Luber).

Erfurt, Stadttheater: conductor Friedrich Walter, director Hermann Pfeiffer, designer Walter Schröter; with Albert Johannes (Severin), and Sieglinde Riesmann (Fennimore).

Note 1

Der Silbersee was the last work that Weill completed in Germany, and the last to have had its world premiere there. The success of the first three productions was considerable, despite political opposition; but it is clear from the press notices that the demands of a long and complex play were not easily reconciled with those of a score that is by no means simple even for professional singers.

Posthumous dramatic versions

1955: Version for the Schlosspark-Theater, West Berlin; first performed on 19 September 1955, as part of the Berlin Festival; the score somewhat shortened, and arranged for five players by Boris Blacher (and others).

1971: Concert version by Josef Heinzelmann and David Drew; first performed on 25 June 1971 in The Hague, as part of the Holland Festival; Residentie orchestra conducted by Gary Bertini; with Lotte Lenya as narrator. This version consisted of the entire score in its original orchestration, linked by narrations and semi-staged dialogue scenes. Duration, approximately 90 minutes.

1980: *Silverlake*: version for the New York City Opera, book and lyrics by Hugh Wheeler, freely adapted from the original; musically continuous score devised by Lys Symonette, incorporating the music for Strindberg's *Gustav III* (1927) and the 'Muschel-Song' from *Konjunktur* (1928), with new lyrics.

Concert Suites

By Karel Salomon (*c.* 1952), for orchestra, closely based on the original score, and comprising six numbers: *1a* (+ introduction to *14*), *4*, *11*, *12*, *7a*, *16* (*i*) + (*iv*).

By David Drew (1975), for five soloists, chorus, and orchestra, comprising sixteen numbers in their original scoring, arranged in an order designed for concert listening without narrations or dialogue; the only significant omissions are the two melodrama-and-chorus scenes (*5* and *6a*) and the Severin–Olim duet (*7*). Duration, 50 minutes; first performed 10 September 1975, Berlin Festival: with Anja Silja (soprano), Günter Reich (baritone), and the Radio-Symphonie-Orchester, Berlin, conducted by Gary Bertini.

January 1933 – February 1934, Berlin/Paris/Louveciennes

Symphony [No. 2]

Commissioned by, and dedicated to, the Princesse Edmond de Polignac

1　*Sostenuto – Allegro molto*
2　*Largo*
3　*Allegro vivace – Presto*
Duration: 25 minutes
Orchestra: 2 (2 picc.).2.2.2.　2.2.2.0.　timp. str.

Autographs

SKETCHES

Nothing has survived apart from three memos, all of them adjacent to drafts of other compositions dating from the early autumn of 1933. The opening of the *Largo* appears on the last of the four sides of D^{24} that carry the draft of the song 'Der Abschiedsbrief'; a 12-bar memo for the second theme of the movement is at the foot of the single side of D^{24} carrying the rough draft of *La grande complainte de Fantômas*. The third memo relates to the wind band episode in the Symphony's finale; it is on the same D^{24} leaf as the rough draft of the Cocteau song 'Es regnet'.

DRAFT

Missing.

FULL SCORE

The manuscript, which is in the possession of the heirs of the Princesse Edmond de Polignac, is on seventy-nine sides of D^{28}, with autograph pagination, and a title page reading: 'Dédié à la Princesse Edmond de

Polignac/Kurt Weill/Symphonie Nr. 1'. The first movement has the end date 'Berlin Januar 1933', the second is undated, and the third has the end date 'Louveciennes Februar 1934'. While the first of these dates can refer only to the completion in Berlin of the draft, the second certainly refers to the full score, for the draft of the finale was completed on 16 December 1933. The numbering of the Symphony reflects the fact that Weill's first symphony (see p. 128) remained unpublished and unperformed.

ADDITIONAL MATERIAL

A photographic copy (on glossy paper) of the professionally copied full score has been used by Weill as a means of recording, in soft pencil, numerous minor revisions and one major addition – a percussion part (triangle, cymbal, side-drum, tenor drum, bass drum) for the second and third movements. Bruno Walter, who conducted the premiere and two subsequent performances (in Vienna and in New York), had insisted on the percussion parts, much against Weill's inclination. Not surprisingly, the result is heavy-handed, and the unadorned original far superior.

Publication

Heugel et Cie, 1934: score and parts for hire only.

First Performance

11 October 1934, Amsterdam, Concertgebouw Orchestra conducted by Bruno Walter.

Notes

With strong encouragement from Erwin Stein among others, Weill had started thinking about an orchestral work in his post-*Mahagonny* style as early as 1929. Traces of that may well have found their way into *Der Lindberghflug*; but the Second Symphony unmistakably presupposes *Die Bürgschaft* and *Der Silbersee*, with which it has thematic and characteristic links. Yet Weill insisted, very rightly, that the Symphony was not programmatic. Bruno Walter tried in vain to persuade him to give the Symphony a descriptive title, but prior to the world premiere had succeeded only in extracting from him the Schumannesque 'Symphonische Fantasie' or 'Fantaisie Symphonique'. Embarrassed, perhaps, by the almost uniformly contemptuous reception of the work in Amsterdam, Walter performed it with the New York Philharmonic Orchestra on 13 December 1934 under the title *Three Night Scenes*. Whether or not Weill had agreed to this, the title was of no avail; the critics were as hostile as they had been in Amsterdam.

Posthumous Publication

Schott/Heugel, 1966: study score, edited, with a preface and notes, by David Drew.

16 April – May 1933, Paris

Die sieben Todsünden
(*The Seven Deadly Sins*)

'Spectacle in nine scenes'
Text: Bertolt Brecht
Commissioned by Edward James for Les Ballets 1933
Dedication: the Vicomte and Vicomtesse Charles de Noailles
Duration: 35 minutes
Cast: Anna I (high voice), Anna II (dancer), the Family (2 tenors, 2 basses), dancers and corps de ballet *ad libitum*
Orchestra: 2(2 picc.).1.2.2.   2.2.1.1.   timp. perc. harp pno. bjo. str.

1a	Introduktion: *Andante sostenuto* 'Meine Schwester und ich stammen aus Louisiana' (Anna I)	
1	Faulheit [Sloth]: *Allegro vivace* 'Müssiggang ist aller Laster Anfang' (Family)	
2	Stolz [Pride]: *Allegretto, quasi andantino – Schneller Walzer* 'Als wir aber ausgestattet waren' (Anna)	
3	Zorn [Anger]: *Molto agitato* 'Das geht nicht vorwärts!' (Family); 'Jetzt geht es vorwärts!' (Anna)	
4	Völlerei [Gluttony]: *Largo* 'Das ist ein Brief aus Philadelphia' (Family)	
5	Unzucht [Lechery]: *Moderato* 'Und wir fanden einen Mann in Boston' (Anna); refrain: 'Ach ich sagte ihr oft' (Anna)	
6	Habsucht [Avarice]: *Allegro giusto* 'Wie hier in der Zeitung steht' (Family)	
7	Neid [Envy]: *Allegro non troppo – Alla marcia, un poco tenuto* 'Und die letzte Stadt der Reise war San Franscisco' (Anna); refrain: 'Schwester, wir alle sind frei geboren' (Anna)	
7a	Finaletto: *Andante sostenuto* 'Darauf kehrten wir zurück nach Louisiana' (Anna)	

Although the text of *The Seven Deadly Sins* contains nothing to indicate that it was intended for the stage, it resembles the *Mahagonny-Songspiel* in that its descriptions of actions and reactions develop a certain narrative momentum. In *The Seven Deadly Sins* this is heightened by an element of characterization and quasi-dramatic conflict. The following summary is based on the texts Brecht wrote for the composer (and not on the 'official' scenario, which was the work of other hands – see *Note 2*).

Introduction: Anna I, who sings and is 'practical', introduces herself and her 'beautiful' sister, Anna II, who dances. They set out from Louisiana, to seek their fortune. Their journey will last seven years and take them to seven cities, in each of which they will earn their contribution to the 'little house' which the Family is to build beside the Mississippi.
    Sloth: the Family pray that Anna II will soon learn to get a move on.
    Pride: Anna II has found herself a job as a cabaret dancer. Proudly she demonstrates to the patrons all she knows of the 'art' of dancing; but catcalls and

Weill photographed by Hoyningen-Huene (see p.44) in Paris in 1933,
at the time of *Die sieben Todsünden*.

Holograph of 'Maikaterlied', 1917(?); text by Otto Julius Bierbaum, underlaid in German script.

'Klops Lied', 1925; text traditional.

Sketch of the closing bars of the *Mahagonny Songspiel*, from the
original in the O.W. Neighbour Collection.

Mahagonny Songspiel: © copyright 1963 by Universal Edition A.G., Vienna. All rights reserved.
Used by permission.

Snapshot of Weill by Lotte Lenya, c.1930, in their Berlin apartment
(Bayern-Allee 19).

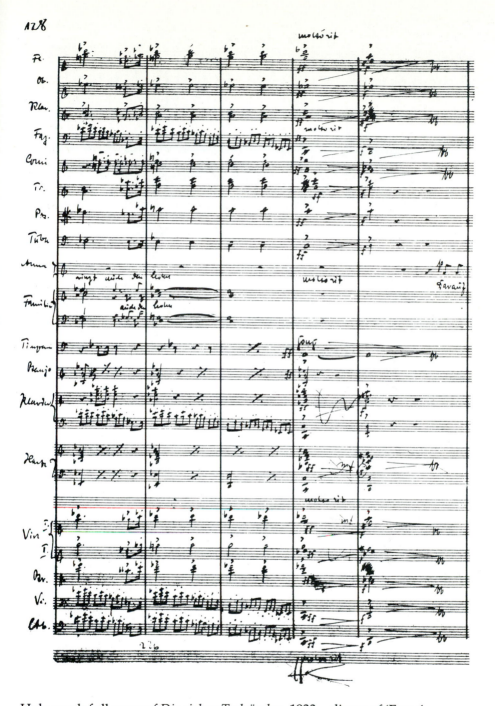

Holograph full score of *Die sieben Todsünden*, 1933 – climax of 'Envy'.

Holograph full score of *Railroads on Parade*, 1937.

'Schickelgruber', 1942; lyrics by Howard Dietz.

Draft of the refrain of 'Trouble Man' *(Lost in the Stars)*, 1949; lyrics by Maxwell Anderson.

Weill rehearsing *Lost in the Stars* with Maxwell Anderson *(left)* and Rouben Mamoulian.

The famous Karsh portrait of Weill (at the time of *Street Scene*) which is discussed and deplored on p.44.

whistles are her only reward. Anna I tells her to forget her pride and her art and show the patrons what they want. She complies.

Anger: Anna II is much too forthright in her protests about the world's injustices; Anna I advises her that if she doesn't learn to curb her temper she'll soon be out of a job.

Gluttony: Anna II has a healthy appetite, but her Family remind her that her present contract stipulates a slim figure and appropriate diet.

Lechery: Anna II is kept by a wealthy roué in Boston, but gives all the money she gets from him to her true love, a penniless layabout. This, explains her sister, is unethical and tactless. Anna II is persuaded to renounce her lover.

Avarice: Anna II is the toast of Baltimore. The Family are delighted to see her name in the papers. But now that she has nearly reached the top and people are actually shooting themselves for her, the Family wonder if she is not perhaps exhibiting her greed rather too flagrantly. A little restraint here, a veil or two there, might, they suggest, bring dividends.

Envy: the sisters have reached San Francisco, the last of the seven cities. Anna II is growing weary, and envies those who can afford to be slothful, who are too proud to sell themselves, and who are free to rage against injustice and to share their beds only with those they love. Rebuked by Anna I for her self-indulgence and sentimentality, Anna II repents the error of her ways.

Epilogue: the sisters rejoin their Family, now snugly installed in the 'little house' that has been built from the wages of virtue and self-righteousness.

Autographs

SKETCHES AND DRAFTS

Missing; believed by the late Edward James to have been in his private collection, but yet to be traced.

REHEARSAL SCORE

The score is in the collection of the heirs of the Vicomtesse de Noailles. Fifty-three numbered pages of D^{16} are gathered in a title sheet of 29-line paper. The title page reads: 'Für Marie-Laure u. Charles de Noailles/in herzlicher Freundschaft/Die sieben Todsünden/(les sept péchés capitaux) Spectâcle [sic!] in 9 Bildern/mit Gedichten von Bert Brecht/Musik von Kurt Weill/Erste Niederschrift des Klavierauszuges'. The score is dated at the end: '16. April–4. Mai 1933. Paris, 1 Place des Etats-Unis'. As the rehearsal score predates the full score, it is not a 'Klavierauszug'.

FULL SCORE [LPA]

131 numbered pages of D^{24}. The score has been disbound, and comprises seven gatherings (with the original stitching) plus the Finaletto on a separate sheet. Soon after Weill's arrival in America, the binding was replaced by a title sheet of American manuscript paper (Sch^{16}), now badly damaged. The title reads: 'Kurt Weill/Die sieben Todsünden/(Anna–Anna)/Ballett in 8 Teilen/Tous droits réservés)'. There are numerous non-autograph markings in various hands throughout the score–bar numberings, nuances, and occasional excisions of doublings.

The score of 'Völlerei' (4) is not included. In 1955, when performance material was prepared for Lenya, it was thought to be missing and was therefore orchestrated from a non-autograph copy of the rehearsal score. However, it is clear from the holograph rehearsal score (which was not accessible in 1955) that the accompaniment was written for guitar only. Weill had no reason – and no time – to write it out again for the sake of making a 'complete' full score.

Note 1

Brecht scholars have had some difficulty in dating the genesis of *The Seven Deadly Sins*, owing to uncertainty about Brecht's exact movements during this unsettled period. Fortunately, Weill's situation was simpler than Brecht's and is better documented with regard to *The Seven Deadly Sins*. The key dates indicate a strong probability that Brecht arrived in Paris at the beginning of the second week in April 1933, and that he started writing the texts for *The Seven Deadly Sins* on or around 10 April. Weill is known to have moved from his hotel to the Noailles' home at the beginning of the third week in April, which could well have been when Brecht left Paris and returned to Switzerland. The Noailles had invited Weill expressly in order that he could work undisturbed: within less than five weeks he had to compose a 30-minute work (which turned out longer) and produce a rehearsal score as well as the orchestral one. Although a few preliminary sketches may have been made before Brecht had finished the text, it was obviously the composition, and not the rehearsal score, that was begun on 16 April.

Universal Edition were too preoccupied with the disastrous effects on their business of the Nazi seizure of power in March 1933 to concern themselves with *The Seven Deadly Sins*, and in July 1933 formally declined to publish it. The production of performance material was therefore undertaken by Les Ballets 1933. Weill's rehearsal score was recopied and duplicated.

First Performance

7 June 1933, Paris, Théâtre des Champs-Elysées; choreographer George(s) Balanchine, designer Caspar Neher, conductor Maurice Abravanel; with Lotte Lenya (Anna I), Tilly Losch (Anna II), Otto Pasetti and Albert Peters (tenors), Erich Fuchs (baritone), and Heinrich Gertler (bass). On 28 June 1933 the same cast performed the work at the Savoy Theatre in London, where the title was changed to *Anna–Anna* after the Lord Chamberlain's Office had remarked that the original title might offend religious susceptibilities. The text itself caused no offence, as it was sung in German on the first night and in Lenya's phonetically learned English thereafter. (The translation was by Edward James, with help from the composer, who spoke 'school English' at that time.) The

only other production in Weill's lifetime or Brecht's was by Harald Lander at the Royal Theatre, Copenhagen, on 12 November 1936. It was withdrawn after the second performance, in response to a formal protest from the German Ambassador.

Note 2

The scenario Balanchine used for his original choreography (and his revival of it with the New York City Ballet in the early 1960s) has naturally acquired quasi-official status, and has exerted a strong influence on most subsequent productions. Frequently attributed to Brecht, it was in fact written by Edward James and his artistic director Boris Kochno. (A carbon copy of their original typescript is in WLA.) The need for a scenario was probably not discovered until Balanchine, who was under great pressure, had received the score and begun to study it in conjunction with the text (of which a reading translation had been prepared by Georges Ribemont-Dessaignes, the surrealist writer and poet, and one-time Dadaist). By then, time was short and Brecht was far away; he was not to return until shortly before the premiere.

Posthumous Publications

1955: privately published by Lotte Lenya (Karoline Weill-Davis) through her own company, Brookhouse Music. (1) Full score, arranged by Wilhelm Brückner-Rüggeberg, with all solo sections transposed downwards (generally a fourth), to suit Lenya's vocal requirements, and with some changes of orchestration, either because of the transpositions or in order to uncover or support the vocal line. Brückner-Rüggeberg scored the guitar accompaniment in 4 for orchestra. (2) Vocal score, reduction by Brückner-Rüggeberg.

Suhrkamp Verlag, Frankfurt-am-Main, 1959: libretto. Title page reads: 'Bertolt Brecht/Die sieben Todsünden/der Kleinbürger/Suhrkamp'. The extended title (*The Seven Deadly Sins of the Petty-Bourgeois*) was evidently proposed by Brecht's widow, Helene Weigel-Brecht; the scenario in this edition is freely adapted from the original James–Kochno one, unattributed.

Schott Verlag, Mainz, 1960: (1) Reprint of 1955 vocal score, with pictorial cover by Hein Heckroth and title page reading 'Kurt Weill/Die sieben Todsünden/ Ballett mit Gesang in acht Teilen/Text von Bert Brecht/ Klavierauszug von Wilhelm Brückner-Rüggeberg'. No editorial notes or reference to the transpositions. (2) Reprint, hire only, of 1955 full score.

1968: full score, hire only, of Weill's original version, partly edited by David Drew; with English adaptation by W. H. Auden and Chester Kallman.

1972: vocal score of the original version, with an appendix containing the solo sections, as transposed in the 1955 vocal score by Brückner-Rüggeberg.

Note 3

The 1968 full score was prepared specifically for the first performance since 1936 of Weill's original version (given by Evelyn Lear, with the BBC Symphony Orchestra under Colin Davis, at a Henry Wood Promenade Concert in London that same year). Because of the pressure of time, the editing of the full score was not completed in a publishable form, though it had a bearing on the 1972 vocal score. Publication of a study score, with introduction and editorial notes, was planned at that time but has yet to be authorized and carried through. The interpretation of the work that Lenya recorded commercially in 1956, and which she performed numerous times in Germany and America until the mid-1960s, established a preference for the transposed version. But even in those literary and theatrical circles where arguments based on the claims of the composer's own score would be regarded as the merest pedantry – especially if the box-office is making strong counter-claims – there may be some agreement that the high-voice version obviates dangerous comparisons with Lenya's mature interpretation and frees the soloist from the ties of hallowed tradition. Technically and musically the role is, however, beyond the reach of most present-day diseuses, chansonnières, and rock stars. The notion that modern microphone techniques will come to the rescue (irrespective of the effect on the male quartet and the general balance) has by now been proved false on countless painful occasions. Even for trained singers who really understand what the score requires of them, and what it does not require, *Die sieben Todsünden* is far from simple.

[September] 1933, Paris

Der Abschiedsbrief

[*The farewell letter*]

For voice and piano
Text: Erich Kästner

Autographs

SKETCHES

Missing

DRAFT

Four sides of D²⁴; on the last side is a sketch of the opening of the *Largo* of the Second Symphony; inverse, in ink, is an abortive start (one bar only) for the full score of the 'Zorn' number in *Die sieben Todsünden*.

FAIR COPY

Blue ink on sides *a–g* of a folding of four sheets of 14-line paper (measuring 35 × 27 cms). Weill has added in pencil the note 'Einen Ton tiefer transponieren!' (transpose down a tone!). A French translation by André Mauprey, entitled 'La Lettre d'adieux' (and, alternatively, 'On vous laisse tomber' – 'Lettre d'adieu de Mélanie') is underlaid in pencil in other hands.

Notes

The song is one of two that arose from a meeting with Marlene Dietrich in the summer of 1933. Together with its companion piece – which was probably 'Es regnet' (see next entry) – it was written in response to a request for revue and recording material. The project came to nothing, ostensibly because Dietrich found that 'Der Abschiedsbrief' did not suit her voice, but probably also (if not principally) on account of the text, which Weill had selected in preference to the conventional popular-song lyrics Dietrich had offered him. The song might also be read as an ironic farewell to Erik Charell's plan for a Weill–Kästner collaboration (see p. 393).

Posthumous Publication

EAM, 1982: in *The Unknown Kurt Weill: A Collection of 14 Songs*, edited by Lys Symonette.

[September] 1933, Paris

Es regnet

For voice and piano
Text: after Jean Cocteau
(Partly missing)

Autographs

SKETCHES

Missing

DRAFT

Partly missing. A rough draft of the song fills both sides of a leaf of D^{24} (which also carries a sketch for the wind-band episode in the finale of the Second Symphony). The draft is still far from complete at the end of the second side. Title and attribution to Cocteau have been added in Lenya's hand, *c.* 1954.

FAIR COPY

Missing.

Text

Apart from Lenya's addition to the draft, there is no evidence in WLA of Cocteau's authorship. On a separate sheet of paper Weill has neatly written out the first section of the text, in ink, without giving Cocteau's name. Assuming that Cocteau was in fact the author, there are two possibilities: either that Weill translated the French original, or that he revised Cocteau's attempt at a German text.

Notes

In its drafted form the song is in two distinct parts. The first part breaks off without cadencing, after an open-ended refrain; the second, in contrasted character, is headed, just above the start of the vocal line, 'Der Lügner' ('The Liar'), as if the piece were a dialogue scene for male and female voices. As a musico-dramatic answer to the first part it promises well; but the page ends before the music and the text have reached a point from which it would be possible to foresee and forehear a formal rejoinder. The musical and textual evidence, as well as the actual appearance of the manuscript, tend to suggest that 'The Liar's' intervention was the continuation of an interior dialogue, or the branching out of a duet, rather than the start of a separate song. Whether the piece was conceived for Dietrich is impossible to determine from internal evidence. There is little sign of its having been conceived as a companion piece for 'Der Abschiedsbrief' – another Kästner poem would have been more logical, and a more striking contrast of tone and tempo desirable. It is perhaps worth noting – though it proves nothing either way – that the (often sketchy) accompanimental texture is notably less pianistic than that of 'Der Abschiedsbrief' at comparable draft stage. The tango feeling, and the harmony, cries out for the *Silbersee* orchestra; and like the *Silbersee* 'Gnossienne', the first section of 'Es regnet' was to be resuscitated in orchestral form as incidental music for *The Eternal Road*.

Posthumous Publication

EAM, 1982: a version of the first section of the draft, edited and completed by Lys Symonette, was published for the first time in *The Unknown Kurt Weill: A Collection of 14 Songs*.

[October] 1933, Paris

La grande complainte de Fantômas
Ballad for Radio

Text: Robert Desnos
Commissioned by French Radio (Paris station)
(Mostly missing)
Duration: 15 minutes

Note 1

Nothing is known of the instrumentation, or of the relationship between the music and the production, which was exceptionally elaborate for so short a programme: the announcements and the press reports indicate that there was a cast of approximately one hundred, including cabaret and music-hall artists, buskers, accordionists, whistlers, and clowns – with a few opera singers and recitalists thrown in for good measure.

Text

Fantômas, the crooked hero of an immensely popular pulp-fiction series by Pierre Souvestre and Marcel Allin, was adopted as a kind of mascot by the Paris surrealists during the inter-war period (rather as Superman and his like were adopted by the American Pop Art movement in the 1950s). Desnos, who died in Terezin concentration camp in 1944, was one of the most original poets associated with the circle of André Breton and Louis Aragon, and an early convert to the art of broadcasting. His *Grande complainte de Fantômas* chronicles the exploits of Fantômas in twenty-five quatrains, and does so in a manner presumably intended to appeal to the composer of *L'Opéra de quat' sous*, a work best known in France through the French-language version of Pabst's *Dreigroschenoper* film, and a powerful influence on the writers and composers associated with the literary cabarets of Montmartre and Montparnasse.

Autographs

A leaf of D^{24} carries a sketch of two stanzas (and a 12-bar sketch of the second theme of the *Largo* of the Second Symphony). There is no title or heading, but the text is legible enough for purposes of verification. *Verso*, a 7-bar sketch for piano, headed 'English Waltz', clearly related to *Fantômas*.

First Performance

3 November 1933, Radio Paris; director Antonin Artaud, producer Paul Deharme, conductor Alejo Carpentier.

Note 2

Paul Deharme was the leading innovator in French Radio before the war – a counterpart of Alfred Braun in pre-Hitler Berlin radio, and Lawrence Gilliam in the BBC. It was entirely characteristic of him that he brought together not only Desnos and Weill but also Artaud and Carpentier (remembered today as an eminent novelist). The *Fantômas* production was also typical in that material attractive to a wide listening public was treated in a manner that was highly experimental (though surely not 'cerebral', as one impressed but bemused critic remarked). In view of the complexities of the production and the relative primitiveness of studio conditions, at least some of the musical elements must have been prerecorded. No trace of recordings, or of the vocal parts and rehearsal scores (which must have been widely distributed) has been found in the archives of French Radio. Yet it is in the nature of such apparently trivial relics of transient collaborations that their true value – in this case, their historic value – is more readily appreciated by private collectors than by official institutions. Sure enough, *Fantômas* re-emerged after Weill's death as an item on the programme of the Rose Rouge cabaret in the Rue de Rennes, alongside Raymond Queneau's *Exercices de style* (see Jacques Damase, *Les Folies du Music-Hall*, London, 1962, p. 87). It is easy to understand how this unauthorized use of unpublished music passed unnoticed at the time, and how the manuscript or recording that made it possible then vanished once again into limbo. Less understandable is the unauthorized recording of a *Fantômas* song made by Catherine Sauvage for the French Philips Company in the early 1970s (label number B 77 936 L). In this case, attempts to discover what material had been used and who owned it proved fruitless. The instrumental backing used in the recording has no claims to authenticity, but is a typical attempt at a commercially acceptable version of what is commonly thought to be the 'Weill sound'. The melody sung by Sauvage is a smoothed-out and popularized version of the one sketched by Weill, which is a waltz-time descendant of the *Silbersee* 'Ballad of Caesar'. The differences are not so great as to rule out the possibility that Weill himself was responsible for the popularization. If a vocal part (without indications of harmony or texture) was all the arranger had to go by, that would explain much. But it is just within the bounds of possibility that no authentic score of any kind was used for the recording, or for the Rose Rouge performances: the tune and a few harmonic guidelines could have been written down from imperfect but fond memory, and passed from friend to friend. Of that at least, Weill would scarcely have disapproved.

February–June 1934; November–December 1934, Louveciennes

Der Kuhhandel

[*Shady Business*]

Operetta in two acts – unfinished German version

Book and lyrics by Robert Vambery

Musical comedy version, with book by Reginald Arkell and lyrics by Desmond Carter, completed in 1935 and produced in London under the title *A Kingdom for a Cow* (see p. 271)

Cast: singing roles: Juanita Sanchez (soprano), Juan Santos (tenor), Bimbi (boy soprano), President Mendez of Santa Maria (high baritone), Ximenes (tenor), Leslie Jones (tenor), General Garcia Conchas (bass baritone), Bailiff (tenor), Schoolmaster, Emilio Sanchez (tenor), Juan's mother (mezzo), Mme. Odette (mezzo), Footmen; chorus (villagers); packers; high society; soldiers; citizens; other roles: P. W. Waterkeyn, Ucquan Minister, Lieutenant, whores, the cow

Orchestra: See *A Kingdom for a Cow*.

The action is set in the fictitious republic of Santa Maria, which controls half of a fictitious (but plainly Caribbean) island. The neighbouring republic of Ucqua has already been visited by Leslie Jones, a roving representative of the Waterkeyn Armaments Corporation of Cleveland. Jones has instructions to start an armaments race and service the requirements of both sides, but learns to his dismay that the President of Santa Maria is not only a University Professor infected by liberal ideas, but also a confirmed pacifist. Fortunately for Jones, the President turns out to be a sentimental duffer. Not above accepting an ill-concealed bribe so long as it benefits his son Bimbi, he soon finds himself ordering a shipment of arms which he has no intention of using. Jones now spreads alarmist reports on both sides of the border, and with the aid of bellicose editorials in the easily corruptible press, increases tension to the point where Ucqua is about to invade Santa Maria. But the President, faithful to the vestiges of his principles, calls a Peace Conference, and invites the representatives of Ucqua to a gala dinner. Jones promptly organizes a *coup d'état* by General Conchas, the Santa Marian War Minister, and leader of the paramilitary 'Strong Hand Fellowship'. Within moments of Conchas's seizure of power, war between the two republics seems certain. Meanwhile the star-crossed romance of the two villagers, Juan and Juanita, illustrates the effect that such mighty events can have on the lives of ordinary people. The cow, which is Juan's chief means of livelihood, is twice distrained upon, in lieu of extraordinary taxes (for military expenditure) which Juan has neglected to pay. Eventually, as an unwilling conscript in the General's army, Juan becomes the symbol of militant opposition. He is saved from the firing squad, and Santa Maria from war, by the discovery that none of the weaponry supplied by Waterkeyn is in working order. Jones flees, while the General proclaims to the defenceless Santa Marians the virtues of peaceful coexistence. Amid popular rejoicing he pardons Juan and gives a vote-winning blessing to the happy couple.

Note 1

The following list of numbers includes two (in square brackets) for which the libretto provides the only source. An unusual feature of Weill's rehearsal scores is the use of generic titles in the Offenbach manner. Where these occur, they are reproduced here at the end of each number entry. First lines appear within quotation marks; descriptive titles do not. *4a* is a slightly varied repeat of *2*, with, of course, a different text; *9* is a significant development of *7*.

ACT I

Scene i: A Mountain Stream
  1a 'Siehst du keine?' (Juan–Juanita)
  1b 'Denn Einer ist Keiner'

Scene ii: President's Office
[2a 'Wenn der Husar zu Pferde sitzt' (Bimbi)]
  2   Friedensrede (President) – Recitative
  3   'Leise, nur leise' (President–Ximenes–Jones) – Terzettino
  4   'Schockschwerenot!' (General) – Auftrittslied
  4az 'Die Wohlfahrtsteuer' (President) – Recitative

Scene iii: A Village Street
  5   Der Mädchenraub (Juan, Juanita, Schoolmaster, Mother, villagers)
  6   'Auf Wiedersehen' (Juan–Juanita)

Scene iv: Baloma Railway Station
  7   Die Ballade vom Pharao, 1. Teil: 'Pharao! Lasst das Volk jetzt frei!' (Juan and packers) – Arbeitslied
  8   'Seit ich in diese Stadt gekommen bin' (Juan) – Ariette
  9   Die Ballade vom Pharao, 2. Teil (Juan and packers)

Scene v: President's Bedroom
  10   Das Erlebnis im Café: 'Heute abend ging ich ins Café' (General) – Cancan
  11   'Schlafe, Santa Maria' (Ximenes–President–General) – Berceuse

Scene vi: A Village Street
  12   'Triffst du mich abends in der Schenke' (Bailiff) – Gerichtsvollzieherslied
  13   'O trüber Tag' (Juanita, Mother, Juan, Schoolmaster) – Quartetto
  14   'Es zog zu Salomon' (Juanita)

Scene vii: Gala Dinner
  15   First Finale (full company)

ACT II

Scene viii (a): Open Country, Night
  16z Soldatenmarsch und Zwischenspiel (orchestra)

Scene viii (b): Mme Odette's Establishment
  17z Nationalhymne: 'Wehe über Land und Meer' (Mme Odette, whores, General)
  18   Ballade vom Räuber Esteban: 'Wenn der Wind geht' (Juanita)
  19z Trinklied: 'Schön war die erste Flasche' (General) – Fandango

20   Nationalhymne (reprise)

Scene viii (c): Open Country, Night
21   'Ich habe eine Kuh gehabt' (Juan) – Kuhlied

Scene ix: General's Bedroom
[22   'In der Zeitung steht geschrieben' (Ximenes)]

Scene x (a): In Front of the Arsenal
23z   'Fünf hab' ich und fünf hast du' (Juan–Juanita)

Scene x (b): The Market Place in Baloma
24   Second Finale

Note 2

The fate of *Der Kuhhandel* was indicative of Weill's new situation as an exiled composer working in the field of musical theatre: for the first time in his career the combined effect of adverse circumstances and box-office requirements prevented him from completing a work in the form and style in which it had originally been conceived. By the spring of 1934 he had sketched about half the music for *Der Kuhhandel* and was already investigating possibilities for a premiere in Paris or in Zurich. In a letter of 19 April 1934 to his friend Hans Curjel, who was then in charge of the Corso theatre in Zurich, he described the work as 'weit weg von dem Wiener-Operetten-Schund'. Renewing his advocacy four days later, he claimed 'dass es an die beste Tradition der Operette, die seit Jahrzehnten verschüttet war, endlich wieder anknüpft'. Such a work clearly reflected something of the discussions he had had with Karl Kraus in 1931–2; but as such it was never completed.

Nothing came of Weill's Zurich endeavours, nor was any progress made in Paris, despite René Clair's interest in directing a production there. But an introduction to theatre circles in London led to discussions during the early summer of 1934 with Charles B. Cochran and his associate Eric Wollheim. Cochran had admired *Die sieben Todsünden*, and although he now warned Weill that the operetta might be too 'satirical' for a public nurtured on Ivor Novello and Vivian Ellis, he advised him to commission a rough translation, and gave him some reason to hope that he might produce the work when it was finished.

There matters rested until November, owing to the more urgent claims of *Der Weg der Verheissung* and *Marie Galante*. Weill then managed to snatch a little more time for *Der Kuhhandel*. By the end of the year he had sketched several new numbers and revised one or two old ones. But the English version had not advanced beyond Wollheim's suggestion of a title: *A Kingdom for a Cow*.

Early in January 1935 Weill went to London with the intention of staying until he had finished the rehearsal score and negotiated a production. His hopes of a Cochran production were dashed almost at once, and the next three or four weeks were given over to increasingly discouraging meetings with entrepreneurs in the British theatre and film

world. It seemed that Cochran was not alone in his fears about the work
and its suitability for London audiences. But in mid-February the chances
of a London production suddenly improved.

It was at this point that Weill was persuaded that some music in a
lighter and more 'romantic' popular style could profitably be introduced,
if only to reassure London audiences. His first step was to append to the
opening duet scene an adaptation of the music of 'Le roi d'Aquitaine',
one of the musical 'hits' in the otherwise ill-starred and already forgotten
Paris production of *Marie Galante*. An 'English Waltz' in the *thé dansant*
style of the day, the song had little bearing on 'the best tradition of
operetta', or indeed on the style of the *Kuhhandel* music. But it was not
inappropriate to the task of completing *Der Kuhhandel* in the form and
likeness of a West End musical comedy; and that task became paramount
when the contract was signed in March for a production of *A Kingdom for
a Cow* at the Savoy Theatre in May (later postponed to June). During the
next weeks several important numbers were cut or completely rewritten
in a much lighter style, and more material was borrowed from *Marie
Galante*.

The important task of distinguishing between the numbers originally
intended for *Der Kuhhandel* and those designed to meet the exigencies of
the London version is complicated by various lacunae in the manuscript
collection. In cases where there are no German-language holographs of
any kind, and where the English lyrics precisely follow the German ones,
musical style may be the only clue. On the other hand, an underlaid
German text is not necessarily proof that the music belongs to *Der
Kuhhandel*. Several numbers were sketched, or copied out, during the
period between the signing of the production contract and the delivery of
the translation. The black-ink rehearsal scores of Juanita's 'Es zog zu
Salomon' (*14*) and of the General's Fandango (*19*) undoubtedly date from
that period, since the German text has been underlaid in pencil. But this
does not mean that both numbers were composed in the same period, for
their differences of musical character argue a gap of several months. The
Fandango unquestionably belongs to the world of *Der Kuhhandel* despite
the fact that it replaced the typically Weillian 'Trinklied' – a witty but
perhaps somewhat undramatic parody in 'Schweizerdeutsch' style,
sketched early in 1934 while there were hopes of a Zurich premiere. The
Fandango probably dates from the end of that year, whereas the extant
version of Juanita's song is redolent of 1935 and *A Kingdom for a Cow*.
Displaying a studied disregard for the tone of Vambery's excellent lyrics,
'Es zog zu Salomon' prepares itself for the English adaptation by
attempting to emulate the accents of Shaftesbury Avenue. The result is
an acceptable companion piece for the English arrangement of 'Le roi
d'Aquitaine', but so far removed from the style of *Der Kuhhandel* as to be
almost inconceivable except as a substitute for some earlier and more
appropriate setting.

Juanita's 'Ballade vom Räuber Esteban' reveals similar problems in a more acute form, further emphasized by the dramatic importance of the song. No trace has yet been found of the setting that Weill sketched in the early weeks of 1934 and referred to, with some pride, in a contemporary letter to Lotte Lenya. The only holograph source for the extant version is one of a group of sketches made in London early in 1935. The style is an uncomfortable mixture of German beer-garden and English music-hall, with the former predominating and standard Weillian accompaniments underpinning it. Even if the 1934 version used some of the same material, the form must have been different, in view of the structural differences between the German and the English lyrics. But it is not the form so much as the discrepancies of tone that make the extant version of the 'Ballade vom Räuber Esteban' sound out of place beside the authentic *Kuhhandel* numbers.

Autographs

SKETCHES AND DRAFTS

The following descriptions of loose sheets and separate foldings are in a chronological order determined by ascertainable or inferable dates of composition.

A   A sheet of D^{28} carries first drafts of 2 and 21, together with a 22-bar waltz in Viennese Schrammel-ensemble style. There are also unrelated sketches for a new and more 'commercial' setting of 'Es regnet' (see p. 249).

B   A second D^{28} sheet (discovered in 1970 among the orchestral material for *A Kingdom for a Cow*) is filled with sketches relating to Act II. It includes, among other things, the only known sources for 16, 17, 19, and 23. A letter from Weill to Lenya (WLRC), describing several of these sketches as a recent achievement which had pleased him, dates from March 1934. The reminder of 'Le roi d'Aquitaine' (from *Marie Galante*), which appears at the foot of the fourth side, must therefore have been added some nine months later.

C   A third sheet of D^{28} carries the whole of 7 and as much of 9 as can be accommodated (the rest is missing).

D   Sides *a* and *b* of another D^{28} sheet carry 8 complete, together with a sketch for an orchestral transition to 9; sides *c* and *d* carry 13 complete, but with a simpler (tonic) cadence than in the final version.

E   A folding of D^{28} carries on its first six sides an almost complete draft of 5. The seventh and eighth sides carry a complete draft of 12; the ninth side is blank; and the tenth has a sketch for 'Je ne t'aime pas', a sketch for 12, and seven bars of recitative, without text, but evidently an early version of one of the President's or the General's recitatives. The presence of 'Je ne t'aime pas' indicates that this folding dates from April–May 1934. The following items are of much later date.

F   Two versions of 4 (without text) are on a sheet of D²⁸ together with some sketches for *Marie Galante* – indicating composition after September 1934.

G   A folding of twenty-four pages of 28-line paper measuring 27 × 34.8 cms (Ku²⁸), headed 'Nr 1' and initialled, contains the following: *1a*, up to fermata, and an 8-bar introduction to *1b*; *24* (Second Finale) without heading and possibly continuing *attacca* from *23*; and finally a sketch of *18* (sixteen bars only, plus fragments). On the page where *1a* ends Weill has scribbled the address of Muir Mathieson, who was to conduct the first performance of *A Kingdom for a Cow*; the introduction to *1b* confirms that all the music on this folding was drafted in London early in 1935, before the translation had been embarked on, and after the composition and debâcle of *Marie Galante*.

REHEARSAL SCORE

All the material known to have survived is in the Weill legacy. The numbers are in separate foldings, paginated separately in another hand, and numbered in pencil in various hands (including the composer's) according to various provisional plans for *A Kingdom for a Cow*. These numberings, where they occur, are given below in parentheses.

1a		seven sides of Ku¹⁶, on detached leaves
1b		missing or never composed; but see *A Kingdom for a Cow*
2a		missing
2		missing (sketch only)
3		four sides of Ku¹⁶ sheet damaged and repaired
4		four sides of D¹⁶, text in pencil; see also *A Kingdom for a Cow*; an alternative version corresponding to one of the sketches, and again without text, is written on three pages of Ku¹², and has the title 'Lied des Generals'
4az		missing (see sketches)
5	(5)	sixteen sides of D¹⁶; the final side carries some fragmentary pencil sketches evidently of later date and almost certainly made in America
6		missing (see *A Kingdom for a Cow*)
7	(7)	seven sides of Ku¹⁶, carrying both parts of the Ballad
8	(8)	four sides of Ku¹²
9		see 7
10	(9)	four sides of Ku¹⁶, on two leaves
11		missing
12	(11)	four sides (divided and badly damaged) of Ku¹⁶
13	(12)	four sides (plus pasted-on insert) of Ku¹⁶
14	(13)	missing, but see *A Kingdom for a Cow*
15	(14)	twenty-eight sides of Ku¹⁶ in a 30-page folding; signed 'Weill' in pencil
16z		missing (see sketches and full score)

17z   missing (see sketches; music also in 14)
18   missing (see sketches and *A Kingdom for a Cow*)
19z (16) four sides of D^{16}, text in pencil; badly damaged
20   see 17
21 (17) four sides of Ku^{16}
22   missing; not composed?
23z   missing; see sketches
24 (20) forty pages of Ku^{16}

ORCHESTRAL SCORE

Weill did not start orchestrating until *Der Kuhhandel* had been transformed into *A Kingdom for a Cow*. But although the general character of the orchestration was affected by the more popular character of the added numbers, there is no reason to suppose that the demands of the London theatre significantly influenced the orchestration of those *Kuhhandel* numbers that were transferred to *A Kingdom for a Cow*. The four numbers that were not transferred – 6, 7, 9 and 23 – are among the most important, but were considered too serious for the London production, and were never scored. The 'Kuhlied' (21) narrowly escaped the same fate: it was cut from *A Kingdom for a Cow* and replaced by a more popular number, but fortunately not before Weill had scored it. As for the interludes and entr'actes which the form cried out for, none of these advanced further than first-sketch stage. The related question of an Overture or Prologue is discussed in the following summary of lacunae and defects.

Note 3

LACUNAE AND DEFECTS

Overture/Prologue
Some form of choral or vocal prologue seems to have been in mind for *Der Kuhhandel* but the relevant pages (2–4) are missing from the copy of the libretto in WLA. *A Kingdom for a Cow* has an orchestral introduction and choral prologue strictly in the *Kuhhandel* style; but since Robert Vambery has disclaimed responsibility for the English lyrics (which are on a notably higher level than any of those which the English lyric-writer devised independently from Vambery) and as he has no recollection of a German-language original, the basis for the English text may have been a German one sketched by Weill himself, perhaps in collaboration with his designer Hein Heckroth (or even with Erik Charell, who was at one time interested in producing the operetta).

1b   'Denn Einer ist Keiner': no German lyrics apart from cue lines; no
         music apart from borrowing of 'Le roi d'Aquitaine'
2a   Bimbi's Song: no music
2   Friedensrede: no extant setting of the German text, which is
         slightly longer than the English one

4   Auftrittslied des Generals: shortened version only; original missing?

4az   Wohlfahrtsteuer-Rezitativ: sketches only

6   'Auf Wiedersehen': English version only, with text not coinciding exactly with the German; at least part of the number may have been recomposed for *A Kingdom for a Cow*

7/9   Die Ballade vom Pharao: no orchestral score

13   'O trüber Tag': no orchestral score

16z   Soldatenmarsch und Zwischenspiel: only fragmentary sketches

14   'Es zog zu Salomon': stylistic discrepancy; original version lost?

17z   Nationalhymne: separate version missing – but quoted in First Finale

18   Ballade vom Räuber Esteban: English version only, apart from fragmentary sketch of German; stylistic discrepancies in the music and formal discrepancy between the English text and the German original

22   'In der Zeitung steht geschrieben': no music

23z   Duett 'Fünf hab' ich': sketch only, of preliminary and shorter version without transition to Second Finale

Posthumous Editions

1970: (1) The four *Kuhhandel* numbers which Weill left unorchestrated, together with additional material derived by the present writer from Weill's sketches, were orchestrated in 1970 by Christopher Shaw. Exemplary though these orchestrations are in their fidelity to the principles of Weill's orchestration, they have remained unpublished owing to their association with libretto revisions, by Josef Heinzelmann and the present writer, which did not meet with Robert Vambery's approval. (2) Vambery himself revised the libretto in 1970; an edition of the score, with new orchestrations of those numbers already orchestrated by Christopher Shaw, was prepared during the late 1970s under the supervision of Lys Symonette.

Publication

(Hire only)
1935: music, book and lyric assigned to Heugel.
1978: revised version reassigned to Schott–Mainz.

May 1934, Louveciennes

Complainte de la Seine

For voice and piano
Text: Maurice Magre

Autographs

SKETCHES AND FAIR COPY

Missing

DRAFT

Two sides of a sheet of D²⁸; the remaining sides carry rough drafts for *Der Kuhhandel* and *Marie Galante*. The draft version has a darker and more dramatic character than the published one. (It ends in D minor, without a return to the initial strain.)

Publication

Editions Coda (Heugel), 1934.

Note

The song was written at the suggestion of Weill's French publisher, Heugel, for the *diseuse* Lys Gauty, and for the firm's popular-music imprint. Its success prompted Lys Gauty to ask for a companion piece in order that she could make a commercial recording of both.

[Summer] 1934, Louveciennes

Je ne t'aime pas

For voice and piano

Text: Maurice Magre

Autographs

Missing: but see 'Wie lange noch' (p. 340)

Publication

Editions Coda (Heugel), 1934

Note

There is no evidence or likelihood that Weill was responsible for the (conventional but effective) orchestrations used by Lys Gauty in her recordings of this song and its predecessor.

---

21 August–3 November 1934/January–March 1935/August 1935, Louveciennes/London/Salzburg; October–December 1935, New York

Der Weg der Verheissung
(*The Road of Promise*)

Biblical Drama in four parts by Franz Werfel
Commissioned by Meyer W. Weisgal for production by Max Reinhardt
Duration: full evening; 160 minutes music
(Unperformed; orchestration not quite finished)

American version by Ludwig Lewisohn entitled *The Eternal Road*; abridged in three parts with musical interpolations (see p. 280) and added lyrics by Charles Alan, first performed in January, 1937.

Cast: singing roles in order of appearance: Rabbi (baritone), Eleiser, White Angel, Dark Angel, Abraham, Sarah, Isaac, Jacob, Rachel, Joseph and his brothers, Moses, Miriam, Voice of God, Angel of Death, Ruth and Boaz, Reaper, Saul, David, The Witch of Endor, Solomon, Chananjah, Jeremiah, Zedekiah, Voice of the Angel of the End of Days; double chorus SATB; speaking roles: The Pious Man, Other Pious Men, President of the Congregation, The Estranged One and his Son, The Adversary, The Timid Soul, The Rich Man, The Watchman, The Youth, The Strange Girl.
Orchestra: 2.1.2.1   4.3.3.1.   2 pno. harp org. gtr. timp. perc. str.

'The scene of this biblical mystery play is the timeless community of Israel; its Time is the equally timeless night of Israel's persecution.'* The lowest of the five stage levels represents a Synagogue. The second and third stages are linked by the Road, which leads to the fourth stage – the sacred level of Mount Moriah, of Sinai, of the Temple's altar place – and thence to the fifth stage, the threshold of Heaven. The Jewish community has gathered in the Synagogue during a time of persecution. Returning from a fruitless discussion with the authorities, the Rabbi calls for the scrolls of the Torah, and begins (*recitativo*) the readings which are

---

*From the prefatory notes to *The Eternal Road* (Viking Press, New York, 1936, p. ix).

designed to give the community a heightened understanding of their present situation and duties. The readings give rise to the biblical scenes, which are framed and punctuated by the Synagogue scenes, and at crucial points combined with them. Throughout, the Rabbi's teaching is challenged by the Adversary, and questioned by doubters. When at last the community is driven from the Synagogue by armed men – after a vision of the decadence of Jerusalem under Zedekiah – the lamentations are mingled with, and then overwhelmed by, the joy of the Estranged One's Son, who, in that night of extreme darkness, has seen the Messiah.

The following outline of the music is greatly simplified, and for the sake of clarity does not include the very numerous brief recitatives for the Rabbi.

PART I: THE PATRIARCHS

Abraham

1	Recitative and Chorus: 'Denn ich will segnen' (Rabbi, chorus)
2	Narrative and March: 'Die Stunde kam' (Eleiser, Rabbi)
3	Abraham and Sarah (White Angel, Dark Angel, Abraham, Sarah)
4	Sodom and Gomorrah (Rabbi, Angels)
5	Scene: Abraham and Isaac
6	'Gott schuf im Anfang Himmel und Erde' (chorus)

Jacob and Rachel

7	Pastorale (orchestra)
8y	'Wieder kommst du in Gedanken' (Jacob, Rachel); replaced by:
8	'Like a dream thou comest' (Jacob, Rachel) – English version only, for *The Eternal Road*

Joseph and his Brothers

9	Scene: Jacob, Joseph, Brothers, Angel, chorus

PART II: MOSES

10	Narrative, Israel in Egypt (Rabbi)
11	Miriam's Song: 'Die Königstochter sah unten im Rohr'
12	The Burning Bush (Moses and Voice)

In the Wilderness

13	Dance round the Golden Calf: 'Das ist ein Gott' (double chorus)
14a	Scene (The Voice of God)
14b(y)	Aria: 'Euch stand die Herrlichkeit Gottes' (Moses) Finale: March to Zion
15a	March: 'Wir zagen nicht und wir fürchten uns nicht' (male chorus)
15b	Aria I: 'Merkt auf, ihr Himmel' (Moses)
15c	Aria II: 'O König der Welt' (Moses)
15d	Scene: 'Steh und erzitt're' (Angel of Death)
15e	Death of Moses (two angels, chorus)

PART III: THE KINGS

Ruth

16a	Narrative and Song: 'Nein, wo du hingehst' (Ruth)
16b	Scene (Ruth and Boaz, Reaper, chorus)

Saul

17a	Psalm: 'Als der Ewige uns aus Ägypten geführt hat' (David, Rabbi, chorus)

17b   Scene (David, Adversary, Saul, chorus)
17c   Scene (Saul and David)
17d   Scene: The Witch of Endor (Saul, Witch, Samuel)
17e   Psalm: 'Ihr Berge Gilboas' (David)

David
18a   Scene and Aria; 'Zwei Männer lebten im Lande' (The Dark Angel)
18b   Building of the Temple (orchestra)

Solomon
18c   Dedication of the Temple (Solomon)
18d   'Die Völker klatschen in die Hände' (chorus)

PART IV: THE PROPHETS

Jeremiah
19a   'Wächter, wie weit ist die Nacht schon?' (Jeremiah)
19b   'Tröste, tröste mein Volk' (Jeremiah)
19c   Scene and Adversary's Song, 'Kauf Götter'
19d   Song of the False Prophet Chananjah, 'Erwache, Tochter Zion'
19e   'Steiniget ihn!' (chorus)
19f   Chorale: 'In Fron und Falsch' (Jeremiah)
19g   'Entscheide!' (double chorus)

20   Narrative and Scene: Destruction of the Temple
21   Chorale (as *19f*): 'O König der Welt' (Voice of Rachel)
22   'Ihr Schläfer des Schmerzes!' (Voice of the Messiah)
23   Psalm: 'Wenn der Herr die Gefangenen' (chorus)

Autographs

SKETCHES

Missing except for one sheet of Ch^{24} devoted to the new Jacob scene.

DRAFT

In the possession of the Library of Congress, Washington, DC. Ninety-three pages of D^{24} are wrapped in a title sheet of Sch^{16} with the autograph inscription, 'Skizzen zur Musik für/'The Eternal Road'/(Erste Niederschrift)/Für Max Reinhardt/in grosser Verehrung/und mit den schönsten Wünschen/für 1936/Kurt Weill/New York/Weihnachten 1935'. The manuscript is dated at the end '21 August–3 November 1934'. The pagination (on alternate pages) is in another hand. The first five pages carry preliminary sketches. Page 1 is headed '"Der Weg der Verheissung"/1.u.2. Teil' and carries two sketches – a chorale (not used) and music for Part IV. Another chorale and some sketches for the Joseph scene (9) follow on the next page; page 3 carries several items that found their way into the final draft, but also includes a 14-bar bridge missing from the final version of the Abraham and Isaac scene. The draft proper begins on page 6 with the heading 'Anfang', and proceeds in much the same order as the final score. A few afterthoughts (including an unused fragment) are sketched at the end, and a substantial one (*15c* and *15d*) is inserted at the appropriate place. The only important passage not transferred to the rehearsal score is a link between *21* and *22*.

REHEARSAL SCORE

No title page. The first page is headed 'Der Weg der Verheissung / (Werfel)/I. Teil:/Die Erzväter', and has the composer's signature. Part I is in two foldings of an unnamed 16-line paper measuring 35 × 27 cms. The pages are numbered 1–61 in another hand. Pages 62–4 are unnumbered, as is a single page insert on Sch[16]. Part II is a single folding of Ch[16], on forty-one pages numbered 108–49. (There is no trace of, and no evident *raison d'être* for, pages 65–107.) Most of Part III is on another such folding, but its fifty-four pages include an 8-page insert on a folding of Sch[16]. The pagination continues from Part II and is continued throughout Part IV, which is in a single folding of Sch[16], containing thirty-four manuscript pages. Parts II–IV have a draft of the English translation underlaid in pencil in another hand.

Rehearsal scores of the music added for *The Eternal Road* are missing, except for two sides of a leaf of Sch[16] headed 'Bath-Sheba'. Presumably the other additions were on the same paper as this and the inserts.

FULL SCORE

Unbound, no title page. The manuscript is in poor condition, not only because it served as a conductor's score but also because it was repeatedly raided for the Ben Hecht pageants with which Weill was associated in the 1940s. Numerous markings relate to these pageants.

Part I is in two foldings of Ch[24] (outer pages badly damaged), and Part II in a third folding of the same paper. The pages of Parts I and II have been numbered by the composer 1–73. Part III has the heading 'III / "Ruth"/Solo elektr. Orgel', but begins with *17a*. Pages 174–85 are written on Ch[24], but the remainder (pp. 186–230) is on F[24]. Part IV was apparently never finished in full score. A 12-page collection of Ch[24] is headed in pencil 'IV Part', but it begins with the *allegro vivace* section of *19c* and breaks off before the ensuing aria of Chananjah. A detached leaf of Sch[24] – from which the other half is missing – contains the first twenty-nine bars of Chananjah's aria, written in pencil with a bowing slur from the end of the last bar to the beginning of the missing leaf. (An orchestral arrangement of this aria was incorporated in *A Flag is Born*, see p. 356.) Another detached leaf of Sch[24] contains scorings of two short passages of recitative from the Jeremiah scene. The final section of the score – that is, from the music for the destruction of the Second Temple to the close – is on eighteen pages of F[24]. In sum, the main lacunae in Part IV are *19c* (second half of aria), *19e* and *19g*.

Three important sections from earlier parts were never orchestrated: *8y*, because Reinhardt demanded something simpler and more 'popular'; *14b* and the first section of *18a*, because Reinhardt decided to suppress them.

For *The Eternal Road* in 1936 Weill orchestrated the Ruth scene (which, as we have seen, he had originally intended to be accompanied on an electric organ). It is written in ink on a 20-page folding of F^{24}; a sheet of Sch^{24} carries a transposition of part of it, in pencil.

Some of the additions for the purposes of that production are missing. The seven extant items are described on pp. 280–2.

At some point between 1975 and 1981, and in unknown circumstances, the entire holograph score was lost (see p. 436).

Publication

Heugel, subpublished by Chappell Inc., 1936: hire material only

Heugel, subpublished by Chappell Inc., 1937: vocal selections (Chappell Inc.). The album was intended primarily to be sold to theatregoers. It contained six numbers: 'Promise' (brief extract from *1*); 'Song of Miriam' (*10*); 'Dance of [*sic*] the Golden Calf' (popularized and simplified version of *12*); 'Song of Ruth' (refrains from *16a*); 'David's Psalm' (simplified and shortened versions of *17a*); 'March to Zion' (*23*). The title page reads: THE ETERNAL ROAD/MUSIC BY/KURT WEILL/PLAY BY/FRANZ WERFEL/SETTINGS AND COSTUMES BY/NORMAN BEL GEDDES/ DIRECTION BY MAX REINHARDT/PRODUCED BY MEYER W. WEISGAL/AND/ CROSBY GAIGE/AT THE MANHATTAN OPERA HOUSE/Chappell.

Since there is no further information, this 14-page album has often been listed and catalogued as if it were the complete vocal score. The dedication 'To my father' appears on the first page.

First Performance of The Eternal Road

4 January 1937: New York, Manhattan Opera House; director Max Reinhardt, conductors Isaac van Grove and Leo Kopp, designer Norman Bel Geddes, production supervisor Charles Alan, associate director Francesco von Mendelssohn, choreographer Benjamin Zemach, artistic adviser Harry Horner; with Myron Taylor (Rabbi), Sam Jaffe (Adversary), Harold Johnsrud (Estranged One), Sidney Lumet (Estranged One's Son), Ben Cutler (Voice of God, and Second Dark Angel), Thomas Chalmers (Abraham), Bertha Kunz-Baker (Sarah and Naomi), John Uppman (White Angel and Solomon), Edward Cane (First Dark Angel), Ralph Jameson (Jacob and Boaz), Sarah Osnath-Halevy (Rachel), Earl Weatherford (Joseph and David), Samuel Goldenberg (Moses), Lotte Lenya (Miriam and the Witch of Endor), Noel Cravat (Aaron), Florence Meyer (Priestess of the Golden Calf), Joseph Macauley (Angel of Death), Katherine Carrington (Ruth), Walter Gilbert (Saul).

Notes

The Eternal Road is related to *Der Weg der Verheissung* much as *A Kingdom for a Cow* is related to *Der Kuhhandel*. The most striking differences are those of scale and aspiration. Whereas *Der Kuhhandel* stemmed from, and broadly speaking remained within, the family of *Die Dreigroschenoper* and *Der Silbersee, Der Weg der Verheissung* began somewhat nebulously, but developed, during the course of composition, a powerful tendency towards certain areas beyond *Mahagonny* and *Die Bürgschaft*. This was not at all what Werfel and Reinhardt had been looking for, and their resistance to Weill's 'operatic' pretensions, as Reinhardt called them, partly accounts for the eventual mutilation of the score. Equally influential, however, were the financial and commercial constraints. Originally the production had been conceived by Meyer H. Weisgal as a means of raising funds for the victims of Nazi persecution (and was to have begun its world tour at the Royal Albert Hall in London). For various reasons, that intention was progressively undermined, and the production increasingly became an end in itself. After several costly postponements, *The Eternal Road* opened on Broadway amid critical and public acclaim. Unlike *A Kingdom for a Cow* it attracted considerable audiences and for some weeks had at least the outward appearance of success. But the burden of costs and running expenses was immense, and far in excess of receipts. When the production closed, it left a trail of debts unprecedented in the history of Broadway. *The Eternal Road* has not been seen or heard again from that day to this; *Der Weg der Verheissung* remains, in effect, unperformed.

In that respect the parallel with the Vambery operetta seems to hold good. There are, however, significant divergencies. While the Broadway production of *The Eternal Road* was perhaps even further removed from Weill's musical intentions than the London production of the operetta, and certainly less within his control, the critical and musicological problems are relatively slight, thanks to the survival of the entire draft score and rehearsal score. But the crucial advantage *Der Weg der Verheissung* has over *Der Kuhhandel* is that the score is complete, and not ultimately dependent on its theatrical context.

What Weill had in mind during the early stages of composition was not opera, as Reinhardt supposed, but popular oratorio in the nineteenth-century sense – Mendelssohn of course, but also, perhaps, Gounod. Yet it was a twentieth-century work that offered him the closest precedent – the oratorio *Le roi David* by Arthur Honegger, whose friendship and advice had been important to him during his residence in France. The first version of Honegger's score was likewise written for a play. Although Honegger adapted it for the concert hall with little regard for the kind of musical and narrative continuity that Weill's score already possessed, it has remained one of his most widely performed works, and deservedly so.

The fact that Weill did not undertake a comparable adaptation of his score for *Der Weg der Verheissung* may seem almost incomprehensible in view of the disproportion between the time he had devoted to composing the score and the two or three weeks he would have needed for making a definitive concert version. For him it would have been a simple task, apart from the contractual and psychological obstacles. For someone else, nearly half a century later, it would be far from simple; it is none the less a task worth considering.

---

27 August – September 1934, Louveciennes

Marie Galante

Play by Jacques Déval adapted from his novel of the same name
Lyrics by Déval and Roger Fernay
Duration: 30 minutes music
Cast: singing roles: Marie, Mamouille, Soledad, Mercédès, Staub, Josiah, chorus of blacks; other roles: Letuvier, Pastolle, Vigouroux, Crawbett, Tsamatsui, Poldine, Tapia, Gloria.
Orchestra: fl. (sax.) cl. (sax.) tenor sax.   0.2.1.0.   pno. acdn. gtr. perc. including ship's siren; 2 vlns. vla. db.

Marie, a pure-hearted and fastidious prostitute, is abducted by Captain Letuvier, and taken on his cargo ship to South America. Having refused his advances throughout the voyage, she is unloaded at Carupano, the first port of call. Her only thought is of returning to her beloved France. She finds her way to Panama, occupies a *casa* in the local red-light district in order to earn the price of a steamer ticket to Bordeaux, but spends her meagre savings caring for an old and dying black, Josiah. Made the unwitting accomplice of a canal-zone espionage plot, she at last earns enough for her fare, but is murdered on the eve of her departure.

  1   Introduction

Scene i (a): Cargo Pier, Bordeaux
  2a Les filles de Bordeaux (Mamouille)
  2b ditto, chorus
  3   Intermezzo (orchestra)

Scene i (b): The Deck of Le Cormoran *at Carupano*
  3a Chant des Matelots: 'Je ne suis pas un ange'

Scene ii: Staub's Shop, Panama
  4   Marche de l'armée panaméenne

Scene iii: Dance Hall in Panama
  5a Introduction (orchestra)
  5b Scène au Dancing (orchestra)
  6   Tango (orchestra)

Scene iv: A Panama Street
  7   J'attends un navire (Josiah, Marie)

Scene v: Isabel Tapia's House
  8a Complainte (orchestra)

8b   L'arreglo religioso (Mercédès, Soledad), 'Voici Señora l'histoire'
9   'Tengo quatince ce años' (Soledad)

Scene vi: Marie's casa on the Chorillo
10   Le roi d'Aquitaine (Marie)
11   Choeur nègre (Chorus)
12   Train du ciel (chorus)

Scene vii: French Consulate in Panama

Scene viii: Staub's Shop
13   'Yo le dije al caporal' (Staub)

Scene ix: Marie's casa
14   Le Grand Lustucru (Maria)

Scene x: Departure Pier, Bilbao
15   Reprise of 7

Autographs

SKETCHES AND FIRST DRAFTS

Mostly missing. There are three items in WLA, all written on D^{28}. One side of a leaf carries a sketch of 7 (the *verso* side is blank). An intact sheet headed '*Marie Galante*' at the top-left corner of *a* carries a complete short-score draft of a 56-bar orchestral interlude. (Sides *b–d* carry sketches for *Der Kuhhandel* and a draft of 'Complainte de la Seine'.) The expressive character and descriptive implications of the interlude are such as to suggest that it was intended for the first scene change – Marie's ill-fated voyage from Bordeaux to South America. The interlude is based on two fragments originally sketched for *Der Silbersee* – the C sharp minor music in the manner of Satie's *Gnossiennes*, and the E major music in more popular style. These two ideas are now linked together, and the second of them has a minor-mode development that achieves considerable intensity. If in fact the interlude was meant to depict Marie's voyage, it is significantly more serious and more ambitious than the Intermezzo (3) that fulfils that function in *Marie Galante*. Equally interesting in this respect is the third item in WLA. Likewise written on the first side of an intact sheet, with the non-autograph heading '*Marie Galante*' partly erased, it is the complete piano-score draft of a 107-bar dance precisely modelled on the form, rhythm, and tone of the Mandelay Song from *Happy End*, but using different melodic and harmonic materials. Unlike the three direct borrowings from the same score (see *Notes*) the 'Mandelay' imitation was discarded – not, presumably, because it was too 'serious' but because it was unconvincing in itself and inferior to the original. There are no further *Marie Galante* sketches on the sheet – the remaining three sides are devoted to *Der Kuhhandel*.

FINAL DRAFTS [WLA]

Mostly missing. A sheet of D^{16} has the main section of 5b in pencil on the first two sides, and sketches for the introductory section on the third; the fourth carries a draft of 7. A leaf of D^{28} carries *recto* a definitive piano score of *5a*, and *verso* a draft of *13* (part ink, part pencil, and incomplete at the end of the side).

REHEARSAL SCORE

5–7 and *12–14* are in the Heugel archive, each on separate foldings of D^{24} and D^{28}. WLA has a pencil fair copy of *10* on the first three sides of a sheet of D^{16} (with sketches of *2a* and *12* on the fourth side); also in WLA are the unaccompanied melodies of *2a*, *9* and *13*, each written in ink on a small fragment of unidentifiable paper.

FULL SCORE

1–5, *7*, *10*, *12* and *14* are in WLA, each in a separately paginated folding and each titled (generally with signature). The papers are mixed D^{24} and D^{28}, totalling 75 pages of manuscript. On the last page of the folding containing *1* there is the score of *2a*, which is for voice and accordion. In the Heugel archive are three further numbers on D^{28}: *6* (six sides); both parts of *8* (four sides); and an alternative version of *5a* (pencil, two sides). Also in the Heugel archive is a copyist's score of *7* with autograph corrections pasted over passages on pages 6, 10 and 11. If there was any score of *13*, it is missing; but the vocal score suggests the possibility of a guitar accompaniment. The 'Chant des Matelots' and Soledad's song (*9*) were probably unaccompanied; if not, the contexts and style suggest, respectively, an accordion and a guitar.

First Performance

22 December 1934, Théâtre de Paris; director H. Henriot, designer André Lefaur, conductor Edmond Mahieux; with Florelle (Marie), Alcover (Staub), Inkijinoff (Tsamatsui), H. Lesur (Letuvier), Leda Swan (Poldine), Yvonne Yona (Tapia), Nita Raya (Gloria), Junie Astor (Soledad), Micheline Cheirel (Mercédès), Serge Nadaud (Crawbett), Gallet (Massoubre), Joé Alex (Josiah), Rolls (Manouille), Glenat (Pastole); Trio Marino, Norris, Zoïga & Rachel (dancers)

Publication

Heugel, 1934: *2a*, *4*, *5b*, *7*, *10*, *12* and *14* were issued as sheet music, and also collected in an album, repaginated but using identical plates, and therefore without names or dramatic context. *6*, entitled 'Marie Galante/Tango' was engraved and copyrighted 1934, but apparently never published; a vocal version of it, with lyrics by Roger Fernay, was published by Heugel in 1946 under the title 'Youkali/Tango Habanera'. *14* was arranged for voice and ensemble in the 1970s by Luciano Berio, and in that form is published by Universal Edition.

Notes

Marie Galante reflects the straitened circumstances in which Weill found himself in 1934, for it was the result of a commission which he accepted only because he could not afford to reject it. As if to cover the break with his past which it represented, he drew on some of his music for *Happy End*: 1 and 2 are founded on the Salvationist's Song 'In der Jugend goldenem Schimmer' (*Happy End*, 7); 5b on 'Das Lied von der harten Nuss' (*11*); and both parts of 8 on 'Das Lied vom Branntweinhändler' (*8*). As was the case with *Happy End*, the score was assembled piecemeal during the course of the production; and because the production failed, no attempt was made to collate the material or publish a definitive score. The numberings given above are editorial.

January–May 1935, London

A Kingdom for a Cow

Musical play in three acts
Book by Reginald Arkell; lyrics by Desmond Carter – after R. Vambery
Unpublished and withdrawn English adaptation of the operetta *Der Kuhhandel* (see p. 253)
Cast: as in *Der Kuhhandel*, but with the addition of a dancer (sc. viii b)
Orchestra: 2.1.2 (2sax.).1. 2.2.2.1. harp, gtr. mdln. bjo. timp. SD, TD, BD, cym. gong, str.

Apart from a change of tone, which broadens the ironies and softens the asperities of the original, and a change of title, which (in deference, perhaps, to British susceptibilities) misleadingly suggests that Santa Maria has become a monarchy, the text follows Vambery faithfully enough, and the plot is identical. The numbers in square brackets in the following list refer to the corresponding numbers in *Der Kuhhandel*, and carry a question mark where the original German setting is missing, or the extant one is perhaps not the original.

1	[–]	Prologue (tenor and chorus)
1a	[1a]	Fishing scene
1b	[–]	Duet; 'Two Hearts' (adapted from *Marie Galante 10*)
2y	[2]	Peace Speech
3	[3]	Trio: 'Hush, not a word'
3ay	[4a]	The Public Welfare Tax
4y		(General Conchas's Song – untitled, no lyrics) replaced by:
4	[?4]	A Military Man
5	[5]	Wedding Scene
6	[?6]	'Goodbye my love'

7	[–]	'San Salvatore' (Juan and porters)
8	[8]	Arietta: 'Since first I left my home'
9	[11]	'Sleep on, Santa Maria'
10	[12]	'If you should meet me'
11	[?14]	'As long as I love'
12	[15]	First Finale
13	[16]	Soldier's March (shortened)
14	[?18]	Ballad of the Robber Esteban
15	[–]	'A Jones is a Jones' (Jones)
16	[19]	'Life is too sad' (General)
16a	[–]	Fandango and Tango (orchestral arrangements of 16 and of the *Marie Galante* Tango)
17	[–]	'A year ago I had a cow' (Juan and Chorus); replaces 'Kuhlied'
18	[22]	Second Finale

Autographs

(post-*Kuhhandel* numbers)

SKETCHES

Missing. Weill presented a collection of holographs, which may have been these very sketches (possibly including some *Kuhhandel* ones), to his English friend Frank Cahill, the business manager of the London production. The collection was destroyed during the bombing of London in 1940–1.

DRAFTS

Unusually, all drafts are written in black ink, as if they were rehearsal scores. The following are in WLA: *1b*, on both sides of a leaf of Ki^{12}; *7*, on both sides of a Ch^{24} leaf; *11* and *13*, on sheets of an unnamed paper measuring 35 × 26.6 cms, slightly damaged and foxed, with red crayon markings in another hand; and *17*, with incomplete underlay of text on four sides of an unnamed 16-line paper measuring 36.5 × 27 cms. In the Heugel archive is a draft of *3ay*, on both sides of a leaf measuring 31 × 24 cms. Muir Mathieson, the conductor, has added (in pencil) to the first five bars a tentative version of the voice part and text of *2*; at the foot of the second side Weill has added a definitive version, also in pencil.

REHEARSAL SCORES

1b is written on 5 sides of Ki^{12}, and inserted in a set of rehearsal scores (partly hand copied in London and partly processed in Paris by Heugel) belonging to Frank Cahill. There are some non-autograph annotations in pencil. Weill has struck out the modulation to the D minor central section and indicated that it should be sung a major third lower. *7* is on two sides of a leaf of unnamed paper; *11* (headed 'No. 13') is on three sides of a damaged and foxed sheet of 20-line paper (measuring 35 × 26.5 cms), and *15* (headed 'Couplet Jones') on a similar sheet. *17* is on four sides of an unnamed 16-line paper measuring 36.5 × 27 cms, and has only partial text underlay.

FULL SCORE

There is no title page. Each number is in a separately paginated folding. The non-autograph pagination 1–302 has been added latterly for purposes of photography, and ignores two numbers (discovered in the Heugel archive) which bring the total to 317 pages. Various types of paper are used. The Prologue, *1a*, *1b*, *2*, *4* (in part), *6*, *11*, *14–16*, *17* and *18* are on Ch²⁴; *3*, *5*, *8*, *9*, *14* on Ku²⁸; *12* and part of *16* on D²⁸; *7* on an unnamed 20-line paper measuring 37 × 27 cms, and *13* (in pencil) on an unnamed 12-line paper measuring 30 × 24.8 cms. All numbers – including 'Song of the Cow' – are heavily marked in pencil and in blue and red crayon, in various hands but predominantly that of the conductor, Muir Mathieson. Much of the English text has been underlaid in red ink by Muir Mathieson.

Note 1

The title on the copy of the book and lyrics submitted to the Lord Chamberlain's Office was *My Kingdom for a Cow*. Weill himself wrote the same title in pencil on a folder in which some sketches were kept.

First Performance

28 June 1935, Savoy Theatre, London; conductor Muir Mathieson, designer Hein Heckroth; directors Ernst Matray and Felix Weissberger; with Jacqueline Francell (Juanita), Webster Booth (Juan), George Gee (Leslie Jones), Edward Dalby (P. W. Waterkeyn), Hay Petrie (Ximenes), Aubrey Mather (President), Bobbie Comber (General Conchas), Vivienne Chatterton (Mother), Norman Williams (Bailiff), Joan Hay (Madame Odette), Colin Cunningham (Prologue), La Jana (Dancer).

Publication

Chappell, London; under licence from Heugel, 1935: sheet-music versions of *1b* and *11*; a 'vocal gems' album was announced but did not appear.

Note 2

Though favourably received by the press, *A Kingdom for a Cow* was a disaster at the box office. This, for Weill, was a much more serious reverse than the failure of *Marie Galante*, in which he had invested relatively little time or effort. For a while he discouraged interest in the operetta from elsewhere – including the Soviet Union – on the grounds that he was contemplating an extensive revision. Soon after his arrival in

America he informed his French publisher, Heugel, that he was discussing a new version with two American writers. Nothing came of these discussions (if indeed they had any substance). Instead he borrowed extensively from the score during the next ten years.

Aside from incidental uses – notably in the rejected film score *The River is Blue* – the chief borrowings were these:

1	Song of the Goddess (*Johnny Johnson*) refrain only
4y	The Scars (*Knickerbocker Holiday*)
4	The Greatest Show on Earth (*Lady in the Dark*)
6	head motive, September Song (*Knickerbocker Holiday*)
7	*High Wind in Jamaica*
10	'We need a man' (*Johnny Johnson*)
11	'We'll man the trains' (*Railroads on Parade*)
12	National Anthem: Alessandro the Wise (*The Firebrand of Florence*)
12	Waltz: The Best Years of His Life (*Lady in the Dark*)
16	*High Wind in Jamaica*
17	The Song of the Guns (*Johnny Johnson*)
18	Mme Odette's Theme: Very, Very (*One Touch of Venus*)
18	Juan/Juanita Duet: Columbus (*Where Do We Go From Here?*)

Spring 1936, New York

High Wind in Jamaica

Two songs, without texts, for voice and piano
(Unpublished)

Autographs (LOC)

Each song is neatly written in black ink on a sheet of Sch[14], numbered '1' and '2' respectively and bearing the main title only. (The first is on three sides, the second on four.) There is no reference to the fact that the title is that of Richard Hughes's famous novel, published in 1929. Both holographs are date-stamped 'June 18, 1936'.

Notes

The two songs are almost literal transcriptions from *A Kingdom for a Cow*. The first is the porters' chorus 'San Salvatore', with only the finale cadence changed; the second is identical with General Conchas's drinking song 'Life is too sad', apart from a foreshortening of the basic figure, which converts the entire piece into 5/4 time. Two questions arise: first, why was Weill unwilling or unable to produce any new ideas, and secondly, why was the evidence solemnly registered in Washington? The probable answer to both questions is that the songs were commissioned as audition material for a film production that never materialized, and were registered automatically by the company concerned. Presumably time was short, and Weill's main concern was merely to demonstrate the type of music he had in mind. The one benefit is a variant of the drinking song which may well derive from something Weill had had in mind for an orchestral 'reminiscence' in *Der Kuhhandel*, where there is already some comparable play with irrational metres.

Summer 1936, New York

The Fräulein and the Little Son of the Rich

'A song drama' for Lenya and piano, with text by Robert Graham
(Unpublished and unperformed)
Duration: 15 minutes

Autographs

DRAFT

$1\frac{1}{2}$ sides of Ch²⁴; side *b* carries a first sketch for 'The Laughing Generals' (*Johnny Johnson*).

FAIR COPY

Four sides of Ch²⁴, in ink.

TEXT

Four pages (author's manuscript).

Notes

The number owes its existence to Lenya's hoped-for engagement – which did not materialize – in Leonard Sillman's 1936 Broadway revue *New Faces*. Graham's intended satire is of such unsurpassable naivety that the absence of any distinctive musical response is less puzzling than Weill's reasons for preserving the manuscript. The text, however, may be seen as a remote ancestor of the Lullaby in *Street Scene*.

June–November 1936, Nichols (Connecticut)/New York

Johnny Johnson

Musical play in three acts by Paul Green
Written for the Group Theatre at the suggestion of Cheryl Crawford
Duration: full evening; 65 minutes music
Cast: singing roles: Mayor, Minny Belle Tompkins, Grandpa Jo, Johnny
    Johnson, Aggie Tompkins, Captain Valentine, Sergeant Jackson,
    Private Hardwood, Chief of Allied High Command, a French Nurse,
    American Priest, German Priest, Dr Mahodan; speaking roles:
    Anguish Howington, Dr McBray, Johann Lang, Brother George,
    photographer, messenger, villagers, orderlies, generals, officers, sol-
    diers, politicians, madmen.
Orchestra: Reed I (cl. E flat cl. bcl.). Reed II (alto sax. cl. baritone sax. bcl.).
    2 tpt. tbn. timp. perc. gtr. (bjo.), Hammond org. (pno. *ad lib*), 2 vln.
    vlc.

America, 1917. The village stonemason Johnny Johnson has no sooner completed
his monument to Wilsonian peace than Wilson declares war. On the understanding that this is to be the 'war to end wars' promised by the President, he
enthusiastically presents himself at the recruiting office, and before long is on his
way to the Western Front. Faithful as ever to Wilson's pious words, and spurred
on by his experiences in the trenches, he risks his life promoting the cause of
peace among the lower ranks on both sides of no man's land. After a surreal scene
in which even the Allied High Command is momentarily converted to Johnny's
cause, he is arrested, returned to America, and committed to an asylum. He and
his fellow inmates later form a debating society modelled on the League of
Nations. As chairman, he conducts the meetings in accordance with his
principles; so it is not for another decade or more that he is finally certified as
harmless, and released. His songs of peace and goodwill are now scarcely audible
amid the mounting din of Fascist oratory.

ACT I

Scene i: A Hill in the American South
1   Introduction
2   Over in Europe (Mayor and Villagers)
3*y*   Epitaph (Minny Belle); replaced by:
3   Democracy's Call (Minny Belle, Mayor and Villagers)
4   The Battle of San Juan Hill (Grandpa Jo and Villagers)
5   Johnny's Melody (orchestral anticipation of 23)

Scene ii: Minny Belle's Home
6   Aggie's Song: 'My husband is dead'
7*y*   Minny Belle's Song; replaced by:
7*x*   'Farewell, Goodbye' (Minny); replaced by:
7   'Oh Heart of Love' (Minny)

Scene iii: Recruitment Office

8y   'We need a Man' (Sergeant, Captain, Doctor); replaced by:
8   Captain Valentine's Song: 'What are you coming for?'
8a   *Allegro vivace* (orchestra)

Suppressed Scene: Training Camp

9ax   Sergeant's Chant
9bx   The West Pointers (male chorus)

Scene iv: New York Harbour

9   Song of the Goddess (mezzo-soprano solo): 'He calls on me'

ACT II

Scene i: The French Front

10   Song of the Wounded Frenchmen (male chorus): 'Nous
       sommes blessés'
10x   *Alla marcia* (orchestral variation of *3*); replaced by coda to *10*

Scene ii: A Trench

11   The Tea Song (English sergeant, male chorus): 'All hail Britannia
       and her crown!'
12   'Oh the Rio Grande' (Private Hardwood)
12a   Johnny's Dream (orchestral version of *8*)
12b   Interlude (trumpet and organ)
13   Song of the Guns (male chorus): 'Soldiers! Soldiers! Sleep softly now
       beneath the sky'

Scene iii: A Ruined Churchyard

14   The Stricken Redeemer (orchestra)

Scene iv: A Hospital

15   Mon Ami, My Friend (Nurse): 'My Madelon of Paree'
15a   Reminiscence of *15*

Scene v: The Allied High Command

16   The Allied High Command (Marshal, Generals, Brigadiers)
17   The Laughing Generals (orchestra)

Scene vi: Battlefield

18   The Battle (orchestra)

Scene vii: Battle Scenes

19   In Times of War and Tumults (German and American Priests):
       'Almighty God, the supreme governor of all things'

Scene viii: No Man's Land; Scene ix: New York Harbour

19a   Reminiscence of *10*; anticipation of *23* (orchestra)

ACT III

Scene i: A State Hospital

20   The Psychiatry Song (Dr Mahodan): 'Back in the ages primitive'

Scene ii: Asylum

21   Asylum chorus (male chorus): 'How sweetly friendship binds'
22   Hymn to Peace (male chorus): 'Come let us hymn a hymn to peace'

Scene iii: A Street Corner

23   Johnny's Song (Johnny): 'When man was first created'

Autographs

SKETCHES AND DRAFTS

Intermingled pencil sketches and ink drafts for most of the numbers are on forty sides of Ch²⁴ (sheets and leaves). Two crucial numbers, 'The Laughing Generals' (*17*) and 'Johnny's Song' (*23*), underwent extensive changes. In its sketch form *17* is a vocal number. The draft version retains fragments of the lyrics, but is predominantly instrumental and has a 54-bar interpolation in waltz time (of which there is no trace in the final and almost entirely instrumental version). Whereas these prototypes have the same musical character and dramaturgic function as the published version, *23*, which became the 'theme song' of the entire work, was inspired by lyrics of quite another sort, and began with a sombrely critical F minor verse to the words:

> *Please don't tell a soul*
> *I'll run away from home*
> *I'm going to Paris today,*
> *I'm going to Paris where*
> *The streets are paved with gold.*

This is so far removed from the world of 'Johnny's Song' that one must presume that it was intended for another character – perhaps for a predecessor of the French Nurse who sings 'Mon Ami, My Friend' (*15*). Of less importance, but still worth noting, are the three sketches that were not used in the final score: *24z* is based on the *Gnossienne*-like idea first sketched for *Der Silbersee*; *25z* was to be resurrected in *The Firebrand of Florence* (1945); and *26z* is distantly related to the closing chorale in *The Threepenny Opera*.

REHEARSAL SCORE

All items in WLA are written on Sch¹⁴, and apart from *21* – which is entitled 'The Asylum Senate Chorus (Canon in 4 parts)' – they are either superseded versions or discarded numbers. The superseded versions of *9*, *11* and *12* (entitled 'Cowboy Song') differ only in minor respects from the definitive ones. Except for *8y*, which is a reworking of the Bailiff's Song in *Der Kuhhandel* and adds nothing to its brilliant model, and *9ax*, which is an unremarkable Tchaikovsky spoof, each of the discarded numbers is, in its own way, masterly; indeed, three of them (*3y*, *7x* and *9bx*) are among the best Weill wrote for *Johnny Johnson*.

The fact that the only rehearsal scores in the legacy are those for numbers or versions of numbers excluded from the published vocal score – with the sole exception of the *a cappella* chorus (*21*) of which there were doubtless several copies (including, perhaps, one or two by Weill himself) – acquires added significance in the light of similarly depleted holdings for two later Broadway scores, and reminds us that *Johnny*

Johnson is the first of Weill's scores to be written, produced, and published under American conditions. There can be little doubt that in this case, as in the later ones, the holograph rehearsal scores were used as production masters for the printed scores, and that engravers or copyists, rather than business executives, may have been the last to handle them officially.

FULL SCORE

The score is unbound, and has been separated from the manila folder (32.5 × 26 cms) which at one time served as a rough cover and title page. A printed label with the address of the Playwrights' Company has been attached to the front of the folder. On it, Weill has signed his name; beneath it he has written: 'Johnny Johnson/Orchestral Score/(Manuscript/All rights reserved'. The score itself is written on Ch^{24} sheets which may once have been gathered in foldings but have since been neatly divided into single leaves for photographic purposes. There are two separate non-autograph paginations, one at the top, the other at the foot of the page. Neither is altogether complete or consistent. The first relegates the cut numbers to the end, where a 9-page gap in the pagination may indicate the loss of an orchestral score of at least one of the cut numbers that exist only in rehearsal score – for instance, 'Epitaph' (*3y*) or Minny Belle's Song (*7y*). There are three small lacunae in the main body of the score: *10ay*; the end of *7a*; and coda to *18* (the holograph of *18* ends at the foot of a *recto* page; *verso* is blank).

First Production

19 November 1936, New York, the Group Theatre at the 44th Street Theatre; director Lee Strasberg, designer Donald Oenslager, conductor Lehman Engel; with Russell Collins (Johnny), Phoebe Brand (Minny), Bob Lewis (Mayor), Roman Bohnen (Grandpa Jo and American C.-in-C.), Grover Burgess (Anguish), Sanford Meisner (Captain Valentine), Lee J. Cobb (Dr McBray, French Major-General), Elia Kazan (Private Kearns), Luther Adler (English Sergeant and Belgian C.-in-C.), John Garfield (Johann Lang), Morris Carnovsky (Chief of Allied High Command, and Dr Mahodan)

Publication

Samuel French/Chappell, 1936: Book and lyrics (Samuel French); Chappell published sheet music versions of 7, 12, and 23 in a would-be hit-song arrangement, entitled 'To love you and to lose you' (for which Chappell supplied new lyrics by Edward Heyman, much to Paul Green's displeasure).

Samuel French, 1940: vocal score. Several numbers and subsections are in different keys from the orchestral scores. Wartime publication may account for the fact that the German text of *19* has been suppressed without explanation, as have the two training-camp numbers (*9a* and *9b*). Altogether inexplicable is the omission of a 29-bar prelude (for trumpet and organ) to *14*, and of a continuation of *8*.

Dramatic licences and performance materials: present (1986) availability – Samuel French (USA), KWF (Britain), Felix Bloch-Erben (German-speaking territories).

Posthumous Arrangement

A *Songspiel* incorporating all the *Johnny Johnson* music relating to the themes of war and peace – and including an orchestration of 'Epitaph' (*3y*) by Christopher Shaw together with two other discarded numbers (*7x* and *9bx*) that Weill himself orchestrated – was devised by the present writer in 1974, and first performed on 13 September 1975, under the title *War Play*, at the Akademie der Künste, West Berlin. The singers were Mary Thomas (soprano), Meriel Dickinson (mezzo-soprano), Philip Langridge (tenor), and Michael Rippon (baritone), with the London Sinfonietta conducted by David Atherton. It calls for six singers (soprano, mezzo-soprano, 2 tenors, baritone, bass), uses the same orchestra as the original, and lasts approximately 40 minutes.

November–December 1936, New York

The Eternal Road

(Interpolations: see pp. 262–8 for details of the parent work, *Der Weg der Verheissung*, and of the January 1937 premiere of its American adaptation, *The Eternal Road*.)

Note 1

To judge from the surviving material (see *Autographs* below) most of the interpolations owed their existence to last-moment expediencies of production, and were not intended as musico-structural 'improvements' to *Der Weg der Verheissung* (whose rehearsal score Weill had completed in the summer of 1935). The scoring of each interpolation is suited to the small stage orchestra that the production company had reluctantly agreed to employ in return for union consent to the use of pre-recorded accompaniments for full orchestra in most of the vocal and orchestral music. Since the full orchestra had been recorded in the RCA studios a year beforehand, the stage orchestra was the only available medium for interpolations, so each interpolation also served to strengthen the stage orchestra's somewhat tenuous *raison d'être*.

Orchestral Parts

Neither the set of parts extracted from the full score of the parent work during the last weeks of 1935, nor the interpolated set of parts extracted a year later, has yet come to light. Without the latter, the interpolations can be listed only provisionally on the basis of the surviving autographs.

Autographs

SKETCHES AND DRAFTS

Missing.

FULL SCORES

The (unbound) full score of the parent work was not repaginated to include the interpolations, nor was it furnished with clear or complete cross-references to them – some markings confusingly refer to subsequent uses. In later years *The Eternal Road* became a convenient source of incidental music for Ben Hecht's Jewish manifestations (see, for example, pp. 329 and 356). Several interpolations borrowed for such purposes were eventually awarded an unmarked resting place among Weill's miscellaneous manuscripts. Others were reunited with the parent score, but incorrectly placed. Although there is no means of telling exactly how many interpolations are missing, the number is unlikely to have been large. The ten surviving in WLA are clearly contemporary with each other. All are in good condition and neatly written in pencil on leaves or sheets of Sch²⁴. Altogether, there are twenty-one sides of manuscript. The items have no formal titles, but are identified by the headings given below in inverted commas:

1 *'Rachel's Death'*
   Incorporates a variant of the melodic shape common to the 'Epitaph' and 'Democracy's Call' in *Johnny Johnson*.

2 *'Saul Scene'*
   Non-autograph heading for a recitative without text.

3 *'David and Goliath'*
   The autograph heading is partly erased; more prominent, and in another hand, is the German heading 'Einlage' ('insert'). There is a blank stave for the Rabbi's part in the first system, but no further indication that this is intended as a vocal number. The ensuing music is markedly East European in character, and may well be based on authentic folk material. Whether it is intended as incidental music for David's fight with Goliath, or – more probably, in view of the orchestration – whether it is a song accompaniment (with the melody doubled throughout), it differs from the other interpolations in that it bridges a gap in the musico-dramatic structure and is therefore, in principle, an improvement.

4 *'Bath-Sheba'*
   Though based on the main idea of the first setting of 'Es regnet' (see p. 249) the piece is not orchestrated as if it were a song accompaniment; a non-autograph piano score in WLA seems to confirm that it was not intended as such.

5   'Caravan'
    This is certainly incidental music. It is based on the *Gnossienne*-like idea
    that began life in the *Silbersee* sketches and then vainly attempted to find
    its way into *Marie Galante* and *Johnny Johnson*.

6   'Einlage'
    Non-autograph heading for a short orchestral *allegro* incidental to the
    Goliath scene.

7   'Fugato I, Fugato II, Fugato III, Fugato VI'
    Brief orchestral interjections in the *Bürgschaft* manner, to be inserted at
    unspecified points in the 'Joseph' scene. Fugatos IV and V are missing.

Note 2

The following credit line in the souvenir programme may be relevant to
these or to other interpolations: 'Lyrics for the Rachel scene, the Goliath
Ballad, and the Witch of Endor scene are by Charles Alan.' Alan does not
seem to have contributed to the Lewisohn version of *The Eternal Road* –
which was published by the Viking Press in New York in January 1936 –
nor is he known to have been part of the original production team. But
the 1937 programme credit leaves so much unexplained that there is no
certainty that any of his lyrics involved musical interpolations. What for
instance is meant by 'the Rachel scene' as distinct from the Rachel–Jacob
duet? Weill had made two musically independent settings of the duet
(*8y, 8*) – the first one in Werfel's original German, the more 'popular' one
in Lewisohn's English translation. Unless Alan provided a replacement
for the Lewisohn text, the programme credit is confusing, and unfair to
Lewisohn. One could, however, argue that 'Rachel's Death' is not the
inserted slice of incidental music it appears to be, but is in fact the
orchestral accompaniment of an elegiac song for which Alan wrote lyrics.
While a similar reading would allow the main section of 'David and
Goliath' to be identified as the orchestral accompaniment for the missing
'Goliath Ballad', the musical structure of the Witch of Endor scene
precludes the insertion of 'lyrics'. If Weill's masterly amalgamation of
recitative and melodrama in this scene was rejected by Reinhardt, it can
only have been on the grounds that it was too 'serious' or – like the first
version of the Rachel–Jacob duet – too 'classical'. In that event, the
disappearance of any substitute gives no great cause for regret.

March–April 1937, Hollywood

The River is Blue
(*Castles in Spain*)

Unrecorded and unorchestrated film score for a screenplay after Ilya
Ehrenburg by Lewis Milestone and Clifford Odets
Commissioned by Walter Wanger Productions

Note 1

The distinguished film director Lewis Milestone was a supporter of the Group Theatre and one of the backers of *Johnny Johnson*. He was engaged to direct *The River is Blue* (or *Castles in Spain* as it was first called), and persuaded his producer Walter Wanger that it must be cast principally from the Group Theatre. He and Odets adapted their screenplay from Ilya Ehrenburg's novel *The Loves of Jeanne Ney* (of which G. W. Pabst had made an important silent film for the German Ufa company in 1927). In the Milestone–Odets screenplay the setting is changed from post-revolutionary civil war in the Crimea to the contemporary civil war in Spain, and the romance between the bourgeois French heroine and a young communist is depoliticized in the interests of universalizing a thinly disguised plea for the Republican cause.

Weill had no sooner begun composition than Walter Wanger fell out with Milestone and commissioned a new script from John Howard Lawson. Weill was contractually obliged to complete the score, but did so in the knowledge that the film as discussed with Milestone and Odets would never be made. Before long Wanger had found a new director in William (Wilhelm) Dieterle, who duly filmed the Lawson screenplay and then, after a piano audition of Weill's score, promptly commissioned a new one from Werner Janssen. In its final piano version – as prepared by the studio copyist – Weill's score runs to forty numbered entries. The following list includes, in parentheses, the cues indicated in the copyist's score:

1	*Vivace assai, molto agitato*	(title music)
2	*Andante non troppo*	(train; woman's voice)
	Più mosso	(people evacuating city)
	Tempo I	(eyes on peepholes)
3	*Allegro non troppo*	(open field; Marco singing)
4	*Vivace assai*	(hand fighting)
5	*Alla marcia*	(empty street)
6	*Andante non troppo*	(walking feet)
7	*Andante non troppo*	(Bonnard exits; Norma's head)
8	*Lento*	(funeral scene)
9	*Andantino*	(Marco and Norma)
10	Tango	(love scene)
11	*Agitato*	(Norma walking rapidly; ruins of her house)
12	*Allegro moderato*	(Luis goes to bed)
13	*Allegro moderato, tempo di tango*	(Norma in armchair)
14	*Molto tranquillo*	(hall in hotel)
15	*Allegretto*	(Marco and Luis awaken)
16	*Moderato assai*	(Norma asleep in chair)
17	*Andante*	(Luis talking of Marco's father)
18	*Allegro agitato*	(street war activity)
19	*Tempo di tango*	(Marco's room; scene on the roof)
	Valse lente	(music-box)
20	*Allegro non troppo*	(scene with rooster)

21	*Allegro marcato*	(popular song, for Luis, Marco, Norma)
22	*Andantino*	(Luis on a donkey)
23	*Molto tranquillo*	(Norma and Marco walking to the station)
	Valse lente	(music-box)
24	*Vivace assai*	(train at platform)
25	*Molto tranquillo*	(Norma and Marco)
26	*Valse lente*	(music-box)
	Tempo di tango	
27	*Tempo di tango*	
28	[No tempo given]	(poster: torch)
29	*Allegro giocoso – tempo di cancan*	(Norma in Paris)
30	*Vivace*	(mountain pass)
31	*Moderato assai*	(Ney's gallery)
32	*Moderato assai*	(gallery; cherubs among clouds)
33	*Tempo di cancan*	(French music from the radio)
33a	*Andante misterioso*	(Marco at the French border)
34	*Lento*	(Renoir scene)
35	*Lento*	(fountain basin)
36	*Allegro non troppo – chorus a cappella*	(soldiers on a rear platform of train)
37	*Vivace assai*	(Luis appears in the gallery)
38	*Andantino*	(engagement dinner)
39	*Molto tranquillo*	(Norma with Max watching clock)
40	*Molto tranquillo*	(Norma with Max watching clock)
	Montage and combination of three tempi, tonalities and musical characters: Viennese waltz, tango, and cancan	(amusement park with montage Vienna/Spain/Paris)
	Alla marcia	(hotel room and end titles)

Note 2

Weill set out with the intention of writing a 'serious' score in an appropriately popular but potentially symphonic idiom. This is clear not only from his correspondence with Lenya (WLRC) but also from the extensive 'title music'. But his growing sense that the score had only a contractual significance is reflected in the increasing reliance on borrowed material. Already in the third entry there is a borrowing from *Der Kuhhandel* (General's Song); the Bailiff's Song from that work later recurs, note for note, as the cancan in entries 29, 33, and 40. Entries 7, 8 and 38 are similarly borrowed from *Der Silbersee* – the first two from the Funeral March and the last from Fennimore's 'Song of the Poor Relation', here arranged in Palm Court style for violin, cello and piano. Ideas sketched for *Johnny Johnson* but not included in the final score appear in entries 23 and 34. The 'love theme' introduced in entry 10 and insistently returned to thereafter is the tango originally written for *Marie Galante* and then transferred to *A Kingdom for a Cow*. Of the ideas for which there is no known precedent in an earlier work the most substantial and developed is the Waltz, first heard in a music-box arrangement in entry 19.

Unmistakably Central European in style, it reads as if it were a transcription of a vocal duet. If it is not one of the lost items from *Der Kuhhandel*, it is probably a remnant from the abortive Spewack musical (see p. 286). Two musically significant ideas were to recur in later works, and both, to judge from their style and texture, may have originated several years before the film score. The first is an organum-like motif of superimposed fifths and fourths which is reminiscent of the final song in Hindemith's *Das Marienleben*. In the film score it depicts the art gallery (*31*); and that association, including its Hindemithian background, may have prompted Weill to use it as the opening motif of *One Touch of Venus* (which begins in a New York gallery of modern art). Of similar stylistic origin is a canonic passage (*andante misterioso*) in the Phrygian mode. It has no definable relationship to its cue (*33a*, Marco at the French border). Nearly ten years later Weill remembered it during a fraught rehearsal of *Love Life* and used it, then and there, as incidental music for the Magician's entry (see p. 358).

Autographs

SKETCHES

The earliest known sketches are on a sheet of Ch^{24} – the Chester paper Weill bought in London in 1935 and last used for *Johnny Johnson*. The first side carries a complete draft of a tango song, 'Sweet World', whose introduction – borrowed from the *Marie Galante* tango – was to become one of the 'theme tunes' in the score. (Its refrain is borrowed from the 1933 setting of 'Es regnet'.) The remainder of the sheet carries sundry fragmentary sketches for the film score, including the second 'theme tune'.

DRAFT

A near complete draft, following the script's cues precisely, begins on a sheet of Sch^{24}, and continues on a 12-page folding of Sch^{20}. Written for the most part on two staves, and containing occasional instrumental indications, it is legible enough for the composer's own purposes – which included playing the music to the producer – but was certainly not intended as a presentable score. An autograph fair copy must therefore have been made at an early date, but has not been traced.

Non-autograph Short Score

Black ink on sixty-six numbered pages of K^{12} originally stapled together and taped to a light board cover, but now disbound. Front cover and title page have identical legends: 'By KURT WEILL/COMPLETE MUSICAL SCORE / for/"THE RIVER IS BLUE"/screenplay by Clifford Odets'. The score contains various non-autograph pencil and crayon markings. Notable among these is an incomplete and roughly underlaid text for entry *31*, identified as 'Popular Song'. It is a typical Russian folk song, both in its modality and in its rhythmic–metrical structure (alternating 2/4 and 3/4 time). The lyric writer – probably Ann Ronell (see *Arrangements* below) – responds to this with explicit Cossack references in the refrain.

Arrangements

NON-AUTOGRAPH

In 1938 copies of two songs with lyrics by Ann Ronell were deposited for copyright purposes in the Library of Congress, Washington. The first, entitled 'Soldier's Song', is based on the march tune that dominates the title music and the closing entries. The second, entitled 'The River is Blue', is a version of the Tango tune. Also in the Library of Congress are chorus parts (registered on 17 March 1938) for *21, 36* and *40* listed as follows:

1   The Soldier's Song: 'Will she let me give her this?'
2   March: 'Shout the answer men'
3   Finale: 'At last we know our throats can cheer you'

March–June 1937, Hollywood

[Musical play: The Opera from Mannheim]

Book: Bella and Samuel Spewack
Lyrics: E. Y. Harburg
(Unfinished and lost)

Notes

The Weill–Spewack–Harburg project is the missing connection between Weill's last experiences as a German composer and the work with which he made his full-scale Broadway debut in 1938 – *Knickerbocker Holiday*. The project belongs to the transitional period in which he was exploring the practicability of a quadrilateral career structure that could be upturned, inverted, or reshaped according to requirements. Although his main hopes for the future were still centred on the Federal Theatre (KW.AS, p. 85), he had found, through the Group Theatre and through Clifford Odets, a convenient short-cut between the 'progressive' sectors of Broadway and Hollywood. In Hollywood especially there were no clear lines of demarcation between the intelligentsia and the entertainers. According to Ronald Sanders (RS.DGS, p. 260), it was in the Beverly Hills villa of George and Ira Gershwin that Weill first met Harburg and the Spewacks (the Gershwins he had already met at the 1935 premiere of *Porgy and Bess*). The producer Max Gordon (see p. 346) was involved in the project from the start, and was soon seeking the necessary financial backing for a Broadway production during the season 1937–8. He did not succeed.

There are two widely different but to some extent complementary accounts of the subject matter. The earlier by some forty years was by Weill himself, in a letter to Lenya written (in German) from Hollywood on 29 March 1937:

The action begins in the Mannheim opera house. The rehearsal is suddenly interrupted by a Nazi, who dismisses everyone from their posts because they are non-Aryans. They all go to New York. We now show their experiences – naturally with much humour, but also, for instance, in a scene where they receive a letter from a Mannheim friend which was to be mailed only in the event of the friend's death.

Eventually another friend arrives from Germany, and tells them that everything has been arranged so that they can return. But they reply that they will not return. At the end, in the cinema of a small American country town, they perform the opera that they had been rehearsing at the start of the first act.

Never before had Weill agreed to a subject that directly reflected his personal experience (nor was he to do so again in so overt a manner). It is hard to judge how far he expected Lenya to grasp what he was driving at, but the choice of Mannheim was surely intended to deflect the kind of questions that would have been prompted by Berlin or even Hamburg – the two major cities in which productions of Die Bürgschaft and Der Silbersee were being actively prepared at the time of the Nazi seizure of power. The present writer, in his forthcoming Weill biography, argues that the Mannheim location enabled Weill to merge his own experience with that of his slightly younger contemporary Berthold Goldschmidt (born in Hamburg, in 1903). Goldschmidt's opera Der gewaltige Hahnrei was published by Universal Edition and first performed in Mannheim a month before the Berlin premiere of Die Bürgschaft.

Although the musical style and dramatic content of Der gewaltige Hahnrei were far removed from his own preoccupations of the time, Weill took a fraternal interest in the work and according to Goldschmidt (at the Kurt Weill Conference in Yale in November 1983) vigorously defended it, at some risk to his own professional interests. The last successful operatic debut in pre-Hitler Germany, Der gewaltige Hahnrei was for political reasons shunned by the opera houses that had expressed an interest in producing it during the season 1932–3. In the summer of 1932, when the political situation in Germany seemed to be improving, Mannheim began negotiations for Die Bürgschaft, while the Städtische Oper in Berlin resolved to give further performances of Die Bürgschaft during the 1932–3 season and to present Der gewaltige Hahnrei during the following season. Mannheim's negotiations for Die Bürgschaft hung fire and were never completed, and Berlin's further performances were postponed from month to month for security reasons until there was no security left – whereupon virtually every German opera manager and conductor who would have wished, let alone dared, to advocate such works as Die Bürgschaft and Der gewaltige Hahnrei was 'released' from his duties.

For all their differences, the two operas, like the two cities in which they were first performed, were interchangeable symbols of the culture that was destroyed in 1933. Given that Weill was now beginning to settle down in America and was soon to take the first formal step towards acquiring American citizenship, the passage in his account of the Spewack–Harburg project that deals with the company's decision not to return to Germany is again charged with personal significance. Returning to France would for him have been the only practical course at that time; but nothing would alter the fact that his roots were in Germany.

By 1937 Weill knew quite enough about Broadway to realize that the fate of twentieth-century German opera was not a topic likely to endear his project to prospective backers, and that in human terms the same story might be acceptable on the level of light entertainment. We can be sure that by the time Max Gordon began his unsuccessful quest for financial backing Weill's 'opera' company had been converted into something rather less forbidding (and perhaps closer to the Shakespeare company that figures in the Spewack–Cole Porter musical *Kiss Me Kate*). Some such development is implicit in the story outline given to Ronald Sanders by Harburg in the late 1970s (RS.DGS, pp. 260–1):

The story concerned a Jewish theatrical troupe that, in better days, had regularly toured Germany giving musical comedies that they themselves had written. At the beginning of the play they have fled Nazi Germany and are on their way to the United States; they are first seen aboard ship trying to rehearse and prepare their favourite show for its new American career. But since they have been forced to leave the score behind in their hurried escape from Germany, they have to rely on memory to reconstitute the music. Most of it comes back quickly, but the waltz that always climaxed the show resists their recollections. In the end they put on their show in America, and the waltz gradually emerges through the course of it, coming out fully defined at last in the finale.

The notion of a 'forgotten' music that has somehow to be recovered seems relevant to Weill's psychological condition in 1937 and was to reappear in *Lady in the Dark* (see p. 315). Here, its personal associations are enhanced by the score which is 'left behind' by the musicians 'in their hurried escape', just as Weill had left many of his own scores behind (see p. 436). The closest match between Harburg's recollections and Weill's personal experience is, however, in a supplementary passage concerning the letter song: 'a letter from a member of the troupe to the "Aryan" occupant of his apartment back in Germany, asking how all the old things – the books, pictures, furniture, and so on – were doing.' In Paris in 1933 Weill was writing to Lenya in Berlin about the contents of his house, the settling of his debts, and the details of their divorce.

Autographs

No lyrics and no musical sketches or drafts are known to have survived. Weill's letters to Lenya from Hollywood of April–May 1937 confirm that the project was very much alive during that period; and on 7 June he claimed to have composed five 'very good songs' for it. Sanders (RS.DGS, p. 261) gives the impression, without actually stating, that Harburg had remembered Weill writing music prior to the arrival of the few lyrics Harburg sketched. It is unlikely that Max Gordon would have begun his search for financial backing without several playable numbers, of which one would have had to be the *valse oubliée*. Among the few personal ideas in *The River is Blue* that is not a borrowing from a known Weill score is a large-scale waltz with variations. Although redolent of *Der Kuhhandel*, it fits neatly into the musical area between Weill's and Harburg's accounts of the story outline. But unless and until a direct connection is established, we are left with the irony that all the music Weill managed to write for an unfinished play about a lost score has itself been lost.

April–June 1937/December 1937/Spring 1938, Hollywood

You and Me

Music for the Paramount film produced and directed by Fritz Lang
Story by Norman Krasna, screenplay by Virginia van Upp
Lyrics by Sam Coslow and Johnny Burke

America in the 1930s. Joe Dennis (George Raft) is a convict working on parole as a floorman in a department store. He falls in love with Helen (Sylvia Sidney), a fellow employee, and is moved to confess his criminal past, little knowing that she too is on parole. The conventional complications that arise when he discovers the truth about her are resolved in a conventional happy end.

Note 1

Unusually and perhaps uniquely in a film of this kind – which is not a musical and contains no 'production numbers' – the score was planned and partly composed before shooting began. Adaptations and additions were made at the various editing stages, and eventually the score was entrusted to staff arrangers and orchestrators. After the first dubbing sessions (in April 1938), the score underwent ruthless surgery and was bandaged together with strips of ready-made or newly manufactured material provided by the music department (see *Final Dubbing* below). The music Weill himself wrote for the film – as much of it as has been traced – is listed below in a conjectural order. The numberings of unused items are parenthesized.

1   Title music
2   The Song of the Cash Register (Coslow): 'You can't get something for nothing'
3   The Knocking Song (Coslow): 'Do you hear me?'

(4)   The Song of the Lie (Burke)
 5   The Right Guy for Me (Coslow)
(6)   Too much to dream (Coslow)
(7)   Barbershop Quartet (Coslow)
 8   The Romance of a Lifetime (Coslow)
(9)   Jiggaboo (dance music)
(10) We're the kind of people who sing Lullabies (Burke)
 11   Honeymoon Scene (incidental)
 12   The Robbery (incidental)
(13) I set my heart on sable (author unknown)
 14   End titles

Autographs

SKETCHES

The first side of a 6-sided sheet of K¹² carries (left) a column of notes on music cues and (right) a subsequently added column of partly cryptic footnotes. The numbering, orthography, and layout are reproduced below (with editorial comments in square brackets).

[*lh* column]	[*rh* column]
1 Main title Cash register	5 Do not marry (?) (Song of the Lie)
2 First dance tune Second dance tune	6 Walk in the rain (stop sign) (Theme in minor)
3 Introduction for torch song	
	7 It's you and me
Torch song Third dance tune	8 Fight with electric piano. Sylvia [Sidney] standing alone after George [Raft] walked out Leading into dive (Do you hear me)
4 Song of the Lie Information (Theme)	
5 Honeymoon	
6 —	[at the foot of the column is a notation of a chordal motif marked 'Rain']
7 Reminiscence Song of the Lie Knocking Song	
8 Knocking Song continued	
9 Robbery	
10 —	
11 George [Raft] alone in department store. George coming home. Search for Helen. End.	

The fourth and fifth sides of the triple sheet are blank. On the second, third and sixth sides are sketches of various motifs including 'China', 'Italy' and 'Sweden' (from the Honeymoon sequence, *11*), all of these being variations of the title tune *1*; also a variation of *2* for the robbery sequence.

A sheet of Sch²⁰ carries finished sketches and rough drafts on each side. *a* has a wordless foxtrot in E flat major (incorporating ideas from *Marie Galante* and *Der Kuhhandel*); *b* a torch song in E minor (see Weill's note for entry *3*) with an incomplete lyric beginning, 'I set my heart on sable'; *c* has sketches for *3*; and *d* has various sketches for *The River is Blue* (including the canonic episode that ten years later was incorporated in *Love Life*).

DRAFTS (with Sketches)

Sixteen pages of P¹² carry the remains of what must have been a sizeable collection of drafts and sketches. Among the noteworthy items are: a page of short score, giving what looks like the end titles; a sketch of the 'Vienna' waltz for the Honeymoon sequence; a 25-bar reminder of 'San Salvatore' (*A Kingdom for a Cow*); a 32-bar refrain in jazz rhythm based on the 'Ruth' theme (*Der Weg der Verheissung*, *16a*) and several pages of incidental music thematically connected with the 'Robbery' theme. There are further drafts on ten sides of Sch¹² and six of K¹² – the latter including a passage of short score for the Robbery scene, a 32-bar arrangement of the title theme, and a reminder (also thirty-two bars) of the refrain of 'Der Mädchenraub' (*Der Kuhhandel*). A sheet of 12-line paper measuring 31.5 × 24 cms carries a torch song (see Weill's note for his music entry *3*) entitled 'Too much to dream', with lyrics by Sam Coslow.

VOCAL AND SHORT SCORES

No comprehensive score – whether autograph or non-autograph – has been traced. Apart from fragmentary sketches, *1, 2, 11, 12* and *13* are missing altogether; the holographs of *4y* and *10y* are also missing. The following material is in WLA:

'Knocking Song' (*3*)
First version for voice and piano, in pencil on nine sides of a 3-sheet folding of AB¹², with the first side stamped '22 December 1937'; second version for voices, chorus and percussion, in pencil on thirteen sides of a 4-sheet folding of K¹² which also contains a sketch for *Knickerbocker Holiday* (*30*) – indicating composition in spring 1938. A fragment of another arrangement for solo voice and unison chorus is on a sheet of K¹²; a copyist's score of the second version is prefaced by the autograph sketch of a 9-bar 'knocking rhythm' for six pitched and three (or more) unpitched percussion, evidently intended to continue, with variations, throughout the number. Details of the relationship between the percussion instrumentation and the visual images are given in a note made by the composer on a torn sheet of AB¹². 'Table = low marimba (struck with hands), Glasses = tuned glasses, Bottles = tuned bottles, Radiator = glissando bells, Pipe = chimes, Keys = Timpani, low xylophone.'

'The Right Guy for Me'   *(5)*
First version in pencil on five sides of AB^{12}; second version (with different accompanimental figuration) is in pencil on five sides of AB^{12}; the third (final) version, which has a new refrain, is sketched on two sides of P^{12}; the fair copy is in ink on five sides of K^{12}.

'Too much to dream'   *(6y)*
Pencil, on four sides of Sch^{12}.

Barbershop Quartet   *(7y)*
Ink, on four sides of Cp^{12}.

The Romance of a Lifetime   *(8)*
Ink, on four sides of K^{12}.

Jiggaboo   *(9y)*
Pencil, on two sides of K^{12}.

NON-AUTOGRAPH FAIR COPIES

2, 3 and 4y in (presumably) the composer's versions, and 2, 3 and 5 in the studio arrangements.

Film Credits

Cast: George Raft (Joe Dennis), Sylvia Sidney (Helen), Robert Cummings (Jim), Gwinn Williams (Taxi), Carol Paige (Torch Singer), Barton Maclane (Mickey), Roscoe Karns (Cuffy), Ray Middleton (One of the Gang)
Music credits: director Boris Morros; arrangements and orchestrations by Gordon Jenkins, Phil Bootelje, Max Terr, Al Siegel.

Final Dubbing

The first dubbing sessions took place in April 1938. To judge from Weill's contemporary correspondence, the Music Department was not enthusiastic and radical changes were ordered. Little of Weill's original score, and nothing of his formal conception, survived in the final dubbing. 4, 6, 7, 8, 9, 10, 13 and 14 were discarded; 2 was 'arranged' out of recognition and 3 was reduced to an insignificant fragment. Of the twenty-five entries only nine are credited to Weill alone in the final dubbing sheets:

1   Prelude (KW)
2   Honeymoon scene (KW)
3   Song of the Cash Register (KW/Boutelje)
4   Entry to dance hall (Shuken)
5   Dance Hall (Shuken)
6   Two fanfares (Bradshaw)
7   Introduction to 'The Right Guy for Me' (Bradshaw)
8   The Right Guy for Me (KW)
9   Big Apple (Frey)

10   It's been a Whole Year (Yacht Club Boys)
11   Honeymoon scene (KW)
12   Honeymoon scene (KW)
13   Christmas Party (Leipold)
14   Jingle Bells (Leipold)
15   Silent Night (Gruber)
16   We won't get home till morning (trad.)
17   Hail! Hail! the Gang's all here (Sullivan)
18   The Robbery (KW)
19   Song of the Cash Register (KW/Boutelje)
20   A timely regeneration (KW/Harling)
21   Honeymoon scene (KW)
22   The Search (KW/Harling)
23   Honeymoon scene (KW)
24   End title (Shuken)
25   Honeymoon scene (KW)

Publication

Famous Music Corp., New York, 1938: 'The Right Guy for Me'.

August 1937, New York

[Two Chansons for Yvette Guilbert]

For voice and piano
Texts: Yvette Guilbert
  1   'Tu me démolis'
  2   'Pauv' Madam' Peachum!' (*Tempo di Minuetto*)
(Unpublished; 1 missing; unperformed?)

Written for the 1937 Paris production of *Die Dreigroschenoper* (as *L'Opéra de quat' sous*) in which Yvette Guilbert played the part of Mrs Peachum (Théâtre des Etoiles, 29 September 1937; producer, Ernst Josef Aufricht).

Autographs

SKETCHES AND FINAL COPIES

1, missing; 2, sketched on P^{12}, with fragmentary sketch for *The River is Blue*; final copy in black ink, on three sides of AB^{12} headed 'Chanson II pour "L'Opéra de Quat' Sous"/Texte d'Yvette Guilbert, Musique de Kurt Weill'.

Note 1

Yvette Guilbert provided her own music for her texts; there is no evidence (and little likelihood) that she sang Weill's settings, which were made at the suggestion of Ernst Josef Aufricht. In a covering letter to Aufricht written (in German) from New York on 18 August 1937, Weill stated:

I enclose the two songs for Yvette Guilbert. Both texts are excellent, and I think they have turned into two very good *Dreigroschenoper*-chansons. The first chanson ('Ah Polly, Polly, tu me démolis') must be taken fairly fast, the rhythm has a slightly Spanish colouring; the third verse (where she is already very drunk) is composed as a kind of funeral march, but then in the refrain suddenly goes back into the cheerful tempo. The second song I have composed as a minuet. To set this rather obscene text to music that is very graceful and charming is very much in the style of *Die Dreigroschenoper*. I have built the song round the question 'Qui?', and allow this 'Qui?' to interrupt the song at certain points – which of course must each time be given a different expression. Then the reply is always an outburst of despair and grief.

Weill has cleverly avoided suggesting that the music – as distinct from the attitude – of the minuet-song is 'very much in the style of *Die Dreigroschenoper'*. In truth it has no musical affinity with that work, but belongs somewhere between *A Kingdom for a Cow* (the added numbers) and the more European sections of *Knickerbocker Holiday*. The fact that Weill does not even mention the possibility of orchestrating his voice-and-piano scores (although Aufricht's musical director was the eminent conductor Selmar Meyerowitz) seems to confirm that so far from intending to integrate the two songs, he was content that they should be identified as the interlopers they are.

August–December 1937, Chapel Hill/Manhattan

The Common Glory

Musical Pageant
Text: Paul Green
Commissioned by the Federal Theatre
(Unfinished)

A lifelong proponent of regional and open-air theatre (as opposed to Broadway) Paul Green was a member of the board of directors of the Federal Theatre, which had been created in October 1935 as a federally sponsored and nationwide theatre under the aegis of the New Deal's 'Works Progress Administration' (WPA). Weill's decision to collaborate with him on a large-scale musico-dramatic portrayal of the beginnings of the American Constitution followed on from Max Reinhardt's previous interest in an American *Everyman* by Weill and Green (RS.DGS, p. 206), and was intimately associated with his first step towards American citizenship, which he took at the end of August 1937. Earlier that month he had visited Paul Green at his home in Chapel Hill, North Carolina, and discussed with him a dramatization of the American Revolution. On 19 August he wrote a long and serious letter to Green, quoting two passages from a recent Roosevelt speech. In the second of these he had found what he described as 'the complete ideological outline of our play'. Roosevelt had declared that if 'certain modern Americans who protest loudly their devotion to American ideals were suddenly to be given a comprehensive view of the earliest American colonists and their methods of life and government, they would probably label them as socialists'. Taking his cue from this, Weill continued:

> It is this 'comprehensive view' which we have to give – a picture of early America, completely different from the one we are used to read in schoolbooks and chronicles; the socialist idea in early America, its fight against the followers of European feudalism, and its final triumph in the Constitution.

Weill's conception of the work was, at this stage, clearly indebted to the non-Aristotelian epic forms of *Die Bürgschaft*. The pageant was to be in three parts: 'An introduction in the form of a chorus symphony, showing [. . .] with a reporting chorus the great events which shake the old world, wars, revolutions, persecutions [. . .] leading from the early days up to the seventeenth century.' The central part should show 'the birth of the Constitution as the drama of an idea'; and the third part should continue 'the symphonic report of the first part [. . .] right up to Hitler and Mussolini'.

It was a dauntingly ambitious plan for a work which the Federal Theatre intended to stage in February 1938 – only six months hence. Green was not, however, attracted by the European panels in Weill's triptych, and in September persuaded him that they should concentrate on the central section and build it round the figure of Samuel Adams (1722–1803), a figure discussed at their previous meeting. Weill returned to Chapel Hill in October, and was distressed to find that Green was still immersed in his historical studies, and by no means clear about the next steps. After further consultations in New York with the Federal Theatre authorities Weill wrote to Green (13 October) suggesting three different ways out of the present impasse. Green plumped for the idea of introducing a fictional 'common man' as counterpart to Sam Adams, but before long was in difficulties once again. The Federal Theatre's December deadline was missed. Weill turned to a new Federal Theatre venture (see p. 297) and Green continued with *The Common Glory*. The collaboration with Weill was not resumed.

Autographs

The draft of a 62-bar choral hymn, 'Almighty and everlasting God', is all that survives (on three sides of a sheet of AB^{12}). During the three months between the inception of the work and the point at which he must have realized that Green would not meet the deadline, Weill had no conflicting musical obligations that we know of. Although his own reading and research for *The Common Glory* must have been extensive, it seems most unlikely, in view of his initial enthusiasm and the proximity of the February 1938 premiere, that he composed nothing apart from the hymn.

---

7 November 1937, New York

Albumblatt für Erika

For piano
(Unpublished)

Autograph: (heirs of Caspar and Erika Neher)

Ink fair copy, on a leaf of S¹⁴, headed 'Albumblatt für Erika/Kurt Weill/ 7.11.1937'.

Notes

This birthday present for Caspar Neher's wife Erika is a transcription of the 'Pastorale' (7) from *Der Weg der Verheissung*.

1938, New York

Two Folksongs of the New Palestine

Arranged for voice and piano

   1   Havu l'venim (Bring the Bricks); melody by Seira
   2   Baa M'nucha (There comes Peace unto the Weary); melody by Samburski

Autographs

Missing.

Publication

Nigun Press, 1938: in the collection *Folksongs of the New Palestine* (1 in First Series, No. 3; 2 in First Series, No. 5) edited and annotated by Hans Nathan, with an English translation by Harry H. Fein. Other contributors to the series included Copland, Dessau, Honegger, Milhaud, Saminsky, Toch, and Wolpe.

January–April 1938, Suffern/Hollywood

Davy Crockett

'Musical play by H. R. Hays and Kurt Weill'
Unfinished project for the Federal Theatre
Duration: *c.* 45 minutes music in rehearsal-score draft

The play is a much idealized chronicle of the life of the folk hero and
congressman Davy Crockett (1786–1836). The action begins *c.* 1800 with the
eviction of the Crockett family from their log cabin in Tennessee by
government surveyors, and ends with Davy's death in the battle of the
Alamo. Davy's principal adversary is Job Spindle, an archetypal capitalist.
Davy marries Sarah, sister of his best friend Josh Hawkins – to the fury of
Spindle, who had fancied her for himself. Throughout the play, Spindle's
progress from rags to riches, and Davy's from the backwoods to Congress,
are identified as representative of, respectively, the negative and the positive
sides of American life and politics.

ACT I

1   Introduction (orchestra)

Scene i: The Woods
2   I'm a rolling stone (Josh Hawkins)
3   (continuation of 2)

Scene ii: The Crockett Cabin
4   Where the green pines shadow the ground (Davy and chorus)
5   Interscene I (Hillbilly narrative song)

Scene iii: The Woods
6   Song of the Trees (chorus, with Davy)
7   Interscene II (Hillbilly narrative song)

Scene iv: Sarah Hawkins's Home
8   Look your partner straight in the eye (Davy's square-dance song)
9   Interscene III (Hillbilly narrative – Davy's and Sarah's marriage)

Scene v: Job Spindle's Office
10   The Hand is quicker than the eye (Job Spindle)

Scene vi: Davy's and Sarah's Home
11   Letter Song – The death of Josh Hawkins (solo voice, Davy)
12   Watch out for me (Davy, Sarah and chorus)

Scene vii: Tucsonville, Tennessee
13   March (orchestral version of 12)
         Finale 1
14a When I'm in Congress (Davy, chorus)
14b Unfinished

ACT II

Scene viii: Buffet in a Washington Theatre
15   Politics (stage singer)
16   Polka (orchestra)

17   Interscene IV (Hillbilly narrative)

Scene ix: President Jackson's Office in the White House
18   All goes badly (chorus)

Scene x: Outside the White House
19   Time is standing still (Sarah and chorus)

Scene xi: The Alamo
20   Battle of the Alamo (orchestra)
21   Closing music

Autographs

SKETCHES

Missing, except for two pages of Paramount film-studio paper (P^{12}) with notations for *6* and *8*.

DRAFTS

Six pages of P^{12} contain: a discarded song, 'I'll cook them corn and taters', headed 'Beginning 1st scene'; *2*; *9*; and *20*, headed 'Indian Battle', incomplete on three numbered pages. The main collection of drafts is on a 20-page folding of another Paramount film studio paper – AB^{12}. There are also three sheets of the same paper, each with one number or more. The song beginning 'You cannot buy love' covers three pages of a sheet of K^{12} whose fourth side has sketches for *20*. A note in the WLA playtext, 'Sarah: You can't buy love' may indicate that the song was intended for Scene iv though its tone has more in common with that of *You and Me* in its later stages. Revised and adapted to fit new lyrics, the song became 'It never was you' in *Knickerbocker Holiday*.

REHEARSAL SCORE

The score is wrapped in a title page inscribed by the composer: 'H. R. Hays and Kurt Weill/*Davy Crockett*/Piano Score/(first, *incomplete* draft ,/ only for rehearsal purpose)'. There are forty-one unnumbered pages of manuscript, very neatly written in black or blue-black ink, with the song texts recopied in upper case throughout, in another hand; all on K^{12}, except for *9* and *10*, which are on film-studio paper (AB^{12}). There is no pagination, but each number is headed (in another hand) by a pencilled and encircled numeral. (Most of the numbers also have cross-references to the libretto, in red crayon in another hand.) This numbering is reproduced in the list given above, with slight modifications. *16* is signified merely by a pencilled note in the composer's hand: 'On page 8– 12 [i.e. scene 8 page 12] there is another music back-stage which is a

Polka (like "Madelon of Paree") [*Johnny Johnson, 15*]. Follows Interscene IV (not finished).' That this is a German-English way of saying that Interscene IV follows the Polka is confirmed by a note at the head of *18* ('Here follows Interscene IV'). No material for Interscene IV has been traced, but there are no other claimants for the number *17*. At the end of *19* appears another pencilled note in the composer's hand: 'Here follows Battle of Alamo (not finished)'; for 'Battle of Alamo' see *Drafts* above. The music was completed as 'The Dance of the Tumblers' in *Lady in the Dark*.

The numbers in the rehearsal score appear to be complete in themselves apart from the following: *4* (a choral reprise and coda is indicated), *14b* (marked 'to be continued, building up to a big Finale') and *15* (marked 'etc.' before cadential bars).

Notes

Hoffmann Reynolds Hays (1904–1980) was well known as a writer, translator, and polemicist. Together with Arnold Sundgaard (and others) he was responsible for *Medicine Show* (1940), the first privately sponsored 'Living Newspaper'. Hanns Eisler, who had worked with him for the first time in 1935 (*A Song about America*) and went on to write the score for *Medicine Show*, introduced him to Brecht in 1941; Hays collaborated with Brecht and Auden on the adaptation of Webster's *The Duchess of Malfi* for Elisabeth Bergner, and was translator and editor of Brecht's *Selected Poems* (New York, 1947).

Davy Crockett began as a straight play, *The Ballad of Davy Crockett*, produced by the Columbia University Players and then by the Federal Theatre in 1937. It attracted the attention of Weill's friends Burgess Meredith and Charles Alan, who suggested that Hays and Weill collaborate on a musical version for the Federal Theatre (the copy of the text in WLRC is entitled 'One Man from Tennessee/By/H. R. Hays and Kurt Weill'). John Wildberg of the Federal Theatre planned to produce the play with Henry Fonda as Crockett (and presumably Meredith as Job Spindle), but the financial backing was not immediately forthcoming. When Weill returned from Hollywood in June 1938 he found, to his consternation, that Maxwell Anderson had not only written most of the book and lyrics for *Knickerbocker Holiday* during his absence, but had arranged for a production in late September. *Davy Crockett* – about which Weill evidently had reservations – was therefore put to one side. But the time spent on it was not wasted. Much simpler in style than *Johnny Johnson*, and also more 'American' – or at least, less obviously European – the Crockett score was a necessary step towards *Knickerbocker Holiday*. In its folksiness it belongs more to the world of the Federal Theatre than to Broadway, and in no sense looks forward to *Oklahoma* or *Annie Get Your Gun*. Nor does it anticipate Weill's own *Down in the Valley*, apart from the (eighteenth-century European) Vaudeville device of narrative songs (Interscene I, etc.) based on the same tune – in this case the melody of

Josh Hawkins's hillbilly song, 'I'm a rolling stone'. The music of this song
and its three derivatives was reincarnated in *Knickerbocker Holiday*, where
it appears in a much strengthened form as 'There's Nowhere to go but
Up'. A modified version of one of the ideas from *8* – Davy's square-dance
song – also appears in that score, as a Dutch Dance for orchestra.

Although *Davy Crockett* has some good moments, Weill was surely
right to abandon it. Compared to *Johnny Johnson* on the one hand and
Knickerbocker Holiday on the other, it seems undernourished and lacking
in both vitality and conviction. For that, the play must certainly bear part
of the blame.

Spring 1938/Winter 1938–9, Suffern

Railroads on Parade
'Fantasia on Rail Transport'

For locomotives, actors, dancers, soloists, chorus, and orchestra
Planned and written by Edward Hungerford
Commissioned by the Eastern Railroad Presidents' Conference
Duration: 70 minutes; 45 minutes music
(Unpublished)
Cast: singing roles: female narrator (soprano), male narrator (tenor),
   numerous soloists from chorus; other roles: historic locomotives,
   historical figures, financiers, businessmen, workers, travellers
Orchestra: 1.1.3.(3sax.)o. 0.3.2.1. novachord, Hammond org. pno. gtr.
   perc. str. 5.3.3.2.1.

PROLOGUE

1   Narration: 'Once was the time' (narrator, soprano, chorus)
2   Narration, The Rocket: 'Here's a brave beginning' (narrator, chorus)

ACT I: NEW YORK – GATEWAY OF THE NEW EMPIRE

Scene i: The Erie Canal, the Battery, New York, 1825
3   *Allegro moderato* (orchestra, with narrator)
4a   *Alla marcia* (brass band)
4b   'The British Grenadiers' (brass band)

Scene ii: The First Railroad, Massachusetts, 1826
5   *Sostenuto – allegro grazioso* (orchestra, with narrator)

ACT II: THE COMING OF THE IRON HORSE

Scene i: The Stourbridge Lion – Honesdale, Pennsylvania, 1829
6   'Low Bridge' (bass, chorus)
7a   *Allegro assai* (orchestra)

Scene ii: The Iron Horse – Parade of Locomotives
7b   *Allegro assai*, continued

Scene iii: The Tom Thumb – City Dock, Baltimore, 1829
8a   'Heave away' (male chorus)
8b   *Allegretto moderato* (orchestra)
9a   *Allegro assai* (orchestra)
9b   'This train is bound for glory' (chorus)

ACT III: THE RAILROAD REACHES THE WEST

Scene i: Overland Trail, Road to the West, 1849
10a   'Westward Ho!' (female narrator and chorus)
10b   *Allegro giocoso* (orchestra)
10c   *Andante non troppo* (orchestra)

Scene ii: Lincoln Rides the Railroads, New York 1861

Scene iii: The Golden Spike – Promontory Point, Utah, 1869
11   'I've been working on the railroad' (chorus)
12   Song: 'What the Engine Said' (tenor, chorus)

ACT IV: RIDING ON THE CARS IN THE 1870s

Scene i: Yesterdays – The Depot of a Small Town in the 1870s
13   Waltz ensemble: 'Riding on the Railroad' (tenor, chorus)
13a   *Alla marcia* (brass band)

Scene ii: The Old-time Day Coach of the 1870s
14   'Riding on the Cars' (poem by John Godfrey Saxe)

Scene iii: And Still They Ride – New York in the 1930s
15a   Station 'Ensemble': 'Oh Mister, where's the train' (six soloists)
15b   Commuters' Chorus: 'We're city men of sober mien'
15c   Through-travellers' Chorus: 'We're Travellers Through and Through'

ACT V: SWIFT PERFORMANCE

Scene i: Orange Grove, Southern California

Scene ii: Pounding the High Iron

Scene iii: The Little Red Caboose

Scene iv: Railroad under Test

Scene v: In a Small Suburban Home

EPILOGUE

16   Song of the Railroad Workers: 'We man the trains' (narrator, soloists, chorus)

Additions, 1939

After the completion of the full score, and probably at rehearsal stage, the items listed below were added (*17* for production reasons, *18b* in order to supply a contemporary pop-song element otherwise missing). Texts and lyrics are by Charles Alan.

17a   Our Lincoln comes (female chorus)
17b   This Train is bound for glory (black chorus)
18a   Pullman Scene (narrators)
18b   Wheels through the Night (tenor and chorus)

1940 version

As the outstanding success at the 1939 World's Fair, *Railroads on Parade* was revived at the 1940 Fair, in a simplified production, with the dialogue shortened and modified, and various musical changes and additions, as well as cuts. The additions were mostly arrangements of folk songs and ballads. The evidence of the manuscripts suggests that with the possible exception of 24 this music was composed in 1939, soon after the premiere. The additional numbers are:

19   The Sailor's Wife (chorus) for Act II, scene ii
20   'Tell ol' Bill' (baritone and male chorus) for Act II, scene iii
21   'Snagtooth Sal', and 'Sacramento' (soloists and chorus) for
          Act III, scene i
22   new Lincoln Scene
23   Waltz, Cakewalk, and Ballad: 'Two little girls in Blue' (orchestra, with
          tenor) for Act IV, scene ii, as conclusion to 'Riding on the Cars'
24   Pullman Blues, as substitute for 17
25   Orange Farm (orchestral arrangement of *Marie Galante* tango) for
          Act V, scene i

Autographs

SKETCHES

Mostly missing. Eight sides of P^{12} contain notations of folk songs as well as fragmentary sketches and a rough draft of *17b*. A leaf of MM^{24} carries sketches for 22 and (*verso*) a scoring of a fanfare for *Knickerbocker Holiday*; a sheet of Sch^{12} carries a reminder of the *Marie Galante* tango; a leaf of Sch^{14} (with a few bars' ink fair copy of the closing chorale in *Knickerbocker Holiday*) carries a sketch for *18*.

Most of the 1939/40 additions are sketched on twelve pages of a spiral-bound notebook (Fsp^{12}). As there are only six more pages left in the book – see *Songs of Discovery*, p. 308 – it is obvious that many have been removed. (At least one sheet was removed by Weill himself: folk-song notations are written upside-down on both sides of a leaf found among his miscellaneous papers.)

DRAFT

The 1939 version is drafted in structural sequence, from start to finish. The score is written on forty-five unnumbered pages of K^{12}, wrapped in a title sheet on whose second side the Prologue begins.

REHEARSAL SCORE

107 consecutively numbered pages (MM[14], F[12], K[12] and O[12]) are arranged in two foldings within a title sheet of F[12] inscribed 'Railroads on Parade/ by/Edward Hungerford/Music/by/Kurt Weill/Piano Score'. Two sheets (17–18/23–4 and 35–6/60–1) are missing, as are pages 60–7 and 83–90. Only the last-moment additions are written on O[12]; a sheet of O[12] headed 'End of Lincoln Scene' is not included in the pagination. The Pullman Scene (18) exists in two forms: first as a popular song 'Wheels through the Night' – written on a sheet of O[12] and inserted at the appropriate place in the page order – and secondly as a fully composed scene incorporating 'Wheels through the Night' and written on a 10-page folding of O[12] which has its own pagination. Two further sheets of O[12] give alternative versions of the popular song, and appear to have been intended as master copies for the sheet-music publication (though the latter is musically simplified, and has different lyrics). The supplementary numbers composed for the 1940 version of the score are separate, each on a sheet or folding of Sc[14], totalling thirty-two pages. The Pullman Blues (24), without lyrics, is on a leaf of Fsp[12] torn from the spiral-bound manuscript book.

FULL SCORE

The original version of the score is arranged in three foldings of Sch[20] comprising 185 numbered pages, with one unnumbered sheet inserted at page 85 and another at 112. The Lincoln scene is in a separate 8-page folding of Sch[20]; the Pullman scene, together with an arrangement of Sousa's 'Anchors Aweigh', is in a 20-page folding of the same paper. With one exception, the supplementary numbers for the 1940 versions are likewise on separate foldings of the same paper. The Pullman Blues (or Pullman Song) is on six sides of Psp[24].

Publication

Crawford, 1939: 'Mile after Mile' – sheet-music version of 17b, lyrics by Buddy Bernier and Charles Alan.

First Performance

30 April 1939, New York World's Fair. Director Charles Alan, designer Harry Horner, choreographer Bill Matons, conductor Isaac van Grove; with members of the WPA Theatre Project, Ballet Caravan, and the Ted Shawm Dance Company; with Mary Drayton and Wallace Walter Folmer (soprano and tenor narrators), and soloists (in chorus) including Robert Rounseville, Earl Wetherford and Bernice Tyler. Chorus of 18, corps de ballet of 32, and theatre ensemble of 130, including Michael Kidd, Don DeFore, Elizabeth Barrett, Margaret Chaffee Kent.

Note

Musically, *Railroads on Parade* is the culmination of Weill's first period in the USA – a period dominated, for him, by the Group Theatre, the Federal Theatre, and the social and political climate of the New Deal. While paying lip-service to its official role as a hymn to pioneering capitalism and the development of America's industrial might, it becomes, through its strikingly personal treatment of folk song, a truthful and touching expression of 'the common glory', in Carl Sandburg's sense as well as Paul Green's.

June–September 1938, Suffern

Knickerbocker Holiday

Musical play [quasi-operetta], after Washington Irving's *The History of New York by Diedrich Knickerbocker*
Book and lyrics: Maxwell Anderson
Duration: full evening; 70 minutes' music
Cast: singing roles: Washington Irving, Brom Broek, Tina Tienhoven, Peter Stuyvesant, Tienhoven, Tenpin, councillors, citizens, soldiers; other roles: Vanderbilt, Roosevelt, de Peyster, de Vries, Van Rensselaer, Van Cortlandt Jr, Schermerhorn, General Poffenburgh
Orchestra: fl.(picc.). ob. 3cl.(3sax.).2tpt. 2tbn. org. pno. gtr. str. (without violas in manuscript, but added by Irving Schlein).

Manhattan Island, 1647. The new Governor, Peter Stuyvesant, informs the corrupt and inefficient Council that he will now take charge of everything – including their various illicit practices. He appoints Councillor Tienhoven as his pay-off man and is much delighted when Tienhoven offers him the hand of his daughter Tina. But Tina's true love is the cheerfully penniless knife-grinder Brom Broek, who has made no secret of his scorn for the Council, and now seems almost alone in refusing to welcome Stuyvesant's New Order. Exercising his democratic rights, Brom tells Stuyvesant what he thinks of him and is promptly clapped in gaol. He escapes, and soon manages to play upon the growing disaffection of the Council, who resent the way Stuyvesant is usurping their 'Ancient Liberties' and establishing a monopoly in graft, extortion and chicanery. In the end, Washington Irving steps into his own story, to remind Stuyvesant that none of his actions or decisions will escape the judgement of posterity. An instant convert to democracy, the Governor introduces the recommended reforms, and graciously consents to the marriage of Brom and Tina.

Introduction: Washington Irving's Study
1   Melodrama and Song: 'I'll sing of a golden age' (Washington Irving)

ACT I

Scene i: The Battery, 1647

2	Clickety-Clack (Tina and girls)
3	Entry of the Council (Irving)
4x	It's a Law (Councillors); replaced by:
4	Hush Hush (Roosevelt and Councillors)
5x	'I Do Business in my Hat' (Brom, Tenpin, chorus); replaced by:
5	'There's Nowhere to go but Up' (Brom, Tenpin, chorus)
6	It Never Was You (Brom, Tina)
7y	Brom's Complaint (Brom); replaced by:
7	How Can You Tell an American? (Irving, Brom)
8x	Another Law (Councillors)
9	Will You Remember Me? (Tina, Brom, chorus)
9a	The Hanging (orchestra)
10x	The Consequence is Awful (Stuyvesant and chorus); replaced by:
10	Stuyvesant's Entrance (orchestra)
11	One Touch of Alchemy (Stuyvesant and chorus)
12	Exit of the Council (orchestra)
13	The One Indispensable Man (Stuyvesant, Tienhoven)
14	Young People Think About Love (Brom, Tina, Councillors, chorus)
15	September Song (Stuyvesant)
16x	Clump! Clump! Swish! (Tina and Dutch girls); replaced by:
16	Dutch Dance (orchestra)
17	All Hail the Political Honeymoon (Councillors and chorus)

ACT II

Scene i: Interior of the Gaol

18x	Old Pete is in the City (Irving) – music of *10*; replaced by:
18	Ballad of the Robber (Irving)
19	Sitting in Gaol (Stuyvesant)
20	We Are Cut in Twain (Tina, Brom)
21	Reprise of *5* (Irving)

Scene ii: The Battery

22	The Army of New Amsterdam (orchestra)
23	To War! (Soldiers)
24	Our Ancient Liberties (Councillors)
25	Exit of Council (orchestra)
26	May and January (Bridesmaids and chorus)
27ya	The Scars, version 1 (Stuyvesant); replaced by:
27b	The Scars, version 2 (Stuyvesant)
28	Algonquins from Harlem (battle music for orchestra)
29	Dirge for a Soldier (Chorus)
30	We Want to Make the Laws (Councillors and Crowd)
30a	Incidental music
31y	Epilogue (Stuyvesant and chorus); replaced by:
31	Reprise of *5* (All)

Unlocated numbers:

32y	How far will you go with me? (Tina)
33x	Bachelor Song (Tenpin)

Autographs

SKETCHES

Mostly missing. Eight sides of P^{12}, six of MM^{24}, carry sketches for a few of the numbers and some unused material. A leaf of AB^{12} carries *Crockett*-style battle music incorporating a motif from 'The Ballad of Pharaoh' (*Der Kuhhandel*), and a dissonant harmonization of the melody of $5x$. A sketch for the start of 'Will You Remember Me?' is on side c of a sheet of Cp^{12}, and is the only means of dating the remaining workings, which are biographically and critically of considerable interest. Whether they relate to *Knickerbocker Holiday*, or to contemporary work in Hollywood during the spring of 1938, or to nothing in particular, is immaterial; they are simply exercises in the use of conventional popular-song and jazz formulae. Side a is headed 'Themes', and carries five such formulae, numbered as if they had been copied from a song writer's textbook (see *Music Library*, p. 433). Side b is headed 'Breaks' and carries two more formulae, together with a third item which is remarkable enough in itself, but quite astonishing in the context: a memo of the last three bars of the *Mahagonny-Songspiel* (of which Weill possessed no score in America). Neither rhythmically nor harmonically does this echo from 1927 have the slightest bearing on the 'Breaks' or the so-called 'Themes' – the third of which is developed on side c (and the fifth of which crops up seven years later on an Sch^{20} sheet otherwise devoted to sketches for *Where Do We Go From Here?*).

DRAFTS

Twenty-two sides of P^{12} and twenty-three of MM^{24} carry drafts of most of the numbers; 4, 14, 15, and the final versions of 7 and 29 are missing. When the extant drafts were first examined by the present writer, rather more than half of them were gathered together in an MM^{24} title sheet on which the composer had written: 'Complete first manuscript/of the "Knickerbocker Holiday" music/to Mab and Max/as a token of my undying affection./Kurt'. On the b side of the cover sheet is a complete draft of a simple 2-part invention in classical style. On c and d – that is, the last two sides presented to the Andersons – is a sketch for a quasi-*maestoso* variation of 5, with a solemn introduction – presumably planned for 31, which in the final version is a literal reprise of 5.

REHEARSAL SCORE

4 is missing; otherwise complete on 173 unnumbered and unbound pages; predominantly Sch^{14} but with some MM^{14}, Cp^{12} and F^{12}; choral arrangements added to 5 and 9 are on M^{12} – the earliest known instance of Weill's use of ozalid paper. Except for these single sheets, the score is divided into separate foldings for each number. It was originally wrapped in a sheet (now a detached leaf) of Sch^{24} inscribed in pencil

'Maxwell Anderson – Kurt Weill/Knickerbocker Holiday/Complete Vocal Score/Manuscript'. A few items are written in pencil, and these are evidently late additions to the score: introduction to 6, 10, 12, 15, 19, dance coda to 27, and choral arrangements for 5 and 9. The score is marked throughout in other hands, having been used at auditions, in rehearsal, and as the publisher's production master. Several numbers have a note to the effect that they must be transposed because the orchestration is in a different key.

FULL SCORE

Unbound and without title page. Each number is written in a separate folding of Sch²⁰, except for 30a in pencil on Pa²⁰ and an incomplete scoring of 32 on Ss²⁰. In all there are 361 pages of manuscript. 12 (one page), and four pages of an unlocated insertion using the music of 5, are in pencil. The end of 8x is missing, as is part of 27b (which has a pencilled note by the composer, 'four pages missing'). Nos. 7y and 31y were evidently left unscored.

Except for the omitted numbers, the entire manuscript is heavily annotated by other hands. Pencil is used for cuts, and red crayon for instructions to the copyist. Here and there – notably in 15 – extra doublings have been neatly added in red crayon. The most important addition, which affects all but the cut numbers, is in the string section: a viola part has been added throughout. (This was doubtless for contractual reasons, since artistic ones would scarcely have outweighed the financial cost.) The viola part is written out, or, where possible, simply indicated, in the hand of Weill's assistant, Irving Schlein.

First Performance

28 September 1938 (try-out), Hartford (Connecticut), Bushnell Memorial Theatre; 19 October 1938, New York, Ethyl Barrymore Theatre. Produced by the Playwrights' Company and staged by Joshua Logan; conductor Maurice Abravanel, designer Jo Mielziner (costumes Frank Bevan), choreographers Carl Randall and Edwin Denby; with Ray Middleton (Irving), Richard Kollmar (Brom), Jean Madden (Tina), Walter Huston (Stuyvesant), Mark Smith (Tienhoven) and Clarence Nordstrom (Tenpin). Chorus including Erika Zaranova, Bruce Hamilton and Robert Rounseville.

Publication

Chappell, 1938: vocal score; vocal album (containing 1, 7, 9, 14, 15 and 24); sheet music: 5, 6, 9, 15
Dramatic licences and performance materials: present (1986) availability – Rodgers & Hammerstein Music Library (USA), KWF (USA and Britain).

Film

United Artists, released 20 April 1944; produced and directed by Harry Joe Brown; screen adaptation by Thomas Lennon, screenplay by David Boehm and Rowland Leight; additional musical numbers by Jule Styne and Sammy Kahn, Forman Brown, Werner R. Heymann, and Fritz Steininger. 'Musical score' by Werner R. Heymann, conducted by Jacques Samousoud. With Nelson Eddy (Brom Broek), Charles Coburn (Peter Stuyvesant), Constance Dowling (Tina Tienhoven), Ernest Cossart (Tienhoven), Otto Kruger (Roosevelt), Carmen Amaya and her company.

Note

When the film rights were acquired in 1939, Weill tried to persuade the producers to commission a screenplay that developed and emphasized the anti-Nazi satire in Anderson's play, and excluded the anti-New Deal satire. To this end he made various concrete proposals, and offered to write additional songs. Even at that time it was not, perhaps, very likely that his serious intentions would be taken seriously (there is no record in WLA or WLRC of any response to his proposals). By the time the film went into production, United Artists had excluded Weill and Anderson from their calculations. To all intents and purposes the film is independent of the musical play; and as the film credits proclaim, Weill had been supplanted by Werner R. Heymann, a contemporary of his from Berlin, and already in those pre-Hitler years a successful contributor to revues, cabarets, and films.

1939

[Songs of Discovery]

(Incomplete and partly missing)

1 [Columbus Song] – incomplete
2 [Peregrine White and Virginia Dare]

Autographs

The only known source for the 'Columbus Song' is a substantial fragment (109 bars) drafted on the first five pages of the spiral-bound manuscript book (Fsp^{12}) that contains the 1939 drafts for the supplement to *Railroads on Parade*. The draft ends at the foot of the fifth page with a harmonic shift presaging a further development; the sixth page is blank. 'Peregrine White and Virginia Dare' is complete on two loose leaves of the same paper, first found among a collection of unidentified manuscripts. The scribal and bibliographic evidence that it belongs to the same unit as the 'Columbus Song' is confirmed by the music and the text.

Notes

The absence of any clue as to the origin of these songs is itself a clue: whatever the nature of the project, it is unlikely to have been commissioned for, or to have been designed for, some metropolitan medium or market. A relatively informal origin, without attendant correspondence and negotiations, would be in keeping with both the music and the text – whose light-footedness and spontaneity of invention invite favourable comparisons with any of the *Davy Crockett* numbers. The tone is not that of Broadway, but closer to the requirements of the Federal Theatre and progressive radio. The young audience which is clearly in mind is approached without condescension. Fragments though they are, the songs share with *Railroads on Parade* a marked tendency towards forms of popular expression alternative to those generally favoured in areas of high capital investment, and show Weill at a crossroads from which he and his collaborators could have taken a path parallel to that which led Britten and Auden to their operetta *Paul Bunyan* (1940–1). Among his associates, Charles Alan was perhaps the one most likely at that time to have envisaged such a development, given that any further collaboration with H. R. Hays was by then unlikely. Although it is not altogether impossible that the author of the present song texts was Maxwell Anderson (see p. 399), their style and tone are not typical of him.

March–August 1939, Suffern-Malibu/[?]July 1945

Ulysses Africanus

Unfinished Musical
Book and lyrics by Maxwell Anderson

Note 1

The project was based on Harry Stillwell Edwards's *Aeneas Africanus* (1919), an epistolary novel concerning the wanderings of a faithful 'Negro' slave who is separated from his devoted owners during the American Civil War. He tries to rejoin them (and return the family silver which they had entrusted to him), but for eight years is prevented from doing so by a variety of confusions that lead him on a 3000-mile journey back and forth across the American South. During his wanderings he marries, begets children, and encounters more kindness than prejudice.

Ronald Sanders (RS.DGS, pp. 285–7, and 343) describes how in March 1939 Anderson offered the title role to Paul Robeson, who declined it on account of what Sanders calls an 'innate condescension in the story'. According to Sanders, Anderson's interest already began to wane, as he needed the security of a 'major star'. However, a provisional commitment from Bill Robinson, a somewhat lesser star who was then appearing in Broadway's all-black Gilbert and Sullivan show, *The Hot Mikado*, encouraged Anderson to start work again. In June Weill joined Anderson for a working holiday in California, where most of the sketches and drafts were made. Progress was sufficient to justify plans for a production during the coming season; but Robinson was not, after all, available, and Anderson lost heart.

Apparently on the basis of newspaper reports, Sanders maintains that a (very belated!) sign of interest from Robeson in July 1945 induced Anderson and Weill to reconsider the *Ulysses* material. (Sanders does not mention Weill's own connections with Robeson, which went back at least as far as meetings in London in 1935 for discussions about the role of General Conchas in *A Kingdom for a Cow*, which Robeson declined on the understandable ground that it was too 'negative' for a black.) The final destination of the *Ulysses* material is set out in *Note 2* below.

Autographs

SKETCHES AND DRAFTS

Twenty-one loose sheets of RM^{12} carry a few fragmentary sketches and (unnumbered) rough drafts of the following:

1a	Introduction (*agitato*) and Melodrama
1b	White Folks (chorus and dance)
1c	White Folks (solo)
2	When I was a pickaninny (bass solo, chorus)
3	Lady, you drop yo' feminine wiles (solo)
4	The Little Tin God (solo)
5	Ku Klux Klan meeting (speech, chorus and orchestra)
6	The Little Grey House (duet)
7a	Lover Man (solo; first version)
7b	Lover Man (solo; second version)
8	Lost in the Stars
9	Going Down Hill

A sheet of O^{12} has earlier workings than any of these. Sides *a* and *b*, and the first half of *c* carry transcriptions of traditional blues (including 'Death Valley', the model for several of Weill's C minor blues). The lower part of *c* has some fragmentary jottings, while *d* carries the unharmonized melodies of *1b*, *2* and *6*, and the complete melody (in G major) of a song that became 'Stay Well' in *Lost in the Stars*.

FAIR COPIES

7 and *8* are each on a sheet of F^{14}, in ink. The fourth side of each sheet carries pencil sketches.

EXTRA LYRICS

Typescripts of 'In an old time far away and long ago' and 'Here's how it is when you're going away' are in WLRC.

Publication

Chappell, 1942: 7 and 8 only, as sheet music.

Note 2

The music of 3 was drawn upon for the song 'Huxley' in *Lady in the Dark*. If, as Sanders suggests (see *Note 1* above), there was some revision of the *Ulysses* material in July 1945, it was probably confined to the draft libretto. Certainly there is no sign of it in the surviving musical holographs. However, there is evidence in a letter of 1945 from Anderson to Weill (WLA) that 'Lost in the Stars' had already been selected as a suitable title song for a musical, which at that stage may well have been envisaged as a new *Ulysses*. It was Alan Paton's novel *Cry the Beloved Country*, published in 1947, that finally provided Anderson and Weill with a framework suitable for their title song, and for the music and lyrics of 6 and 7b (renamed 'Trouble Man' because of a rival claimant). The *Lost in the Stars* material (p. 368) also includes the lyrics of 4, 'The Little Tin God', but the setting is quite different from the one drafted for *Ulysses* – or at least from the one that survives. The *Ulysses* material in WLA may well be incomplete. It is for instance hard to imagine that the melody that became 'Stay Well' in *Lost in the Stars* remained without accompaniment in *Ulysses*.

_____

November 1939, Suffern

Madam, will you walk?

Music for the Night Court scene in Act III of Sidney Howard's Faustian
    comedy
(Unpublished)
Duration: 4½ minutes
Orchestra: 0.0.3.(3sax.).0.   0.2.1.0.   pno. novachord, perc. db.

Autographs

SKETCH

Introductory (blues) section only, on a single side of RM^{12}; *verso*, a sketch of *Nannas Lied* (in the same key and similar mood).

DRAFT

Four sides of RM[12].

FULL SCORE

Missing.

Additional Material

Set of instrumental parts in copyist's hand, and a copy of the recording used in the production.

First Performance

13 November 1939, Baltimore; director Margaret Webster, designer Robert Edmond Jones; with Peggy Conklin, George M. Cohan, Sara Allgood, Keenan Wynn, Arthur Kennedy; recorded music conducted by Maurice Abravanel.

Notes

Sidney Howard (1891–1939) was one of the most gifted American playwrights of his generation. Weill liked and admired him and wrote the music for the Night Court scene – a blues linked to a charleston – as a personal favour. The production was poorly received at its 'try-outs' in Baltimore and Washington, and was therefore not transferred to Broadway. Weill subsequently contemplated a musical adaptation of the play.

December 1939

Two on an Island

Incidental music to the comedy by Elmer Rice
For novachord solo
(Missing)

First Performance

20 January 1940, New York, Broadhurst Theater. Production by the Playwrights' Company directed by Elmer Rice and designed by Jo Mielziner. With Martin Ritt, Betty Field, Robert Williams, Luther Adler and Howard da Silva.

Notes

According to the brief (and unfavourable) mention by Marc Blitzstein in *Modern Music* (New York: vol. XVII no. 3, March–April 1940 p. 184), the score consisted largely of folk song arrangements.

22 December 1939, Suffern

Nannas Lied

'Meine Herren, mit siebzehn Jahren'
Song for voice and piano
Text: Bertolt Brecht
Dedication: Lotte Lenya

Autographs

SKETCHES

A leaf of RM¹² carries the first section only; on the reverse is the blues
from *Madam, Will You Walk?*

FAIR COPY

Four sides of F¹⁴, with the dedication 'Für Lenya Weihnachten 1939', and
the end date 'Suffern NY Dec. 22 1939'.

Note

According to Ronald Shull (RS.MWB) the poem was introduced into the
script of Brecht's play *Die Rundköpfe und die Spitzköpfe* in 1936, probably a
few months before the premiere (4 November 1936). Hanns Eisler set it to
music in the late summer of that year.

Posthumous Publication

EAM, 1982: in *The Unknown Kurt Weill: A Collection of 14 Songs.*

December 1939, Suffern

Stopping by Woods on a Snowy Evening

Song for voice and piano
Text: Robert Frost
Dedication: Maxwell and Mabel Anderson
(Missing)

Autographs

SKETCH

A sheet of RM¹² carries a sketch of the first twelve bars.

FAIR COPY

Missing, except for a title sheet (of F¹⁴) bearing the dedication 'For Max and Mab Christmas 1939'.

January 1940, Suffern

The Ballad of Magna Carta

Cantata for tenor and bass soloists, chorus and orchestra
Text: Maxwell Anderson
Commissioned by the Columbia Broadcasting System for Norman
  Corwin's radio series, *The Pursuit of Happiness*
Duration: 15 minutes
Orchestra: 2.1.0.4sax.1.   0.3.2.0.   timp. pno. harp, gtr. str.

Autographs

SKETCHES

Missing.

FINAL DRAFT

Eighteen pages of Sch¹⁴, with the end date '16 January 1940'; complete except for the start.

REHEARSAL SCORE

The score is in WLRC – a single folding of F¹⁴ comprising twenty-six numbered pages of ink manuscript, with cue numbers in red and blue crayon. Pages 23–4 are on a leaf of F¹². The score is titled 'The Magna Charta', and has the end date 21 January 1940. This means that Weill had precisely fourteen days in which to complete the full score, and that the orchestral parts must have been extracted concurrently.

FULL SCORE

Sixty-six numbered pages of Sch²⁴, bound with a strip of brown paper, without cover or title page. The underlaid text is non-autograph.

Publication

Chappell, 1940: vocal score, piano reduction unattributed.

First Performance

4 February 1940, New York, CBS; conductor Mark Warnow; with Burgess Meredith (narrator), Julius Huehn (bass), the Mark Warnow Orchestra, and the Lynn Murray Choir.

February–November 1940, Suffern

Lady in the Dark

Play in two acts by Moss Hart, lyrics by Ira Gershwin
Duration: full evening; 65 minutes music
Cast: singing roles: Liza Elliott, Miss Foster (as Sutton in Dream 1), Russell Paxton (as Beckman and Ringmaster in Dream 3), Kendall Nesbitt (as Pierre), Charley Johnson (as Marine), Randy Curtis (as Randy Curtis in Dream 2), chorus; other roles: Miss Bowers, Miss Stevens, Alison Du Bois, office boys, models, dancers, etc.
Orchestra: Flute (fl. picc.). Reed I (cl. alto sax.). Reed II (cl. bcl. alto sax. baritone sax.). Reed III (cl. tenor sax. ob.). 0.3.1.0. Hammond org. pno. perc. str. (no vla.)

New York, early 1940s. Although she has fought her way to the top and become editor of a celebrated fashion magazine, Liza Elliott still feels threatened by a male-dominated and success-oriented society. Apparently on the verge of a breakdown, she consults her psychiatrist. At each of her sessions she recounts a dream – of glamour, of marriage, and finally of a mock trial in a circus. The psychiatrist duly analyses her dreams, and at the final session finds the clue to her problems in a repressed childhood memory and in the song, 'My Ship', which she has been trying to recall. At peace with herself at last, she recognizes that the 'right man' for her is her colleague Charley Johnson, with whom she has been at odds, and that her lover, Kendall Nesbitt, and her ideal, the film star Randy Curtis, are unsuitable companions.

The music is confined to the dream sequences. Though divisible into separate sections as listed below, Dreams 1–3 (and the discarded Hollywood Dream) are through-composed, in the manner of large-scale operetta finales.

ACT I

1 *Glamour Dream: Park Avenue – Liza's Apartment – A Night Club*

  1a Prelude (orchestra)
  1b Oh Fabulous One (six suitors)
  2   Huxley (Sutton, Liza)
  3   One Life to Live (Liza, Beckman)
  4   The Girl of the Moment (Pierre)

2 *Wedding Dream*

  5   Mapleton High Chorale (chorus)
  6   This is New (Randy)
  7   The Princess of Pure Delight (Liza)
  8x It's Never too late to Mendelssohn (Paxton and chorus)

ACT II

9a   Overture

3 *Circus Dream*

9   The Greatest Show on Earth (chorus)
10   Dance of the Tumblers (orchestra)
11   The Best Years of His Life (ringmaster)
12   Tchaikovsky (ringmaster)
13z The Zodiac Song (Liza): 'No matter under what star you're born';
       replaced by:
13   The Saga of Jenny (Liza)

4 *Hollywood Dream*
(Unfinished)

14z The Boss is Bringing Home the Bride
15z Our Little San Fernando House
16z Hollywood party

Childhood Dream

17   My Ship

Unlocated songs:
18x Bats About You
19z You are Unforgettable

Autographs

SKETCHES AND FIRST DRAFTS

Fourteen loose leaves of Fsp^{12} (probably torn from the spiral-bound notebook containing the sketches for the 1940 version of *Railroads on Parade*) carry numerous memos and early sketches; almost all were discarded.

Further preliminary sketches are on four leaves of Psp^{22}; most of the material was later incorporated.

Ten pages of F^{14} sketches contain three noteworthy items: a complete draft of an E major setting of 'My Ship' which is unrelated to the published version and sufficiently striking to suggest that it was rejected only because of its somewhat introspective and European character; a tune without words, which was to be used for 'Westwind' in *One Touch of Venus*; and a second tune without words, which was to be used for 'Love Song' in *Love Life*.

Short-score drafts of *1a* and *9a* are in a folding of Cp^{12}.

The main group of sketches and early drafts is on seventy pages of Sch^{14}. It includes complete first drafts of *16z* and *19z*, four evolutionary drafts of *17*, and, surprisingly, a brief memo of the 'Muschel-Song' from *Konjunktur*.

DRAFTS

A hardback sketchbook (Psk^{12}) contains extensive drafts of Dreams 1 and 3 and fragmentary ones of the remainder, interspersed with preliminary sketches. 'The Saga of Jenny' (13), which was a late addition, appears towards the end. Many leaves have been removed from the sketchbook, and although some have now been restored, others (especially towards the end and hence from Dream 4) are missing. No draft of 13az has been traced. In all there are sixty-two pages of music manuscript, plus twelve blank pages. At the end of the book three loose leaves of plain paper, measuring 28 × 21.5 cms, carry Ira Gershwin's pencil and ink drafts for the lyrics of 8x and 13; a fourth page carries Weill's draft of a stanza about Napoleon – also intended for 13z.

REHEARSAL SCORE

Missing, except for thirty-four pages of discarded and supplementary items: 8x; a preliminary version of the first part of Dream 3; and two wordless arrangements of 3 and 17. All these are on F^{14}. A choral arrangement of 6 is on a sheet of Cp^{12}, as is an alternative version of 8x. A manuscript 'Piano score' (so titled) in various hands contains a few autograph passages, and amounts to 81 + 42 + 75 pages for the three dream sequences, plus some twenty pages of miscellanea. Though used as the basis for the published vocal score, it differs widely from it (see 'CRITICAL EDITION').

FULL SCORE

The score is written on Sch^{20} and finely bound, with title and authors' names in gilt on the spine. The title page reads: 'Kurt Weill "Lady in the Dark"/Complete Orchestration/Original Manuscript of the composer'. Various paginations occur at the top of the pages, and some are autograph. A continuous non-autograph pagination at the foot reaches 375 on the last page; it includes the eight pages of a dance arrangement of 3 by Ted Royal, and the twenty pages of Royal's orchestration of 19x. There are 129 autograph pages for Dream 1, 82 for Dream 2, 103 for Dream 3, seven for Dream 4, and four for the 'ending' of the show. The score, which has been used in performance, is heavily marked in other hands, with numerous cuts indicated in pencil and in crayon. Some autograph additions and rescorings are in pencil. Three items are not bound. The first is 4c, originally headed 'Overture/"Lady in the Dark"' but with the words 'before 2nd Act' subsequently added by the composer in parenthesis after 'Overture'. The pages are numbered 1–34 by the composer, and 206–49 in another hand. A single page of pencil score headed 'Music for light changes in flashbacks' is numbered 342, and 4 pages of pencil score numbered 104–7 carry a much shortened version of the chorale variation of 4.

A manuscript footnote to the score reads: 'The Hammond Organ is used mostly as a fill-in. It should be used very sparingly and should never be noticeable. It can be replaced by a Harmonium.'

First Performance

30 December 1940, Boston, Colonial Theatre.
21 January 1941, Alvin Theatre, New York; production by Sam H. Harris, staged by Moss Hart, conductor Maurice Abravanel, sets by Harry Horner, costumes by Irene Sharaff, choreographer Albertina Rasch, production assistant Hassard Short; with Gertrude Lawrence (Liza), Evelyn Wyckoff (Miss Foster), Danny Kaye (Russell Paxton), Macdonald Carey (Charley Johnson), Victor Mature (Randy Curtis), Bert Lytell (Kendall Nesbitt).

Publication

MUSIC

Chappell, 1941: vocal score, edited by Albert Sirmay; sheet-music versions of *3, 4, 6, 7, 12, 13* and *17*.

PLAY AND LYRICS

Random House, New York, 1941.
Dramatic licences and performance materials: present (1986) availability – Rodgers & Hammerstein Music Library (USA), KWF (UK and German-speaking territories).

CRITICAL EDITION

In collaboration with KWF and the conductor John Mauceri, and with grant support from the National Endowment for the Humanities, David Loud compiled in 1986 a vocal score based primarily on the autograph full score, but with reference to the recently discovered non-autograph rehearsal score. Diverging considerably from the published vocal score and reinstating substantial passages omitted by Sirmay, his edition constitutes the first step towards the essential if distant objective of a complete edition of the entire corpus of Weill's Broadway musicals; the next step will be a set of orchestral parts of *Lady in the Dark*, edited by Mr Loud from the full score.

Film Version

Paramount, released February 1944. Directed by Mitchell Leisen, screenplay by Frances Goodrich and Albert Hackett. Music concocted and conducted by Robert Emmett Dolan and orchestrated by Robert Russell Bennett – themes from Weill's score; 'Artist's Waltz' by Dolan; 'Dream Lover' by Grey and Schertzinger; and 'Suddenly it's Spring' by Burke and Van Heusen. With Ginger Rogers (Liza), Ray Milland (Charley), Mischa Auer (Russell Paxton).

The film owes nothing to the Broadway show apart from the title, the basic plot idea, and the opportunity it wasted. Weill was not involved.

Autumn 1941, New York

Fun to be Free

Music for a pageant by Ben Hecht and Charles MacArthur
For narrators, chorus and orchestra
Sponsored by Fight for Freedom Inc.

Autographs

SKETCHES

Missing.

DRAFTS

'Introduction' on seven sides of a double folding of C^{12}.

FULL SCORE

Missing.

First Performance

5 October 1941, New York, Madison Square Garden; director Brett
Warren, designer S. Syrjala, conductor Simon Rady; with the chorus and
orchestra of the International Ladies' Garment Workers' Union, and
Tallulah Bankhead, Melvyn Douglas, Burgess Meredith, Franchot Tone
(narrators).

Notes

Twenty-nine cues are listed on a typescript page (27.5 × 21.5 cms)
headed 'Music Cue Sheet for Pageant'. It is clear from this that the music
was purely incidental, and that some of it was founded on versions of the
march theme from *Davy Crockett*. There were various so-called 'cadenzas'
and some passages of traditional melody. Borrowings from *The Eternal
Road* are not indicated in the list, but would readily have suggested
themselves. The possible (but doubtful) inclusion of the so-called 'Red
Army Song' is discussed on p. 330.

   Fight for Freedom Inc. was a Broadway-based organization dedicated
to the fight against isolationism, and hence to the cause of America's total
involvement in the European war – already implied by the Lease–Lend
Act of March 1941 and by the public statements of Roosevelt and his
aides. *Fun to be Free* was a benefit production (one performance only), to
which all concerned gave their services.

January 1942
(date of orchestration unknown)

Three Walt Whitman Songs

    (a)   for voice and piano
    (b)   for voice and orchestra (with Irving Schlein)
Written for Fight for Freedom Inc.
Dedication: Max and Mab Anderson
Duration: 12 minutes
Orchestra 2.1.3.1. 2.2.2.0. timp. perc. harp, str.
    1   Oh Captain! My Captain!
    2   Beat! Beat! Drums!
    3   Dirge for Two Veterans

Autographs

SKETCHES AND DRAFTS

Missing, except for 2 on four sides of K^{12}.

VOICE AND PIANO SCORE

1 – pencil on five sides of C^{12}; *2* – ink on seven sides of C^{12}; *3* – ink on six sides of C^{12}. No title page or binding.

FULL SCORES

The numbers are in separate gatherings, each bound with Scotch tape. *1* (sixteen pages) and *2* (twenty pages) are on Ns^{22}. Only the first seven pages of *3* (to the words 'I hear the great drums pounding') are scored by Weill; the remaining eleven pages are in the hand of his assistant Irving Schlein. All are on Ns^{22}.

Publication

Chappell, 1942: voice and piano score.

First Performance

Not known.

Notes

See p. 357 for a fourth Whitman setting, and for details of the first recording of all four. The 1942 set was intended for Paul Robeson – whose reactions to it are not documented in WLA – and was offered to the Fight for Freedom organization (see preceding entry). In the aftermath of Pearl Harbor, Fight for Freedom had necessarily changed its programme, and was now involved in the new national task of morale-boosting. That purpose, with its essentially popular implications, is reflected in the very nature of Weill's settings, which are clearly not intended as 'art songs' in the European sense. The orchestral version has yet to be dated precisely. In March 1942 Weill arranged 2 for speaker, chorus and orchestra, and included it in the album commissioned by Helen Hayes and Victor Records for Fight for Freedom (see p. 324). Perhaps the Whitman settings had been destined for a similar record album, with Robeson as soloist. But see *Notes* for *Propaganda Songs* (p. 322) for another possibility.

February 1942

Your Navy

Incidental music for a half-hour radio programme by Maxwell Anderson
Commissioned by the Columbia Broadcasting System and NBC
(Largely missing)
Five entries, including 'Shanty Music' and 'Horn Call'

Autographs

SKETCHES

Sides *a* and *b* of a sheet of C¹² carry notations of sea shanties (including 'O Santy Anna', 'Shenandoah', 'Heave Away') and of the ballad 'John Paul Jones'. *a* and *d* carry memos of harmonic and rhythmic motifs.

DRAFTS

Largely missing. A leaf of C¹² carries an arrangement of 'John Paul Jones' in the style of a chorale. A sheet of the same paper carries arrangements of 'Santy Anna' and 'Heave Away', a fugal variation of 'Santy Anna' (identified as the seventh entry), and a further arrangement of 'John Paul Jones'. Another variation of 'Santy Anna', with the tune on three muted trumpets, is on one side of a leaf of C¹².

FULL SCORE

Missing.

First Broadcast

28 February 1942, NBC Radio, New York; director Norman Corwin, conductor Don Vorhees; with Frederic March, Douglas Fairbanks Jr (narrators).

[February–April 1942]

[Propaganda Songs]

1   Song of the Free (Archibald MacLeish)
2   Schickelgruber (Howard Dietz)
3   [One Morning in Spring] (St Clair McKelway)
4   The Good Earth (Oscar Hammerstein)
5   Buddy on the Nightshift (Oscar Hammerstein)
6   Song of the Inventory (Lewis Allan)
7   We don't feel like surrendering today (Maxwell Anderson)
8   Oh Uncle Samuel! (Maxwell Anderson); melody by
        Henry C. Work (1832–1884)
9   Toughen up, Buckle down, Carry on (Dorothy Fields)

Autographs

SKETCHES

According to Weill's correspondence with Lenya, *1, 2,* and *3* were sketched on 5 February 1942. The only sketches in WLA are of *3* and *5,* both in alternative versions. *3* is untitled; it begins: 'Walked through the Country/One Morning in Spring'.

FAIR COPIES (piano/vocal)

3 is missing; all other copies are written on C^{12}, and all but *4* and *8* are in ink. *1* and *2* (five sides each) were both finished on 15 February 1942. *4,* finished on 26 February, is on two sides; the lyrics have been erased, and the title 'The Good Earth' added in Lenya's hand. (Pearl Buck's famous novel of that title was published in 1931.) *5–7* are on four sides, *8* on three; an earlier version of *5* is on four sides of K^{10}.

First Performances

The 'Song of the Free' was included in a revue that opened at the Roxy Theatre New York, on 4 June 1942. The singer was Bob Hannon, with choral backing.

Publications

Chappell, 1947: 'Song of the Free'; EAM, 1982: *2* and *5*

Notes

A letter to Weill from a Lieutenant Marvin Young of the 'Headquarters, Army Service Forces, Entertainment section' is dated 24 August 1944. Young thanks Weill for his 'efforts in connection with the Soldier Shows

Production Three Days Pass', and ends: 'I feel certain that the songs you have written for Three Days Pass will prove a tremendous incentive to our fighting men here and over seas in staging their own shows.' (Copies in WLRC and WLA.) Unless the songs are missing, they were almost certainly drawn from those listed here. However, Marvin Young also writes in his letter (my italics): 'The complete script, *full orchestral score*, and designs for improved costumes and scenery, will be sent to military installations all over the world.' This raises the possibility that the orchestration of the *Three Songs of Walt Whitman* was made for *Three Days Pass*. However, the relatively serious tone of the Whitman settings seems out of keeping with the kind of show *Three Days Pass* was likely to have been.

[March 1942]

Und was bekam des Soldaten Weib?

Ballad for voice and piano
Text: Bertolt Brecht
Duration: 3 minutes

Autographs

The sketches are missing. The definitive version is neatly written in pencil on four sides of a double sheet of C^{12}, signed and with the title 'Und was bekam des Soldaten Weib?' ('And what did the soldier's woman receive?'). There are no indications of dynamics or phrasing. A slightly modified version of the piano part only, transposed from B minor to B flat minor, has been (swiftly) written in pencil on sides *b* and *c* of another sheet of C^{12}, the first side of which carries the same title, but is unsigned. The two sheets have been roughly folded to pocket-size, presumably at the time of one or other of the two known performances. Since Weill himself played the piano part in both, there was no need for him to produce a definitive copy; and it is most unlikely that he did so at any later date.

First Performance

3 April 1943, Hunter College, New York; Lotte Lenya, with the composer at the piano. The programme gives the title 'Die Ballade vom Soldatenweib'.

Notes

Brecht sent the poem to Weill on 12 March 1942. Weill replied next day, thanking him for the 'marvellous song', and saying that he would make a setting of it and offer it to the War Department unit responsible for shortwave broadcasts to Germany. The swiftness and enthusiasm of his response are consistent with his reactions to every opportunity of this kind during the early months of 1942 and suggest the likelihood that he composed the song there and then. The downward transposition may well date from the preparations for the first performance a year later. The context of the performance itself sheds some light on Weill's reference to shortwave broadcasts. The programme at Hunter College was an anti-Nazi literary cabaret produced by Ernst Josef Aufricht and Manfred George (who for many years edited New York's highly respected German-language weekly *Aufbau*). Its title, *We Fight Back*, was the one used for the radio series that Aufricht had been producing since 1942, with support from George and the Office of Strategic Services in Washington. It was not until a year after the Hunter College performance that another government department provided the means of broadcasting the song to Germany. For further details, see 'Wie lange noch?' (p. 340). Three other settings of the ballad were made during Brecht's lifetime: the first by Hanns Eisler, with whom Brecht discussed the text on 9 May 1942 (see Brecht's *Arbeitsjournal* and also Hans Bunge, *Fragen Sie mehr über Brecht*, Munich, 1970, pp. 227–9); the second by Paul Dessau; and the third by Mischa Spoliansky, who had been one of the leading revue and cabaret composers in Berlin before 1933, and had written the songs for Georg Kaiser's *Zwei Krawatten*.

Posthumous Publication

EAM, 1982: in *The Unknown Kurt Weill: A Collection of 14 Songs*.

March 1942

Mine Eyes Have Seen The Glory

Four patriotic melodramas
For speaker, chorus and orchestra
Commissioned by Helen Hayes and Victor Records for Fight for
    Freedom Inc.
Duration: 12 minutes
Orchestra: 2.2.3.(4sax.).1.   2.2.2.0.   org. timp. perc. harp, str.

1   Battle Hymn of the Republic (Julia Ward Howe)
2   The Star-Spangled Banner (Francis Scott Key)
3   America (Samuel Francis Smith) and Pledge to the Flag (J. B. Upham
     and F. Bellamy)
4   Beat! Beat! Drums! (Walt Whitman)

Autographs

SKETCHES AND DRAFTS

Missing.

SHORT SCORE

Twenty-six pages of pencil manuscript on C^{12}, with some indications of instrumentation in ink. The few non-autograph notes and corrections are presumably by Ted Dreher, who made the full score. A rehearsal score of 4 is incomplete on two sides of a leaf of C^{12}; two non-autograph rehearsal scores of 4 are written on C^{12}, and one of them, headed 'Black and White Song', has autograph notes of instrumentation that correspond precisely to the scoring of 'Beat! Beat! Drums!' in the orchestral version of the *Three Walt Whitman Songs* (see p. 320). Presumably, therefore, the latter postdates the present version. The remaining short scores are non-autograph: 3 is dated 28 March; 1, 31 March.

FULL SCORE

Non-autograph; prepared from the short score by Ted Dreher. 1 is dated 31 March; 2 is dated 29 March; and 3 is dated 28 March.

First Recording

30–31 March 1942, by Helen Hayes, Victor Concert Orchestra and male chorus, conductor Roy Shields, for a 2-disc album issued by Victor under the title *Mine Eyes Have Seen The Glory*.

Note

4 is an adaptation of the second of the *Three Walt Whitman Songs* (p. 320).

April–May 1942

The Pirate

Sketches for a musical based on Ludwig Fulda's play *Der Seeräuber*, in an adaptation by S. N. Behrman, for production as *The Pirate* by the Playwrights' Company and Alfred Lunt

Notes

The German Jewish playwright Ludwig Fulda (*b*. Frankfurt 1862) enjoyed considerable success in the middlebrow entertainment theatre of his day. Elected president of the literary section of the Prussian Academy of Arts in 1928, he was dismissed after the Nazi seizure of power, and died by his own hand in Berlin in 1939. It was that year and in that tragic context that the idea of adapting one of his 'Spanish Comedies' was first mooted on Broadway. Rights in *Der Seeräuber* were acquired by The Playwrights' Company, largely thanks to the advocacy of S. N. Behrman, one of the playwright-directors of that company, and a close counterpart to Fulda in the Broadway theatre. At that time Weill was already informally linked to the Playwrights through his friendship with Maxwell Anderson and his success with *Knickerbocker Holiday*. He had been interested in the *Pirate* project from the start – but only, one suspects, as a convenient means of transport to Broadway. An undistinguished romantic comedy of the sort that copy-writers would describe as colourful, it had little to recommend it to Weill apart from a Caribbean setting (which reminded him, as did *High Wind in Jamaica*, of *A Kingdom for a Cow*), and a sentimental connection with Berlin.

The project began to take shape early in 1942, when the celebrated actor and producer Alfred Lunt became interested in the play as a vehicle for himself and his wife Lynn Fontanne, and on that basis negotiated a co-production agreement with The Playwrights' Company. It was not an auspicious development from Weill's point of view: the talents and interests of the Lunts were far removed from his requirements for musical theatre. Adapting himself to the new situation with characteristic ingenuity, Weill proposed a version of *Der Seeräuber* in which the songs and dances, commenting upon and elaborating the action, would be confined to a calypso ensemble posted on stage throughout. Whether out of mere politeness or genuine interest (stimulated, perhaps, by Moss Hart and the success of *Lady in the Dark*), Lunt was sufficiently responsive for Weill to conclude that it was worth his while to start work without a contract. His first notes for the score were made on 22 April 1942. For several weeks he continued working, sketching, and making suggestions, despite the absence of a contract and the increasing inaccessibility of Lunt and of Behrman. Eventually, disheartened by unmistakable evidence that Lunt's ideas were far removed from his own and that Behrman was by no means wedded to the collaboration, Weill withdrew.

The Pirate sailed on. With Behrman at the helm, the Lunts on the quarterdeck, and some nondescript incidental music in the hold, it reached Broadway during the following season. On the strength of its success there it proceeded to Hollywood, where it was re-equipped with songs by Cole Porter, and successfully filmed.

Autographs

SKETCHES AND FIRST DRAFTS

A 6-sheet folding of R^{12} carries the results of Weill's preliminary researches into Latin American and Spanish folk music – which, according to a marginal note, led him to consult (among other sources)

Harcourt's study, *La Musique des Incas*. Notations of folk tunes, and of characteristic rhythms and accompaniment figures, predominate. There are also fragments from Albéniz's *Iberia* and Copland's *El Salón México*, and another fragment attributed to Villa-Lobos but not otherwise identified. The last side of the folding carries a draft of a 43-bar habanera. Further notations, of a purely rhythmic nature, mostly Latin American and all syncopated, are on sides *a* and *d* of a sheet of NBC^{12}; sides *b–c* carry the piano score draft of a 51-bar dance in Latin American style, headed 'Alfred's Entrance' (the Alfred being, of course, Alfred Lunt). A leaf of K^{12}, likewise found among Weill's unsorted and untitled manuscripts, is the only other item that clearly relates to *The Pirate* (but see *Miscellaneous Unidentified Sketches*, p. 372, under the heading '1936–9', for another possibility). It carries three sketches for rumbas, and memos of three ideas from *A Kingdom for a Cow*: the porters' chorus 'San Salvatore', the canonic chorus in the second finale, and the closing duet.

1942[–3]

Six Songs

Arrangements for Lotte Lenya and piano, made for Bost Records
1   Barbara Song (*Die Dreigroschenoper*)
2   Denn wie man sich bettet (*Aufstieg und Fall der Stadt Mahagonny*)
3   Surabaya-Johnny (*Happy End*)
4   'Au fond de la Seine'
5   Kanonen Song (*Die Dreigroschenoper*)
6   J'attends un navire (*Marie Galante*)

Autographs

DRAFTS

1–3 are each on a sheet of C^{12}. Side *d* of *1* carries a sketch of the first eight bars of the song 'Wooden Wedding' (*One Touch of Venus*).

FINAL COPIES

1, 3, 5, and *6* are in ink on K^{12}, *4* in pencil on C^{12}; *2* is missing. Only *4* and *6* have the complete texts. The final page of *4* carries a rapid sketch of an elaborate arrangement of the 'Alabama Song' (*Mahagonny*).

Recording

Lenya's recordings of these songs – with an unnamed pianist who, according to her recollection twenty years later, was Weill – was released in an album of three 10-inch 78 rpm discs, Bost 6 5017–19.

Notes

The arrangements are not only more pianistic than the original published vocal scores, but are harmonically modified in the light of Weill's American experience and with a view to enhancing the coherence of the selection.

June 1942 – February 1943

One Man's Venus

Operetta (unfinished) for production by Cheryl Crawford
Based on F. J. Anstey's *The Tinted Venus*
Book by Bella Spewack
Lyrics by Ogden Nash

Notes

An operetta based on Anstey's novella was one of the many projects for which Weill was trying to find collaborators and producers during the uncertain months that followed the success of *Lady in the Dark*. In February 1942 *The Tinted Venus* headed a list of fifteen possibilities he was considering for Cheryl Crawford. After the break-up of the Group Theatre (where she had initiated the *Johnny Johnson* production – see p. 276) Crawford had established herself as an independent producer and with Weill's encouragement was intending to specialize in musical theatre. The first round of discussions with Crawford took place soon after the February opening of her highly successful revival of Gershwin's *Porgy and Bess*, on which Weill had informally offered her some professional advice. Nothing was decided at that stage. Weill then became involved in *The Pirate* and was not free again until June, when Crawford agreed with him to produce a Venus operetta. She engaged Sam and Bella Spewack (see p. 286) to write the book and Ogden Nash the lyrics; and on 24 July Weill wrote to Marlene Dietrich in Hollywood, offering her the role of Venus. She expressed interest, but would not decide until she had seen something of the Spewack book. During August the Spewacks drafted Act I, and Nash completed some lyrics. By the third week in September, Weill had drafted seven or eight numbers. On 21 September he and Crawford left for Hollywood. There Weill played through the songs with Dietrich, who then read the draft libretto and made various constructive criticisms. These were then discussed with Bella Spewack, who was now to assume sole responsibility for the libretto. But during the next weeks her progress became increasingly uncertain and in February 1943 she withdrew altogether. Any chance of mounting a production that season was now lost, and Dietrich with it. But Crawford persisted, and within a few weeks had obtained an entirely new book from S. J. Perelman, with revised and new lyrics from Nash. Operetta and Victorian London had been abandoned in favour of a musical comedy set in modern New York – *One Touch of Venus* (see p. 333).

Autographs

LYRICS

Ogden Nash's manuscripts of five lyrics – written in pencil on 22-line yellow paper – are in WLA: 'Earthbound'; 'The Fates'; 'Flash Rounds'; 'Fresh Air and Exercise' (two versions) and 'If I could find another rhyme for Love'. There are no known settings of these. That the lyrics relate to the Spewack *Venus* rather than to its successor is a matter for conjecture, but seems probable on internal evidence.

SKETCHES AND DRAFTS

Missing.

REHEARSAL SCORES

Except where a clue is provided by discrepancies in the naming of characters, there is no means of distinguishing between those rehearsal scores in WLA which date from the summer of 1942 and those which are discarded versions of numbers written for *One Touch of Venus*. Were the Spewack drafts to come to light they might provide conclusive evidence. Meanwhile, all extant holographs are here catalogued under *One Touch of Venus*.

August 1942

Russian War Relief

For voice, piano, guitar
Text: J. P. McEvoy
Written for the revue *Rockland Riot* in aid of the Rockland for Russia relief fund

Autographs

SKETCHES

Missing.

FAIR COPY

Ink, on five sides of a 2-sheet folding of C^{12}. A title sheet of K^{12} carries only the pencilled heading 'Russian War Relief'; there is no signature. (Sides *b* and *c* carry non-autograph notations for the guitarist.)

First (and only) Performance

c. 20 August 1942, at the Clarkstown Country Club, Nyack, Rockland County; Lotte Lenya and the composer.

Notes

Rockland Riot was a fund-raising production put together by prominent 'media personalities' from Rockland County, the area some thirty-five miles north of Manhattan that had been Weill's rural retreat since 1939. His contribution to the revue made light of the 'classical' pretensions implicit in its three quotations (from Tchaikovsky's *Romeo and Juliet* Overture, Rachmaninov's C sharp minor Prelude, and Shostakovich's 7th Symphony) by repeatedly interposing the refrain of 'Black Eyes'. The result is somewhat reminiscent of the collectively written numbers favoured by Agitprop revues in the days before 'advanced' composers began to offer their services to the cause: clearly, no such reminder was intended by Weill.

Early 1943

We Will Never Die

'A Memorial'
'Dedicated to the Two Million Jewish Dead of Europe'
Text: Ben Hecht
Sponsored by the Committee for a Jewish Army of Stateless and
   Palestinian Jews
Cast: Rabbi, Cantors (tenor solo), narrators, actors (as victims of
   persecution) and chorus.
Duration: 90 minutes
Orchestra: [?]1.1.1.1.   0.3.3.0.   org. harp, perc. str.
   Episode 1   The Roll Call
   Episode 2   Jews in the War
   Episode 3   Remember Us

After the Rabbi's opening address (which is to be accompanied throughout by 'mourning music', as Weill calls it in his notes), the narrators begin the 'roll call' of Jewish men and women who have won international recognition in the arts and sciences, in philosophy and politics. Episode 2 is a survey of the part played by Jewish servicemen on the various battlefronts of the Second World War. In the introduction to the last episode, the narrator declares: 'Of the 6 million Jews in German-held lands, the Germans have said none shall remain. The 4 million left to kill are being killed – according to plan. When the time comes to make the peace, these will have been done to death.' Representatives of the victims of atrocities appear on stage, one by one and group by group, to give simple, almost colourless, accounts of what occurred, and where. The Memorial ends with a Kaddish for 'the voiceless and the Jewish dead of Europe'.

Autographs

SKETCHES

Missing.

DRAFTS

Mostly missing. The few holographs in WLA were scattered among the unsorted manuscripts. Each item has an individual title, but none bears the main title. A total of fifteen sides of Chappell Musical Comedy paper (CMC²⁵) carry 'Introduction to Episode 1', 'Exit of the twenty rabbis', and two versions of 'Sabbath (Chanukeh)' – one in A flat, the other in C, headed 'Insert 1' and 'Insert 2' respectively. Two further items are both based on material from *The Eternal Road*: 'Rabbi's entrance' (two sides of F²¹) uses the 'March to Zion' (*15a*), and 'Peace Table' (seven sides of F²¹), the closing chorale (*19f*). 'Peace Table' is marked as being intended for Episode 3.

FULL SCORE

Missing; but the full score of an item entitled 'Red Army Song' was found among the miscellaneous unsorted manuscripts. It is written on three sides of the same Chappell Musical Comedy paper as the first three drafts described above. Page 20 of the script (Episode 2) gives the following cue: 'A Russian soldier enters carrying a Russian flag. The organ plays the Soviet march.' Although the 'Red Army Song' would have been equally appropriate to *Fun to be Free*, the cue sheet for that pageant does not refer to it.

Note 1

The melody of 'Red Army Song' is by Lev Knipper (whose name does not appear on the holograph score). Also known as 'Cavalry of the Steppes', it became an international 'hit' after the German invasion of Russia, where it had been a popular favourite ever since its original appearance in the choral finale of Knipper's Fourth Symphony of 1932. (Knipper was two years older than Weill and, like him, had studied in Berlin with Philipp Jarnach. One wonders, idly, whether he and Weill knew each other.)

First Performance

9 March 1943, New York, Madison Square Gardens; producer Billy Rose, director Moss Hart, designer Lemuel Ayers, conductor Isaac van Grove; with the NBC Symphony Orchestra and Kurt Baum (Cantor), Jacob Ben-Ami (Rabbi), Paul Muni, Edward G. Robinson, Luther Adler, and Herbert Rudley (narrators); and ten actors and actresses, including Sylvia Sidney and Eleanora Mendelssohn.

Note 2 (Postscript, January 1987)

See David S. Wyman, *The Abandonment of the Jews. America and the Holocaust 1941–1945* (Pantheon Books: New York, 1984), pp. 90–2, and Ben Hecht, *A Child of the Century* (Primus: New York, 1985), pp. 553–7 and 574–6, for accounts of the origins and history of the pageant, with particular reference to the manner in which the CJA's hopes of presenting it in many cities across the USA were opposed and partially frustrated by the American Jewish Congress and other Jewish organizations. After the two Madison Square Garden performances – of which the second was a matinee hurriedly arranged in response to public demand – the pageant was seen in only five cities: Washington, Philadelphia, Chicago, Boston and Hollywood. It seems, however, that in each of these cities the performance was broadcast by local radio – a medium to which Hecht's script was already related through its affinities with the reportage style of Norman Corwin. A copy of a radio recording made at the Hollywood Bowl performance in May 1943 was acquired by WLRC in November 1986. The conductor of this performance was the well-known film composer Franz Waxmann, and the cast included Joan Leslie, Edward G. Robinson, Edward Arnold, John Garfield, Akim Tamiroff, Paul Henried, and J. Edward Bromberg. Although the radio announcer described the production as 'an exact replica' of the New York original, the text as recorded differs in some respects from Weill's own copy of the script. Whether the changes and additions were made before the New York performance or after remains a matter for investigation. As for the music – which is largely incidental, but occupies almost half the total playing time – there is no reason to suppose that it would have been regarded as sacrosanct, least of all when Weill was safely out of earshot. Cuts and rearrangements could easily have been made according to taste or convenience, since the score is not in fact a composition, but a rough-and-ready conglomeration of pre-existing material and new arrangements. The main source is *The Eternal Road*, from which is derived most of the background music for the spoken texts, and some of the incidental music – notably an orchestral version of 'Miriam's Song'. The closing chorale is used for both background and foreground purposes, and in its religious functions is associated with the two Kaddish-arrangements, 'Yisgadal' and 'Chanukeh'. The other musical elements are: a sequence of routine arrangements of national anthems and melodies for the section in Episode 2 dedicated to 'The Fighting Jew' (including 'Tipperary' for the British army and, as surmised in Note 1, 'Cavalry of the Steppes' for the Soviet army); sundry fanfares; a succession of *sforzando* chords sustained, pp, by tremolo strings for 'underscoring'; and some fragments of Nazi music countered by arrangements of the 'Hatikvah' and the 'Warscha-wianka'. From a musical as from a literary point of view the Warsaw Ghetto sequence stands apart from the rest, and is entirely free from those blemishes of taste which, in the radio recording, sometimes tend to evoke nothing so much as the Hollywood of Evelyn Waugh's *The Loved One*. One or two musical devices in the Ghetto sequence are surprisingly 'advanced' by Weill's standards in the 1940s, and raise the question of a possible contribution by Waxmann.

June–September 1943

One Touch of Venus

Musical comedy
Book by S. J. Perelman and Ogden Nash, after F. J. Anstey's novella *The Tinted Venus*
Lyrics by Ogden Nash
Cast: singing roles: Whitelaw Savory, Molly Grant, Rodney Hatch, Venus, Taxi Black, Stanley, chorus; other roles: Mrs Moat, Mrs Kramer, Gloria Kramer, two Anatolians, salesman, policeman, dancers, etc.
Orchestra: Reed I (cl. alto sax.). Reed II (cl. bcl. alto sax. fl. tenor sax. picc.). Reed III (cl. tenor sax. fl. picc. alto sax.). Reed IV (fl. tenor sax. cl. picc.). 3tpt. tbn. pno. perc. 8.4.3.2.1.

Manhattan. Rodney Hatch, an impeccably nondescript barber from Ozone Heights, L.I., numbers among his clients Whitelaw Savory, the benefactor of the Savory Foundation of Modern Art. While waiting in the Foundation's gallery for his appointment with Savory, Rodney looks with lacklustre eyes at the 3000-year-old statue known as the Anatolian Venus, and decides that his egregious fiancée Gloria Kramer is much more beautiful. But a game with the wedding ring he has just bought for Gloria has the magical effect of bringing the Venus to life and making him the object of her passion. More alarmed by her frankly carnal intentions than by any element of the supernatural, Rodney takes to his heels. The Venus sets off in amorous pursuit, ensnares him with ease, and then rids him and the world of the two remaining obstacles to wedded bliss – Gloria, and her equally disagreeable mother. But a (choreographed) vision of what lies in store for her as a suburban housewife swiftly cures the goddess of her passion. She returns to Olympus; he to Ozone Heights.

ACT I

1   *Overture*

Scene i: Gallery of the Savory Foundation of Modern Art
2y   Who dealt? (four women); first version of:
2   New Art is True Art (Savory and chorus)
3y   Venus Was a Modest Goddess (trio); first version of:
3   One Touch of Venus (Molly and chorus)
3a   Venus Awakening (2 versions)
3b   Curtain music

Scene ii: Rodney's Room
4   How much I love you (Rodney)
4a   Venus enters (reprise of *3a*)
4b   Mrs Moat falls (3 bars orchestral)
5   I'm a Stranger Here Myself (Venus)

Scene iii: Rockefeller Plaza
6   Forty Minutes for Lunch (ballet scene)
6a   Incidental
7z   Love in a Mist; replaced by:
7   West Wind (Savory)

Scene iv: Bus Station Waiting Room
8y   The Jersey Plunk (trio); first version of:
8   Way Out West in New Jersey (Mrs Kramer, Gloria, Rodney)
8a   Reprise of *4*
9   Foolish Heart (Venus)
9a   Foolish Heart Dance (Venus and Rodney)

Scene v: Rodney's Barber Shop
10   The Trouble with Women (Rodney, Savory, Taxi, Stanley)
10a Gloria disappears (3 bars orchestral)
11y Too Soon (Venus and Rodney); first version of:
11   Speak Low (Venus and Rodney)

Scene vi: Roof of Museum
12a Artists' Ball (orchestral development of *11*)
12   Dr Crippen (Savory and dancers)

ACT II

Scene i: Savory's Bedroom
13   Very, Very (Molly)
14x Who am I? (Savory)

Scene ii: New York City Prison
15   Reprise of 'Speak Low' (Rodney)
16y It Must be Ernie (quartet); first version of:
16   Catch Hatch (Savory, Molly and ensemble)

Scene iii: The Sitting Room of a De Luxe Suite
17   That's Him (Venus)
18   Wooden Wedding (Rodney)
19a Venus in Ozone Heights (ballet)
19b Bacchanale (ballet)

Scene iv: The Savory Gallery
20a Reprise of *4* (Rodney)
20b Finaletto (Rodney)

Unlocated numbers:
21x Vive la différence
22x Westwind Dance
23x Reprise 'Westwind'

Sketched numbers:
24z You'll find it on the bill (Private investigator's narrative)
25z Fresh air and exercise
26z Same time, same place

Autographs

SKETCHES

The preliminary sketches are missing. The only sketches in WLA are marginal ones made during the draft stage.

DRAFTS

(1) The earliest collection comprises 108 pages of C^{12}. It includes 24z and 25z.

(2) 111 sides of Pr^{12}, of which forty-three are sketches and drafts for the ballet music (including the ritornello from 'Habsucht' in *Die Sieben Todsünden*).

(3) Two leaves of K^{12}. The first carries notes in another hand – presumably Agnes de Mille's – of musical requirements for the ballet, including two motifs (one described as a reminder of Bach's First Brandenburg Concerto) that Weill made use of. The second leaf has a sketch of 7, based on one of the settings of 7z; also a reminder of 'Der Mädchenraub' from *Der Kuhhandel*.

(4) A sheet of unnamed 20-line paper measuring 34.2 × 27.3 cms carries a draft of 2. A leaf of the same paper carries the introduction to 9.

REHEARSAL SCORE

The definitive versions (presumably used as production masters) are missing. WLA holds preliminary versions of fourteen numbers. Three of them – 4, 6 and 16 – are almost identical with the final ones; six – 5, 7, 10, 11, 12 and 17 – are in versions subsequently transposed and to varying extents revised; and two are cut numbers – 19x and 20x. The remainder – 2y, 3y, 8y (two versions), and 16y – have different lyrics and character names, and must therefore derive from *One Man's Venus* (see p. 328). Altogether there are 122 pages of manuscript, in black or blue-black ink on C^{12} (except for 6, which is on Pr^{12}).

FULL SCORE

Unbound and without title page; each number is in a separate folding of Sch^{20}, some titled, and all clearly identified by number. The pagination is in another hand. The definitive score comprises 423 numbered pages plus a 36-page Overture of which 20 pages are in another hand. There are 68 pages of cut material.

Publication

Chappell, 1943: vocal album containing 7, 9, 10, 11, 17, 18; sheet music versions of 7, 9, 10, 11 and 17; complete vocal score (hire only).

Dramatic licences and performance materials: present (1986) availability – Rodgers & Hammerstein Music Library (USA), KWF (Britain and German-speaking territories).

First Performance

17 September 1943 Boston (Massachusetts) Shubert Theatre; 7 October 1943, New York, Imperial Theatre. Production by Cheryl Crawford, staged by Elia Kazan; conductor Maurice Abravanel, choreographer Agnes de Mille, sets by Howard Bay, costumes by Paul du Pont and Kermit Love, gowns by Mainbocher; with Mary Martin (Venus), Kenny Baker (Rodney), John Boles (Savory), Paula Laurence (Molly), Ruth Bond (Gloria), Helen Raymond (Mrs Kramer) and Sono Osato (dancer).

Notes

For the origins of *One Touch of Venus*, see *One Man's Venus* (p. 328); for the 1948 film version, see pp. 347–8. 'The Trouble with Women' is a companion piece to 'Les filles de Bordeaux' (*Marie Galante*, p. 268), since both are based on the Salvation Army chorus 'In der Jugend gold'nem Schimmer' from *Happy End* (p. 217). The other borrowings are from *The River is Blue* (opening orchestral motif for 2) and *Der Kuhhandel* (second finale, C minor waltz, in the chorus of 'Very, Very', 13).

November 1943 – January 1944, Hollywood

Where Do We Go From Here?

Musical film
Screenplay by Morris Ryskind, story by Ryskind and Sid Herzig
Lyrics: Ira Gershwin
Directed by Gregory Ratoff and produced by William Perlberg
Released by Twentieth-Century–Fox

The USA at war. Bill Morgan yearns to play his part in the war effort, but has been rejected by all three services and fears that until he proves himself in action even his girlfriend will spurn him. Bemoaning his unhappy lot, he joins his fellow rejects in the national drive for scrap metal. Among his early finds are a magic lamp and an obliging genie, who promises to spirit him to the battlefronts forthwith. But the genie's magic proves to be as rusty as the lamp. At the first attempt the hapless Bill finds himself serving under Columbus on the voyage to America; at the second, he is under Washington, fighting the Hessians at Valley Forge. Only at the third does he finally fulfil his heart's desire, as a World War II marine.

   1   (Opening Music)
  1a   That's how it is
  1b   Telephone Call

1c Morale
2 All at once
3y It could have happened to anyone
4a If love remains
4b Minuet (development of 4a)
5 Song of the Rhineland
6 Columbus sequence
7y Manhattan
8 Church scene
9z You are unforgettable
10z Knowing you're there.

Autographs

SKETCHES

Thirty sides of Sch[20] and twenty-two sides of 12-line papers, mostly Sch[12], with some N[12], and one sheet of Ns[12]. The first side of the latter is headed 'Conga (Carnival)' and is musically reminiscent of the presumed sketches for *The Pirate*, some of which were written on the same brand and size of paper. However, sides *b–d* carry sketches for the 'Columbus' scene, including the mock-tragic episode 'If I'm in tears', which uses the quasi-Hungarian theme from the second finale in *Der Kuhhandel*.

DRAFTS

Thirty-eight pages of Sch[12], including ink draft of 4a; 10z is complete on four sides of a sheet of Sch[20].

FINAL COPIES

Complete in separate foldings, or sheets, of Sch[12] ('Columbus' on S[14]) for each number. 102 pages of manuscript; 8, and a *Tempo di conga* interpolation (6), were written on a sheet which has been neatly divided.

Publication

Chappell, 1945: 2, 4a and 5 as sheet music, all somewhat altered, especially 5.
Chappell, 1954: the greater part of 6, arranged for solo, chorus and piano, and published without reference to the source, under the title 'The Nina, The Pinta, The Santa Maria'.

Trade Show

21 May 1945

Cast

Fred MacMurray (Bill Morgan), Joan Leslie (Sally), June Haver (Lucilla), Gene Sheldon (Ali), Anthony Quinn (Indian Chief), Carlos Ramirez

(Benito), Alan Mowbray (George Washington), Fortunio Bonanova (Columbus), Herman Bing (Hessian Colonel).

Music Credits

Music directors Emil Newman and Charles Henderson; additional music composed by David Raksin and David Buttolph; orchestrations and arrangements by Maurice de Packh, Charles Henderson, Herb Taylor, Sonny Burke, Arthur Morton, Urban Thielman, Wallace Wheeler, Alfred Newman, David Buttolph, Sydney B. Cutner, Leo Shuken, Cyril J. Mockridge, Guy Massey and Jack Virgil.

Dubbing

Weill attended many of the dubbing sessions, which took place in Hollywood in August and September 1944. *3y* and *7y* were orchestrated and recorded, but not retained in the final version. Gaps in the numbering of the musical entries in the final dubbing sheets reveal where cuts have been made at the previous edit, while alphabetical suffixes indicate where there have been late additions. These numberings have therefore been reproduced in the following, slightly abbreviated, transcript of the dubbing sheets. Studio jargon has been retained in the interests of authenticity, but requires some explanation. For copyright and other reasons the dubbing sheets distinguish between the invention of motifs or themes, which is termed 'composing' ('comp.' for short), and the processes of 'development' and 'arrangement' ('dev.' and 'arr.'). The latter functions are the responsibility of the music department, not of the official 'composer'. A 'theme dev.' is background music based on the listed material. 'Devising' is a refinement reserved for the title music, which in those far-off days always came first and was intended as an aural advertisement of delights or thrills to come, and an invocation to the box-office victory the producers were praying for. So onerous a task was generally considered to be beyond the reach of a mere composer.

Musical Entries

After the title music, which is treated separately in the dubbing sheets, the entries are numbered reel by reel. In the following list the reel numbers are in **bold** type parenthesized.

Title Music
Devised by David Raksin, orch. Maurice de Packh. Comprises 'Magic' (comp. Raksin), 'The Genie' (comp. Raksin), 'All at once' (comp. Weill), and 'Columbus' (comp. Weill)

(1)
1   'All at once' (vocal arr. Charles Henderson, orch. Herb Taylor)
3   'All at once' (MacMurray solo, orch. de Packh)
4   'All at once' (dev. Raksin, orch. de Packh)

4a 'Chattanooga Choo-Choo' (comp. Harry Warren, arr. Sonny Burke) [contemporary hit song from the Twentieth-Century–Fox film *Sun Valley Serenade*]

5 'Chattanooga Choo-Choo'

(2)

1 'Morale' dance arrangement (dev. Raksin, orch. Burke)
2 'Morale' (June Haver with chorus, arr. Henderson, orch. de Packh)
3 'Good Night Sweetheart' (comp. Ray Noble, Jimmy Campbell, Reg Connelly; arr. Taylor) [hit song of the 1930s]
4 'The Lamp', 'The Genie', 'Magic' (dev. Raksin, orch. de Packh)
5 'Yankee Doodle' (arr. Raksin)
6 Army Bugle Call, and 'Yankee Doodle' (dev. Raksin, orch. Arthur Morton)
7 'Minuet Medley No. 1' – 'All at once' and 'Prudence' (orch. de Packh for harpsichord and strings)

(3)

1 'All at once' (minuet, arr. de Packh)
2 'If love remains' (arr. harpsichord, Urban Thielman)
3 'If love remains' (MacMurray and Leslie; vocal arr. Henderson, orch. de Packh)
5 '1776 Boogie' (comp. and dev. Raksin, orch. Morton)
5a 'Magic' (comp. and dev. Raksin, orch. Morton)
5b 'Ach du lieber Augustin' – 4 bars
6 Theme dev. 3 – 'Magic' and 'The Genie' (dev. and comp. Raksin, orch. Morton)

(4)

1 'The Hessians' (comp. and dev. Raksin, orch. Morton)
2 'The Song of the Rhineland' (Trenton Bierstube) (vocal arr. Henderson, orch. de Packh)
3 Theme dev. 4 – 'Rhineland Waltz' (comp. David Buttolph)

(5)

1 Theme dev. 5 – 'Magic', 'The Genie', 'Smoke' (Raksin/Morton)
1a Theme dev. 6 – '1492' (Buttolph); 'Columbus' (Weill); 'Mutiny' (Buttolph)
2 'Columbus' part 1 (vocal Charles Henderson, orch. de Packh) 'Columbus' parts 2 and 3 (orch. de Packh and Wallace Wheeler)

(6)

2 Cuban Drums
3 'Columbus' and 'Big Chief' (Buttolph and Alfred Newman)
4 Theme dev. 8 – 'The Genie', 'Magic', and 'Big Chief', 'Traffic Lights' and 'Indian Maid' (dev. Buttolph, orch. Sydney B. Cutner and Leo Shuken)

(7)

1 Theme dev. 9 – 'Smoke' (Raksin), 'If love remains' (dev. Cyril J. Mockridge, orch. Cutner)
1a Theme dev. 10 – 'Magic', 'The Genie', 'Smoke' (Raksin, dev. Mockridge, orch. Cutner)
1b 'If love remains' – Dutch Street scene (Weill, dev. Mockridge, orch. Cutner, arrangement based on 'Anvil Chorus' from *Il Trovatore*)
1d Theme dev. 11 – 'If love remains' and 'All at once' (dev. Mockridge, orch. Cutner)

1e 'All at once' (dev. Mockridge, orch. Cutner)
2   'All at once' – reprise Dutch scene (orch. de Packh)
2a 'All at once' – (dev. Mockridge, orch. Cutner)
2b 'All at once', 7/2 with lyrics
2c 'If love remains' (dev. Mockridge, orch. Cutner)

(8)

1   'The Prisoner's song' – 6 bars unaccompanied (comp. Guy Massey)
2   Theme dev. 12 – 'Magic', 'The Genie' (comp. and dev. Raksin, orch. Morton)
2a 'Smoke' (comp. Raksin)
2b 'Catrina's Wedding', 'Smoke' (Raksin)
3   Theme dev. 14 – 'Genie', 'Up in the Air', '18th Century' (Raksin), '20th Century Trademark' (comp. Newman), 'Entering 20th Century' (comp. Raksin), 'You're in the Army now'
4   9 bars slide-whistle
5   Brass band and voice medley – 'Morale', 'Smoke', 'Genie', etc. (dev. Buttolph, arr. Jack Virgil)
6   Field Drum
7   'The Genie' (comp. Raksin, dev. Buttolph, orch. Jack Virgil)
8   Brass band and vocal finale: 'Smoke' (Raksin); 'Morale' (Weill)
9   'The Genie' (comp. and dev. Raksin, orch. Morton)

Notes

The 'Columbus' sequence was at the time reputed to be the longest vocal number ever recorded for a Hollywood musical. (Its three sections ran for a total of just over nine minutes.) Weill regarded it as a first step towards his ideal of a through-composed musical film. Like the satirical 'Song of the Rhineland', it belies its Hollywood scoring and inclines towards a post-Offenbachian European operetta style. The borrowing from *Der Kuhhandel* is representative of that.

Spring 1944

Wie lange noch?

Song for voice and piano
Text: Walter Mehring
Written for the Office of War Information in Washington
Duration: 3 minutes

Autograph

Ink fair copy on four sides of Pr^{12}.

First Performance (Recording)

Spring 1944, New York; Lotte Lenya and the composer

Notes

Apart from its final cadence, the music is almost identical with that of the 1934 chanson for Lys Gauty, 'Je ne t'aime pas' (p. 261). Mehring's text is entirely new: the first stanza ostensibly a lover's complaint, the second an anti-Fascist gloss on it. The song owes its existence to the wartime activities of Ernst Josef Aufricht and Manfred George, who were responsible for the radio series *We Fight Back*, and for the similarly named Hunter College revue at which Lenya and Weill had given the first performance of the 'Soldatenweib' ballad (p. 323). Mehring too had contributed to *We Fight Back*. A key figure in the literary avant garde of pre-Hitler Berlin, and the author of one of Piscator's historic productions (for which Eisler wrote the music), Mehring had by now turned his back on revolutionary politics – like some but not all the émigrés who were working in the New York section of the Office of War Information. Aufricht's friend Robert Vambery, the librettist of *Der Kuhhandel*, had recently joined the section (after a short spell at the Brander Matthews Theater of Columbia University, where he had worked on the 1941 premiere of Britten's and Auden's *Paul Bunyan*). One of his colleagues in the German Office was Brecht's close friend and collaborator Ruth Berlau; Brecht himself would have been another, had his application been successful. Vambery's reaction to his discovery of 'communist' infiltration in the Office of War Information is described in Aufricht's memoirs (*Erzähle, damit du dein Recht erweist*, Berlin, 1966, p. 257). However, Weill dealt directly with Washington over the recording of 'Wie lange noch?' and 'Soldatenweib'. The praise that Manfred George had lavished on the setting of the 'Soldatenweib' ballad after the Hunter College evening in April 1943 is a clue to the genesis of 'Wie lange noch?' a year later. From his Washington office, George could well have promoted the idea of recording the ballad on disc, and transporting copies to Europe for broadcasting to Germany. But the timing of the release must have depended on the course of events in Europe, and especially on the long-awaited attack from the West. In the early spring of 1944 Weill was called to the Office of War Information in Washington. Whatever transpired there has left little trace in WLA, for at the time it was classified information. Almost certainly, Weill was asked to supply, at very short notice, another anti-Nazi song to be recorded at the same time as the 'Soldatenweib' ballad. Undoubtedly he was also commissioned to write the score for Jean Renoir's film *Salute to France* (see next entry). The reason for the urgency and for the secrecy was that the Allied invasion of Normandy was imminent. After 6 June 1944 the question 'Wie lange noch?' would have additional force.

Posthumous Publication

EAM, 1982: in *The Unknown Kurt Weill: A Collection of 14 Songs*.

April–May 1944

Salute to France

Incidental music for a propaganda film
Produced by the US Office of War Information (Robert Riskin, European
    Chief; Philip Dunne in charge of production; executive producer
    Burgess Meredith)
Directed by Jean Renoir and Garson Kanin
Script by Maxwell Anderson
Narrator José Ferrer
Musical director Max Goberman
Duration: *c*. 30 minutes

Note 1

One of a series of OWI films made during the months preceding the
opening of the 'Second Front' in Western Europe on 4 June 1944, *Salute to
France* was a bilingual production designed for American and Free French
forces involved in the liberation of France, and also for the French
populace itself. At the start, a popular song entitled 'Le temps des cerises'
('The Time of the Cherries') serves to evoke images of France in peacetime.
The rustic idyll is then interrupted by newsreel clips and recordings from
Hitler's Germany. After a parenthetical reminder of the 1914–18 War, the
Horst Wessel Song introduces a *Blitzkrieg* sequence. A fictional curé takes
up the story from there, reflecting upon France's defeat and its
consequences. The ignominies of Pétain and Laval are then contrasted
with the fighting spirit of de Gaulle's Free French, and the valour of the
Resistance. *Salute to France* ends with the capture and trial of a Resistance
hero, and his vision of France's imminent liberation and regeneration.

   The film was made in conditions of top secrecy and looks as if it has
been cobbled together under pressure of time, on a tight budget. At no
point does it transcend its purely utilitarian purposes, let alone reveal,
either in the direction or in the editing, the hand of Renoir, one of the
finest film directors of his day or any other. Emphatically not a film for
cinéastes, it even lacks distinction within its own genre: historians and
students of film propaganda in the Second World War are unlikely to
linger over its attempted fusion of documentary and fictional material, or
to probe the worthy sentiments embodied in Anderson's script. Whether
Weill's score deserves better than the verdict passed on it by Lawrence
Morton in *Modern Music* (vol. XXII, no. 1, November–December 1944, p.
65) is a question that must await the discovery of missing manuscripts.
Meanwhile the copy of the film housed in the National Archive in
Washington (video copy in WLA) is the best available means of checking
the final dubbing, though the soundtrack is markedly inferior to that of

the copy seen by the present author in 1960, and lacks the elaborately elegiac variation (on the theme song) that accompanied the curé's account of the French defeat. Since many of the musical entries are too brief to merit separate listing, the following numberings denote only the principal sections in the score:

1   Title music
2   Peacetime: 'The Time of the Cherries' (song, with variations)
3   The Master Race
4   War
4a   1914–18 (Verdun, the Marne, Chemin des Dames, etc.)
4b   Horst Wessel
4c   1939–40
5   The Curé's Story (Defeat; Vichy)
6   The Free French
7   The Resistance: 'Chant de Libération' (chorus)
8   Trial Scene
9   End titles

Arrangements of 'Le temps des cerises' (words by J. B. Clement, music by A. Renard) and of the 'Chant de Libération' (words and music by Anna Marly), and simple variations on these songs, dominate, respectively, the opening stages of the score and the final ones. The remainder of the score relies either on arrangements and quotations (e.g. the Horst Wessel Song and a typical band march for a Nazi rally, obviously pre-recorded) or on self-borrowings. The title-music's juxtaposition of a conventional fanfare with a version of the *Marseillaise* lifted directly from *Johnny Johnson* prepares for the extensive quotation from the *Johnny Johnson* battle music that accompanies the first *Blitzkrieg* shots – a passage followed immediately by a stretto in tarantella rhythm borrowed from *The River is Blue*. The Free French are introduced by the *Railroads on Parade* version of the band march that opens the *Kuhhandel* finale; and the end titles repeat the *Marseillaise* quotation from the start. On the evidence of the soundtrack alone, sympathetic observers might conclude that pressure of time prevented Weill from availing himself of the musical opportunities latent in a non-commercial undertaking of this sort, and unsympathetic ones (like Lawrence Morton) either that he was incapable of doing so, or that he was downright irresponsible. It seems possible that the true explanation of the debâcle – for that indeed is what the soundtrack represents, in relation to comparable film-music achievements of such contemporaries as Milhaud and Eisler – lies somewhere between the two extremes. If the difference between the draft Weill made for a rhythmically notated melodrama surveying the battles of the First World War and the pitiful fragments which are all that is audible on the National Archive copy is anything to go by – and the fate of the elegiac variation on 'The Time of the Cherries' suggests that it is – Weill's intentions were better than the final results suggest, and some interference at OWI level must be allowed for. The discovery of a copy of the French version of the film would certainly be helpful.

July–December 1944, Hollywood/Brook House

The Firebrand of Florence

Operetta in two acts
Book by Edwin Justus Mayer, based on his play *The Firebrand*
Lyrics by Ira Gershwin
Cast: singing roles: Benvenuto Cellini, Angela, Emilia, Duke, Duchess, Ottaviano, Clerk, Hangman, Tartman, Ascanio, Maffio, Captain of the Guard, Marquis, Page, chorus; other roles: Arlecchino, Columbina, Pierrot, Flomina, Major Domo, Pantalone, Fiorinetta, Gelfomino, models, apprentices, poets, ladies-in-waiting
Orchestra: 1(picc.).1(ca.).2.1.   2.3.1.0.   harp, perc. gtr.   8.4.2.2.1.

Florence, in the year 1535. The plot – which is distantly related to passages in Cellini's memoirs – is a series of intertwined amorous intrigues. The Duke fancies Cellini's model Angela, and the Duchess fancies Cellini; Cellini has the best of both worlds, and contrives to escape hanging.

1*ax*	Overture; replaced by:
1	Prelude

ACT I

Scene i: A Piazza in Florence
2	Opening
2a	'The bell of doom is clanging' (Hangman, assistants)
2b	Ensemble: 'Come to Florence' (Hangman, chorus, dancers)
2c	Aria and ensemble: 'Life, Love, and Laughter' (Cellini, apprentices, chorus)

Scene ii: Street Scene

Scene iii: Cellini's Workshop
3	Duet: 'Our Master is Free Again' (Emilia, Ascanio)
4	Arietta: 'I had just been pardoned' (Cellini)
5	Waltz duet: 'You're far too near me' (Cellini, Angela)
6	Duke's entry-song: 'Alessandro the Wise' (Duke, chorus)
7	Finaletto (Angela, Emilia, Ottaviano, Cellini, Duke, chorus)

Scene iv: The City Gates
8	Duchess's Entrance (Blackamoor)
9	'Sing Me Not a Ballad' (Duchess, four courtiers)

Scene v: The Gardens of the Summer Palace
10	Madrigal: 'When the Duchess is Away' (Captain of the Guard, Duke, Emilia, chorus)
11	Duet (reprise of 2c): 'Life, Love, and Laughter' (Angela, Cellini)
12	Trio: 'The Nozy Cook' (Angela, Duke, Cellini)
13	Finale alla Tarantella (Emilia, Angela, Duke, Duchess, Cellini)

ACT II

Scene i: Cellini's Workshop
14   'The Duchess's Letter' (Cellini)
15   'The Little Naked Boy' (Angela and models)

Scene ii: The Palace Gates
16   March chorus: 'We're Soldiers of the Duchy' [sometimes listed as 'Just
        in Case']

Scene iii: A Loggia in the City Palace
17   Song: 'A Rhyme for Angela' (Duke, Poets, Ladies-in-Waiting)
18   Procession – partial reprise of *2a*

Scene iv: Grand Council Chamber of the Palace
19   Trial Scene
19a   'Hear Ye! Hear Ye!' (Clerk)
19b   'The World is Full of Villains' (three judges)
19c   'You Have to Do What You Do Do' (Cellini, Duke, chorus)
19d   'How wonderfully fortunate!' (Angela)
19e   Duet: 'Love is my Enemy' (Cellini, Angela)
20   Ensemble: 'Come to Paris' (Marquis, two girls, chorus)

Scene v: Versailles
21   Finale
21a   Sarabande (orchestral version of *19e*)
21b   Gigue (dancers)
21c   Reprise of *2a* (full company)

Autographs

SKETCHES

Missing, except for those interspersed with the drafts.

DRAFTS

To judge from the manuscript, the score was drafted at great speed and in
no particular order. Headings are few, and only rarely are sheets gathered
into foldings. There are 113 pages of K^{12}, sixty-four of Sch^{12}, ten of Cp^{12}
and four of Sch^{24}. Almost all the material was incorporated in the final
score. Among the few discarded fragments are a waltz song ('I have lived, I
have loved, I have laughed') based on the 'music-box' waltz from *The River
is Blue*, a 'Serenade' based on the *Marie Galante* tango, three borrowings
from *Der Kuhhandel*, and a 40-bar pastiche of Lehár and Puccini.

REHEARSAL SCORE

The score is complete on 239 unnumbered sides of Sch^{12}, plus ten pages
of C^{12} (containing *13a*, which alone is written in ink). *1x*, *1* and *21b* are in
short score.

FULL SCORE

Unbound, without title page, on 493 pages of single-sided scoring paper
(C^{22}); each number paginated separately. The score was apparently used

only by the copyist, and is therefore in good condition, with few non-autograph markings. The precise location of late additions (mostly in pencil) is seldom clear, but not of great importance. Far more significant is the fact that the holograph score is supplemented by 164 pages of score by Weill's assistant Ted Royal: *1x*, *1*, and *21b* are realized from Weill's short score, and the remainder – *7*, *20*, and 'encores' of *9*, *16*, and *17* – are based on his examples. In *9*, Weill has made corrections to Royal's score.

Publication

1945: sheet music of *2c*, *5*, *9* and *17*. The first printings bear the work's original title, *Much Ado About Love*.
Dramatic licences and performance materials: present (1986) availability – KWF (USA, Britain, German-speaking territories).

First Productions

23 February 1945, Colonial Theatre, Boston, under the title *Much Ado About Love*; 22 March, Alvin Theatre, New York, under the present title; production by Max Gordon, staged by John Murray Anderson; conductor Maurice Abravanel, designer Jo Mielziner, costumes by Raoul René DuBois, choreographer Catherine Littlefield; with Earl Wrightson (Cellini), Beverly Tyler (Angela), Melville Cooper (Duke), Lotte Lenya (Duchess), Randolph Symonette (Hangman), Don Marshall (Tartman), Ferdie Hoffman (Ottaviano), James Dobson (Ascanio).

Notes

Like *A Kingdom for a Cow* (p. 271), *The Firebrand of Florence* is a finished work only in a cataloguing sense; and like that ill-founded condominium of operetta and musical comedy, it was a box-office failure. Were the sketches to come to light, they could well reveal more borrowings from the Vambery operetta than occur in the drafts. But such a discovery would merely emphasize the distance between the first conception and the final work. Significantly, only one of these borrowings reached the final score, where a fragment of the Santa Maria national anthem has embedded itself in 'Alessandro the Wise' (much as the funeral march discarded from the *Johnny Johnson* sketches has invaded the Hangman's music in *2a*). *The Firebrand* is very different in character from the Vambery operetta, and quite without its innovatory impulse. To the extent that it inherited the ambitions towards operetta that had been frustrated by the collapse of the Spewack *Venus* (p. 328) it was representative of that phase in Broadway history when the initiatives and the popular appeal of the soprano Grace Moore were starting to make the names of Strauss and Offenbach almost respectable. It is in *The Firebrand* that Weill begins to show what he might have achieved with Shaw's *Pygmalion* had he managed to follow through his interest in that play, and thus to forestall

Lerner and Loewe. In that sense it was a precursor to Bernstein's *Candide* rather than *My Fair Lady*, and a successor to *Knickerbocker Holiday* rather than *Lady in the Dark*. With *One Touch of Venus* it has almost no audible connection. While the freshness of invention, the sheer musicality, of its best passages are quite unmatched in the earlier score, the stylistic and structural unity of music, book, and lyrics is much weaker. Thus the Act I finale, after a lively beginning in classical operetta style, dissolves into a succession of ill-motivated reprises, and the opening of Act II is as sketchy as its counterpart in Act I is elaborate and effective. This loss of grip – already portended by the very appearance of some of the drafts and rehearsal scores – has its gravest consequences in the last finale, where all pretence of musico-dramatic form is abandoned. The fact that so much of the orchestration was handed over to a professional Broadway arranger tells its own story. What prevented Weill from completing the score as he had begun it was neither the pressure of time nor a failure of invention: it was a growing awareness of limits to the amount of 'purely' musical substance he could hope to convey to a Broadway audience in the 1940s. The 'Zodiac Song', which he and Ira Gershwin rescued from the discard tray of *Lady in the Dark* and incorporated in *The Firebrand*, achieves its peculiar authenticity by parodying a real predicament: 'You have to do what you do do, it isn't up to you at all'.

April 1945 [. . .] 1948

One Touch of Venus

Film version
Released (October 1948) by Universal-International
Produced by Lester Cowan
Directed by William A. Selter
Screenplay by Harry Kurnitz and Frank Tashlin
Musical director Ann Ronell

Autographs

To judge from the time and effort he was obliged to devote to the film, Weill must have written a considerable quantity of material. All that survives in WLA is two sheets of AB^{12}. The first carries the complete pencil fair copy of a song entitled 'The Picture on the Wall', with lyrics by Ann Ronell; the second has a complete pencil draft of an untitled song whose lyrics feature the repeated tag 'Love rhymes with you' – presumably the intended title. This draft is followed by a banal version of 'Westwind' in 6/8 time.

Notes

According to the original plan, *One Touch of Venus* was to have been a film musical. Weill was engaged to write the score, and managed to negotiate a contract ensuring, for the first time in his American career, that no music other than his own would be included or interpolated. Already at that stage he was given to understand that the music department considered his Broadway score too 'sophisticated' for general consumption, and that the 'romantic' element should be strengthened at the expense of the parodistic one. To that end he spent several weeks of the Hollywood spring and summer of 1945 unhappily sketching additional material. His only ally, or so he felt, was Ann Ronell, whom he had known and respected since they first worked together on *The River is Blue*. Once he had fulfilled his contractual responsibilities he returned to New York, leaving Ann Ronell with the unenviable task of fending off the 'philistines' in the music department. He even urged her to rescue as much as she could from his original orchestrations, when the time came for the dubbing sessions.

But the time never came. After several changes of producer, and two years of indecision about the very nature of the film, the studio decided to shed the burden of production numbers, and settle for a romantic comedy starring Ava Gardner and Robert Walker. Background music was all that was needed for this, and Weill was duly invited to provide it. Being otherwise engaged, he subcontracted the work to Ann Ronell. Completed at last, the film was released amid a chorus of complaints that Hollywood had successfully obliterated a well-loved Broadway musical. After *Knickerbocker Holiday* and *Lady in the Dark*, Weill had hoped for better treatment. But only the film was better; the treatment was identical.

Cast

Ava Gardner (Venus), Robert Walker (Eddie [*sic*] Hatch), Dick Haymes (Joe Grant), Eve Arden (Molly Stewart), Olga San Juan (Gloria), Tom Conway (Whitfield [*sic*] Savory), and Sara Allgood (Landlady).

August–September 1945/November 1945

Down in the Valley

Folk-opera
(trial version for radio; withdrawn)
Libretto: Arnold Sundgaard
Duration: 25 minutes
Cast: singing roles: Brack Weaver (tenor or high baritone), Jennie Parsons

(lyric soprano), Thomas Bouché (bass), Leader/Preacher (baritone); SATB chorus; speaking roles: Guard, Peters, Jennie's father, two men, two women

Orchestra: 2.1.2(2sax.).1.   2.3.2.1.   gtr. pno. perc. str. (no violas)

Note 1

This first version of the celebrated 'folk-opera' (p. 363) was written for Frontiers Unlimited, a production company formed by Charles McArthur and Olin Downes with a view to launching a sponsored series of short radio operas, each specially commissioned, and each based on a folk song or popular ballad. McArthur was a senior advertising executive, and a keen music-lover whose job gave him direct access to radio stations throughout the USA. Downes had been music critic of the *New York Times* since 1924, and, as music director of the New York World's Fair in 1938– 9, had shared some of the responsibility and credit for *Railroads on Parade* (p. 300). Conditioned in his attitude to modern music by a mistrust of (Central) European 'intellectualism', he tended to champion those national schools or individuals that retained links with folklore. (For him, as for many critics of his generation, Sibelius, Kodály, and even Bartók provided relatively safe routes on either side of Schoenberg and Stravinsky.) Though Broadway was not in his professional line of duty nor entirely to his taste, his own brand of populism allowed him to take a sympathetic interest in it. Frontiers Unlimited owed much to his view of folk song as a respository of humane and democratic values, if not of the commercial ones that were McArthur's professional concern. Weill and Maxwell Anderson were brought in as fellow directors, and a constitution was drafted and approved. The first objective was now to find sponsors, by commissioning a sample product and distributing a so-called 'auditions recording' to potential advertisers. *Down in the Valley* was conceived and written as the sample; and after a try-out with piano, it was orchestrated, and then produced and recorded as if for broadcasting. Duly distributed along the frontiers of Madison Avenue, the recording failed to convince prospective sponsors that the project as a whole had sufficient popular appeal. Frontiers Unlimited was therefore disbanded, and the score shelved. Although the stage version of 1948 is differently orchestrated and contains two new settings that add some five minutes to the playing time, music and libretto are essentially unchanged. They are described on pp. 363–4 below. The following details relate only to the 1945 version.

Autographs

SKETCHES AND DRAFTS

Missing.

REHEARSAL SCORE

The score is unbound and has no title page, but is complete (apart from the introductory bars) on fifty-six numbered pages of K^{12}.

FULL SCORE

119 numbered pages of Cs^{22}, unbound but gathered in four sections by string ties, in punched holes. The voice parts and text have been inserted in red ink in another hand.

Auditions Recording

December 1945, New York; conducted by Maurice Abravanel and produced by Andrew Allen of the Canadian Broadcasting Corporation.

Note 2

Unlike most original versions of operas that have become celebrated in later versions, the 1945 *Down in the Valley* is entirely contained by its successor, and is wholly superseded by it. Musicologically it is therefore of little interest. What is certainly interesting – indeed, of the essence – is its genesis; and the effects of that are, of course, equally audible in the stage version.

January–November 1946, Brook House

Street Scene

'An American Opera'
Book by Elmer Rice, adapted from his play of the same name (1929)
Lyrics: Langston Hughes
Dedication: 'To the Memory of My Brother Hanns Weill'
Duration: full evening
Cast: singing roles: Anna Maurrant (dramatic soprano), Frank Maurrant (bass-baritone), Willie Maurrant (child), Rose Maurrant (lyric soprano), Sam Kaplan (tenor), Abraham Kaplan (tenor), Harry Easter (light baritone), Henry Davis (high baritone), Dick McGann (dancer–singer), Mae Jones (dancer–singer), Lippo Fiorentino (tenor), Gossips – Mrs Fiorentino, Mrs Jones and Mrs Olsen (soprano, mezzo, alto), Daniel Buchanan (buffo tenor), Jennie Hildebrand (mezzo), Nursemaids (soprano, mezzo), three children; other roles: Steve Sankey, Shirley Kaplan, Emma and Vincent Jones, Charles and Laura Hildebrand, Milkman, City Marshall, Officer Murphy, Old Clothes Man, Interne, Ambulance Driver, Married Couple, Neighbours.
Orchestra: 2.2.2(bcl.).2. 2.2.2.0. timp. perc. pno. harp, cel. str.

A tenement block in a run-down district of New York; its windows, doorways and sidewalk are the 'frames' for an action that preserves the classical unities. Two narrative elements bind together various 'slices of life' from a 24-hour period. The first concerns the unhappy marriage of Frank and Anna Maurrant, which ends with his murdering her in a fit of jealousy; the second concerns the relationship between their daughter Rose and the young student Sam Kaplan who hopes to marry her. Influenced by the tragedy of her parents' marriage yet consoled by reminders of Walt Whitman and his 'Lilacs', Rose sadly renounces Sam and sets off in search of a new and better life, responsible to none but herself.

The score is virtually continuous. More or less self-contained numbers are linked by spoken dialogue, most of which is 'underscored' in the manner of film music. In the published vocal score, the numbers carry generic titles whose classical or Verdian origins are sometimes at odds with the musical character. The titling and the numbering adopted here are taken from the vocal score (with editorial adjustments in square brackets).

ACT I

A New York Sidewalk, Towards Evening

1[a]	Introduction
1[b]	'Ain't it Awful, the Heat?' (Gossips, Kaplan, Olsen, Neighbours)
2	Blues: 'I Got a Marble and a Star' (Henry Davis, the Janitor)
[3a]	Scene: 'Come in, come in' (offstage voices)
3	[Gossips'] Trio: 'Get a Load of That' (Gossips)
4	'When a Woman Has a Baby' (Buchanan and women)
[5a]	Scene (Mrs Maurrant, Mrs Fiorentino, Maurrant)
5	Aria: 'Somehow I Never Could Believe' (Mrs Maurrant)
6[a]	Scene (Jones, Sankey, Mrs Maurrant, Mrs Fiorentino)
[b]	Gossips' Quartet (Gossips and Olsen)
7	Ice-Cream Sextet (Lippo, Henry Jones, Olsen, Gossips)
8	Aria: 'Let Things Be Like They Always Was' (Maurrant)
[9a]	Scene and Song: 'Hail to the School'
9	Ensemble: 'Wrapped in a Ribbon' (Jennie and Neighbours)
10	Arioso: 'Lonely House' (Sam)
11	Scene and Song: 'Wouldn't You Like to be on Broadway?' (Easter)
[11a]	Scene (Rose and Maurrant)]
12	Cavatina: 'What Good Would the Moon Be?' (Rose) and Scene (Rose, Easter, Maurrant)
13	Song: 'Moon-faced, Starry-eyed' (Dick and Mae); Scene and Dance (Dick and Mae)
14	Duet: 'Remember That I Care'; 'In the dooryard fronting an old farmhouse' (Sam and Rose)
[14a]	Finaletto (Sam, Rose, Henry)

ACT II

Scene i: Same, The Next Morning

15[a]	Introduction (orchestra)
15[b]	Children's Game: 'Fat, Fat, the Water Rat'; 'Catch Me if You Can'
16	Scene and Trio: 'There'll be Trouble' (Maurrant, Mrs Maurrant, Rose)
17	Song: 'A Boy Like You' (Mrs Maurrant)
18	Duet: 'We'll Go Away Together' (Sam and Rose) and Scene (Rose, Easter, etc.)
19	Chorus Scene and Lament: 'The Woman Who Lived Up There'
[19a]	Interlude (orchestral reprise of *18*)

Scene ii: The Same Afternoon

20	Lullaby: 'Sleep, baby dear' (Nursemaids)
21	Scene (Officer Murphy, Rose, Sam, etc.)
22	Finale
[22a]	'I Loved Her Too' (Maurrant, Rose, Ensemble)
[22b]	'Remember that I care' (Sam and Rose)
[22c]	Reprise of 1b (Gossips)

Cut numbers:

24y	Horoscope Song: 'That's where our horoscopes lie'
25y	'Italy in Technicolor'
26x	'Rose's Goodbye to Easter'

Unfinished numbers:

27z	'The Great Big Sky'
28z	'Street Light is my Moonlight'
29z	Melting Pot Ensemble: 'A Nation of Nations'
29za	'Colombo'
29zb	'It's the Irish'
29zc	'A Little Swing for Swinging'
29zd	'Hot-Dog Waltz'
29ze	'The Kids in School'
30y	Gossip Trio III

Autographs

SKETCHES

Fragmentary sketches and rough drafts cover sixty-two sides of F^{12}, twenty-eight of K^{12}, and seven of Sch^{12}. The order of sketching is seemingly random. The leaf of F^{12} carrying part of 29zb has a text beginning 'It's the Reillys and the Kellys', and has been headed by Lenya (c. 1955) 'Love Life'; just legible above the text is the name of the singer, 'Mrs Jones'. This discovery led to the identification and piecing together of the other sketches for the 'Melting Pot' ensemble, which had also been associated with the *Love Life* holographs – understandably so in the case of an F^{12} sheet whose *b* side (headed 'Love Life' in Edward Cole's hand) carries a piano-score sketch of a tune that re-emerged in *Love Life* as 'You understand me so'; the *a* side of this sheet carries 29zb, three staves to a system without text, while *c* has unidentified fragments, and *d* is blank.

DRAFTS

Weill's diary for January 1946 gives the following dates of composition: 12 January (11); 13 January (1b, etc.); 19 January (3); 20 January (27z); 25 January (7). These numbers are all drafted on F^{12}, which is one of the three papers Weill used for drafting *Street Scene* (apart from a leaf of Cp^{12} on which he sketched one of half-a-dozen abortive versions of 8). Internal evidence, musical and textual, suggests that the 209 pages of drafts on F^{12} paper represent the earlier stages, and the sixty-eight pages on K^{12} the later ones. Twelve pages of Sch^{12} (carrying drafts of 17 and 25x), and two pages of a 20-stave paper (measuring 34 × 27 cms, and carrying a sketch for 7 and a draft of an extended dance in 6/8) cannot be precisely dated, but are certainly earlier than the K^{12} material. Throughout, final drafts – or those begun as such – are distinguished from the rest by titles. There are two such drafts of 'The Great Big Sky' (27z). No final draft of 'Street Light is my Moonlight' (28z) has been traced; of the two earlier drafts of this excellent song, one breaks off before the end of the page, and the other – on both sides of a leaf of K^{12} – lacks a conclusion. The draft of 'A Nation of Nations' (29z) – referred to in Weill's correspondence as the 'Melting Pot Ensemble' – is incomplete on twenty pages of F^{12}. The transitions are in some cases unfinished, and in others partly missing. As the pages are not numbered, the order of 29zb–d above is conjectural.

REHEARSAL SCORE

The entire score is on ozalid paper (M^{12}) from which dyeline copies were made for rehearsal purposes. It is therefore unbound and without editorial or other markings. The numbers are paginated separately. Neither originals nor copies of 27–30 have been traced; presumably these numbers were left in draft form. There are 293 pages of manuscript.

FULL SCORE

The score is written in various inks on 556 pages of Sch^{24}, and is heavily marked in other hands (with numerous indications of cuts). There is no title page or binding and each number is in a separate folding, separately paginated. A continuous pagination in the Act I manuscript has a 6-page gap after 6b – insufficient to account for either 24y or 25y, both of which are missing, if indeed they were orchestrated. Two further numbers were orchestrated by, and are in the hand of, Ted Royal: 9 (thirty-four pages) and 13 (twenty-nine pages).

First Performance

16 December 1946, Philadelphia, Shubert Theatre; same cast as for New York. 9 January 1947, New York, Adelphi Theatre. Production by Dwight Deere Wiman and the Playwrights' Company, staged by Charles Friedman; conductor Maurice Abravanel, sets by Jo Mielziner, costumes by Lucinda Ballard, choreography by Anna Sokolov; with Norman Cordon (Maurrant), Polyna Stoska (Mrs Maurrant), Anne Jeffreys (Rose Maurrant), Brian Sullivan (Sam Kaplan), Sydney Rayner (Lippo), Hope Emerson (Emma Jones), Irving Kaufman (Kaplan), Don Saxon (Easter), Beverly Janis (Jennie), Randolph Symonette (City Marshall).

Publication

Chappell, 1947: vocal score; sheet-music versions of *10, 12, 13, 17, 18.*
Dramatic licences and performance materials: present (1986) availability –

Rodgers & Hammerstein Music Library (USA), KWF (Britain and German-speaking territories).

Notes

Weill made no secret of his special regard for *Street Scene*. In his notes for the 1947 commercial recording he presents it not only as the fulfilment of an ambition to write 'an American opera', which he traced back to his first days in the USA, but also as the achievement of a goal towards which *all* his stage works had been striving since the early twenties: 'a special brand of musical theatre which would completely integrate drama and music, spoken word, song and movement'. Adequately to consider the justice of such momentous claims is a task that would warrant a book to itself. The bibliographer will perhaps be content merely to note how the two ambitions (or 'dreams' in Weill's terminology) are reflected, first, in the work's official subtitle – to which Weill himself offered a more modest alternative in the shape of 'A Broadway Opera' – and then in the somewhat ostentatious pluralism of the generic titling used in the vocal score. These details may distract attention from the debt *Street Scene* owes to Cheryl Crawford's commercial success with a version of Gershwin's *Porgy and Bess* (see p. 328) that played down the work's operatic ambitions, and removed most of the recitative (a strategy that Weill proposed and about which, indeed, he offered Crawford some professional advice). Less clear is the basis for Weill's claim (in his 1947 notes) that *Die Dreigroschenoper*, *Mahagonny*, and *Der Silbersee* were but steps on the path to *Street Scene*. He did not mention, and perhaps was not even conscious of, the one indisputable link with his European past: the orchestral introduction to Act II is borrowed, with only slight modifications, from his music for Erwin Piscator's 1928 production of *Konjunktur* (p. 190). The inner motivation of this borrowing is fascinating, whether Weill had been combing through his untidy and mostly unlabelled collection of European manuscripts – which would have been highly uncharacteristic, according to Lenya – or whether (as the otherwise almost superfluous sketches for the *Street Scene* passage suggest) he was prompted by an unconscious memory. So averse was he to raking over the past that the borrowing cannot even be explained by reference to his friendly relationship with Piscator during the American years.

The *Konjunktur* borrowing is exceptional in itself as well as in its implications: even if the entire collection of sketches and drafts is taken into account, it is *Street Scene*'s only borrowing from a European work. No previous Broadway score of Weill's had staked so great a claim to independence in that respect, nor is there any, before or after, that seems so remote from his European experience. If, even in the narrow torchlight of bibliography, his remarks about the long lineage of *Street Scene* seem questionable, it is only fair to add that at least part of his fierce faith in the work has been vindicated by recent history. Of all his

American stage works it is the one that seemed best suited to the very different circumstances of the 1970s and early 1980s. Musicians, critics, and historians of the musical theatre may continue to prefer – indeed, greatly to prefer – other Broadway works of his. But the sacrifices *Street Scene* exacted from him, and the courage he and his producer Dwight Deere Wiman showed in the face of a disastrous try-out in Philadelphia, have been rewarded by the applause and affection of posterity.

16 March 1946, Brook House

Kiddush
(Sanctification)

[Hebrew prayer for the sanctification of wine]
For cantor, SATB chorus, and organ
Commissioned by Cantor David J. Putterman for the 75th Anniversary of
    the Park Avenue Synagogue, New York
Dedication: Albert Weill
Duration: 5 minutes

Manuscripts

ROUGH DRAFT

Five sides of a 2-sheet folding of F^{12} (remainder blank).

SCORE

Missing; ozalid copies of the holograph score show eleven sides of M^{12},
    headed: 'To my father/Kiddush/for/Tenor Solo, Chorus and Organ
    /by/Kurt Weill'; end date, 'Purim 1946/Brookhouse'.

Publication

Schirmer, 1951: in *Synagogue Music by Contemporary Composers*, an
    anthology of thirty-eight compositions for the Sabbath Eve Service
    (including works by Arthur Berger, Leonard Bernstein, Paul Dessau
    and Roy Harris), most of them commissioned by Cantor Putterman.

First Performance

10 May 1946, New York, Park Avenue Synagogue; Cantor, David
Putterman. This 75th Anniversary concert also included specially
commissioned works by Milhaud, Bloch, and David Diamond.

August 1946

A Flag is Born

'Palestine is Ours' – a Pageant
Text: Ben Hecht
Commissioned by the American League for a Free Palestine
(Unpublished)
Approximately fifteen musical numbers for standard orchestra, arranged
  by Isaac van Grove

A vision of the Jewish homeland is experienced by three survivors from the Nazi persecution – an elderly couple and a 16-year-old boy. They set forth in search of the reality. In the manner of *The Eternal Road* (p. 281) their experiences in the modern world are linked to, and explained by, biblical scenes.

Autographs and Other Sources

Mostly missing. No performance material has been traced, nor any holographs. The Library of Congress, Washington, has non-autograph piano–conductor scores (date-stamped 21 November 1946) of four numbers: 'Opening', 'Temple Music', and 'Interlude' are arrangements from *The Eternal Road*; 'Temple Music' is labelled 'No. 13', and 'Interlude' 'No. 14'. The fourth item, 'Partisan Finale', has no number.

Sole Performance

5 September 1946, New York, Alvin Theater; director Luther Adler, designer Robert Davison, conductor Isaac van Grove; with Paul Muni, Quentin Reynolds, Mario Berini, Celia Adler, Marlon Brando (as the boy), George Baxter, Gregory Morton, Tom Emlyn Williams, Jonathan Harris, and Steve Hill.

Notes

The souvenir programme includes the credit 'Music arranged by Isaac van Grove' beneath the main credit to Weill. Only one of the four piano–conductor scores in the Library of Congress gives the composer's name: 'Temple Music' bears the legend 'Music by Kurt Weill arranged by Isaac van Grove'. The question of authorship arises only with the 'Partisan Finale', an admirable piece, which treats ideas of obviously ethnic origin in a manner somewhat akin to that of Bartók in his early piano pieces *For Children*. It has no parallel in Weill's music of the 1940s. Considering that whatever time he devoted to *A Flag is Born* had to be snatched from *Street Scene* – which he was in the midst of – he could well be forgiven for taking to *The Eternal Road* yet again. References in Hecht's copy of the script to traditional Jewish music include the Kaddish Yisgadal, which Weill had already arranged in 1943 for *We Will Never Die*.

July 1947

Come up from the Fields, Father

For voice and piano
Text: Walt Whitman
(Unpublished)
Duration: 3 minutes

Autographs

SKETCHES

Eight sides of K^{12} and F^{12}.

FINAL COPY

Eleven sides of C^{12}; various pencil annotations in another hand.

First Performance (Recording)

William Horne (tenor) and Adam Garner (piano) recorded the song for
Concert Hall Records in 1947. The recording was released on the fourth
side of a 2-disc album; the first three sides carried the *Three Walt Whitman
Songs* (see p. 320). The song was written specifically for the recording.

Posthumous Arrangement

In 1956 Carlos Surinach orchestrated the song for the same forces Weill
had used in his orchestration of the *Three Walt Whitman Songs*.

July 1947 – January 1948/July–August 1948, Brook House

Love Life

Vaudeville in two parts
Book and Lyrics: Alan Jay Lerner
Cast: in Act I: Susan Cooper, Sam Cooper, Elizabeth Cooper, Mary Jo,
    George Crockett, Jonathan Anderson, Charlie Hamilton, Hank; in later
    acts: their descendants and counterparts; throughout: vaudevillians
Orchestra: Reed I (cl. alto sax.). Reed II (cl. bcl. alto sax.). Reed III (fl. cl.
    tenor sax. picc.). Reed IV (tenor sax. cl. ob.). Reed V (baritone sax. bsn.
    fl. cl.) 3tpt. 2tbn. tba. pno. glock. vib. mdln. gtr. bjo. acdn. timp.
    perc. str. without vlas

Love Life examines the life-cycle of an American marriage by dividing it into seven
'phases' and transposing each phase one historical era (or more) ahead of its

predecessor. Developments on the personal level can thus be shown as consequences or reflections of those on the social and economic levels. When Susan and Sam Cooper first set up home in the New England of 1791, their values are those of the close-knit, hard-working, and God-fearing community to which they belong. The disruption of that multiple harmony begins with the transition from a rural to an industrial economy. It continues, stage by stage and era by era, until the mid-twentieth century finds Susan and Sam divorced, alienated, and seemingly blind to the realities of their own situation and that of the society to whose opportunism and vulgar materialism both have surrendered. Each step in their downward progress has been introduced and commented upon by a vaudeville act that purports to be ironically detached from dramatic time and place. Yet the very nature of the song-and-dance routines involves the vaudevillians in the social and market forces they decry; for theirs is the voice of popular culture, and the debasement of that culture is part of the story. The decisive collapsing together of vaudeville and drama occurs in the penultimate 'Locker Room' scene, where the confined space and the highly combustible subject matter ensure that the explosive effect of the satire is very much greater than the force applied. With the partition walls demolished, the protagonists of the drama can themselves enter the final Minstrel Show, and see it for the cynical confidence trick it is. Recognizing in its stridently advertised panaceas a startling resemblance to their own illusions and fantasies, they begin, in the dawning light of reality, to edge towards the rediscovery of long-forgotten truths, as the curtain falls.

1   Overture

PART I

Vaudeville 1
  2a   Magician's entrance
  2b   The Magician
  2c   Magician's exit

Scene i: The Coopers, Mayville, Connecticut, 1791
  3a   'Who is Samuel Cooper?' (Mary Jo, Jonathan, Charlie, Hank, Women)
  3b   'My name is Samuel Cooper' (Sam)
  4   'Here I'll Stay' (Susan and Sam)

Vaudeville 2
  5   'Progress' (The Go-Getters)

Scene ii: The Farewell, Mayville, 1821
  6   'I Remember it Well' (Susan and Sam)
  7a   'A Home of Our Own' (Susan and Men)
  7b   'Green-up Time' (Susan and Women)
  7c   'Green-up Time' Polka

Vaudeville 3
  8   'Economics' (Black quartet)
  9   'Susan's Dream' (Black quartet)

Scene iii: The New Baby, Mayville, 1857
[No music]

Vaudeville 4
  10   'Mother's Getting Nervous' (Trapeze Artist and The Three Tots)
  10a   Foxtrot variations of 10

Discarded Scene: Mayville Square, 1896 (replaced by Scene iv)

11z   Suffragette Meeting (Joe the Cop; Kate Burgess, the Curator's
          daughter; Susan, Lonella, Mrs Vander, her maid Jane, Burgess,
          Suffragettes, Men)
11za   'Cop's Serenade' (Joe, Kate)
11zb   Plotting Scene (Susan, Jane, Mrs Vander and maid, Lonella, Men)
11zc   'Can't we have a rally?' (Susan)
11zd   'Viva the women!' (Suffragettes, Men)
11ze   'Cop's Lament' (Joe)
11zf   'We're Taking Over Now' (Suffragettes)

Scene iv: The Coopers' Home, Early 1890s

12   'My Kind of Night' (Sam)
13y   Csárdás (Susan and Women's Club);
          replaced by 14y 'Love'; replaced by:
14   'Women's Club Blues' (Susan and Women)

Vaudeville 5

15x   Love Song (Hobo); replaced by:
15   Reprise of 8 (Ventriloquist and dummy)

Discarded Scene: Temperance League

16y   Drinking Song

Scene v: Cruise Liner during Prohibition

17   'There's nothing Left for Daddy but the Rumba' (Night Club Singer)
18   'I'm Your Man' (Sam and Men)
19   'You Understand Me So' (Susan, a Lover, Sam)
19a   Ending (reprise of 18)

PART II

Vaudeville 6

20   Madrigal: 'Ho, Billy O!'

Scene vi: Radio Night in the Coopers' New York Apartment

21z   'Where do I belong?' (Susan); replaced by:
22   'Is it him or is it me?' (Susan)

Vaudeville 7

23x   The Locker Room (four soloists, quartet, masseur, tumblers);
          replaced by:
24   Punch and Judy Divorce (ballet)

Scene vii: A Hotel Room

25   'This is the Life' (Sam)

Finale: A City Street – A Minstrel Show

26   The Minstrel Show
26a   'We're sellin' sunshine' (Interlocutor and Minstrels)
26b   'Madame Zuzu' (The Misses Horoscope and Mysticism)
26c   'Takin' No Chances on Nothing'' (Mr Cynic)
26d   'Mr Right' (Girl and Susan)
26e   'Reality!' (Interlocutor and Minstrels)
26f   Ending (Sam and Susan)

FURTHER UNPUBLISHED MATERIAL

27z   'Baby' [adapted from *Street Scene 29zc*; unlikely to have been intended
      for Scene iii, which is very different in tone]
28z   'Mr Right and Miss Dream' [titled but without text; possibly an early
      version of *26d*, but musically unrelated to it]

Note 1

A typed draft of the lyrics of 'Love Song' (*15x*) bears the original title,
'Ocean Song'. Though it is not a love song in the conventional sense it
has more claim to its new title than does the show itself to the title *Love
Life* (though Lerner's working title, *A Dish for the Gods*, was hardly
preferable).

Autographs

SKETCHES AND DRAFTS

The first of two large batches of intermingled sketches and drafts covers
224 pages of Sch^{12}. The draft of 'Here I'll Stay' (*4*) is dated 23 August, and
that of 'Progress' 26 August. The second batch, comprising 80 pages of
F^{12} and three of Sch^{24}, includes the following datings:

28 August	'Cop's Serenade' (*11a*)
31 August	'Cop's Serenade', refrain (*11a*)
3 September	Plotting Scene [false start] (*11b*)
4 September	Plotting Scene (*11b*)
5 September	'Viva the women!' (*11d*)
5 September	'Cop's Lament' (*11e*)
8 September	'You Understand Me So' (*19*)
10 September	'Green-up Time' (*7b*)
17 September	'Baby' (*27*)
20 September	'Susan's Dream' (*9*)
1 October	'Economics' (*8*)
10 October	'We're Taking Over Now' (*11f*)
17 October	'Mother's Getting Nervous' (*10*)

The six items comprising the discarded number *11* (Suffragette Scene) are
nearly complete, in general outline and most details, on 41 pages. Item
11zc is the only one without a date or title, and is on different paper
(Sch^{12}); the notation of the first bar indicates that some preceding music
is missing, though the continuity is clear from one of the sketches. The
lyrics throughout the scene are not fully written out, but a complete text
is in WLA.

A batch of sketches on 20 pages of K^{12} includes some jottings for the
1948 version of *Down in the Valley*, and a square-dance setting of 'Green-
up Time' (*7c*), which is closely related to the arrangement of 'Hop up, my
ladies!' in *Down in the Valley*. Conversely, the sketches for the 1948
version of that work include a few jottings for *Love Life*.

The ballet scene 'Punch and Judy Get a Divorce' postdates the try-out.
Nine pages of a 12-page folding of Sch^{12} carry a pencil draft headed

'Ballet-Music'. It bears little relation to the final version (which was assembled by Irving Schlein). It is, however, a unique patchwork of borrowings:

'Organum' motif from *The River is Blue* (*31*) and *One Touch of Venus*;
Canonic 'hurry music' from *The River is Blue* and 'Salute to France';
Beginning of the 'Faulheit' section of *Die sieben Todsünden*;
Cancan (*10*) from *Der Kuhhandel*; 'War Music' (*18*) from *Die Bürgschaft*.

All these items are in their original keys. The appearance of the manuscript suggests that the entire compilation was written from memory; and this impression seems to be confirmed by a rough sketch (two pages of Sch^{12}) of the oldest of the five quotations – the *Bürgschaft* music, composed some fifteen years earlier. A similar feat of memory produced the 4-part invention for solo violins in *2b*, which was sketched, during rehearsal, on two pages of Sch^{12}: it is identical with a passage (probably already a quotation) in *The River is Blue* (*33a*). Among a collection of *Love Life* sketches was found a page of Pr^{12}, apparently torn from the notebook containing the drafts for *Lady in the Dark*. It carries a wordless version of *18x* ('Bats About You') from that work – a song of a type parodied in the *Love Life* 'Minstrel Show'.

REHEARSAL SCORE

With the exceptions noted below, the entire score is on M^{12}, without title page, signatures, or consecutive pagination. There are 278 pages of manuscript. *2a* and part of *23x* are missing, but exist in dyeline copies. There are two versions of *7b* – the earlier of them copyright 1947 and written on Cb^{12} (as is *19*), with a heading in another hand, giving the work's original title, *A Dish for the Gods*. Of the three versions of *13y*, the first has no title or lyrics, the second is entitled 'Csárdás', and the third, entitled 'Love', has a lengthy middle section based on the *Marie Galante* tango. The introduction to *10* is written on a leaf of F^{12}, and that to *22* on a leaf of Sch^{12}. The music for the 'Punch and Judy' ballet (*24*) was compiled by Irving Schlein and a piano score is in his hand. Apart from using section 5 of Weill's draft (with the result that the war music from *Die Bürgschaft* received its first and, to date its only, American stage performances, incognito, in a Broadway theatre) it is entirely based on motifs from *Love Life*.

FULL SCORE

The score is written on M^{20} ozalid paper. Neither the original nor any copies of *15* have been traced. The remainder of the autograph is complete on 595 pages. Numbers *7c*, *10a*, and *23*, and the central Boogie-woogie section of *14*, were orchestrated by Irving Schlein, and are in his hand on a further 126 pages.

First Performances

13 September 1948, Boston, Shubert Theatre; 7 October 1948, New York, 46th Street Theater; production by Cheryl Crawford, staged by Elia Kazan; conductor Joseph Littau, designed by Boris Aronson, costumes by Lucinda Ballard, choreography by Michael Kidd; with Nanette Fabray (Susan), Ray Middleton (Sam), Cheryl Archer (Elizabeth), Johnny Stewart (Johnny), Jay Marshall (Magician), Victor Clarke (Interlocutor), Sylvia Stahlman (Miss Ideal), and dancers including Melissa Hayden and Arthur Partington.

Publication

Chappell, 1948: sheet-music versions of *4, 7b, 8, 9, 15x, 22, 25* and *26d*. *Dramatic licences and performance materials*: present (1986) availability – KWF (USA, Britain, German-speaking territories).

Note 2

A mere list of scenes and numbers, together with a synopsis of the action, already help convey a salient fact that is not to be gleaned from the contemporary press or from the few scattered references in Broadway histories and the recent Weill literature: dramaturgically, *Love Life* is much the most ambitious of Weill's Broadway shows, *Street Scene* included. Although it does not seek to emulate the continuity or the operatic pretensions of *Street Scene*, it represents a formidable challenge to every claim that Weill made for that work, not least in its relationship – indeed, its intimate relationship – to his European experience; but also, paradoxically, in its Americanness, which in thought and feeling is as far removed from what Weill was seeking in *Street Scene* as it was from the ethos of Maxwell Anderson or, for that matter, Moss Hart. Without presuming to enter the world of 'serious' music as defined by the various factions in the American League of Composers, the Weill of *Love Life* approaches, for the first and only time, the narrowest section of that almost uncrossable borderland between his notions of Broadway and those of Marc Blitzstein. Significantly, it was beyond Broadway that the influence of *Love Life* first made itself felt, and, moreover, in a work dedicated to Blitzstein – the one-act opera *Trouble in Tahiti* by Leonard Bernstein. In Broadway terms *Love Life* was perhaps twenty-five years ahead of its time, even after it had been stripped of the crucial Locker Room number and its lyrical counterpart 'Love Song' – not to mention the remarkable 'Suffragette' scene. Without such sacrifices, and a catchpenny title to compensate for them, *Love Life* would surely never have reached Broadway. That it was even moderately successful reflects great credit on all concerned.

19 November 1947, Brook House

Hatikvah

Arrangement for orchestra of the Israeli National Anthem
Commissioned by the American Committee for the Weitzmann Institute
  of Science
(Unpublished)
Orchestra: 3.2.3.2.   4.3.3.1.   timp. harp. perc.(SD, BD, cym. tam-tam).
  str.

Autograph

SKETCH

Two pages Sch^{12}, short score.

FULL SCORE

In the possession of the Jewish National and University Library,
Jerusalem; nine pages of Sch^{24}, end date 'Nov. 19 1947'; the title sheet
(also Sch^{24}) reads 'Hatikvah/Orchestrated by Kurt Weill'.

First Performance

25 November 1947, at the Waldorf-Astoria Hotel, New York, by the
Boston Symphony Orchestra, conductor Serge Koussevitzky, as part of a
concert at a Testimonial Dinner on the occasion of Chaim Weizmann's
73rd birthday.

April 1948

Down in the Valley

[Folk-opera in one act, mainly for non-professional production]
Libretto: Arnold Sundgaard
Duration: 35 minutes
Cast: singing roles: Brack Weaver (tenor or high baritone), Jennie Parsons
  (lyric soprano), Thomas Bouché (bass), Leader/Preacher (baritone);
  SATB chorus, narrating and commenting; other roles: Peters, Jennie's
  father, two men, two women
Orchestra: 2.1.2(2sax.).1.   2.2.2.0.   gtr. pno. perc. str. without vlas

A village in the American South, time unspecified. Jennie is in love with Brack,
but is fancied by the sinister Bouché – to whom her father is looking for help in his
present financial difficulties. Arriving drunk at a village dance, Bouché becomes

involved in a fight with Brack, and is killed. Brack is tried and condemned for murder. On the eve of his execution he escapes from prison to spend his last hours with Jennie.

Note

The eight scenes are linked by narrative choruses, each based on the folk melody 'Down in the Valley'. The spoken dialogue, which was unaccompanied in the 1945 version (p. 348), has the same kind of underpinning as in *Street Scene*. These melodramas and narrative choruses frame the eight set pieces listed below. 2 and 3 are additions to the 1945 version; all revisions are tabulated by John Graziano in KK.ANO, pp. 317–19.

1   Introduction and Chorus: 'Down in the Valley'

Scene i: Birmingham Gaol
2   'Where is the one who will mourn me when I'm gone?' (Brack)

Scene ii: Parsons's House
3   'Brack Weaver, my true love' (Jennie)
4   'The Lonesome Dove' (Jennie)

Scene iii: In the Church
5   'The Little Black Train' (chorus)

Scene iv: Outside the Church
6   'Hop up, my ladies' (Brack, Jennie)

Scene v: In front of Parsons's House

Scene vi: The Shadow Creek Café
7   'Hoe-Down' (Jennie, Brack, Bouché, chorus)

Scene vii: In front of Parsons's House
7a   Reprise of 4

Scene viii: Birmingham Gaol
8   'Down in the Valley' (Jennie, chorus)

Autographs

SKETCHES AND DRAFTS

Missing (see p. 349) except for 1948 additions. These are sketched on twelve sides of K^{12} and F^{12}, and five of Sch^{24} (where they are intermingled with jottings for the 'Minstrel Show' in *Love Life*).

FULL SCORE [LPA, New York]

165 pages of C^{22}, dated at the end, '22 April'.

Publication

Schirmer, 1948: vocal score, with preface by the composer.

First Performance

15 July 1948, Bloomington, Indiana University Auditorium; conductor Ernst Hoffmann, director Hans Busch, designer Wolfgang Roth; with James Welch (Brack), Marion Bell (Jennie), Charles Campbell (Bouché).

February–March/August–September 1949, Brook House

Lost in the Stars

A Musical Tragedy
After Alan Paton's novel *Cry the Beloved Country*
Book and Lyrics by Maxwell Anderson
Duration: full evening; 60 minutes music
Cast: singing roles: Leader, Stephen Kumalo, Linda, Irina, Alex, Villager, chorus; other roles: Grace Kumalo, Absalom Kumalo, James Jarvis and his sons Edward and Arthur
Orchestra: Reed I (alto sax. fl. cl.). Reed II (tenor sax. ob. ca. cl.). Reed III (alto sax. cl. bcl.)   tpt.   pno. harp, perc. 2vla. 2vlc. db.

South Africa, 1949. The Reverend Stephen Kumalo's search for his son Absalom, who has gone to Johannesburg to earn money for his education, but has fallen into bad company; Absalom's involvement in a burglary and his arrest for the murder of Arthur Jarvis; the agony of Stephen and of Arthur's father James, a lifelong supporter of the black people; Absalom's repentance and his refusal to perjure himself; his unfair trial, and his execution; the final understanding reached by Stephen and James Jarvis.

In the following schedule, the scenes follow the 1950 edition.

ACT I

1   The Hills of Ixopo' (Leader and chorus)
1a   Chorus exit

Scene i: Stephen Kumalo's House
2x   'The Little Tin God'; replaced by:
2   'Thousands of Miles' (Stephen)
2a   Incidental music

Scene ii: Ndotsheni Railway Station
3   Train to Johannesburg (Leader and chorus)
3a   Change of Scene

Scene iii: John Kumalo's Tobacco Shop in Johannesburg

Scene iv: Factories, Houses and Parole Office in Johannesburg
4   The Search
4a   Change of Scene

Scene v: Stephen's Shantytown Lodging
5   'The Little Gray House' (Stephen and chorus)

Scene vi: A Dive in Shantytown
6   'Who'll Buy?' (Linda)
7x   'Gold' (chorus and dancers)
8a   Change of Scene

Scene vii: Irina's Hut
8   'Trouble Man' (Irina)

Scene viii: Arthur Jarvis's Kitchen
9a   'Murder in Parkwold' (chorus)

Scene ix: Arthur Jarvis's Library
9b   Change of Scene

Scene x: Street
9c   Fear! (pantomime; chorus)
9d   Change of Scene

Scene xi: Prison
10a   Change of Scene

Scene xii: Stephen's Shantytown Lodging
11x   'The Shadowy Glass' (Stephen and chorus); replaced by:
12   'Lost in the Stars' (Stephen and chorus)

ACT II

13   Entr'acte (orchestral reprises of 12 and 6)
Drop: Johannesburg
14   'The Wild Justice' (Leader and chorus)

Scene i: Kumalo's Tobacco Shop

Scene ii: Stephen's Soliloquy
15x   Soliloquy (Stephen); replaced by:
15   'O Tixo, Tixo, Help Me!' (Stephen)

Scene iii: Arthur Jarvis's Doorway
      [No music]

Scene iv: Irina's Hut
16   'Stay Well' (Irina)
16a   Change of Scene

Scene v: The Courtroom
17a   Change of Scene (reprise of 14)

Scene vi: The Prison
17   'Cry the Beloved Country' (Leader and chorus)

Scene vii: Stephen's Chapel
18   'Big Mole' (Alex)
19a   Incidental Music
20   'A Bird of Passage' (Villager and congregation)

Scene viii: Stephen's Home
21   'Four o'clock' (melodrama)
22a   Reprise of 2

Autographs

SKETCHES AND ROUGH DRAFTS

None of Weill's previous musicals left so few sketches and so little unused material. Twenty-two sides of Po^{12}, eight of Sch^{24} and Sc^{24}, and one each of K^{20} and O^{12} contribute only one idea that is not in the final score: on the O^{12} sheet is the rough draft of a 'valse lente' (so headed). This, like several numbers in the final score, is a borrowing from *Ulysses Africanus* (see p. 309).

DRAFTS

Eight sides of Po^{12} and ten of F^{12} carry drafts that are intermediate, rather than preliminary or final. The main draft (with interspersed sketches) covers 118 sides of Sch^{12}. It contains most of the final score, but little extra – doubtless a reflection of the fact that much of the groundwork had been done ten years earlier, for *Ulysses Africanus*. There are no drafts of 15 ('O Tixo, Tixo, Help Me!') and none of the final versions of 2 ('Thousands of Miles'), 5 ('The Little Gray House'), or 20 ('A Bird of Passage'). Weill's correspondence indicates that 15 was composed after discussions with the director, and according to his prescriptions; presumably the same was the case with the final versions of 2, 5 and 20, which were to be made more popular in style – very much more, in the case of 20, which is here a dignified and somewhat austere piece in a modal idiom far removed from that of the outer sections of the final version.

A sketch for *10a* on the first page of a sheet of Km^{10} was made during or immediately after a late rehearsal with orchestra; on side *d* are a few notes about the rehearsal.

REHEARSAL SCORE

248 pages of M^{12}, unbound and without title page or signatures, give all the main numbers as published, together with earlier versions, discarded numbers and a few incidental passages. The autographs of the remaining incidental music and the reprises are written in pencil on various papers (mostly MM^{14}), and inserted in the dyeline master copy of the vocal score, as used by the engraver. This dyeline score, which is in WLA, has autograph corrections and emendations throughout. Weill completed his work on it in hospital shortly before his death, and that, of course, lends it a special interest. Nevertheless the M^{12} transparencies are much the more important document. Vocal and choral numbers *1–8* and *10–11* have been numbered (and titled) by the composer as in the above list, except that 'The Little Tin God' is No. 2, and 'Thousands of Miles', which replaced it, is unnumbered, as are the remaining numbers. Presumably the complex of ostinato pieces that forms the present *9* is a substitute for an earlier and missing number. Additions to the score can be deduced from the pagination (red crayon, non-autograph), which includes only

the original numbers, and resorts to supplementary systems for interpolations. Numbers *4*, *5*, *8*, *11x*, *12*, *15* and *22a* each exist in two versions. A non-autograph insertion in *8* alters the final cadence of the introduction and transposes the entire refrain down a tone. There are three versions of *22a* (the closing reprise): one as published, and two using 'Lost in the Stars'. *15x* (Soliloquy) follows the predominantly meditative tone of both versions of *11x* – which in effect it replaced. But in response to the director's request for a more 'dramatic' number, Anderson converted the philosophical text into a prayer and Weill recomposed it as *15*. A further suggestion – this time from the conductor – led to a 3-bar change at the climax, inserted in the master copy.

FULL SCORE

Missing, except for *2x*, *7x*, fragments of a reprise of *12*, and the first version of *4* – all written on K²⁰ (eighty-seven pages). A photostat copy of the entire score as used for the first production is in WLA. There are 359 autograph pages. The jazz song 'Who'll Buy?' is in the hand of Irving Schlein, and was presumably scored by him.

First Production

30 October 1949, New York, the Music Box Theatre; production by the Playwrights' Company, staged by Rouben Mamoulian; conductor Maurice Levine, sets by George Jenkins; with Todd Duncan (Stephen), Leslie Banks (James Jarvis), Inez Matthews (Irina), Warren Coleman (John Kumalo), Herbert Coleman (Alex), Sheila Gayse (Linda).

Publication

Chappell, 1949: sheet-music versions of *2*, *5*, *8*, *12*, *16*, *18*.
Chappell, 1950: vocal score.
Dramatic licences and performance materials: present (1986) availability – Rodgers & Hammerstein Music Library (USA), KWF (Britain, German-speaking territories).

Notes

Musically, *Lost in the Stars* owes at least five of its numbers, (*2x*, *5*, *8*, *12* and *16*), and much of its character, to the abortive *Ulysses Africanus*. Despite its serious theme and its classicizing choruses, it was addressed to a broad public, and reached it.

January–March 1950

Huckleberry Finn

Unfinished musical play after Mark Twain's novel
Book and lyrics: Maxwell Anderson

Note 1

According to the composer's diary, Weill and Anderson drafted the
scenario between 7 and 9 January 1950. The lyrics for the opening chorus
were finished four days later. Musical sketches for that number (and for
others) may have been made later in the month, but the date of
composition is given in the diary as 15 February – two days after the
diary's only other composition date, that of the song 'Come In, Mornin''.
Towards the end of February Weill had a severe attack of psoriasis. His
health remained poor during the early part of March. When Anderson
visited him on 16 March he was in bed, but had finished the 'Catfish
Song'. That night, however, his heart condition became acute. Transferred to a local hospital on the 19th, he made a slight recovery, but on the
23rd he was moved to a major New York hospital for intensive treatment.
After another relapse there was a marked improvement. Anderson
visited him again and there were further talks about *Huckleberry Finn*.
According to Lenya, Weill had time to add some further sketches before
the final crisis. He died on 3 April, leaving the following (unnumbered)
items in rough draft:

1. 'River Chanty'
2. 'Come In, Mornin'' ('Come in, Sun')
3. 'Apple Jack'
4. 'This Time Next Year'
5. 'Catfish Song'

Autographs

SKETCHES

Sides *a* and *d* of a sheet of Sch²⁴ carry preliminary memos and sketches,
all of which are taken up in the drafts. Further sketches follow each of the
drafts of *2*; and a second version of *4* is fully sketched on *c* of the sheet
carrying the draft of that number.

DRAFTS

There are thirteen sides of manuscript, all with the appearance of having
been very swiftly written. Each number is on a separate sheet of Sch²⁴,
and is titled. There are two versions of *2* (which Anderson titled 'Come
in, Sun'); the first consists only of the refrain, the second has a variant of

the same refrain followed (side *b*) by a 24-bar paragraph on the words 'Never was a place more comfortable than a raft'. Anderson's ink holograph of the lyrics (in WLA) gives this as the second of the two 'verses', to which 'Come in, Mornin'' acts as refrain. What appears to be a double bar at the 'end' of Weill's holograph – that is, at the end of the 'verse' – is deceptive, and all the more so since no other draft ends with a double bar. In general, comparison with any final drafts of numbers for earlier Broadway shows confirms that the *Huckleberry Finn* drafts were meant to appear tentative, and are so.

ADDITIONAL LYRICS

Anderson's 2-page pencil manuscript of lyrics entitled 'Our Private Spring' has a note in ink in Lenya's hand indicating that it belongs to *Huckleberry Finn*, though on internal grounds this seems questionable. Anderson's draft of the opening river scene is also in WLA, and is written in ink on the *verso* sides of two leaves of Playwrights' Company letterhead.

Posthumous Publication

Chappell, 1954: separate sheet-music edition; all five numbers, edited by Lys Symonette, issued separately under their individual titles and with no reference to *Huckleberry Finn* either on the cover or within – only in the back-page listing.

Note 1

The published versions of the songs are transposed to more convenient keys. They also and necessarily undergo varying degrees of creative editing:

'River Chanty'

The final return of the opening strain is editorial.

'Come in, Mornin''

The two slightly different versions have been amalgamated.

'Apple Jack'

Harmonic alterations in the penultimate bars of both the verse and the refrain; first melody note in bar 5 is misprinted F sharp instead of G sharp.

'This Time Next Year'

The first four bars are editorial, as is the added sixth in the final chord.

'Catfish Song'

The first four bars are editorial, as is the added second in the tonic harmony of the next two bars.

Posthumous Orchestrations and First Performance

In 1951 Robert Russell Bennett arranged three of the songs for voice and orchestra. The first performance was given in New York on 22 March 1952 by the orchestra of the Young Men's Hebrew Association conducted by Maurice Levine. The two remaining songs were orchestrated some years later.

Note 2

The aura conventionally associated with the last work of notable artists is of just the sort that Weill disavowed in everything he wrote after the Second Symphony and *Die sieben Todsünden*. To look for it in the *Huckleberry Finn* songs would be especially futile. It is true that for the first time in his career he had actually embarked on the musical adaptation of a literary classic, rather than merely considered doing so (as he frequently had). But the qualities that account for the novel's great popularity are – as Hollywood was quick to discover – easily detachable from those complexities of tone and meaning that have earned it such high esteem in literary circles. The latter were not Weill's immediate concern. In an interview published in a Rockland County newspaper on 4 March 1950 he disclaimed any operatic ambitions, and described the work as 'essentially a light musical comedy'. Such, indeed, is the impression left by the few numbers he drafted (though it is important to remember that a collection of attractively 'light' numbers was a priority with regard to financial backing, and that early press interviews are part of the search for such backing, and therefore not an appropriate place for advertising any serious intentions). If there is any musical hint of the darker side of Twain's novel, it is in the opening 'River Chanty'; and if the E flat minor ostinato of the published version seems also to convey some kind of valediction on Weill's part, it is perhaps because of a very distant echo from *Die Bürgschaft* and the E flat minor music of the death scene in Act III. But in such cases Weill's unconscious memories seldom played him false, least of all with regard to key-colour and its expressive connotations. For him the river's timeless ostinato was not – as the printed page would have it – in E flat, but in C.

Miscellaneous
Unidentified Sketches

(Approximate datings are inferred from musical and scribal evidence.)

1927–8

A leaf of B³⁰ carries, *recto*, a complete (36-bar) foxtrot refrain in C major, and verso a 14-bar introduction based on the notes H–E–D–D–A, ending with a slurred upbeat to what was presumably to be a G major refrain.

1936[–9]

A much-folded sheet of onion-skin paper measuring 38 × 29 cms carries eleven unharmonized tunes, of which three are entitled respectively 'Dutch Polka', '3 Tambours' and 'Matrosen-Song – Curaçao'. The prevailing folk idiom of the tunes, the absence of any contemporary popular-song inflexions, and the recurrent rhythmic and metrical irregularities (one untitled tune having the mixed time signature 5/4, 6/4) suggest a date soon after Weill's arrival in America, as does the lapse into German. Only in *Knickerbocker Holiday* is Weill known to have used onion-skin paper before it came into general use after the Second World War, and neither the handwriting nor the musical content are consistent with a postwar date. At the earliest, the sketches might have been studies for *High Wind in Jamaica* (see p. 274); at the latest, for the 1939 'Songs of Discovery' (p. 308).

1937

A leaf of P¹² carries a 32-bar foxtrot in strictly commercial style; it is based, note for note, on 'The Song of Ruth' (*16a*) in *Der Weg der Verheissung*, and was probably intended for *You and Me* (to judge by the musical tone and the brand of manuscript paper).

1937[–9]

Ten sides of a folding of Pa¹⁴ (including one separated leaf) carry numerous brief sketches in popular style, and a complete refrain of a popular song beginning with the words 'It might have been another tale' and ending with what was presumably the title motif, 'Love being what it is'. Despite the presence of a musical motif used in *The River is Blue*, anticipations of *Davy Crockett* (*14a*) and *Knickerbocker Holiday* (*24*) suggest that these sketches belong to the early weeks of 1938 and contain at least some material relating to *You and Me*.

A leaf of F¹⁴ carries a 6-bar introduction and a 9-bar setting of the words 'Master of earth and waves, we have no altar . . . but accept from us this prayer'. Possibly intended for *The Common Glory*. A similar leaf – not the other half of the same sheet – carries, *recto*, two piano sketches, including an E flat major tune entitled 'Oh Mariner', and *verso*, four bars in C minor, headed 'Soldier'.

1943–8

(a) A leaf of K¹² carries *recto* a rough sketch for a dance and, *verso*, a 4-bar bridge formula. Although the dance is based on the melody of 'Farewell, Goodbye' (*Johnny Johnson*) the style and one musical motif suggest *One Touch of Venus*.

(b) A leaf measuring 30 × 24 cms, with staves on one side only, carries two sketches in popular style. Further sketches of a similar kind are on a leaf torn from a sheet of K¹² and headed in another hand (Edward Cole's?) 'Love Life?'

(c) A sheet of K¹² has the autograph heading 'Dinner Table' and then, in Lenya's hand, 'J'attends un navire'. It is in fact a complete arrangement of that song, for solo accordion. Possibly intended for a discarded scene in *Salute to France*, but certainly dating from the 1940s, to judge by the paper and the handwriting.

Doubtful and
Chimerical Works

The 'lost' Symphony of 1920 noted in the work-list that follows the present author's Weill entry in *Grove's Dictionary of Music and Musicians* (Sixth Edition) is not lost: it existed only in the minds of those of us whose first attempts to decipher the German script of Weill's postcard to his father of 10 December 1920 (WLRC) led to the conclusion that it was 'meine Sinfonie' which Weill had just finished and was pleased with. The recently discovered correspondence in RWC, and a further inspection of the postcard, confirm that Weill was in fact announcing the completion of 'mein Vortrag', 'my talk'. Although he says he has been working in the Staatsbibliothek 'to keep warm', and for the same reason could equally well have been writing music there, the library's official purposes were better served by a talk than by a symphony. In a letter to his brother Hanns from Berlin of 3 July 1919, Weill mentions the 'Mahler talk' he is planning, and the problem that he can work on it only in holiday time, but will then be in places (including Dessau) where he will not have access to the material he needs – 'especially the symphonies'. Like the Beethoven talk he prepared eighteen months later, the Mahler one would have been intended for the Jewish cultural circle in Halberstadt. His brother was responsible for the circle's musical activities.

In interviews with American journalists during the period 1937–41 Weill occasionally alluded to his musical beginnings, but the details in their published form are unreliable. One example is the 'opera' supposedly based on Sudermann's *Das hohe Lied* (see p. 125), which is mentioned by Louis M. Simon in his *New York Times* feature 'Up the Rungs from Opera' (13 April 1941). Another, from the same source, is Weill's reported claim to have orchestrated parts of Engelbert Humperdinck's opera *Gaudeamus*. Weill studied composition with Humperdinck at the Berlin Hochschule für Musik in 1918–19, and *Gaudeamus* was his master's last opera. The holograph full score (in the Humperdinck Archive in the music library of Frankfurt University) has the end date 4 August 1917 – some six months before Weill left Dessau for his studies in Berlin. There is no sign of any other hand than Humperdinck's in the score of the opera, or in the Overture that he wrote in Berlin (Wannsee) in the summer of 1919.

One would hardly expect otherwise, even if the dates matched. Humperdinck was a fine craftsman, and it is inconceivable that he would have entrusted the orchestration of part of an opera to a young composer whose orchestral technique was as rudimentary as Weill's demonstrably was at the time when he began his studies at the Hochschule (see p. 112) or as fallible as it still was a year later (in the Suite in E – see p. 115). Weill's remark to Louis Simon was surely misreported: no doubt Humperdinck had given him the exercise of orchestrating one or two passages from the vocal score of *Gaudeamus* and comparing the results with his own versions.

Both for personal reasons and because of the cultural climate, Weill did not encourage serious interest in his European work during the 1940s – his few references to it in public are pointedly casual. After his death, Lenya became his apologist and brave advocate in countless interviews for the media. Her recollections of Weill's work during the two periods of their life together – that is, from 1925 to 1930, and again from 1937 to the end – were always vivid, and generally consistent with the facts. There is, however, one case where she is the sole authority for the existence of a particular score: in discussions with the present writer during the 1960s she maintained that Weill had written incidental music for Karlheinz Martin's staging of Büchner's *Dantons Tod* in September 1929 – a historic and, in Büchner's spirit, revolutionary production for the Berlin Volksbühne, with Hans Ruhmann as Danton and Walter Franck as Robespierre. Music is not mentioned in any press notices traced so far, but Lenya was not relying on hearsay, as she was obliged to do in her accounts of the opening night of *Happy End* on 2 September 1929: she was unable to attend that premiere (or the few performances that followed) because she was playing the role of Lucille in *Dantons Tod*, which opened one day earlier. It is just possible that Weill contributed to the Volksbühne production two or three anonymous arrangements of historically authentic material – for instance 'La Carmagnole' (see p. 187). But he would not have had much time to spare in August: it was only in that month that he began the orchestral score for *Happy End* (or so a letter to Hans Curjel of 2 August suggests).

Another Berliner Volksbühne production to which Weill is said to have contributed and in which Lenya played a supporting role was *Das Lied von Hoboken*. Directed by Heinz Dieter Kenter and designed by Caspar Neher, with Albert Hoerrmann, Leonhard Steckel, Hermann Speelmanns and Dolly Haas in the principal roles, it opened at the Theater am Bülowplatz on 30 March 1930 – just three weeks after the premiere of *Aufstieg und Fall der Stadt Mahagonny*. *Das Lied von Hoboken* was a free adaptation by Günther Weisenborn (1902–1969) of a play by Michael Gold, one of the many American writers who openly associated themselves with the struggles of the American Communist Party during the inter-war years. Weisenborn had made his name in 1928 with a pacifist play *U-Boot S 4*, and was an early recruit to Brecht's circle in Berlin.* In adapting Gold's play he followed the current post-*Dreigroschenoper* fashion and interpolated a few topical songs.

According to Lenya's recollections in the early 1960s, Weill had written the score for the play and composed one of the songs expressly for her. On 24 September 1963 Weisenborn replied to the present author's inquiry, and confirmed that Weill had written 'ein langes Chanson' entitled 'Tango Locarno', and that it had indeed been performed by Lenya. Further inquiries from Lenya prompted a letter of 28 November 1963 in which Weisenborn declared that there had been a misunderstanding, and that the song she had sung was 'Das Lied vom blinden Mädchen' (from which he quoted two verses from memory). Later in the letter he quoted a couplet from another of her songs, and declared that he had written 'only a few Chansons' for the play, and held out hope of finding 'das Manuskript der Lieder und des Stücks'. That was the end of the correspondence (of which copies are in WLA), but not of the problem, which was transformed if not entirely solved when the present author's researches in newspaper files and at the University of Cologne's Institut für Theaterwissenschaft revealed that the music for *Das Lied von Hoboken* had from the start been attributed to the Austrian-born composer and conductor Wilhelm Grosz (1894–1939), and that there was no mention of Weill's name in the press or in the Volksbühne programme.

It is possible – even, in the circumstances, probable – that Weill was the first composer whom the Volksbühne approached. In view of the pressure of work created by the *Mahagonny* premiere (and its aftermath), and in the light of his recent experiences over the Grossmann–Hessel *Apollo–Brunnenstrasse* (see p. 383), he may have declined immediately; or else he may, for Lenya's sake, have given his provisional assent. The latter possibility would increase the likelihood of a confusion in Lenya's mind and in Weisenborn's thirty years later. But in either case Grosz was a logical alternative. A pupil of Franz Schreker who had followed the tonal path of his younger contemporary Křenek and become increasingly

---

*The adaptation of Gorki's *Mutter* on which Weisenborn had collaborated with the Dramaturg of the Berliner Volksbühne, Günther Stark, was the basis of Brecht's *Die Mutter* (on which Weisenborn then collaborated, together with Eisler and Slatan Dudow). Weisenborn left Germany in 1933 but returned two years later and continued writing under a pseudonym. As a member of the Communist Resistance Movement 'Die rote Kapelle' he was arrested in 1942. After three years of imprisonment and extreme hardship he was freed by Russian troops. He settled in the Federal Republic, and in 1953 he published his classic account of the German Resistance Movement, *Der lautlose Aufstand* (Rowohlt, Hamburg). A different route was taken by Heinz Dieter Kenter, the director of *Das Lied von Hoboken*; see Joseph Wulf, *Theater und Film im Dritten Reich. Eine Dokumentation* (Hamburg, 1964), p. 154, for notes, and for an excerpt from Kenter's 1936 article 'Über Regieführung aus nationalsozialistischem Geist'.

influenced by American jazz, Grosz had settled in Berlin, where he collaborated with the left-wing writer and film critic Béla Balász on the dance-pantomime *Baby in der Bar*. Prior to his emigration in 1933 he was artistic director of the Ultraphone recording company. His works, like Weill's, were published by Universal Edition – not without success, especially in circles where Grosz was admired as an outspoken opponent of Schoenberg and his school. Having started his career several years earlier than Weill and taken a quite different path towards popular idioms, Grosz – to judge from his published works – was immune from his influence, but likely to be sympathetic to his aims, and unlikely to have written for *Das Lied von Hoboken* anything so far removed in style from Weill's jazz number in *Happy End*, 'Das Lied von der harten Nuss', that confusions between the two could not eventually have arisen in Lenya's mind, and Weisenborn's also.

Adjacent to every area of potential doubt about the authenticity of missing 'Weill' scores there is the near-certainty that the music itself would give the answer – provided it is not earlier than 1918, and provided it does not date from either of the two brief periods when Weill was experimenting – that is, with non-tonal structures in 1924–5, and with 'Tin Pan Alley' idioms in 1937–8. Identification might also be difficult whenever he was working strictly to order – as in a film studio – or when his decisions were influenced by an omnipotent director (e.g. Max Reinhardt) or a complaining producer (e.g. in *A Kingdom for a Cow*).

Today there is perhaps a greater chance of doubtful works being discovered than fictional ones being invented. Two songs credited to the mysterious team 'Jary/Weill' have been included in a recent two-disc Electrola album (IC 134–31 782/83M) devoted to archive recordings of Hilde Hildebrand, the star of Rudolf Nelson's last two pre-Hitler revues, *Es hat geklingelt* and *Etwas für Sie*. The two songs – 'Liebster' and 'Einsamkeit' – were recorded in 1935. A third Hildebrand number, 'Lächle noch einmal', is listed under 'Weill, Kurt' in Clough and Cuming's *The World's Encyclopaedia of Recorded Music*, vol. 1 (London, 1952). To judge from a copy examined in the BBC's Record Library in 1960 it belongs to the same period; and again the credit to Weill is without forename or initial. In the absence of any official, circumstantial, or autograph connection between Weill and the Hildebrand songs, we can either exclude all three songs from the Weill canon on the grounds of probability, or accept the challenge of deciding for or against their authenticity on the evidence of our ears.

In the latter case allowance must be made for the dance-band accompaniments, which are in the standard metropolitan revue and night-club idiom of the day. Similar examples from the repertory of Weill recordings show that such arrangements generally remove the more idiosyncratic harmonic and figurative detail, but preserve a recognizable melodic skeleton. In each of the Hildebrand songs there are cliché phrases that Weill himself might have used (and not only in a weak moment). But as soon as two or more phrases are strung together the dissimilarity is complete. The Hildebrand songs are effective examples of their kind; but their kind is Rudolf Nelson's or Mischa Spoliansky's, not Weill's.

The differences of character, language, and gesture between the Hildebrand songs and any song, however popular, that Weill released for publication or recording are far greater than the differences between, say, the 'September Song' and the 'Alabama Song', or indeed between the 'Alabama Song' and the chorale theme in the finale of the First Symphony. To distinguish the American Weill from the European is of critical importance so long as the process is confined to questions of musical language, tone, structure, and expressive aim. Once it ignores the elements in Weill's creative character that were ineradicable, the composer of the *Kleine Dreigroschenmusik* becomes indistinguishable from the composer of *Baby in der Bar*, and the Weill who wrote 'September Song' in New York in 1938 is upstaged by the 'Willy Grosz' who wrote 'The Isle of Capri' in London in 1934. In other words: incontrovertible evidence that the Hildebrand songs were by Weill would call for a more radical reassessment of his creative character than comparable evidence that every one of the *Dreigroschenoper* numbers was based on models dictated by Brecht to Franz Servatius Bruinier.

Projects:
An Outline*

With Weill, the shadowplay of projects discussed but never begun is framed by the fallen masonry of those begun but never completed, and the drama it conveys is quite distinct from that of the finished and unfinished works. Yet the entrances and exits must have been so numerous, and the appearances often so fleeting, that there can be no definitive record of them, nor any certainty that those of which a record exists were more significant than those of which we may never learn.

The beginnings are not quite as obscure as they were before 1983, when the Weill–Lenya Research Center acquired duplicates of part of a hitherto unknown collection of letters from Weill to his family – notably to Hanns, his musical brother. In a letter written to Hanns in 1917 (the rest of the date is not legible from the photostat copy) Weill comments as follows:†

> The poems by Franz Werfel (is he a Jew?) are really good. Admittedly, Bing advises me against setting them, but I want to have a try at it; perhaps it will be my first 'philosophical composition' in the manner of [Pfitzner's] *Palestrina*.

Werfel's first volume of verse, *Der Weltfreund* (Berlin, 1911), is one of the key works in the early history of Expressionist poetry, and like its two successors, *Wir sind* (Leipzig, 1913) and *Einander* (Leipzig, 1915), it contained much that was consciously oriented towards music. But the volume most likely to have attracted Weill and his brother in 1917 was a more substantial one, published in Leipzig that same year – Werfel's first retrospective collection, *Gesänge aus den drei Reichen. Ausgewählte Gedichte*.

At present we have no firm evidence that Weill proceeded with his plan, and at least one indication that he may not have done: memories of an early Werfel cycle would surely have been stirred by the collaboration

---

*Weill's projects are discussed in more detail, with fuller background and source references, in the author's forthcoming *Kurt Weill: A Documentary Biography*.
†The Kurt Weill Foundation for Music owns the copyright in Weill's letters. All quotations in the present essay appear by kind permission of the Foundation. Translations are the author's.

with Werfel on *Der Weg der Verheissung* and *The Eternal Road* during the mid-1930s, and yet there is no mention of anything of the kind in the numerous articles and interviews the collaboration gave rise to. While an idea that never took root could easily have been forgotten, even a half-finished work would surely have been called to mind two decades later and reported as some kind of anticipatory validation for the actual collaboration.

The reference to Werfel is the first sign of Weill's early acquaintance with Expressionist literature. The next is in an undated letter of 1919, where he compares a recent social drama *Das Gesetz* (Galsworthy's *Justice*?) to Else Lasker-Schüler's *Die Wupper*, much to the latter's advantage and rather as if it was an old favourite of his. While there is no implication that he had ever thought of it in a musical connection, *Die Wupper* is a logical link between Werfel and Johannes R. Becher, for whose 'Festspiel', *Arbeiter Bauern Soldaten*, Weill hoped in November 1920 to provide a score (see p. 129).

Nothing as yet is known of any unfulfilled projects during Weill's three years in Busoni's Masterclass. His first letter to Universal Edition (16 February 1924) mentions plans for a comic opera and a new string quartet. The 'opera' seems very swiftly to have become the *Pantomime* (see p. 154), but the quartet project remained in the air for more than a year: on 7 July 1925 Weill reported to UE that he was working on *Der neue Orpheus*, and that he would next write some piano pieces for Claudio Arrau and a string quartet for (Féri) Roth and his colleagues. But on 15 October – with *Der neue Orpheus* already finished – he tells UE that he is already working on *Royal Palace*, and has also 'begun' a ballet entitled *Maschinen* for Max Terpis, the ballet master at the Staatsoper unter den Linden in Berlin. There is no further word of *Maschinen* in the correspondence, and no trace of it elsewhere – except perhaps in a few motoric passages in the dance sections of *Royal Palace*, which Terpis choreographed.

The collaboration with Goll provided Weill with a bridge from the literary and musical salons of Berlin – notably Helene von Nostitz's – to those of Paris, where he already had an entrée thanks to Henri Prunières and his ISCM circle. If the bilingual Goll was the leading literary representative of the Paris–Berlin axis, the central one, and the *éminence grise*, was the diplomat, patron, and diarist Count Harry Kessler (1868–1958). Kessler had been a friend of Busoni, and may already have met Weill during the Masterclass years. Except perhaps through Goll, no further opportunity would have been likely to arise before April 1926, when Kessler left Germany for some fourteen months. The evidence suggests that the decisive meeting occurred soon after Kessler returned to Berlin in the second week of June 1927; for it was in that month that Weill reported to his publishers that Goll had talked to Diaghilev about *Royal Palace* and *Der neue Orpheus*, had given him the published scores, and was now proposing to discuss both works with Kessler (who had been a friend and adviser of Diaghilev since his collaboration in 1914 with Hofmannsthal on the scenario for Richard Strauss's *Josephslegende*).

Although Kessler had not been in Berlin during the brief period in March–April 1927 when the two Weill–Goll works were staged at the Staatsoper as part of a triple bill with Falla's *Master Peter's Puppet Show*, the manifest incongruity of the Falla was probably his excuse for suggesting to Diaghilev that he write a scenario for a new ballet by Weill. According to Richard Buckle in his *Diaghilev* (London, 1979, pp. 492, 581) Weill wrote to Diaghilev on 1 July 1927, expressing interest in the project.*

In his Weill biography *The Days Grow Short* (New York, 1980, pp. 101–3), Ronald Sanders overlooks the Goll connection and obscures the whole picture by confusing two separate episodes from Wolfgang Pfeiffer-Belli's edition of the Kessler diaries (*Tagebücher 1918–1937*: Frankfurt, 1961) – a fascinating volume, but highly selective, and furnished with only the barest minimum of editorial annotations. The opening episode cited by Sanders contains no mention of Weill, and is confined to two diary entries from February 1926. The first of these, dated 13 February, describes a voyeuristic evening in the Berlin home of the playwright Carl Vollmoeller, where Max Reinhardt and other eminent figures enjoy the company of half-a-dozen unclothed girls and the self-absorbed quasi-oriental dancing of Josephine Baker, wearing nothing but a pink muslin apron. Vollmoeller's girlfriend, dressed as a boy in dinner-jacket, then joins Baker in a dance – to the accompaniment of jazz records – which ends, horizontally, in an idyllic embrace.

Although Vollmoeller has already announced that he will, that very night, write a ballet for Baker and offer it to Reinhardt, Kessler now declares that the final embrace has inspired him to devise a pantomime based on the *Song of Songs*, with Baker ('dressed, or not dressed, in the manner of oriental antiquity') as the Sulamite, and Vollmoeller's girlfriend (in dinner-jacket) either as Solomon or as the Sulamite's young lover. The music for this pantomime, Kessler suggests, will be partly jazz and partly in the oriental style, 'perhaps by Richard Strauss'.

On 24 February Kessler invites Reinhardt, Vollmoeller and others to dinner, and describes to them the first scene of the pantomime, which he has already written. (Baker arrives at midnight, and is expected to dance for them in the library, but is embarrassed to do so in front of the ladies.) Four days later Kessler meets Strauss after a performance of *Die Frau ohne*

---

*There is no copy of the letter in WLA or WLRC. Footnote 72 on p. 581 of Buckle's *Diaghilev* gives the location of the original as follows: 'Bibliothèque Nationale, Opéra, Kochno collection'. Neither the Bibliothèque Nationale itself nor the library of the Paris Opéra were able to trace the letter when the author visited them in 1985; a year later the Kochno archives were acquired by the University and Cantonal Library in Lausanne.

Schatten, discusses *Josephslegende* with him (but not, it seems, his *Song of Songs*) and declines to join him for dinner as he is already expected *chez* Vollmoeller – where he arrives after midnight. Another *louche* scene awaits him, but this time Baker is sitting on a sofa munching Bockwurst and stoutly refusing to dance for anyone. Kessler leaves at 3 am, rather disgruntled. And apart from a solitary recollection of the initial evening, that is the end of Baker and the *Song of Songs* as far as the published diaries are concerned.

The first mention of Weill in the published diaries is dated 14 November 1927: Kessler writes that he had attended Helene von Nostitz's soirée that evening specifically in order to talk with Weill about what he calls 'my ballet' (but for some reason does not identify). Weill, however, sent word that he had been delayed by a rehearsal in Leipzig and could not see him until the following day. Helene von Nostitz invited them to tea on that day, but once again Weill was delayed, and the meeting finally took place in Kessler's own house at 7.30 the same evening. Weill told him that he would like to write the ballet score, but first would have to ask his publishers, as he had a commission from them(!) to write a large-scale opera, and would need permission to borrow two or three months for the ballet. Weill must already have known something about the ballet, for Kessler reports him as saying that he intended to have most of the music *sung* from behind the stage, with only a handful of instruments ('flute, saxophone' adds Kessler uncommunicatively). The instrumentation seems to have some bearing on the topic of the ballet, for Kessler went on to talk about the popular wind bands of Catalonia, and to play recordings of authentic sardanas which Weill had not heard before and was much impressed by. Was this a legacy of *Master Peter*, perhaps?

There is no further mention of the ballet project in the published diaries until 29 December 1928, when Diaghilev (who has not figured in the earlier diary entries about Weill) is said to have rejected 'as before' the idea of Weill as a suitable collaborator for Kessler, and to have added, 'Il faudra vous trouver un musicien.' That is the last the published diaries tell us about the project; eight months later, Diaghilev was dead.

Interesting though they are in their musical context, Kessler's references to Weill are not the stuff of which popular biographies are made. On the other hand every threadbare preconception about Weimar Berlin and Weill's relationship to it heightens the attractions of the previous Baker–Vollmoeller episodes, not least in the eyes of prospective film-makers, who are seldom concerned with niceties of textual interpretation. Sanders, however, attaches no importance to the lapse of twenty-one months between the two episodes, glosses lightly over the replacement of Strauss by Weill, and ignores altogether the shift from pantomime to ballet, from Reinhardt to Diaghilev, and not least from the *demi-monde* of Vollmoeller's salon to the *haut-monde* of Helene von

Nostitz's. Whereas the Baker project, for all its *Jugendstil* aspirations, was ephemeral in its very essence, the Weill one was certainly in Kessler's mind for at least a year and a half, and the sardanas that were somehow bound up with it were a reflection of a fascination with Catalonia and the Balearics that lasted to the end of his days. Once the Josephine Baker phantom has been banished, it becomes possible to imagine what might have been going on in Weill's musical mind that November evening in 1927; thus alerted, we may even catch distant echoes of sardana in the wind music of the *Mahagonny* opera, and again in the *Kleine Dreigroschenmusik*.

1927–33

The much-acclaimed premiere of the *Mahagonny-Songspiel* in July 1927 established Weill and Brecht as a marketable combination. On the strength of it, their friend Karl Koch – the film-maker and the husband of Lotte Reiniger – persuaded the Social Democrat council in Essen to collaborate with local industrialists and commission from Brecht and Weill a so-called *Ruhrepos*, which would portray the industrial complex of the Ruhr district in words, music, stage action, and documentary film (the latter to be directed by Walter Ruttmann). Weill and Brecht were duly introduced to the local dignitaries and businessmen, flown in a chartered plane over the entire Rhine–Ruhr industrial belt, and taken on a guided tour of a coalmine. Weill described the mine in an impassioned letter to Lenya (WLRC) and declared that he and Brecht must somehow find a way of expressing their sense of outrage. At this stage Weill was fully occupied with the composition of the *Mahagonny* opera; but Brecht found time to write several song texts before the Essen authorities predictably took fright and the project collapsed. In 1930 the song texts were set to music by Hanns Eisler.*

The success of *Die Dreigroschenoper* in 1928 greatly improved Weill's personal circumstances but in no way impaired his judgement. A year later he reacted to the failure of *Happy End* in a way that commands respect even if it was misguided. Sensing that a temporary escape from Brecht's America was necessary in view of the coming premiere of *Mahagonny*, he became interested in writing some songs for *Apollo-Brunnenstrasse*, a recently completed *Volksstück* by Stefan Grossmann with lyrics by Franz Hessel. (Grossmann was a prominent political journalist and editor, Hessel a noted translator remembered today for his collaborations with Walter Benjamin.) The project would certainly have gone ahead but for the misgivings expressed by Hans Heinsheimer, the

---

*See Eckhardt Köhn: *Das Ruhrepos, Dokumentation eines gescheiterten Projekts*. In: *Brecht-Jahrbuch 1977* (Berlin/Frankfurt).

head of the opera department of Universal Edition.* Bowing to Heinsheimer's judgement, Weill entrusted the task to Theo Mackeben. The production was a failure.

If *Apollo-Brunnenstrasse* had momentarily distracted Weill's attention from Brecht, it was perhaps only because the *Mahagonny* opera, which had loomed in the background of their collaboration for the past two years, was now complete, and the arduous preparations for its premiere were about to begin. However, Brecht himself provided, via Arthur Waley, an alternative and far more rewarding escape route from the *Mahagonny* world. The success of *Der Jasager* in the summer of 1930 resolved at least some of the problems created by the earlier *succès de scandale* of the *Mahagonny* opera, and prompted discussions about a companion piece. Significantly – in view of the abortive Grossmann project – the one that Brecht (but not Weill) made a start on, *Der Moabiter Pferdehandel*, was set in working-class Berlin. Possibly because of his experience with the Grossmann project Weill does not mention *Der Moabiter Pferdehandel* in his correspondence with Hans Heinsheimer, but merely the intention to provide *Der Jasager* with a light-hearted companion piece.

Whatever else prevented *Der Moabiter Pferdehandel* from materializing it was not personal or ideological differences between Weill and Brecht. Weill's main concern after *Mahagonny* was to write his first large-scale serio-comic opera, and for this he had in mind Jaroslav Hašek's epic novel *The Good Soldier Švejk*. Brecht had worked on Piscator's immensely successful stage version of 1927, and Weill's first hope was that he could be lured into writing the libretto. Brecht, it seems, was not averse to the idea, but Weill was by now experienced enough to know that detailed discussions would be risky until he had himself secured the rights from Hašek's publisher.

The task proved more difficult than he had anticipated, for Hašek's Estate was divided between two widows, of whom his publisher was rightly in awe and between whom there was no apparent possibility of agreement about anything in this world or the next. Although the Estate's lawyer, Jan Loewenbach, was a well-known amateur of music who admired Weill greatly and was in no doubt about the importance of his Schwejk project, the negotiations were bedevilled from the start by grievances stemming from the unruly Piscator production and by the existence of an 'official' stage version by Max Brod and Hans Riemann.

---

* The correspondence between Weill and Heinsheimer regarding *Apollo-Brunnenstrasse* is quoted and discussed by Christopher Hailey in his paper 'Creating a Public, Addressing a Market: Kurt Weill and Universal Edition', delivered at the Kurt Weill Conference at Yale in November 1983. A version of the paper is in *A New Orpheus: Essays on Kurt Weill* (ed. Kim H. Kowalke, Yale University Press, 1986). A translation of Weill's response to Heinsheimer was published in *Kurt Weill Newsletter* 3, Spring 1985.

Not only did Weill find the proposed artistic restrictions and production timetable unreasonable, but the terms first proposed to him were such that any author's share likely to be acceptable to Brecht would have left Weill with such a pitiful reward for two years' work that he even considered undertaking the libretto himself. Despite Loewenbach's undoubted good will, the correspondence dragged on for months. Eventually, with great reluctance and forgivable bitterness, Weill renounced the project, at least for the time being. His enthusiasm for it had certainly not been misplaced, for a major dramatic work in the comic mode was exactly what the arches of his creative development seemed to call for at this point; and it was also something the modern repertoire was sorely in need of.

From his hopes of a comedy that would show up the tragic farce of militarism Weill turned to the wholly serious *Bürgschaft*. Brecht, meanwhile, had written *Die Massnahme* (the Leninist sequel to *Der Jasager*) which Eisler later set to music. But contrary to today's popular notion, neither Weill nor Brecht took the view that their collaboration had ended. Its survival was already implicit in the history of a project proposed to Weill in April 1931 by David Joseph Bach (1874–1947), a pioneer of the Austrian 'Workers' Music' movement, and a close associate of Schoenberg and his school. In his official capacity as director of the all-powerful arts section of the Austrian Social Democratic Party (at that time a strictly socialist organization, far to the left of its latterday namesakes), Bach asked Weill to consider writing a large-scale composition for the workers' music associations, and suggested a suitably prominent premiere – either at the next year's May Day Festival, or else in November of that same year at a huge Republican pageant to be staged in Vienna. Weill seemed to welcome the idea, and proposed, for an example of the kind of thing he had in mind, a work inspired by Jack London's *General Strike*. (He had already been considering a Jack London project during the period following the completion of *Mahagonny*, at which stage its opposite pole, so to speak, was a Kafka project of which nothing else is known, though some link with Walter Benjamin may perhaps be surmised.) Bach reacted favourably to the Jack London idea.

Once Weill had returned to Berlin and resumed work on *Die Bürgschaft* he is unlikely to have had much time for thinking about Bach's project. It was not until August that he heard further news from UE. On the 14th and again on the 25th Hans Heinsheimer wrote in some excitement about Bach's plans for a May Day 'Festspiel' in the 60,000-seat Vienna Stadium. Bach's committee had decided to award the Festspiel commission to the composer who submitted the most promising scenario; and the deadline for that was 30 September 1931. According to Heinsheimer, Bach's colleagues were inclined to choose an Austrian composer, but Bach himself was determined to win a majority for Weill and confident that he could do so provided Weill sent him some kind of outline, or, at the very least, a provisional title.

On 27 August Weill wrote to Heinsheimer asking whether Bach would allow a collaboration with Brecht. Heinsheimer cabled an affirmative reply, adding only a word of caution – allegedly from Bach – regarding the party-political orientation. According to Weill (in a letter to UE of 8 September) Brecht was unperturbed by this, and declared that Bach's acceptance of the Jack London idea implied that there were no real constraints.

There the matter had to rest until *Die Bürgschaft* was finished, which Weill hoped would be at the end of September. But unforeseen difficulties over the close of the opera cost him an extra three weeks. On 19 October he told Heinsheimer that there was now insufficient time for composing a large-scale choral work, and he was therefore proposing in its stead a set of choruses on existing texts – provided suitable ones could be found.

This relatively modest alternative prompted an enthusiastic intervention from Erwin Stein. At that time Stein was, among other things, editor in charge of UE's orchestral catalogue – in which capacity he had for some while been urging Weill to write a purely orchestral work for the concert hall. On the choral side Stein was able to draw on his experience as conductor of Typographia, the choir of the Viennese print workers. Aside from D. J. Bach's immediate purposes he saw a long-term need for new repertory that was technically simple enough for the workers' choirs yet musically interesting. He advised Weill against polyphonic textures, and suggested that he restrict the instrumental accompaniments to a small wind orchestra or else – in the event of performances by massed choirs – a percussion ensemble.

Stein's practical rather than party-political concerns seem to have struck a sympathetic chord. Weill promised to do his best, and months later was still giving Stein grounds for hope that something would be forthcoming.

By then the May Day project had long since faded from view. On 12 December 1931 Weill had informed Heinsheimer that he was still trying to come to an agreement with Brecht, and as a last resort was considering a revised and expanded version of *Das Berliner Requiem*. An end-of-year reminder from D. J. Bach elicited nothing but a promise that he would continue to look for a suitable text.

That was the end of the May Day project as far as the UE correspondence is concerned and, indeed, as far as we need to know. Whether or not the quarrel between Weill and Brecht during the December rehearsals for the Berlin *Mahagonny* was the decisive event, it is clear from the drift of the correspondence that Weill had never been entirely happy about the idea of associating a large-scale composition with the interests of any political party, however congenial. The contrast with his manifestly conscientious commitment to the *Ruhrepos* in 1927 speaks for itself, but is further emphasized by the fact that the material

Brecht had written for that ill-fated venture is never mentioned in his correspondence with UE, despite the fact that it was eminently suited to the character and purposes of the May Day Festspiel.

Bach's and Stein's initiatives were not, however, without consequences. Weill would certainly have had discussions with both men* during his brief visit to Vienna in April. After attending the premiere, at the Raimundtheater on the 26th, of a shortened version of *Mahagonny* staged by Heinsheimer and Max Brand, he then made his way back to Berlin by way of Munich, where he visited Caspar Neher. In an undated letter to Lenya written at the end of April, he reported that he and Neher had decided to start work on a cantata – defined as a cantata for workers' choirs in a letter to UE of 17 June – as soon as Neher returned to Berlin at the end of May, and then to embark on a small-scale opera designed for performance in non-subsidized theatres.

Announcing the latter project to UE in a letter of 29 May, Weill reports that he and Neher had started work on a new operatic genre, *Laienoper* (opera for amateurs), which he believes will be particularly suitable for the workers' choral movement. Five days later he is speculating about a complementary genre of small-scale operas without chorus, designed for production in commercial theatres (or 'private theatres', as he called them).

Now that reactionary trends in Germany were affecting the economic basis of his relations with Universal Edition, Weill is proceeding with due caution. Neither in his letter of 29 May nor in its successor of 3 June is there mention of any subject matter considered by him and Neher. The impression he surely intends to leave is that his publishers are to help him decide on the strategy before he determines his next move. The *Laienoper* idea obviously takes account of the fact that his slightly older contemporary Hanns Eisler had already established a commanding position on the left wing of the workers' choral movement – where he had set new standards with his contributions to UE's new series of 'proletarian' choruses – but was relatively inexperienced in the musico-dramatic field. If Eisler's scores for *Die Massnahme* and *Die Mutter* represented a challenge for Weill as far as the workers' movement was concerned, it was one that had more bearing on concert conditions, and hence on his projected cantata, than on the theatre as he understood it.

The commercial theatre was quite another matter, and it was shrewd of Weill to devote a separate letter to his current thoughts about it. In the harsh circumstances of 1932 the foothold *Die Dreigroschenoper* had unexpectedly won him three years earlier had taken on a new significance. Without that fortunate precedent the privately funded

---

*Especially with Stein, who had conducted the Viennese premiere of *Der Jasager* in February 1932.

productions of *Mahagonny* at the Theater am Kurfürstendamm and the Raimundtheater would not have happened. Yet the extent to which they demonstrated that his operas and suchlike were producible outside the state-supported system was strictly limited. In both cases, and especially in Vienna, conditions for which *Mahagonny* had not been designed necessitated artistic compromises that Weill found regrettable. Both experiences must have helped him define the formal and stylistic problems any new work for the commercial stage would have to solve if it was to continue his creative development rather than weakly hark back to an earlier success.

Weill's speculations about commercial theatre in his letter of 3 June were by no means as detached as they seemed. They were in fact a judiciously timed preliminary to the announcement of what might otherwise have seemed an abrupt change of tack. Very soon afterwards Weill must have informed his publishers, by telephone or personally, that he had just been approached by the internationally successful impresario and director Erik Charell. On the 11th he told UE that Charell wanted to commission a major theatre work from him, and that there had also been separate approaches from Max Reinhardt and from Carl Vollmoeller. 'But in this area,' Weill concluded, 'Charell is the best man.'

With the 54-year-old Vollmoeller Weill had nothing in common apart from no doubt unwelcome memories of Humperdinck via the music that master had written in 1914 for Reinhardt's production of Vollmoeller's *Das Mirakel*, a 'Mysterienspiel' which conquered London and New York after the First World War. With Reinhardt there were much stronger connections. An early admirer and supporter of Brecht, Reinhardt had obtained an option on *Mahagonny* for production at his Berlin Deutsches Theater during the 1930–1 season – an option Weill had gladly agreed to now that there was no remaining chance of a production at one of Berlin's opera houses.

While Vollmoeller had some slight claim to intellectual respectability and Reinhardt a substantial one, Charell belonged strictly to the world of high-class show business. Producer of Berlin's most sumptuous revues, director of *Congress Dances* – the German cinema's first great international success in the sound-film era – and co-author as well as director of the immensely lucrative musical comedy *The White Horse Inn*, Charell entered Weill's life like the Lottery Agent in *Der Silbersee*. Combining as he did something of the various talents of a C. B. Cochran, a Billy Rose, and a Rouben Mamoulian, he was nothing if not an alluring figure.

In his paper 'Creating a Public, Addressing a Market: Kurt Weill and Universal Edition' (KK.ANO), Christopher Hailey rightly attaches crucial importance to the Charell project. Linking it with the earlier correspondence regarding the Grossmann–Hessel *Apollo-Brunnenstrasse*, he argues that the encounter with Charell marked a decisive shift in Weill's sympathies – a shift, that is, away from a subsidized theatre system enshrining the principles of classical Weimar and towards the kind of theatre Weill was to discover in New York in its quintessential and most technically advanced form. Powerfully supported by John Rockwell's more general observations in his KK.ANO paper 'Kurt Weill's Operatic Reform, and its Context in Berlin', Hailey encourages a reading of the correspondence about the Charell project that is not perhaps unaffected by the seductions of hindsight.

Weill's first assessment of the Charell project, in his letter of 11 June 1932, deserves careful reading. Charell, he says, 'promises himself an international success (*Welterfolg*) through collaboration with me'. However, he continues (my italics):

> Up to now it seems almost impossible to find a subject matter that is accessible to the public he is working for but which at the same time observes *the standards and boundaries I regard as indispensable*. The subject he is recommending to me is so far removed from anything I have previously worked on that I would be painfully interrupting the consistent development of my previous work. On the other hand this collaboration could be extremely attractive, *not only financially but also artistically*.
>
> We [Weill and Neher?] will now try to incorporate in a subject that seems possible to him something that could raise it to my level. But it is very difficult.

Why, then, is the collaboration 'artistically' so attractive? This is the one nebulous area in what is otherwise a clear and sensible account.

Any suspicion that Weill might be equivocating is, however, removed by his next letter – a long and very important one dated 15 June. Two of its three pages were in reply to a letter bearing the same date in which Heinsheimer had pointed out that 'from a purely financial point of view' Weill's prospects for the coming year were 'anything but rosy in the present situation'. Allowing that such economic considerations should not be the only ones to determine attitudes towards offers from Charell and others of his kind, Heinsheimer goes on to argue, with some subtlety, that the virtual boycott of *Die Bürgschaft* – after a major success with press and public, and an intensive promotion campaign – left no reasonable alternative but to come to terms with Charell and then, on the strength of a popular success in Charell's sense, to demonstrate 'with documents' exactly why it had proved impossible to move forward with *Die Bürgschaft*, and forward from it.

Weill opens his reply by accepting that the 'catastrophic' situation in the German theatre has to be taken into account in all his planning. Nothing would please him more, he declares, than to expose the German Intendants as the 'shameful cowards they are'. Indulging himself in the 'fantasies of one thirsting for revenge' he imagines writing a 'hit' so desirable to backsliding Intendants that the rights to it would be obtainable only on signature of a performance contract for *Die Bürgschaft*. 'Naturally', he continues, financial considerations also play their part. You know me well enough to believe me when I say that I would be very happy, not only for myself but also for UE, were we to find ourselves a tasty morsel. On the other hand I would not like to renounce my firm and prescribed line. Were I to develop that line precisely and straight as a die, the next thing due from me would be a piece for the workers' movement, though not – in the light of my recent experiences and thoughts – a choral piece for the workers' choirs, but rather a musical *Volksstück* with a clear political tendency, which I would specifically offer to proletarian audiences. For that I already have various clearly outlined plans which I'm very pleased about. But it seems to me very questionable whether such pointedly left-wing pieces are at all performable in present-day Germany.

Another and already quite far advanced plan is for a school opera, *Naboths Weinberg* [Naboth's Vineyard], which would present a social theme in a biblical context. Here too the question arises whether they will allow a school opera by me into the schools. Apart from these two projects, which I will in any case proceed with, the offers from major theatre people of international standing (Reinhardt, Charell) become increasingly prominent. Here there seems to be a real need for my music. The commercial composers [*Industrie-Komponisten*] are completely written out, and apparently there is no one apart from me who can write music that is artistically valuable, yet understandable to all. At least, that's what these people always assure me.

Weill had been heartened by Charell's attitude at their most recent meeting, only a day before. Charell had opened the discussion by declaring that after long reflection he had decided that it was up to him to find common ground with Weill, rather than vice versa. Taking that as an assurance that the preservation of his own 'artistic standards' (*Niveaugrenze*) would be implicit in any further discussion, Weill now felt that he could, 'with a quiet conscience', entrust to Charell four of the subjects on which he had been working during the past weeks. There is no mention of a literary collaborator at this stage, but numerous references in earlier letters to his work with Neher* leave no doubt as to whom he had in mind.

The four subjects to be offered to Charell are described as follows ('all in strict confidence'):

1 A Volksoper, *Romeo und Julia*, played in a market hall; conflict between two families of fruit sellers, a love story of simple young people, with a happy ending.
2 *Uncle Tom's Cabin*, a simple Volksoper based on the famous novel [by Harriet Beecher Stowe], moral tableaux (*Sittengemälde*) from the age of slavery (which is one of my most important topics for an opera).
3 A 'Play with Music' based on a true event at the 1920 Peace Conference in Geneva – a very amusing story whose background is the ping-pong game between the Russian outlook on the world and the West European.
4 Georg Kaiser's *Die jüdische Witwe* as an opera.

---

*See for example the letter of 29 May, which ends with the news that he will now collaborate with Neher on two of the three opera subjects he has selected for the workers' movement.

Remarking that Reinhardt had nothing to offer him but a Berlin *Volksstück* – a kind of 'Berliner Leben' – and that in any case he was not someone with whom he had any 'real contact', he applauded Charell's 'fresh and youthful enterprise, his enormous sense of the theatre, and his great cultivation'.

It is towards the end of his letter of 15 June that Weill achieves the maturity of judgement his native astuteness called for but his impulsiveness sometimes endangered. The contention that Charell offered him more artistic security than Reinhardt had always been crucial to his argument, but until this late point it had seemed, in the light of Charell's previous record, to lack objective justification. This he provides, with masterly skill, in his closing paragraph.

He begins by noting the essential difference between undertaking a work at Charell's behest and inducing Charell to select one of the subjects he had already decided on for a future work. Preferable though the latter arrangement would be, it still entailed a decision which, he pointed out, was not to be taken lightly. Whatever Charell's decision, he would therefore insist on UE's involvement and agreement. Meanwhile he counselled UE against judging the affair simply from the standpoint of 'the present and very unfavourable situation'. 'I am optimist enough', he continued,

> to believe that the present situation cannot last all that long, and in no event do I want to take an over-hasty step which I will live to regret. I shall therefore do my utmost, in the Charell affair also, to keep to my line as closely as possible. I believe – and he too seems to have understood – that he as well as I will be better served if he does not exact concessions from me that could destroy the artistic position I have now attained after *Die Bürgschaft*.

So far from being prophetic, these words and this conclusion are inconceivable in the context of Weill's life and work after 1933; and nothing in the subsequent history of the Charell project throws any shadow of doubt on them.

With this letter Weill won from his publishers the unconditional support he was no doubt seeking and certainly deserved. In his reply of 21 June Heinsheimer rose magnanimously to the occasion and contrived to dissociate himself from any unfortunate impressions that might have been left by his previous letter. On no account was Weill to suppose that after a sorrowful glance at the royalty statements UE was intending to force him into a 'shameful money-marriage with Charell'.

Be that as it may, Charell was not susceptible to the charms of Weill's four projects. Although none of them is mentioned again in the UE correspondence, Weill's serious commitment to each of them, and also to *Naboths Weinberg*, is demonstrable: *Romeo und Julia* re-emerges soon after Weill's emigration in March 1933, when it is the subject of discussions and correspondence with Marlene Dietrich (undated letters from 'M.D.' in WLRC); *Uncle Tom's Cabin* is the direct predecessor of *Ulysses Africanus* (see p. 309); the Geneva Peace Conference idea recurs several times in Weill's project notes of the late 1930s; and both *Die jüdische Witwe* and *Naboths Weinberg* were under consideration during the same period – the former as an opera for the Federal Theatre, the latter as a radio opera.

On 29 June 1932 Weill devoted another long letter to the Charell project. The negotiations had now reached 'a very critical point'. On a 'purely superficial' level they appeared to be 'very favourable', with a series of international productions beginning in Vienna and proceeding via Paris and London to Berlin. But in the meantime the project's artistic credentials had, in his view, become increasingly suspect. Without alluding to Charell's rejection of his four ideas – which must have been a considerable blow to his pride – Weill scornfully announces that Charell has had his 'final inspiration' and has decided on a stage version, 90 per cent musical, of Robert Wiene's classic film of the silent era, *The Cabinet of Dr Caligari*. 'Yesterday,' he tells UE on the 29th,

> I had the film shown to me, in Charell's and Neher's company. For me this film offers nothing, apart from its title, that one can use in a theatre piece. Charell sees it purely in terms of atmosphere. He sees fairground, hypnosis, somnambulism, mysticism – always private, abnormal, bourgeois, phenomena which I cannot all of a sudden turn into the content of a work after having, for years past and with the greatest obstinacy, taken the standpoint that the theatre must dedicate itself to the major and enduring ideas of the time.

If only to provide a slight adjustment to the views of Christopher Hailey and John Rockwell, it is perhaps helpful to remind ourselves that these words are completely foreign to the composer who eight years later began his collaboration with Moss Hart on *Lady in the Dark*, a large-scale musical about psychoanalysis and other private, not to say bourgeois, phenomena.

According to Weill, the *Caligari* film showing was followed by a six-hour debate which left both sides with the feeling that 'between his attitude to the theatre and mine there is a wide gulf, and one that it will not be altogether easy to bridge'. While it is legitimate to argue that eight years later Weill triumphantly succeeded in bridging it, there is no evidence that in 1932 he wished or intended to do so. On the contrary, his first practical step after the *Caligari* showing was to introduce a fourth member to the production team, in the formidable person of Georg Kaiser. Although Kaiser was not entirely a stranger to the commercial theatre, one can well imagine with what disquiet Charell must have viewed his arrival. Nevertheless he allowed the discussion to proceed to a point where Weill, Kaiser, and Neher felt confident enough to devote three whole days to working on a scenario suitable 'not only for a Charell production but also for developing a philosophical and artistic line on a high level' (letter to UE of 7 July). Further discussions, including the not unimportant question of Charell's royalty share in relation to three other shares, ensued during the next fortnight. On the 20th Weill sent UE the news that just when all concerned were ready to sign an agreement Charell had suddenly cried off – partly, it seemed, because of worries about the subject matter, and partly because he had become anxious about what for him was an entirely new team of collaborators. Soon after, Charell suggested to Weill that they postpone the *Caligari* project and embark alone on 'an entirely new plan for a purely musical work'.

This plan, Weill declared, pleased him more than any that had previously been discussed. What it amounted to – if indeed it amounted to anything more than the idea of a through-composed work – he did not reveal. Before the month was over Charell left Berlin on doctors' orders and was taking the cures at Bad Gastein – where he fondly hoped Weill would join him for yet more discussions. Weill declined, for the excellent reason that he, Kaiser, and Neher had already started work on *Der Silbersee*. Three months later Charell was back again, pressing Weill to collaborate with Erich Kästner. But Kästner's financial demands struck Heinsheimer as excessive (letter to Weill of 8 December 1932) and Weill was still fully occupied. Not until he was looking for a production of *Der Kuhhandel* did he again become closely involved with Charell.

The lessons to be learned from a study of the Charell project are equalled in importance only by the inversely related ones to be learned from the history of Weill's abortive collaboration with Brecht in America. The Weill of 1932 is never in doubt about where he stands as an artist, and where his ultimate responsibilities lie. In almost all of his letters about Charell – and they are numerous – he stresses the necessity of creative continuity and the artistic standards it implies. With singular adroitness he acknowledges the interplay of artistic and pecuniary interests on both sides of the publishing fence, but loads the case in such a way that his UE colleagues, being who they are, have no choice but to offer the unqualified moral support he needed but might not have obtained had he openly solicited it. Without such support the leap from Charell to *Der Silbersee* – a notably less 'commercial' undertaking than either *Die Dreigroschenoper* or *Happy End* – would have been foolhardy; and without it the very essence of Weill's relationship with Universal Edition would have been called in question.

At once pragmatic and idealistic, Weill's basic attitude throughout the Charell debate was wholly consistent with his bearing since the day he signed his first contract with UE. To suggest otherwise – as even Christopher Hailey's perceptive account is in danger of doing – is not merely to misjudge the inner dynamics of the debate; it is to underrate the intellectual and spiritual content of the entire relationship between Weill and his Viennese publisher, and hence to overlook the profound consequences of the collapse of that relationship in 1933. The history of Weill's music, as of his unfulfilled projects, before and after that fatal break, belongs, among other things, to the history of music publishing in the twentieth century, and hence to the diagnosis of cultural and industrial ailments on both sides of the Atlantic.

Neither Weill nor Heinsheimer could have guessed how close they were to the precipice in 1932. As work on *Der Silbersee* progressed, so did the political climate seem to improve, and with it, the prospects for *Die Bürgschaft* and a renewal of Weill's operatic career. *Der Silbersee* was by its very nature an interim work with two distinct aspects – on the one side an idealistic, post-Charell, enlargement of the old 'play-with-music' concept which incorporated some of the energy from Weill's recent discussions with Neher about *Volksstücke* for the private theatres, on the other, an expedient reduction of the 'epic' forms of *Die Bürgschaft*. It was the kind of work that imposed no conditions on the next project other than those implicit in the 'philosophical and artistic' principles it continued to uphold.

A letter from Heinsheimer to Weill of 12 October 1932 refers for the first and only time to a discussion with Kaiser's publisher regarding the rights – presumably the musical rights – to Bernard Shaw's *Caesar and Cleopatra*. Written on the assumption that Weill had already been informed about the matter by Felix Bloch-Erben – with whom he was in continual contact regarding the forthcoming premieres of *Der Silbersee* – Heinsheimer's letter reaffirmed that it was almost impossible to come to an agreement with Shaw. The reference is valuable, not only as a footnote to the highly effective but dramatically inapposite 'Ballade von Cäsars Tod' in *Der Silbersee*, but also as the first known step in Weill's long and ultimately unsuccessful quest for this particular Shaw play (and indeed for others). Given Kaiser's involvement it is not hard to imagine a development from *Caligari* to *Caesar* under the continuing aegis of Charell. But the next Weill–Kaiser project we know of, and the last before Hitler's seizure of power, was not for the theatre but for the concert hall. In a letter to UE dated 6 January 1933 Weill reports that 'Kaiser is busy with a plan for a major choral work for me, and has a very fine idea for it.'

The same letter contains an equally cryptic reference to an opera subject, which he has been considering 'for a long time', and about which he is now having preliminary discussions with Neher. Like the Kaiser project this is mentioned as evidence that he is gradually preparing himself for 'a new large-scale work'. That his long-considered opera subject was none other than *Švejk* is just within the bounds of possibility, given the reference to a further year's consideration he made in a letter to Heinsheimer of 4 May 1932. The 'suitable librettist' he was then looking for could hardly have turned out to be Kaiser, but might have been Neher – by a margin still too narrow for Weill to have risked telling UE.

There is a third name in Weill's letter of 6 January, and an unexpected one: that very evening Weill was to meet Brecht and hear his suggestions regarding a new companion piece for the *Mahagonny–Songspiel* which was now urgently needed after the work's great success at the Salle Gaveau in Paris a month before.

During the year that elapsed between the Berlin production of *Mahagonny* and the Weill Concert in Paris, relations between Weill and Brecht had reached a nadir. According to Weill's account in a letter to Lenya of 9 January (WLA), the January meeting had come about only because Brecht had repeatedly pestered Ernst Josef Aufricht and finally persuaded him to invite them both to his apartment. Unmoved by Brecht's apparent eagerness to please, Weill returned home without any clear idea of what Brecht had in mind. But at 2 am Brecht telephoned him and suggested 'dramatizing' *Der Lindberghflug* so that it would serve as a companion piece for the *Mahagonny-Songspiel* – an idea Weill describes, with good reason, as 'idiotic'. Since then Brecht had phoned several times, anxious to arrange another meeting. Weill clearly was not; but he ended his account to Lenya by remarking that he had read Brecht's version of *Measure for Measure* – the forebear of *Die Rundköpfe und die Spitzköpfe* – and found it 'partly very fine'.

Only perhaps in his perception that one of the roles in *Mass für Mass* was ideal for Lenya would Weill have had any incentive at this moment to renew his collaboration with Brecht. But his heart was not in it, and circumstances were against it. That fateful January he had much to attend to. Not only was the Second Symphony beginning to take shape, but he was embroiled in preparations for the three forthcoming productions of *Der Silbersee*, while at the same time discussing, investigating, and negotiating the basis for his first musical film.

The film project was in itself very recent, though something of the kind had been in view ever since Weill's successful lawsuit against Tobis-Warner over the liberties taken with his music in their production of Pabst's *Dreigroschenoper* film. In lieu of damages, he had demanded and obtained from Tobis an agreement assuring him a minimum of three major film commissions, together with such far-ranging artistic rights and powers that even the director would have to defer to him. Together with the right of approval to the subject matter and to the choice of director, screenwriters, and designer, Weill was to be involved in the planning of each film from the outset.

The first offer under this unprecedented and unparalleled agreement was one that Weill accepted with alacrity: a film of Hans Fallada's novel *Kleiner Mann – was nun?* First published in Berlin in 1931, the novel was already enjoying a well-merited international success. For Weill's purposes it had the supreme merit that it dealt in strictly realistic terms with the same phenomena that *Der Silbersee* had shown in legendary form – the social and political consequences of economic recession.

The producers, led by Rudolf Neppach (a relative of Bruno Walter), struck Weill as intelligent and sympathetic. He had no difficulty in securing the engagement of Caspar Neher as designer, and he accepted without reservation a team of screenwriters that included Fallada himself. The choice of director proved more problematic. Weill recommended René Clair, sought out Josef von Sternberg, and had talks with Lupu Pick. None was available. But the final choice was one that pleased him greatly: Berthold Viertel, the Austrian-born poet and director (best known in the English-speaking world through Isherwood's *Prater Violet*). He was a close friend of Karl Kraus, and an independent-minded member of Brecht's circle.

An unexplained delay in the arrival of Viertel's contract caused Weill some concern, not least because Viertel had already been working long hours with him on the scenario. In the climate created by the appointment of Hitler as Chancellor on 30 January, delays of that kind did not seem trivial. Moreover it was clear that Neppach and his colleagues were anxiously awaiting the premieres of *Der Silbersee* in mid-February.

No sooner had they congratulated themselves on the resounding success of *Der Silbersee* in Leipzig, and the friendly receptions in Magdeburg and Erfurt, than their worst fears were confirmed by anti-Semitic and expressly anti-Weill demonstrations at the second Magdeburg performance. On 25 February they warned Weill that they might have to ask him to withdraw from the film. He was not inclined to oblige, but after the burning of the Reichstag two days later there was no alternative. At the beginning of March came news of Fallada's arrest; and on the 14th Weill was heading for Paris with Caspar and Erika Neher. He had been given to believe that he would find alternative film work in France, either with René Clair or with Jean Renoir. But circumstances were changing from day to day, and neither Clair nor Renoir could promise anything. Though still convinced that conditions in Germany would improve before long, Weill was now trapped in Paris, with belongings and resources sufficient for only a brief stay. In these circumstances the sudden appearance of Edward James with the offer of a ballet commission was indeed providential.

While James was proposing a collaboration with Brecht, Weill secretly approached Jean Cocteau – who had become a passionate devotee of his music – and tried to bring him into the project before Brecht could be reached. But Cocteau preferred to wait until Weill was free to collaborate with him on a work of their own. Soon after, they agreed to write a Faust opera with a modern setting.

Cocteau began work shortly before the premiere of *Die sieben Todsünden*. In a letter to Weill (WLRC) written immediately after the premiere he deplored the production and the occasion – apart from the performances of Lenya and Tilly Losch – but expressed profound and manifestly sincere admiration for a score that had generally been underrated and misunderstood. In difficult times, it had given him a new incentive to press on with the *Faust* libretto.

A short undated letter reporting progress and reaffirming his devotion is the last known trace of the project. Given the emotional and other upheavals in Cocteau's life during a period when the French police were interesting themselves in his opium smoking, one can imagine that any sketches he may have made for the *Faust* were lost or unwittingly destroyed. (The project is not mentioned in Francis Steegmuller's definitive biography of Cocteau, nor indeed in any other Cocteau literature.) There is no reason to suppose that there was any formal breach between Weill and Cocteau: events were carrying them in opposite directions long before that moment in the winter of 1933–4 when Weill finally awoke to the fact that he was no longer the darling of the Paris salons. If the *Faust* project was not doomed from the start, its chances of survival were always slender.

1933–50

There are no records of any other unfulfilled project until the early weeks of 1936, when Weill found himself stranded in New York with only his royalty advances from Heugel to rely upon. A promised commission from René Blum for a Toulouse-Lautrec ballet for the Ballets Russes de Monte Carlo would have required him to return to Europe forthwith, but it came to nothing. Of much greater importance, however, was the commission offered by Eugene Meyer, the publisher of the *Washington Post*, for a ballet on any subject of his choice, for the American Ballet Company. After an exchange of letters with Lenya, Weill settled for Wedekind's two-act pantomime *The Empress of Newfoundland*, an almost forgotten work so perfectly suited to his creative and professional needs at that critical stage that no living writer could have hoped to match it, and now that Alban Berg was dead, no living composer could challenge his singular claim to it. Whereas Hašek's *Švejk* had for him been a natural and almost obvious choice, Wedekind's *Empress* was an inspired one. But the rights had yet to be obtained from Wedekind's heirs and publishers in Nazi Germany. Approaches were made to them on Weill's behalf by his and Lenya's old friend Richard Révy, a noted actor, stage director and screenwriter who was then living in Munich. For reasons not divulged but easy to imagine, permission was not forthcoming. The loss is incalculable.

Two other dance projects were mooted during the pre-war years in America. The first was concurrent with the Wedekind, and entailed a scenario to be written by the Austrian émigré writer Franz Hoellering, who promised to tackle it as soon as his work-in-progress was finished. As far as we know there were no further developments. The impatience with which Weill awaited news from Hoellering was representative of a period dominated by the short-term need to earn his keep in the USA until the postponed production of *The Eternal Road* was reconstituted.

First the Group Theatre and then Hollywood helped secure his position and hence diminished the conscious and unconscious attractions of Europe. He was therefore already in a more confident frame of mind when the choreographer and dancer Ruth Page begged him to write a score for her new company (her letter, dated 20 July 1938, is in WLA). Having studied in Berlin during Weill's heyday there, she knew precisely to whom she was talking, and what she wanted. Weill later tried to recommend Milhaud in his stead, but Page would accept no alternatives.

To be seen at his true worth was not, for Weill, so common an experience in the New World that he could afford to dismiss such an approach. How far he went to meet it, despite the other claims on his time, is not clear; but there is in the legacy a two-page typescript of a scenario, written in German and bearing his name, for a ballet or dance drama entitled *Jephthas Tochter*. By the standards of the time it is amazingly old-fashioned: Handel and *Idomeneo* notwithstanding, it reads like a footnote to the tradition of Strauss's *Josephslegende*, and could almost be mistaken for a relic of Weill's conversations with Kessler.

Consciously or otherwise, Weill may well have seen the dance theatre as a last refuge for any symphonic ambitions that may have survived the contemptuous dismissal of his Second Symphony on both sides of the Atlantic. While the old Ballets Russes tradition implicit in the Toulouse-Lautrec material had never been an enthusiasm of his (and was never to become one), Modern Dance, as developed by Laban, Wigman, Jooss, and their American disciples, was not without links with the kind of musical theatre he was seeking to develop during his first three years in the USA. The poet, librettist, dancer and ballet critic Edwin Denby, with whom he was friendly, provided a valuable link of that sort during the period when the Federal Theatre and its dance wing were flourishing.

From the European point of view that was still very much his own, Weill's whole-hearted commitment to the ideals of the Federal Theatre during his first two years in the USA was as logical as his contemporary affiliations with the Group Theatre, the Welles–Houseman Mercury Theatre, and the more progressive spirits in the Theatre Guild and in broadcasting. If the legend of his instant Americanization and immediately consequent espousal of Broadway were not partly of his own making, its popularity today on both sides of the Atlantic would be hard to explain. While the masterly sleight-of-hand by which he created the illusion of an 'American' idiom in *Johnny Johnson* is demonstrable only in terms of the musical syntax, the unmasked reality is immediately apparent in some of the lists of possible projects he made for himself during the last fifteen years of his life. Their nature and provenance require some explanation.

Weill did not gather together or file his project memos. Widely scattered among his papers and effects, they came to light, one by one, during the course of the present author's investigation of the legacy. A few memos were preserved in notebooks and diaries, the rest on loose scraps of paper – about fifty separate items, including cablegram forms, gin-rummy score cards, hotel stationery, and compliments slips.* Generally scribbled in pencil, and only in one or two cases intended for other eyes, they are immeasurably more revealing, as well as more numerous, than the press interviews, announcements, and gossip-column entries arranged by his Broadway and Hollywood agents. With the rare exception of reading lists, the memos identify titles or topics that have already been selected for project status. The names of prospective producers and adapters are specified, but seldom those of the original authors. Only exceptionally, and then only in his last years, did Weill date the memos.

One of the early memos – written in pencil on a 10 × 8 inch sheet of typing paper – gives a remarkably broad picture of Weill's first interests and tendencies during his Group Theatre period (1936–7). In the following transcription, editorial additions are in square brackets; otherwise the layout and orthography are as in the original.

Group: Germinal Zola
            Caesar (Bellum Gallicum) Hermannsschlacht [Kleist; or perhaps
                Grabbe?]
            Coepenick (Howard Dietz) [i.e. Zuckmayer's play]

Dietz   Coepenick
            Marlborough [Marcel Achard's *Malbrouk s'en va t'en guerre*]
            Serena Blandish [S. N. Behrman's comedy, after Enid Bagnold]

Anderson: Klaus Mann
            Kinderoper (Columbus)
            Silbersee?

Defraudant [Valentin Katayev's satire *The Embezzlers*]
Russische Novelle
Silbersee
Maurois-Novelle
Candide
Geschäft ist Geschäft [Mirbeau, *Les Affaires sont les affaires*]
Tagebuch eines Dienstmäderls [Mirbeau, *Le Journal d'une femme de chambre*]
Waiting for Lefty (*Oper*) [Odets]
Joseph
Jüdische Witwe [Georg Kaiser]
Alkibiades [Kaiser, *Der gerettete Alkibiades*]

Except for S. N. Behrman's successful comedy *Serena Blandish* (1929), which was presumably intended for a musical or a film with lyrics by Howard Dietz, the list is irrelevant to normal Broadway/Hollywood considerations. On internal evidence it probably dates from the first weeks of 1937 – that is, from Weill's first visit to Hollywood, where he

---

* The collection is now in WLA.

joined Clifford Odets, Lewis Milestone, and members of the Group Theatre, to work on *The River is Blue*. If so, it contains the first known reference to a possible collaboration with Maxwell Anderson (Sherwood cannot have been in mind), and must have preceded Weill's discussions with Odets about a possible stage adaptation of *Der Silbersee* featuring the German-born actress Luise Rainer – to whom Odets was then married – as Fennimore.

The association of Howard Dietz's name with that of the Group Theatre is not one that would readily occur to admirers of that gifted and successful lyric writer, but it is another clue to the dating of Weill's memo. His friendship with Dietz was consolidated in Hollywood during that first visit. Before he left California in June 1937 he and Dietz made plans for a series of radio operas based on literary classics.

A draft list of titles for the series is in the Weill legacy. Though typewritten and unsigned, it bears all the marks of Weill, and is unmistakably a counterpart to the handwritten list transcribed above. Just as that list had revived one of the four projects offered to Charell in 1932 – Kaiser's Wedekindian biblical comedy *Die jüdische Witwe* – so does the radio draft revive the project with which Weill and Neher had been occupied immediately prior to the approach from Charell: *Naboths Weinberg*. To this Weill now adds three other Old Testament subjects: *Job, Susanna and the Elders,* and *Jepthas Tochter*.

The Old Testament group is oddly counterbalanced on the New Testament side by Balzac's *Christ in Flanders* (from the *Etudes philosophiques*) and *A Passion in the Desert* (from *Scènes de la vie politique*) and Zola's *The Feast of the Fisherman*. Finally come two great novellas by Kleist. The first, *Michael Kohlhaas*, was said by Lenya (in conversation with the present author) to have been one of Weill's most cherished opera projects in Germany. Although there is no word of it in his correspondence, the relevance of *Kohlhaas* to the worlds of *Die Bürgschaft* and *Der Silbersee* is so striking that it could hardly have failed to be a topic of discussion in 1932–3, either with Neher, who would have taken a Brechtian view of it, or with Kaiser, who had been a devotee of Kleist since his beginnings as a playwright. The second novella is *The Marquise of O.*, which is closer to Kaiser than to Neher, and is to recur in several later memos.

Even allowing for the New Deal era's discovery of the European concept of 'public service' broadcasting, the opera list seems almost aggressively high-minded, and quite foreign to the practical and cultural assumptions on which Weill was later to base his contributions to American radio. Nevertheless the list is too weighty to be dismissed as some idealistic aberration brought on by the Californian sunshine and who knows what congenial company. In excluding the modern world it acquired a modernity quite distinct from that of the contemporary project memos, yet consistent and at certain points contiguous with them.

On the practical level the Weill–Dietz scheme served as a link between

the 1937 project memo reproduced above and another memo from later
the same year in which there is evidence that Weill was actively involved
with plans for a Federal Opera project – a venture with which Virgil
Thomson, among others, was involved. Written on two pages, this
memo intermingles notes for Weill's own projects with others presumably intended for repertory discussions:

Hollywood – Living Newspaper [i.e. The Federal Theatre's documentary
   series]
White Wings [Philip Barry]
Davy Crockett [see p. 297]
Dreigroschenoper [repeated attempts to promote new adaptations]
Johnny Johnson [plans for Federal Theatre productions?]
Paul Green (Common Glory) [see p. 294]
Lawson (Spain) [John Howard Lawson]
Toller [Weill attended a Spanish Aid rally at which Ernst Toller and Malraux
   were principal speakers]
Joseph [sic]
Offenbach Périchole (Virgil Thomson) [n.b. Kraus version produced at the
   Kroll in 1931]
Mute of Portici [Auber's opera, produced at the Kroll by Piscator in 1930]
John Brown's Body [Stephen Vincent Benét's narrative poem]
Copland–Denby [The Second Hurricane, libretto by Denby]
Froissart [n.b. Neher and Wagner-Régeny's contemporaneous opera after
   Froissart and Kaiser, Die Bürger von Calais]
Arabian Nights [Stevenson]
Irwin Shaw
THE DEVIL AND DANIEL WEBSTER [S. V. Benét story filmed by William Dieterle
   in 1941; folk opera by Douglas Moore, with libretto by Benét, 1939]
Corners Four
[page 2]
Joseph
American Revolution (Paul) [Green]
Twelve Chairs? [Soviet Russian comedy by Ilf and Petrov]
Ghengis Khan (Harold Lamb)
Embezzlers [Katayev]
Acropolis

The role played by Behrman's *Serena Blandish* in the previous list is here
fulfilled, with more distinction perhaps, by Philip Barry's comedy *White
Wings* – not, in fact, a notable success in its Broadway production of 1929,
but a play to which Weill was attracted, and one whose musical future he
persistently tried to promote over the next seven or eight years, always in
vain. It concerns the last in a family firm of street cleaners – the 'White
Wings' of the title – at the close of the era of the horsedrawn carriage. A
friend, though never actually a member of the Playwrights' Company,
Barry was wholly in sympathy with its democratic and middlebrow
ideals. In that sense *White Wings* – or, for that matter, *Serena Blandish* –
had much more bearing on Weill's future associations in the American
theatre than the rest of those two early project memos – not to mention
the projects he was discussing in 1937 with Charles Alan and Burgess

Meredith, which included the hobo-fantasy *The Heavenly Express* by the
self-styled proletarian playwright Albert Bein, Auden's and Isherwood's
The Ascent of F6 and H. R. Hays's *Davy Crockett*. In November 1937 Weill
proposed to Bein a co-authorship agreement, but despite Alan's
assurances, Bein was unhappy about the prospect of interference with
his play. Hays's acceptance of a similar agreement ensured the
supersession of *The Heavenly Express* by *Davy Crockett*.

The predominant influence throughout the early project memos is that
of Weill's theatrical experience in Berlin. German titles – always without
author's name attached – are in this respect an infallible guide wherever
they concern non-German plays or novels. Thus, for example, the social
satires of Mirbeau became something of a cult in Weimar Berlin (and *La
Chienne*, the first of Jean Renoir's two film versions of *The Diary of a
Chambermaid*, was seen there in 1932), while those of Katayev – one of the
rare court jesters in Stalin's Russia – were a discovery of Aufricht's
Theater am Schiffbauerdamm. Gogol's *The Government Inspector* appears
again and again in memos of the late 1930s and early 1940s, often in
conjunction with Zuckmayer's Köpenick play – its modern counterpart –
and always under the title *(Der) Revisor*, whose Moscow production by
Meyerhold was one of Weimar Berlin's most influential theatrical
imports. Theodore Dreiser's tragedy *The Hand of the Potter* (1918) appears,
again without author's name, as *Ton in Töpfers Hand* – another important
Berlin production of the pre-Hitler years.

Max Reinhardt (who in 1935 had Weill in mind for the wretched task,
later delegated to Korngold, of adding to Mendelssohn's *Midsummer
Night's Dream* score some numbers specifically designed for Reinhardt's
Hollywood film) was responsible for introducing Weill to Thornton
Wilder. After the successful premiere of *Our Town* in January 1938 – in a
production directed by Jed Harris, whose acquaintance Weill had already
cultivated in Paris – Wilder set to work on an adaptation of Nestroy's
Einen Jux will er sich machen (1842), which Reinhardt was due to direct
during the following season, with Herman Shumlin (yet another key
figure in the American theatre with whom Weill was consorting during
this period) as his producer. At an early stage if not at the very start,
Reinhardt encouraged Wilder to discuss with Weill the possibility of
introducing musical numbers, after the manner of Nestroy himself.
Wilder wrote to Weill expressing keen interest but also some anxiety
about his as yet untried abilities as a writer of lyrics. Weill was then
sidetracked by Maxwell Anderson and *Knickerbocker Holiday*. *The Merchant
of Yonkers* – for such the Nestroy became – was duly produced by
Shumlin and directed by Reinhardt as a straight play, in December 1938.
It was not successful. Nine years later Weill listed it in one of his project
memos; but the kind of musical he might then have had in mind was not
to be (Jerry Herman's *Hello Dolly!*, a hit show of 1966 based on *The
Merchant of Yonkers* via *The Matchmaker*, is surely of another kind); and an

attempt, during the same period, to wrest from Wilder permission to make a musical version of his novel *Heaven's my Destination* (1935) was fruitless.

Of the exclusive options Weill obtained during the late 1930s, the one from which he stood to gain most in the long term was for a musical version of Arthur Schnitzler's *Reigen*. Heinrich Schnitzler, the playwright's son and the executor of his estate, was an active member of the émigré community in California, a professor of German, and a keen supporter of modern music. (It was he who introduced Roger Sessions to the H. R. Hays version of Brecht's *Trial of Lucullus*, having previously spoken to Stravinsky about it.) Weill's good fortune in obtaining the rights to *Reigen* owed much to Heinrich Schnitzler's knowledge and experience of his music up to and including *Der Silbersee* (which Heinsheimer had discussed with Schnitzler prior to the first performance). But in the late 1930s and in the following decade *Reigen* was by no means as valuable a 'property' as might be imagined from today's standpoint. Written in 1896–7 and privately printed in 1900, it had had to wait until 1920 – that is, until the abolition of the Wilhelmine censorship – for its first performance in Germany. Twenty years later the censorships that still held sway throughout the English-speaking world were such that *Reigen* was at best suited for experimental theatre clubs, and in no foreseeable circumstances likely material for a major film sale. But Heinrich Schnitzler may well have reckoned that a musical version would (almost by definition) leave more to the imagination than the dialogues of Schnitzler's sexual rondo, and might therefore escape the censor on the back of *Der Rosenkavalier*, so to speak.

Whether in fact the supposed impropriety of the play was the principal obstacle seems questionable. The failure of Weill's attempts over a period of several years to find willing collaborators was surely due to the play's tone and to its wider social implications. Unlike the Mayerling material which Weill was considering during the same period – probably because of renewed contacts with Erik Charell, who had made a successful film of that hunting-lodge drama – *Reigen* offered nothing in the way of romantic idealism. Analytical and unsentimental, it would surely have been poison for the public that in 1940 rejected as merely unappetizing Rodgers's and Hart's *Pal Joey*.

For superficially different yet basically similar reasons, Weill was equally unlucky with the idea of a musical adaption of Georg Kaiser's satirical comedy *Kolportage*, to which he gave the working title *Trash*. His loyalty to Kaiser's work in general during these years is a recurrent feature of his project memos and correspondence, and it even extended to the Expressionist movement as a whole. Sternheim's *Der Snob* appears next to Kaiser's *Zweimal Oliver* in a remarkable list, c. 1937, that also embraces three plays by the once-fashionable Russian dramatist Leonid Andreyev (*He Who Gets Slapped*, *King Hunger*, and *The Life of Man*); and in

1937 Weill was corresponding with the émigré Expressionist playwright Ferdinand Bruckner regarding his play *The Enchantress* and Burgess Meredith's interest in it.

At the top of the list containing the Kaiser, Sternheim, and Andreyev titles was *Donogoo*, a play by Jules Romains which in broad outline anticipates *Mahagonny*. It was one of the many possibilities Weill was discussing in the late 1930s with Cheryl Crawford. Among the other French works were André Obey's *Noah* and Anatole France's *La Révolte des Anges* – the latter a special favourite, which he tried in vain to press on Ogden Nash after the success of *One Touch of Venus*.

The outbreak of the Second World War had so immediate and powerful a significance for Weill that the change it wrought in the character of his project notes was great enough to absorb the further impact of America's eventual entry into the war. That the change was not extreme – except with regard to socially critical material – owed much to Weill's continuing collaboration with Cheryl Crawford. Her musical and literary interests were close enough to his own to ensure that a few projects were carried over from the pre-war to the wartime periods and that new ones that were not entirely unrelated to earlier aims were still discussable. The ten ideas listed against the name 'Cheryl' in a memo of (winter) 1941–2 are representative of Weill's thinking in the war years:

> Tinted Venus
> Pirate
> Aristophanes
> Valentine
> James Barrie
> Caesar and Cleopatra
> Noah
> Arabian Nights in an air-raid shelter
> Tobias and the Angel
> Mary and the Fairy

F. J. Anstey's novella *The Tinted Venus* has been mentioned in several previous memos. The fact that it has now reached the top suggests that the 'Cheryl' list immediately anticipates her decision to go ahead with the project that eventually became *One Touch of Venus*. In this context the reappearance of Obey's *Noah* may mean that it was not in Paris but in London that Weill first encountered that remarkable play (which was staged at the New Theatre in 1935 with Gielgud in the title role). While the entry 'Arabian Nights in an air-raid shelter' must be a reverberation from the Battle of Britain and was probably linked with R. L. Stevenson's *New Arabian Nights* (listed in a memo of the late 1930s), James Bridie's *Tobias and the Angel* was an abiding interest: it has already been mentioned in several much earlier memos and is still being noted as late as November 1945 (when it is paired with Bridie's *Susanna and the Elders*).

The name 'James Barrie' almost certainly denotes *What Every Woman Knows*, the Barrie play in which Helen Hayes (the actress wife of Charles

MacArthur and a neighbour of Weill and Lenya) had a notable Broadway success. Jerome K. Jerome's *The Passing of Third Floor Back* was another warhorse from the pre-1914 British theatre. Successfully filmed in the 1930s, it had been staple fare of amateur dramatic societies ever since Forbes-Robertson had captured the public's imagination with his portrayal of the Christ-like stranger who takes a room in a poor lodging house and transforms the lives of the inhabitants. Its appearance in a project memo would be inexplicable but for the streak of vestigial messianism that surfaces from time to time in the series of memos and was finally embodied in *Lost in the Stars*.

With a Shaw play thrown in for good measure – and of that, more later – the British bias of the memo for Cheryl Crawford is as pronounced as the break with the Group Theatre ethos. Influenced by his own personal links with London at a time when it was under continued aerial bombardment, and by his new friendship with Gertrude Lawrence, the Weill of 1942 was especially mindful of the long-standing financial and artistic connections between the American theatre and the British. To the evidence of the Crawford memo must be added the detailed plans for a *Nell Gwyn* operetta, which Weill outlined in correspondence with the producer Russell Davies in the late summer of 1942. A post-Offenbachian vehicle for the popular soprano Grace Moore, *Nell Gwyn* was intended as a satire on monarchs and imperialism. But for the connection with Miss Moore – which Weill owed to Abravanel – *Nell Gwyn* would surely have been included in the Crawford memo, beside *The Tinted Venus*.

If *Lady in the Dark* may be seen as a substitute for *Reigen* or *Kolportage* – both of which Weill had offered to Moss Hart – the Crawford memo may be read as a practical replacement for those earlier memos in which German, French, and Russian literature had predominated. In its Anglophile leanings it complements the opening group in a 1941 memo destined for Moss Hart: Minstrel Show/Harriet Beecher Stowe/O. Henry (*Gentle Grafters*)/*Uncle Remus*.

After the success of *Lady in the Dark*, the Hart and Crawford memos each had their part to play; but neither was as broadly representative as the more eclectic list for S. N. Behrman that forms the greater part of a memo dating from June 1942. An added column on the right-hand side repeats the O. Henry title already given twice in the left-hand column:

Pirate	
Julius Caesar	
The Gentle Grafters	
The Beggar's Opera for negroes	
Horst Wessel	
The Trojan Horse	Negro Beggar's opera
The Gentle Grafters	Harriet Beecher Stowe
Ghengis Khan	Minstrel Show
Twelve Chairs	Julius Caesar
	Gentle Grafters

At the head of the memo that contains this 'Behrman' list stands once again the 'black *Dreigroschenoper*' idea – with the names of Moss Hart, Ben Hecht and Charles MacArthur against it. Beneath are seven names and titles, including *Der Silbersee*, and the cryptic 'Borchardt', which appears in no other memo.

The playwright and novelist Hans Hermann Borchardt (1891–1951) had worked with Piscator, and is named by Brecht as one of his collaborators on *St Joan of the Stockyards*. Disillusioned by his experiences in Stalin's Russia and subsequently maltreated in a Nazi concentration camp, Borchardt and his family had arrived on Ellis Island in 1940, and obtained entry permits thanks to the intercession of Georg Grosz. By profession a teacher as well as a writer, he spoke little English and was now penniless. Weill first learned of his plight from Rudolph Kommer in 1941, and promptly took up the cudgels on his behalf. Not only did he write a long and eloquent letter to the Guggenheim Foundation recommending – in vain – a grant to Borchardt, but he made a rough translation of his anti-Nazi play *Der verlorene Haufe*, and offered it to Maxwell Anderson as the basis for an adaptation in which there would be an important role for music. (The translation has not been traced.*) Predictably Anderson found the dramatic and intellectual structure of the play alien, and discounted any possibility of a successful Broadway adaptation. Kommer then approached Thornton Wilder, who read the play with sympathy, and was impressed by its authenticity, rigour, and integrity. But America had by now entered the war, and the national mood was such that Wilder came to the same conclusion as Anderson, if for different reasons.

Meanwhile Weill had introduced Borchardt to Ernst Josef Aufricht, whose entrepreneurial gifts were now directed towards émigré German literature and drama, especially in connection with New York's numerous German-language radio programmes. It was, however, to Kommer's legendary influence that Borchardt owed the publication in 1943 of his novel *The Conspiracy of the Carpenters*, a translation of a vast manuscript originally intended as a film treatment. Despite cuts so extensive as to render some passages almost incomprehensible, the book enjoyed a critical success. This may well have helped Aufricht's efforts on behalf of Borchardt's play *Die Brüder von Halberstadt*. But having raised approximately half the backing required for a Broadway production, he ran into the same obstacle as Weill had done with *Der verlorene Haufe*: unlike the authors of anti-Nazi plays and films written, however sincerely, for the wartime propaganda market, Borchardt was concerned to distinguish

---

* A typescript of *Der verlorene Haufe* is in WLRC, together with the Kommer–Borchardt–Weill correspondence and the text of Weill's recommendation of Borchardt to the Guggenheim Foundation. For further details of the episode, see the present author's paper 'Weill, Borchardt, und Kaiser' in: Lothar Schirmer (ed.), *Theater im Exil 1933–45. Ein Symposium der Akademie der Künste*. Berlin (West) 1979.

between Nazis and the German people as a whole. It was not a popular theme at that time. Indeed, the only public receptive to it was the small, isolated and fractious community of exiled German and Austrian intellectuals. Typical in that respect if in few others was Borchardt's erstwhile colleague and future sparring partner Bertolt Brecht.*

Brecht, together with his wife and children and Ruth Berlau, had landed in California in July 1941, after a journey that had taken them from Finland to Vladivostok and thence across the Pacific Ocean. Weill had already been in touch with him before he left Finland about American plans for *The Threepenny Opera*, and had sent a contribution towards his travelling expenses. In February 1942 Brecht writes from Santa Monica asking whether he had received *Der gute Mensch von Sezuan* from Finland, and whether there had been developments with *The Threepenny Opera*. In a second letter (2 March) he broaches the topic of an all-black production of *The Threepenny Opera* to be mounted in California, with Paul Robeson as Peachum and Katherine Dunham as Polly, and then brought to Broadway.

Weill was far from happy with the idea. But Brecht's account of Weill's reaction in his journal entry of 15 April 1942 is thoroughly misleading, and mischievously so if it was intended for any eyes but his own. Brecht does not mention Weill's sensible warnings about the folly of attempting to initiate a Broadway production on the West Coast, nor his insistence on proper and fair contractual arrangements. Instead he simply says that because Weill was 'making difficulties' he asked T. W. Adorno to write to him, and that Weill's response was abusive.

Adorno's letter to Weill of 31 March 1942 (WLA 48.18) was remarkably ill-advised: a legitimate appeal for understanding in the light of Brecht's straitened circumstances was combined with a brilliantly maladroit plea that the *Threepenny Opera* score was due for 'refunctioning' in terms of contemporary jazz improvisation. Weill did not keep a copy of his reply, but told Lenya (in a letter of 5 April) that it was one Adorno would not forget in a hurry. He was right; but Brecht, who notes on 15 April that it was 'full of attacks on me', seemed eager to forget it when he met Weill (for the first time in seven years) in Hollywood five months later. By then the *Threepenny Opera* project had died a natural death, as Weill had predicted (though his own project notes confirm the evidence in his correspondence that he appreciated its worth and took it seriously, despite all his justifiable reservations).

The main purpose of Weill's September visit to Hollywood was to introduce Cheryl Crawford to Marlene Dietrich, and play Dietrich some

---

*For Brecht's views on Borchardt, see the entry dated 30.9.43 in Brecht, ed. Werner Hecht, *Arbeitsjournal* (Frankfurt, Suhrkamp 1974). The entry was prompted by the publication of *The Conspiracy of the Carpenters*.

of his music for the *Venus* show in the hope of persuading her to undertake the title role. He saw Brecht only towards the end of his visit, and on 1 October reported to Lenya that he was 'just as dirty and unshaven as ever, but somehow much nicer and rather pathetic'. The letter continued:

> He wants to work with me badly, and the way he talks about it sounds very reasonable – but you know how long that lasts. Anyway, I will try to see him once more before I leave. [. . .] if I don't have to go into the army I think I will do a show with Brecht *for you*.

There is no word of that meeting in Brecht's journal, from which Weill is banished for twelve months after the black *Threepenny Opera* episode; he is not allowed to return until Brecht is in New York during the spring of 1943. In a single long entry covering the period March to May 1943 Brecht records various meetings with old friends and acquaintances. A characteristic awareness of posterity looking over his shoulder is particularly discernible in his remarks about Weill. Lest his future readers forget what he had written a year before, he notes that Weill has had a great success on Broadway. But this time he goes on to claim that Weill is 'no longer sure about his future here', and does so in order to imply that this is why he and Weill have now been 'brought together' by Ernst Josef Aufricht, their old manager at the Theater am Schiffbauerdamm.

Had Brecht recorded his October 1942 meeting with Weill in his work diary it would have been self-evident that their rapprochement was not dependent on Aufricht's intervention the following spring. A graver omission from his work diary is any mention of the spring days (a whole week according to Lenya) that he and Ruth Berlau spent in Brook House working with Weill on two separate projects – the *Sezuan* play, which had surely been a topic of discussion the previous October, and a new *Schweyk* (which was the one in which Lenya was to be given a role). In the work diary the first sign of Brecht's renewed interest in *Schweyk* is dated 15 July 1942 – some three months before his meeting with Weill. So that too may already have been discussed in October.

The 1943 *Švejk* project and its ultimate fate were to an uncanny extent predetermined by the project's long and complex ancestry. We have already seen that a *Švejk* opera, with or without Brecht, was to have been the immediate successor to *Mahagonny*. Weill's very first suggestion to Cheryl Crawford and the Group Theatre in 1936 had been *Švejk* as a play-with-music. From that idea, he and Paul Green had then developed *Johnny Johnson*, and thus circumvented the rights problem. A year later Brecht had attended Aufricht's Paris production of *Die Dreigroschenoper* – the production for which Weill had composed, in vain, the two Guilbert songs (see p. 293) – and while he was there, had talked with Erwin Piscator (who also attended Aufricht's production) about a Julius Caesar play and a *Švejk* film, which Piscator was now seeking to set up in France.* Aufricht would certainly have wished to involve himself with such projects, since he was at that time seeking a secure position for himself as a producer in Paris. But circumstances were against him, and neither his plans nor Piscator's came to anything. After the French collapse in 1940 Aufricht and his family made their escape by way of Spain and Portugal, arriving in New York in time to witness Weill's triumph with *Lady in the Dark*. When Weill wrote to Brecht on 13 March 1942 to thank him for the 'marvellous' *Ballade vom Soldatenweib* (see p. 323) and declared that he would set it to music immediately and 'offer it to the people who do the short-wave broadcasts to Germany', the 'people' he surely had in mind were Margot Aufricht and her colleagues at the Office of War Information.

Towards the end of 1942 Ruth Berlau began working for the OWI's short-wave Danish station, and in March Brecht joined her in New York, where he was to remain, as we have seen, for three months. On 3 April Aufricht presented at Hunter College the anti-Nazi programme in which Weill and Lenya gave the first public performance of *Die Ballade vom Soldatenweib*. The programme ended with a sketch given by the Czech comedians George Voskovec and Jan Werich, entitled 'Schweyk's spirit lives on'. Brecht was delighted with the sketch and so was Weill (who later became friends with Voskovec and Weric, and in 1947 seriously considered a collaboration with them).

Aufricht relates in his memoirs† how he had tried in vain to interest Weill in Joseph Roth's novel *Hiob* (Job), but now succeeded with the idea of a *Švejk* with Brecht, and, what is more, obtained the necessary rights from the 'agency in New York of the Czech Government-in-exile'. Aufricht does not mention, and may well have been unaware, that the legal representative of the agency was the selfsame Jan Loewenbach with whom Weill had been negotiating for *Švejk* thirteen years earlier; nor does he allude to Piscator's precisely contemporary discussions with the Theatre Guild regarding a possible production of the 'collective' adaptation of *Švejk* which he, Leo Lania, Brecht, and Gasbarra had made in 1927. Brecht knew of Piscator's plan, and John Willett is surely right in suggesting that since Piscator had involved Brecht in his plan, the arrangement between Aufricht and Brecht must have been made behind Piscator's back in order to secure the rights from Loewenbach.

---

* The indispensable source for all students of the *Švejk* project is Herbert Knust (ed.), *Materialien zu Bertolt Brechts 'Schweyk im zweiten Weltkrieg'* (Frankfurt, Suhrkamp, 1974). See also John Willett's introduction and notes to his edition of Brecht, *The American Plays 1942–46* (New York) and the same author's paper 'Piscator and Brecht. Closeness Through Distance' (*I Carbs*, Carbondale, vol. 1 no. 2, 1974) for many important details about the background to the Weill–Brecht *Schweyk* project; Klaus Völker's *Brecht-Chronik* (Munich, Hanser, 1971) and his *Brecht. A Biography* (London, Boyars, 1979) have also been helpful sources for the following account.

† E. J. Aufricht, *Erzähle, damit du dein Recht erweist* (Frankfurt/Berlin, 1966, p. 256).

Brecht's typescript of a scene-by-scene outline of *Schweyk* is dated '140 h, May 1943/New City (N.Y.)'.* On 23 May Brecht left by train for California. Having reread Hašek's novel during the journey, he wrote to Berlau on the 28th saying he had already started work on the play, and a day later he talked to Peter Lorre about the leading role. (Lorre had been a member of Aufricht's company in Berlin.) Within a fortnight he had finished the first act. By 25 June he could report to Berlau that apart from some of the song-texts the play was more or less complete. Weill – who by now had started the new Perelman–Nash version of the *Venus* show – arrived in Hollywood on 20 June or thereabouts, and visited Brecht on the 28th. After reading the *Schweyk* draft he made various suggestions which Brecht decided to adopt, noting in his journal that Weill's 'dramaturgic judgement was sound'. But meanwhile there had appeared in the *New York Times* of 22 June an announcement to the effect that Piscator was planning a production of *Švejk* in an adaptation by Arthur Kreymborg. Two days after Weill's visit, Brecht asked Berlau whether Kreymborg might be persuaded to undertake the translation of his play; Aufricht, he told her, would intercede with Piscator on his behalf, and would emphasize that although Brecht intended his *Schweyk* for Piscator, he and Aufricht were dependent on Weill.

By 7 July Brecht wrote again to Berlau saying that Aufricht had agreed to Kreymborg as translator. In a long and friendly letter to Weill – undated but clearly from the beginning of July (*Materialien*, p. 292) – Brecht announces that his work on *Schweyk* is almost done and that the first finished scenes will be on their way soon.† He recommends Kreymborg warmly, on the grounds that he is a poet, can write lyrics for music (or so he told Berlau), understands German, and 'ist gesinnungsmässig in Ordnung ['liberal']'. According to Brecht's letter to Berlau of 9 July, Weill replied that Kreymborg should be engaged only as a *translator*. Perhaps because of his parallel commitment to *Sezuan* but more probably because he was unhappy about Kreymborg's involvement, Weill did not (as far as we know) take any financial responsibility for the translation; it was paid for by Peter Lorre.

Early in August – according to a letter of the 13th from Brecht to Berlau – Weill reported that unspecified American writers had expressed the view that the *Schweyk* play (which he had already been discussing with them on the basis of the original outline of May) was unsuitable for Broadway, and that Aufricht, who also seemed to have doubts about it,

---

* The complete outline is published in Herbert Knust's *Materialien* volume; a translation of it is in John Willett's edition of the American plays.

† WLA lacks the originals of much of the *Schweyk* correspondence, including this important letter and the equally important (and again wholly amicable) letter pertaining to the contract with Weill (*Materialien*, 292–3). Nor does WLA have the *Schweyk* typescript that Brecht sent Weill later in July.

was alone capable of bringing about an 'experimental' production. Aufricht, indeed, had already found adequate backing for a production, and may well have had Piscator's Theatre Workshop in mind.* If so, he was unaware of the true state of affairs.

It was not until 12 August that Kreymborg wrote to Piscator to explain, as best he could, why he was now translating a *Schweyk* play of Brecht's instead of making his own Hašek adaptation for Piscator. Kreymborg completed his translation that same month. In September a typescript of it, bearing on the title page the proud legend 'Musical Score by Kurt Weill', was submitted to the Theatre Guild as if in ignorance of Piscator's previous negotiations about his own *Švejk*. (George Grosz, a friend of Aufricht, Brecht, and above all Piscator, had first approached the Theatre Guild about *Švejk* in 1935 – see Knust, *Materialien*, p. 138.) On 18 September 1943 Brecht wrote to Berlau in anticipation of the possibility that Weill would withdraw from the project, and wondered how far his participation was actually needed (Knust, *Materialien*, p. 296): after all, Eisler was ready to start work at once (having already composed two numbers), and he, Brecht, was not in principle opposed to the idea of officially sharing with Piscator the role of director. But five days later Piscator wrote to Brecht (in English – having drafted a very much angrier letter in German) saying that he was 'amazed to read in the newspapers an item that you, in collaboration with Kurt Weill, Mr Alfred Kreymborg, and Mr Aufricht were contemplating the production in the United States of *The Good Soldier Schweik*' (Knust, *Materialien*, p. 296). Piscator insisted on his prior claim, reminded Brecht of their discussions many months before, and declared that he was instructing his attorney to protect his rights. Weill – who had surely spoken to Piscator long before this – was sent a copy of the letter (which is not in WLA). On 12 October John Gassner of the Theatre Guild formally rejected the Brecht–Kreymborg play on the grounds that neither the form, nor the subject matter, nor the treatment, were suitable.

That, one might expect, would have been the end of the matter as far as Weill was concerned: during the five months it had taken to reach an impasse with *Schweyk*, *One Touch of Venus* had been written, composed, and finally, on 7 October, produced on Broadway. Rewarded by his second 'smashing box-office success' (*Variety*, 20 October 1943), Weill was not, to all outward appearances, someone of whom even Brecht could still have written that he was 'no longer sure of his position here'. Yet on 5 December 1943 he wrote to Brecht a letter that was entirely consistent with the spirit in which he had worked with Brecht and Berlau

---

*Piscator and Kreymborg do not figure in Aufricht's brief account of the *Schweyk* project. According to his recollection, he and Weill simply rejected as unproducible and irredeemable the play that Brecht sent them some six weeks after the signature of the contract (which would indeed have been early July).

in May. About *Sezuan*, as we shall see, he was wholly positive. 'With regard to *Schweyk*,' he continued,

> I would like to reaffirm my position: I do not think the present [Kreymborg] version has any chance of success on the American stage without decisive alterations. It's possible that a leading American writer – such as Ben Hecht – would find a way of translating the humour of your original text into American. But I doubt if the contractual situation [cf. Piscator's letter] is sufficiently clear for the financing of a first-class Broadway production. [. . .] My own collaboration would depend on three things. First, that the play is adapted by a top-flight American writer and directed by a top-flight American director; second that Lenya plays the role of the landlady [a condition heartily endorsed by Brecht – see his letter to Berlau of 19 July]; and third, that the play is written as a 'musical play' with more openings for music than the present version [which nevertheless contained numerous songs and two finales]. In no event will I write 'incidental music'.

Brecht was undeterred. In the summer of 1947 he wrote to Weill from California informing him that Walter Langhoff, the new Intendant of the Deutsches Theater in the Russian sector of Berlin, had invited him to form a company, and that *Schweyk im zweiten Weltkrieg* would be among its first productions. Brecht urged Weill to undertake the score for Berlin. Weill, who had just embarked on *Love Life* with Alan Jay Lerner, replied on 3 September 1947:

> I'm afraid that I'm so heavily committed for the next five to six months that I would have no time for the *Schweyk* music. But if you are not planning to have the performance until the 1948–49 season, I could perhaps do it next summer.

Brecht appeared at the HUAC hearings in Washington at the end of October, left for Europe immediately afterwards, and spent most of the next year in Switzerland. It was not until December 1948 that he reached Berlin, and began his discussions with Langhoff. The world premiere of *Schweyk* (with Peter Lorre in the title role) was indeed one of the topics of discussion. But a production did not materialize in Weill's lifetime; nor even in Brecht's.

It would be unrealistic to equate the loss of a *Švejk* opera by Weill in 1930 with the loss of a musical play by Brecht and Weill in 1943 or even 1948. The 1930 project arose from Weill's own creative requirements, and the ultimate responsibility was his alone. Its successor of 1943 arose from Aufricht's and Brecht's keen interest in a Broadway production, and whatever the extent of Weill's contributions, both at the planning stage in Brook House and at the revision stage in Santa Monica, the end result was a play by Brecht (for which Eisler in due course provided an admirable score).

From Weill's point of view the topicality of the new *Schweyk* must have seemed its most attractive and at the same time its most dangerous feature. His project memos of 1937–42 repeatedly approach the phenomenon of Hitlerism, either by way of history (Julius Caesar, Genghis

Khan, Napoleon) or through contemporary satire. In that sense Brecht's 'Interludes in the Higher Regions' and the final confrontation between Schweyk and Hitler himself* would have answered a long-felt need. But the victory that was already in sight in 1943 promised an early end to that kind of topicality. References to Hitler and his forebears vanish from Weill's project memos after 1942.

Whereas the agreement with Aufricht over *Schweyk* was by its very nature ephemeral, the underlying and unwritten agreement between Brecht and Weill was of quite another order, as is clear from the partly contemporaneous *Sezuan* project (and even from the fact that Brecht entrusted his *Kinderkreuzzug* to Weill during his stay in Brook House, and noted in his *Arbeitsjournal* that Weill would make a setting of it). It is *Sezuan* not *Schweyk* that reveals how close were the bonds between the two men.

In a letter to Weill written from Denmark on 23 March 1939 Brecht reports that he is now working on *Sezuan*, the parable play 'which I told you about in New York'. The significance of this apparently casual reminder derives from the following facts: (1) the first entry concerning *Der gute Mensch von Sezuan* in Brecht's *Arbeitsjournal* is dated 15 March 1939 – just eight days before his letter to Weill – and it states that he has been re-examining the 'old draft' of the *Sezuan* begun in Berlin as *Die Ware Liebe* (*The Commodity, Love*); (2) the New York meeting with Weill took place in November–December 1935; (3) *Die sieben Todsünden* had been staged in Copenhagen on 12 November 1936, and until there is clear evidence to the contrary we can surely assume that Brecht and Berlau attended the performance, for they were both living in Denmark during that period; (4) *Die Ware Liebe* dates from 1930, the year of Weill's *Švejk* opera project, and derives from *Fanny Kress*, a play project of 1927, the year in which the Weill–Brecht collaboration was established.†

Not only does the New York meeting precisely bisect the span from *Die Ware Liebe* of 1930 to *Der gute Mensch* of 1939, but it followed closely on the consolidation of Brecht's relationship with Ruth Berlau. Berlau's crucial role during the years of Brecht's exile in Denmark is well documented, and her involvement with the 1939 *gute Mensch* plan can safely be taken for granted in view of Brecht's formal acknowledgement of her collaboration on the play. How far the Shen Te/Shui Ta antinomy reflected Brecht's perception of her character at that stage – as it

---

*The final confrontation has a satirical function comparable to that of a work that appears in one of Weill's memos (*c.* 1941) as 'English book about Hitler landing (Low)' – clearly *The Flying Visit*, a satirical novella by Peter Fleming, with illustrations by David Low, published in 1940. Fleming has the 'Eagle Führer' ignominiously parachuted into rural England, where he cuts so absurd a figure that the incredulous villagers take him for an escaped lunatic.

†See *Materialien zu Brechts 'Der gute Mensch von Sezuan'* (ed. Werner Hecht: Frankfurt, 1974) for much useful documentation – though not a word about Weill.

demonstrably did in later years – is of purely psychological interest, and not a question that significantly colours the result of the week's discussions between Weill, Brecht and Berlau in the spring of 1943. Of far greater relevance is the casual-seeming reference to the 1935 discussion of *Sezuan* in Brecht's 1939 letter to Weill from Denmark and the fact that he troubled to mail the completed play to Weill from Finland in 1941.*

Collaboration – on his own terms if humanly possible, and flexible ones if not – was a matter of fundamental creative importance to Brecht, and something about which his intentions and actions were never, in any circumstances, casual. As subsequent events showed, his 1939 reference to a discussion four years earlier was strictly functional. If, as seems likely, the 1935 discussions about *Sezuan* harked back at least five years to joint consideration of *Die Ware Liebe*, the *Sezuan–Schweyk* agreement of 1943 was precisely symmetrical in its retrospective aspects. The essential difference was that *Schweyk* had yet to be written and was a quasi-commercial venture, whereas *Sezuan* had already been performed (in Zurich in February 1943) and was manifestly a work of central importance in Brecht's output.

In his letter of 5 December 1943 – written from Hollywood to Brecht in New York – Weill declared:

> You write that you would now like to come to an early agreement about *Sezuan*. I could come to terms with you at once, pay you an advance and commission a rough translation, if I had the agreement or at least the honourable interest of a writer who would prepare the American book.

On 19 January 1944 Weill cabled his New York lawyer about an announcement in the *New York Times* indicating that Brecht was exploring alternative possibilities for a Broadway *Sezuan*.† On the 22nd he wrote as follows to his lawyer:

> You will have gathered from my wire that I feel a strong resentment against Brecht's attitude in the matter of *Sezuan*. I have known Brecht for years. He has always been the most difficult man to work with. I hoped that he had changed his attitude. [. . .] Unfortunately I was mistaken. Instead of seizing his opportunity with both hands, he kept stalling, made impossible demands, and all kinds of difficulties. [. . .] The next thing I heard was the announcement in the newspapers that somebody else is doing the play. He is playing his old tricks again – and I just don't feel like going through all this again. Life is too short – and the finest American playwrights would be only too happy to give me their plays or to collaborate with me. Of course this feeling would not be enough for me to dismiss an interesting project. [. . .] In the meantime, if Brecht thinks he should go ahead with the other

---

* It was not in legacy in 1958–60. On his arrival in America in 1941 Brecht asked Weill (undated letter, WLRC) whether he had received the copy he had sent from Finland. If the answer was no, he would presumably have sent another.
† No edition of the *New York Times* containing such an announcement has yet been traced. The gist of it, apparently, was that Aufricht was planning a (workshop?) production. Note also Brecht's discussions of the play with Elisabeth Bergner.

production, I don't want to be in his way. But I do want to make sure that he cannot use any of my ideas for that other production.

News of Weill's reaction prompted Brecht to write an apologetic letter to Weill, assuring him that he was not responsible for the *Times* announcement. 'Be that as it may,' wrote Weill to his lawyer on 30 January,

the damage has been done. Some people who were important to me are no longer interested in the project because they are afraid of getting involved in something that looks like a lot of headaches. [. . .] But I don't want to use this incident to withdraw from my promise. Brecht seems to need money badly, and I might just as well give him something. If I get the show together, so much the better. If not, I have helped a very talented (and very difficult) man a little bit. With the signing of our contract I am willing to pay Brecht the sum of $600 representing a payment of $100 monthly, six months in advance. If after six months I did not succeed in lining up a production, it is up to me either to cancel the contract or to continue it, in which case I would have to continue to pay $100 monthly for another six months. If, on the other hand, I am able to line up a production during the first six months I am willing to pay Brecht an additional $400 – so that in this case he has an advance of $1000 as well as a production coming up.

These terms were accepted by Brecht, and a contract for what Brecht describes in *Arbeitsjournal* (p. 370) as a 'semi-operatic' version was duly signed. What transpired in the ensuing six months can only be guessed from a letter Weill wrote to his New York lawyer on 25 October 1944. Weill, who was again in Hollywood, thanked his lawyer for 'winding up the Brecht affair', and continued:

I have tried very hard to get somebody interested in this property, but nobody who would be talented enough to do the job caught fire. So I had to give it up. Maybe at a later date I will find somebody.

The irony of describing *Sezuan* as a 'property' was certainly unintentional, for in Broadway terms that is exactly what it was – an unmarketable one. When we recall that the period of Weill's main engagement with the *Sezuan* idea is bounded at the one end by the New York opening of *One Touch of Venus* in October 1943 and at the other by the start of his work with Edwin Justus Mayer and Ira Gershwin on *The Firebrand of Florence*, his efforts on Brecht's behalf are seen in their proper context. The extent to which Mayer may have been involved in them merits some investigation.

Mayer, who had made a name for himself as a Broadway playwright in the 1920s but was now firmly ensconced at MGM, had been introduced to Weill by Ira Gershwin, who had doubtless noted the accidental affinities between *The Threepenny Opera* and Mayer's *The Children of Darkness* – a play involving among other historical figures the highwayman Jonathan Wild immortalized by Fielding in his eponymous novel. *The Children of Darkness* appears on a project memo dating from the immediate aftermath of *Lady in the Dark* (though *Jonathan Wild* itself had already appeared in a memo of the late 1930s). In the course of his unceasing search for an American writer or team of writers capable of making a new *Threepenny Opera* adaptation – a search that began in the Group Theatre days and continued throughout the 1940s* – Weill would surely not have neglected a collaborator who combined the right sort of background with ready access to the film industry.† The only evidence in the Weill legacy of a connection between Mayer and Brecht is a cable from Mayer dated 18 April 1944:

> Dear Kurt, having your manuscript typed, sending copy to Brecht as you requested and rest of copies to you. [. . .] Are you going to do the Billy Rose thing‡ or are you going to do *The Firebrand* with me?

As nothing else is known about the transaction, the most likely inference from the date and content of the cable is that 'your manuscript' was the rough translation of *Sezuan* which Weill had told Brecht he would commission.

If such indeed it was, Mayer had presumably been offered first refusal, but had telephoned Weill after reading the manuscript, and was now acting as a disinterested intermediary. Brecht had returned to Santa Monica in mid-March. On 29 April he notes in the *Arbeitsjournal* that Charles Laughton had been feasting himself on the 'rough translation' of *Schweyk* (a new one). Weill left New York in the third week of June for a three-month spell in Hollywood, during which *The Firebrand* claimed much of his attention and *Where Do We Go From Here?* the remainder. Of *Sezuan* no more is heard for eighteen months.

One of the themes of Weill's letters to Lenya during the weeks in Hollywood when he was composing *The Firebrand* was his desire to return to opera. By this he meant opera for Broadway or even Hollywood, a distinction already implicit in the inverted commas he had placed around the word in a project memo dated 15 March 1942. Of the three subjects he then had in mind for 'operas', the first, identified

---

* The most distinguished writer whom Weill approached – indirectly, through Cheryl Crawford in 1945 – was Thornton Wilder, who had seen and been greatly impressed by *Mother Courage* in Zurich in 1941. As quoted by Cheryl Crawford in her letter to Weill of 9 August 1945, Wilder found the *Threepenny Novel* very striking and the play (which he seems to have seen in the theatre, but not to have read before) 'superb'. Nevertheless he felt that the play was not for him – 'It's a criticism of society, not human all-too-human.'

† The entry of 1 June 1942 in Brecht's *Arbeitsjournal* lists four 'chances', of which the first is a *Threepenny Opera* film deal with MGM, the second a film with Jean Renoir, and the third a Broadway *Sezuan* starring Anna May Wong.

‡ This was a revue entitled *The Seven Lively Arts* which Billy Rose was planning to present at the Ziegfeld Theater in New York in December 1944. Rose had engaged Maurice Abravanel as his musical director, and had asked Weill to write a ballet score for Anton Dolin (with sets by Norman Bel Geddes). Weill declined, and suggested Stravinsky or, failing him, Milhaud. (Stravinsky accepted, and composed *Scènes de Ballet*.)

simply as 'Walt Whitman', does not appear again and was obviously prompted by the Whitman settings he was then composing. But the other two, '*Marco Millions* or *Fountain*', were a pair that had begun to thread their way through the project memos in the 1930s, and continued to do so until at least the mid-forties. Whatever the personal grounds for Weill's long-standing interest in these resolutely old-fashioned examples of O'Neill's dramatic art, it is clear from *The Firebrand* that he regarded historical romances as a necessary part of his contribution to Broadway. How else to account for no fewer than three references in the project memos to *Gone with the Wind*? An international bestseller that had first met its match in the film music of Max Steiner, Margaret Mitchell's by no means negligible novel might perhaps have been suitable material for a Deems Taylor or a Korngold, but for Weill it has no obvious attractions. The context in which he first mentions it is a memo of fifteen titles dating from the summer or early autumn of 1945. The background to it was the failure of *The Firebrand* in February of that year. It had been Weill's first major reverse since arriving in the USA, and in blaming it (as he did in his correspondence with Lenya) on Mayer's 'book' he was implicitly blaming himself for accepting such a book. At the beginning of May he was talking with René Clair about a musical version of Labiche's *The Italian Straw Hat* – which he had just been reading at the Milhauds' – and also corresponding with Paul Robeson, for whom he wanted to write a black *Oedipus*. Obviously seeing it as a substitute for the abortive *Ulysses Africanus*, he discussed it with Maxwell Anderson, who was initially enthusiastic. On 18 May 1945 Weill wrote to Lenya from Hollywood:

> As was to be expected, Max's enthusiasm for a coloured *Oedipus* opera died a very quick death. He didn't find a 'meaning' in it. I tried to call Paul Robeson in Chicago but couldn't reach him, so I'll see him in New York. Otherwise nothing interesting has shown up yet with regard to the new show. It will be a hard grind to find a book because it has to be darned good this time – and I'll have to find it all by myself.

That surely is the inner sense of the long memo in which *Gone with the Wind* first appears. It begins with three old favourites: Gogol's *Revisor* (still with its German title), Molière, and *White Wings*. Others appear further down the list, including Ben Jonson, of whom he had been reminded by a performance of *Volpone* given by actors mostly from the old Group Theatre ('What a wonderful play!' – Weill to Lenya, 16 June 1945) and Bridie's *Tobias* (together with *Susanna and the Elders*).

In studying any memo made in Hollywood it is important to remember that Weill is also looking for possible material for film musicals – a distinction of aim he seldom troubles to specify. However, a memo dated April 1945 has the heading 'Pictures', and includes *White Wings*, *The Italian Straw Hat*, *The Gentle Grafters*, Maxwell Anderson's *High Tor* (a very old favourite), and Marc Connelly's *The Farmer Takes a Wife*. The Hollywood emphasis in the memos of 1945 makes the first appearance of

Gone with the Wind doubly surprising, since the prospect of a film sale
would have to be discounted in any approach to potential backers of a
stage version. (The same applied to *How Green was my Valley*, another
recently filmed novel that appears on the fifteen-part list, and probably
also to Frank Capra's classic film comedy of 1934, *It Happened One Night*,
which is also listed there.)

Whereas it had taken Weill some eighteen months to establish the basis
for a new show after the success of *Lady in the Dark*, it took him only half
that time to achieve the same result after the failure of *The Firebrand*. The
key that unlocked the door is in a memo written on the same paper as its
fifteen-part predecessor, and dated 7 November 1945. It comprises only
eight titles, of which, however, the first and third have been struck out:

Robeson show
Street Scene
Don Juan
Gone with the Wind
School for Wives
Farmer Takes a Wife
Sezuan (Hughes)
The Blue Danube

The most immediately striking title is *Sezuan*, reappearing just a year after
Weill had officially surrendered his option. (It is not the last we shall hear
of it.) Two of the three titles that have not appeared in any previous
memo or correspondence are never to reappear – *Don Juan* (Molière
again? Or E. T. A. Hoffmann? Or even Sternheim?) and *The Blue Danube*
(which perhaps speaks for itself). The third is *Street Scene*.

The 7 November memo is thus one of the crucial documents in the
study of Weill's selection processes during the American years. Were
some earlier evidence of an interest in *Street Scene* to come to light, it
would support Weill's contention – in interviews and elsewhere – that a
musical version of *Street Scene* was an old and cherished ambition of his.*
But it would not alter the significance of the contents and the date of the
memo. The deletion of 'Robeson show' may well be a clue to the
appearance, for the first time in any memo, of the name of Langston
Hughes. Once Maxwell Anderson had declined the black *Oedipus* and
Weill had discussed the project again with Robeson, the name of
Langston Hughes was bound to present itself. As the leading black poet
of his generation, and like Robeson a militant campaigner for black
rights, Hughes was the obvious choice as lyricist of any 'show' that Weill
might have in mind for Robeson. While Robeson's numerous wartime

---

* A production of Elmer Rice's play, starring Albert Bassermann, Grete Mosheim and
Rosa Valetti, was staged by Heinz Hilpert in Berlin in 1930. Like the precisely
contemporary *Apollo–Brunnenstrasse* by Grossmann and Hessel, it was not well
received. There is no record of Weill having seen it.

engagements were probably responsible for the demise of the project, his connection with Brecht's black *Threepenny Opera* project of 1942 would have been sufficient to prompt the idea of transposing Brecht's *Sezuan* to Harlem with the expert assistance of Hughes.

If some such thought was in Weill's mind, the member of the Playwrights' Company whose collaboration he was most likely to have solicited was the one whose political views were furthest to the Left (though far short of Brecht's), and the only one who had first-hand experience of the theatre of pre-Hitler Germany and post-Revolutionary Russia – Elmer Rice, the author of *Street Scene*.

In The Playwrights' Company and the votes of its six playwright members lay Weill's surest hope of financial backing for a Broadway musical in the 1940s. Since Elmer Rice in November 1945 would have had even less to gain from adapting a play by Brecht than E. J. Mayer would have had eighteen months earlier, the rapidity with which events overtook the memo of 7 November is scarcely surprising. On the 28th of that month Weill wrote to his agent in Hollywood:

> For the theatre I have started working on a musical version of *Street Scene* as a Broadway Opera, book by Elmer Rice, lyrics by Langston Hughes. It looks very exciting. The Playwrights' Company will produce it next fall. I am also working on a show project with Maxwell Anderson as a possibility for spring.

Yet it was to S. N. Behrman – another member of the Playwrights' Company – that Weill was speaking on 14 December, with a view to securing his collaboration on an opera buffa version of *The Inspector General* (as he calls it, at long last, in his diary). Behrman was not interested. Neither was Anderson, to whom Weill spoke on 12 January – the day on which he initiated the composition of *Street Scene* with the song 'Wouldn't you like to be on Broadway?' On the 21st he dangled in front of Anderson a play that was certainly among those he was to discuss with Alan Jay Lerner a year or two later – *Pygmalion*.

Weill's presentiments of Broadway hits, whether Lerner's and Loewe's with *My Fair Lady* in 1956 or Frank Loesser's with *The Most Happy Fella* that same year,* lend an occasional piquancy to the grand procession of his project memos, but are misleading with regard to general character and tendency. So far from being success-oriented, the majority of his American projects is manifestly at odds with prevailing box-office criteria. A European bias continually asserts itself and is then subject to the same form of over-correction that can lead Weill from some favourite

---

* *The Most Happy Fella* is based on *They Knew What They Wanted*, a comedy by Sidney Howard noted in a project memo of 1946. Howard and Weill had a high regard for each other, and before his tragic death in 1939 Howard was in correspondence with Weill about several projects. His last play, finished shortly before his death, was *Madam Will You Walk?* (see p. 311); it too figures among Weill's project memos of the 1940s.

but hopelessly recondite project* to another so overweeningly 'commercial' as to be, in practice, unrealizable.

Gone with the Wind belongs, of course, in the latter category. *Pygmalion* does not. Like *Heartbreak House*, *Captain Brassbound's Conversion*, and *Caesar and Cleopatra* – all of which, and especially the latter, figure in Weill's plans from 1937 onwards – *Pygmalion* was a choice determined not only by the immediate box-office attractions (heightened as they were by the success of the film version made in 1938 by Anthony Asquith, with whom Weill had been on friendly terms in London) but also and fundamentally by the considerations that had led his and Brecht's generation in Germany (and Georg Kaiser's generation before it) to accord Shaw a special place of honour among modern dramatists.

In that sense Weill's interest in Shaw was distinct from his interest in O'Neill – or for that matter Ferenc Molnár, whose perennial *Liliom* he was ardently pursuing in 1937 with a view to a Theatre Guild production that would certainly have come about had the musical rights been obtainable.† With Shaw, however, the aversion experienced by every successful playwright to the prospect of sharing royalties with a composer was intensified by a peculiarly strong sense of the sanctity of his work, coupled with a wide knowledge, and lively understanding, of music. Shaw had been so incensed by *The Chocolate Soldier* – the highly successful Oscar Straus operetta based on *Arms and the Man* – that he refused to license any further musical adaptations of his plays. However, his equally intransigent view of the film industry had proved susceptible to change: in 1937 he was persuaded to grant exclusive film rights to Gabriel Pascal, a French-born producer whom Weill had met in Paris two or three years before. *Pygmalion* was Pascal's first venture under the new dispensation, and Shaw was delighted with it. If everything had gone according to Pascal's well-publicized plans, a start would then have been made on *Caesar and Cleopatra*. But the war intervened, and in due course Pascal came to Hollywood in search of funds and resources. It was there that Weill renewed his acquaintance, not without hope of gaining a musical entrée to *Caesar and Cleopatra* by way of the cinema. (The score for the *Pygmalion* film had been written by Arthur Honegger, who was now trapped in France.) Pascal was apparently amenable, and assured Weill that he would be his first choice not only for *Caesar and Cleopatra* but for

---

*E.g. the 'Multatuli' noted in a memo of 7 September 1946. Multatuli was the pseudonym of the Dutch writer Eduard Douwes Dekker (1820–1887). His central work is the two-volume novel *Max Havelaar*, a denunciation of colonialism based – like most of Dekker's writings – on his experiences in Indonesia. Weill's interest in Multatuli dates back to 1930 if not before. In 1933 he wrote from Paris to Lenya in Berlin, asking her to send him his Multatuli edition. (See p. 438.)

†Two less celebrated Molnár plays figure in a memo of the early 1940s. As for *Liliom*, Richard Rodgers and Oscar Hammerstein succeeded where Weill failed, and produced from it their hit show *Carousel* (1945).

all his Shaw films. After delays and crises worthy of *The Eternal Road*, *Caesar and Cleopatra* was filmed in England under the auspices of J. Arthur Rank, and released in 1945 with a score by Honegger's colleague Georges Auric.

It was not until several weeks after the successful Broadway opening of *Street Scene* that Weill continued his ill-fated overtures to the film industry. On 17 March 1947 he instructed his Hollywood agent to offer the studios musical versions of Maxwell Anderson's *High Tor* and John Galsworthy's short story 'The Apple Tree' – the latter to be presented first as a stage show, possibly with book and lyrics by Alan Jay Lerner. Meanwhile Weill was in correspondence with William Saroyan about a possible stage collaboration, and on 18 April he received news that Tennessee Williams would be 'thrilled with the idea of doing a play' with him. But the idea of a musical *High Tor* thrilled no one in Hollywood: and the Galsworthy Estate could offer Weill only the stage rights in 'The Apple Tree', as the film rights had already been sold.

On returning to New York in June 1947 from his visit to Europe and Palestine, Weill opened discussions with the director Charles Friedman and the 31-year-old novelist Herman Wouk regarding a musical adaptation of Wouk's *Aurora Dawn*, a satire on the American radio business. Although Wouk was enthusiastic, the project had to be postponed as he had just embarked on his third novel, *The Caine Mutiny*. A month later Lerner and Weill were at work on *Love Life* for Cheryl Crawford.

Lerner accompanied Weill on his last foray to Hollywood, in November 1948. They had collaborated on a film story entitled *Miss Memory*, and were hoping to find a buyer for it (correspondence in WLA). A film story by Weill himself, entitled *I Married a King* (typescript in WLA), reads very much as if it dated from the same period. On 2 December 1948 – a few days after he had received a letter from his agent saying there was no longer a market in Hollywood for the kind of musical films he wanted to write – Weill cabled Alexander Korda in England, offering him a musical version of René Clair's British-made film *The Ghost Goes West*, to be directed by Lewis Milestone. Korda replied that he was very much interested, whereupon Weill wrote to him at some length, and recommended Alan Lerner as screenwriter and lyricist.

Perhaps because Weill's main concern was how to consolidate his collaboration with Lerner, the flow of new project ideas seems sharply to diminish during the last year of his life. In January 1949, just as he was about to begin *Lost in the Stars*, he sent Lerner a few lines about a version of the Lorelei legend set in 1944 at the time of the Rhine crossings. Three months later he was much moved by Stephen Vincent Benét's short story 'Too Early Spring', which he had been reading in an anthology entitled *First Love*. This too he suggested to Lerner, at the same time as announcing that he would shortly be talking to the actor–producer José Ferrer about O'Neill's *Marco Millions*.

After his first heart attack in July 1949, Weill reserved most of his energies for *Lost in the Stars*; and as soon as the show was successfully launched he turned again to Maxwell Anderson, for *Huckleberry Finn*. But Lerner was not forgotten: in his diary entry of 1 February 1950 – six weeks before the start of his final illness – Weill records that he had telephoned Gertrude Lawrence to tell her that he and Lerner had decided to go ahead with *Ruth*, a project they had first discussed as an 'opera' during their abortive visit to Hollywood in 1948. It was to be based on the Book of Ruth, and like *Lost in the Stars* was to incorporate music written many years before – in this case, the 'Ruth' scene in *The Eternal Road*.

The chronological sense in which *Ruth* is, or appears to be, the last of Weill's declared projects is misleading, in that it ignores the continual and complex overlapping characteristic of Weill's decision-making during his last fifteen years. Significantly, *Ruth* does not figure in what is surely the last and perhaps the most revealing of all Weill's project memos. Dated 15 January 1950 – that is, towards the end of his first week with Maxwell Anderson on *Huckleberry Finn* – it bears the heading 'Opera Ideas', and comprises nine swiftly written titles, six of which have appeared more or less frequently in memos going back as far as the 1930s. The list reads as follows:

Spoon River Anthology [Edgar Lee Masters]
Dulcinea [Elmer Rice?]
The Grapes of Wrath [Steinbeck]
Green Mansions [W. H. Hudson]
Good Maiden of Sezuan [Brecht]
Gone with the Wind [Mitchell]
John Brown's Body [Benét]
Winterset [Maxwell Anderson]
Moby Dick [Melville]

The first idea is certainly one of the oldest – it appears in a project memo of 1938 – and the last is perhaps the newest; as for *Winterset* (Anderson's third Saccho and Vanzetti drama) it was the first play Weill and Lenya saw in New York in 1935; and *The Grapes of Wrath* is a legacy from early attempts to establish a collaboration with Steinbeck. There is no previous record of the cryptic *Dulcinea*, nor is there any sign of previous interest in the towering figure of Herman Melville. And yet on 2 February 1950 Weill noted in his diary a meeting with Mrs Francis Pain 'who offers me to do *Moby Dick* for Met'.

One senses in the 'Opera Ideas' a conscious effort on Weill's part to confront the post-war world and signal the start of his own and his century's sixth decade by gathering some of the threads from the past fifteen years. Yet their heterogeneity is at first glance almost incomprehensible, and much more so than that of the project memos of the 1940s which manifestly provide for the elements of chance and random selection inherent in the Broadway production system. Although the generic title firmly distinguishes the memo from those of the previous decade, the comparison it suggests with the proposals for the 1937 radio opera project is only helpful in so far as it highlights the relative homogeneity and the somewhat impersonal character of the radio list. Altogether more telling is the comparison with the four-part list offered to Charell in 1932 (and its two adjacent projects, *Naboth's Vineyard* and *Caligari*). In 1932 Weill was still evaluating every project in terms of the creative 'line' he had maintained since the early 1920s; and the standards implicit in that evolution continued to hold sway until the sudden intervention of *Marie Galante*.

Although at the time *Marie Galante* may not have signified anything more than a temporary surrender to expediency, the precedent had been set for the oscillations that soon superseded the linear progression and became characteristic of Weill's Broadway career. The nine 'Opera Ideas' begin to reveal their secrets only when read as two alternating series.*

Annotations in the margins of Weill's troubled hopes during the last weeks of his life, the 'Opera Ideas' have an air of unreality that recalls the symphonic project mentioned, with studied nonchalance, in a letter to Ira Gershwin of 28 May 1941.† In the complex of emotions that drew Weill to George Gershwin's younger brother, the need to inform did not always take precedence over the desire to impress. The fact that the American section of Weill's legacy contains not even the briefest sketch for concert music of any kind is, in its own way, singularly impressive; but it is not conclusive. More important, and more relevant to the substance of the 'Opera Ideas', is the speed with which Weill had distanced himself during the late 1930s from all musical conventions appropriate to the construction of abstract forms. A folksong symphony in the manner of say, Virgil Thomson, might have been conceivable at the time of *Railroads on Parade*; but surely not after *Lady in the Dark*. Likewise the idioms appropriate to a *Spoon River Anthology* or even a *Grapes of Wrath* had been far more readily accessible in the era of *Johnny Johnson* and the Federal Theatre – when Weill first noted these projects – than in the aftermath of *Down in the Valley* and *Lost in the Stars*.

Thanks to the self-analysis so painfully begun in *Love Life*, the journey to *Spoon River* might nevertheless have been accomplished in due course. Immeasurably longer and more arduous for Weill in 1950 was the road to Brecht's *Sezuan*. Students of the collaboration who take the short side path indicated by the *Arbeitsjournal* are spared even a glimpse of the real obstacles, and very soon reach the pre-ordained conclusions about Weill and the crass commercialism of Broadway. The fact that Weill devoted so

---

* If the 'Dulcinea' Weill had in mind was the creation of Cervantes rather than Elmer Rice the alternative series begins with a new colour, but not, as *The Man from La Mancha* demonstrated in 1965, with one that is necessarily incompatible with Broadway.
† Copy in the Weill–Lenya Research Center; see also letter to I.G. of 4 September 1941.

much time and effort to furthering the project, and persisted with it long after Broadway had rejected his approaches, is yet another warning that where Weill is concerned the truth is seldom as simple as Brecht and his more trusting disciples would have us believe. On the other hand it would be irresponsible to assume that Weill's evident awareness of the musical, intellectual, and personal problems inherent in the *Sezuan* project took full account of their complexity, let alone presupposed a feasible solution.

If, like the final number in *The Lindbergh Flight*, the 'Opera Ideas' of 1950 may be read as a 'Report on the Unattainable' their true epitome is not *Sezuan* but *Moby Dick*. Ishmael and Ahab have more to tell us about Weill and the projects he never began than have Brecht's *gute Mensch* or the Bible's Ruth about those he never completed. But since there is no 'last project', just as there is no 'last work', it seems appropriate to close this survey by returning, with Melville, to the one moment of apparent finality in Weill's American career – the moment when Europe and the seven *Wanderjahre* seemed safely behind him, and *Lady in the Dark* had publicly celebrated his nuptials with Broadway and the American way of life.

While Brecht was sailing from Vladivostock to Los Angeles, his and Weill's one-time father-figure Georg Kaiser was gazing longingly across the Atlantic from his exile in Switzerland, and dreaming of a collaboration with Weill that was as far removed from the world of *Lady in the Dark* as either *Sezuan* or *Schweyk*. On 7 July 1941 Kaiser wrote to his American representative Paul Gordon about Melville's last work and his decision to base a musical play on it. 'Some time ago,' he recalled,

> you asked if I would be willing to produce something together with Kurt Weill. The novel *Billy Budd* ends with a ballad. After I had read this ballad, the style of the play came clear to me. It would have to be a play with music. This music should be written by Kurt Weill. Therefore I ask you to read Melville's novel and then have a confidential discussion with Kurt Weill.*

In the letters from Gordon to Weill (WLA) there is no mention of *Billy Budd*. But in the lines of Billy's ballad there was indeed a music that Weill might have contrived to hear in 1950, if not in 1941:

> *I feel it stealing now. Sentry, are you there?*
> *Just ease those darbies at the wrist,*
> *And roll me over fair,*
> *I am sleepy, and the oozy weeds about me twist.*

END OF BOOK April 19, 1891

---

*Georg Kaiser, *Briefe* (Frankfurt-am-Main, Propyläen Verlag, 1980), pp. 628–9. Quoted in Ernst Schürer, *Georg Kaiser* (New York, Twayne, 1971), p. 139.

Brook House Library

Most of Weill's important books and all his printed scores remained in his studio for some twelve years after his death. George Davis's large library of American, English, and (predominantly) French literature was kept in other rooms and on stairway bookshelves; its character was so distinct that there was no risk of confusion with Weill's library. In 1963, Lenya's third husband, the painter Russell Detwiler, rearranged the old studio for his own work, and added a number of books to the shelves. Pressure of space and other practical exigencies took their toll over the next decade. Nevertheless most of the music and perhaps two-thirds of Weill's studio library survived and are now housed in the Weill–Lenya Research Center.

The purpose of the following notes is to give an outline of the library as it existed ten years after Weill's death. Music and books that had obviously been added during the 1950s are ignored, as of course are subsequent additions (which are numerous).

From Weill's thirty-five years in Europe little had survived. It is important to remember that when Weill left his Klein-Machnow home for the last time in 1933, it was in the belief that he would soon return to it. He therefore took to Paris only what was needed for a short stay. Two years later he left his new home in Louveciennes with every intention of returning at the end of his four-month engagement with Weisgal's *Eternal Road* company in New York. But that, too, was not to be. On two occasions, therefore, the responsibility of transporting his belongings, or disposing of them, had to be left to others: to Lenya, to Weill's family, and to his Berlin lawyer, in 1933; to Madeleine Milhaud in 1936–7.

HOLOGRAPH AND AUTOGRAPH WORKS BY OTHER COMPOSERS

Ferruccio Busoni, *Brautwahl-Suite*
The score is part autograph and part engraved, and is bound in a blue board cover inscribed in another hand: 'F. Busoni/"Brautwahl-Suite "/ Partitur'. The autograph title page is arranged thus:

an Herrn Curt Sobernheim
in herzlicher Freundschaft
*

Orchester-Suite
aus der Musik zur Oper
"die Brautwahl"
von
Ferruccio Busoni
*

Fünf Stücke:
1. Spukhaftes. 2. Lyrisches.
3. Mystisches. 4. Hebraeisches.
5. Heiteres.
*

(original-Partitur)

Dem lieben Kurt Weill
mit den freundschaftlichsten
Wünschen.
herzlichst. F. Busoni

The score comprises 110 pages of a 24-stave manuscript paper measuring 35.5 × 25.7 cms. Pages from the engraved full score of the opera, with autograph emendations where necessary, have been pasted on to most of these pages. The few recomposed passages – notably the entire *Valse lente* of No. 3 – are written in black ink directly on the backing manuscript paper. The first page of the score is signed, and dated August 1912.

Busoni probably gave the score to Weill at the end of his three years in the Masterclass at the Prussian Academy of Arts – that is, in December 1923. The score's survival, when almost everything else from Weill's Berlin library was lost, seems to indicate that it was stored in a place of its own.

Arthur Honegger, *Fièvre Jaune* (Nino)
A copy of the first edition of this rather Weillian *chanson* – published in Paris in 1935 by Sirène Musicale – is inscribed in Honegger's hand: 'Jusqu'où votre influence va, je niche' ('As far as your influence is concerned, I'm nesting').

Darius Milhaud, *Médée*
Opera in three acts, text by Madeleine Milhaud
A copy of the vocal score of Milhaud's 3-act opera, published by Heugel in 1938, is inscribed by the composer and his wife: 'à Kurt Weill/souvenir de ses amis/Milhaud/Madeleine'.

Aaron Copland, *The Second Hurricane*
School Opera in two acts, text by Edwin Denby
A copy of the first edition of the vocal score, published by C. C. Birchard and Co. in 1937, is inscribed: 'Für Kurt und Lenja/in Freundschaft/Edwin Denby'.

PRINTED MUSIC

Piano Music and Art Songs

The small Broadwood upright piano now owned by the Weill Foundation was the instrument Weill used in Brook House for post-compositional checking. When Lenya showed it to the present author for the first time in 1958 she remarked that the only music she ever heard Weill playing on it recreationally was Mozart. Though not perhaps an uncoloured memory, it was to some extent corroborated by the contents of the Brook House music library: apart from a few trifles which may not even have belonged to Weill, the only piano music was the Moscheles edition of the Mozart Piano Sonatas (in two battered volumes that looked as if they had been family heirlooms). An American collection of early Italian music clearly belonged to quite another category and was as pristine in condition as the companion volume of 'Songs and Airs' from the time of Caccini to that of Bononcini. Both volumes were presumably acquired during the period when Weill was preparing to write *The Firebrand of Florence*. Since there is no reason to suppose that he would have concerned himself with strict historical accuracy in such matters, a modern collection of eighteenth-century English song may likewise have been part of his preparatory work for the projected Nell Gwyn operetta of 1942.

The absence of German *Lieder* and ballads, or indeed of any relics of Weill's early professional experience as an accompanist, emphasized the incongruity of a solitary volume of *Mélodies* by Chabrier – a gift, perhaps, from the Milhauds during one of Weill's Californian trips. During the Dessau years Weill probably relied on his father's and Albert Bing's music libraries for most of the vocal literature with which he was actively involved; but it is inconceivable that he then spent thirteen years in Berlin without a single example from the entire *Lieder* repertoire. After 1933 there was much music he might have thrown away without a qualm. But Schubert or Mahler? Surely not.

Sacred Music, Cantillations, etc.

In response to a request from Weill in 1934 for traditional Jewish material relevant to the composition of *Der Weg der Verheissung*, Albert Weill had sent a number of collections. Together with compositions for synagogue use by members of the Weill family, including Albert Weill himself, this material was part of the legacy and has been safely preserved.

Orchestral and Chamber Music

The thirteen pocket scores and study scores that were in the legacy in 1960 are now in WLRC. At least seven of them clearly date from Weill's adolescence in Dessau and Berlin. An Eulenburg score of Schubert's

'Trout' Quintet is dated on the front cover '1915/16'; but on the title page it is signed, and dated simply '1916'. Eulenburg scores of Schubert's 'Unfinished' Symphony and Mozart's K. 543 were bought in a music shop in what was still the kingdom of Württemberg – that is to say, before November 1918, and probably on a visit to a branch of the Weill family that was still living there. An Eulenburg score of Mozart's G minor Piano Quartet (K. 478) bears Weill's signature and the date 1917. (In view of the 'Trout' dating, one wonders whether the development of Weill's pianistic abilities under Bing's tutelage allowed him to contemplate and even undertake the performance of both works with local string players.) Clearly from the same period is another Eulenburg score – that of Haydn's 'Drumroll' Symphony. The signature of one 'Ludwig Brau' (of which nothing is known) and the non-autograph date '1913' are inscribed on an older but clean Eulenburg score of Brahms's Fourth Symphony. A well-used study score of Mahler's *Das Lied von der Erde* bears the stamp of a Dessau music dealer, and would scarcely have been acquired before Weill's eighteenth year. A clean pocket score of Mahler's *Kindertotenlieder*, in Universal Edition's Philharmonia series, is a much later acquisition. Deriving from stock first printed in 1923, it looks as if it were acquired at the same time as the three Haydn symphonies in the same series – Nos. 45 ('Farewell'), 85 ('La Reine'), and 101 ('Clock'). Given that one of these is from stock printed in August 1931, it seems reasonable to conclude that all three, together with the *Kindertotenlieder*, were acquired from Universal Edition (there is no dealer's stamp on any of them) during the year that saw the composition of the Second Symphony and *Die sieben Todsünden*.

The one pocket score that unquestionably dates from Weill's years in Berlin is that of Bartók's First String Quartet of 1909; it contains various annotations in Weill's hand that relate to an analytical talk he gave for Berlin Radio in March 1926, as introduction to a broadcast performance of the work by the Roth Quartet. (See Kurt Weill, *Ausgewählte Schriften*, Frankfurt, 1975, pp. 132–4.) There are indications of no fewer than sixteen excerpts, which presumably were played by the Roth Quartet during the course of the talk.

The notion of a 'pocket' or 'study' score of a work for the concert hall was so remote from the musical life Weill led in America that there is little cause for surprise in the fact that his music library contained in 1960 only one such score of American origin – a post-war Kalmus edition of *The Rite of Spring*, doubtless given to him at the same time as the recording (see below). To view that as evidence that the score of Bartók's First Quartet might likewise have been a unique acquisition in the 1920s would plainly be absurd, however accurate Lenya's recollection that Weill's Berlin music library was 'very small'. It is already hard enough to accept the seven scores from the Dessau years as more than a fragment of his student library. Even assuming that he had free access to Albert Bing's no doubt extensive library, are we to believe that in the very years when he was first encouraged to learn the craft of composition and indeed consider himself at least an apprentice composer, he failed to equip himself with a single orchestral or chamber music score by Bach or Beethoven, Mendelssohn or (for modernity's sake) Richard Strauss? What is quite unthinkable is that he then spent three years in Busoni's Masterclass with absolutely nothing to show for it on his library shelves: not one of the twelve Mozart piano concertos which became a focal point for the Masterclass while Busoni was preparing to play the complete set, for the first time, with the Berlin Philharmonic Orchestra under Gustav Brecher; nothing of Bach–Busoni (which, of course, included the Goldberg variations and the '48'); and nothing whatsoever by Busoni himself – not even the Divertimento for flute and strings of which Weill made the piano reduction!

Allowances must of course be made for Weill's penurious circumstances during the years of the Masterclass, which coincided with the collapse of the German economy. If we assume, however, that Weill emerged from the Masterclass with at least a small library of Busoni's favoured classics and a number of the master's own works (interspersed with a few by his erstwhile friend and teacher Jarnach), it is clear that there must, before long, have been considerable additions. The year 1924 saw the stabilization of the German economy and the beginning of Weill's close involvement with the music department of Berlin radio and with the International Society for Contemporary Music (both in Berlin and abroad). It is inconceivable that a solitary score of Bartók's earliest and most traditional quartet was all he acquired during a period when he was joining forces with Hindemith and Křenek, when Schoenberg was important to him (and became more so as Busoni's successor in Berlin), when the neo-classical Stravinsky was looming large, and finally when he identified himself with Klemperer's passionately progressive policy for concerts, as well as opera productions, at the Kroll.

It is, however, when we turn to Klemperer's main sphere of responsibility, opera, that the poverty of the main library, as it stood in 1960, is most starkly revealed.

Opera

Four of the six operatic full scores in the 1960 library obviously date back to the Dessau years – a pre-1914 *Rigoletto* with Albert Bing's signature on the fly-leaf, and three much older German editions of Mozart: *Die Entführung aus dem Serail*, *Don Giovanni*, and *Die Zauberflöte*. Full scores of *Der Rosenkavalier* and *Ariadne auf Naxos* were acquired in the USA, but reflect a lifelong affection for Strauss's music whose constancy may have owed something to Weill's wisdom in never publicly testifying to it.

These full scores were supplemented by eight vocal scores, of which only two were acquired in the USA – Verdi's *Otello* and Puccini's

Turandot, the latter a gift inscribed 'To Giacomo Weill/from/Gabriele Gershwin /Chappell/Jan 22 1941'. The remaining operas were *Idomeneo* and *The Marriage of Figaro*, *Fidelio*, *Norma* (two copies), *La Juive*, and *Falstaff*.

With the sole exception of *Turandot*, every one of these operas had either been in the repertory of the Dessau Court Opera during Weill's childhood and adolescence, or in principle could have been. In that sense the one glaring absentee from Weill's library shelves was Wagner; and it is as hard to picture the young Weill without a single Wagner score on his shelves as it is to imagine a friend or relative being so tactless as to send him so unwelcome a memento from Hitler's Germany.

That apart, the little collection of opera scores that survived in Brook House ten years after Weill's death was a curiously accurate representation of Weill's operatic upbringing, and hence of a culture that ended with the November revolution and the Armistice. By contrast, the entire era from 1918 to 1933 – as it were, from Schreker's *Das Schatzgräber* through *Wozzeck* and *Jonny* to Goldschmidt's *Gewaltige Hahnrei* (to mention just four works which in various ways had been of special concern to Weill) – has vanished without a trace. Weill's career and celebrity in Germany were such as to ensure that numerous opera scores would have come his way. Many of them might have struck him as wholly dispensable after 1933. But simple loyalty, if nothing else, would surely have induced him to retain at least one token of his youthful faith in the operas of Busoni. It is the absence of *Arlecchino* or *Doktor Faust*, not of *Cardillac* or *Jonny spielt auf*, that points to mere contingency as the most likely explanation of the fact that in Weill's little library of operas the most 'modern' work is *Ariadne auf Naxos*.

Operetta and Musicals

Weill's admiration for Offenbach, and his occasional tendency – mistakenly regarded by Adorno and others as habitual – to see himself as a successor of that master, did not, it seems, lead him to possess any of his scores, at least in the last years. Vocal scores of *The Yeomen of the Guard* and the Austin version of *The Beggar's Opera* – both obtained in the USA – stood for the lighter side of the European musical theatre. The only American composers in this (or any other) category were Gershwin and Richard Rodgers: vocal scores of *Strike up the Band* and *Porgy and Bess* were significant possessions for the composer of *Knickerbocker Holiday* and *Street Scene*, while the vocal score of *Allegro* was perhaps a welcome reminder that the composer whom Weill latterly regarded as his one major rival could try his hand at an 'experiment' comparable to *Love Life* and be rewarded for his pains by a box-office disaster.

Folk Music*

Botkin, B. A., ed., *A Treasury of American Folklore: Stories, Ballads, and Traditions of the People*, New York, Crown Publishers, 1944

Downes, Olin, and Siegmeister, Elie, *A Treasury of American Song*, 2nd ed., New York, Alfred A. Knopf, 1943

Handy, W. C., ed., *A Treasury of the Blues: Complete Words and Music of 67 Great Songs From 'Memphis Blues' to the Present Day*, New York, Charles Boni, Simon and Schuster, 1946

Hare, Walter Ben, *The Minstrel Encyclopedia*, Boston, Walter Baker Company, 1926

Henry, Mellinger Edward, ed., *Folk-Songs from the Southern Highlands*, New York, J. J. Augustin, 1938

Johnson, James Weldon, and Johnson, J. Rosamond, *The Book of American Negro Spirituals: Including 'The Book of American Negro Spirituals' and 'The Second Book of Negro Spirituals'*, New York, Viking Press, 1942

Jordan, Philip D., and Kessler, Lillian, *Songs of Yesterday: A Song Anthology of American Life*, Garden City, NY, Doubleday, Doran & Co., 1941

Kaser, Arthur LeRoy, *The Screamline Minstrel Book*, Boston, Baker's Plays, 1940

Loesser, Arthur, *Humor in American Song*, New York, Howell, Soskin, Publishers, 1942

Lomax, John A., and Lomax, Alan, *Negro Folk Songs as Sung by Lead Belly*, New York, Macmillan, 1936

Lomax, John A., and Lomax, Alan, *Our Singing Country: A Second Volume of American Ballads and Folk Songs*, New York, Macmillan, 1941

This book was in the possession of Arnold Sundgaard and returned to the Foundation in 1984. Weill signed the cover. Sundgaard confirms this book was the source for 'Little black train' and 'Did you ever go to meetin' Uncle Joe?' from *Down in the Valley*.

Peat, Frank E., and Smith, Lee Orean, *Legion Airs: Songs of 'Over There' and 'Over Here'*, New York, Leo Fiest, 1932

Rice, Edw. Le Roy, *Monarchs of Minstrelsy: From 'Daddy' Rice to Date*, New York, Kenny, 1911

Sandburg, Carl, *The American Songbag*, New York, Harcourt, Brace & Co., 1927

The Southern Harmony Songbook, New York, Hastings House, 1939

Thomas, Jean, and Leeder, Joseph A., *The Singin' Gatherin': Tunes from the Southern Appalachians*, New York, Silver Burdett, 1939

Wheeler, Mary, *Steamboatin' Days: Folk Songs of the River Packet Era*, Baton Rouge, LA, Louisiana State University Press, 1944

Work, John W., ed., *American Negro Songs and Spirituals: A Comprehensive Collection of 230 Folk Songs, Religious and Secular*, New York, Crown, 1940

---

*List compiled by David Farneth, 30 June 1985.

Related, but not folksong:

Ruby, Harry, *Songs My Mother Never Sang*, New York, Random House,
1943

Popular Song

'La vie en rose' and a handful of other *chansons* were the only European
elements in a collection amounting to about a hundred songs from the
twenties, thirties, and forties. Except in so far as it might have been
relevant to Weill's wartime work for 'Lunch Hour Follies', the collection
had the air of being a random accretion from day-to-day contacts with
publishers, song-pluggers, and show-business personalities. Most of the
successful song-writers of the day were represented, but without any
critical or personal bias, even with regard to the two song-writers who
happened to belong to Weill's circle of friends – Arthur Schwartz and
Burton Lane. One can only conclude that sheet music was not Weill's
primary means of acquainting himself with the idioms and trends in
American popular music. For that purpose he listened to the radio,
followed the hit parade, and bought recordings.

RECORDINGS

The nature and extent of any record collection Weill left in Klein-
Machnow in March 1933 are unknown. Commercial recordings of his
own music were few enough for them to have been subsequently
exported by Lenya in her personal luggage, but by 1957 the only pre-
Hitler recordings surviving in the legacy were foreign pressings that
could have been bought from the specialist dealers in New York in the
1930s or 1940s. Of the genuine rarities – not to mention priceless
collector's items such as the 1933 recordings by Lenya and Ernst Busch of
songs from *Der Silbersee* – none was left, if indeed any had reached Weill
in New York, as Lenya believed. On the other hand the pre-war
recordings made in France – the *chansons* for Lys Gauty, the two *Marie
Galante* discs, and various Left Bank renderings of Weill–Brecht songs –
were safely preserved in albums. These were much less likely to have
been obtainable in New York, and were presumably sent from Louveciennes by Madeleine Milhaud.

Whereas Weill apparently had no interest in original-cast recordings of
Broadway shows by his contemporaries, he assembled a large collection
of pop songs, boogie-woogie and swing. Like the recorded folk songs,
ballads, and assorted Americana from the end of the New Deal era and
the onset of wartime nationalism, these were part of a process of self-
education, and a direct contribution to his own work. In that sense they
were quite separate from his few recordings of operatic and concert
music, which were found in an attic in 1958, and could well have been

there for ten years and more. Typically gifts rather than his own purchases, they must nevertheless have owed their survival to some degree of genuine appreciation. The Bruno Walter *Rosenkavalier* was the only album of historic interest, *The Rite of Spring* the only classic of modernism, and Milhaud's *Suite française* – surely a gift from the composer himself – the only work by one of Weill's immediate contemporaries.

BOOKS ON MUSIC, TUTORS, ETC.

Neither in their totality nor in detail did the books on Weill's shelves betray the fact that they had once belonged to a composer. Astonishingly, there were no manuals of orchestration, even for the 'commercial' sector where conventionally trained composers are most in need of guidance. Among the biographies there were, it is true, several of composers; but none that might not have found a place on the shelves of a general reader. Apart from Siegfried Kracauer's *Jacques Offenbach und das Paris seiner Zeit* (Amsterdam, 1937), all were in English. Sacheverell Sitwell's *Mozart* (London, 1932) and Sir Richard Terry's *Bach. A Biography* (London, 1933) probably dated from Weill's London visits of 1934–5, a period when there may have been connections with the Sitwells through Edward James and his circle. Alfred Einstein's *Mozart* (London, 1945) was no doubt acquired irrespective of Weill's acquaintance with that noted scholar and critic, or his renewed contact with him in New York. Giuseppe Adami's *The Letters of Puccini* (New York, 1931), Francis Toye's *Rossini. A Study in Tragi-Comedy* (New York, 1934), and Franz Werfel's *Verdi. The Man in his Letters* (New York, 1942) covered complementary aspects of Weill's involvement with the ideals of Italian opera.

These, indeed, were the ideals that helped sustain Weill's operatic ambitions in the 1940s. At the opposite extreme, but strictly relevant to the theory and practice of his work for Broadway, was the following collection of tutors discovered in a pile of miscellaneous popular music:

Anon, *Count Basie's Piano Styles*
Anon, *Five Boogie-woogie and blues piano solos featured by Woodie Herman*
Garnston, David, *Improvising simplified. The Melody Way to Hot playing for all instruments*
King, Stanford, *Here's boogie woogie*
King, Stanford, *Here's more boogie woogie*
King, Stanford, *Swingy Fingers – twelve studies in popular music for piano solo*
Potter, Harold, and Wheeler, C. E., *Breaks, Fillers, Endings, and Introductions for piano*

GENERAL LITERATURE

The books Weill chose to live with and work beside during his ten years
in Brook House were to a large extent mirrors of his American persona.
The majority had been acquired after he moved to that American first
home, and very few of the others predated his original application for
citizenship. Americans of longer standing than he found the atmosphere
of Brook House beguilingly 'European';* but that was not the impression
Weill himself wanted it to give, nor was it substantiated by any part or
aspect of Brook House, least of all its bookshelves.

The coherences were in no sense contrived: Weill would not have been
the man he was, nor Brook House the home he and Lenya so
spontaneously and hospitably made it, had he been prone to affectations
of any sort, whether literary or aesthetic, mandarin or moronic. None of
the joint works of his last years was more truly 'composed' that his and
Lenya's Brook House. But it was in the special seclusion of his studio that
he could best construct his own world; and so he assembled around him
a library that affirmed his American loyalties as surely as the oath he took
in 1943. Yet there was space enough for fleeting acknowledgements of
his earlier life and distant origins. Scattered among the library's manifold
previsions of a decent future embodying the democratic truths of the
Founding Fathers were a few relics of the past: Heinrich Mann's *Der Hass*
of 1933; the two volumes, well-thumbed, of Brecht's *Gesammelte Werke* in
the Malik Verlag edition of 1938; and (mysteriously, since the edition was
published by Allert de Lange in Amsterdam in 1940 and the copy
purchased in Budapest) B. Traven's *Ein General kommt aus dem Dschungel*.
Hardly less remote from the wooded enclave of South Mountain Road
were comparable relics from the early and still politicized months in
America: Lincoln Steffens's *Autobiography* (New York, 1931); two copies
of Matthew Josephson's *The Robber Barons* (New York, 1934); Ernst
Toller's *Seven Plays* (a volume of translations published in New York
1936); and Auden–Isherwood's *The Ascent of F6* (a copy belonging to
Charles Alan).

In the context of a library that for the most part corresponded faithfully
to the ethos and outlook of The Playwrights' Company in the 1940s,
these few volumes were strikingly incongruous, but perhaps no more so
than the surprising evidence of Weill's interest in the work of the first
and greatest of America's literary decadents, Edgar Allan Poe. As well as
two collected editions of his works, there was an old German edition of
poems and stories, which suggests that the interest was deep-seated.

Equally remote from the world of Maxwell Anderson and S. N.
Behrman was a copy of the first English translation of Thomas Mann's

---

*E.g. Goddard Lieberson, in his introduction to the CBS recording of *Die Dreigrosch-
enoper*.

Doktor Faustus (New York, 1947). Unread though it visibly was, it signified by its very presence in the studio a conscious link with the tradition to which the complete *Wilhelm Meister*, in German, and a Kleist collection, also in German, paid tribute.

The Lacunae:
A Résumé

Weill's (Lenya's) papers were acquired by the Yale University Music Library in 1981, and were subsequently the subject of a 300-page register (AN.WL) compiled for the library by Adrienne Nesnow with support from the Research Resources Program of the National Endowment for the Humanities. In November 1983 Ms Nesnow informed the present author that three holographs listed in his 1974 catalogue of the legacy were missing. None has yet been found (1987). By far the most important is the entire full score of *Der Weg der Verheissung / The Eternal Road.* (see p. 265) Fortunately WLRC has a photostat of this score (in the edition edited during the late 1970s by Lys Symonette), and likewise one of the fragmentary holograph piano-duet arrangement of the 1921 Symphony. The third loss is that of the piano/vocal holograph of the 'Matrosen- Tango' (*Happy End*).

The present author completed his last comprehensive reappraisal of the holographs in the Weill legacy in 1974. The publication of Adrienne Nesnow's meticulous register ten years later was therefore a prerequisite for the present catalogue, since it confirms that with the three exceptions noted above the legacy is intact – and has indeed been added to since 1975. But the catalogue does not, of course, reflect changes made since 1974 in the ordering of the holographs of each individual work – an ordering that had been gradually evolved with a view to establishing the basis for a complete and rational foliation. Sample checks during the course of brief visits to WLA in 1984–6 have revealed that while some holographs remain exactly as they were left in 1974, others – for example, the elaborate sketches for *Love Life* – are no longer in an order that corresponds to the descriptions given in the present catalogue. But these are minor problems compared to the loss of the *Der Weg der Verheissung* score; and that in turn loses some of its impact when it is seen in the context of those works that were lost during Weill's lifetime.

The composition of the symphonic poem *Die Weise von Liebe und Tod* marked the beginning of a sixteen-year period that ended with Weill's departure for New York. Of those sixteen years, the equivalent of at least four must have been spent on works or parts of works that have since been lost:

Die Weise von Liebe und Tod (1919)
Sulamith (1920)
Sinfonia Sacra (1922)
Zaubernacht (1922) – full score
Pantomime (1924)
Stundenbuch (1924)
Royal Palace (1926) – full score
Na und ? (1926–7)
Herzog Theodor von Gothland (1926)
Das Leben Eduards II von England (1928)
Katalaunische Schlacht (1928)
Petroleuminseln (1928)
additions to the *Mahagonny* opera (1931)
full scores of additions to *Die Bürgschaft* (1932)
La grande complainte de Fantômas (1933)

The salient fact is that with the exception of the 1921 Symphony – whose survival, as we have seen, was due to sheer accident – the holographs of every score composed in Germany and left unpublished in Weill's lifetime have disappeared (including, of course, the holograph of the *Recordare*). The significance of this is inseparable from that of the equally comprehensive losses in other categories. From the same sixteen-year period are missing: all books, and all printed music apart from the Bartók quartet and three vocal scores of Weill's own works (*Die Dreigroschenoper, Aufstieg und Fall der Stadt Mahagonny*, and *Die Bürgschaft*); all diaries, address books, and notebooks; and all business correspondence.

This, surely, is the proper context for any inquiry into the disappearance of the unpublished manuscripts that Herbert Fleischer posted from Italy in 1933 (see p. 10). Fleischer did not explain – and the present author failed to ask – why he decided to send the unpublished manuscripts to the Universal Edition office in Berlin. The only answer obvious enough for him to have regarded it as self-evident is one that allows for a series of dependent hypotheses: (1) in his Italian retreat Fleischer had no knowledge of Weill's whereabouts and no easy means of quickly finding out; (1.1) so he chose UE's Berlin office as the most convenient forwarding address; (1.2) the parcel duly arrived, but being addressed to Weill it was neither opened nor recorded in a ledger, but was simply redirected to Weill's home in Klein-Machnow; (1.3) someone authorized to open Weill's mail during the months before his house was sold put the Fleischer scores in what seemed to him or her an appropriate place, but unfortunately it was not the one where Weill kept the handful of manuscripts that eventually reached him in New York – that is, the two Busoni autographs, the draft of *Die Bürgschaft*, and the miscellaneous sketches, drafts and scores; (2) from the probability that the Fleischer manuscripts were bound in stiff covers and neatly labelled – which seems to have been customary for Weill in the years before he found a publisher – we could conclude that they were more likely to be shelved beside printed music than deposited with loose manuscripts (such as the missing sketches and drafts for the Brecht works and *Der Silbersee*); (2.1) in either event, their journeys would not have been over.

There is one element missing from this explanation, and it may well be fatal: every step in it presupposes normal conditions, and conditions in Germany after March 1933 were in no respect normal. Fleischer may well have used the Universal Edition address because he assumed that an Austrian firm would be to some degree exempt from postal censorship and police raids. If that assumption was wrong, his parcel may never even have reached the Berlin office, let alone Weill's home address.*

Before drawing any conclusions, let us turn for a moment to the remnants of Weill's pre-1920 music library that were in Brook House in 1960. If, as seems likely, these came from a single branch of the family, they may be only part of what has survived even to this day – the part, that is, that has been identified. Any books or music that Weill left with his parents, or with his brothers or sister, when he settled in Berlin in 1920 would have tended, with the passage of time and also under the pressure of one or more emigrations, to have been increasingly assimilated with family belongings.

There is no such hope for the Berlin library. Although Weill's parents remained in Germany until 1935, they do not seem in any way or at any time to have been involved with the disposal of the contents of Weill's home. As for Lenya, her involvement was bound to be limited by the nature of her own circumstances in 1933, which was hardly of a kind to enhance her sense of personal commitment to the survival of a cumbersome collection of books and scores.

Weill himself would surely not have considered that collection negligible. If the character of his American library is anything to go by it would have contained numerous books associated with future projects, some of which would have been annotated accordingly. (One of them, as we know from an undated letter of 1933 to Lenya, was his Multatuli edition.) Since it is unlikely that he would have trusted his memory sufficiently, at the time of the sale, to send a selective list of what he wanted, the most practical course of action would have been to arrange for the entire library, together with correspondence files and the like, to be forwarded to him in France as soon as the necessary export licences were obtained. Although there is little reason to suppose that the official obstacles to such a licence would have been as great as they were in the case of capital assets – we know that Weill was able to rescue his beloved

---

* Before finalizing the German translation of the present section, Ken Bartlett wrote to me at some length about its contents. The main part of his letter – dated Munich, 12 March 1986 – appears on p. 440.

German sheepdog from Berlin, but unable to draw on his main deposit account – allowance must be made for interminable bureaucratic delays, and hence for the possibility that the crates of books were put into storage for some while, or even entrusted to a close friend (Caspar Neher and his wife being the obvious choice). If the crates remained in Berlin, there could have been little chance of their contents surviving the ravages of war. But if in due course they reached Paris, Weill would probably not have taken them to his apartment in Louveciennes, where space was limited. One must therefore ask whether the score of the *Recordare* that appeared in the racks of a Parisian music dealer in 1970 was flotsam from an unidentified treasure that may still be lying near the banks of the Seine.

By the time Weill had decided to remain in America and had arranged for the transfer of his effects from Louveciennes to New York, his orientation was such that he could easily have forgotten, or even ceased to care about, books, music, and other remnants of his Berlin life that had been given a temporary home in Paris by some friend or friends with whom, perhaps, he had since lost touch. Left in the lumber room or attic of a family home in Paris, a few boxes containing books and scores would probably be discovered after the death of their original trustee, but might gather dust for generations.

By far the least likely possibility is that the Berlin library reached Weill in America during the late 1930s – perhaps before his remarriage to Lenya, certainly before he had a home of his own. If that had happened, we can be sure only that the Fleischer manuscripts were not involved, for it is clear from the legacy that Weill's studied indifference to most of his European music was never so great that he was ready to destroy its holograph remains. As for literature, Weill's friend Hans Curjel testified (to the present author in 1960) that after the burning of the Reichstag, Weill had driven him and two friends to a suitably remote spot in Berlin and dumped a collection of books and periodicals from Weill's library which Weill feared might be politically compromising. While it is possible to imagine a comparable housecleaning in America four or five years later – with regard to those books which, in the light of his American experience, might have seemed a painful testimony to the extent to which, as an assimilated Jew, he had once steeped himself in German culture – circumstances that would explain the disappearance in America of the entire Berlin library are so hard to imagine that the postulate of its arrival there can virtually be discounted.

Perhaps the truth will one day, or even soon, be discovered. Meanwhile the continuing search for missing material belongs to that greater quest for each and every inner meaning that Weill himself, by the end of the third decade of our century, had deliberately or forgetfully left behind in Europe.

24 November 1985

An exchange of letters
in lieu of a conclusion

from Ken W. Bartlett to the author

The conditions after January 1933 in Germany were so incredible that probably only someone who had lived through that nightmare could really grasp the true impact on the lives of the intellectual circles and the Jewish population in particular.

As to the Fleischer parcel: I am more and more inclined to assume that the parcel never reached even the Universal Edition office in Berlin, and that it was destroyed as *entartete Kunst* by the omnipresent censors, particularly if it arrived in Berlin after 10 May 1933, the night when the *Bücherverbrennung* took place on the square outside Berlin University (to be followed up in almost every larger German town). This at once changed the whole cultural climate. Thereafter, if you were found to possess books by (for instance) Thomas or Heinrich Mann, by Zweig, Einstein, Wells, Gide, Freud or Proust, you were labelled as *politisch unzuverlässig* and could even be arrested for subversive activities. If the censors found out – and this is more likely than not – that the contents of a parcel were music by a Jew, it was automatically *entartete Kunst*, and to destroy it would have been a patriotic duty.

It does not surprise me in the least that there has been no trace of Weill's diaries, address books, correspondence, etc.; it would almost have been suicidal for him to keep them, or even to try to get them across the frontier. He must have been badly shaken by his experience of the Nazi-organized riots during the Magdeburg *Silbersee* and of having been sacked from the film project. After all, he was a sensitive young man of only 33 – the much older 'Aryan' and probably 'stronger' Fritz Busch left the country after booing SA hordes interrupted a performance he was conducting in Dresden. Weill, or whoever looked after his belongings after his departure, would have behaved most irresponsibly had he not got rid of such incriminating items as address books, diaries, etc., which might have endangered relatives, friends, even business partners. He would not have dared to take anything of the sort across the frontier on

440

his drive to Paris, because the luggage controls, particularly with 'suspicious elements' like Weill (or perhaps even the 'non-conformist' Nehers) were unbelievably strict.

If Weill ever attempted to get his library to Paris after he had left Berlin, he would have had to be doubly careful not to have in the crates any books that were on the Nazi Index. They would have been confiscated; and I would imagine that this would have applied to a large number of books and music in his library. I doubt whether he would have attempted to get an export licence at all. (I have heard of cases where applications were turned down or whole consignments confiscated if any 'incriminating' materials were found.)

Being half Jewish myself I have come to these conclusions from recalling my own situation in Germany at the time. Of course, it was not nearly as precarious as that of the already prominent Weill. I was only a 21-year-old music student, and by no means 'dangerous'. But after my Jewish father, who had been a judge, was dismissed in 1933, I destroyed any personal things like address books, photographs, letters which could have become dangerous for myself, my family and friends. My father and I began searching our libraries for 'forbidden' books: the caretaker, the electrician or plumber could have been an informer and reported us to the Gestapo for owning forbidden books or music. This is why I have hardly any from my many pre-war books on my shelves.

Judging from what I felt like after having finally got to England in 1938, I could well understand if Weill should not have bothered any more about his German (or European) past, about books and music left behind in Berlin or elsewhere. That complete change or relief results in a feeling – especially when one is young – that one does not want to remember or to be reminded, when one has made up one's mind to build a new life.

K.W.B.
Munich, 12 March 1986

from the author to Ken W. Bartlett

When I said to you all those months ago how moved I'd been by your letter and how grateful I was for your agreement to the idea of including it in the *Handbook*, I already had the feeling that a mere telephone call was scarcely an adequate response to such a letter. I was soon reminded of that by a conversation with Berthold Goldschmidt – he, as you may know, remained in Berlin until 1935, composing little but mainly occupied with the Jewish orchestra which, thanks to Hubermann, formed a nucleus for the Palestine Philharmonic Orchestra. With just the kind of ironic laughter you can hear in the last movement of his second string quartet of 1935, Berthold recalled that in Berlin during the first two years of the Nazi regime, the processes of *Gleichschaltung* were sometimes mercifully slow, thanks to a combination of local resistance and bureaucratic muddle. Moreover, he was able to leave for England in 1935 with all his belongings, including his library of books and scores.

Naturally those recollections helped me recover a thread of hope for Weill's lost manuscripts that I'd let slip after reading your letter. But you as well as Berthold had made me ask myself once again why I set such store by these missing items. Although they are clearly of immense interest to students of Weill, they concern the musical world at large only in proportion to the value currently placed on Weill's work as a whole. Yet it is in the context of his output's singular lack of wholeness that these missing fragments acquire their singular interest. In writing this, I recognize myself as a product of *my* generation, which is to say, a generation that went to school with the experiences of your generation and of his.

If it is possible, let alone desirable, to distinguish between the enormities of Hitler and those of Stalin, it is surely in the sense that the former were perpetrated in the name of 'culture' and, what's more, of a culture that is one of the prides of Western civilization. For that reason it seems to me that although Weill was never in any sense an ideologue, any writer about him is willy-nilly embroiled in fundamental political and moral issues. Thus a catalogue of Weill's work becomes among other things a catalogue of some representative fragments of our own riven culture.

To publish such a catalogue today would be imprudent without recognition of the fact that ours is a time when the eternal forces of reaction are parading themselves at every political, social and artistic level more confidently, and on a far wider front, than in any era since the 1930s. Behind these *parades sauvages* of bigotry and worse there now marches the all-too-real embodiment of the metaphorical epidemic described by Camus in *La Peste*. It is characteristic of the present climate that Camus's famous warning in his final paragraph is being trotted out again – and quoted as a prophecy about to be fulfilled. But some earlier lines have always struck me more forcibly. Written in the light of the world's rejoicings in 1945, they even have a bearing on the life and work of Weill, who of course shared those rejoicings and had surely by then suppressed all memory of the authoritarian perspectives illuminated by the 'Krankheit' scene in *Die Bürgschaft*. I'm sure you remember the Camus passage, and especially the last six words of it:

> It was doubtful if this could be called a victory. All that could be said was that the epidemic seemed to be leaving as unaccountably as it had come. Indeed, one's chief impression was that the enemy had called a retreat after having reached all its objectives.

That of course is an image that merges precisely with George Steiner's baleful vision of the ninety-year-old Hitler's jubilation at the speed and efficiency with which posterity was realizing 'all his objectives'.

The other day, when I again finished re-reading our catalogue from beginning to end, I was suddenly reminded of a phrase in Hermann Broch's letter to Carl Seelig of 2 December 1945: 'Was er gemacht hätte, wenn er nicht die Gnade gehabt hätte, Jude zu sein' ['What would he have done if he had not had the honour to be a Jew']. If I, who do not have that honour, dare to suggest to you that Broch's rhetorical question might be turned inside out and used as a means of enquiry about the life and work of Weill, it is because I see that it could be the start of a whole series of questions which we have yet to discuss.

D.D.

Fulham, 22 January 1987

Appendix I
Kurt Weill Foundation for Music

The Kurt Weill Foundation for Music, Inc., is a not-for-profit, private foundation chartered to preserve and perpetuate the legacies of Kurt Weill and Lotte Lenya. In pursuit of these goals, the Foundation maintains the Weill–Lenya Research Center to serve scholars and performers, administers Weill's copyrights worldwide, provides information regarding availability of performance materials and clearance of performance rights, awards grants to support excellence in research and performance, and sponsors an expanding publication programme.

Founded in 1962, the Foundation initially served as an advisory group to assist Lenya in her lifelong mission to bring Kurt Weill's music to the world. After her death in 1981, when it was bequeathed Lenya's ownership of Weill's literary and musical copyrights, the Foundation has been able to take an active and meaningful role in the continuance of that mission.

INFORMATION SERVICE

The staff of the Weill–Lenya Research Center in New York stands ready to assist all interested persons with information pertaining to published and unpublished materials, current performances, research efforts, availability of translations, and clearance of performance rights. They can advise which publisher controls each composition, whether performance materials are available for sale or rental, and whether performance rights need to be licensed. They welcome the opportunity to discuss possible works for future programming and to assist in providing materials for programmes and publicity.

In addition, information is available from European American Music Inc., the sole US representative of the major publishers of Weill's European compositions. EAM also serves as the Foundation's American agent for selected stage rights. Inquiries may be addressed to: Mr Ronald Freed, President, European American Music Distributors Corporation, PO Box 850, Valley Forge, PA 19482. Telephone: (215) 648–0506.

444

PUBLICATIONS

The Foundation publishes the semi-annual *Kurt Weill Newsletter*, a free-subscription journal featuring news, reviews, and analysis of major works and performance trends. In addition, the Foundation is preparing a guide to Weill's music to assist performers, producers, and scholars in locating musical materials around the world. Publications currently in progress include an annotated, bilingual edition of the Weill–Lenya correspondence.

FUNDING ASSISTANCE

The Foundation solicits proposals from individuals and non-profit organizations for funding of Weill- or Lenya-related projects in one or more of the following categories: Research, Performance and Production, Travel, Translations and Adaptations, Dissertation Fellowships, and Publication Assistance.

Selection criteria include: (1) quality of the project; (2) evidence of the applicant's potential, motivation, and ability to carry out the project successfully; (3) evidence of the applicant's prior record of achievement in the field covered by the project; (4) relevance and value of the proposed project to the Foundation's purposes. Preliminary applications must be received each year by 15 December and should contain the following information: (1) a detailed description of the project; (2) an up-to-date résumé for individuals; a profile of purposes, activities, and past achievements for organizations; (3) an itemized statement of how the amount requested would be used.

All applications and correspondence should be addressed to Mr David Farneth, Director of Programs, at the Foundation's New York address. Applicants will be informed of awards by 1 February.

Appendix II
Weill–Lenya Research Center

The Weill–Lenya Research Center has been established at the Foundation's headquarters in New York City to promote scholarly study and publication and to assist in the research needs of conductors, performers, and producers. The collection includes printed music, photocopies of musical manuscripts, performance materials, scripts, correspondence, audio recordings, video tapes, programmes, photographs, posters, press clippings, published reference materials, dissertations, business records, and memorabilia.

Access to the Research Center's collections is open to all qualified and properly accredited researchers and should be arranged in advance by appointment. Photocopy services are available on location with the approval of the archivist. Permission to publish protected information and documents from the collections must be secured from the Foundation and any other copyright holder.

Unlike similar collections in major research institutions, the Research Center is attempting to assemble a comprehensive collection on Weill and Lenya as well as relevant information about collaborators and secondary sources dealing with the musical, theatrical, and social history of the time. Access to the collection will be achieved by means of a computerized cataloguing and indexing system which will feature a wide variety of reference points.

ACQUISITIONS

The Research Center is actively searching for materials to add to its collections. Any person wishing to donate or make available photocopies of relevant materials is encouraged to contact the Foundation. All contributions are greatly appreciated and will be duly acknowledged.

ORAL HISTORY

The work of Weill and Lenya is being further documented through a series of oral history interviews with friends and collaborators. The interviews are transcribed and made available to researchers and selected interviews videotaped.

Appendix III
Weill/Lenya Archive at Yale University

In accordance with Lenya's bequest, many of Weill's original manuscripts have been deposited with the Yale University Music Library. The Foundation has donated additional materials which it felt would most appropriately be placed at Yale to ensure their security and preservation and to reinforce the intellectual integrity of Yale's collection. With a grant from the National Endowment for the Humanities, a formal register of the collection has been prepared and is available for purchase from the library. All inquiries regarding the collection may be addressed to: Yale University Music Library, PO Box 2104A, Yale Station, New Haven, CT 06520–7440. Telephone: (203) 436–8240.

Weill's Music and his Projects

Bold type indicates principal works and page references to main catalogue entries.

Abendlied, 39, 54, **108–10**, 111, 121, 124

Aber dieses ganze Mahagonny, (*Aufstieg und Fall* and *Mahagonny-Songspiel*), 182

Abschiedsbrief, Der, 242, **248–9**, 250

Ach bedenken Sie, Herr Jakob Schmidt, *see* Havanna-Lied

Alabama Song (*Aufstieg und Fall* and *Mahagonny-Songspiel*), 187, 327, 378

Albumblatt für Erika, **296**

Alessandro the Wise (*The Firebrand of Florence*), 274, 346

All at once (*Where Do We Go From Here?*), 338, 339, 340

Almighty and everlasting God (*The Common Glory*), 295

Als sie ertrunken war und hinunterschwamm, *see* Ballade vom ertrunkenen Mädchen

Andante aus der A-dur-Sonate von C. M. v. Weber, **112**

Anna-Anna, *see* Die sieben Todsünden

Anstatt-dass Song (*Die Dreigroschenoper* and *Kleine Dreigroschenmusik*), 191, 192

Apollo-Brunnenstrasse (project), 383, 384, 388

Apple Jack (*Huckleberry Finn*), 370

Arie der Lucy (*Die Dreigroschenoper*), 198

Au fond de la Seine, 327

Aufstieg und Fall der Stadt Mahagonny, 2, 13–17, 33, 39, 40, 41, 57, 58, 164, 165, 166, 167, 168, 171, 172, 174, **175–85**, 186, 187, 188, 202, 208, 214, 217, 220, 227, 231, 267, 354, 375, 376, 383, 384 386, 387, 388, 395, 404, 408, 437

Baa M'nucha, *see* Two Folksongs of the New Palestine

Baby (*Love Life*), 360

Ballade vom ertrunkenen Mädchen (*Das Berliner Requiem*), 210

Ballade vom Pharao (*Der Kuhhandel*), 306

Ballade vom Räuber Esteban (*Der Kuhhandel*), 256

Ballade vom Soldatenweib, *see* Und was bekam des Soldaten Weib?

Ballade von Cäsars Tod (*Der Silbersee*), 240–1, 252, 394

Ballade von der sexuellen Hörigkeit (*Die Dreigroschenoper*), 196

Ballad of Magna Carta, The, 314

Ballad of the drowned girl, *see* Ballade vom ertrunkenen Mädchen

Barbara Song (*Die Dreigroschenoper*), 196, 198, 202, 204, 327

Barbarischer Marsch (*Die Bürgschaft*), 237

Barbershop Quartet (*You and Me*), 292

Bastille Music (*Gustav III*), 189

Bath-Sheba (*The Eternal Road*), 281

Bats About You (*Lady in the Dark*), 361

Beat! Beat! Drums! (*Mine Eyes Have Seen The Glory* and *Three Walt Whitman Songs*), 325

Beharre night auf der Welle, *see* Lied vom Fluss der Dinge, Das

Begbick Song, *see* Lied vom Fluss der Dinge, Das

Bekehrte, Die, **130–1**, 132, 153
Benares Song (*Aufstieg und Fall* and *Mahagonny-Songspiel*), 182, 185
Berceuse (*Der Kuhhandel*), 278, 284
Berliner Requiem, Das, 2, 17, 27, 187, **207–11**, 214, 223, 386
Berlin im Licht, **205–6**
Best Years of His Life, The (*Lady in the Dark*), 274
Bilbao Song (*Happy End*), 201
Bills Ballhaus in Bilbao, *see* Bilbao Song
Bird of Passage, A (*Lost in the Stars*), 367
Blue Danube, The (project), 418
Brandy Merchant, Song of the, *see* Lied vom Branntweinhändlers
Bring the Bricks, *see* Two Folksongs of the New Palestine
Brothel Scene (*Aufstieg und Fall*), 182, 187, 188, 189
Buddy on the Nightshift, **322–3**
Bürgschaft, Die (*The Pledge* or *The Surety*), 3, 6, 7, 14, 16, 17, 18, 23, 27–8, 38, 58, 67, 124, 153, 185, 228, 229, **229–36**, 240 243, 267, 287, 295, 361, 371, 385, 386, 389, 391, 394, 400, 437, 442

Cabaret Number, **129–30**, 141
Cabinet of Dr Caligari, The (project), 392, 393, 423
Caesar and Cleopatra (project), 394, 404, 420
Caesar's Death, Ballad of, *see* Ballade von Cäsars Tod
Candide (project), 399
Caravan (*The Eternal Road*), 282
Carmagnole (*Gustav III*), 375
Castles in Spain, see The River is Blue
Catfish Song (*Huckleberry Finn*), 369, 371
Chant de Libération (*Salute to France*), 343
Chanukeh, *see* Sabbath
Columbus sequence (*Where Do We Go From Here?*), 274, 339, 340
Come In, Mornin' (*Huckleberry Finn*), 369, 370
Come up from the Fields, Father, **357**
Common Glory, The, 62, 63, **294–6**, 373, 401
Complainte de la Seine, **261**, 269
Concerto for Violin and Wind

Instruments, op. 12, 2, 17, 57, 151, 153, 155, **156–7**, 158
Conga (Carnival) (*Where Do We Go From Here?*), 337
Cop's Lament (*Love Life*), 360
Cop's Serenade (*Love Life*), 360
Cowboy Song (*Johnny Johnson*), 278
Cranes' Duet, *see* Kraniche-Duett

Dance of the Tumblers (*Lady in the Dark*), 299
Das ist der Mond über Soho, *see* Anstatt-dass Song
David and Goliath (*The Eternal Road*), 281
Davy Crockett, 109, **297–300**, 309, 319, 373, 401
Death Valley, 310
Democracy's Call (*Johnny Johnson*), 281
Denn wie man sich bettet, so liegt man (*Aufstieg und Fall*), 327
Dinner Table, 373
Dish for the Gods, A, see Love Life
Divertimento, op. 5, 18, 56, 131, **132–3**, 135, 143, 146
Divertimento for flute and orchestra (Busoni–Weill), **134–5**, 158, 429
Don Juan (project), 418
Down in the Valley, 67, 299, **348–50**, 360, **363–5**, 423
Dreigroschenoper, Die (*The Threepenny Opera*), 1, 6, 8, 25, 41, 57, 58, 67, 83, 89, 103, 111, 124, 145, 183, 192, **194–205**, 211, 214, 215, 251, 267, 294, 354, 376, 378, 383, 387, 393, 395, 401, 406, 407, 408, 416, 419, 437
Drowned Maiden, Ballad of, *see* Ballade vom ertrunkenen Mädchen
Dulcinea (project), 422

Earthbound (*One Man's Venus*), 329
Economics (*Love Life*), 360
Edis Kebsweib hat einen Bart auf der Brust (*Lebens Eduards des Zweiten von England*), 190
Eifersuchtsduett (*Die Dreigroschenoper*), 103
Einsamkeit, 377
Embezzlers, The (project), 399, 401
Epitaph (*Johnny Johnson*), 281
Erlebnis im Café, Das (*Der Kuhhandel*), 284

Es blühen zwei flammende Rosen,
96–7, 105
Es regnet, 242, **249–50**, 257, 281, 285
Es schienen so golden die Sterne, *see*
Sehnsucht
Es zog zu Salomon (*Der Kuhhandel*),
256
Eternal Road, The, 61, 62, 104, 240,
250, 262–8, **280–2**, 319, 331, 332,
356, 380, 397, 421, 422, 436, *see also*
Der Weg der Verheissung

Fandango (*Der Kuhhandel*), 256
Fantasia, Passacaglia and Hymnus *see*
Sinfonia Sacra
Fantômas, *see* grande complainte de
Fantômas, La
Farewell, Goodbye (*Johnny Johnson*),
373
Farmer Takes a Wife, The (project), 417,
418
Fates, The (*One Man's Venus*), 329
Faust opera (project), 396–7
filles de Bordeaux, Les (*Marie
Galante*), 336
Firebrand of Florence, The, 278,
344–7, 415, 416, 417, 418, 427
Flag is Born, A, 46, 265, **356**
Flash Rounds (*One Man's Venus*), 329
Foxtrot and Ragtime, 156, **157–8**
Frauentanz, op. 10, 56, 147, **148–50**,
153
*Fräulein and the Little Son of the Rich,
The*, **275**
Fresh air and exercise (*One Man's
Venus* and *One Touch of Venus*), 329
Fugatos I–IV (*The Eternal Road*), 282
Fun to be Free, **319**

Gang zum Galgen (*Die
Dreigroschenoper*), 196
Gebet, **99–100**
Gentle Grafters, The (project), 405, 417
Genghis Khan (project), 412–13
Gone with the Wind (project), 417, 418,
420, 422
Good Earth, The, **322–3**
Good Person of Sezuan, The (project),
412, 413–15, 418, 419, 422, 423, 424
Good Soldier Schweyk (Švejk), The
(project), 384, 394, 408–12, 414
Grabschrift 1919 (*Das Berliner
Requiem*), 210, 211
Grabschrift (*Die Dreigroschenoper*), 211

grande complainte de Fantômas, La,
242, **251–2**
Grapes of Wrath, The (project), 422,
423
Great Big Sky, The (*Street Scene*), 353
Greatest Show on Earth, The (*Lady in
the Dark*), 274
Green Mansions (project), 422
Green-up Time (*Love Life*), 360
Gustav III, 165, 171, **187–9**, 241

Habanera (*The Pirate*), 327
Happy End, 2, 3, 40, 58, 83, 201, 215,
217–22, 269, 336, 375, 383, 393, 436
Hard Nut, Song of the, *see* Lied von
der harten Nuss
Hatikvah, 363
Havanna-Lied (*Aufstieg und Fall*),
172, 180, 184
Havu l'venim, *see* Two Folksongs of
the New Palestine
Heilsarmeelieder, *see* Happy End
Herr, den ich tief im Herzen trage,
see Gebet
Herzog Theodor von Gothland, 165,
168–9
Heute abend ging ich ins Café, *see*
Das Erlebnis im Café
Hier ruht die Jungfrau Johanna Beck,
see Marterl
High Wind in Jamaica, 274, **274–5**, 326,
372
Hinter Gläsern, an den Schanktisch,
see Lied vom Branntweinhändlers,
Das
Horst Wessel, (project), 405
Hosianna Rockefeller (*Happy End*),
221
Huckleberry Finn, 369–71, 422
Huxley (*Lady in the Dark*), 311
Hymne von Santa Maria, *see*
Berceuse
Hymnus, *see* Sinfonia Sacra

Ich bin dir mehr als Sonnenglanz,
102
Ich habe eine Kuh gehabt *see* Kuhlied
Ich schlaf, ich wach, 148
Ich sitze da un' esse Klops, **161–2**
Ich war jung, Gott, erst sechzehn
Jahre, *see* Surabaya-Johnny
Ich weiss wofür, **97–8**, 98, 99, 100,
104
Ich will ihn preisen, 135

Ich will trauern lassen stehn, 148
If I could find another rhyme for
    Love (*One Man's Venus*), 329
If love remains (*Where Do We Go From
    Here?*), 339
I'm a rolling stone, 297
I Married a King (film story), 421
Im Volkston, 98, **104–6**, 106–7
In der Jugend gold'nem Schimmer
    (Heilsarmeelied IV, *Happy End*,
    271, 336
In Margate bei der Promenade, *see*
    Muschelsong
Intermezzo, 100, **110–11**, 114, 116, 121
I set my heart on sable (*You and Me*),
    291
It Never Was You (*Knickerbocker
    Holiday*), 298

Ja da kann man sich doch nicht nur
    hinlegen, *see* Barbara Song
Ja, das Meer ist blau, so blau, *see*
    Matrosen-Tango
Der Jasager (*The Yes-Sayer*), 58, 59, 60,
    67, 174, 177, **226–9**, 233, 384, 385,
    387n
J'attends un navire (*Marie Galante*),
    327, 373
Je ne t'aime pas, 257, **261–2**, 341
Jephthas Tochter (project), 398, 400
Jiggaboo (*You and Me*), 292
Job (project), 400
John Brown's Body (project), 422
Johnny Johnson, 25, 29, 61, 62, 109,
    240, 275, **276–80**, 283, 285, 299,
    300, 328, 343, 346, 398, 401, 408,
    423
Johnny's Song (*Johnny Johnson*), 278
Jonathan Wild (project), 415–16
jüdische Witwe, Die (project), 390, 392,
    399, 400
Julius Caesar (project), 405, 408,
    412–13

Kanonen Song (*Die Dreigroschenoper*
    and *Kleine Dreigroschenmusik*), 198,
    327
Katalaunische Schlacht, **193**
Kiddush, **355**
Kingdom for a Cow, A, 19, 60, 61,
    253, 266, 267, **271–4**, 284, 294, 310,
    326, 327, 346, 377; *see also der
    Kuhhandel*
Kleine Dreigroschenmusik (*Little*

Threepenny Music), 191, 198,
    211–12, 378, 383
kleine Mahagonny, Der, *see*
    Mahagonny-Songspiel
Klops-Lied, *see* Ich sitze da un' esse
    Klops
Knickerbocker Holiday, 63, 109,
    190, 286, 291, 294, 298, 299, 300,
    302, **304–8**, 326, 347, 348, 373, 402,
    430
Knocking Song, The (*You and Me*),
    291
Komm heraus, du Schönheit von
    Soho, *see Eifersuchtsduett*
Konjunktur, **190–3**, 211, 241, 354
Kraniche-Duett (*Aufstieg and Fall*),
    181, 182, 184, 185
Kuhhandel, Der (*Shady Business*), 19,
    20, 28, 44, 60, 72, 109, 190, **253–60**,
    266, 267, 269, 275, 284, 289, 291,
    335, 336, 337, 340, 341, 343, 345,
    361, 393, *see also A Kingdom for a
    Cow*
Kuhlied (*Der Kuhhandel*), 259

Lächle noch einmal (attrib. KW), 377
Lady in the Dark, 25, 45, 64, 83, 125,
    288, 299, 311, 315–18, 326, 347,
    348, 361, 392, 405, 409, 415, 418,
    423, 424
Lady Lili You, *see* Shimmy-song
Laienoper (project), 387
Lasst euch nicht verführen (*Aufstieg
    und Fall*), 184
Laughing Generals, The (*Johnny
    Johnson*), 275, 278
**Lebens Eduards des Zweiten von
    England**, **189–90**
Legende vom toten Soldaten, Die, 209,
    and see Workers' Choruses
Leise, nur leise, *see Der Kuhhandel*
Let's go to Benares, *see* Benares Song
Lettre d'adieux, La, *see* Der
    Abschiedsbrief
Liebeslied (*Die Dreigroschenoper*), 197
Liebster (attrib. KW), 377
Lied vom blinden Mädchen, Das
    (attrib. KW), 376
Lied vom Branntweinhändler, Das
    (*Happy End*), 218
Lied vom Fluss der Dinge, Das
    (*Mann ist Mann*), 236, 237
Lied von der harten Nuss, Das
    (*Happy End*), 218, 271, 377

Lied von der Unzulänglichkeit menschlichen Strebens (*Die Dreigroschenoper*), 211

Life, Love, and Laughter, *see The Firebrand of Florence*

Lindbergh Flight, The, see Der Lindberghflug

Lindberghflug, Der (*The Lindbergh Flight*), 125, 177, 186, 243, 395, 424; original version, **212–17**; Vorstellung des Fliegers Charles Lindbergh; cantata, **223–6**

Little Gray House, The (*Lost in the Stars* and *Ulysses Africanus*), 367

Little Swing for Swinging, A, *see Street Scene*

Little Threepenny Music, see Kleine Dreigroschenmusik

Little Tin God, The (*Lost in the Stars* and *Ulysses Africanus*), 311, 367

Locker Room, The (*Love Life*), 362

Lost in the Stars, 46, 67, 68, **365–8**, 405, 421, 422, 423

Lost in the Stars (*Lost in the Stars* and *Ulysses Africanus*), 311, 368

Love Life, 67, 285, 291, 352, **357–62**, 373, 412, 421, 423, 430, 436

Lover Man (*Ulysses Africanus*), 311

Love Song (*Love Life*), 316, 362

Lucy's Aria, *see Arie der Lucy*

Lullaby (*Street Scene*), 275

Mack the Knife (*Die Dreigroschenoper*), 200, 202

Madam, Will You Walk?, **311–12**, 313

Mädchenraub, Der (*Der Kuhhandel*), 291, 335

Mahagonny-Songspiel, 2, 13, 18, 41, 57, 59, 60, 89, 167, **171–5**, 180, 182, 185, 186, 188, 189, 220, 225, 306, 383, 394–5; *Der kleine Mahagonny*, 174, 175; Paris version, 174, 184

Maikaterlied, 54, **108–110**, 111, 116

Mandelay Song (*Happy End*), 218

Mann ist Mann, **236–7**

Marco Millions (project), 417

Marie Galante, 60, 61, 240, 255, 256, 257, 258, **268–71**, 271, 284, 285, 291, 302, 327, 336, 345, 361, 423, 432

Marschmusik (*Mann ist Mann*), 236, 237

Marterl (*Das Berliner Requiem*), 209, 210

Maschinen (project, ballet), 380

Master of earth and waves, 373

Matrosen-Tango (*Happy End*), 217, 436

May Day *Festspiel* (project), 385, 386, 387

Mayerling (project), 403

Meine Herren, mit siebzehn Jahren, *see Nannas Lied*

Meine Herrn, heut sehn Sie mich Gläser aufwaschen, *see Seeräuberjenny*

Melting Pot Ensemble (*Street Scene*), 352

Mensch lebt durch den Kopf, Der, *see Lied von der Unzulänglichkeit menschlichen Strebens*

Mi addir, **96**, 96–7, 98, 106, 120

Mile after Mile (*Railroads on Parade*), 303

Mine Eyes Have Seen The Glory, **324–5**

Minstrel Song, The (*Love Life*), 364

Miss Memory (film story), 421

Moby Dick (project), 422

Mon Ami, My Friend (*Johnny Johnson*), 278, 299

Morale (*Where Do We Go From Here?*), 339, 340

Morgenchoral des Peachum (*Die Dreigroschenoper*), 211

Mother's Getting Nervous (*Love Life*), 360

Much Ado About Love, see The Firebrand of Florence

Muschelsong (*Konjunktur*), 192, 241, 316

Muschel von Margate, Die, *see Muschelsong*

Musical play: The Opera from Mannheim, 286–9

Mussel of Margate, The, *see Muschelsong*

Mutter Goddams Puff in Mandelay, *see Mandelay Song*

My Ship (*Lady in the Dark*), 316

Naboths Weinberg (project), 390, 391, 392, 400, 423

Nachtmusik (*Mann ist Mann*), 236

Nannas Lied, 311, **313**

Napoleon (project), 413

Nation of Nations, A, *see Melting Pot Ensemble*

Na und?, 160, **163–8**, 176, 177, 189

Nell Gwyn operetta (project), 405, 427

neue Orpheus, Der, 25n, 57, 158, **160**, 161, 162, 163, 380

Nichts ist die Welt mir (*Ofrah's Lieder*), 204

Nina, The Pinta, The Santa Maria, The (*Where Do We Go From Here?*), 337

Ninon von Lenclos, 124–5, 126

Noah (project), 404

No matter under what star you're born, *see* The Zodiac Song

Nur die Nacht darf nicht aufhör'n, *see* Wenn der Himmel hell wird

Ocean Song, *see* Love Song

Ofrah's Lieder, 38, 39, 54, 100, 101, **101–4**, 104, 105, 106, 107, 109, 111, 114, 124, 126, 204

Oh Mariner, 373

Oh meine Tochter, warum kommst du nicht zurück? (*Die Bürgschaft*), 237

Oh Moon of Alabama, *see* Alabama Song

Oh show us the way to the next whiskey bar, *see* Alabama Song

Oh the shark has pretty teeth, dear, *see* Mack the Knife

Oh Uncle Samuel, **322–3**

Oil Islands, The, see Petroleuminseln

One Man from Tennessee, see Davy Crockett

One Morning in Spring, **322–3**

One Indispensable Man, The, *see* Knickerbocker Holiday

One Man's Venus, 328–9, 335, 346

One Touch of Venus, 3, 65, 89, 285, 316, 327, 329, **333–6**, 361, 373, 404, 408, 410, 411, 415

One Touch of Venus (film), **347–8**

Opéra de Quat' Sous, L', *see Die Dreigroschenoper* and Two Chansons for Yvette Guilbert

Opera from Mannheim, The, *see* Musical play: The Opera from Mannheim

O Tixo, Tixo, Help Me! (*Lost in the Stars*), 367

Our Lincoln comes (*Railroads on Parade*), 302

Ozeanflug, Der, see Der Lindberghflug

Pantomime, op. 14, 141, 142, **154–6**, 380

Partisan Finale (*A Flag is Born*), 356

Passacaglia, *see Sinfonia Sacra*

Pastorale (*Der Weg der Verheissung*), 296

Pauv' Madam' Peachum!' *see* Two Chansons for Yvette Guilbert

Petroleuminseln (*The Oil Islands*), **206–7**

Pharaoh, Ballad of, *see* Ballade vom Pharao

Picture on the Wall, The (*One Touch of Venus*, film), 347

Pirate, The, 325–7, 372

Pledge, The, see Die Bürgschaft

Polka, **130**, 149

Propaganda Songs, 321, and *see individual entries*: Song of the Free, Schickelgruber, One Morning in Spring, The Good Earth, Buddy on the Nightshift, Song of the Inventory, We don't feel like surrendering today, Oh Uncle Samuel!, and Toughen up, Buckle down, Carry on

Protagonist, Der, 13n, 57, 155, 156, **158–9**, 160, 162, 170

Psalm VIII, **134**, 143

Pullman Blues (*Railroads on Parade*), 302, 303

Pullman Scene (*Railroads on Parade*), 302

Punch and Judy Get a Divorce (*Love Life*), 360

Pygmalion (project), 420

Quodlibet, 115, 130, 137, 141, 147, **147–8**

Rachel's Death (*The Eternal Road*), 281

Railroads on Parade, 63, **300–4**. 309, 316, 343, 349, 423

Recordare, 20–1, 146, 147, **150**, 151, 152, 437, 439

Red Army Song (Lev Knipper's Cavalry of the Steppes), 319, 331

Reiche den Reichtum den Reichen, *see* Hosianna Rockefeller

Reiterlied, **98**, 105, 120

Right Guy for Me, The (*You and Me*), 292, 293

Rilkelieder, 131–2, 136, 137, 151

Rise and Fall of Mahagonny City, see Aufstieg und Fall

River Chanty (*Huckleberry Finn*), 370, 371

River is Blue, The, 274, **282–6**, 289, 291, 293, 343, 345, 348, 361, 373, 400

Road of Promise, The, see Der Weg der Verheissung

Roi d' Aquitaine, Le (*Marie Galante*), 256, 257

Romance of a Lifetime, The (*You and Me*), 292

Romeo und Julia (project), 390, 391

Rom hiess eine Stadt, *see* Ballade von Cäsars Tod

rote Rosa schon lang verschwand, Die, *see* Grabschrift 1919

Royal Palace, 13, 19, 20, 57, 89, 149, 156, **162–3**, 164, 167, 170, 176, 380

Ruf aus der Gruft (*Die Dreigroschenoper*), 211

Ruhrepos (project), 383, 386

Russian War Relief, **329–30**

Ruth (project), 422

Sabbath (Chanukeh) (*We Will Never Die*), 331

Sacramento (*Railroads on Parade*), 302

Saga of Jenny, The (*Lady in the Dark*), 317

Sailor's Wife, The (*Railroads on Parade*), 302

Salomon Song (*Die Dreigroschenoper*), 196

Salute to France, **342–3**, 361, 373

San Salvatore (*A Kingdom for a Cow*), 291, 327

Scars, The (*Knickerbocker Holiday*), 274

Scheiden, ach das Scheiden, Das, *see* Im Volkston

Schickelgruber, **322–3**

Schilflieder, **119–20**

Schlachtmusik (*Mann ist Mann*), 236

Schlafe, Santa Maria, *see* Berceuse

schöne Kind, Das, 106, **107**, 109

Schön war die erste Flasche, *see* Fandango

School for Wives (project), 418

Schweyk, *see* The Good Soldier Schweyk

Seeräuberjenny (*Die Dreigroschenoper*), 202, 203, 204

Sehnsucht, 100, **101**, 105, 107, 204

September Song (*Knickerbocker Holiday*), 274, 378

Seven Deadly Sins, The, see Die sieben Todsünden

Shady Business, see Der Kuhhandel

Shimmy-song (*Na und?*), 164, 165

Shanty Music, see Your Navy

sieben Todsünden, Die (*The Seven Deadly Sins*), 10, 13, 17, 21, 43, 44, 59, 83, 89, 149, **244–8**, 248, 255, 335, 361, 371, 396, 413, 428

Sieh jene Kraniche, *see* Kraniche-Duett

Siehst du den Mond über Soho?, *see* Liebeslied

Silbersee, Der (*The Silver Lake*), 20, 25, 33–4, 59, 62, 72, 83, 84, 89, 149, 185, 233, **238–42**, 243, 250, 267, 269, 278, 284, 287, 354, 388, 393–4, 395, 396, 399, 400, 403, 406, 432, 438, 439

simple Leben lebe, wer da mag!, Das, *see* Ballade vom angenehmen Leben

Sinfonia Sacra, op. 6, 18, 56, 133, **135–7**, 142, 146, 153

Six Songs, see individual entries: Barbara Song, Denn wie man sich bettet, Surabaya-Johnny, Au fond de la Seine; Kanonen Song; J'attends un navire

Sleep, baby dear, *see* Lullaby

Snagtooth Sal (*Railroads on Parade*), 302

So kamen sie zu den rier Toren (*Die Bürgschaft*), 240

Soldaten wohnen auf die Kanone, *see* Kanone Song

Soldier's Song, The (*The River is Blue*), 286

Soldier's Woman [Wife], Ballad of, *see* Ballade vom Soldatenweib

Sonata for Cello and Piano, 10, 113, **120–2**, 124, 126, 129

Song of the Cash Register, *see* You and Me

Song of the Emek, *see* Two Folksongs of the New Palestine

Song of the Free, **322–3**

Song of the Goddess (*Johnny Johnson*), 274

Song of the Guns, The (*Johnny Johnson*), 274

Song of the Inventory, **322–3**

Song of the Rhineland (*Where Do We Go From Here?*), 340

Songs of Discovery, 302, **308–9**

Spoon River Anthology (project), 422, 423

Stay Well (*Lost in the Stars*), 310, 311

stille Stadt, Die, 39, 109, 121, **123–4**, 152

Stopping by Woods on a Snowy Evening, **313–4**

Street Light is my Moonlight (*Street Scene*), 353

Street Scene, 44, 66, 72, 83, 193, 275, 362, 364, 418, 419, 421, 430

String Quartet in B minor, **112–15**, 116, 117, 121, 141, 145

String Quartet, op. 8, 56, 133, 134, 141, 142–3, **144–7**, 153, 155

Stundenbuch, op. 13, 132, **151–4**

Suffragette Meeting (*Love Life*), 362

Suite in E for Orchestra, **115–17**, 117, 118, 121, 147, 375

Sulamith, 125–6

Surabaya-Johnny (*Happy End*), 218, 327

Surety, The, see Die Bürgschaft

Susanna and the Elders (project), 400, 417

Susan's Dream (*Love Live*), 360

Švejk, *see* The Good Soldier Schweyk

Symphony (1920), 374

Symphony [No. 1, in one movement], 10, 11, 17, **128–9**, 131, 132, 137, 146, 154, 378, 436, 437

Symphony [No. 2], 17, 18, 25n, 44, 59, 60, 83, 124, 128, **242–3**, 248, 249, 251, 371, 395, 398, 428

Tag und Nacht marschiert die Armee, *see* Barbarischer Marsch

Tango (*Marie Galante*), 284, 285, 302, 345, 361

Tango Locarno (attrib. KW), 376

Tell ol' Bill (*Railroads on Parade*), 302

Temple Music (*A Flag is Born*), 356

There comes peace into the weary, *see* Two Songs of the New Palestine

There is no money in this land, *see* Benares Song

There's Nowhere to go but Up (*Knickerbocker Holiday*), 300

This Time Next Year (*Huckleberry Finn*), 370

This train is bound for glory (*Railroads on Parade*), 302

Thousands of Miles (*Lost in the Stars*), 367

Three Night Scenes, see Symphony [No. 2]

Threepenny Opera, see Die Dreigroschenoper

Three Walt Whitman Songs, **320–1**, 323, 325, 357

Tobias and the Angel (project), 404, 417

To love you and to lose you (*Johnny Johnson*), 279

Too much to dream (*You and Me*), 291, 292

Toughen up, Buckle down, Carry on, **322–3**

Toulouse-Lautrec ballet (project), 397, 398

Triffst du mich abends in der Schenke (*Der Kuhhandel*), 278, 284

Tröste, tröste mein Volk, *see* Der Weg der Verheissung

Trouble with Women, The (*One Touch of Venus*), 336

Tsar has his photograph taken, The, see Der Zar lässt sich photographieren

Tu me démolis, *see* Two Chansons for Yvette Guilbert

Two Chansons for Yvette Guilbert, **293–4**, 408

Two Folksongs of the New Palestine, **296**

Two little girls in Blue (*Railroads on Parade*), 302

Two on an Island, **312**

Ulysses Africanus, 63, **309–11**, 367, 368, 391, 417

Uncle Tom's Cabin (project), 390, 391

Und ein Schiff mit acht Segeln, *see* Seeräuberjenny

Und gibt es kein Schriftstück vom Standesamt, *see* Liebeslied

Und was bekam des Soldaten Weib?, **323–4**, 341, 409

Very, Very (*One Touch of Venus*), 274, 336

Viva the women! (*Love Life*), 360

Volkslied, 98, **106–7**

Vom Tod im Wald, op. 23, **186–7**, 208, 209

Waiting for Lefty (project), 399
Walked through the Country, *see*
    One Morning in Spring
Was soll ich essen in der
    Morgenfrühe? (*Der Silbersee*), 239
Weber, Die, 126–7
We don't feel like surrendering
    today, 322
Weg der Verheissung, Der (*The Road
    of Promise*), 43, 44, 60, 61, 89, 104,
    124, 185, 255, **262–8**, 280, 291, 372,
    380, 427; *see also The Eternal Road*
Weise von Liebe und Tod, Die,
    118–19, 120, 121, 436
We'll Go Away Together, *see Street
    Scene*
We'll man the trains (*Railroads on
    Parade*), 274
We need a Man (*Johnny Johnson*), 274
Wenn der Himmel hell wird (*Aufstieg
    und Fall*), 166, 185
Wenn der Wind geht, *see* Ballade
    vom Räuber Esteban
We're Taking Over Now (*Love Life*),
    360
Wer will einen grossen Mann hab'n,
    see Das Lied von der harten Nuss
West Wind (*One Touch of Venus*), 316,
    347
We Will Never Die, 46, 65, **330–3**,
    356
Wheels through the Night (*Railroads
    on Parade*), 302, 303
Where do I belong?, *see Love Life*
Where Do We Go From Here?, 65,
    306, **336–40**, 416
White Wings (project), 401, 417
Who'll Buy? (*Lost in the Stars*), 368

Wie lange noch?, 324, **340–1**
Wie staunenswert, 102
Wie war ich doch so wonnereich, *see
    Das schöne Kind*
Winterset (project), 422
Wooden Wedding (*One Touch of
    Venus*), 327
Workers' Choruses, **222–3**
Wouldn't You Like to be on
    Broadway? (*Street Scene*), 419

year ago I had a cow, A (*A Kingdom
    for a Cow*), 272
Yes-Sayer, The, see Der Jasager
Yisgadal, 332
You and Me, 63, **289–93**, 298, 372,
    373
You cannot buy love (*Davy Crockett*),
    298
Youkali/Tango Habanera (*Marie
    Galante*), 271
Your Navy, **321**
You Understand Me So (*Love Life*),
    352, 360

Zar lässt sich photographieren, Der
    (*The Tsar has his photograph taken*),
    2, 13n, 57, 165, 168, **169–70**, 187,
    188, 190
Zaubernacht (*Magic Night*), op. 7, 56,
    57, 115, 117, 119, 130, **137–42**, 146,
    147, 148, 153, 156; Suite, 56
Zodiac Song (*Lady in the Dark*), 347
Zriny, **104**
Zu Potsdam unter den Eichen (*Das
    Berliner Requeim*), 208, *and see
    Workers' Choruses*

Index of Weill's literary collaborators and authors set by him

The names of Weill's collaborators are shown in **bold** type. The first part of these entries, before the oblique, relates to the Weill collaborations, and refers solely to the main catalogue entries. The second part of these entries, after the oblique, comprises general references.

Aiste, Dietmar von, 148
Alan Charles, *The Eternal Road,*
   262–8 / 262, 266, 282, 299, 301,
   303, 309, 401, 434
Allan, Lewis, Song of the Inventory,
   322–3 / 322
Anderson, Maxwell, *The Ballad of*
   Magna Carta, 314; *Huckleberry Finn,*
   369–71; *Knickerbocker Holiday,*
   304–8; *Lost in the Stars,* 365–8;
   Ulysses Africanus, 309–11; *Salute to*
   France, 342–3; We don't feel like
   surrendering today, 322–3; *Your*
   Navy, 321 / 47, 63, 64, 67, 68, 299,
   304, 306, 307, 308, 309, 310, 311,
   313, 314, 320, 321, 322, 326, 342,
   349, 362, 365, 368, 369, 370, 400,
   402, 406, 417, 418, 419, 421, 422,
   434; *High Tor,* 417, 421; *Winterset,*
   422
Anstey, F. J., 64, 328, 333, 404; *The*
   Tinted Venus, 64, 328, 333, 404, 405
Arkell, Reginald, 253, 271

Behrman, S. N., 325, 326, 399, 401,
   405, 406, 419, 434; *Serena Blandish,*
   399, 401
Bellamy, F., 324
Bierbaum, Otto Julius, 108, 123
Boritsch, Wladimir, *Zaubernacht,*
   137–42 / 56, 57, 137, 140, 141, 142
Brabant, Herzog Johann von, 148
Braun, Alfred, 168, 252
Brecht, Bertolt, *Aufstieg und Fall der*
   Stadt Mahagonny, 175–85; *Das*

Berliner Requiem, 207–11; *Die*
Dreigroschenoper, 194–205; *Happy*
End, 217–22; *Lebens Eduards des*
Zweiten von England, 189–90; Die
Legende vom toten Soldaten,
222–3; *Der Lindberghflug,* 212–17,
223–6; *Mahagonny-Songspiel,*
171–5; *Mann ist Mann,* 236–7;
Nannas Lied, 313; *Die sieben*
Todsünden, 244–8; Und was bekam
des Soldaten Weib?, 323–4; *Vom*
Tod im Wald, 186–7; Zu Potsdam
unter den Eichen, 222–3 / 1–2, 7,
9, 15, 16, 17, 26, 30, 31, 35, 39–43,
44, 45, 57, 58, 59, 61, 64, 65, 66–7,
68, 128, 153, 166, 171, 172, 175,
182, 184, 185, 186, 187, 189, 190,
192, 194, 196, 200–4, 206, 207, 208,
209, 210, 212, 213, 214, 216, 217,
219, 220, 222, 223, 225, 226, 227,
228, 229, 236, 244, 245, 246, 247,
299, 313, 323, 324, 341, 376n, 378,
383–8, 394–5, 396, 403, 406–16,
419, 422, 423, 432, 434, 438;
Arbeitsjournal (BB.AJ), 181, 324, 413,
415, 416, 423; *Badener Lehrstück vom*
Einverstandnis, 214, 215; *Fanny*
Kress, 413; *Der Flug der Lindberghs,*
225; *Galileo,* 66; *Das grosse*
Brecht-Liederbuch (BB.GBL), 202; *Der*
gute Mensch von Sezuan, 65, 407,
408, 412–16, 419, 422, 423, 424;
Hauspostille, 172, 173, 175, 187, 223;
Die heilige Johanna der Schlachthöfe
(*St Joan of the Stockyards*), 220, 406;

Der Jasager, 226–9, 384, 385, 387n; *Kinderkreuzzug*, 413; *Mass für Mass*, 395; *Die Massnahme*, 227, 385, 387; *Der Moabiter Pferdehandel*, 384; *Mother Courage*, 416n; *Die Mutter (The Mother)*, 61, 376n, 387; *Der Neinsager*, 229; On the use of music in the Epic Theatre, 1; *Der Ozeanflug*, 225; *Die Rundköpfe und die Spitzköpfe*, 313, 395; *Schweyk im 2. Weltkrieg*, 66, 67, 408–14, 416, 424; *Selected Poems*, 299; *The Threepenny Novel*, 416n; *Trial of Lucullus*, 403; *Trommeln in der Nacht*, 223; *Die Ware Liebe*, 413, 414

Bronnen, Arnolt, *Katalaunische Schlacht*, 193 / 193

Burke, Johnny, 289, 318

Carter, Desmond, *A Kingdom for a Cow*, 253–60, 271–4 / 253, 271

Cocteau, Jean, Es regnet, 249–50 / 242, 249, 250, 396, 397

Coslow, Sam, *You and Me*, 289–93 / 289, 291

Dehmel, Richard, 109, 121, 123; Die stille Stadt, 121

Desnos, Robert, *La grande complainte de Fantômas*, 251–2 / 251, 252

Déval, Jacques, *Marie Galante*, 268–71 / 60, 268

Dietz, Howard, Schickelgruber, 322–3 / 322, 399, 400

Edwards, Harry Stillwell, 309; *Aeneas Africanus*, 309

Ehrenburg, Ilya, 282, 283; *The Loves of Jeanne Ney*, 283

Eichendorff, Joseph Freiherr von, 101, 110, 204; Sehnsucht, 204

Fernay, Roger, *Marie Galante*, 268–71 / 268, 270

Feuchtwanger, Lion, *Lebens Eduards des Zweiten von England*, 189–90; *Petroleuminseln*, 206–7 / 189, 206

Fields, Dorothy, Toughen up, Buckle down, Carry on, 322–3 / 322

Frost, Robert, 313

Fulda, Ludwig, 325, 326, 372; *Der Seeräuber*, 325, 326, 372

Gasbarra, Felix, *Konjunktur*, 190–3 / 190, 192, 193, 409

Gay, John, 57, 194, 197; *The Beggar's Opera*, 57, 194, 197

Geibel, Emanuel, 99–100

George, Stefan, 39; Die stille Stadt, 39

Gershwin, Ira, *Lady in the Dark*, 315–18; *The Firebrand of Florence*, 344–7; *Where Do We Go From Here?*, 336–40 / 61, 62, 65, 286, 315, 317, 336, 344, 347, 415, 423, 430

Goethe, Johann Wolfgang von, 2, 130, 131, 153, 435; Die Bekehrte, 130, 131, 153

Gold, Michael, 375–6; *Das Lied von Hoboken*, 375

Goll, Iwan, *Der neue Orpheus*, 160; *Royal Palace*, 162–3 / 2, 57, 73, 160, 162, 380, 381

Grabbe, Christian Dietrich, *Herzog Theodor von Gothland*, 168–9

Graham, Robert, 275

Green, Paul, *The Common Glory*, 294–6; *Johnny Johnson*, 276–80 / 61, 62, 276, 279, 294–5, 304, 401, 408

Guilbert, Yvette, 293–4

Güllhausen, Guido von, 97, 100

Halevi, Jehuda, 101; *Ofrah's Lieder*, 101–4, 110, 204

Hammerstein, Oscar, Buddy on the Nightshift, 322–3; The Good Earth, 322–3 / 322, 420n

Harburg, E. Y., Musical play: The Opera from Mannheim, 286–9 / 62, 286, 288, 289

Hardt, Ernst, 124, 125, 216; *Ninon von Lenclos*, 124–5

Hart, Moss, *Lady in the Dark*, 315–18 / 45, 63, 315, 318, 326, 331, 362, 392, 403, 405, 406

Hauptmann, Elisabeth, *Die Dreigroschenoper*, 194–205; *Happy End*, 217–22; *Der Jasager*, 226–9 / 57, 58, 194, 197, 217, 219, 220, 226

Hauptmann, Gerhart, 126, *Die Weber*, 126–7

Hays, H. R., 63, 297, 298, 299, 309, 402, 403; *The Ballad of Davy Crockett*, 299, 402

Hecht, Ben, *A Flag is Born*, 356; *Fun to be Free*, 319; *We Will Never Die*, 330–2 / 46, 65, 265, 319, 330, 332, 356, 406, 412

Herder, Johann Gottfried, 2, 229
Herzig, Sid, 336
Holz, Arno, 104, 105, 106, 107, 123
Howard, Sidney, Madam, will you
　walk?, 311–12 / 311, 312, 419n;
　They Knew What They Wanted, 419n
Howe, Julia Ward, 324
Hughes, Langston, Street Scene,
　350–5 / 350, 418, 419
Hughes, Richard, 274; High Wind in
　Jamaica, 274
Hungerford, Edward, Railroads on
　Parade, 300–4 / 300, 303

Irving, Washington, 63, 304; The
　History of New York by Diedrich
　Knickerbocker, 304

Jackson, Felix (Felix Joachimson),
　Na und?, 163–8 / 163, 164, 166–7,
　168, 189; Fünf von der Jazzband, 166
Jacobsen, Jens Peter, 133; Frau Marie
　Grubbe, 133

Kaiser, Georg, Pantomine, 154–6; Der
　Protagonist; 158–9; Der Silbersee,
　238–42; Der Zar lässt sich photo-
　graphieren, 169–701 / 2, 9, 13, 16,
　33, 56, 59, 73, 153, 154, 155, 156
　158, 162, 169, 176, 238, 324, 390,
　392, 393, 394, 399, 400, 403, 404,
　420, 424; Die jüdische Witwe, 390,
　399, 400; Kolportage, 403, 405; Der
　Silbersee, 4, 33; Zwei Krawatten, 324;
　Zweimal Oliver, 403
Kästner, Erich, 248, 249, 393
Key, Francis Scott, 324
Klabund, see Grabbe
Körner, Theodor, 104
Krasna, Norman, You and Me,
　289–93 / 289
Kürenberg, Der von, 148
Kurnitz, Harry, 347

Lania, Leo, Konjunktur, 190–3 / 190,
　193, 215, 409
Lenau, Nikolaus, 119, 120
Lerner, Alan Jay, Love Life,
　357–62 / 66, 67, 68, 347, 357, 360,
　412, 419, 421, 422
Lewisohn, Ludwig, 262, 282
Löns, Hermann, 98, 105

MacArthur, Charles, Fun to be Free,
　319 / 319, 349, 404–5, 406
McEvoy, J. P., Russian War Relief,
　329–30 / 329
McKelway, St Clair, One Morning in
　Spring, 322–3 / 322
MacLeish, Archibald, Song of the
　Free, 322–3 / 322
Magre, Maurice, Complainte de la
　Seine, 261; Je ne t'aime pas,
　261–2 / 261
Marlowe, Christopher, 189; Edward
　II, 189–90
Mayer, Edwin Justus, The Firebrand
　of Florence, 344–7 / 65, 344, 415,
　416, 419; The Children of Darkness,
　415; The Firebrand, 65, 344
Mehring, Walter, Wie lange noch?,
　340–1 / Gedichte, 215
Milestone, Lewis, The River is Blue,
　282–6 / 62, 282, 283, 400

Nash, Ogden, One Man's Venus,
　328–9; One Touch of Venus,
　333–6 / 64, 328, 329, 333, 404, 410
Neher, Caspar, Die Bürgschaft,
　229–36 / 14, 16, 58, 59, 67, 166,
　173, 182, 183, 184, 190, 197, 207,
　219, 220, 229, 234, 235, 237, 240,
　246, 296, 375, 387, 389, 390, 392,
　393, 394, 395, 396, 400, 401, 439

Odets, Clifford, The River is Blue,
　282–6 / 62, 282, 283, 285, 286, 399,
　400; Waiting for Lefty, 399

Paton, Alan, Lost in the Stars,
　365–8 / 67, 311, 365; Cry the Beloved
　Country, 67, 311, 365
Perelman, S. J., One Touch of Venus,
　333–6 / 65, 329, 333, 410

Rice, Elmer, Street Scene, 350–5; Two
　on an Island, 312 / 66, 312, 350,
　418n, 419, 422, 423n; Street Scene,
　66, 350, 418, 419
Rilke, Rainer Maria, 2, 118, 123, 131,
　151, 152–3; Ich will ihn preisen,
　135; Das Stundenbuch, 131, 135, 151;
　Die Weise von Liebe und Tod des
　Cornets Christoph Rilke, 118
Ritter, Anna, 106
Ryskind, Morris, Where Do We Go
　From Here?, 336–40 / 336

Smith, Samuel Francis, 324
Spewack, Bella, Musical play: The
  Opera from Mannheim, 286–9;
  One Man's Venus, 328–9 / 62, 64,
  65, 285, 286, 288, 328, 346
Spewack, Samuel, Musical play: The
  Opera from Mannheim,
  286–9 / 62, 64, 65, 285, 286, 288,
  328, 346
Strindberg, August, 166, 187, 188;
  Gustav III, 166, 187–9
Sudermann, Hermann, 125, 374; Das
  hohe Lied, 125, 374
Sundgaard, Arnold, Down in the
  Valley, 348–50, 363–5 / 299, 348,
  363

Tashlin, Frank, 347
Twain, Mark, 369, 371; Huckleberry
  Finn, 68, 369

Upham, J. B., 324
Upp, Virginia van, 289

Vambery, Robert, Der Kuhhandel,
  253–60, 271–4 / 19, 28, 253, 259,
  260, 271, 341

Waley, Arthur, 226, 384
Werfel, Franz, Der Weg der
  Verheissung, 262–8; The Eternal
  Road, 280–2 / 60, 61, 126, 262, 266,
  282, 379, 380, 433; Einander, 379;
  Gesänge aus den drei Reichen.
  Ausgewählte Gedichte, 379; Der
  Weltfreund, 379; Wir sind, 379
Whitman, Walt, 320, 324, 357
Work, Henry C., 322

General index

For theatres and institutions see the relevant town or city; for books, plays, etc, see under author.

Abbott, Geoffrey, 199
Abendroth, Martin, 225
Abravanel, Maurice, 34, 50, 56, 60, 170, 172, 174, 246, 307, 312, 318, 336, 346, 350, 353, 405, 416
Accademia di Santa Cecilia, Rome, see Rome
Achaz, Karl-Ludwig, 188
Adami, Giuseppe, 433
Adams, Samuel, 295
Adelphi Theatre, New York, see New York
Adler, Celia, 356
Adler, Luther, 279, 312, 331, 356
Adorno, Theodor W., 5, 13, 16, 45, 146, 184, 199, 407, 430; *Philosophy of New Music*, 5
Aiste, Dietmar von, *see Author Index*
Akademie der Künste, Berlin, *see* Berlin
Alan, Charles, *see Author Index*
Albéniz, Isaac, 327; *Iberia*, 327
Alcover, 270
Aldeburgh, 25
Allan, Lewis, *see Author Index*
Allen, Andrew, 350
Allgood, Sara, 312, 348
Allin, Marcel, 251
Alpar, Gitta, 163
Altes Theater, Leipzig, *see* Leipzig
Alvin Theatre, New York, *see* New York
Amar, Licco, 145
Amar Quartet, 143, 144, 145, 153
Amaya, Carmen, 308
American Ballet, 61, 397
American Committee for the
   Weizmann Institute of Science, 363
American League for a Free Palestine, 356
American League of Composers, 362
Anderson, John Murray, 346
Anderson, Mabel, 306, 313, 314, 320
Anderson, Maxwell, *see Author Index*
Andreyev, Leonid, 403, 404; *He Who Gets Slapped*, 403; *King Hunger*, 403; *The Life of Man*, 403
Anrooy, Piet van, 152
Anstey, F., *see Author Index*
Antheil, George, 62, 225
Aravantinos, Franco, 163
Archer, Cheryl, 362
Arden, Eve, 348
Arkell, Reginald, *see Author Index*
Armstrong, Louis, 200, 202
Arnold, Edward, 332
Aronson, Boris, 362
Arrau, Claudio, 56, 380
Artaud, Antonin, 251, 252
ASCAP, 9, 129
Asquith, Anthony, 420
Astor, Junie, 270
Atherton, David, 25, 189, 193, 221, 280
Auber, Daniel, 401
Auden, W. H., 247, 299, 309, 341, 402, 434; *The Ascent of F6*, 402
Auer, Mischa, 318
Aufbau, 324
Aufricht, Ernst Josef, 58, 176, 183, 184, 198, 214, 293, 294, 324, 341, 395, 402, 406, 408, 409, 410, 411, 412, 413; *Erzähle, damit du dein Recht erweist*, 214, 341

Aufricht, Margot, 409
Auric, Georges, 421
Austrian National Library, Vienna, 75
Ayers, Lemuel, 331

Bach, David Josef, 235, 385, 386, 387
Bach, Johann Sebastian, 429; Brandenburg Concerto No. 1, 335; Brandenburg Concerto No. 6, 212
Baden-Baden: Deutsche Kammermusik, 57, 58, 171, 212, 213, 214, 215; Kurhaus, 173, 216
Bahn, Roma, 192, 197
Baker, Josephine, 381, 382, 383
Baker, Kenny, 336
Balanchine, George(s), 246, 247
Balász, Béla, 377
Baldor, Ruth, 241
Ballard, Lucinda, 353, 362
Ballet Caravan, 303
Ballet Rambert, 198
Ballet Theatre, New York, 198
Ballets 1933, Les, 246
Ballets Russes de Monte Carlo, Les, 61, 397
Balser, Ewald, 192
Baltimore, 312
Balzac, Honoré de, 400; Christ in Flanders, 400; A Passion in the Desert, 400
Bankhead, Tallulah, 319
Banks, Leslie, 368
Bard, Maria, 193
Barnowsky, Victor, 188
Barrett, Elizabeth, 303
Barry, Philip, 401; White Wings, 401, 417
Bartlett, Ken W., 17, 33, 36, 37, 50
Bartók, Béla, 144, 161, 349, 356, 428, 429, 437; For Children, 356; Tót nepdál, 161
Bassermann, Albert, 418n
Baum, Kurt, 331
Baumann, Helmut, 38
Baxter, George, 356
Bay, Howard, 336
BBC, 15, 66, 217, 377
BBC Chorus, 134
BBC Symphony Orchestra, 17, 248
Beethoven, Ludwig van, 12, 374, 429
Becher, Johannes R., 128, 380; Arbeiter, Bauern, Soldaten, 128, 380
Behrend-Lehmann-Verein, 55, 114

Behrman, S. N., see Author Index
Bein, Albert, 403; The Heavenly Express, 402
Beinert, Paul, 183
Bel Geddes, Norman, 266, 416n
Bell, Marion, 365
Bellamy, F., see Author Index
Ben-Ami, Jacob, 331
Benét, Stephen Vincent, 401, 421, 422; John Brown's Body, 401, 422; Too Early Spring, 421
Benjamin, Walter, 383, 385
Bennett, Robert Russell, 318, 371
Bentley, Eric, 41, 201, 202, 203; The Brecht Memoir, 41; Homage to BB, 41, 201, 202, 203
Berg, Alban, 8, 39, 184, 397
Berger, Arthur, 355
Berglund, Ruth, 235
Bergner, Elisabeth, 299, 414n
Berini, Mario, 356
Berio, Luciano, 270
Berlau, Ruth, 65, 341, 407, 408, 409, 410, 411, 412, 413, 414
Berlin, 10–11, 12, 16, 25, 26, 54, 55, 56, 58, 59; Akademie der Künste, 4, 7, 8, 13, 18, 23, 24, 26, 30, 33, 75, 82, 98, 114, 122, 154, 161, 189, 192, 221, 280; Deutsches Theater, 62, 66, 388, 412; Hochschule für Musik, 54, 55, 112, 114, 116, 117, 126, 374, 375; Lessing Theater, 192; Philharmonie, 133, 136, 152, 186; Schiller Theater, 38; Schlosspark-Theater, 241; Singakademie, 133; Staatoper am Platz der Republik (Kroll-Oper), 167, 205, 211, 225, 237, 401; Staatsoper unter den Linden, 57, 160, 163, 380, 381; Staatstheater, 193, 207, 236; Städtische Oper, 7, 38, 58, 176, 234, 287; Theater am Bülowplatz, 375; Theater am Kurfürstendamm, 56, 58, 140, 180, 183, 388; Theater am Schiffbauerdamm, 57, 58, 184, 197, 214, 215, 217, 402, 408; Theater des Westens, 38; Theater in der Königgrätzerstrasse, 188; Viktor Barnowsky theatre, 166
Berliner Ensemble, 25, 174, 175
Berliner Festwochen, 7, 21, 23, 24, 26, 31, 32
Berliner Funkstunde, 217
Berliner Volksbühne, 222, 375, 376

Berlin Festival, 189
Berlin im Licht Exhibition, 205
Berlin Philharmonic Orchestra, 56,
    133, 136, 152, 186, 429
Berlin Radio, 220, 428
Berlin University, 112
Berndt, Gretel, 241
Bernier, Buddy, 303
Bernstein, Eduard, 2
Bernstein, Leonard, 46, 200, 347, 355,
    362; Candide, 347; Trouble in Tahiti,
    362
Bertini, Gary, 17, 163, 241, 242
Bertolt Brecht Archive, 75
Bevan, Frank, 307
Bierbaum, Otto Julius, see Author
    Index
Bing, Albert, 53, 54, 55, 103, 104, 109,
    111, 112, 120, 121, 122, 123, 129,
    147, 148, 427, 428
Bing, Herman, 338
Bing, Peter, 10, 116, 120, 151, 153,
    159, 169
Birtwistle, Harrison, 24, 28; Silbury
    Air, 28
Blacher, Boris, 4, 7, 23, 24, 36, 38, 48,
    241
Blitzstein, Marc, 61, 200, 201, 202,
    312, 362
Bloch, Ernest, 355
Bloch, Ernst, 30, 103n, 204
Bloch-Erben, Felix, 220, 394
Blum, René, 397
B'nai B'rith Children's Home, 55
Boehm, David, 308
Bohnen, Roman, 279
Bois, Curt, 192
Boles, John, 336
Bonanova, Fortunio, 338
Bond, Ruth, 336
Bononcini, Giovanni, 427
Boosey & Hawkes, 27, 67
Bootelje, Phil, 292
Booth, Webster, 273
Borchardt, Hans Hermann, 220,
    406–7; Die Bruder vom Halberstadt,
    406; The Conspiracy of Carpenters,
    406; Der verlorene Haufe, 406
Boritsch, Mrs, 140, 142
Boritsch, Wladimir, see Author Index
Bost Records, 327
Boston: Colonial Theatre, 318, 346;
    Shubert Theatre, 336, 362
Boston Symphony Orchestra, 363

Bour, Ernest, 17, 133
Boustead, Alan, 221
Brabant, Herzog Johann von, see
    Author Index
Brand, Max, 220, 387
Brand, Phoebe, 279
Brandeis University, 200
Brando, Marlon, 356
Braun, Alfred, see Author Index
Brecher, Gustav, 170, 183, 226, 227,
    241, 429
Brecht, Bertolt, see Author Index
Brecht, Stefan, 35
Brecht Archive, see Bertolt Brecht
    Archive
Breitkopf & Härtel, 134
Bridie, James, 404, 417; Susanna and
    the Elders, 404, 417; Tobias and the
    Angel, 404, 417; What Every Woman
    Knows, 404
British Museum, 6
Britten, Benjamin, 25, 29, 39, 46,
    309, 341; Paul Bunyan, 309, 341
Broadhurst Theatre, New York, see
    New York
Broch, Hermann, 443
Brod, Max, 384
Bromberg, J. Edward, 332
Bronnen, Arnolt, see Author Index
Brookhouse, Music, 247
Brown, Forman, 308
Brown, Harry Joe, 308
Brückner, Albert, 54
Bruckner, Ferdinand, 404; The
    Enchantress, 404
Brückner-Rüggeberg, Wilhelm, 247
Brügmann, Walter, 170, 172, 173,
    183
Bruinier, Franz Servatius, 202–4, 378
Brüchner, Georg, 375; Dantons Tod,
    222, 375
Buck, Pearl, 322
Buckle, Richard, 381; Diaghilev, 381
Buckwitz, Harry, 13
Burgess, Grover, 279
Burgwinkel, Josef, 234
Burke, Johnny, see Author Index
Burke, Sonny, 338, 339
Burkhard, Heinrich, 57
Burri, Emil, 220
Burth, Jürg, 38
Busch, Ernst, 197, 241, 432
Busch, Fritz, 57, 67, 159, 440
Busch, Hans, 67, 365

Bushnell Memorial Theatre, Hartford, *see* Hartford (Connecticut)
Busoni, Ferruccio, 7, 56, 82, 120, 126, 128, 129, 131, 134–5, 141, 143, 145, 146, 149, 152, 153, 154, 156, 164, 380, 425, 426, 429, 430; *Die Brautwahl-Suite*, 425–6; *Doktor Faust*, 135; *Entwurf einer neuen Ästhetik der Tonkunst*, 152; *Fantasia Contrappuntistica*, 145
Busoni Archive, *see* Ferruccio Busoni Archive
Butting, Max, 145
Buttlar, Freiherr von, 7
Buttolph, David, 338, 339, 340
Byrns, Harold, 198

Cabinet of Dr Caligari, The (film), 392
Cahill, Frank, 272
Camden Festival (1986), 13n
Campbell, Charles, 365
Campbell, Jimmy, 339
Cane, Edward, 266
Capalbo, Carmen, 200
Capra, Frank, 418
Carey, Macdonald, 318
Caridis, Miltiades, 210
Carl Lindström AG, 170
Carnovsky, Morris, 279
Carousel (musical), 420n
Carpentier, Alejo, 251, 252
Carrington, Katherine, 266
Carstens, Lina, 241
Carter, Desmond, *see Author Index*
Caspar, Walter, 145
Cassirer, Ernst, 54
CBS (Columbia Broadcasting System), 314, 321
Cervantes, Miguel de, 423n
Chabrier, Emmanuel, 427
Chalmers, Thomas, 266
Chappell, 9
Charell, Erik, 249, 259, 388–9, 390, 391, 392, 393, 394, 400, 403, 423
Chatterton, Vivienne, 273
Cheirel, Micheline, 270
Chienne, La (film), 402
Chomsky, Noam, 16
Chopin, Frédéric, 54
Clair, René, 65, 255, 396, 417, 421
Clarke Victor, 362
Clarkstown Country Club, 330
Clement, J. B., *see Author Index*

Clifford, Hubert, 66
Clurman, Harold, 61
Cobb, Lee J., 279
Coburn, Charles, 308
Cochran, Charles B., 255, 256, 388
Cocteau, Jean, *see Author Index*
Cohan, George M., 312
Cole, Edward, 8, 352, 373
Coleman, Herbert, 368
Coleman, Warren, 368
Collins, Russell, 279
Colonial Theatre, Boston, *see* Boston
Columbia Broadcasting System, *see* CBS
Columbia University: Brander Matthews Hall, 341
Columbia University Players, 299
Comber, Bobbie, 273
Committee for a Jewish Army of Stateless and Palestinian Jews, 330
Concertgebouw Orchestra, 243
Concert Hall Records, 357
Congress Dances, 388
Conklin, Peggy, 312
Connelly, Marc, 417; *The Farmer Takes a Wife*, 417
Connelly, Reg, 339
Conway, Tom, 348
Cooke, John, 198
Cooper, Melville, 346
Copland, Aaron, 1, 296, 327; *The Second Hurricane*, 426; *El Salón México*, 327
Cordon, Norman, 353
Corso Theatre, Zurich, *see* Zurich
Corwin, Norman, 314, 321, 332
Coslow, Sam, *see Author Index*
Cossart, Ernest, 308
Cowan, Lester, 347
Cravat, Noel, 266
Crawford, Cheryl, 61, 62, 63, 64, 65, 66, 276, 328, 336, 354, 362, 404, 405, 407, 408, 416n, 421
Crockett, Davy, 297
Cummings, Robert, 292
Cunningham, Colin, 273
Curjel, Hans, 167, 168, 172, 174, 189, 216, 255, 439
Curtis Chamber Ensemble, 143
Cutler, Ben, 266
Cutner, Sydney B., 338, 339, 340

Dahlhaus, Carl, 42
Dalby, Edward, 273

Dannenberg, Marga, 183
Darmstadt, 5, 6, 20; Kranichsteiner Musikinstitut, 13; Landestheater, 13, 14; Fereinkurse für Neue Musik, 13, 14
Darrieux, Marcel, 157
Davies, Peter Maxwell, 28; *A Mirror of Whitening Light*, 28
Davies, Russell, 405
Davis, Colin, 15, 17, 248
Davis, George, 7, 8, 9, 10, 13, 35, 47, 48, 135, 425
Davison, Robert, 356
DeFore, Don, 303
Deharme, Paul, 251, 252
Dehmel, Richard, *see Author Index*
Deman, Rudolf, 160
Denby, Edwin, 307, 398, 401, 426; *The Second Hurricane*, 401
Desnos, Robert, *see Author Index*
Dessau, 53, 54, 99, 374; Court Theatre, 54, 123; Friedrichs-Theater, 55, 147, 148; Opera, 55, 121, 124, 430; Orchestra, 121
Dessau, Paul, 40, 175, 199, 296, 324, 355
Dessoir, Max, 54
Detwiler, Russell, 425
Deutsche Grammophon, 26, 28
Deutsche Kammermusik, Baden-Baden, *see* Baden-Baden
Deutsche Rundfunk, Der, 56
Deutsches Theater, Berlin, *see* Berlin
Déval, Jacques, *see Author Index*
Diaghilev, Serge, 203, 381, 382
Diamand, Peter, 20
Diamond, David, 355
Dickinson, Meriel, 193, 221, 280
Dicks, Harro, 13, 14
Dieterle, William (Wilhelm), 283
Dietrich, Marlene, 64, 249, 250, 328, 391, 407
Dietz, Howard, *see Author Index*
Dobbri Saxophone Orchestra, 170
Döblin, Alfred, 215; *Die drei Sprünge des Wang-lun*, 215
Dobson, James, 346
Dolan, Robert Emmett, 318; Artist's Waltz, 318
Dolin, Anton, 416n
Donaueschingen Neue Musik festival, 143, 145
Doone, Rupert, 66
Dortmund, 19–20

Douglas, Melvyn, 319
Dowling, Constance, 308
Downes, Olin, 349
Drabek, Kurt, 228
Drayton, Mary, 303
Dreher, Ted, 325
Dreiser, Theodore, 402; *The Hand of the Potter*, 402
Dresden State Opera, 57, 159
Drese, Dr, 23
Drew, David, 31, 39, 129, 133, 154, 173, 184, 189, 192, 210, 221, 235, 241, 242, 243, 247, 260, 287, 374; Reflections on the Last Years, 44n; *Über Kurt Weill* (DD.UKW), 24, 25, 26, 28, 31, 118, 119, 125, 128, 133, 151; Weill and his Critics, 24
DuBois, Raoul René, 346
Dudow, Slatan, 376n
Duke, Vernon, 84
Dümling, Albrecht, 42, 202–3; *Lasst euch nicht verführen. Brecht und die Musik* (AD.BM), 42, 181, 202–3
Duncan, Todd, 368
Dunham, Katherine, 407
Dunne, Philip, 342
Durieux, Tilla, 192
Düsseldorf, 234, 235

Eastern Railroad Presidents' Conference, 300
Eaton, John, 13n
Ebert, Carl, 7, 14, 38, 234, 235
Eckhardt, Ulrich, 21, 23, 24, 26, 38
Eddy, Nelson, 308
Eden, Irene, 172, 173
Edinburgh: Traverse Theatre, 222
Edwards, Harry Stillwell, *see Author Index*
Ehrenburg, Ilya, *see Author Index*
Eichendorff, Joseph Freiherr von, *see Author Index*
Einem, Gottfried von, 48, 235
Eisinger, Irene, 234
Eisler, Hanns, 17, 26–7, 31, 34, 40, 43, 46, 58, 61, 63, 67, 175, 188, 223, 227, 299, 313, 324, 341, 343, 376n, 383, 385, 387, 411, 412; *Die Massnahme*, 58, 227, 387; *Die Mutter*, 387; *A Song About America*, 63, 299
Einstein, Alfred, 433
Ellis, Vivian, 255
Elsendoorn, Jo, 20, 21

Emerson, Hope, 353
Engel, Erich, 166, 197, 219
Engel, Lehman, 279
Engelbert Humperdinck Archive, 75, 374
Engelhardt, Jürgen, 32
English National Opera, 15
Erdmann, Edward, 143
Erfurt, 59, 396; Stadttheater, 241
Es hat geklingelt (revue), 377
Es liegt ein Schloss in Oesterreich (folk song), 127
Essen Opera, 163
Esslin, Martin, 51
Ethel Barrymore Theatre, New York, see New York
Etwas für Sie (revue), 377
European American Music Inc., 76
European Broadcasting Union (EBU), 17–18

Faber and Faber, 29
Fabray, Nanette, 362
Fagin, Gary, 221
Fairbanks, Douglas, Jr, 321
Falla, Manuel da, 381; Master Peter's Puppet Show, 163, 381, 382
Fallada, Hans, 395, 396; Kleiner Mann – was nun?, 395
Farneth, David, 36, 37, 38, 49, 445
Federal Opera, 401
Federal Theatre, 62, 63, 286, 294, 295, 297, 299, 304, 392, 398, 401, 423
Feher, Paul, 234
Fehling, Jürgen, 207
Fein, Harry H., 296
Fein, Maria, 188
Feingold, Michael, 221
Fernay, Roger, see Author Index
Ferrer, José, 342, 421
Ferruccio Busoni Archive, 75
Feuchtwanger, Lion, see Author Index
Feuge, Elisabeth, 39, 55, 102, 108, 109, 123, 124
Feuge, Emilie, 54, 108
Field, Betty, 312
Fielding, Henry, 415; Jonathan Wild, 415
Fields, Dorothy, see Author Index
Fight for Freedom Inc., 319, 320, 321, 324
Fischer-Dieskau, Dietrich, 27
Fitelberg, Jerzy, 198, 205
Fleischer, Hans, 183

Fleischer, Herbert, 10, 12, 18, 20, 168, 437, 438, 439, 440
Fleisser, Marieluise, 215
Fleming, Peter, 413n; The Flying Visit, 413n
Flesch, Hans, 57
Florelle, 270
Folmer, Wallace Walter, 303
Fonda, Henry, 299
Fontanne, Lynn, 326
Forbes-Robertson, Johnston, 405
Forster, Rudolf, 188
46th Street Theatre, New York, see New York
France, Anatole, 404; La Révolte des Anges, 404
Francell, Jacqueline, 273
Franck, Walter, 375
Frank, Maurits, 145
Frank, Nelly, 148
Frank, Walter, 193
Frankfurt, 5, 13, 145, 183
Frankfurter Kammermusikwoche Neue Musik, 144
Frankfurt Radio, 207, 209
Frankfurt Radio Orchestra, 209, 216
French Institute, London, 222
Frenkel, Stefan, 158, 160, 198
Friedman, Charles, 353, 421
Friedrich of Anhalt, Duke, 54
Friedrichs-Theater, Dessau, see Dessau
From Berlin to Broadway, 24
Frontiers Unlimited, 349
Frost, Robert, see Author Index
Fuchs, Erich, 246
Fulda, Ludwig, see Author Index
Füssl, Karl Heinz, 210

Gaige, Crosby, 266
Galsworthy, John, 380, 421; The Apple Tree, 421; Justice, 380
Garbe, Albert, 241
Gardner, Ava, 348
Garfield, John, 279, 332
Garner, Adam, 357
Garrick Theatre, New York, see New York
Garten, Hugo F., 16
Gasbarra, Felix, see Author Index
Gassner, John, 411
Gauty, Lys, 261, 262, 341, 432
Gay, John, see Author Index
Gayse, Sheila, 368

Gazzelloni, Severino, 134
Gee, George, 273
Geibel, Emanuel, *see Author Index*
Geliot, Michael, 15, 33, 222
Gellhorn, Peter, 134
Gelsenkirchen (Musiktheater im Revier), 13
GEMA, 9
Georg Kaiser Archive, 23
George, Manfred, 324, 341
George, Stefan, *see Author Index*
Georges, Horst, 235
Gera: Reussisches Theater, 170
Gerhard, Roberto, 5, 6; *The Duenna*, 5
Gerron, Kurt, 197, 219
Gershwin, George, 45, 46, 61, 62, 84, 286, 328, 354, 423, 430; *Porgy and Bess*, 61, 286, 328, 354
Gershwin, Ira, *see Author Index*
Gertler, Heinrich, 246
Gesetz, Das (play), 380
Ghost Goes West, The (film), 421
Giebel, Karl, 173
Gielen, Josef, 159
Gielgud, John, 404
Gilbert, Michael John Tyler, 39–40; *Bertolt Brecht and Music. A Comprehensive Study*, 39–40
Gilbert, W. S., 310
Gilbert, Walter, 266
Gilbricht, 181
Gilliam, Lawrence, 252
Gingold, Norbert, 183, 196, 197, 209, 210, 225
Glenat, 270
Glock, Sir William, 15, 17
Goberman, Max, 342
Goehr, Walter, 187, 188, 207, 210; *Pep*, 207
Goethe, Johann Wolfgang von, *see Author Index*
Goethe House, New York, 143
Gogol, Nikolai, 402, 417; *The Government Inspector*, 402, 417, 419
Gold, Michael, *see Author Index*
Goldenberg, Samuel, 266
Goldschmidt, Berthold, 235n, 287, 430, 441, 442; *Der gewaltige Hahnrei*, 287
Goll, Iwan, *see Author Index*
Golling, Alexander, 241
Gombert, Wilhelm, 235
Gonszar, Rudolf, 235
Goodrich, Frances, 318

Gordon, Max, 62, 288, 289, 346
Gordon, Paul, 424
Gorki, Maxim, 376n; *Die Mutter*, 376n
Götze, Helmut, 241
Gounod, Charles, 267
Grabbe, Christian Dietrich, *see Author Index*
Graetz, Paul, 205
Graham, Roberts, *see Author Index*
Grahl, Hans, 209
Gramholtz, Elsa, 141
Granach, Alexander, 236
Gratenau, 129
Graziano, John, 364
Green, Paul, *see Author Index*
Greissle, Felix, 181
Grey, Madeleine, 60
Gronostay, Uwe, 98
Grossmann, Stefan, 376, 383, 384, 388, 418n; *Apollo-Brunnenstrasse*, 376, 383, 384, 388, 418n
Grosz, George, 406, 411
Grosz, Wilhelm, 376, 377, 378; *Baby in der Bar*, 377, 378; *The Isle of Capri*, 378
Group Theatre (London), 66
Group Theatre (New York), 61, 276, 279, 283, 286, 304, 328, 398, 399, 400, 405, 408, 416
Grove, Isaac van, 266, 303, 331, 356
Grove's Dictionary of Music and Musicians, 374
Gruber, Heinz Karl, 34; *Frankenstein!!*, 34
Guggenheim Foundation, 406
Guilbert, Yvette, 198, 293, 294, 408, *see also Author Index*
Gulbenkian Foundation, 17
Güllhausen, Guido von, *see Author Index*
Gutheim, Karlheinz, 200n

Haas, Dolly, 375
Hackett, Albert, 318
Hailey, Christopher, 384n, 388–9, 392, 393
Halberstadt, 55, 374
Halevi, Jehuda, *see Author Index*
Hamburg Staatsoper, 14, 15
Hamburg-Altona, 235
Hamilton, Bruce, 307
Hammerstein, Oscar, *see Author Index*
Handel, George Frideric, 398

Hannon, Bob, 322
Hanns Eisler Choir, 27, 32, 42
Happe, Frau E., 113
Harburg, E. Y., *see Author Index*
Harcourt, 327; *La Musique des Incas*, 327
Harden, Erich, 219
Hardt, Ernst, *see Author Index*
Harris, Jed, 61, 402
Harris, Jonathan, 356
Harris, Margo, 27, 28, 29, 34, 35
Harris, Roy, 355
Harris, Sam H., 318
Hart, Moss, *see Author Index*
Hart, Walter, 24
Hartford (Connecticut): Bushnell Memorial Theatre, 307
Hartmann, Ernst, 16
Hartmann, Karl-Amadeus, 7, 200
Hašek, Jaroslav, 384, 397, 410, 411; *Die Abenteuer des braven Soldaten Schweyk*, *The Good Soldier Švejk*, 193, 384, 397, 408–12
Hauptmann, Elisabeth, *see Author Index*
Hauptmann, Gerhart, *see Author Index*
Hauschild, Hanns, 183
Haver, June, 337
Haverstraw, 68
Hawkes, Ralph, 67
Hawkins, Josh, 297, 300; I'm a rolling stone, 300
Hay, Joan, 273
Hayden, Melissa, 362
Haydn, Franz Joseph, 428
Hayes, Helen, 321, 324, 325, 404
Haymes, Dick, 348
Hays, H. R., *see Author Index*
Hecht, Ben, *see Author Index*
Hecht, Werner, 199
Heckroth, Hein, 247, 259, 273
Heg, Hans, 21
Heine, Heinrich, 2
Heinsheimer, Hans, 51, 67, 167, 184, 220, 383–4, 385–6, 387, 389, 391, 394, 403
Heinz, Wolfgang, 236
Heinzelmann, Josef, 19, 20, 241, 260
Hello Dolly!, (musical), 402
Henahan, Donal, 30
Henderson, Charles, 338, 339
Hennenberg, Fritz, 197, 199, 202
Henried, Paul, 332

Henriot, H., 270
Henry, O., 405; *The Gentle Grafters*, 405, 417
Henschke, Grete, 241
Henze, Hans Werner, 25
Herbert, Victor, 84
Herder, Johann Gottfried, 2
Herder, Johann Gottfried, *see Author Index*
Herman, Jerry, 402
Hermanns, Heinrich, 186
Hertling, Nele, 26
Hertzka, Emil, 63, 147, 161, 162, 167
Herzig, Sid, *see Author Index*
Hessel, Franz, 376, 383, 388, 418n
Hesterberg, Trude, 184
Heugel et Cie, 9, 19, 28, 59, 60, 61, 270, 274, 397
Heyman, Edward, 279
Heymann, Werner R., 308
Heyworth, Peter, 189, 212; *Otto Klemperer. His life and times* (PH.OK), 167, 189
Hildebrand, Hilde, 377, 378
Hill, Steve, 356
Hilpert, Heinz, 193, 418n
Hindemith, Paul, 1, 43, 57, 58, 128, 144, 145, 153, 167, 212, 213, 214, 215, 216, 224, 225, 285, 429; *Hin und Zurück*, 167; *Kammermusik* no. 1, op. 24, 145; *Kammermusik*, op. 6 no. 2, 212; *Das Marienleben*, 144, 153, 285; *Mathis der Maler*, 153; *Neues vom Tage*, 167; *Sämtliche Werke*, 213, 216; *Tuttifäntchen*, 145, 153
Hindemith Foundation, *see* Paul Hindemith Foundation
Hindemith Institute, *see* Paul Hindemith Institute
Hinton, Stephen, 51, 199
Hinz und Kunz collective, 25, 26
Hitler, Adolf, 15, 16, 59, 63, 295, 341, 342, 394, 396, 413, 442
Hitlerism, 412–13
Hochschule für Musik, Berlin, *see* Berlin
Hoder, Johanna, 168
Hoellering, Franz, 397
Hoerrmann, Albert, 219, 375
Hoffman, Ferdie, 346
Hoffmann, Ernst, 365
Hoffmann, E. T. A., 418
Hofmannsthal, Hugo von, 381; *Jedermann*, 294

Holl, Karl, 144
Holländer, 1
Hollander, Alfred, 183
Holland Festival, 20–1
Holloway, Robin, 25, 28; Concertino No. 3, 'Homage to Weill', 25, 28
Holz, Arno, see Author Index
Homolka, Florence, 44
Homolka, Oskar, 219
Honegger, Arthur, 13, 267, 296, 420–1, 426; Antigone, 13; Fièvre Jaune, 426; Le roi David, 267
Hopf, Otto, 228
Horand, Theodor, 170, 183
Horenstein, Jascha, 235
Horne, William, 357
Horner, Harry, 266, 303, 318
Horst Wessel Song, 342
Hörth, Franz-Ludwig, 140, 163
Hosalla, Hans-Dieter, 175, 225
The Hot Mikado (musical), 310
House Committee on Un-American Activities (HUAC), 67, 412
Houseman, John, 398
Howard, Sidney, see Author Index
Howe, Julia Ward, see Author Index
How Green was my Valley (film), 418
Hoyningen-Huene, 44–5
Huder, Walter, 23, 48
Hudson, W. H., 422; Green Mansions, 422
Huehn, Julius, 314
Hughes, Langston, see Author Index
Hughes, Richard, see Author Index
Hugo Holles Madrigal Society, 216
Humperdinck, Engelbert, 54, 55, 116, 119, 374–5, 388; Gaudeamus, 374, 375
Humperdinck Archive, see Englebert Humperdinck Archive
Hungerford, Edward, see Author Index
Hunter College, New York, 323, 324, 341
Huston, Walter, 307

Ihering, Herbert, 166, 193
Imperial Theatre, New York, see New York
Indiana University, 365
Inkijinoff, 270
Institut für Theaterwissenschaft, Cologne, 376
International Ladies' Garment Workers' Union, 319

Irving, Washington, see Author Index
ISCM (International Society for Contemporary Music), 380, 429
Isherwood, Christopher, 396, 402, 434; The Ascent of F6, 402; Prater Violet; 396
It Happened One Night (film), 418
Ito, Micho, 141

Jackson, Felix, see Author Index
Jacobsen, Jens Peter, see Author Index
Jaffe, Sam, 266
James, Edward, 59, 244, 245, 246, 247, 396, 433
Jameson, Ralph, 266
Jana, La, 273
Janis, Beverly, 353
Janowska, Maria, 170
Janssen, Werner, 283
Jarnach, Philipp, 56, 129, 132, 135, 143, 145, 331, 429; Quartet, 145
Jarry, Alfred, 57
Jeffreys, Anne, 353
Jenkins, George, 368
Jenkins, Gordon, 292
Jerome, Jerome K., 405; The Passing of Third Floor Back, 405
Joachimson, Felix, see Jackson, Felix
Johannes, Albert, 241
Johnsrud, Harold, 266
Joken, Karl, 163
Jones, Robert Edmond, 312
Jonic, Bettina, 222; The Ladies, 222
Jonson, Ben, 417; Volpone, 417
Jooss, Kurt, 398
Judgement of Paris, The (ballet), 198

Kaempfer, Walter, 129
Kafka, Franz, 385
Kagel, Mauricio, 21
Kahn, Sammy, 308
Kaiser, Georg, see Author Index
Kaiser, Margarethe, 9
Kaiser Archive, see Georg Kaiser Archive
Kaiser-Wilhelm-Gedächtniskirche choir, 133
Kallman, Chester, 247
Kalman, Oskar, 216
Kandl, Eduard, 235
Kanin, Garson, 342
Karge, Manfred, 174
Karl-Marx School, Berlin, 228, 229
Karns, Roscoe, 292

Karsh, Yousuf, 44–5
Kassel, 13n
Kassel Tonkünstlerfest, 150
Kassowitz, Gottfried, 184
Kästner, Erich, see Author Index
Kastner, Rudolf, 119, 120
Katayev, Valentin, 399, 401, 402; The
  Embezzlers, 399, 401
Kaufman, Irving, 353
Kaye, Danny, 318
Kazan, Elia, 279, 336, 362
Keller, Hans, 17, 29
Kemp, Ian, 189
Kennedy, Arthur, 312
Kent, Margaret Chaffee, 303
Kenter, Heinz Dieter, 375, 376n
Kern, Leonhard, 163
Kessler, Harry, 380, 381, 382, 383,
  398; Tagebucher, 381
Kestenberg, Leo, 227
Key, Francis Scott, see Author Index
Kidd, Michael, 303, 362
King, William, G., 45
Kipling, Rudyard, 197
Kistenmacher, Arthur, 119
Kleiber, Erich, 57, 160, 163
Klein, Erika, 141
Kleist, Heinrich von, 400, 435; The
  Marquise von O., 400; Michael
  Kohlhaas, 400
Klemperer, Otto, 167, 189, 211, 212,
  225, 429
Klöpfer, Eugen, 207
Knappertsbusch, Hans, 55
Knipper, Lev, 203, 331; Cavalry of
  the Steppes, 203, 331; Symphony
  No. 4, 331
Knust, Herbert, 409n, 410n, 411
Koch, Karl, 383
Koch, F. E., 54, 116
Kochno, Boris, 247
Kodály, Zoltán, 349
Kogel, Ilse, 170
Kolisch, 6
Kölling, Rudolf, 163
Kollmar, Richard, 307
Koltai, Ralph, 15
Kommer, Rudolph, 406
Königsberg, 235
Kontarsky, Aloys, 122
Kopp, Leo, 266
Koppenhöfer, Maria, 207
Korda, Alexander, 60, 66, 421
Körner, Theodor, see Author Index

Korngold, Julius, 402, 417
Kotschenreuther, Helmut, 21
Koussevitzky, Serge, 363
Kowalke, Kim, 33, 34, 35–6, 37, 38,
  40, 48–9, 95, 97, 199n, 364, 388, 389
Kracauer, Siegfried, 433
Kranichsteiner Musikinstitut,
  Darmstadt, see Darmstadt
Krasna, Norman, see Author Index
Krasselt, 54
Kraus, Clemens, 235
Kraus, Karl, 255, 396, 401
Krauss, Werner, 168
Krebs, Anna, 22
Krenek, Ernst, 13, 167, 376, 429;
  Jonny spielt auf, 167; Das Leben des
  Orestes, 13
Krenn, Fritz, 225
Kretzschmar, 116
Kreutzberg, Harald, 163
Kreymborg, Arthur, 410, 411, 412
Kroll-Oper, see Berlin, Staatsoper am
  Platz der Republik
Kronacher, Alwin, 190
Kruger, Otto, 308
Kühl, Kate, 197
Kunz-Baker, Bertha, 266
Kürenberg, Der von, see Author Index
Kurhaus, Baden-Baden, see Baden-
  Baden
Kurnitz, Harry, see Author Index
Kurt Weill Conference (1983), 36, 95,
  235n, 287
Kurt Weill Foundation for Music, 22,
  28, 30, 31, 34, 35, 36, 38, 75, 95,
  221, 379n, 444–5
Kurt Weill Newsletter (KWN), 36, 95,
  118, 445

Laban, 398
Labiche, Eugène, 417, The Italian
  Straw Hat, 417
Lander, Harald, 246
Landestheater, Darmstadt, see
  Darmstadt
Lane, Burton, 432
Lane, Dorothy, see Hauptmann,
  Elisabeth
Lang, Eugen, 186
Lang, Fritz, 63, 289
Langhoff, Matthias, 174
Langhoff, Wolfgang, 66, 412
Langridge, Philip, 161, 221, 280
Lania, Leo, see Author Index

Lasker-Schüler, Else, 380; *Die Wupper*, 380
Lasoli, 129
Lasto, Rafael, 145
Laughton, Charles, 66, 416
Laurence, Paula, 336
Laval, Pierre, 342
Lawrence, Gertrude, 318, 405, 422
Lawson, John Howard, 283, 401
League of Composers (USA), 61
Lear, Evelyn, 17, 248
Lefaur, André, 270
Legal, Ernst, 237
Lehár, Franz, 345
Lehmann, R. O., 161
Leibelt, Hans, 188
Leichtentritt, Hugo, 151
Leight, Rowland, 308
Leipzig, 55, 58, 59, 396; Altes Theater, 190, 241; Neues Theater, 170, 183, 190
Leipzig Gewandhaus orchestra, 170
Leipzig Opera, 57, 170, 190
Leisen, Mitchell, 318
Lenau, Nikolaus, *see Author Index*
Lennartz, Elisabeth, 241
Lennon, Thomas, 308
Lenya, Lotte, 6–36 *passim*, 41, 46, 47, 56, 57, 58, 60, 61, 62, 65, 68,75, 82 135, 154, 158, 168, 173, 174, 184, 197, 198, 200, 207, 210, 219, 220, 222, 226, 235, 241, 245, 246, 247, 248, 250, 257, 266, 275, 284, 287, 288, 313, 322, 323, 327, 330, 340, 346, 352, 354, 370, 373, 375, 376, 377, 383, 387, 395, 396, 397, 400, 405, 407, 408, 412, 416, 417, 420n, 422, 425, 427, 428, 432, 434, 438, 439; *Six Songs* (recording), 198, 327–8
Leonard, Lotte, 159, 160
Leonhardt, Rudolph, 57
Lerner, Alan Jay, *see Author Index*
Leslie, Joan, 332, 337, 339
Lessing Theater, Berlin, *see* Berlin
Lesur, H., 270
Levine, Maurice, 368, 371
Lévi-Strauss, Claude, 16
Lewandowsky, Manfred, 152
Lewis, Bob, 279
Lewisohn, Ludwig, *see Author Index*
Lewis Ruth Band, 207, 219
Library of Congress, Washington, 38, 75, 102, 264, 286, 356

Library of the Performing Arts, New York, 75
Lincoln Center, New York, *see* New York
Lindemann, Otto, 205
Lingen, Theo, 219, 236
Liszt, Franz, 54, 55; *Liebestraum* no. 3, 54
Littau, Joseph, 362
Little, Brown and Co., 23
Littlefield, Catherine, 346
Loesser, Frank, 419
Loewe, Ferdinand, 101, 104
Loewe, Frederick, 347, 419
Loewenbach, Jan, 384–5, 409
Logan, Joshua, 307
London, 12, 60; Mercury Theatre, 198; Queen Elizabeth Hall, 28; Royal Albert Hall, 267; Royal Court Theatre, 222; Savoy Theatre, 256, 273
London, Jack, 385, 386; *General Strike*, 385
London, Sinfonietta, 25, 26, 27, 28, 32, 161, 189, 193, 221, 280
Löns, Hermann, *see Author Index*
Loos, Theodor, 168
Lorre, Peter, 219, 236, 410
Losch, Tilly, 64, 246, 396
Losey, Joseph, 66
Loud, David, 318
Love, Kermit, 336
Low, David, 413n
Lüdenscheid, 55, 113; Stadttheater, 113, 119
Lumet, Sidney, 266
Lunch Hour Follies, 64, 432
Lunt, Alfred, 325, 326
Luxemburg, Rosa, 210
Luxon, Benjamin, 193, 221
Lynn Murray Choir, 314
Lytell, Bert, 318

MacArthur, Charles,*see Author Index*
Macauley, Jospeph, 266
McDaniel, Barry, 26, 98, 154
MacDonald, Malcolm, 23, 154
McEvoy, J. P., *see Author Index*
Mackeben, Theo, 197, 199, 219, 384
McKelway, St Clair, *see Author Index*
Maclane, Barton, 292
MacLeish, Archibald, *see Author Index*
MacMurray, Fred, 337, 338, 339

Madden, Jean, 307
Maderna, Bruno, 20
Madison Square Gardens, New York, *see* New York
Magdeburg, 59, 396; Stadttheater, 241
Magre, Maurice, *see Author Index*
Mahieux, Edmond, 270
Mahler, Gustav, 8, 29, 104, 106, 114, 117, 121, 374, 427, 428
Mahnkes, Adolf, 159
Mainbocher, 336
Malraux, André, 401
Mamoulian, Rouben, 368, 388
Man from La Mancha, The (musical), 423n
Manhattan Opera House, New York, *see* New York
Mann, Heinrich, 434
Mann, Thomas, 45, 435
Mannheim, 287
Manzi, 129
March, Frederic, 321
Marcuse, Herbert, 16
Marker-Wagner, Frau, 140
Mark Warnow Orchestra, 314
Marlowe, Christopher, *see Author Index*
Marly, Anna, 343; Chant de Libération, 343
Marseillaise, 343
Marshall, Don, 346
Marshall, Jay, 362
Martin, Karlheinz, 222, 375
Martin, Mary, 336
Marx, Josef, 55
Massey, Guy, 338, 340
Masters, Edgar Lee, 422
Mather, Aubrey, 273
Mather, Bruce, 22
Mathieson, Muir, 66, 258, 272, 273
Matons, Bill, 303
Matrai, Ernest, 273
Matthews, Inez, 368
Mature, Victor, 318
Mauceri, John, 318
Mauprey, André, 249
Mayer, Edwin Justus, *see Author Index*
Medicine Show (Living Newspaper), 299
Mehlich, Ernst, 172, 173
Mehring, Walter, *see Author Index*
Meisel, Edmund, 192

Meisner, Sanford, 279
Melchett, Lord, 60
Melos-Quartett of Stuttgart, 114
Melville, Herman, 422; *Billy Budd*, 424; *Moby Dick*, 422, 424
Mendelssohn, Eleanora, 331
Mendelssohn, Felix, 101, 104, 107, 114, 117, 267, 402, 429; *A Midsummer Night's Dream*, 402
Mendelssohn, Francesco von, 266
Mendelssohn, Moses, 2, 99
Mendelssohn Prize, 55, 116
Menotti, Gian Carlo, 46, 164
Mercury Theatre, London, *see* London
Mercury Theatre (New York), 398
Meredith, Burgess, 63, 64, 299, 314, 319, 342, 402, 404
Mergler, Betty, 216
Merten, Reinhold, 209
Messiaen, Oliver, 5–6; *Livre d'orgue* (1951), 5
Metropolitan Opera, New York, *see* New York
Meyer, Eugene, 397
Meyer, Florence, 266
Meyerbeer, Giacomo, 55
Meyerhold, Vsevolod, 402
Meyerowitz, Selmar, 294
Middleton, Ray, 292, 307, 362
Mielziner, Jo, 307, 312, 346, 353
Mikorey, Edith, 53
Mikorey, Franz, 53
Milan: La Scala, 15
Milestone, Lewis, *see Author Index*
Milhaud, Darius, 22, 296, 343, 355, 398, 416n, 417, 428, 429, 433
Milhaud, Madeleine, 62, 417, 425, 428, 429, 432
Milland, Ray, 318
Mille, Agnes de, 335, 336; *Médée*, 426
Milva, 24, 26
Mirbeau, Octave, 402
Missner, Martin, 113, 122
Mitchell, Donald, 29–30, 49
Mitchell, Margaret, 417, 422; *Gone with the Wind*, 417, 422
Mockridge, Cyril J., 338, 339, 340
Molière, 417, 418; *Don Juan*, 418
Molnár, Ferenc, 420; *Liliom*, 420
Monk, Egon, 14
Moore, Grace, 346, 405
Mopp, 240
Morros, Boris, 292

Mortimer, Myra, 152
Morton, Arthur, 338, 339
Morton, Gregory, 356
Morton, Lawrence, 342, 343
Mosheim, Grete, 418n
Most Happy Fella, The (musical), 419
Mowbray, Alan, 338
Mozart, Wolfgang Amadeus, 427, 428, 429; *Idomeneo*, 398
Muller, Charlotte, 234
Müller, Traugott, 188, 192, 193
Multatuli (Eduard Douwes Dekker), 420n 438; *Max Havelaar*, 420n
Muni, Paul, 331, 356
Munich Kammerspiele, 200
Murrill, Herbert, 66
Music Box Theatre, New York, *see* New York
Mussolini, Benito, 295
Müthel, Lothar, 168, 193, 207
My Fair Lady (musical), 347, 419

Nabokov, Nicholas, 21
Nadaud, Serge, 270
Naharia, Palestine, 66
Nash, Ogden, *see Author Index*
Nathan, Hans, 296
NBC, 321
NBC Symphony Orchestra, 331
NCRV Vocal Ensemble, 150
Neher, Carola, 219
Neher, Caspar, *see Author Index*
Neher, Erika, 59, 296, 396
Neighbour, O. W., 6, 20, 150
Neighbour Collection, *see* O. W. Neighbour Collection
Nelson, Rudolf, 377, 378
Neppach, Rudolf, 395, 396
Nesnow, Adrienne, 37, 436
Nestroy, Johann, 89, 215, 402; *30 Jahre aus dem Leben eines Lumpen*, 215; *Einen Jux will er sich machen*, 402
Neue Musik Berlin, 226, 227
Neues Theater, Leipzig, *see* Leipzig
New Faces (revue), 275
Newman, Alfred, 338, 339
Newman, Emil, 338
New York, 64· Adelphi Theatre, 353; Alvin Theatre, 318, 346, 356; Broadhurst Theatre, 312; Broadway, 12, 65, 66, 84–5; Ethel Barrymore Theatre, 307; 46th Street Theatre, 362; Garrick

Theatre, 57, 141; Imperial Theatre, 336; Lincoln Center, 143; Madison Square Gardens, 319, 331; Manhattan Opera House, 62, 266; Music Box Theatre, 368; Roxy Theatre, 322; Theatre de Lys, 200
New York City Ballet, 247
New York City Opera, 33, 241
New York Philharmonic Orchestra, 243
New York World's Fair (1939), 63, 303, 349
Nigun Press, 296
Nikisch, Arthur, 53, 119
Noailles, Vicomte Charles de, 59, 227, 244, 245, 246
Noailles, Vicomtesse Marie-Laure de, 59, 227, 244, 245, 246
Noble, Ray, 339
Noë, Marcel, 163
Nono, Luigi, 5
Nordstrom, Clarence, 307
North-West German Radio, 129
North-West German Radio Symphony Orchestra, 129
Nostitz, Helene von, 380, 382–3
Novello, Ivor, 255

Obey, André, 404; *Noah*, 404
Odets, Clifford, *see Author Index*
Oenslager, Donald, 279
Offenbach, Jacques, 19, 89, 254, 346, 430
Office of War Information (OWI), Washington, 340, 341, 342, 343, 409
Ogdon, John, 18, 136
Ohent, Clara, 108
Oklahoma, 299
O'Neill, Eugene, 417, 420, 421; *Marco Millions*, 417, 421
Orchestre des Concerts Straram, 157
Orff, Carl, 46, 200
Osato, Sono, 336
Osnath-Halevy, Sarah, 266
Osterkamp, Ernst, 183
O. W. Neighbour Collection, 75, 188

Pabst, G. W., 199, 283, 395
Packh, Maurice de, 338, 339, 340
Padilla, Lola Artôt de, 150
Page, Ruth, 398
Paige, Carol, 292
Pain, Mrs Francis, 422

Palestine Philharmonic Orchestra, 441
Palestine Symphony Orchestra, 66
Pal Joey (musical), 403
Palm, Siegfried, 122
Pan, 123
Paramount, 64, 289, 318
Paris, 12, 43, 59, 60, 66; Salle Gaveau, 59, 172, 174; Théâtre de l'exposition des arts décoratifs, 157; Théâtre de Paris, 270; Théâtre des Champs-Elysées, 59, 246; Théâtre des Etoiles, 198
Paris Opéra, 235
Park Avenue Synagogue, New York, 355
Partington, Arthur, 362
Pascal, Gabriel, 420
Pasetti, Otto von, 174, 184, 246
Paton, Alan *see Author Index*
Paul Hindemith Foundation, 22
Paul Hindemith Institute, 75, 216
Paulsen, Harald, 184, 197
Pechner, Gerhard, 173
Perelman, S. J., *see Author Index*
Perlberg, William, 336
Pétain, Henri, 342
Peters, Albert, 246
Petrie, Hay, 273
Pfeiffer-Belli, Wolfgang, 381
Pfieffer, Hermann, 241
Pfitzner, Hans, 53, 55, 116, 123; *Der arme Heinrich*, 123
Philadelphia: Shubert Theatre, 353
Philharmonie, Berlin, *see* Berlin
Phoebus-Film, 163
Pick, Lupu, 396
Pierpont Morgan Library, New York, 161
Piscator, Erwin, 59, 192, 193, 341, 354, 384, 401, 406, 408–11, 412; *Das politische Theater*, 193
Piscator-Bühne, 192
Pisling-Boas, Nora, 149
Playwrights' Company, The, 22, 66, 279, 307, 312, 325, 326, 353, 368, 370, 401, 419, 434
Poe, Edgar Allan, 434
Polignac, Princesse Edmond de, 59, 242–3
Pont, Paul du, 336
Ponto, Erich, 197
Porter, Cole, 1, 288, 326; *Kiss Me Kate*, 288

Presley, Elvis, 16
Preussisches Staatskapelle, 211
Prinzler, Gertrud, 108
Prunières, Henri, 380
Prussian Academy of Arts, 44, 56, 325, 426
Prussian Academy of Church and School Music, 58
Puccini, Giacomo, 345, 429
Pursuit of Happiness, The, 314
Putterman, David J., 355

Queen Elizabeth Hall, London, *see* London
Queneau, Raymond, 252; *Exercices de style*, 252
Quinn, Anthony, 337

Rachmaninov, Sergey, 330; Prelude in C sharp minor, 330
Radio Berlin, 168, 228
Radio Paris, 217, 251
Radio-Symphonie-Orchester, Berlin, 242
Rady, Simon, 319
Raft, George, 289, 290, 292
Raimund, Ferdinand, 89
Raimundtheater, Vienna, *see* Vienna
Rainer, Luise, 62, 400
Raksin, David, 338, 339
Ramirez, Carlos, 337
Ramthun, Herta, 190, 237
Randall, Carl, 307
Rankl, Karl, 223, 235
Rasch, Albertina, 318
Ratoff, Gregory, 336
Ray, Man, 44
Raya, Nita, 270
Raymond, Helen, 336
Rayner, Sydney, 353
Reger, Max, 55, 114, 116, 117, 123, 135; Suite, op. 125, 116; Suite op. 130, 116
Reich, Günter, 242
Reichstag fire, 396, 439
Reimann, Aribert, 24, 26, 98, 154
Reiner, Fritz, 119
Reinhardt, Delia, 160, 163
Reinhardt, Max, 60, 61, 176, 262, 264, 265, 266, 267, 294, 377, 381, 382, 388, 390, 391, 402
Reininger, Lotte, 383
Reinmar, Hans, 234

Renard, A., 343; Le Temps des Cerises, 342, 343
Renoir, Jean, 65, 341, 342, 396, 402, 416n
Residentie orchestra, 20, 152, 241
Reussisches Theater, Gera, see Gera
Révy, Richard, 397
Reynolds, Quentin, 356
RIAS Kammerchor, 98
Ribemont-Dessaignes, Georges, 247
Rice, Alfred, 27, 28, 35
Rice, Elmer, see Author Index
Richter, Marga, 8
Riemann, Hans, 384
Riesmann, Sieglinde, 241
Rilke, Rainer Maria, see Author Index
Ripperger, Georg, 173
Rippon, Michael, 280
Riskin, Robert, 342
Rita Weill Collection (RWC), 38, 95, 97
Ritt, Martin, 312
Ritter, Anna, see Author Index
Robeson, Paul, 63, 65, 309, 310, 320, 321, 407, 417, 418
Robinson, Bill, 309, 310
Robinson, Edward G., 331
Rockland Riot (revue), 329–30
Rockwell, John, 389, 392
Rode, Wilhelm, 234
Rodgers, Richard, 403, 420n, 430
Rogers, Ginger, 318
Romains, Jules, 404; Donogoo, 404
Rome: Accademia di Santa Cecilia, 60
Ronell, Ann, 286, 347, 348
Roosevelt, Franklin D., 295, 319
Rose, Billy, 331, 388, 416
Rossini, Gioacchino, 55
rote Kapelle, Die (Communist Resistance Movement), 376n
Roth, Dr Ernst, 181
Roth, Féri, 380
Roth, Joseph, 409; Hiob, 409
Roth, Wolfgang, 365
Roth Quartet, 145, 380 428
Rother, Arthur, 235
Rottenberg, Ludwig, 209
Rounseville, Robert, 303, 307
Roxy Theatre, New York, see New York
Royal, Ted, 317, 346, 353
Royal Albert Hall, London, see London

Royal Court Theatre, London, see London
Rudley, Herbert, 331
Rufer, Ernst, 241
Rufer, Josef, 4, 6, 7, 9, 123; The Works of Arnold Schoenberg, 123
Ruhmann, Hans, 375
Rupprecht, Fritz, 120, 121, 122, 129
Rushby-Smith, John, 222
Rüth, Ludwig, 219
Ruttmann, Walter, 383
Ryskind, Morris, see Author Index

Sadler's Wells Opera, 15, 33
St-Cyr-sur-Mer, 194
Salle Gaveau, Paris, see Paris
Salomon, Karel, 242
Salute to France, 341
Samburski, 296
Saminsky, Lazare, 296
Samousoud, Jacques, 308
Samuel, Harold E., 37
Sandburg, Carl, 304
Sanders, Ronald, 37, 286, 288, 289, 309, 310, 381, 382; The Days Grow Short. The Life and Music of Kurt Weill (RS.DGS), 37, 286, 289, 309, 381
San Francisco Opera, 19, 163
San Juan, Olga, 348
Saroyan, William, 421
Satie, Erik, 130, 240, 269; Gnossiennes, 240, 269, 278
Sattler, Ernst, 241
Sauvage, Catherine, 252
Saxe, John Godfrey, 301
Saxon, Don, 353
Scala, La, Milan, see Milan
Schapiro, Margaret, 54
Schebera, Jürgen: Kurt Weill (JS.KW), 109
Scherchen, Hermann, 127, 144, 205, 216, 217, 235
Schiffer, Marcellus, 167
Schiller, Johann Christoph Friedrich von, 34; Die Räuber, 34
Schiller Theater, Berlin, see Berlin
Schillings, Max von, 235
Schirmer, 67
Schlee, Alfred, 11, 63
Schlein, Irving, 307, 320, 361 368
Schlosspark-Theater, Berlin, see Berlin
Schmitt, Florent, 59

Schneider, Hans, 147n
Schnitzler, Arthur, 403; *Reigen*, 403, 405
Schoenberg, Arnold, 4–5, 6, 7, 9, 13, 21–2, 24, 43, 44, 45, 46, 55, 82, 109, 111, 118, 121, 123, 161, 188, 349, 377, 385, 429; *Das Buch der hängenden Gärten*, 144; *The Dance Around the Golden Calf*, 5; Four Songs, op. 2, 123; *Friede auf Erden*, 144; 'Gigerlette', 109; *Gurrelieder*, 123; *Israel Exists Again*, 46; Letters, 144; *Pelleas und Melisande*, 118; Piano Concerto, 5; *Pierrot lunaire*, 4–5; Six Songs, op. 3, 123; *A Survivor from Warsaw*, 46; Symphony for soloists, chorus and orchestra, 123; Tapfer sind solche, die Taten vollbringen, 161; Three Pieces, op. 11, 5; *Verklärte Nacht*, 111, 123
Schöffler, Paul, 159
Scholz, Friedrich, 225
Schöpflin, Adolf, 159
Schott, 17, 167, 168
Schreker, Franz, 55, 125, 126, 376, 430
Schröter, Walter, 241
Schubert, Franz, 104, 105, 130, 427, 428
Schubertchor, 223
Schüchter, Wilhelm, 129
Schuller, Gunther, 19, 163
Schultz-Dornburg, Rudolph, 163
Schultze-Rohr, Peter, 225
Schumann, Robert, 104, 135
Schützendorf, Leo, 163
Schwartz, Arthur, 432
Seelig, Carl, 443
Seghers, Anna, 59; *The Revolt of the Fishermen of St Barbara*, 59
Seidler-Winkler, Bruno, 168, 219
Seira, 296
Selo, Alexander, 136
Selter, William A., 347
Sender Freies Berlin, 24, 25
Sérénade, La, 174
Sessions, Roger, 403
Seven Lively Arts, The (revue), 416n
Shakespeare, William, 288
Sharaff, Irene, 318
Shaw, Christopher, 18, 19, 28, 133, 154, 260, 280
Shaw, George Bernard, 346, 394, 405,

420–1; *Arms and the Man*, 420; *Caesar and Cleopatra*, 394, 404, 420, 421; *Captain Brassbound's Conversion*, 420; *Heartbreak House*, 420; *Pygmalion*, 346, 419, 420
Sheldon, Gene, 337
Sheriff, Noam, 163
Shields, Roy, 325
Short, Hassard, 318
Shostakovich, Dmitri, 330; Symphony No. 7, 330
Shubert Theatre, Boston, *see* Boston
Shubert Theatre, Philadelphia, *see* Philadelphia
Shuken, Leo, 338, 339
Shull, Ronald K., 213, 313; *Music and the Works of Bertolt Brecht* (RS.MWB), 190, 213, 313
Shumlin, Herman, 402
Sibelius, Jean, 349
Sidney, Sylvia, 289, 290, 292, 331
Sidney Kay's Fellows, 207
Siedl, Erhard, 241
Siegel, Al, 292
Sierck, Detlef, *see* Sirk, Douglas
Silja, Anja, 25n, 242
Sillman, Leonard, 275
Silva, Howard da, 312
Simon, Louis B., 104, 125, 374, 375
Singakademie, Berlin, *see* Berlin
Sirk, Douglas, 241
Sirmay, Albert, 318
Sitwell, Sacheverell, 433
Skalkottas, Nikos, 56
Smith, Mark, 307
Smith, Samuel Francis, *see* Author Index
Sobernheim, Curt, 426
Sokolov, Anna, 353
Sorel, Felicia, 57
Sousa, John Philip, 303; Anchors Aweigh, 303
Souvestre, Pierre, 251
Speelmanns, Hermann, 375
Spewack, Bella, *see* Author Index
Spewack, Sam, *see* Author Index
Spinelli, Nicola, 170; *A basso porto*, 170
Spoliansky, Mischa, 324, 378
Staatoper am Platz der Republik, Berlin, *see* Berlin
Staatsoper unter den Linden, Berlin, *see* Berlin
Stadlen, Peter, 5

Stahlman, Sylvia, 362
Stahl-Nachbaur, Ernst, 188
Stalin, Joseph, 402, 406, 442
Stark, Günther, 376n
Steckel, Leonhard, 192, 375
Steegmuller, Francis, 397
Stefan, Rudi, 144; *Musik für Saiten-instrumente*, 144
Stein, Erwin, 144, 170, 223, 234, 240, 243, 386, 387
Steinbeck, John, 422; *The Grapes of Wrath*, 422
Steinberg, Wilhelm (William), 183
Steinecke, Wolfgang, 13
Steiner, George, 442
Steiner, Max, 417
Steinthal, Walter, 229
Steininger, Fritz, 308
Steinsieck, Annamarie, 188
Stephan, Rudolf, 213, 216
Stern, Dietrich, 32
Stern, Jean, 209
Sternberg, Josef von, 396
Sternheim, Carl, 53, 403, 404, 418; *Der Snob*, 403
Steuermann, Eduard, 6
Stevenson, R. L., 404; *New Arabian Nights*, 404
Stewart, Johnny, 362
Stiedry, Fritz, 56, 149, 153, 234, 235
Stiemer, Camilla, 168, 169
Stobrawa, Renée, 192
Stockhausen, Karlheinz, 5
Stokowski, Leopold, 235
Stoska, Polyna, 353
Stowe, Harriet Beecher, 390, 405; *Uncle Tom's Cabin*, 390
Straram, Walther, 157
Strasberg, Lee, 61, 279
Stratas, Teresa, 24, 33, 35
Straus, Oscar, 420; *The Chocolate Soldier*, 420
Strauss, Johann, 89, 346
Strauss, Richard, 107, 110, 176, 381, 398, 429, 430, 433; *Die Frau ohne Schatten*, 381–2; *Josephslegende*, 381, 382, 398; *Der Rosenkavalier*, 164, 403
Stravinsky, Igor, 5, 6, 10, 45, 144, 148, 203, 212, 349, 403, 416n, 428, 429, 433; *The Fairy's Kiss*, 148; *The Firebird*, 203; *L'histoire du soldat*, 145; *Pulcinella* Suite, 212; *Scènes de Ballet*, 416n
Strindberg, August, *see Author Index*

Strobel, 118, 125, 126, 128, 133, 151
Stuckenschmidt, H. H., 44n, 161; *Arnold Schoenberg*, 44n
Stuckenschmidt, Thea, 161
Stünzner, Elisa, 159
Styne, Jule, 308
Sudermann, Hermann, *see Author Index*
Südwestfunk, Baden-Baden, 17, 225; Orchestra, 133
Suhrkamp, Peter, 15, 225
Suhrkamp Verlag, 23, 29, 32, 42
Sullivan, Arthur, 310, 430
Sullivan, Brian, 353
Sundgaard, Arnold, *see Author Index*
Sun Valley Serenade (film), 339
Surinach, Carlos, 357
Swan, Leda, 270
Symonette, Lys, 22, 49, 95, 118, 241, 249, 250, 260, 370, 436
Symonette, Randolph, 346, 353
Synagogue Music by Contemporary Composers, 355
Syrjala, S., 319
Szigeti, Josef, 157

Talbot Library, Princeton, 151, 152
Talén, Bjorn, 234
Tamiroff, Akim, 332
Taniko, 226
Tashlin, Frank, *see Author Index*
Taucher, Kurt, 159
Taylor, Deems, 417
Taylor, Herb, 338, 339
Taylor, Myron, 266
Tchaikovsky, Peter Ilyich, 107, 278, 330; Overture: *Romeo and Juliet*, 330
Ted Shawm Dance Company, 303
Terpis, Max, 380
Terr, Max, 292
Terry, Richard, 433
Thaler, Isko, 198
Theatre Guild, 398, 411, 420
Theatre Union (New York), 61
Theatre Workshop, 411
Thielman, Urban, 338, 339
Thomas, Ambroise, 55
Thomas, Mary, 221, 280
Thomson, Virgil, 401, 423
Three Days Pass, 322–3
Thuille, Ludwig, 116; *Harmonielehre*, 116
Toch, Ernst, 296
Toller, Ernst, 126, 401, 434

Tone, Franchot, 319
Toye, Francis, 433
Traven, B., 434
Traverse Theatre Edinburgh, *see* Edinburgh
Trummer, Mali, 183
Trunk, Richard, 55
Tudor, Antony, 198
Twain, Mark, *see Author Index*
Twentieth-Century–Fox, 336
Tyler, Bernice, 303
Tyler, Beverly, 346
Typographia, 386

Unger, Heinz, 133, 152, 154
United Artists, 308
Universal Edition, 6, 9, 10, 11–12, 16, 17, 27, 56, 59, 63, 67, 75, 76, 140, 141, 142, 147, 153, 154, 156, 160, 164, 165, 167, 168, 170, 172, 177, 183, 198, 205, 211, 216, 218, 219, 220, 223, 224, 235, 236, 240, 246, 270, 287, 377, 380, 384, 386, 387, 388, 391, 393, 394, 437, 438, 440
The Unknown Kurt Weill (recording), 35
Unseld, Siegfried, 23–4
Upham, J. B., *see Author Index*
Upp, Virginia van, *see Author Index*
Uppman, John, 266

Valetti, Rosa, 418n
Vambery, Robert, *see Author Index*
Van Heusen, 318; Suddenly it's Spring, 318
Venice Biennale, 174
Verdi, Giuseppe, 429
Victor Concert Orchestra, 325
Victor Records, 321, 324
Vienna: Raimundtheater, 184, 387, 388; Staatsoper, 235
Viertel, Berthold, 396
Viking Press, 282
Viktor Barnowsky theatre, Berlin, *see* Berlin
Villa-Lobos, Heitor, 327
Virgil, Jack, 338, 340
Vogel, Vladimir, 131
Völker, Klaus, 409n
Vollmoeller, Carl, 381, 382, 388; *Das Mirakel*, 388
Voltaire, 215; *Candide*, 399
Von Bilbao, Youkali und Alabama, 38
Voorberg, Marinus, 150

Vorhees, Don, 321
Voskovec, George, 409

Wagner, Gottfried, 30–2, 35; *Weill und Brecht. Das musikalische Zeittheater*, 31–2
Wagner, Richard, 12, 42, 102, 103, 104, 430; *Tristan und Isolde*, 116
Wagner, Wieland, 30
Wagner, Wolfgang, 30
Waldorf-Astoria Hotel, New York, 363
Waley, Arthur, *see Author Index*
Walker, Robert, 348
Walter, Bruno, 243, 395
Walter, Friedrich, 241
Walter Wagner Productions, 282
Wanger, Walter, 283
Warnow, Mark, 314
Warren, Brett, 319
Warren, Harry, 339
Watzke, Rudolf, 163
Waugh, Evelyn, 333; *The Loved One*, 333
Waxmann, Franz, 332
Weatherford, Earl, 266
Weber, Carl Maria, 104, 112; *Der Freischütz*, 104; *Leyer und Schwert*, op. 42, 104; Second Piano Sonata, 112
Webern, Anton, 5
Webster, John, 299; *The Duchess of Malfi*, 299
Webster, Margaret, 312
Wedekind, Frank, 156, 397; *Der Kaiserin von Neufundland*, 156, 397
We Fight Back (cabaret), 324, 341
Weigel, Helene, 190, 219, 222, 236, 237, 407
Weill, Albert, 53, 55, 100, 115, 144, 355, 427
Weill, Emma, 53
Weill, Hanns, 53, 55, 95, 103n, 109, 111, 114, 117, 118, 120, 121, 122, 124, 150, 154, 350, 374, 379
Weill, Kurt: *Ausgewählte Schriften* (KW.AS), 26, 175; *Song-Album*, 190, 192, 198, 209, 211, 218, 224; 'Über den gestischen Charakter der Musik', 175; American citizenship, 62, 65: composing methods, 82–5; family background, 2; health, 369, 422; homes: Brook House, 7, 8–9, 11, 12, 34, 35, 44, 45, 64, 65, 408,

412, 425–35, 438; Klein Machnow, 425, 432, 437; Louveciennes, 43, 59, 60, 62, 425, 432, 439; Jewish affairs, 281, 330; manuscripts, 8–12, 73, 82; marriages to Lenya, 62, 439; politics, 308, 319, 329–30, 331, 342; projects, 65, 66, 67, 215, 379–424; religion, 99–100; socialism, 295, 385
Weill, Nathan, 53
Weill, Rita, 37, 95
Weill, Ruth, 10, 53, 99–100, 104, 124, 125, 154
Weill Estate, 22, 28
Weill Foundation, see Kurt Weill Foundation for Music
Weill/Lenya Archive, 75, 448
Weill–Lenya Exhibition (1977), 143
Weill–Lenya Research Center, 32n, 36, 37, 38, 75, 95, 379, 425, 444, 446–7
Weill-Holesovsky, Hanne, 37, 95
Weisenborn, Günther, 375, 376, 377; U-Boat S 4, 376
Weisgal, Meyer W., 60, 61, 262, 266, 267
Weissberger, Felix, 273
Weizmann, Chaim, 66, 363
Weizmann Institute of Science, 363
Wekwerth, Manfred, 174
Welch, James, 365
Weller, George, 140
Welles, Orson, 398
Werfel, Franz, see Author Index
Werich, Jan, 409
Wetherford, Earl, 303
Wetzler, Hermann, 55
Wharton, John F., 22, 49
Wheeler, Hugh, 33, 241; Silverlake (Kaiser adaptation), 33, 241
Wheeler, Wallace, 338, 339
White Horse Inn, The (musical comedy), 388
Whitman, Walt, see Author Index
Wiegler, Paul, 198
Wiene, Robert, 392
Wiesbaden, 234, 235
Wigman, Marie, 398
Wild, Jonathan, 415
Wildberg, John, 299

Wilder, Thornton, 402–3, 406, 416n; Heaven's my Destination, 403; The Matchmaker, 402; Our Town, 402
Willett, John, 51, 409
Williams, Gwinn, 292
Williams, Norman, 273
Williams, Robert, 312
Williams, Tennessee, 421
Williams, Tom Emlyn, 356
Willner, Arthur, 160, 162
Willy, Johannes, 209, 216
Wiman, Dwight Deere, 353, 355
Winkler, Georg, 241
Wirl, Erik, 173, 217, 225
Witt, Josef, 216
Wolf, Friedrich, 126
Wolf, Hugo, 99, 131; Die Bekehrte, 131; Spanisches Liederbuch, 99
Wollheim, Eric, 255
Wolpe, Stefan, 296
Wong, Anna May, 416n
Work, Henry C., see Author Index
Wouk, Herman, 421; Aurora Dawn, 66, 421; The Caine Mutiny, 421
WPA (Works Progress Administration), 294
WPA Theatre Project, 303
Wrightson, Earl, 346
Wulf, Joseph, 376n
Wyckoff, Evelyn, 318
Wyman, David S., 332
Wynn, Keenan, 312

Yale University Music Library, 36, 37, 75, 95, 436, 448
Yona, Yvonne, 270
You and Me (film), 63
Young, Marvin, 322–3
Young Men's Hebrew Association, 371

Zaranova, Erika, 307
Zemach, Benjamin, 266
Zemlinsky, Alexander von, 58, 183, 184
Zimmer, Walter, 183
Zimmermann, Mary, 140
Zola, Emile, 400; The Feast of the Fisherman, 400
Zurich, 23; Corso Theatre, 255